COVER & BAKE

A BEST RECIPE CLASSIC

A BEST RECIPE CLASSIC

Cover & Bake

BY THE EDITORS OF

COOK'S ILLUSTRATED

PHOTOGRAPHY

CARL TREMBLAY

DANIEL J. VAN ACKERE

ILLUSTRATIONS

JOHN BURGOYNE

AMERICA'S TEST KITCHEN

BROOKLINE, MASSACHUSETTS

America's Test Kitchen
17 Station Street
Brookline, MA 02445

0-936184-80-9
Library of Congress Cataloging-in-Publication Data
The Editors of *Cook's Illustrated*

Cover & Bake: Casseroles, Pot Roasts, Skillet Dinners, and Slow-Cooker Favorites.
Would you make 35 batches of macaroni and cheese to find the absolute best version? We did. Here are more than 200 exhaustively tested recipes for one-dish meals that cook while you rest.

1st Edition

ISBN 0-936184-80-9 (hardcover): $29.95
I. Cooking. I. Title
2004

Manufactured in the United States of America

10 9 8 7 6 5 4 3 2 1

Distributed by America's Test Kitchen, 17 Station Street, Brookline, MA 02445.

Editorial Manager: Elizabeth Carduff
Senior Editor: Julia Collin Davison
Associate Editors: Matthew Card and Keith Dresser
Test Cooks: Stephanie Alleyne, Sean Lawler, Diane Unger-Mahoney
Assistant Test Cook: Charles Kelsey
Series Designer: Amy Klee
Jacket Designer: Julia Sedykh
Book Production Specialist: Ron Bilodeau
Photographers: Carl Tremblay (color and documentary photography); Daniel J. Van Ackere (silhouette photography)
Food Stylist: Catrine Kelty
Illustrator: John Burgoyne
Production Manager: Jessica Lindheimer Quirk
Copyeditor: Cheryl Redmond
Proofreader: Holly Hartman
Indexer: Cathy Dorsey

Pictured on front of jacket: Baked Macaroni and Cheese (page 18)
Pictured on back of jacket: Chili Mac (page 81), Chicken with White Wine, Tarragon, and Cream (page 320), Skillet Lasagna (page 238), Beef Pot Pie (page 127), Chicken Tagine with Olives and Lemon (page 202), Cheese Soufflé with Spinach (page 291)

Contents

PREFACE

SOME OLD-FASHIONED FOODS REALLY DESERVE to be obsolete. Many heirloom varieties of apple, for example, had tough, bitter skins and flesh that was no better. Others tasted great but didn't keep more than two or three weeks and so were impractical. A neighbor of mine in Vermont recently told me about an aunt who used to store raw sausage patties in pig fat (an American version of "confit," I suppose) and then take them out as needed, frying them up for breakfast. (Freezers brought an end to these sorts of country recipes.) However, some of my favorite foods—corned beef, watermelon pickles, and applesauce—are children of necessity, as none of these foods would last very long without pickling or canning. Yet they retain their appeal because they are delicious in their own right. Here necessity and culinary appeal found common ground.

Another classic American tradition, the meat-and-potato diet, is also based on purely practical considerations. Anyone who has ever spent time on a mountain farm can tell you that poor, hilly soil is ideally suited to two crops. You guessed it: meat and potatoes. Cattle graze on ground that would not support any crop other than grass, including steep hillsides that can't be worked with a tractor. Potatoes, as any brown-thumbed gardener will tell you, grow (thankfully) under almost any conditions. Yet the two ingredients have a deep affinity for each other, one that has survived the original, pragmatic reasons for their early pairing.

Of course, this is a book about another old-fashioned category of recipes: casseroles, pot pies, braises, slow-cooked meals, and skillet dinners. Why have casseroles and their cousins retained their appeal, even in this modern age of quick, microwaved food? I can think of two reasons. One, they are practical, as most of the work can be done long before supper, and two, many foods simply taste better when prepared in this manner. Flavors meld, tough meats soften, and the perfect balance of ingredients may be achieved through slow cooking. But, as in gardening, much depends on technique.

The bane of covered-dish suppers is overabundance and overcooking. Simplification of recipes, a light hand with ingredients, and the notion of treating each addition individually are the keys to success. After all, some of the great culinary traditions from France and Italy are nothing more than casseroles. Few would deny the appeal of lasagna or vegetable gratin.

So, like good anthropologists, we set out to investigate the past in an effort to make a better future. We tweaked popular recipes that needed only slight alterations, while others—those lost to the pages of culinary history—were completely rehabilitated. We hope you will find what you are looking for in *Cover & Bake,* whether it's Chili Mac or Slow-Cooker Asian-Spiced Pork Ribs with Noodles. We offer a place where the past and future meet over the dinner table. Not a bad place to visit with old and new friends alike.

Christopher Kimball
Founder and Editor
Cook's Illustrated

WELCOME TO AMERICA'S TEST KITCHEN

THIS BOOK HAS BEEN TESTED, WRITTEN, AND edited by the folks at America's Test Kitchen, a very real 2,500-square-foot kitchen located just outside of Boston. It is the home of *Cook's Illustrated* magazine and is the Monday through Friday destination for close to two dozen test cooks, editors, food scientists, tasters, and cookware specialists. Our mission is to test recipes over and over again until we understand how and why they work and until we arrive at the "best" version.

We start the process of testing a recipe with a complete lack of conviction. By that I mean that we accept no claim, no theory, no technique, and no recipe at face value. We simply assemble as many variations as possible, test a half dozen of the most promising, and taste the results blind. We then construct our own hybrid recipe and continue to test it, varying ingredients, techniques, and cooking times until we reach a consensus. The result, we hope, is the "best" version of a particular recipe, but we realize that only you can be the final judge of our success (or failure). As we like to say in the test kitchen, "We make the mistakes, so you don't have to."

All of this would not be possible without a belief that good cooking, much like good music, is indeed based on a foundation of objective technique. Some people like spicy foods and others don't, but there is a right way to sauté, there is a "best" way to cook a pot roast, and there are measurable scientific principles involved in producing perfectly beaten, stable egg whites. This is our ultimate goal: to investigate the fundamental principles of cooking so that you become a better cook. It is as simple as that.

You can watch us work (in our actual test kitchen) by tuning into America's Test Kitchen (www.americastestkitchen.com) on public television or by subscribing to *Cook's Illustrated* magazine (www.cooksillustrated.com), which is published every other month. We welcome you into our kitchen, where you can stand by our side as we test our way to the "best" recipes in America.

Reinventing Casseroles:
An Introduction

IT'S EASY TO UNDERSTAND THE UNIVERSAL appeal of casseroles, ever present at family gatherings, church suppers, school fundraisers, and parties of almost every stripe. But it seems that all too often the promise of a warm and comforting meal pulled hot and cheesy from the oven falls far short of our expectations. Tired of lackluster dishes made with jarred sauces and boring ingredients? Well, so were we, and with this book we set out to prove that the venerable casserole, once the manifestation of the best sort of American home cooking, could be revived and re-imagined.

In this collection of recipes, we've taken some liberties with the traditional casserole in our effort to develop recipes for a broad range of one-dish meals that will allow you put a fresh, savory meal on the table with a minimum of prep work and pot watching. In the first chapter of this book, "Assemble and Bake," you will find "true" casseroles, that is to say you'll find pasta, rice, and meat dishes that are meant to be layered in a Pyrex dish, topped with cheese or savory bread and nuts, and then baked for a short time in a hot oven. Moving through the book you'll find pot pies, oven-braised "casseroles," skillet "casseroles," and slow-cooker "casseroles," all of which are designed to help you build flavorful and substantial meals from readily accessible ingredients—often using only one or two pots. And since we know that this kind of cooking often appeals to busy families, we've spent time figuring out exactly how and when these recipes can be made ahead. Wherever possible we've provided make-ahead instructions along with storage and reheating specifics.

Along the way, the test kitchen learned a lot about the art of the casserole, since most of these recipes had traditionally taken either hours and hours to prepare or, at the other end of the spectrum, become associated with processed convenience products that could be dumped together at the last minute and then baked. Our goal was to find a happy middle ground and give you the best recipe, whether it's an adaptation of an old favorite, like Chicken Divan, which we turned into a true casserole with a rich and creamy sauce (instead of using canned cream of mushroom soup), or an entirely new invention like Baked Ravioli Puttanesca, where easy-to-find frozen ravioli is paired with a robust tomato sauce and simple topping and then baked. We've also adapted some of our own stovetop recipes to be suitable for a longish stay in the oven, freeing busy home cooks from the need to watch and stir the pot.

We developed many tricks as we experimented with these recipes, from how to bake rice without drying it out to how to prepare skillet casseroles for which meat, chicken, vegetables, and rice must all be cooked to perfection in one pan. The one thing uniting all these recipes is a reliance on fresh ingredients, including high-quality cheeses, herbs, and spices. And it helps enormously to have a well-stocked pantry and a well-equipped kitchen. Here is a list of the equipment and ingredients we use regularly in the test kitchen when making these casseroles, along with some tips we learned from all our trial and error in developing this book.

1

Casserole 101:
Tips for Success

1. UNDERCOOK YOUR PASTA Starches like pasta and rice should be cooked so that they are slightly underdone. Once they are assembled with the other casserole ingredients and baked, they will finish cooking.

2. PAY ATTENTION TO SIZE Be sure to follow recipe instructions with respect to cutting chicken into strips or bite-size pieces since, in many cases, we have constructed the recipes so that the chicken will cook directly in the sauce before the casserole goes in the oven. Improperly cut pieces will overcook or undercook and also look unappealing in the finished casserole. The same principle holds true for vegetables.

3. STORE CASSEROLE FILLINGS AND SAUCES SEPARATELY WHEN MAKING RECIPES AHEAD We've provided detailed make-ahead instructions for all appropriate recipes. As a general rule, we find that storing toppings, fillings, and sauces separately helps maintain the integrity of the final dish. There are a few casseroles that can be fully assembled in advance but they are the exception.

4. BRING MADE-AHEAD CASSEROLES TO ROOM TEMPERATURE BEFORE BAKING Assembled casseroles stored overnight in the refrigerator should be brought to room temperature before baking. Cold casseroles take too long to come up to temperature in the oven and are prone to drying out.

5. USE THE SPECIFIED SIZE OF BAKING DISH If a baking dish is under- or overfilled, the casserole will cook improperly.

6. MAKE SURE YOUR OVEN IS THE CORRECT TEMPERATURE It takes at least 15 minutes for a standard oven to reach the desired temperature (it's also good to use an oven thermometer for accuracy). Many of the casseroles in this book are meant to spend a short time in the oven at high heat because all the ingredients have already been cooked and just need to meld in the oven. Casseroles that spend too much time in the oven will lose their texture and bright flavors.

7. ALLOW CASSEROLES TO COOL BRIEFLY BEFORE SERVING Casseroles need a few minutes of repose before they are sliced, to allow the layers to bind and the sauce to cool. Five to 10 minutes is generally sufficient.

8. PROPER SEASONING IS IMPORTANT Fresh herbs can make all the difference between a great casserole and a mediocre one.

9. TOPPINGS MAKE A DIFFERENCE A good crumb topping makes a big difference in many recipes in this book. Dried crumbs are usually stale and powdery so we recommend using the food processor to grind fresh sandwich bread with melted butter for a crispy and appealing topping. You can add nuts and cheese as well to vary your toppings.

Casserole Basics:
Equipment and Ingredients

A PROPERLY PROVISIONED KITCHEN HELPS TAKE THE CHALLENGE OUT OF COOKING. Nothing is more frustrating than getting halfway through a recipe before realizing that you're missing a key ingredient or you don't have a pan large enough to accommodate the casserole that you are preparing. There are a few pieces of basic equipment we think every kitchen should have and some foodstuffs we think should be in every pantry or refrigerator.

But as any cook knows, not all skillets or brands of chicken broth are created equal. Some skillets perform better than others and some cans of chicken broth are tastier than others. Over the years, we have evaluated hundreds of pieces of equipment and food items in the test kitchen. Equipment is put through rigorous, real-life kitchen tests to find the sharpest knives, the most accurate thermometer, and the handiest garlic press. We have summarized these tests in the list that follows and offer specific recommendations on brands that have fared well in these tests. In addition, we evaluate ingredients in blind taste-tests. We not only taste products as is but we cook with them. For example, we taste diced tomatoes straight from the can but also make a quick sauce with them. By the time we are done evaluating a category of food items, we can confidently recommend specific brands, as we have done in the ingredient list that follows.

Equipment

DUTCH OVENS: Dutch ovens are large (generally 6 to 8 quarts), heavyweight pots squatter in stature than they are tall. They are one of the more versatile pots in the kitchen and can be used for everything from sautéing and searing to braising. We use them for dozens of recipes in this book and find them an indispensable piece in any well-equipped kitchen. After rigorously testing a dozen different Dutch ovens, we came up with a few favorites, like the models from Le Creuset and All-Clad. For more information about Dutch ovens and testing results, see page 147.

SKILLETS: The only pan we use more than a Dutch oven is a skillet. A sloped-sided, flat-based skillet is the best choice for sautéing, searing, browning, and pan-frying, not to mention for cooking a grilled cheese sandwich or Sunday morning pancakes.

Depending on the manufacturer, a sloped-sided pan may be called everything from an omelet pan to a sauté pan or fry pan. For the sake of standardization, we refer to them all as skillets. (Technically, a sauté pan has straight sides and is most frequently used for pan-frying or shallow braising. The straight sides inhibit evaporation, which is important to sautéing or searing.)

A large, 12-inch skillet is the most practical size. Measured outer lip to outer lip, it can easily accommodate a large quantity of ingredients without overcrowding, which can prevent adequate browning and thereby affect flavor and texture.

Skillets are available as "traditional" or "nonstick." The latter is covered with a Teflon-based coating that prevents food from sticking. While manufacturers claim that the coating lasts a lifetime, we have found otherwise. (See pages 211–212 for testing results on both traditional and nonstick skillets.)

Which style should you own? Ideally, you should own one of each, as both have their merits. Nonstick skillets are easy to clean and require less fat for cooking than traditional pans. However, they don't develop a fond—the browned bits that adhere to the pan's bottom during cooking and contain a good deal of flavor. We recommend a traditional skillet for dishes in which browning contributes an essential flavor base, like the many oven-braised dishes in chapter 3 of this book, where the meat and aromatics are browned on the stovetop first.

SAUCEPANS: A relatively large, 3-quart saucepan is ideal for preparing a variety of the sauces that bind together many of the casseroles in this book. After testing eight popular brands, we found that the merits of a good saucepan aren't all that different from those we require of other pots and pans. It should be sturdily constructed, have a solid heft for even heat distribution, and have a tight-fitting lid. All-Clad's saucepan hit all the marks—as their cookware generally does. But given its high price tag (around $140), it should perform flawlessly.

If spending that much on a saucepan seems like overkill, a decent pan can be had for much less. The Sitram Professional Induction Saucepan is about $57 and works nearly as well as the All-Clad in most tasks. The pan's major flaw is a lightweight lid that allows steam to escape (so it is not the best choice for making rice).

ALL-CLAD
Stainless Steel
3-Quart Saucepan

SITRAM
Professional Induction
3.17-Quart Saucepan

SPLATTER SCREEN: To keep mess to a minimum when browning meats on the stovetop, cover the pan with a splatter screen. This fine-mesh screen will trap escaping grease without retaining steam or affecting the cooking time. Most grocery stores carry inexpensive splatter screens, though check your local gourmet store for a heavier-weight version that will survive a trip through the dishwasher.

BAKING DISHES: A true workhorse for making desserts and casseroles alike, a 9 by 13-inch baking dish is indispensable for making many of the recipes in this book. We tested a dozen different baking dishes made from steel, aluminum, glass, and ceramic and the classic glass Pyrex dish easily outshone them all. Time after time, it browned casseroles evenly and released food easily. And priced at around $9, the Pyrex dish is a real bargain.

As for the other types of dishes we tested, metal dishes performed well, but they can react with acidic ingredients in sauces and affect the flavor of the food. Another strike against them is that they cannot be scrubbed with abrasive pads (an almost certain necessity considering the sticking power of some casseroles) and food cannot be cut in them. Ceramic dishes also performed well, but were more fragile than either Pyrex or metal and were fussy to clean.

When removing hot Pyrex dishes from the oven, it is important to cool them on a clean, dry cooling rack. If placed on a cool or wet surface, they can shatter—a dangerous situation we have experienced in the test kitchen on more than one occasion. It is also important to never place Pyrex dishes over direct heat because they can crack.

Pyrex dishes work for everyday casseroles, but when company comes, you may want to use a fancier casserole dish for presentation's sake. But how do you know if the dish you want to use is a sufficient size for the recipe? It's easy: Simply fill the dish with water and measure the volume of the water. A 9 by 13-inch baking dish (virtually every casserole recipe in this book is written for a 9 by 13-inch dish) has a capacity of 3 quarts (all Pyrex dishes have the volume marked on the bottom, so it is easy to substitute). While casserole dish substitutions are fine, it is important to be very close in volume. Underfilled dishes will bake too quickly and dry out while overfilled dishes may bubble over the confines of the dish, leaving a real mess on your oven floor.

KNIVES: Sharp, comfortable knives are one of the true joys of cooking. While those big, chunky knife blocks studded with purposeful-looking cutlery may look good on the kitchen counter, the truth of the matter is that all you really need are just three basic knives: a chef's knife, a paring knife, and a serrated knife.

CHEF'S KNIVES: A razor-sharp chef's knife can get you through 90 percent of your cooking tasks, from mincing and chopping to slicing the Sunday roast. So what separates a great chef's knife from an inferior one? We tested eight knives to find out.

Chef's knives can vary in price from a paltry $10 for a hardware-store special to well over $100 for a razor-honed import. This vast gulf in price can be attributed to the material from which the knife is made and the manufacturing process. Inexpensive knives are generally produced from a low grade of stainless steel that is durable but tends to dull easily. Once they lose the factory edge, stainless knives can be quite hard to resharpen.

Higher-end knives are generally made from high-carbon stainless steel: a steel alloy laced with carbon and other trace metals like chromium and nickel. The blended nature of the steel enables the knife to take a razor-sharp edge and allows it to be resharpened easily. But if there is too much carbon in the mix, the knife can discolor and rust easily (full carbon steel knives, requiring diligent attention, were, until recently, the norm in most kitchens and some cooks still swear by them despite their flaws). So, in the end, material choice is always a compromise between durability and sharpness.

Most commercially manufactured knives are either stamped or forged. Stamped knives are punched from a sheet of steel—not unlike cookie dough being cut by a cookie cutter—and tend to be fairly inexpensive. Forged knives are formed from molten steel and pounded into shape with brute force. They are generally tempered, or quickly heated and cooled to improve the molecular structure of the alloy from which the knife has been made. These knives take a good deal of effort to make and tend to be expensive.

While experts have long argued that forged knives are better than stamped ones, our testing did not fully support this position. We liked some forged knives and did not like others. Likewise, we liked some stamped knives and did not like others. The weight and shape of the handle (it must be comfortable to hold and substantial but not too heavy), the ability of the blade to take an edge, and the shape of the blade (we like a slightly curved blade, which is better suited to the rocking motion often used to mince herbs or garlic than a straight blade) are all key factors in choosing a knife.

When shopping, pick up the knife and see how it feels in your hand. Is it easy to grip? Does the weight seem properly distributed between the handle and blade? In our tests, we liked knives made by Henckels (the Four Star) and Wüsthof-Trident (the Grand Prix), both priced around $80. An inexpensive knife by Forschner (Victorinox), called the Fibrox, with a stamped blade, also scored well and sells for around $30.

Even the best knife grows dull and requires routine maintenance. For day-to-day touch up, we recommend a steel. This long rod, when used properly, effectively hones the blade by realigning the hair-thin edge. Routinely steeling a knife—at least a couple of times a week—will prolong the

HENCKELS Four Star Chef's Knife

WÜSTHOF-TRIDENT Grand Prix Chef's Knife

FORSCHNER (VICTORINOX) Fibrox Chef's Knife

life of the edge for months. Simply slide the knife along the length of the steel with a light touch—heel to tip—at a 20-degree angle a few times on each side.

When the edge grows dull despite steeling, it is time to sharpen the knife. While a sharpening stone is the traditional choice, it can be tricky to maintain the exact angle necessary to restore the edge. Instead, we prefer an electric sharpener, notably one made by Chef's Choice, which takes any guesswork out of sharpening and leaves you with a finely tuned edge. If you prefer to leave your knives in the hands of a professional, contact your local kitchen store. They may provide a sharpening service or can recommend one.

PARING KNIFE: A short, nimble paring knife can accomplish all the small, close work that a chef's knife cannot. Coring tomatoes, slivering garlic, trimming potatoes—it does it all. But which paring knife is best? Prices range from a modest $5 plus change to a grand $50, which invites the obvious question for a home cook: Is the most expensive knife really 10 times better than the cheapest model? To find out, we put seven all-purpose paring knives through a battery of basic kitchen tests to assess their capabilities.

As with the chef's knife testing, construction method wasn't necessarily indicative of capability: Inexpensive stamped knives fared as well as forged. The way the handle felt in testers' hands was much more important. Most testers preferred medium-size, ergonomically designed plastic handles. Slim wooden handles were harder to grasp.

Testers also preferred paring knives with flexible blades, which make it easier to work in tight spots. Stiffer blades were found to be slightly better at mincing and slicing, but these are secondary

tasks for paring knives. Among the knives tested, expensive forged knives from Wüsthof and Henckels performed well, as did an inexpensive stamped knife made by Forschner.

SERRATED KNIFE: For slicing bread or tough-skinned tomatoes, a serrated knife is absolutely essential. After testing 10 different models, we found that our ideal bread knife consists of a long, rigid blade with gently pointed serrations—as opposed to the jagged teeth of some models—and a comfortable handle. Forschner (Victorinox) produces a model that easily surpassed the competition for a price that was hard to beat. At under $40, we think it's a bargain.

Coming in a close second, the LamsonSharp Offset bread knife has a handle that is raised above the height of the blade, meaning no more banging your knuckles on the cutting board. Its blade was a little more aggressive than the model from Forschner, making it a poor choice for delicate tomatoes. The LamsonSharp is also reasonably priced at around $40.

FORSCHNER (VICTORINOX) Bread Knife

LAMSONSHARP Offset Bread Knife

CUTTING BOARDS: Even the best knife is utterly useless without a cutting board beneath it. What separates good cutting boards from bad ones? Is it material, size, thickness, or weight? Whether the board warps or retains odors with use? And what about the possibility of bacteria retention?

To sort all of this out, we tested boards made from wood, polyethylene (plastic), acrylic, glass, and Corian (the hard countertop material) for eight weeks in the test kitchen and found the two most important factors to be size and material.

In terms of size, we favored large boards because they provide ample workspace. The disadvantage

WÜSTHOF-TRIDENT
Grand Prix
Paring Knife

FORSCHNER (VICTORINOX)
Fibrox
Paring Knife

HENCKELS
Four Star
Paring Knife

of really large boards is that they may not fit in the dishwasher, a sacrifice we are willing to accept. If you're not, buy the largest board that will fit in your dishwasher. No matter the dimensions, a board should be heavy enough for stability but not so heavy (or thick and bulky) that it's hard to carry around the kitchen.

Material is important primarily in terms of the way the board interacts with the knife, but it is also relevant to odor retention and warping. We disliked cutting on hard acrylic, glass, and Corian boards because they don't absorb the shock of the knife strike (and they also dull the blade's edge). Plastic and wood boards are softer and therefore cushion the knife's blow, making for more controlled cutting. In the end, both wood and plastic have their merits, so choose whichever you prefer. Just remember, unless specified, wood cutting boards cannot go into the dishwasher because they will warp.

To remove strong odors and bacteria from cutting boards, wash with hot soapy water after each use and then sanitize with a light bleach solution (1 tablespoon of bleach to 1 gallon of water). Wood boards should be dried immediately after washing.

FOOD PROCESSOR: A food processor can make quick work out of any number of kitchen tasks, from slicing potatoes and shredding cheese to pureeing sauces and chopping bread into uniform crumbs. We have evaluated food processors for their ability to handle a wide variety of cooking jobs and found two brands that easily surpassed the others. Both Cuisinart and KitchenAid make sturdy, stable machines that work like draft horses. Priced around $200, a food processor is a serious investment, but one that will last for years and save you invaluable time.

FOOD STORAGE CONTAINERS: Sturdy, effective food storage containers are indispensable to the busy home cook because they allow food to be prepared ahead of time without spoiling and maintain the freshness of leftovers for days. There is a dizzying array of containers on the market that vary wildly in price, but how do

they all work? We tested a dozen and found big discrepancies in quality and effectiveness. Some failed to seal properly, others absorbed odors, and some broke during the dreaded "drop test" (from a countertop). Our favorites from the tests included moderately priced Tupperware Rock 'N Serve and Rubbermaid Stain Shield.

If you are particularly frugal (like many of us in the test kitchen), a 1-quart yogurt container can hold its own against the purpose-built storage containers, effectively sealing in foods and odors with the best of them. The yogurt container's life span, however, is limited; it turned squishy in the microwave and failed the drop test. But for free, it's hard to beat.

TUPPERWARE
Rock 'N Serve Medium
Deep Container

RUBBERMAID
Stain Shield
Square Container

PLASTIC WRAP: Most cooks rarely pay much attention to which plastic wrap they use, but a recent test in the test kitchen proved that some brands are certainly better than others. Because of the concerns over plasticizers (softening agents added to plastic wrap to promote clingability), two types of plastic wrap are commonly marketed: those especially designed for microwaving (they won't melt) and those designed for clinging. After testing six varieties, including both styles of wrap, with a few simple tests, we found that Glad ClingWrap and Saran Cling Plus were the best for all-around use.

NONSTICK ALUMINUM FOIL: Relatively new to the market, Reynolds Wrap Release Nonstick Aluminum Foil is traditional heavyweight foil that has been coated on one side (the matte side) with a food-safe nonstick surface. During testing in the test kitchen, it released foodstuffs effortlessly in a variety of situations. Normally tenacious mozzarella atop lasagna slid right off it, as did sticky cookies. The nonstick foil costs a little more than conventional foil, but we certainly recommend keeping a roll around for topping casseroles. It also works fine as conventional aluminum foil.

HEATPROOF RUBBER SPATULAS:

A wide-bladed, stiff-handled heatproof rubber spatula will do all the work of a wooden spoon but also a much better job of scraping stuck-on bits of food from pans and getting every last bit out of a mixing bowl. After testing 10 popular brands (with a variety of basic cooking tasks), we found Rubbermaid's High Heat Scraper to be the best of the bunch.

RUBBERMAID
13.5-Inch High Heat Scraper

INSTANT-READ THERMOMETER:

A thermometer takes the guesswork out of cooking meats and guarantees moist chicken, tender pork, and medium-rare beef every time. There are several types of thermometers on the market, but our absolute favorite is the Thermapen, an instant-read digital thermometer. Every station in the test kitchen is provisioned with one and we strongly recommend that you follow suit. For more information on the Thermapen, see page 314.

GARLIC PRESS:

Ask any cook and they will tell you how they hate mincing garlic. It takes a lot of time to chop it fine and it leaves a stinky blight on both the cutting board and your hands. Ultra-convenient garlic presses make clean, efficient work of processing garlic into a fine paste. And despite protestations from many a restaurant chef, we have found that a garlic press does not detrimentally affect the garlic's flavor.

Most garlic presses are pretty similar in design, but they definitely differ in capability. We tested 10 and were surprised by how much better some

worked than others. Cleaning was another important factor in testing; these things have to be easy to clean. Our favorite of the bunch was a fairly traditional looking model from Zyliss. It has a comfortable handle, turns cloves into a very fine puree, can accommodate two cloves at once, and is a breeze to clean.

ZYLISS SUSI DeLuxe Garlic Press

POTHOLDERS:

There is a lot of shuttling of hot dishes in and out of the oven in the recipes in this book, so a good set of potholders is of particular value. Potholders come in a variety of materials and sizes and, as we found, some work decidedly better than others. The LamsonSharp Leather Handiholder, made from washable leather, won praise for its unique suppleness, which allowed for a firm grasp on even the most slippery casserole dish. A close second, the plain-Jane, classic terrycloth mitt from Ritz is the potholder most of us are familiar with for a good reason: it's cheap and works well. It easily surpassed potholders costing twice as much.

LAMSONSHARP Leather Handiholder

MEASURING CUPS AND SPOONS:

Incorrect measuring can scuttle even the best recipe, so accurate, easy-to-use measuring cups are absolutely fundamental to a well-stocked kitchen. After testing eight different sets of measuring cups, we found that they are remarkably consistent as far as accuracy goes and the differences boil down to design. We favor relatively long-handled stainless measuring cups for their ease of use and quick clean-up. A set from Amco retails for about $13. For measuring spoons, we also favor the heavyweight durability of stainless steel. A set from Progressive International sells for just $4.

COLANDER: Ever try to strain a pound of cooked pasta or a head of blanched cauliflower in a wimpy, flexible colander? Chances are half of it ended up down the drain. Dozens of recipes in this book require the draining of hot pasta, rice, or vegetables, so a good-quality colander is a solid investment. After putting 10 colanders through rigorous trials (pounds and pounds of spaghetti, orzo, and frozen peas), we favored two: a stainless steel model from Endurance and a sturdy plastic model from Hoan. The Endurance has a unique micro-perforated bowl that drains quickly and holds up to 5 quarts. At $25, we think it is a deal. Despite its plastic composition, the Hoan was very sturdy and held up to 7 quarts. And at $4, the price is hard to beat.

ENDURANCE
Colander/Strainer

HOAN
7-Quart Colander

MICROPLANE CHEESE GRATER: Without a doubt, the Microplane grater/zester is the best on the market (see page 19 for more details). We use it to grate hard cheeses like Parmesan, as well as to zest lemons and grate everything from garlic and ginger to nutmeg and chocolate. Its secret is the tiny rasp-like, razor-sharp teeth that make quick work of just about anything. They come in several styles these days—short and fat to long and thin. Priced around $12, we think the Microplane grater—whichever style you prefer—is a kitchen essential.

POT SCRUBBERS: Casserole dishes, with cheese and pasta stuck to the edges, can be really difficult when it comes to clean-up. When elbow grease and a sponge won't suffice, it's time to pick up a pot scrubber. Made from plastic, steel, copper, brass, or nylon, pot scrubbers come in a variety of shapes and varying degrees of abrasiveness. After putting eight through their paces, we found we liked the copper-coiled model from Chore Boy the best. Tenacious and durable, this copper pad was unbeatable at scouring away the most stubborn stains.

CHORE BOY Copper Scouring Pads

Ingredients

IT IS HARD TO MAKE A GREAT-TASTING meal without top-notch ingredients. We taste-test dozens of products every year—including everything from canned tomatoes to vinegar—to uncover the best of what's out there. In this section, we've included the tasting results for the ingredients most commonly used in the recipes in this book. We also added certain ingredients we think of as pantry staples, ingredients that can lend character to an otherwise bland dish or serve as the defining flavor for an impromptu meal. When dinner is running late and the kitchen is otherwise barren, a couple of key ingredients can make all the difference.

SALT: Grocery stores are packed with innumerable varieties of salt in all shapes, sizes, and colors. From bone-white salt as fine as silt to dirty gray chunks as large as pebbles, there are a lot of options to choose from. We tasted nine different salts—basic iodized table salt to $36-a-pound hand-harvested French sea salt—in a variety of foods and found the results somewhat surprising. For the most part, flavor and textural differences were virtually undetectable in most cooked foods (outside of baked goods, in which case the coarse salts did not completely dissolve). So for the majority of your cooking needs, feel free to use your basic table or kosher salt. Coarser textured, more mineral-rich sea salts are best reserved for finishing dishes or sprinkling at the table where their flavor and texture can best be appreciated. One variety that stood out was Maldon Sea Salt, a uniquely flaky, delicately crunchy salt from England.

It is important to keep in mind that fine-grained table salt and coarse kosher salt are not equivalent. Table salt is roughly twice as strong as kosher salt. (Morton coarse kosher salt, however, has a denser texture and is thus saltier—about 1½ teaspoons is equivalent to 1 teaspoon table salt.)

MALDON Sea Salt

BLACK PEPPER:

For a spice we use virtually every day, we rarely give black pepper much thought. However, without it our casseroles would be bland and our roasts boring. Like coffee or tea, black pepper is grown throughout the temperate regions of the world. After tasting 11 different brands from different regions, we realized that location (what the French term *terroir*) most certainly affects flavor. Indian-grown Tellicherry pepper, for instance, has a distinctly different flavor than Malaysian-grown Sarawak pepper. Is one better than the other? We found that each different style had a flavor all its own and couldn't rate one above the other.

The bigger issue, we found, was freshness. Pepper that was purchased pre-ground had little of the kick or nuanced flavor of pepper ground freshly for the tasting. As a rule, we recommend that you buy peppercorns whole and grind them as needed.

MCCORMICK/ SCHILLING
Whole Black Pepper

As for peppercorns, much of what we tasted were from specialty stores, but we can highly recommend a supermarket staple, McCormick/Schilling Whole Black Pepper (depending on the part of the country, this pepper is labeled either McCormick or Schilling), as flavorful and fresh tasting.

CHICKEN BROTH:

Homemade stock is great when you have it, but who has the time to babysit a simmering pot for hours? More often than not, we use commercial chicken broth, which we find perfectly acceptable in just about every instance (excluding broth-based soups, where the broth is the soup).

But that said, we are really picky about the brand we choose because, for the most part, we've found commercial broths to be pretty bad. Many we tasted lack even a hint of chicken flavor. (Since there are no U.S. Food and Drug Administration standards for chicken broth, the amount of chicken actually used in broth can be minuscule.)

Interestingly, the four broths we rated best were all products of the Campbell Soup Company, of which Swanson is a subsidiary. In order, they were Swanson Chicken Broth, Campbell's Chicken Broth, Swanson Natural Goodness Chicken Broth (with 33 percent less sodium than regular Swanson chicken broth), and Campbell's Healthy Request Chicken Broth (with 30 percent less sodium than regular Campbell's chicken broth). The remaining broths were decidedly inferior and hard to recommend.

SWANSON Natural Goodness Chicken Broth, can and aseptic carton

So why do these four taste so much better? Campbell's claims that its recipes and cooking techniques are considered proprietary information, but the can's label betrays its dark secret. The top two broths happen to contain the highest levels of sodium out of the 13 we tasted, as well as the controversial seasoning monosodium glutamate (MSG), a highly effective flavor enhancer. The other broths simply didn't stand a chance.

A few national brands of chicken broth have begun to offer their products in aseptic packaging (cartons) rather than cans. Compared with traditional canning, in which products are heated in the can for up to nearly an hour to ensure sterilization, the process of aseptic packaging entails a flash heating and cooling process that is said to help products better retain both their nutritional value and their flavor.

We decided to hold another tasting to see if we could detect more flavor in the products sold in aseptic packaging. Of the recommended broths in the tasting, only the two Swanson broths are available in aseptic packaging. We tasted Swanson's traditional and Natural Goodness chicken broths sold in cans and in aseptic packages. The results fell clearly in favor of the aseptically packaged broths; both tasted cleaner and more "chickeny" than their canned counterparts. So if you are truly seeking the best of the best in commercial broths, choose one of the two Swanson broths sold in aseptic packaging. An opened aseptic package will keep in the refrigerator for up to two weeks (broth from a can will keep, refrigerated, for only a few days).

CANNED TOMATOES: Ten months out of the year, canned tomatoes easily surpass any fresh tomato you may be able to find. Picked at the peak of ripeness, they are sweet, flavorful, and succulent. But as we have found, there is a huge difference in the quality of different brands of tomatoes.

Whole tomatoes, either plum or round, are steamed to remove their skins and then packed in tomato juice or puree. We prefer tomatoes packed in juice; they generally have a fresher, livelier flavor than tomatoes packed in puree, which has a cooked tomato flavor that imparts a slightly stale,

tired taste to the whole can.

To find the best canned whole tomatoes, we tasted 11 brands, both straight from the can and in a simple tomato sauce. Muir Glen (an organic brand available in most supermarkets and natural-food stores) finished at the head of the pack. Progresso was a close second in the tasting and is also recommended.

Diced tomatoes are simply whole tomatoes that have been roughly chopped during processing and then packed with juice. For sauces, we prefer diced tomatoes because they save time and effort. Why chop canned tomatoes (a messy proposition at best) if you don't have to? There are not as many brands of diced tomatoes to choose from, although this seems to be changing as more companies realize that consumers want this product. Among the brands we tested, Muir Glen was again our favorite. S&W, a West Coast brand, and Redpack (called Red Gold on the West Coast) came in close behind. Unless otherwise indicated, use the entire contents of the can (both the diced tomatoes and juice) in recipes.

MUIR GLEN
Organic Diced
Tomatoes

S&W
Ready-Cut Premium
Peeled Tomatoes

SANDWICH BREAD: Bread crumbs are a common casserole topping and one we use frequently in this book. We make our crumbs from fresh bread because commercially produced dried breadcrumbs tend to be stale and flavorless. Our favorite choice for bread from which to make crumbs is dense-crumbed white bread, like the sandwich loaves from Pepperidge Farm. In general, we leave the tender crust on, rip the slices into coarse pieces, and then pulse the pieces in the food processor until coarsely ground.

11

NUTS: For a bit of extra flavor and a crunchy texture, we add nuts to many of our casserole toppings. Because of their high fat content, most nuts turn rancid quickly and should be stored in the freezer in freezer-safe, zipper-lock bags. Frozen nuts will keep for months and there's no need to defrost them before toasting or chopping.

VEGETABLE OIL: Vegetable oil is a catch-all phrase for oils processed from plants, nuts, seeds, etc. As a general rule, we use canola oil for its high smoke point and neutral flavor. Olive oil has a lower smoke point, making it inappropriate for browning or searing meats.

OLIVE OIL: Olive oil comes in a variety of styles that are best used for different purposes. The highest grade of olive oil is called extra-virgin, which means it is from the first pressing of the olives and that nothing but pressure has been applied to extract the oil from the olives. Extra-virgin is available at a wide range of prices, depending on a number of factors. At the upper end are the boutique oils that sell for astronomical prices; one we have tried sells for $80 a liter. Boutique oils are best reserved for drizzling atop finished dishes, like grilled or roasted meats, bruschetta, or a simple green salad. Cheaper extra-virgin olive oils are available at the supermarket and, truth be told, can hold their own against boutique oils. DaVinci brand extra-virgin olive oil was our favorite in a recent tasting of supermarket oils and scored well when compared against the boutique oils. For complete tasting results on supermarket extra-virgin oils, see page 243. Supermarket extra-virgin oils can be used for cooking, though they have a low smoke point so should not be used for high-heat searing or sautéing.

The next grade of oil is virgin olive oil, which is from the second pressing. This is followed by pure olive oil and olive pomace. Pure olive oil is what is most commonly available and can be used for virtually any cooking need. Pomace is the lowest grade and may have chemicals added to aid in oil extraction.

PARMESAN CHEESE: Nutty and tangy, smooth yet sharp, Parmigiano-Reggiano cheese has a flavor and texture that no other cheese comes close to replicating. We use it throughout this book in toppings, fillings, and sauces. After trying a variety of nonauthentic, bargain-priced "Parmesans" (both whole and pre-ground), we can unequivocally say that nothing comes close to the real deal. While it isn't cheap, around $15 a pound, we think the real stuff is worth every penny. The only nonauthentic version we could deem acceptable is a Wisconsin-produced version from DiGiorno that's about $8 a pound.

For the best-tasting Parmesan, buy it from a reputable source and try to have it cut fresh from the wheel. Stored too long in plastic wrap, it will dry out and pick up off-flavors and odors. Purchase an amount that you can use within a few weeks. We have tried many ways of storing Parmesan and found that a small zipper-lock bag works just as well at maintaining freshness as anything more complicated.

CHEDDAR CHEESE: Tangy, sharp cheddar cheese is also used in many of the casseroles in this book. What makes it "sharp"? The cheese must be aged for a minimum of 60 days (and up to one year). But this isn't a guarantee of flavor: From brand to brand, the flavor of sharp cheddar can range from as mild as mozzarella to as full as Parmesan. After tasting a broad range of supermarket sharp cheddars (both raw and melted in sandwiches), we found a couple favorites. From

CABOT Sharp Vermont Cheddar Cheese

CRACKER BARREL Sharp-White Cheddar Cheese

Vermont, Cabot's Sharp Cheddar had a "clean" and "buttery" flavor tasters enjoyed. The surprise of the tasting was Kraft's Cracker Barrel Sharp-White Cheddar. It was the bargain-priced cheese of the tasting and roundly appreciated.

BACON: Bacon is used in a large number of recipes in this book because it adds rich, deep flavor with a minimum of effort. You may think that one supermarket bacon tastes just like any other, but we found that to be far from the truth. After tasting 10 different national brands, we found that three were head and shoulders above the rest: Farmland Hickory Smoked Bacon, Boar's Head Brand Naturally Smoked Sliced Bacon, and Hormel Original Black Label Bacon.

FARMLAND
Hickory Smoked Bacon

BOAR'S HEAD BRAND
Naturally Smoked Sliced Bacon

HORMEL
Original Black Label Bacon

SUN-DRIED TOMATOES: Packing big flavor in a small package, sun-dried tomatoes are a great ingredient to keep on hand. We use them in a variety of recipes throughout this book, as well as in quick pasta dishes or even stirred into polenta or mashed potatoes. As a general rule, we prefer the flavor and texture of jarred, oil-packed sun-dried tomatoes above the dry, cellophane-packed tomatoes. They cost a little more, but their quality tends to be higher and they are easier to prepare because they do not need to be hydrated. That said, we generally rinse off the oil or marinade in which they are packed because it can be bitter and astringent.

DIJON MUSTARD: The pungent kick of Dijon mustard is an essential addition to a large number of sauces, vinaigrettes, and fillings. Once only produced in the French town of Dijon, it is now also produced in the United States. After tasting nine different brands (a mix of French and American), we found that provenance had little to do with flavor or quality. Instead we discovered that freshness and spiciness had the biggest impact on tasters' comments. The two are inextricably related: The older a mustard becomes, the milder its flavor because the active ingredient in mustard seeds (allyl isothiocyanate) dissipates. Despite such a finding (quantified by laboratory testing), only the second place finisher, American-made Grey Poupon, has a "best if used by" date on the label.

ROLAND
Extra-Strong
Dijon Mustard

GREY POUPON
Dijon Mustard

First place went to French-made Roland Extra Strong Dijon, which tasters thought had "the right amount of spice" and a thick, smooth texture.

Whichever mustard you purchase, try not to store it too long. Purchase small jars and replace them often for the freshest flavor.

LEMONS: Fresh lemon juice can make all the difference between a good meal and a great dinner. A splash of lemon juice brightens almost any dish and brings to the fore flavors that might otherwise be buried in the mix. While there are many bottled lemon juices on the market, none come close to that of fresh-squeezed and they are not suitable substitutions. We recommend that you keep a couple of lemons in the refrigerator at all times.

DRY AND FRESH HERBS: As a general rule, we much prefer the flavor of fresh herbs over dried. Through extensive side-by-side testing, we have found that many of the subtleties and nuances of fresh herbs seem to be lost during drying. Fresh herbs may require a little more effort to use and they certainly cost more, but we think they are well worth it.

That said, there are certain situations in which certain dried herbs are serviceable. Oregano, rosemary, thyme, and sage can all be used effectively if the recipe is long-cooked, which gives the dried herbs a chance to mellow. If you are substituting dried herbs for fresh, 1 part dried is roughly equivalent to 2 parts fresh (unless it is ground, like sage, in which case it is equal to 3 parts).

1

ASSEMBLE AND BAKE

WHILE CASSEROLES HAVE BEEN AROUND FOR hundreds of years, it wasn't until 50 years ago that Americans really took hold of the idea of the baked, one-dish meal. Unfortunately, as processed convenience foods became more widespread and people's devotion to spending time in the kitchen waned, the tasty casserole dish took a turn for the worse. What was once a comforting dish eagerly consumed at family events and potluck dinners disintegrated all too often into a woeful amalgam of canned soup, frozen vegetables, and prepackaged meat topped with soggy bread crumbs. In this chapter, we've striven to rescue the great American casserole. Focusing on fresh ingredients and sound cooking principles, our recipes may require a little more effort and time than most, but we feel that in not taking shortcuts, we've created something far superior. We've provided recipes for casseroles that revive our old favorites, like Chicken Divan and Baked Ziti with Tomatoes and Mozzarella (see pages 56 and 22), and created completely new dishes, like Beef Teriyaki Casserole and Soy-Glazed Salmon with Shiitake Mushrooms and Bok Choy (see pages 83 and 95), that will add new spark to your casserole repertoire.

The biggest challenge we discovered when testing these recipes was bringing all the different ingredients together to form a cohesive and well-cooked dish, since we learned that each ingredient needed to be handled in a specific manner. For example, in the casseroles that contain pasta, such as Baked Macaroni and Cheese and Baked Penne with Chicken, Broccoli, and Mushrooms (see pages 18 and 25), it was necessary to undercook the pasta so that when the casserole was fully baked, the pasta would be cooked just right. But in the case of the casseroles that contained rice, such as Creamy Chicken and Rice Casserole with Peas, Carrots, and Cheddar (see page 52), we found that the rice needed to be fully cooked before going into the casserole, or else the rice would emerge from the oven crunchy and starchy.

We also discovered that we could throw out the notion that casseroles need to cook in the oven for a long period of time. Nothing ruined casseroles more than a long, torturous stay in the oven;

ingredients were often overcooked and insipid. We realized that since most of the ingredients that are going into these casseroles are already cooked, they don't need to be subjected to any more time in the oven than is absolutely necessary. By using a relatively hot oven (upward of 400 degrees), the casseroles don't take much time to heat through and yet the flavors meld perfectly.

Not wanting to lose sight of the fact that casseroles are meant to be a timesaver for the busy family, we developed these recipes so they can be prepared in advance and then cooked in a flash whenever you're ready for them. Many of the casseroles in this chapter can be fully assembled in the baking dish and then baked, while others can be prepared in "components," quickly assembled, and then baked. When making a casserole destined to be baked at a later date, closely follow the instructions under the heading "Planning Ahead." Also, while it may be tempting to forgo the step of reheating components or bringing the assembled casserole up to room temperature, we found this step to be very important. Placing cold food in the oven extends the cooking time, which invariably leads to soggy, overcooked casseroles.

BAKED MACARONI AND CHEESE

BAKED MACARONI AND CHEESE IS THE KING of all casseroles, to which thousands of recipes have tried to pay homage. At its finest, it emerges from the oven with a golden crumb topping, underneath which a creamy cheddar cheese sauce gracefully cloaks tender pasta elbows and fills their curves. More often, however, it is pulled out of the oven with a texture so dense and dried out that it has be cut into squares and served like lasagna. Our goal was clear—to find a way for the sauce to remain creamy as it baked, and to return the glory to this casserole king.

Before diving into the testing, however, we tried several existing recipes to get the lay of the land. Most recipes use a similar technique: a flour-and-milk-based sauce (a.k.a. béchamel) is made, then enriched with the cheese, mixed with the cooked pasta, and baked. A few nontraditional recipes use eggs rather than flour to thicken the sauce (making it more like a custard), or replace the milk with evaporated milk. Although none of these recipes produced the baked mac and cheese of our dreams, we did learn a thing or two. First, casseroles cook very unevenly in the oven—the edges of the casserole are often done long before the center is even warm. Because of this phenomenon, we noted that egg-thickened recipes just don't work. The egg at the edges becomes overcooked and solidified by the time the center is hot. Second, the hot air of the oven will quickly dry out a casserole unless it is either covered with foil or has quite a loose texture to begin with. Therefore it is no surprise that the sauces made with evaporated milk, which is essentially milk with some of the water taken out, baked up to a dry, gloppy mess; using foil to protect it simply prevented the bread-crumb topping from toasting. The most promising recipes from this initial testing used a béchamel, yet none of them turned out great either. Overall, they tasted bland, dry, and grainy. We clearly had our work cut out for us.

Setting the issue of flavor aside, we began by focusing on the béchamel. Testing how much béchamel we needed for 1 pound of pasta (which fills a 9 by 13-inch casserole dish perfectly), we made three sauces using 3, 4, and 5 cups of milk. Although they produced casseroles that were decreasingly dry, we found that even the sauce made with 5 cups of milk was not enough. Increasing the amount of milk seemed the obvious answer, yet as we added more we noted that the sauce began to turn sticky and taste, well, too milky. As the casserole baked in the oven, the sauce lost some of its moisture but none of the milkfat or flavor. We then tried replacing some of the milk with water or chicken broth. While eliminating some of the milk loosened the sauce up significantly so that it could withstand the evaporation in the oven, the water made the sauce taste somewhat bland. However, the chicken broth was fantastic. It helped the sauce remain creamy without adding or losing any significant flavor.

Testing various amounts of milk and broth to flour (the sauce thickener), we found 3½ cups of milk and one can of chicken broth (about 1¾ cups) to 6 tablespoons of all-purpose flour was perfect.

Up until now, we had been adding a pound of cheddar to the sauce as a baseline, but wondered if either less or more would be better. Testing casseroles with amounts of cheese ranging from 12 to 24 ounces, we found the tasters' penchant for cheese was simply insatiable. At 24 ounces (8 cups), we cried uncle—the casserole tasted sufficiently cheesy. A problem that had been annoying us since the beginning, however, was now impossible to ignore—the grainy texture of the cooked cheddar. To get around this, many recipes mix cheddar with other types of cheese. We tried replacing some of the cheddar with Gruyère, but its potent flavor—an acquired taste—did not sit well with all the tasters. Monterey Jack helped to smooth out the sauce, but it also was too bland for a dish where the cheese was so critical. Gouda, Havarti, and fontina were all given a shot; however, none tasted just right. Last, we tried colby and hit the jackpot. Offering a cheddar-like flavor, and an unbelievably silky texture when melted, colby was the clearly the answer. Trying various ratios of colby to cheddar, we found that the best balance of flavor and texture was 2 parts colby to 1 part extra-sharp cheddar. Adding a pinch of cayenne, dried mustard, and a single clove of garlic also did wonders to enhance the cheddar flavor.

As for the topping, we immediately canned the idea of using store-bought bread crumbs, finding their flavor stale and lifeless. Rather, we preferred the fresh, somewhat sweet flavor of sliced sandwich bread when ground into crumbs using a food processor. Tossed with a little melted butter, these crumbs brown nicely in a 400-degree oven in about the same time it takes for the sauce and macaroni to bind together.

Baked Macaroni and Cheese

SERVES 6 TO 8

Although the classic pasta shape for this dish is elbow macaroni, any small, curvaceous pasta will work.

PLANNING AHEAD: Assemble the casserole as directed in step 4, but do not sprinkle with the bread-crumb topping or bake. Wrap the dish tightly with plastic wrap and poke several vent holes with the tip of a paring knife. Refrigerate the macaroni and cheese until cool, about 3 hours, then wrap tightly with another sheet of plastic wrap. Refrigerate the topping and casserole separately for up to 3 days, or freeze, tightly wrapped with an additional layer of foil, for up to 2 months. (If frozen, thaw in the refrigerator for at least 24 hours.)

TO BAKE: Allow the casserole to sit at room temperature for about 1 hour. Adjust an oven rack to the middle position and heat the oven to 400 degrees. Remove the plastic wrap and sprinkle evenly with the bread-crumb topping. Wrap the dish tightly with foil and bake until the casserole is moderately hot, about 25 to 30 minutes. Remove the foil and continue to cook until the bread crumbs are brown and the mixture is bubbling, 25 to 30 minutes longer. Cool for 10 minutes before serving.

TOPPING

4	slices white sandwich bread, torn into quarters
2	tablespoons unsalted butter, melted

MACARONI AND CHEESE

	Salt
1	pound elbow macaroni
6	tablespoons unsalted butter
1	medium garlic clove, minced or pressed through a garlic press
1	teaspoon dry mustard
1/4	teaspoon cayenne pepper
6	tablespoons all-purpose flour
1¾	cups low-sodium chicken broth
3½	cups whole milk
16	ounces colby cheese, shredded (about 5⅓ cups)
8	ounces extra-sharp cheddar cheese, shredded (about 2⅔ cups)
	Ground black pepper

1. FOR THE TOPPING: Process the bread and butter in a food processor fitted with the steel blade until coarsely ground, about six 1-second pulses; set aside.

2. FOR THE MACARONI AND CHEESE: Adjust an oven rack to the middle position and heat the oven to 400 degrees. Bring 4 quarts of water to a boil in a Dutch oven over high heat. Stir in 1 tablespoon salt and the macaroni; cook, stirring occasionally, until al dente, about 5 minutes. Drain the pasta and leave it in the colander; set aside.

3. Wipe the pot dry. Add the butter and return to medium heat until melted. Add the garlic, mustard, and cayenne; cook until fragrant, about 30 seconds. Add the flour and cook, stirring constantly, until golden, about 1 minute. Slowly whisk in the chicken broth and milk; bring to a simmer and cook, whisking often, until large bubbles form on the surface and the mixture is slightly thickened, 5 to 8 minutes. Off the heat, whisk in the colby and cheddar gradually until completely melted. Season with salt and pepper to taste.

4. Add the drained pasta to the cheese sauce and stir, breaking up any clumps, until well combined. Pour into a 9 by 13-inch baking dish (or a shallow casserole dish of similar size) and sprinkle with the bread-crumb topping. Bake until golden brown and bubbling around the edges, 25 to 30 minutes. Remove from the oven and cool for 10 minutes before serving.

CREAMY BAKED FOUR-CHEESE PASTA

PASTA AI QUATTRO FORMAGGI, THE CLASSIC Italian pasta dish with four cheeses and heavy cream, is a great idea in theory. In reality, however, it often turns into an inedible mess: tasteless, stringy, heavy, and greasy. We wanted to discover what made this dish great in the first place, delivering a pasta dinner that was silky smooth and rich but not heavy—a grown-up, sophisticated version of macaroni and cheese with Italian flavors.

Of course, the cheese was the first issue in terms of both flavor and texture. We were committed to Italian cheeses, but this barely diminished our choices—research turned up varying combinations and amounts (1 cup to 6½ cups cheese per 1 pound pasta) of Asiago, fontina, Taleggio, Pecorino Romano, mascarpone, mozzarella, Gorgonzola, Parmesan, and ricotta. Initial testing reduced the scope quickly: Mascarpone and ricotta added neither flavor nor texture, and Asiago was bland. Pasta tossed with mozzarella was gooey and greasy, whereas Taleggio was not only difficult to obtain but also made the pasta too rich and gluey. After testing numerous combinations of the remaining cheeses, tasters favored a 2½-cup combination of Italian fontina (which is creamier and better-tasting than versions of this cheese made elsewhere), Gorgonzola, Pecorino Romano, and Parmesan.

Both heating the cheeses and cream together and adding the cheeses separately to the hot pasta produced nasty messes. Each attempt caused the cheeses to curdle, separate, and/or turn greasy. Some recipes solve this problem by beginning with a *balsamella* (known in French as a béchamel). This basic white sauce starts with cooking butter and flour and then adding milk or cream. The cheeses can then be added to the white sauce, which because of the flour doesn't separate. As we soon found out, although the flour kept the sauce from breaking, it also had an unintended side effect: The flavor of the cheeses was diminished. The solution was to radically reduce the amount

---

EQUIPMENT: Cheese Graters

In the old days, you grated cheese on the teeth of a box grater. Now, cheese graters come in several distinct designs. Unfortunately, many of them don't work all that well. With some designs, you need Herculean strength to move the cheese over the teeth with sufficient pressure for grating; with others, you eventually discover that a large portion of the grated cheese has remained jammed in the grater instead of going where it belongs, on your food. Whether you are dusting a plate of pasta or grating a full cup of cheese to use in a recipe, a good grater should be efficient and easy to use.

We rounded up 15 models and set about determining which was the best grater. We found five basic configurations. Four-sided box graters have different-sized holes on each side to allow for both fine grating and coarse shredding. Flat graters consist of a flat sheet of metal that is punched through with fine teeth and attached to some type of handle. With rotary graters, you put a small chunk of cheese in a hopper and use a handle to press it down against a crank-operated grating wheel. Porcelain dish graters have raised teeth in the center and a well around the outside edge to collect the grated cheese. We also found a model that uses an electric motor to push and rotate small chunks of cheese against a grating disk.

After grating more than 10 pounds of Parmesan cheese, we concluded that success was due to a combination of sharp grating teeth, a comfortable handle or grip, and good leverage for pressing the cheese onto the grater. Our favorite model was a flat grater based on a small, maneuverable woodworking tool called a rasp. Shaped like a ruler, but with lots and lots of tiny, sharp raised teeth, The Microplane Zester/Grater (as it is called)

can grate large quantities of cheese smoothly and almost effortlessly. The black plastic handle, which we found more comfortable than any of the others, earned high praise, too. Other flat graters also scored well.

What about traditional box graters? Box graters can deliver good results and can do more than just grate hard cheese. However, if grating hard cheese is the task at hand, a box grater is not our first choice.

We also had good results with rotary graters made from metal, but we did not like flimsy versions made from plastic. A metal arm is rigid enough to do some of the work of pushing the cheese down onto the grating drum. The arms on the plastic models we tested flexed too much against the cheese, thus requiring extra pressure to force the cheese down. Hand strain set in quickly. A rotary grater can also chop nuts fine and grate chocolate.

The two porcelain dish graters we tested were duds; the teeth were quite ineffective. And the electric grater was a loser of monumental proportions. True, the grating effort required was next to nothing, but so were the results. A child could have grated cheese faster and more efficiently.

THE BEST GRATER
This Microplane grater has very sharp teeth and a solid handle, which together make grating cheese a breeze.

of flour and butter to 2 teaspoons each instead of the usual 3 to 4 tablespoons each. Now the sauce was silky and smooth and allowed the flavor of the cheeses to stand out.

After making this recipe a half dozen more times, we were bothered by the notion of heating the cheeses ahead of time with the béchamel. We wanted to cook the cheeses as little as possible for the best flavor, so we put the prepared cheeses in a large bowl and added the hot pasta and hot béchamel. A quick toss melted the cheeses without cooking them. We had now both simplified the recipe and produced a cleaner-tasting, more flavorful dish.

Tubular pasta shapes (we found penne to be ideal) allow the sauce to coat the pasta inside and out and are the best choice. Many recipes suggest cooking the pasta fully and then baking it for 30 minutes. Besides making the dish time-consuming to prepare, this approach is a recipe for mushiness. To keep the pasta from overcooking in the oven, we found it necessary to undercook it by several minutes and then minimize the baking time. Just seven minutes in a 500-degree oven (in a shallow baking dish so it heats more quickly) is enough to turn the pasta and sauce into a casserole.

Many recipes add a bread-crumb topping that browns and crisps in the oven. We tried this casserole with and without the crumb topping, and tasters voted unanimously for the topping. It contrasts nicely with the creamy pasta and helps balance the richness of the sauce.

Creamy Baked Four-Cheese Pasta

SERVES 4 TO 6

To streamline the process, prepare the bread-crumb topping and shred, crumble, and grate the cheeses while you wait for the pasta water to come to a boil. This dish can be on the table in about half an hour.

PLANNING AHEAD: Follow the recipe through step 3. Refrigerate the topping, cooked pasta, and cream sauce in separate bowls, tightly wrapped with plastic wrap, for up to 2 days.

To Bake: Adjust an oven rack to the middle position and heat the oven to 400 degrees. Transfer the pasta to a colander and rinse quickly under hot tap water. Poke several vent holes in the plastic wrap covering the sauce and microwave on high power until hot, 3 to 5 minutes. Continue to assemble and bake the casserole as directed in step 4, extending the cooking time to 20 to 30 minutes.

TOPPING

4	slices white sandwich bread, torn into quarters
2	tablespoons unsalted butter, melted
1/2	ounce Parmesan cheese, grated (about 1/4 cup)

PASTA

	Salt
1	pound penne
1	tablespoon olive oil
2	teaspoons unsalted butter
2	teaspoons all-purpose flour
2	cups heavy cream
1/4	teaspoon ground black pepper
4	ounces Italian fontina cheese, shredded (about 1 1/3 cups)
3	ounces Gorgonzola cheese, crumbled (about 3/4 cup)
1	ounce Pecorino Romano cheese, grated (about 1/2 cup)
1/2	ounce Parmesan cheese, grated (about 1/4 cup)

1. FOR THE TOPPING: Process the bread and butter in a food processor fitted with the steel blade until coarsely ground, about six 1-second pulses. Transfer to a bowl and toss with the Parmesan; set aside.

2. FOR THE PASTA: Adjust an oven rack to the middle position and heat the oven to 500 degrees. Bring 4 quarts of water to a boil in a Dutch oven over high heat. Stir in 1 tablespoon salt and the pasta; cook, stirring occasionally, until al dente. Drain the pasta, return it to the pot, and toss with the oil; set aside.

3. Meanwhile, melt the butter in a small saucepan over medium-low heat. Add the flour and cook, stirring constantly, until golden, about 1 minute. Slowly whisk in the cream; bring to a simmer and cook, whisking often, until slightly thickened, about 1 minute. Off the heat, add 1/4 teaspoon salt and the pepper. Cover to keep warm.

4. Combine the cheeses in a large bowl. Add the cooked pasta to the cheeses. Pour the hot cream mixture over the pasta and cover immediately with foil or a large plate; let stand for 3 minutes. Uncover the bowl and stir with a rubber spatula, scraping the cheese from the bottom of the bowl, until the cheeses are melted and the mixture is thoroughly combined. Transfer the pasta to a 9 by 13-inch baking dish (or a shallow casserole dish of similar size) and sprinkle with the bread-crumb topping. Bake until the topping is golden brown, 5 to 10 minutes. Serve immediately.

➤ VARIATIONS

Baked Four-Cheese Pasta with Tomatoes and Basil

Follow the recipe for Creamy Baked Four-Cheese Pasta, adding one (14.5-ounce) can diced tomatoes, drained, to the pasta along with the cream in step 4. Add ¼ cup chopped fresh basil leaves to the pasta just before transferring to the baking dish.

Baked Four-Cheese Pasta with Prosciutto and Peas

Follow the recipe for Creamy Baked Four-Cheese Pasta, omitting the salt from the cream mixture in step 3, and adding 4 ounces prosciutto, chopped, and 1 cup frozen peas to the pasta along with the cream in step 4.

BAKED ZITI

WHAT CHURCH SUPPER OR POTLUCK DINner would be complete without baked ziti? The dish sounds simple enough. Take cooked pasta, add tomato sauce, cheese, and maybe some meatballs, sausage, or even eggplant. If this dish is so easy to prepare, then why are most versions so dry, so bland, and so downright unappealing? We knew good baked ziti, which is an Italian-American classic (arguably more American than Italian), was possible. We just had to figure out how.

Mozzarella binds the noodles together and makes this baked casserole incredibly rich and gooey. Fresh mozzarella packed in water makes the texture of the finished dish especially moist

and creamy and is recommended. Besides adding moisture, we found that fresh mozzarella lent this dish far more flavor than bland, rubbery supermarket mozzarella.

Eight ounces of mozzarella was just right for a pound of pasta. More made this dish too heavy and too rich. In fact, we realized that many American recipes for baked ziti simply add too much cheese, sauce, and other goodies. These ingredients overwhelm the noodles and make the casserole too thick, which extends the cooking time and makes the pasta mushy. We were learning that less is more when it comes to baked ziti.

Even good mozzarella is a bit bland, so we added an ounce of Parmesan to perk up the flavor. To ensure that the cheese was evenly distributed throughout the casserole, we layered half the pasta into the baking dish, sprinkled it with half the cheeses, and then added the remaining pasta and cheeses.

The mozzarella is the binder in baked ziti, but it's the tomato sauce that must keep things moist. A smooth sauce made with crushed tomatoes does the job most effectively. Diced tomatoes tasted good but tasters did not like the chunks of tomato, which tended to dry out in the oven. Crushed tomatoes coated the pasta evenly and thoroughly.

Although it seems obvious, the pasta for these dishes should be slightly undercooked (it's going to soften further in the oven). Too many recipes start with overcooked pasta. By the time the pasta is baked, it's soft and squishy. We also found it helpful to reserve some of the pasta cooking water to help spread the tomato sauce and keep the pasta moist.

Our recipe was coming together. We tested a variety of baking dishes and decided on a relatively shallow 9 by 13-inch dish because it allowed the pasta to heat through quickly. More time in the oven only dries out the noodles or makes them overly soft. With that in mind, we found that a hot 400-degree oven was best. Just 20 minutes in the oven (not the hour called for in many recipes with too much cheese, sauce, and other filling ingredients) yields a casserole with pasta that you still want to eat.

Although the dish needs only cheese and sauce, many recipes throw in the kitchen sink, adding sliced sausage, meatballs, and more. We found that this Italian-American dish is best made with some restraint. Just a few really fresh ingredients are all it needs. In addition to the classic version made with mozzarella, basil, garlic, and tomatoes, we developed two simple variations—one with crumbled sausage and another that pairs eggplant with smoked mozzarella.

Baked Ziti with Tomatoes and Mozzarella

SERVES 4 TO 6

Melted mozzarella cheese provides the binder for the pasta and the other ingredients in this dish. Use fresh mozzarella if possible—it will provide extra creaminess and moisture.

PLANNING AHEAD: Follow the recipe through step 2, adding the reserved pasta water to the sauce before adding the basil. Refrigerate the cooked pasta and tomato sauce in separate bowls, tightly wrapped with plastic wrap, for up to 2 days.
TO BAKE: Adjust an oven rack to the middle position and heat the oven to 400 degrees. Transfer the pasta to a colander and rinse quickly under hot tap water. Poke several vent holes in the plastic wrap covering the tomato sauce and microwave on high power until hot, 3 to 5 minutes. Continue to assemble and bake the casserole as directed in step 3, extending the cooking time to 30 minutes.

Salt
1   pound ziti or other short, tubular pasta
3   tablespoons olive oil
2   medium garlic cloves, minced or pressed
    through a garlic press
1   (28-ounce) can crushed tomatoes
2   tablespoons coarsely chopped fresh basil
    leaves
    Ground black pepper
8   ounces mozzarella cheese, shredded
    (about 2²/₃ cups)
1   ounce Parmesan cheese, grated (about
    ¹/₂ cup)

1. Adjust an oven rack to the middle position and heat the oven to 400 degrees. Bring 4 quarts of water to a boil in a Dutch oven over high heat. Stir in 1 tablespoon salt and the pasta; cook, stirring occasionally, until al dente. Reserve ¼ cup of the cooking water. Drain the pasta, return it to the pot, and toss with 1 tablespoon of the oil; set aside.

2. Meanwhile, heat the remaining 2 tablespoons oil and the garlic in a medium skillet over medium heat until fragrant but not brown, about 2 minutes. Stir in the tomatoes and simmer until thickened slightly, about 10 minutes. Off the heat, stir in the basil and season with salt and pepper to taste.

3. Add the tomato sauce and reserved pasta-cooking water to the pasta; stir to combine. Pour half of the pasta into a 9 by 13-inch baking dish (or a shallow casserole dish of similar size). Sprinkle with half the mozzarella and half the Parmesan. Pour the remaining pasta into the dish and sprinkle with the remaining mozzarella and Parmesan. Cover with foil and bake until the cheese melts, about 15 minutes. Remove the foil and continue to bake until the cheese begins to brown, about 5 minutes. Serve immediately.

VARIATIONS

Baked Ziti with Crumbled Italian Sausage

SERVES 4 TO 6

Both sweet and hot Italian sausage will work fine in this recipe. To remove the sausage from its casing, cut it open at the end and simply squeeze out the ground sausage.

PLANNING AHEAD: Follow the recipe through step 2, adding the reserved pasta water to the sauce before adding the basil. Refrigerate the cooked pasta and tomato sauce in separate bowls, tightly wrapped with plastic wrap, for up to 2 days.
TO BAKE: Adjust an oven rack to the middle position and heat the oven to 400 degrees. Transfer the pasta to a colander and rinse quickly under hot tap water. Poke several vent holes in the plastic wrap covering the tomato sauce and microwave on high power until hot, 3 to 5 minutes. Continue to assemble and bake the casserole as directed in step 3, extending the cooking time to 30 minutes.

Salt

1   pound ziti or other short, tubular pasta
2   tablespoons olive oil
1   pound hot or sweet Italian sausage, removed
    from its casing
4   medium garlic cloves, minced or pressed
    through a garlic press
½   teaspoon red pepper flakes
1   (28-ounce) can crushed tomatoes
2   tablespoons coarsely chopped fresh basil
    leaves
    Ground black pepper
8   ounces mozzarella cheese, shredded
    (about 2⅔ cups)
1   ounce Parmesan cheese, grated (about
    ½ cup)

1. Adjust an oven rack to the middle position and heat the oven to 400 degrees. Bring 4 quarts of water to a boil in a Dutch oven over high heat. Stir in 1 tablespoon salt and the pasta; cook, stirring occasionally, until al dente. Reserve ¼ cup of the cooking water. Drain the pasta, return it to the pot, and toss with 1 tablespoon of the oil; set aside.

2. Meanwhile, heat the remaining tablespoon oil in a 12-inch nonstick skillet over high heat until shimmering. Add the sausage and cook, breaking the meat into small pieces with a wooden spoon, until the sausage loses its raw color, about 5 minutes. Stir in the garlic and red pepper flakes; cook until fragrant, about 30 seconds. Stir in the tomatoes and simmer until thickened slightly, about 10 minutes. Off the heat, stir in the basil and season with salt and pepper to taste.

3. Add the tomato sauce and reserved pasta-cooking water to the pasta; stir to combine. Pour half of the pasta into a 9 by 13-inch baking dish (or a shallow casserole dish of similar size). Sprinkle with half the mozzarella and half the Parmesan. Pour the remaining pasta into the dish and sprinkle with the remaining mozzarella and Parmesan. Cover with foil and bake until the cheeses melt, about 15 minutes. Remove the foil and continue to bake until the cheese begins to brown, about 5 minutes. Serve immediately.

Baked Ziti with Eggplant and Smoked Mozzarella
SERVES 4 TO 6

Very small eggplants (weighing less than 6 ounces each) may be cooked without salting. However, we found that larger eggplants generally have a lot of moisture, which is best removed before cooking.

PLANNING AHEAD: Follow the recipe through step 3, adding the reserved pasta water to the sauce before adding the basil. Refrigerate the cooked pasta and tomato sauce in separate bowls, tightly wrapped with plastic wrap, for up to 2 days.

TO BAKE: Adjust an oven rack to the middle position and heat the oven to 400 degrees. Transfer the pasta to a colander and rinse quickly under hot tap water. Poke several vent holes in the plastic wrap covering the tomato sauce and microwave on high power until hot, 3 to 5 minutes. Continue to assemble and bake the casserole as directed in step 4, extending the cooking time to 30 minutes.

2   pounds globe eggplant (about 2 medium), cut
    crosswise into ¼-inch-thick rounds
    Kosher salt
1   pound ziti or other short, tubular pasta
4   tablespoons olive oil
4   medium garlic cloves, minced or pressed
    through a garlic press
½   teaspoon red pepper flakes
1   (28-ounce) can crushed tomatoes
2   tablespoons coarsely chopped fresh basil
    leaves
    Ground black pepper
8   ounces smoked mozzarella cheese, shredded
    (about 2⅔ cups)
1   ounce Parmesan cheese, grated (about ½ cup)

1. Toss the eggplant with 1 tablespoon kosher salt and place in a large colander set inside a large bowl to drain, about 30 minutes.

2. Meanwhile, adjust an oven rack to the middle position and heat the oven to 400 degrees. Bring 4 quarts of water to a boil in a Dutch oven over high heat. Stir in 2 tablespoons kosher salt and the pasta; cook, stirring occasionally, until al dente. Reserve ¼ cup of the cooking water. Drain the pasta, return it to the pot, and toss with 1 tablespoon of the oil; set aside.

3. Spread the salted eggplant evenly over a double layer of paper towels and pat dry with additional paper towels, wiping off any residual salt. Heat the remaining 3 tablespoons oil in a 12-inch nonstick skillet until shimmering. Add the eggplant and cook until it begins to brown, about 5 minutes. Reduce the heat to medium-low and cook, stirring occasionally, until the eggplant is fully tender and lightly browned, 10 to 15 minutes. Stir in the garlic and red pepper flakes; cook until fragrant, about 30 seconds. Stir in the tomatoes and simmer until thickened slightly, about 10 minutes. Off the heat, stir in the basil and season with salt and pepper to taste.

4. Add the tomato sauce and reserved pasta-cooking water to the pasta; stir to combine. Pour half of the pasta into a 9 by 13-inch baking dish (or a shallow casserole dish of similar size). Sprinkle with half the mozzarella and half the Parmesan. Pour the remaining pasta into the dish and sprinkle with the remaining mozzarella and Parmesan. Cover with foil and bake until the cheese melts, about 15 minutes. Remove the foil and continue to bake until the cheese begins to brown, about 5 minutes. Serve immediately.

BAKED PENNE WITH CHICKEN AND BROCCOLI

PENNE WITH CHICKEN AND BROCCOLI IS A well loved and classic combination that we knew could be made into a crowd-pleasing casserole. The cooked pasta, chicken, and broccoli are usually tossed in a rich cream sauce flavored with garlic and cheese. Our goal was to find a way to prevent the sauce from tasting overly heavy, while keeping the chicken from drying out and the broccoli from turning cafeteria green.

To start, we took a look at the traditional method for making a cream sauce. Generally, aromatics such as onions and garlic are sautéed, then cream is added and allowed to simmer, thicken, and reduce before being finished with cheese. Wanting to make the sauce less fatty, we tried replacing some of the heavy cream with chicken broth. This not only made the sauce lighter, but it boosted the chicken flavor as well. A little white wine also helped cut through the sauce's heaviness without lessening its flavor. These additions of broth and wine, however, made the texture of the sauce a bit too loose. Unlike cream, chicken broth and wine don't become dramatically thicker as they reduce. In order to make the sauce thick enough to properly coat the chicken, penne, and broccoli, we found it necessary to add some flour. Onions, garlic, and fresh thyme rounded out the sauce's flavor, as did some cheese. We tried several Italian cheeses, including Parmesan, fontina, and Pecorino, but tasters far preferred the less sour flavor of Asiago. Although tasty, the sauce was still a little bit lackluster until we introduced yet another flavorful component. Finding that mushrooms paired well with the sauce, we used both fresh sautéed mushrooms and some dried porcini in order to achieve a decent mushroom flavor. Alternatively, sun-dried tomatoes also round the sauce out nicely (see the variation on page 26).

Moving next to the chicken, we found it easiest to use boneless skinless breasts and cut them into bite-size pieces that mirror the size of the penne (and are easily skewered with a dinner fork). Simply tossing raw chicken with the broccoli, penne, and sauce and baking it in the oven, however, didn't work. It took far too long for the chicken to cook through, by which time the pasta was overdone, the broccoli was limp, and the sauce was dried out. Testing a variety of ways to precook the chicken, we tried broiling, sautéing, and poaching (in the pasta water). Broiling turned the edges of the chicken unappealingly crisp, while poaching resulted in the blandest flavor. Sautéing the chicken in a skillet with a little oil worked well, but it required an extra pan, which we were loath to use. Working with the poaching idea, we then tried poaching the chicken right in the sauce. This method worked like a charm and gave us chicken that remained tender and juicy without losing any flavor. In order to prevent the chicken from overcooking in the oven, we found it best to cook it only partway in the sauce, and let it finish in the oven. (Of course, when making this dish in advance, it is necessary to cook the chicken completely.)

Turning our attention to the broccoli, we decided right off the bat not to bother with the broccoli stems and to focus only on the florets. We often use the broccoli stems to add additional broccoli flavor; however, we found the difference it made in this particular dish just didn't warrant the extra work. Usually, broccoli florets are cooked briefly in boiling water (called blanching) then plunged into ice water to keep them crisp and green (called shocking). This process is necessary when making the casserole a day in advance; however, we found it unnecessary when baking the casserole right away. By using the pasta water to cook the broccoli, we were also able to eliminate another extra pot. Cooking the broccoli first, we simply skimmed it out using a slotted spoon (or spider, see page 94) before adding the pasta. One minute in the boiling water was all it took to take the raw edge off the broccoli and turn it bright green. One large head of broccoli (about 1½ pounds) provided enough florets for the casserole.

Last we focused on the pasta, the topping, and the baking time. One pound of penne, although easy to measure, unfortunately made too much filling to fit in a standard 9 by 13-inch baking dish. Reducing the pasta to ¾ pound was our only answer. Undercooking the pasta slightly so that it retained a firm (al dente) center helped keep it from turning too mushy in the oven, and tasters

approved of a sprinkling of buttery bread crumbs over the top. Because all of the ingredients in the casserole were pre-cooked, it only took 15 minutes in a 400-degree oven for the bread crumbs to brown and the flavors to meld.

Baked Penne with Chicken, Broccoli, and Mushrooms

SERVES 6 TO 8

The broccoli cooks very quickly, so stand by after adding it to the water.

PLANNING AHEAD: Follow the recipe through step 3, making the following changes: Plunge the broccoli immediately into a bowl of ice water after cooking. Remove the broccoli from the ice water when cool, and pat dry. Cook the chicken through completely in step 3, about 10 minutes, before stirring in the Asiago. Refrigerate the topping, broccoli, pasta, and sauce in separate bowls, tightly wrapped with plastic wrap, for up to 1 day.

TO BAKE: Adjust an oven rack to the middle position and heat the oven to 400 degrees. Place the pasta in a colander and rinse briefly under hot tap water to warm it. Poke several vent holes in the plastic wrap covering the sauce and microwave on high power until hot, 3 to 5 minutes. Continue to assemble and bake the casserole as directed in step 4, extending the cooking time to 30 minutes.

TOPPING

4	slices white sandwich bread, torn into quarters
2	tablespoons unsalted butter, melted

FILLING

	Salt
1	bunch broccoli (about 1½ pounds), stalks discarded, florets trimmed into 1-inch pieces
¾	pound penne
3	tablespoons olive oil
1¼	pounds cremini mushrooms, stems trimmed, brushed clean, and sliced thin
1	medium onion, minced
8	medium garlic cloves, minced or pressed through a garlic press
1	tablespoon minced fresh thyme leaves
¼	cup all-purpose flour
1	cup white wine

SLICING MUSHROOMS QUICKLY

Trim a thin piece from the stem end of each mushroom, then cut the trimmed mushrooms, one at a time, in an egg slicer. The pieces will be even and thin.

¼ ounce dried porcini mushrooms, rinsed and
    re-hydrated, with soaking liquid reserved (see
    page 41)

2   cups low-sodium chicken broth

1   cup heavy cream

1½ pounds boneless, skinless chicken breasts,
    trimmed and prepared according to the
    illustrations on page 51

2   ounces Asiago cheese, shredded (about 1 cup)

¼ teaspoon ground black pepper

1. FOR THE TOPPING: Process the bread and butter in a food processor fitted with the steel blade until coarsely ground, about six 1-second pulses; set aside.

2. FOR THE FILLING: Adjust an oven rack to the middle position and heat the oven to 400 degrees. Bring 4 quarts of water to a boil in a Dutch oven over high heat. Stir in 1 tablespoon salt and the broccoli; cook until bright green, about 1 minute. Remove the broccoli using a slotted spoon or wire spider (see page 94) and spread it out on a baking sheet to cool. Return the water to a boil. Add the pasta and cook, stirring occasionally, until al dente. Drain the pasta and toss with 1 tablespoon of the oil; leave it in the colander and set aside.

3. Wipe the pot dry. Add the remaining 2 tablespoons oil and return to medium heat until shimmering. Add the cremini and ¾ teaspoon salt; cook until the mushrooms have released their juices and are brown around the edges, about 10 minutes. Add the onion and cook until softened and beginning to brown, about 8 minutes. Stir in the garlic and thyme; cook until fragrant, about 30 seconds. Add the flour and cook, stirring constantly, until golden, about 1 minute. Slowly whisk in the wine and the dried porcini with their reserved liquid; cook until the liquid is almost evaporated, about 1 minute. Slowly whisk in the broth and cream; bring to a simmer, whisking often. Add the chicken and cook, stirring occasionally, until no longer pink, about 4 minutes. Off the heat, stir in the Asiago and pepper.

4. Add the cooked pasta and broccoli to the sauce; stir to combine. Transfer to a 9 by 13-inch baking dish (or a shallow casserole dish of similar size) and sprinkle with the bread-crumb topping.

Bake until the casserole is bubbling and the crumbs are lightly browned, about 15 minutes. Serve immediately.

➤ VARIATION

Baked Penne with Chicken, Broccoli, Sun-Dried Tomatoes, and Smoked Mozzarella
Follow recipe for Baked Penne with Chicken, Broccoli, and Mushrooms, making the following changes: Omit the dried porcini and cremini mushrooms. Substitute 3 ounces of smoked mozzarella, shredded (about 1 cup), for the Asiago. Stir 1 cup (one 8-ounce jar) of drained, oil-packed, sun-dried tomatoes, rinsed, patted dry, and cut into thin strips, into the sauce with the Asiago in step 3.

PENNE WITH SUMMER SQUASH

THE TRADITIONAL PAIRING OF PASTA AND the squash of summer (whether zucchini or summer squash) holds the promise of being a lovely, light, and summery casserole. The tricks are preventing the squash from turning mushy, and making a sauce flavorful enough to bind the dish together without dominating or masking the delicate flavors of the vegetables.

First, we decided to tackle the squash. An Italian method of dealing with summer squash involves submerging them whole in either boiling or room-temperature water. This somewhat obscure technique didn't work, but, rather, rendered the squash watery, for lack of a better word. Similarly, boiling and steaming cut-up pieces of the squash resulted in flavorless, sodden pieces of squash. Wondering if peeling the squash would have any effect, we found that it merely turned the consistency so mushy that tasters called it "baby food." Last we tried sautéing slices of squash. While this approached seemed promising at the start, it took only a few minutes before the squash began to get soggy.

The problem was clear enough: Both zucchini and summer squash are about 95 percent water—

more watery than most other vegetables. Leaving the skin on, we had noticed, helped to keep the pieces intact. And we had given up on any water-based cooking method (boiling or steaming); adding moisture to this dish was like bringing coal to Newcastle. Some sort of intense heat, then, preferably dry, seemed logical. On philosophical grounds, however, we rejected grilling and oven roasting because both methods seemed like too much trouble for such a simple summer casserole. We wondered if there was a way to extract some of the water before sautéing and return to what would certainly be an easier method for dealing with the squash. Drawing inspiration from another temperamental and watery vegetable—eggplant—we wondered if salting the squash before cooking would help. So we salted a pound

of sliced squash and let it sit in a colander for 30 minutes, noting that the squash had released almost 3 tablespoons of liquid—a promising sign. We then blotted the squash dry with paper towels and gave it a sauté. Bingo: brown, crisp-edged squash came out of the pan.

Trying this salting and sautéing method a few more times, we made several additional observations. First, we found that the larger grains of kosher salt work best for salting the squash because the residual grains can be easily wiped away. Second, the ratio of squash to pasta that tasters preferred (and that filled a 9 by 13-inch dish correctly) was 2 pounds of squash to ¾ pound of dried pasta. Third, we found it necessary to brown the 2 pounds of squash in two batches to ensure proper browning.

EQUIPMENT: Herb Choppers

There are many herb choppers and mincers on the market, some of which fetch upward of $50. Wondering whether they were all useless gadgets or valuable tools worth clearing room for in a kitchen drawer, we put eight of them to the test.

There are three main types of herb choppers: mills, rolling mincers, and curved rocking blades called mezzalunas. We tested several brands of each type, along with an oddball rip-cord design, using basil, parsley, rosemary, and garlic. Herb mills have a hopper into which you put the herbs, then a series of small blades chops them as you turn a hand crank. At best, they were able to shred leafy herbs and produce shards of garlic. More often than not, however, they choked and the offending herb had to be carefully extracted from the hopper. Herb rollers depend on a row of pizza-wheel-like blades that is pushed back and forth over the item that is to be minced. Although we found these rollers to be comfortable and easy to use, they crushed and bruised parsley and basil leaves into a slimy green mush in about 30 seconds. The newfangled, rip-cord herb chopper consisted of a round plastic case with a rip cord inside that, when pulled and released, turned a blade. It tore up everything we gave it into large, rough, unevenly sized pieces, and we noted that additional tugs on the rip cord did little to even out the mince. A beat-up clove of garlic looked much the same after 75 pulls as it did after 25.

The only worthwhile alternative to a chef's knife was the mezzaluna, a cutting tool named for its half-moon shape that

has been in use for hundreds of years. We tried three styles: one with a single blade and a single handle meant to be used in a wooden bowl, one with a single blade and two handles, and one with two blades and two handles. The first of these minced well but was a bit awkward to use as well as labor-intensive. The latter pair, each with a handle on either end, let us get a rocking motion going that cut through herbs—especially tough, woody rosemary—cleanly and quickly. The double-bladed mezzaluna was faster (usually 30 to 60 seconds faster than the single blade when producing ¼ cup of minced herbs), but it was tough on the basil, bruising it badly. Neither mezzaluna could mince garlic as perfectly as a garlic press. If your knife skills aren't quite what you'd like them to be, try a single-bladed, two-handled mezzaluna. It's not only effective, it's fun. And purchase one with a 7-inch blade rather than a 6-inch blade. The 7-inch really rocks.

THE BEST HERB CHOPPER
This Henckels 7-inch single-blade mezzaluna is a worthwhile investment if your knife skills are weak.

With the squash figured out, we turned our attention to the sauce, which is the main vehicle for flavor in this casserole. Our goal was to make a sauce that was flavorful and summery without tasting either too lean or too fatty. First, we tried making a sauce with chicken broth thickened lightly with flour. Tasting like a wimpy gravy, this sauce needed help, and we found it necessary to replace some of the broth with heavy cream in order to turn it into a proper sauce. Flavored with garlic, shallots, and a little Parmesan, the sauce just needed the added touch of lots of fresh basil and parsley. Tossing this light, creamy, basil-infused sauce with the penne and sautéed squash, we rounded out the casserole by adding a few cherry tomatoes and a bread-crumb topping. Because most of the components are cooked, it only takes 10 to 15 minutes in the oven for the crumb topping to brown and flavors to meld.

Baked Penne with Summer Squash, Tomatoes, and Basil

SERVES 6 TO 8

A combination of zucchini and summer squash makes for a nice mix of color, but either may be used exclusively if desired. Kosher salt works best for salting the squash because residual grains can be easily wiped away. For a vegetarian version, simply replace the chicken broth with vegetable broth.

PLANNING AHEAD: Follow the recipe through step 5, but do not prepare the basil and parsley or add them to the sauce. Refrigerate the topping, cooked pasta, sautéed squash, and sauce in separate bowls, tightly wrapped with plastic wrap, for up to 1 day.

TO BAKE: Adjust an oven rack to the middle position and heat the oven to 400 degrees. Place the pasta in a colander and rinse briefly under hot tap water to warm it. Poke several vent holes in the plastic wrap covering the sauce, and microwave on high power until hot, 3 to 5 minutes. Add the freshly chopped basil and parsley to the sauce and season with salt and pepper to taste. Continue to assemble and bake the casserole as directed in step 6, extending the cooking time to 30 minutes.

BIGGER IS NOT ALWAYS BETTER

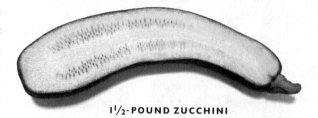

1½-POUND ZUCCHINI

2-OUNCE ZUCCHINI

After cooking more than 40 pounds of squash, we learned that smaller squash are the best choice for pasta sauce. Gardeners may take pride in larger specimens, but we found the flesh in the middle to be soft and spongy as well as loaded with seeds. We prefer squash that weigh 8 ounces or less. If you must use slightly larger squash, quarter them lengthwise and then cut the quarters into the ideal ½-inch-wide pieces.

TOPPING

4	slices white sandwich bread, torn into quarters
2	tablespoons unsalted butter, melted

FILLING

1	pound zucchini, halved lengthwise, sliced ½ inch thick
1	pound yellow summer squash, halved lengthwise, sliced ½ inch thick
	Kosher salt
³/₄	pound penne
4	tablespoons olive oil
6	medium shallots, minced (about 1 cup)
4	medium garlic cloves, minced or pressed through a garlic press
¹/₄	cup all-purpose flour
2¹/₂	cups low-sodium chicken broth
1¹/₂	cups heavy cream
2	ounces Parmesan cheese, grated (about 1 cup)
³/₄	cup chopped fresh basil leaves
¹/₄	cup chopped fresh parsley leaves
	Ground black pepper
1	pint cherry tomatoes, quartered

1. FOR THE TOPPING: Process the bread and butter in a food processor fitted with the steel blade until coarsely ground, about six 1-second pulses; set aside.

2. FOR THE FILLING: Adjust an oven rack to the middle position and heat the oven to 400 degrees. Toss the zucchini and summer squash with 2 tablespoons kosher salt and place in a large colander set inside a large bowl to drain, about 30 minutes.

3. Bring 4 quarts of water to boil in a Dutch oven over high heat. Stir in 2 tablespoons kosher salt and the pasta; cook, stirring occasionally, until al dente. Drain the pasta, return it to the pot, and toss with 1 tablespoon of the oil; set aside.

4. Spread the salted squash evenly over a double layer of paper towels and pat dry with additional paper towels, wiping off any residual salt. Heat 1 more tablespoon oil in a 12-inch nonstick skillet over high heat until smoking. Add half of the squash and cook, stirring occasionally, until golden brown and slightly charred, 5 to 7 minutes. Transfer the squash to a baking sheet. Add 1 more tablespoon oil to the pan and return to high heat until smoking; brown the remaining squash and transfer to the baking sheet.

5. Wipe the skillet clean with a wad of paper towels. Add the remaining tablespoon oil and return to medium-high heat until shimmering. Add the shallots and cook until softened, about 3 minutes. Add the garlic and cook until fragrant, about 30 seconds. Add the flour and cook, stirring constantly, until golden, about 1 minute. Slowly whisk in the broth and cream; bring to a simmer and cook, whisking often, until lightly thickened, about 1 minute. Off the heat, stir in the Parmesan, basil, and parsley. Season to taste with salt and pepper.

6. Add the sauce, tomatoes, and sautéed squash to the pasta; stir gently to combine. Pour the pasta into a 9 by 13-inch baking dish (or a shallow casserole dish of similar size) and sprinkle with the bread-crumb topping. Bake until the casserole is bubbling and the crumbs are lightly browned, about 15 minutes. Serve immediately.

BAKED TORTELLINI WITH PEAS AND BACON

IN THE WORLD OF BAKED PASTA, WHERE hearty, traditional dishes such as lasagna dominate, baked tortellini offers a refreshing and elegant change of pace. When done right, the result is a modern take on the classic baked pasta, with flavors that are more stylish and clean. Almost too chic to be called a casserole, this dish matches the delicate flavor of tortellini with an equally sophisticated sauce and appropriate vegetables.

We found a wide variety of tortellini sold at the supermarket (dried, frozen, and fresh) and began by tasting them side by side. The dried versions, usually found in the spaghetti aisle, were utterly unimpressive, with a stale and lifeless flavor. The frozen tortellini tasted a bit better and were more moist, but even they couldn't hold a candle to the clean flavor and fine texture of the fresh tortellini (found in the refrigerator case). Although the instructions for cooking fresh tortellini say to boil them for just a few minutes, we found it necessary (regardless of brand) to boil them for at least 10 minutes to ensure that all the folds of pasta were thoroughly cooked and tender. Unlike the unfilled pastas used in other pasta casseroles, tortellini don't continue cooking in the oven, so we found that they should be fully cooked on top of the stove.

Moving on to the sauce, we found that a combination of chicken broth and heavy cream produced a respectable flavor that was neither too rich nor too lean. Thickening the sauce with a little flour was necessary to give it the ability to coat the tortellini and vegetables. Flavoring the sauce with shallots, garlic, fresh thyme, and Parmesan gave it a robust flavor, but we were still not satisfied. Starting the sauce off by sautéing a little bacon gave it some necessary oomph, but it wasn't until we added white wine that we knew we were getting somewhere. The wine added a mildly acidic note that helped to cut through the bacon and cream without obscuring their flavors, and gave this sauce its elegance.

With the tortellini and sauce figured out, we still needed to round out the casserole with some vegetables. Wanting to add some interesting flavors yet keep the prep work and cooking to a minimum, we settled on a combination of frozen sweet peas tempered by the slightly bitter taste of radicchio. Neither ingredient requires cooking before being added to the pasta, so they can simply be mixed with the tortellini and the sauce before going into the oven. Topped with a sprinkling of buttery bread crumbs and walnuts, this tortellini casserole is a welcome addition to anyone's baked-pasta repertoire.

Baked Tortellini with Peas, Radicchio, and Bacon

SERVES 6 TO 8

For the best flavor and texture, be sure to buy fresh tortellini sold in the refrigerator case at the supermarket. Avoid buying tortellini that is either frozen or dried.

PLANNING AHEAD: Follow the recipe through step 3, but do not prepare the radicchio. Refrigerate the topping, cooked tortellini, and sauce in separate bowls, tightly wrapped with plastic wrap, for up to 1 day.

TO BAKE: Adjust an oven rack to the lower-middle position and heat the oven to 400 degrees. Place the tortellini in a colander and rinse under hot tap water to warm them. Poke several vent holes in the plastic wrap covering the sauce, and microwave on high power until hot, 3 to 5 minutes. Season the sauce again with salt and pepper to taste. Continue to assemble and bake the casserole as directed in step 4, extending the cooking time to about 30 minutes.

TOPPING

1/2	cup walnuts
4	slices white sandwich bread, torn into quarters
2	tablespoons unsalted butter, melted

FILLING

	Salt
2	pounds fresh cheese tortellini
1	tablespoon olive oil
4	ounces (about 4 slices) bacon, minced
6	medium shallots, minced (about 1 cup)
6	medium garlic cloves, minced or pressed through a garlic press
2	teaspoon minced fresh thyme leaves
4	tablespoons all-purpose flour
1	cup white wine
2	cups low-sodium chicken broth
1	cup heavy cream
2	ounces Parmesan cheese, grated (about 1 cup)
	Ground black pepper
1	large head radicchio (about 9 ounces), cored and chopped medium
1	cup frozen peas

1. FOR THE TOPPING: Process the walnuts in a food processor fitted with the steel blade until they resemble coarse crumbs, about 5 seconds. Add the bread and butter and process to a uniformly coarse crumb, about six 1-second pulses; set aside.

2. Adjust an oven rack to the middle position and heat the oven to 400 degrees. Bring 6 quarts of water to a boil in a Dutch oven over high heat. Stir in 1 tablespoon salt and the tortellini; cook, stirring occasionally, until fully tender, 10 to 12 minutes. Drain the tortellini and return them to the pot. Toss the tortellini with the oil and set aside.

3. FOR THE FILLING: Meanwhile, cook the bacon in a 12-inch nonstick skillet over medium heat, stirring occasionally, until brown and crisp, about 5 minutes. Add the shallots and cook, stirring occasionally, until softened, about 5 minutes. Add the garlic and thyme; cook until fragrant, about 30 seconds. Add the flour and cook, stirring constantly, until golden, about 1 minute. Slowly whisk in the wine and cook until almost evaporated, about 1 minute. Slowly whisk in the broth and cream; bring to a simmer, whisking often. Off the heat, stir in the Parmesan. Season with salt and pepper to taste.

4. Add the sauce, radicchio, and peas to the tortellini; toss gently to combine. Pour into a 9 by 13-inch baking dish (or a shallow casserole dish of similar size) and sprinkle with the bread-crumb topping. Bake until the topping is browned and crisp, about 15 minutes. Serve immediately.

BAKED RAVIOLI

IN OUR RESEARCH FOR THIS CHAPTER, WE encountered just about every sort of pasta casserole imaginable, including recipes for baked ravioli, which we first rejected out of hand since most were just a combination of jarred sauce, frozen ravioli, and shredded cheese. After some debate in the test kitchen, we decided to forge ahead and see if we could concoct a worthy casserole using store-bought ravioli as our starting point. What we wanted was a substantial and comforting dish that had the heft and cheesiness of lasagna but could be put together in a flash. Right off the bat, we knew we wanted to use ricotta ravioli, which we thought would add that same lasagna-like complexity of noodle and cheese without any of the layering.

So our first question was how to build the sauce. We guessed that we'd need 2 pounds of ravioli to fill a standard 9 by 13-inch baking dish, and so we wanted a meaty tomato sauce that would accommodate this quantity and that could be put together quickly, without a long simmering time on the stovetop. Using our simple meat lasagna sauce as a jumping-off point, we tried, for the sake of convenience, replacing the meatloaf mix with Italian sausage removed from its casing. This worked perfectly and we found that both hot and sweet varieties of sausage were equally good. Following our lasagna recipe, we added one 28-ounce can each of pureed and diced tomatoes but found that this created more sauce than we needed for the ravioli, so we settled on one 28-ounce can of pureed tomatoes and a 14.5-ounce can of diced tomatoes.

Looking for the best ravioli, we tried several brands of both frozen and fresh ravioli (the kind sold in the refrigerator case of most supermarkets). Somewhat surprisingly, tasters found that the fresh ravioli tasted too delicate in this application. The hearty, dense texture of frozen ravioli not only worked perfectly when baked, but these ravioli are commonly sold in 2-pound bags to boot. One thing we learned when experimenting with the frozen ravioli was not to follow the cooking instructions printed on the bags, which specify cooking the ravioli for only a couple of minutes; these ravioli turned out tough and starchy. We found that it was better to boil the ravioli for about 10 minutes to rid them of any excess starch and ensure that all corners of every ravioli were thoroughly cooked.

To assemble this casserole, we simply tossed the cooked ravioli with the sauce and poured it into the casserole. We found that sprinkling Parmesan and mozzarella in between the layers was a waste of time; the casserole simply isn't in the oven long enough for the cheeses to melt. Sprinkling both cheeses over the top, however, produced a tasty and attractively browned crust. With minimal preparation and a total cooking time of roughly 25 minutes, this zippy dish is a great, eleventh-hour alternative to lasagna.

Baked Ravioli

SERVES 6 TO 8

For the best texture, do not thaw the frozen ravioli before cooking and be sure to boil the ravioli thoroughly (about 10 minutes).

PLANNING AHEAD: Since frozen ravioli should not be cooked and then chilled and reheated, the only portion of this dish that can be made ahead is the tomato sauce in step 2, which can be cooled and refrigerated for up to 2 days in advance. Reheat the sauce in the microwave on high power until hot, about 3 to 5 minutes, before tossing it with the cooked ravioli and assembling the casserole in step 3.

	Salt
2	pounds frozen cheese ravioli
2	tablespoons olive oil
I	medium onion, minced
I	pound hot or sweet Italian sausage, removed from its casing
6	medium garlic cloves, minced or pressed through a garlic press
1/2	teaspoon red pepper flakes
1/4	teaspoon dried oregano
I	(28-ounce) can tomato puree
I	(14.5-ounce) can diced tomatoes, drained
4	ounces whole-milk mozzarella cheese, shredded (about 1 1/3 cup)
I	ounce Parmesan cheese, grated (about 1/2 cup)

1. Adjust an oven rack to the middle position and heat the oven to 400 degrees. Bring 6 quarts of water to a boil in a Dutch oven over high heat. Stir in 1 tablespoon salt and the ravioli; cook, stirring occasionally, until completely tender, about 10 minutes. Drain the pasta, return it to the pot, and toss with 1 tablespoon of the oil; set aside.

2. Meanwhile, heat the remaining tablespoon oil in a 12-inch skillet over medium-high heat until shimmering. Add the onion and ½ teaspoon salt; cook, stirring occasionally, until softened, about 5 minutes. Add the sausage and cook, breaking the meat into small pieces with a wooden spoon, until the meat loses its raw color but has not browned, about 5 minutes. Add the garlic, red pepper flakes, and oregano; cook until fragrant, about 30 seconds. Add the tomato puree and diced tomatoes; bring to a simmer and cook, stirring occasionally, until the flavors are blended, about 10 minutes.

3. Add the cooked ravioli to the sauce and stir to combine. Pour the mixture into a 9 by 13-inch baking dish (or a shallow casserole dish of similar size) and press gently into an even layer. Sprinkle the mozzarella and Parmesan evenly over the top. Bake until the sauce is bubbling and browned, about 15 minutes. Serve immediately.

BAKED MANICOTTI AND STUFFED SHELLS

MANICOTTI AND STUFFED SHELLS ARE WELL-known dishes consistently plagued by three problems. The filling, for one, often becomes thin and watery as its bakes, turning the pasta mushy. If the pasta escapes this first malady, it often falls prey to the second, in which the heat of the oven dries it out along the edges. Should the casserole manage to avoid these initial two problems, it almost surely gets nailed by the third: a boring sauce and lackluster filling. Stuffed with plain ricotta and coated with a tired red sauce, it's no wonder that these dishes rarely meet our expectations.

We wanted to figure out not only how to avoid these common cooking problems, but also how to infuse these dreary old classics with new life. We started with the ricotta filling, looking into various ways to make it more creamy and less watery. Testing several brands of ricotta, we found that the unwelcome wateriness is largely a result of the ricotta's quality. The high-quality ricotta found at Italian markets and cheese shops has a creamy, luscious texture that supermarket ricotta just can't simulate. Yet because this good ricotta can be hard to find, we focused our attention on how to get the most out of the supermarket brands. We tried draining, whipping, and pureeing in a food processor; however, none of these methods seemed to make a difference. What did work was adding an egg to help bind the filling as it cooked. We tried adding various amounts of egg to the ricotta, and noted that just one did the job without adding any overbearing eggy flavor.

Moving on to the pasta, which can easily dry out in the oven, we tried playing around with oven temperatures and amounts of tomato sauce, but neither of these factors seemed to make a difference. We discovered that covering the casserole dish tightly with foil, so that the trapped steam would keep the pasta pliable, was the key to this dish. (Because the pasta is essentially "steaming" slightly in the oven, we found it necessary to undercook it slightly, until not quite al dente, before filling it.)

Lastly, we focused on the most crucial problem: lack of flavor. Working with the manicotti first, we decided to leave the boring red and meat sauces behind. We opted to pump up the flavor of the sauce with olives, capers, and anchovy—essentially making a puttanesca sauce. Rounding out the flavor of the ricotta filling with Parmesan, mozzarella, and basil, we created a "manicotti puttanesca" that was a unanimous hit with the tasters (and a far cry from the usual steam-table manicotti).

Taking the shells in hand next, we decided to give them a spring-like filling by mixing mint and peas with the ricotta. We wanted to cover these shells with an ultra-smooth tomato sauce, so we processed canned diced tomatoes with their juice in a food processor, which gave us just the right texture. Seeking to give the sauce a little punch, we then added some vodka (making a classic Italian vodka sauce). The heat and intensity of the vodka mellows as the sauce simmers, but it leaves behind a welcome clean, sharp flavor. Rounded out with some garlic, basil, and a little Parmesan, this dish would never be called boring.

Baked Manicotti Puttanesca

SERVES 4 TO 6

When buying manicotti, examine the package to make sure they aren't broken or cracked.

PLANNING AHEAD: Assemble the casserole as directed, but do not bake. Wrap the dish tightly with plastic wrap and refrigerate for up to 2 days.

TO BAKE: Allow the manicotti to sit at room temperature for about 1 hour. Adjust an oven rack to the middle position and heat the oven to 400 degrees. Remove the plastic wrap and wrap the dish tightly with foil. Bake until the sauce is bubbling and the ricotta filling is hot, 40 to 45 minutes. Cool for 5 minutes. Sprinkle with parsley and Parmesan before serving.

Salt
12 manicotti (about 8 ounces)

FILLING
22 ounces whole-milk or part-skim ricotta cheese (2³/₄ cups)
2 ounces Parmesan cheese, grated (about 1 cup)
3 ounces mozzarella cheese, shredded (about 1 cup)
1 large egg, lightly beaten
¹/₄ cup minced fresh basil leaves
Ground black pepper

SAUCE
2 tablespoons olive oil
4 medium garlic cloves, minced to a paste or pressed through a garlic press (see page 35)
¹/₂ teaspoon red pepper flakes
2 anchovy fillets, rinsed, patted dry, and minced
1 (28-ounce) can diced tomatoes
2 tablespoons capers, rinsed
¹/₂ cup black olives (such as Gaeta, Alfonso, or Kalamata), pitted and chopped coarse
¹/₄ cup minced fresh parsley leaves
1 ounce Parmesan cheese, grated (about ¹/₂ cup)

1. Adjust an oven rack to the middle position and heat the oven to 400 degrees. Bring 4 quarts of water to a boil in a Dutch oven over high heat. Stir in 1 tablespoon salt and the manicotti; cook, stirring occasionally, until almost al dente. Drain the manicotti and spread out over a rimmed baking sheet to cool.

2. FOR THE FILLING: Mix the ricotta, 1 cup of the Parmesan, the mozzarella, egg, basil, ¹/₂ teaspoon salt, and ¹/₄ teaspoon black pepper together in a large bowl. Following the illustration below, squeeze a generous 5 tablespoons of the filling into each manicotti and arrange in a 9 by 13-inch baking dish (or shallow casserole dish of similar size). Cover the filled manicotti loosely with damp paper towels and set aside.

3. FOR THE SAUCE: Heat the oil, garlic, red pepper flakes, and anchovies in a 12-inch skillet over medium heat; cook, stirring frequently, until the garlic is fragrant but not brown, about 2 minutes. Stir in the tomatoes with their juice; bring to a simmer and cook, stirring occasionally, until slightly thickened, about 8 minutes. Off the heat, stir in the capers and olives. Season to taste with salt and pepper.

4. Discard the paper towels covering the manicotti and pour the sauce over the top. Wrap the dish tightly with foil. Bake until the sauce is bubbling around the edges and the ricotta filling is hot, 20 to 30 minutes. Cool for 5 minutes. Sprinkle with the parsley and the remaining ¹/₂ cup Parmesan before serving.

FILLING MANICOTTI

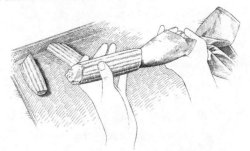

After filling a zipper-lock bag with the ricotta filling, cut a corner of the bag and gently squeeze about 5 tablespoons of the filling into each of the cooked manicotti. Carefully place the manicotti in the baking dish.

Stuffed Shells with Vodka-Tomato Cream Sauce

SERVES 6 TO 8

Some of the shells will inevitably tear as they boil; however, there are usually more than enough shells in a 12-ounce box to accommodate this recipe.

PLANNING AHEAD: Assemble the casserole as directed, but do not bake. Wrap the dish tightly with plastic wrap and refrigerate for up to 2 days.

TO BAKE: Allow the shells to sit at room temperature for about 1 hour. Adjust an oven rack to the middle position and heat the oven to 400 degrees. Remove the plastic wrap and wrap the dish tightly with foil. Bake until the sauce is bubbling and the ricotta filling is hot, 40 to 45 minutes. Cool for 5 minutes. Sprinkle with the basil and Parmesan before serving.

	Salt
1	(12-ounce) box jumbo pasta shells

FILLING

16	ounces whole-milk or part-skim ricotta cheese (about 2 cups)
1½	ounces mozzarella, shredded (about ½ cup)
1	cup frozen peas
2	tablespoons minced fresh mint leaves
1	large egg, lightly beaten
1	medium garlic clove, minced to a paste or pressed through a garlic press (see page 35)
	Ground black pepper

SAUCE

2	(14.5-ounce) cans diced tomatoes
1	tablespoon olive oil
2	medium garlic cloves, minced or pressed through a garlic press
¼	teaspoon red pepper flakes
½	cup vodka
1	cup heavy cream
¼	teaspoon sugar
¼	cup minced fresh basil leaves
½	ounce Parmesan cheese, grated (about ¼ cup)

1. Adjust an oven rack to the middle position and heat the oven to 400 degrees. Bring 4 quarts of water to boil in a Dutch oven over high heat. Stir in 1 tablespoon salt and the shells; cook, stirring occasionally, until almost al dente. Drain the shells and spread out on a rimmed baking sheet to cool. Using a dinner fork, pry apart any shells that have clung together, discarding any that are badly torn (you should have 30 to 33 good shells).

2. FOR THE FILLING: Mix the ricotta, mozzarella, peas, mint, egg, garlic, ¾ teaspoon salt, and ¼ teaspoon pepper together in a large bowl. Following the illustration below, spoon a tablespoon of the filling into each shell and arrange them, seam-side down, into a 9 by 13-inch baking dish (or a shallow casserole dish of similar size). Cover the filled shells loosely with damp paper towels and set aside.

3. FOR THE SAUCE: Puree the canned tomatoes with their juice in a food processor fitted with the steel blade (or in a blender) until smooth, about 1 minute. Heat the oil and garlic in a 12-inch nonstick skillet over medium heat until fragrant but not browned, about 2 minutes. Add the pureed tomatoes, red pepper flakes, vodka, cream, and sugar; bring to a simmer and cook, stirring often, until the flavors have melded and the sauce has thickened, 10 to 12 minutes. Off the heat, season with salt and pepper to taste.

4. Discard the paper towels covering the filled shells and pour the tomato sauce over the top. Tilt the dish to distribute the sauce evenly and make sure each shell is covered with sauce (spoon sauce

STUFFING SHELLS

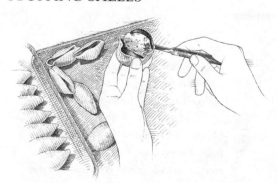

While holding the shell open with one hand, spoon about 1 tablespoon of the ricotta filling into the shell, then arrange seam-side down in the baking dish.

over each shell if necessary). Cover with foil and bake until the sauce is bubbling around the edges and the ricotta filling is hot, about 30 minutes. Cool for 5 minutes. Sprinkle with the basil and Parmesan before serving.

MINCING GARLIC TO A PASTE

1. Mince the garlic as you normally would on a cutting board. Sprinkle the minced garlic with salt.

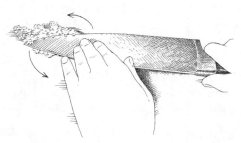

2. Drag the side of a chef's knife over the garlic and salt mixture to form a fine puree. Continue to mince the garlic and drag the knife until the puree is smooth.

EASY MEAT LASAGNA

MOST FAMILIES HAVE HOMEMADE LASAGNA once, maybe twice a year, on holidays (especially if they are Italian) or birthdays. Lasagna is not enjoyed more frequently because it takes the better part of a day to boil the noodles, slow-cook the sauce, prepare and layer the ingredients, and then finally bake it. Although this traditional method does produce a superior dish, we were interested in an Americanized version, one that could be made in two hours or less from start to finish. We would have to sacrifice some of the rich flavors of a traditional recipe, but we were hoping to produce

a lasagna good enough for a family gathering. A bland, watery casserole just wouldn't do.

We knew from the start that to expedite the lasagna-making process we would have to use no-boil lasagna noodles (see page 36). For those unfamiliar or wary of them, relax. After a few initial tests, we discovered that the secret of no-boil noodles is to leave your tomato sauce a little on the watery side. The noodles can then absorb liquid without drying out the dish overall. With this in mind, we got to work on the other components of the lasagna.

Italian cooks build the sauce from the meaty browned bits left in the pan from the meatballs and Italian sausages they cook and later layer into the lasagna. By combining top-quality tomato products with a four-hour simmer, they make a rich, thick, and complex-tasting sauce. We were after the same depth of flavor, but, as time was of the essence, meatballs and a slow simmer were out of the question. We began by concentrating on different kinds of ground meat.

Working with a base of sautéed aromatics (onions and garlic), an all-beef sauce turned out to be one-dimensional and dull. Adding ground pork was an improvement and certainly more interesting. Although the combination of beef and sweet Italian sausage (removed from its casing and browned with the beef) was even better, tasters were still left wanting. Finally, we turned to meatloaf mix, a combination of equal parts ground beef, pork, and veal sold in one package at most supermarkets. The flavor of the sauce this trio produced was robust and sweet. The texture wasn't right, though; it was still too loose and taco-like. We wanted something richer, creamier, and more cohesive, so our thoughts turned to Bolognese, the classic three-hour meat sauce enriched with dairy. Borrowing the notion of combining meat and dairy, we reduced a quarter cup of cream with the meat before adding the tomatoes. The ground meat soaked up the sweet cream, and the final product was rich and decadent. Even better, at this point we had been at the stove for only 12 minutes.

Because no-boil noodles rely primarily on the liquid in the sauce to rehydrate and soften, we had to get the moisture content just right. If the sauce was too thick, the noodles would be dry and crunchy; too loose and they would turn flaccid, limp, and lifeless. We started building the sauce with two 28-ounce cans of pureed tomatoes, but tasters found that this sauce was too heavy for the lasagna and overwhelmed the other flavors. Two 28-ounce cans of diced tomatoes yielded too thin a sauce. We settled on one 28-ounce can of each. The combination of pureed and diced tomatoes yielded a luxurious sauce, with soft but substantial chunks of tomatoes. We added the tomatoes to the meat mixture, warmed it through (no reduction necessary), and in just 15 minutes on the stove the meat sauce was rich, creamy, ultra-meaty, and ready to go.

Most Americans like their lasagna to be cheesy. It was a given that we would sprinkle each layer with mozzarella cheese—the classic lasagna cheese—and after a test of whole-milk cheese versus part-skim we found that whole-milk mozzarella was the best for the job. It had a more intense flavor than its part-skim counterpart and nicer melting qualities, which are crucial to this dish. We also tested shredded, bagged mozzarella, but because it has a very low moisture content, it melted oddly and was somewhat dry, not to mention unappetizing. Shredding a 1-pound block of whole-milk mozzarella on a box grater or in a food processor is the ticket.

Ricotta was the next cheese up for scrutiny. As it turned out, it made little difference whether we used whole-milk or part-skim ricotta. They were both characteristically creamy and rich, and tasters gave them both a thumbs-up. For added sharpness, we tested the ricotta mixed with Parmesan and Pecorino Romano cheeses. Tasters unanimously rejected the Pecorino for giving the lasagna a "sheepy" and "gamey" flavor. Grated Parmesan added a nice little kick to the mild, milky ricotta. An egg helped to thicken and bind this mixture, and some chopped basil added flavor and freshness. Tucked neatly between the layers of lasagna, this ricotta mixture was just what we wanted.

With all the components of the lasagna decided,

INGREDIENTS: No-Boil Noodles

Over the past few years, no-boil (also called oven-ready) lasagna noodles have become a permanent fixture on supermarket shelves. Much like instant rice, no-boil noodles are precooked at the factory. The extruded noodles are run through a water bath and then dehydrated mechanically. During baking, the moisture from the sauce softens, or rehydrates, the noodles, especially when the pan is covered as the lasagna bakes. Most no-boil noodles are rippled, and the accordion-like pleats relax as the pasta rehydrates in the oven, allowing the noodles to elongate.

No-boil lasagna noodles come in two shapes. The most common is a rectangle measuring 7 inches long and 3½ inches wide. Three such noodles make a single layer in a conventional 9 by 13-inch lasagna pan when they swell in the oven. In local markets, we found three brands of this type of no-boil lasagna noodle: Ronzoni (made by New World Pasta, which sells the same product under the American Beauty, Skinner, and San Giorgio labels in certain parts of the country); and Barilla (imported from Italy). Italian noodles made by Delverde came in 7-inch squares.

We made lasagnas with all four noodles to see how they would compare.

Ronzoni and DeFino are both thin and rippled, and although tasters preferred the Ronzoni for their flavor. Barilla noodles tasted great but their texture was sub-par. Two squares of Delverde noodles butted very closely together fit into a 9 by 13-inch pan, but, when baked, the noodles expanded and the edges jumped out of the pan and became unpleasantly dry and tough. The only way to avoid this is to soak these noodles in hot water until tender. You can then cut them with scissors to fit the measurements of the pan. These noodles were no timesaver.

THE BEST NO-BOIL NOODLES

RONZONI OVEN READY LASAGNE
With its "lightly eggy" and "wheaty" flavor and "tender," "perfectly al dente" texture, Ronzoni ($1.79 for 8 ounces) was the tasters' favorite.

it was time to concentrate on the layering procedure. Smearing the entire bottom of a 9 by 13-inch glass dish with some of the sauce was the starting point. Next came the first layer of no-boil noodles, which we topped with ricotta, then mozzarella, and, finally, more meat sauce. We built two more layers using this same process. For the fourth and final layer, we covered the pasta with the remaining meat sauce and the remaining mozzarella and then sprinkled the top with grated Parmesan.

In our tests, we found that covering the lasagna with foil from the outset of baking prevented a loss of moisture and helped soften the noodles properly. Removing the foil for the last 25 minutes of baking ensured that the top layer of cheese turned golden brown. An oven temperature of 375 degrees proved ideal. By the time the top was browned, the noodles had softened.

We found that lasagna made with no-boil noodles takes a little longer in the oven than conventional lasagna. The real time saved is in the preparation. Start to finish, the meat and tomato lasagna took about an hour and a half to make: 40 minutes prep time, 40 minutes in the oven, and 10 minutes to rest. Measuring the final product against an authentic Italian lasagna may not be entirely fair, but having the time to make it on a weeknight, or whenever the craving strikes, is satisfying beyond compare.

MAKING SMALLER BATCHES

For single-serve portions, make lasagna in mini-loaf pans. Pans that measure 5¾ by 3 inches are the perfect size for most standard lasagna noodles, which will fit perfectly if cut in half after cooking. The individual loaf pans can be wrapped, frozen, and baked one at a time as needed.

Easy Meat Lasagna with Hearty Tomato-Meat Sauce

SERVES 6 TO 8

If you can't find meatloaf mixture for the sauce, or if you choose not to eat veal, substitute ½ pound ground beef and ½ pound sweet Italian sausage, casing removed, for the meatloaf mixture.

PLANNING AHEAD: Assemble the casserole as directed in step 4, but do not bake. Wrap the dish tightly with plastic wrap and refrigerate for up to 3 days or freeze, tightly wrapped with an additional layer of foil, for up to 2 months. (If frozen, thaw in the refrigerator for at least 24 hours.)

TO BAKE: Allow the lasagna to sit at room temperature for about 1 hour. Adjust an oven rack to the middle position and heat the oven to 375 degrees. Remove the plastic wrap and wrap the dish tightly with foil that has been sprayed with nonstick cooking spray. Bake for 25 minutes, then remove the foil. Return the lasagna to the oven and continue to bake until the cheese is spotty brown and the sauce is bubbling, about 25 minutes longer. Cool for 10 minutes before serving.

TOMATO-MEAT SAUCE

1	tablespoon olive oil
1	medium onion, chopped fine
6	medium garlic cloves, minced or pressed through a garlic press
1	pound meatloaf mix or ⅓ pound each ground beef chuck, ground veal, and ground pork
½	teaspoon salt
½	teaspoon ground black pepper
¼	cup heavy cream
1	(28-ounce) can tomato puree
1	(28-ounce) can diced tomatoes, drained

RICOTTA, MOZZARELLA, AND PASTA LAYERS

15	ounces whole-milk or part-skim ricotta cheese (about 2 cups)
2½	ounces Parmesan cheese, grated (about 1¼ cups)
½	cup chopped fresh basil leaves
1	large egg, lightly beaten
½	teaspoon salt
½	teaspoon ground black pepper

12   no-boil lasagna noodles from one 8 or 9-ounce
      package (see page 36 for more information on
      no-boil noodles)
 1   pound whole-milk mozzarella cheese,
      shredded (about 5⅓ cups)

1. Adjust an oven rack to the middle position and heat the oven to 375 degrees.

2. FOR THE SAUCE: Heat the oil in a Dutch oven over medium heat until shimmering. Add the onion and cook, stirring occasionally, until softened but not browned, about 2 minutes. Add the garlic and cook until fragrant, about 30 seconds. Add the ground meats, salt, and pepper; cook, breaking the meat into small pieces with a wooden spoon, until the meat loses its raw color but has not browned, about 4 minutes. Add the cream; bring to a simmer and cook, stirring occasionally, until the liquid evaporates and only the fat remains, about 4 minutes. Add the tomato puree and drained diced tomatoes; bring to a slow simmer and cook until the flavors are blended, about 3 minutes; set the sauce aside.

3. FOR THE LAYERS: Mix the ricotta, 1 cup of the Parmesan, the basil, egg, salt, and pepper together in a medium bowl until well combined and creamy; set aside.

4. Smear the entire bottom of a 9 by 13-inch baking dish (or a shallow casserole dish of similar size) with ¼ cup of the meat sauce (avoiding large chunks of meat). Place 3 of the noodles in the baking dish to create the first layer. Drop 3 tablespoons of the ricotta mixture down the center of each noodle and level the domed mounds by pressing with the back of a measuring spoon. Sprinkle evenly with 1⅓ cups of the mozzarella. Spoon 1½ cups of the meat sauce evenly over the cheese. Repeat the layering of the noodles, ricotta, mozzarella, and sauce two more times. Place the 3 remaining noodles on top of the sauce, then spread the remaining sauce over the noodles, sprinkle with the remaining 1⅓ cups mozzarella, and then with the remaining ¼ cup Parmesan.

5. Lightly spray a large sheet of foil with nonstick cooking spray and cover the lasagna. Bake for 15 minutes, then remove the foil. Return the lasagna to the oven and continue to bake until the cheese is spotty brown and the sauce is bubbling, about 25 minutes longer. Cool for 10 minutes before serving.

VEGETABLE LASAGNA

VEGETABLE LASAGNA SOUNDS WONDERful, but the reality is usually quite disappointing. Too often, the dish is bland and watery, nothing like the rich, hearty version made with meat. But Italians certainly make vegetable lasagna and this dish has great appeal for Americans, especially since lasagna is typically served as an "entertaining dish" and more and more cooks need to satisfy guests who don't eat meat. We knew it was possible to make a great vegetable lasagna, but we wondered if we could make one that was fairly quick.

No-boil lasagna noodles are now standard items in most supermarkets and we are big fans of them. Some recipes we ran across in our research suggest soaking these noodles in either cold or hot tap water before layering them with the sauce and cheese. We found that this step made the pasta too soft after baking. After more experimentation, we found that the key to working with them was first to make sure that the sauce was fairly watery (so the noodles had enough liquid to absorb) and second, to cover the pan for part of the baking time to ensure that the sauce didn't dry out and the noodles remained tender. A standard box of noboil noodles contains 12 noodles, which assemble easily into a four-layer lasagna in a 9 by 13-inch casserole dish.

We knew from past experience that precooking the vegetables not only drives off excess liquid but gives us a chance to boost their flavor, either by caramelizing their natural sugars or by adding ingredients such as olive oil, garlic, red pepper flakes, or herbs. The moisture content of the vegetable determines which cooking technique should be used. For example, mushrooms, because of their high moisture content, are best sautéed or roasted. Almost any vegetable can be cooked and assembled into a lasagna, and we found that the flavor of two vegetables is much more interesting than just one. And to keep prep time to a minimum, it helps if both vegetables are cooked in the same manner.

Basing our master recipe (and the bulk of our testing) on a classic combination of mushrooms and spinach, we noted that 3 cups of cooked vegetables sprinkled between the layers of noodles offered plenty of flavor. All too often, vegetable lasagnas are filled to the rim with a hodge-podge of castoffs from the crisper drawer. The resulting lasagna will not only have a schizophrenic flavor but also a messy texture, because when too many vegetables are used, they have trouble binding together physically and the lasagna has to be slopped onto a plate with a spoon. We chose our favorite vegetable combinations here for the master recipe and a variation; however, this recipe is very versatile and you can easily substitute 3 cups of any cooked vegetables you prefer.

During our testing, we discovered that ricotta cheese simply doesn't belong in this lasagna. It turns an unattractive, dirty color as it is spread in between the layers with the precooked vegetables, and its wet, creamy texture tastes completely out of place. Rather, tasters preferred vegetable lasagnas that were bound together with lots of shredded mozzarella. To help give the somewhat bland mozzarella some flavor, we found it necessary to also sprinkle a good dose of grated Parmesan in between the layers.

Covering the lasagna with foil is necessary to keep the noodles from drying out; however, it does present a couple of problems. First, the foil tends to stick to the top layer of cheese. Spraying the foil with nonstick cooking spray is an easy solution. The other issue is browning the top layer of cheese. When you bake a conventional lasagna uncovered in the oven, the top layer of cheese becomes golden and chewy in spots. We found that by removing the foil during the last 15 minutes of baking, we were able to achieve the color and texture we wanted.

Spinach and Mushroom Lasagna with Tomato Sauce

SERVES 6 TO 8

Cremini mushrooms are particularly good in this dish, but any fresh mushroom is fine. Smoked mozzarella, Gruyère, or fontina can be substituted for the mozzarella and Pecorino Romano for the Parmesan. Also, 3½ cups of your favorite prepared tomato sauce can be substituted for the sauce in this recipe. Feel free to substitute 3 cups of your favorite cooked vegetables (roasted, steamed, sautéed, grilled, or broiled) for the mushrooms and spinach.

PLANNING AHEAD: Assemble the lasagna as directed in step 4, but do not bake. Wrap the dish tightly with plastic wrap and refrigerate for up to 1 day or freeze, tightly wrapped with an additional layer of foil, for up to 1 month. (If frozen, thaw in the refrigerator for at least 24 hours.)

TO BAKE: Allow the lasagna to sit at room temperature for about 1 hour. Adjust an oven rack to the middle position and heat the oven to 375 degrees. Remove the plastic wrap and wrap the dish tightly with foil that has been sprayed with nonstick cooking spray. Bake for 25 minutes, then remove the foil. Return the lasagna to the oven and continue to bake until the cheese is spotty brown and the sauce is bubbling, about 15 minutes longer. Cool for 10 minutes before serving.

5	tablespoons olive oil
1	(10-ounce) bag curly-leaf spinach, washed, stemmed, and chopped
	Salt and ground black pepper
1	medium onion, minced
1	pound cremini or white button mushrooms, stems trimmed, brushed clean, and sliced thin
2	medium garlic cloves, minced or pressed through a garlic press
1	(28-ounce) can crushed tomatoes
2	tablespoons chopped fresh basil leaves
12	no-boil lasagna noodles from one 8 or 9-ounce package (see page 36)
1	pound mozzarella cheese, shredded (about 5⅓ cups)
3	ounces Parmesan cheese, grated (about 1½ cups)

1. Heat 1 tablespoon of the oil in a Dutch oven over medium heat until shimmering. Add the spinach in handfuls and cook, stirring, until the spinach is wilted, about 4 minutes. Season with salt and pepper; transfer the spinach to a colander. Gently squeeze any excess liquid from the spinach; set aside (the cooked spinach should measure about 1½ cups).

2. Wipe the pot clean and add 2 more tablespoons oil; return the pot to medium heat until shimmering. Add the onion and sauté until translucent, about 5 minutes. Add the mushrooms and sauté until they have released their moisture and are golden, 8 to 10 minutes. Season the mushrooms with salt and pepper to taste; transfer to a bowl and set aside (the cooked mushrooms should measure about 1½ cups).

3. Add the remaining 2 tablespoons oil and the garlic; return the pot to medium heat until the garlic is fragrant but not brown, about 30 seconds. Stir in the tomatoes; bring to a simmer and cook until thickened slightly, about 5 minutes. Stir in the basil and season with salt and pepper to taste. Pour the sauce into a large measuring cup and add enough water to make 3½ cups.

4. Spread ½ cup of the sauce evenly over the bottom of a 9 by 13-inch baking dish (or a shallow casserole dish of similar size). Lay 3 of the noodles crosswise over the sauce, making sure they do not touch each other or the sides of the dish. Spread 1 cup of the prepared vegetables evenly over the noodles, ⅔ cup of the sauce evenly over the vegetables, and 1⅓ cups of the mozzarella and ⅓ cup of the Parmesan evenly over the sauce. Repeat this layering of the noodles, vegetables, sauce, and cheeses twice more. For the fourth and final layer, lay the last 3 noodles crosswise over the previous layer and top with the remaining 1 cup tomato sauce, 1⅓ cups mozzarella, and ½ cup Parmesan.

5. Adjust an oven rack to the middle position and heat the oven to 375 degrees. Lightly spray a large sheet of foil with nonstick cooking spray and cover the lasagna. Bake 25 minutes; remove the foil and continue baking until the top turns golden brown in spots, about 15 minutes. Cool for 10 minutes before serving.

➤ VARIATION
Roasted Zucchini and Eggplant Lasagna
Adjust two oven racks to the upper- and lower-middle positions and heat the oven to 400 degrees. Toss 1 pound each zucchini (about 2 medium) and eggplant (about 2 small), cut into ½-inch dice, with 3 tablespoons olive oil, 4 minced garlic cloves, and salt and pepper to taste. Spread out the vegetables on two greased baking sheets; roast, turning occasionally, until golden brown, about 35 minutes. Set the vegetables aside. Follow the recipe for Spinach and Mushroom Lasagna with Tomato Sauce, omitting steps 1 and 2. Substitute the roasted zucchini and eggplant for the mushrooms and spinach while assembling the lasagna in step 4.

POLENTA CASSEROLE

POLENTA IS NOTHING MORE THAN DRIED, ground corn cooked until silky and then finished with butter and cheese. Most often served in its soft, velvety form, polenta is rarely thought of as the basis for a casserole. Yet it makes perfect sense—it can withstand being chilled and reheated nicely, and it's stylish, too. The casserole we imagined would have a layer of soft polenta covered with savory toppings and a touch of blue cheese, baked at relatively high heat until the layers were just heated through.

Before focusing on the toppings, however, we had to figure out the best way to make the polenta. After testing a variety of traditional Italian recipes, we realized that making authentic polenta is quite a lot of work. Coarse cornmeal is slowly added to boiling salted water and stirred constantly (to prevent scorching) for 30 to 40 minutes. Within five minutes, you'll feel like you've been arm wrestling Arnold Schwarzenegger. Thirty minutes of such constant stirring is near torture. After making several batches of traditional polenta, we wondered if instant polenta (also called quick-cooking polenta) could be our answer. Instant polenta, like quick-cooking grits and instant rice, has been partially cooked, then dried. All you need to do is reconstitute it with boiling water. Testing several brands we found at the supermarket (all imported from Italy), we found that instant polenta is much easier and takes only about 10 minutes—we were hooked. The downside, however, is that it is not as flavorful as long-cooked polenta.

In our effort to add some flavor to the instant polenta, we disregarded the package instructions, which recommend cooking it in boiling water. Instead we tried cooking it in boiling chicken broth (despite the protests from test-kitchen staff members who felt it was a culinary sacrilege to cook it this way). Unfortunately, this approach gave the polenta a strong chicken flavor that masked the flavor of the cornmeal. So we then tried cooking the polenta in boiling milk, which is somewhat traditional; here we had slightly better luck. The milk rounded out the flavor of the instant polenta nicely, yet it also added an unwelcome, slimy texture. Using a combination of roughly half milk and half water, we were able to add some flavor to the polenta without ruining its creamy texture. Finished with a little butter, which helped keep it smooth and soft, the polenta seemed just perfect. We originally thought we'd need to add cheese for flavor and texture, but the cheese made the polenta too stiff, a problem that would be compounded by its time in the casserole dish.

When it came to the toppings, we were immediately drawn to the idea of using mushrooms in some fashion because their woodsy flavor is classically paired with polenta. Sautéing some sliced mushrooms with a little onion, garlic, and fresh thyme, we found it easy to sprinkle them over the cooked polenta, which had been spread into a casserole dish. After a few tries, we discovered that the key to achieving a good mushroom flavor is to use several different varieties of mushrooms. Portobellos offer a hearty bite, while inexpensive white button mushrooms help to bulk up the yield without costing a fortune. Lastly we found the intense flavor of dried porcini mushrooms (now widely available in supermarkets) really helped to drive home a serious mushroom flavor. Sprinkled with some walnuts and a little blue cheese, this classic duo of polenta and mushrooms was easily turned into a fashionable casserole.

Mildly flavored and very easy to prepare, the polenta can serve as a great backdrop for many simple, company-worthy toppings beyond mushrooms. We included a variation using sautéed sausage and red bell peppers, yet the possibilities don't end there. Polenta is extremely versatile and works with any number of sautéed vegetables, meats, and cheeses, and is an easy way to highlight some of your favorite local or seasonal ingredients.

SOAKING DRIED PORCINI

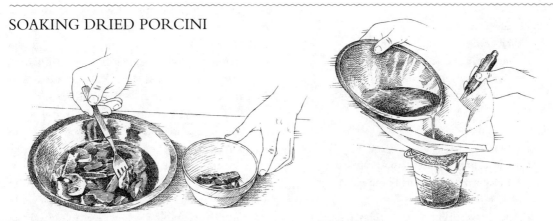

Rinse the dried porcini mushrooms in a small strainer under cool running water. Drain and add the mushrooms with ½ cup tap water to a small microwave-safe bowl. Cover with plastic wrap, cut several steam vents in the plastic wrap with a paring knife, and microwave on high power for 30 seconds. Let stand until the mushrooms soften, about 5 minutes. Lift the mushrooms from the liquid with a fork and mince them. Pour the liquid through a small strainer lined with a coffee filter or a single sheet of paper towel set over a measuring cup. Reserve the mushrooms and strained soaking liquid separately.

Polenta Casserole with Sauteéd Mushrooms, Blue Cheese, and Walnuts

SERVES 6 TO 8

If you do not have a heavy-bottomed saucepan, you may want to use a flame tamer to manage the heat. A flame tamer can be purchased at most kitchen supply stores, or one can be fashioned from a ring of foil (see the illustration on page 44). It's easy to tell whether you need a flame tamer or not. If the polenta bubbles or sputters at all, the heat is too high, and you need one. Properly heated polenta will do little more than release wisps of steam. When stirring the polenta, make sure to scrape the sides and bottom of the pan to ensure even cooking.

PLANNING AHEAD: Assemble the casserole as directed in step 4, but do not bake. Wrap the dish tightly with plastic wrap and poke several vent holes with the tip of a paring knife. Refrigerate the casserole until cool, about 2 hours, then wrap tightly with another sheet of plastic wrap and refrigerate for up to 2 days.

TO BAKE: Allow the casserole to sit at room temperature for about 1 hour. Adjust an oven rack to the middle position and heat the oven to 400 degrees. Remove the plastic wrap and wrap tightly with foil. Bake until the polenta has heated through, about 1 hour. Cool for 10 minutes before serving.

POLENTA

2 1/2	cups whole milk
3	cups water
	Salt
1 1/2	cups instant polenta
2	tablespoons unsalted butter
1	medium garlic clove, minced or pressed through a garlic press
	Ground black pepper

TOPPING

1/4	cup olive oil
12	ounces portobello mushroom caps (about 8 medium caps), brushed clean and sliced 1/4 inch thick
1 1/4	pounds white button mushrooms, stems discarded, brushed clean, and sliced 1/4 inch thick
1	large red onion, halved and sliced thin
	Salt
6	medium garlic cloves, minced or pressed through a garlic press
1	tablespoon minced fresh thyme leaves
1/4	ounce dried porcini mushrooms, rinsed and rehydrated, with soaking liquid reserved (see page 41)
	Ground black pepper
5	ounces Gorgonzola cheese, crumbled (about 1 1/4 cups)
3/4	cup walnuts, coarsely chopped
2	tablespoons minced fresh parsley leaves

1. Adjust an oven rack to the middle position and heat the oven to 400 degrees.

2. FOR THE POLENTA: Bring the milk, water, and 2 teaspoons salt to a simmer in a large, heavy-bottomed saucepan (see the headnote) over medium-high heat. Very slowly, pour the polenta into the boiling liquid while stirring constantly in a circular motion with a wooden spoon (see the illustration on page 43). Reduce the heat to the lowest possible setting and cover. Cook, vigorously stirring the polenta every few minutes, making sure to scrape clean the bottom and edges of the pot, until the polenta has lost its raw cornmeal taste and become soft and smooth, about 10 minutes. Off the heat, stir in the butter and the garlic. Season to taste with salt and pepper; cover the pot to keep the polenta from drying out and set it aside.

3. FOR THE TOPPING: Heat the oil in a Dutch oven over high heat until shimmering. Add the portobellos, white button mushrooms, onion, and 1/2 teaspoon salt; cook, stirring often, until the mushrooms have released their liquid, shrunk dramatically, and browned, about 20 minutes. Add the garlic, thyme, and dried porcini mushrooms with their reserved liquid; cook until most of the liquid has evaporated, about 2 minutes. Season to taste with salt and pepper.

4. Spread the cooked polenta into the bottom of a 9 by 13-inch baking dish (or a shallow casserole dish of similar size). Spread the mushrooms evenly over the polenta and sprinkle with the Gorgonzola and walnuts. Bake until the polenta has heated through and the walnuts have toasted, about 20 minutes. Cool for 10 minutes. Sprinkle with the parsley before serving.

MAKING POLENTA

When the water and milk come to a boil, pour the polenta into the water in a very slow stream from a measuring cup, all the while stirring in a circular motion with a wooden spoon to prevent clumping.

➤ VARIATION

Polenta Casserole with Sauteéd Bell Peppers and Sausage

SERVES 6 TO 8

Planning Ahead: Assemble the casserole as directed in step 4, but do not bake. Wrap the dish tightly with plastic wrap and poke several vent holes with the tip of a paring knife. Refrigerate the casserole until cool, about 2 hours, then wrap tightly with another sheet of plastic wrap and refrigerate for up to 2 days.

To Bake: Allow the casserole to sit at room temperature for about 1 hour. Adjust an oven rack to the middle position and heat the oven to 400 degrees. Remove the plastic wrap and wrap tightly with foil. Bake until the polenta has heated through, about 1 hour. Cool for 10 minutes before serving.

POLENTA
2 1/2	cups whole milk
3	cups water
	Salt
1 1/2	cups instant polenta
2	tablespoons unsalted butter
1	medium garlic clove, minced or pressed through a garlic press
	Ground black pepper

TOPPING
2	tablespoons olive oil
3	medium red bell peppers, stemmed, seeded, and sliced into 1/4-inch-thick strips
1	large red onion, halved and sliced thin
	Salt
1 1/2	pounds sweet Italian sausage, removed from its casing
6	medium garlic cloves, minced or pressed through a garlic press
2	teaspoons minced fresh thyme leaves
1/4	teaspoon red pepper flakes
1	(14.5-ounce) can diced tomatoes
2	tablespoons red wine vinegar
	Ground black pepper
2	ounces Asiago cheese, grated (about 1 cup)
2	tablespoons minced fresh parsley leaves

1. Adjust an oven rack to the middle position and heat the oven to 400 degrees.

2. For the polenta: Bring the milk, water, and 2 teaspoons salt to a simmer in a large, heavy bottomed saucepan (see the note on page 42) over medium-high heat. Very slowly, pour the polenta into the boiling liquid while stirring constantly in a circular motion with a wooden spoon (see the illustration at left). Reduce the heat to the lowest possible setting and cover. Cook, vigorously stirring the polenta every few minutes, making sure to scrape clean the bottom and edges of the pot, until the polenta has lost its raw cornmeal taste and become soft and smooth, about 10 minutes. Off the heat, stir in the butter and garlic. Season to taste with salt and pepper; cover the pot to prevent the polenta from drying out and set it aside.

3. For the topping: Heat the oil in a 12-inch skillet over medium-high heat until shimmering. Add the peppers, onion, and 1/2 teaspoon salt; cook until the peppers are softened and beginning to brown, about 5 minutes. Add the sausage and cook, breaking the meat into small pieces with a wooden spoon, until the meat loses its raw color but has not browned, about 5 minutes. Add the garlic, thyme, and red pepper flakes; cook until fragrant, about 1 minute. Add the tomatoes with their juice; bring to a simmer and cook, stirring occasionally, until the flavors have melded, about 5 minutes. Off the heat, stir in the vinegar. Season with salt and pepper to taste.

4. Spread the cooked polenta into the bottom of a 9 by 13-inch baking dish (or a shallow casserole dish of similar size). Spread the sausage mixture evenly over the polenta and sprinkle with the Asiago. Bake until the polenta has heated through and the Asiago has melted, about 20 minutes. Cool for 10 minutes. Sprinkle with the parsley before serving.

EQUIPMENT: Flame Tamer

A flame tamer (or heat diffuser) is a metal disk that can be fitted over an electric or gas burner to reduce the heat transfer. This device is especially useful when trying to keep a pot at the barest simmer. If you don't own a flame tamer (it costs less than $10 and is stocked at most kitchenware stores), you can fashion one from aluminum foil. Take a long sheet of heavy-duty foil and shape it into a 1-inch-thick ring that will fit on your burner. Make sure that the ring is an even thickness so that a pot will rest flat on it. A foil ring elevates the pot slightly above the flame or electric coil, allowing you to keep a pot of polenta at the merest simmer.

EGGPLANT PARMESAN

TRADITIONAL RECIPES FOR EGGPLANT Parmesan fry breaded eggplant in copious amounts of oil, usually resulting in greasy eggplant with a sodden, unappealing bread-crumb crust. We wanted a fresher, lighter take on this classic Italian dish. Could we eliminate the frying, streamline the dish, and make it taste better than the original?

Most recipes begin by purging (salting) the eggplant to expel bitter juices and prevent the porous flesh from soaking up excess oil. To double-check this theory, we baked some unsalted eggplant. Oil absorption wasn't a problem, but the eggplant did taste bitter, and it had a raw, mealy texture. Thirty minutes of salting remedied the problem. For efficiency's sake, we chose good-size globe eggplants; we didn't want to multiply the number of slices we'd have to prepare. For the best appearance, taste, and texture, we settled on unpeeled ¼-inch-thick crosswise slices, not lengthwise planks.

In our first effort to sidestep deep-frying, we dispensed with the breading altogether, baking naked, salted eggplant slices on a baking sheet coated with cooking spray. (This method is often employed in low-calorie recipes for eggplant Parmesan.) The resulting eggplant earned negative comments from tasters. We concluded that breading was essential and ticked off a list of possibilities. Flour alone wasn't substantial enough. Eggplant swathed in mayonnaise and then bread crumbs turned slimy. Eggplant coated in a flour-and-egg batter and then bread crumbs was thick and tough. A standard single breading (dipping the eggplant first in egg, then bread crumbs) was too messy—the egg slid right off the eggplant, leaving the crumbs with nothing on which to adhere.

A double, or bound, breading proved superior. Dipping the eggplant first in seasoned flour, then egg, then bread crumbs created a substantial (but not heavy) and crisp coating that brought the mild flavor and tender, creamy texture of the eggplant to the fore. The initial coating of flour in a bound breading creates a dry, smooth base to which the egg can cling. We seasoned the bread crumbs with generous amounts of Parmesan, salt, and pepper.

We'd been using fresh bread crumbs and wondered whether we could get away with using store-bought crumbs. The answer was no. Store-bought crumbs were so fine that they disappeared under the blankets of tomato sauce and cheese.

After considerable experimentation, we found that the best way to achieve a crisp coating is to bake the breaded slices on two preheated baking sheets, each coated with a modest 3 tablespoons of vegetable oil (olive oil tasted sour), rotating the pans and flipping the slices partway through. At 425 degrees, the slices sizzled during cooking and became fully tender in 30 minutes. Using this technique, we turned out crisp, golden brown disks of eggplant, expending a minimum of effort (and using very little oil). And now, seeing that we weren't busy frying up four batches of eggplant in hot oil, we had time to grate cheese and whip up a quick tomato sauce while the eggplant baked.

Eggplant Parmesan couldn't be called such without Parmesan cheese, so that was a given. We'd already used some for breading the eggplant, and a little extra browned nicely on top of the casserole. Mozzarella is another standard addition. A modest amount (8 ounces) kept the casserole from becoming stringy.

A few cloves of minced garlic, a sprinkling of red pepper flakes, and some olive oil started off a quick tomato sauce, followed by three cans of diced tomatoes, with just two of them pureed in the food processor to preserve a chunky texture. A handful of fresh basil leaves (we reserved some basil for garnish, too) plus salt and pepper were the final flourishes.

Because breading softens beneath the smothering layers of sauce and cheese, we left most of the

top layer of eggplant exposed. This left us with about one cup of extra sauce, just enough to pass at the table. Another benefit of this technique was that without excess moisture, the casserole was easy to cut into tidy pieces. With the eggplant fully cooked, the dish needed only a brief stay in a hot oven to melt the cheese.

Eggplant Parmesan
SERVES 6 TO 8

Use kosher salt when salting the eggplant. The coarse grains don't dissolve as readily as the fine grains of regular table salt, so any excess can be easily wiped away. It's necessary to divide the eggplant in two batches when tossing it with the salt. To be time efficient, use the 30 to 45 minutes during which the salted eggplant sits to prepare the breading, cheeses, and sauce.

PLANNING AHEAD: Assemble the casserole as directed in step 6, but do not bake. Wrap the dish tightly with plastic wrap and refrigerate for up to 2 days, or freeze, tightly wrapped with an additional layer of foil, for up to 1 month. (If frozen, thaw in the refrigerator for 24 hours.)

TO BAKE: Allow the casserole to sit at room temperature for about 1 hour. Adjust an oven rack to the middle position and heat the oven to 400 degrees. Remove the plastic wrap and cover the dish tightly with foil. Bake until the casserole is moderately hot, about 45 minutes. Remove the foil and continue to cook until the bread crumbs are brown and the mixture is bubbling, 15 to 20 minutes longer. Cool for 10 minutes before serving.

EGGPLANT

2	pounds globe eggplant (about 2 medium), cut crosswise into $1/4$-inch-thick rounds
1	tablespoon kosher salt
8	slices white sandwich bread, torn into quarters
2	ounces Parmesan cheese, grated (about 1 cup)
	Salt and ground black pepper
1	cup all-purpose flour
4	large eggs
6	tablespoons vegetable oil

TOMATO SAUCE

3	(14.5-ounce) cans diced tomatoes
2	tablespoons olive oil

SCIENCE: A Spoonful of Salt

Researchers investigating methods for making bitter medications more palatable have discovered that salt can mask bitter flavors. According to one research group, for example, sodium can reduce the perceived bitterness of acetaminophen, the active ingredient in Tylenol, by more than 50 percent. To see if salt might have the same effect on bitter-tasting foods, we performed a blind taste-test of several, including coffee and eggplant, to which we added either salt or sugar. With the addition of $1/4$ teaspoon salt per pint, the perceived bitterness of the coffee was cut in half. Salt also reduced the perceived bitterness of eggplant.

The tradition of salting eggplant, then, appears to serve two functions. The first, as we have found in kitchen tests, is that it makes eggplant firmer by removing water. The second, as we discovered in the above tests, is that salt can mask bitterness. Indeed, when we had tasters sample previously salted and unsalted batches of sautéed eggplant, most claimed to detect a bitter background flavor in the unsalted batch that they didn't taste in the salted batch. Everybody knows that a spoonful of sugar helps the medicine go down; little did we guess that the same could be true for salt.

4 medium garlic cloves, minced or pressed through a garlic press

1/4 teaspoon red pepper flakes

1/2 cup coarsely chopped fresh basil leaves
Salt and ground black pepper

8 ounces whole-milk or part-skim mozzarella, shredded (about 2 2/3 cups)

I ounce Parmesan cheese, grated (about 1/2 cup)

10 fresh basil leaves, torn, for garnish

1. FOR THE EGGPLANT: Toss half of the eggplant slices and 1½ teaspoons of the kosher salt in a large bowl until combined; transfer the salted eggplant to a large colander set over a bowl. Repeat with the remaining eggplant and kosher salt, placing the second batch on top of the first. Let stand until the eggplant releases about 2 tablespoons liquid, 30 to 45 minutes. Spread the eggplant slices on a triple layer of paper towels; cover with another triple layer of paper towels. Press firmly on each slice to remove as much liquid as possible, then wipe off the excess salt.

2. While the eggplant is draining, adjust two oven racks to the upper- and lower-middle positions, place a rimmed baking sheet on each rack, and heat the oven to 425 degrees. Process the bread in a food processor to fine, even crumbs, about fifteen 1-second pulses (you should have about 4 cups). Transfer the crumbs to a pie plate and stir in the 1 cup Parmesan, ¼ teaspoon salt, and ½ teaspoon pepper; set aside. Wipe out the bowl (do not wash) and set aside.

3. Combine the flour and 1 teaspoon pepper in a large zipper-lock bag; shake to combine. Beat the eggs in a second pie plate. Place 8 to 10 eggplant slices in the bag with the flour; seal the bag and shake to coat the slices. Remove the slices, shaking off the excess flour; dip in the eggs, let the excess egg run off, then coat evenly with the bread-crumb mixture; set the breaded slices on a wire rack set over a baking sheet. Repeat with the

HOW TO BREAD THE EGGPLANT: FOLLOWING A TRAIL OF CRUMBS

WE PREPARED EGGPLANT IN NEARLY A DOZEN WAYS IN OUR EFFORT TO FIND THE perfect method that would eliminate the grease and the frying. Here are the highlights from our testing along with the winning method, which results in a crisp, light coating that stands up to the sauce.

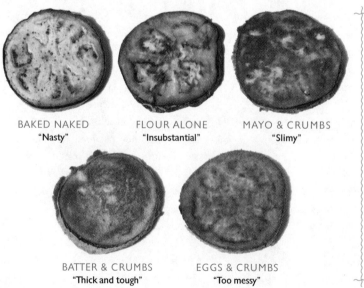

BAKED NAKED
"Nasty"

FLOUR ALONE
"Insubstantial"

MAYO & CRUMBS
"Slimy"

BATTER & CRUMBS
"Thick and tough"

EGGS & CRUMBS
"Too messy"

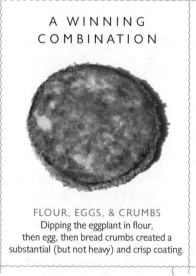

A WINNING COMBINATION

FLOUR, EGGS, & CRUMBS
Dipping the eggplant in flour, then egg, then bread crumbs created a substantial (but not heavy) and crisp coating.

remaining eggplant.

4. Remove the preheated baking sheets from the oven; add 3 tablespoons oil to each sheet, tilting to coat evenly with the oil. Place half of the breaded eggplant slices on each sheet in a single layer. Bake until the eggplant is well browned and crisp, about 30 minutes, rotating the baking sheets front to back and top to bottom after 10 minutes, and flipping the eggplant slices with a wide spatula after 20 minutes. Do not turn off the oven.

5. FOR THE SAUCE: While the eggplant bakes, process 2 cans of the diced tomatoes in a food processor until almost smooth, about 5 seconds. Heat the olive oil, garlic, and red pepper flakes in a large, heavy-bottomed saucepan over medium-high heat, stirring occasionally, until fragrant and the garlic is light golden, about 3 minutes; stir in the processed tomatoes and the remaining can of diced tomatoes. Bring the sauce to a boil, then reduce the heat to medium-low and simmer, stirring occasionally, until slightly thickened and reduced, about 15 minutes (you should have about 4 cups). Stir in the basil and season with salt and pepper to taste.

6. To ASSEMBLE: Spread 1 cup of the tomato sauce in the bottom of a 9 by 13-inch baking dish (or a shallow casserole dish of similar size). Layer in half of the eggplant slices, overlapping the slices to fit; distribute 1 more cup sauce over the eggplant; sprinkle with half of the mozzarella. Layer in the remaining eggplant and dot with 1 more cup sauce, leaving the majority of the eggplant exposed so that it will become crisp; sprinkle with the ½ cup Parmesan and the remaining mozzarella. Bake until the surface is bubbling and the cheese is browned, 13 to 15 minutes. Cool 10 minutes, scatter the basil over the top, and serve, passing the remaining tomato sauce separately.

TURKEY TETRAZZINI

ARE TURKEY TETRAZZINI AND TUNA NOODLE casseroles American institutions or national nightmares? In most cases, the answer is both, no doubt because most versions of these dishes are so bad. Most often made from a canned-soup base (cream of mushroom, cream of celery, and cream of chicken are the usual choices) mixed with soggy noodles, leftover turkey or canned tuna, and a few stray vegetables from the crisper drawer, these casseroles deliver little in the way of flavor or texture, save for the sometimes crunchy topping of bread crumbs. Ready to give these hard-working classics a well-deserved makeover, we began by shutting the cupboard door to all canned soups and focused on making a sauce from scratch.

Tuna noodle casserole and turkey tetrazzini are nearly the same dish, and a little research determined that cream of mushroom soup is the most commonly used sauce base. A mushroom-flavored sauce, therefore, was what we wanted. Testing both a béchamel (flour-thickened milk) and a velouté (flour-thickened broth), we found that neither was perfect. The béchamel sauce tasted too dairy-heavy, while the velouté was simply too light. A sauce made with a combination of milk and broth (thickened with flour) tasted better, but it still lacked some richness. Replacing the milk with half-and-half, we finally landed on the right basic flavor and heft. Four cups of liquid thickened with 4 tablespoons of flour produced enough sauce with the right texture to coat 1 pound of pasta without being either soupy or gummy.

Focusing next on developing the mushroom flavor, we found it necessary to use a whopping 20 ounces of mushrooms. Any less just wouldn't do. Trying both cremini and white button mushrooms in the sauce, we noted that tasters could find no appreciable difference, so we went with the more available and less expensive white button mushrooms. The key to an intense mushroom flavor, we found, is to sauté the mushrooms until they release all their liquid and begin to brown. To round out the flavor of the sauce, onions, garlic, fresh thyme, cayenne, and Parmesan all proved to be absolutely necessary.

Moving on to the vegetables, we noted that many recipes use a lot of celery, which adds crunch but almost no flavor. Interestingly enough, our tasters preferred no celery at all. Bell peppers met a similar fate. We first tried green bell peppers, which were rejected immediately, and while red peppers performed slightly better, tasters preferred to do without them altogether. Frozen peas were the only vegetable given the thumbs-up by the test-kitchen staff, and we found that the peas would not turn soggy if we added them right before baking.

Several recipes we researched call for elbow macaroni; however, we found it too starchy and thick. We preferred fettuccine, linguine, or spaghetti instead, for texture and big structural presence. To make the dish easier to eat, we broke the long pasta in thirds so that there was no need to wind the pasta around a fork.

As for the topping, we decided that store-bought bread crumbs tasted too sandy, while canned, fried onions tasted too much like chemicals. Instead, we found it just as easy to grind our own bread crumbs in the food processor with a little butter; they toast nicely in the oven while the casserole bakes.

Turkey Tetrazzini

SERVES 6 TO 8

Tetrazzini is also great made with leftover chicken. Don't skimp on the salt and pepper; this dish needs aggressive seasoning.

PLANNING AHEAD: Follow the recipe through step 3. Refrigerate the topping, the cooked pasta, and the sauce in separate bowls, tightly wrapped with plastic wrap, for up to 2 days.

TO BAKE: Adjust an oven rack to the middle position and heat the oven to 400 degrees. Transfer the pasta to a colander and rinse quickly under hot tap water. Poke several vent holes in the plastic wrap covering the sauce and microwave on high power until hot, 3 to 5 minutes. Continue to assemble and bake the casserole as directed in step 4, increasing the baking time to 30 minutes.

TOPPING
- 4 slices white sandwich bread, torn into quarters
- 2 tablespoons unsalted butter, melted

FILLING
- Salt
- 1 pound fettuccine, linguine, or spaghetti, broken into thirds
- 1 tablespoon olive oil
- 5 tablespoons unsalted butter
- 20 ounces white button mushrooms, brushed clean, stems trimmed, and sliced 1/4 inch thick
- 2 medium onions, minced
- 4 medium garlic cloves, minced or pressed through a garlic press
- 1 tablespoon minced fresh thyme leaves
- 1/8 teaspoon cayenne pepper
- 1/4 cup all-purpose flour
- 2 cups low-sodium chicken broth
- 2 cups half-and-half
- 2 ounces Parmesan cheese, grated (about 1 cup)
- Ground black pepper
- 4 cups cooked turkey meat, cut into 1/2-inch pieces
- 1 1/2 cups frozen peas

1. **FOR THE TOPPING:** Process the bread and butter in a food processor fitted with the steel blade until coarsely ground, about six 1-second pulses; set aside.

2. **FOR THE FILLING:** Adjust an oven rack to the middle position and heat the oven to 400 degrees. Bring 4 quarts of water to a boil in a Dutch oven over high heat. Stir in 1 tablespoon salt and the pasta; cook, stirring occasionally, until al dente. Drain the pasta and toss with the oil; leave it in the colander and set aside.

3. Wipe the pot dry with a wad of paper towels. Add the butter to the pot and return to medium-high heat until melted. Add the mushrooms and 1/2 teaspoon salt; cook the mushrooms until they have released their juices and are brown around the edges, 7 to 10 minutes. Add the onions and cook until softened, about 5 minutes. Stir in the garlic, thyme, and cayenne; cook until fragrant, about 30 seconds. Add the flour and cook, stirring constantly, until golden, about 1 minute. Slowly whisk in the broth and half-and-half; bring to a simmer and cook, whisking often, until lightly thickened, about 1 minute. Off the heat, whisk in the Parmesan. Season with salt and pepper to taste.

4. Add the pasta, turkey, and peas to the sauce; stir to combine. Pour into a 9 by 13-inch baking dish (or a shallow casserole dish of similar size) and sprinkle with the bread-crumb topping. Bake until the topping has browned and the sauce is bubbly, 10 to 15 minutes. Serve immediately.

➤ VARIATION

Tuna Noodle Casserole

Follow the recipe for Turkey Tetrazzini, substituting two (6-ounce) cans of solid white tuna packed in water, drained and flaked into 1-inch pieces with a fork, for the cooked turkey in step 4.

SOPA SECA

THE NAME OF THIS MEXICAN DISH, LITERally translated, is "dry soup." Don't let the name fool you, however; *sopa seca* is neither dry nor a soup. Although it starts off looking like a soup, when completed it is a distinctive pasta dish with robust flavors.

We started by doing a little research in order to learn more about sopa seca. Of the dozen recipes we found, the one aspect they all shared was the use of *fideos* as a base. Fideos are coils of vermicelli that have been toasted until golden brown. The wonderful nuttiness they bring to this dish underscores all the other flavors. The fideos are placed in a baking dish and topped with an ample amount of liquid (the soup part), then baked until all the liquid is absorbed and the pasta is tender (the dry part). The similarities among the sopa seca recipes stopped there. The liquid and garnish ingredient choices made the search for the perfect sopa seca recipe an adventure.

The use of tomatoes among the recipes varied greatly. Some recipes call for fresh tomatoes, others canned, and still others list jarred salsa as the tomato ingredient. We tried all three variations and found that canned tomatoes worked the best and yielded the most consistent results. The fresh tomatoes, while preferred slightly over canned for their flavor, led to inconsistent results due to the varied moisture content in fresh tomatoes. Jarred

salsa was considered the worst option because it gave the finished dish an artificial flavor. In addition to the tomato base, sopa seca recipes usually include a liquid component, normally chicken broth or water. In our tests, chicken broth was favored slightly over water because of its greater richness.

The use of chiles also varied from recipe to recipe. We tried four options. Our first test used no chiles at all. It was soon obvious, however, that if we wanted multiple dimensions to our sopa seca, chiles were a must. Next up were fresh jalapeños. Although they definitely added a spark, some tasters felt they gave the dish too much raw chile flavor. The third trial used dried ancho chiles. Many testers liked the smokiness of the anchos, but they required a lengthy soaking period that complicated the cooking process and added time. Our final alternative was to use canned chipotle chiles. These turned out to be the best option. They provided a smoky background, like the anchos, without the long preparation time, and they added spiciness, like the jalapeños, without the raw taste.

In addition to the chiles, we liked onions, garlic, and ground cumin for extra flavor. To finish the dish, we topped it with chopped cilantro for freshness and a dollop of sour cream to temper the chile heat.

Sopa Seca

SERVES 4

We used straight vermicelli as opposed to the coiled version because they are more readily available. If you can find the vermicelli in coils, decrease the amount of chicken broth by ¼ cup. If you want a less spicy dish, use only one chipotle chile.

PLANNING AHEAD: Follow the recipe through step 2. Cover the broth mixture tightly with plastic wrap and refrigerate for up to 4 days. Wrap the noodles tightly with plastic wrap and store at room temperature.

TO BAKE: Spread the noodles out in a 9 by 13-inch baking dish (or a shallow casserole dish of similar size). Bring the liquid to a boil in a microwave on high power, 5 to 7 minutes. Continue to assemble and bake the casserole as directed in step 3.

2	tablespoons vegetable oil
½	pound vermicelli, broken in half
I	medium onion, minced
	Salt
2	medium garlic cloves, minced or pressed through a garlic press
½	teaspoon ground cumin
I	(14.5-ounce) can diced tomatoes
2	canned chipotle chiles in adobo sauce, chopped fine
I ½	cups low-sodium chicken broth
	Ground black pepper
2	ounces Monterey Jack cheese, shredded (about ⅔ cup)
¼	cup chopped fresh cilantro leaves
½	cup sour cream

1. Adjust an oven rack to the middle position and heat the oven to 350 degrees. Heat 1 tablespoon of the oil and the vermicelli in a 12-inch skillet over medium-high heat, stirring constantly, until the noodles are golden brown, 4 to 5 minutes. Transfer the noodles to a 9 by 13-inch baking dish (or a shallow casserole dish of similar size).

2. Add the remaining tablespoon oil to the skillet and return to medium heat until shimmering. Add the onion and ½ teaspoon salt; cook, stirring frequently, until softened and beginning to brown, about 8 minutes. Add the garlic and cumin; cook until fragrant, about 30 seconds. Add the tomatoes and their juice, chipotles, and broth; bring to a boil. Off the heat, season with salt and pepper to taste.

3. Pour the tomato mixture over the pasta and cover the dish tightly with foil. Bake until all the liquid is absorbed and the pasta is tender, about 15 minutes. Remove the foil and stir the pasta. Sprinkle the Monterey Jack evenly over the pasta and continue to bake, uncovered, until the cheese is melted, about 3 minutes. Sprinkle with the cilantro. Serve immediately, passing the sour cream separately.

➤ VARIATIONS

Sopa Seca with Chorizo

Adding chorizo to this recipe makes it a more substantial meal. If the chorizo is very spicy, omit the chipotle chiles.

Follow the recipe for Sopa Seca, adding ½ pound diced chorizo sausage to the baking dish with the tomatoes in step 3.

Sopa Seca with Black Beans

Adding black beans and replacing the chicken broth with vegetable broth or water makes this recipe a robust one-dish vegetarian meal.

Follow the recipe for Sopa Seca, adding one (15.5-ounce) can black beans, drained and rinsed, to the baking dish with the tomatoes in step 3. Substitute 1½ cups vegetable broth or water for the chicken broth.

CHICKEN AND RICE CASSEROLE

LIKE A SEASONED PAIR OF HOLLYWOOD B-movie actors, chicken and rice get thrown together in all manner of ill-conceived projects and are expected to make it work. But this stick-to-your-ribs church supper staple is usually an uninspired performance, featuring bone-dry bits of chicken, "blown out" rice, army green vegetables, and a pasty, diet-busting sauce made with gobs of cheese and canned cream soups.

Our goal was to redesign this hearty and convenient weeknight casserole—to give it bright, fresh flavors and a leaner calorie count while preserving its comforting richness.

Existing recipes for this dish were vague and frustrating, calling for "cooked rice" and "cooked chicken," as if these initial cooking steps were trivial details. While we understood the desire to put leftovers to good use, we objected to this approach for two reasons. It squanders an opportunity to build extra flavor into these ingredients, and it ignores the importance of making sure they're done at the same time. We checked the recommended cooking times and immediately saw why most recipes didn't bother to address the issue. In most cases, the casserole was doomed from the outset, sentenced to an hour or so in the oven. When it emerged, the rice had disintegrated and the chicken was unbearably tough—a significantly shorter spell in the oven would have to be a priority in developing our recipe.

For our first tests we parboiled rice in one pot while we built a creamy sauce with chicken in another. Preparing a cooked, flour-thickened sauce (rather than dumping pre-prepared ingredients into a casserole dish) allowed us to incorporate flavors of sautéed aromatics like onions and garlic. The two elements were then combined in a casserole dish and baked in a hot oven until bubbling. The results were good—the chicken imparted a nice flavor to the sauce as it cooked, and vice versa—but did we really need two pots to make this dish? If the rice were also cooked directly in the sauce, it would also be more flavorful, we reasoned.

It was a good plan, but not a simple one, as we discovered when we considered how best to coordinate the various cooking times of the rice, chicken, and vegetables in the sauce. First we tried tossing raw rice into the sauce once the chicken was cooked and placing it in a hot oven. The results were beyond awful. After more than 45 minutes, the chicken was inedibly dry, the vegetables were mushy, the sauce no more than a pasty residue, and the rice, amazingly, was still crunchy, with a few pockets of exploded grains near the edges. Numerous variations on this technique were attempted, with little more success.

Why couldn't we get the rice to finish cooking properly in the oven? One problem was the uneven distribution of heat through the rectangular baking dish. Rice at the center of the dish was the slowest to cook, while grains around the edges blew apart. The problem was compounded by the fact that the cooking liquid was not water, but a thickened sauce. Rice cooks more slowly in a flour-bound sauce because much of the water is trapped by swollen starch granules, so that the rice grains are unable to absorb it.

We began to test recipes in which the rice was almost fully cooked in the sauce before the mixture was transferred to the oven, and immediately saw better results. At first we feared that the rice, already tender going into the oven, would quickly overcook. But the same principle that had prevented the rice from cooking in the oven now protected it from overcooking: There was not enough readily available moisture for the grains to absorb. Any lingering doubts about this theory were dispelled when we set out to determine just how much liquid we needed in order to fully cook the rice in the sauce. For just 1½ cups of raw rice, which would normally take about three cups of liquid to cook, it took a full 7 cups of liquid to both cook the rice and have enough left over for a creamy sauce to bind the casserole. Any less and the dish turned out pasty and dry.

Another reason our casseroles tended to turn out pasty was the excessive amount of flour required to thicken that much liquid—as much as ½ cup or more. We knew that rice grains leached starch when cooked in an abundant quantity of water;

CUTTING UP CHICKEN FOR CASSEROLES

1. Separate the tenderloin from the breast. Starting at the thick end, cut the breast into ¼-inch slices. Stop slicing when you reach the tapered triangle end.

2. With the flat side of a knife, press the tapered end to an even ¼-inch thickness and then cut the slices into 1-inch squares.

3. Use the same technique for the tenderloin, flattening it with the side of the knife and then cutting it into 1-inch pieces.

now we could take advantage of that to thicken our sauce. Reducing the quantity of flour by half resulted in a sauce that started out quite thin—perfect for cooking rice—and thickened as it cooked, thanks to the extra starch released by the rice.

For the sauce, we experimented with chicken stock, milk, and cream in varying proportions and found that tasters preferred a 50/50 mix of milk and chicken stock, thickened with both a roux and a good melting cheese stirred in at the end. The addition of heavy cream made the sauce far too rich—the combined fat from the milk, butter, and cheese was more than sufficient.

Even with 7 full cups of liquid, the mixture looked thick and a little dry when we poured it into the casserole dish. But if we added any more liquid at the outset, the dish turned out soupy. The reason for this was the chicken; as it finished cooking in the oven it released a lot of liquid, which thinned the sauce considerably. This also provided a handy visual cue for when the dish was done: when the dish was bubbling vigorously around the edges, it meant the chicken had released all of its juices, and so was cooked through.

Creamy Chicken and Rice Casserole with Peas, Carrots, and Cheddar
SERVES 6 TO 8

After adding the rice, be sure to stir the sauce often for the first few minutes, using a heatproof rubber spatula; this is when the rice is most likely to clump and stick to the bottom of the pot.

PLANNING AHEAD: Follow the recipe through step 3, cooking the chicken through completely, about 10 minutes, before adding the cheddar and peas. Pour the mixture into a 9 by 13-inch baking dish (or a shallow casserole dish of similar size). Wrap the dish tightly with plastic wrap and poke several vent holes with the tip of a paring knife. Refrigerate the chicken and rice until cool, about 3 hours, then wrap tightly with another sheet of plastic wrap. Refrigerate the topping and casserole separately for up to 3 days.

TO BAKE: Allow the covered dish to sit at room temperature for 1 hour. Adjust an oven rack to the middle position and heat the oven to 400 degrees. Remove the plastic wrap and sprinkle

with the bread-crumb topping. Bake, uncovered, until bubbly and heated through, about 45 minutes. Cool for 10 minutes. Sprinkle with the parsley and serve with the lemon wedges.

TOPPING

4	slices white sandwich bread, torn into quarters
2	tablespoons unsalted butter, melted
1/2	ounce Parmesan cheese, grated (about 1/4 cup)

FILLING

4	tablespoons unsalted butter
1	medium onion, minced
3	medium carrots, peeled and chopped medium
1	teaspoon salt
3	medium garlic cloves, minced or pressed through a garlic press
1/4	cup all-purpose flour
3 1/2	cups low-sodium chicken broth
3 1/2	cups whole milk
1 1/2	cups long-grain white rice
1/8	teaspoon ground black pepper
1/8	teaspoon cayenne pepper
2	pounds boneless, skinless chicken breasts, trimmed of excess fat and prepared according to the illustrations on page 51
8	ounces sharp cheddar cheese, shredded (about 2 2/3 cups)
1 1/2	cups frozen peas
2	tablespoons chopped fresh parsley leaves
1	lemon, cut into wedges

1. FOR THE TOPPING: Process the bread and butter in a food processor fitted with the steel blade until coarsely ground, about six 1-second pulses. Transfer to a bowl and toss with the Parmesan; set aside.

2. FOR THE FILLING: Adjust an oven rack to the middle position and heat the oven to 400 degrees. Melt the butter in a Dutch oven over medium heat. Add the onion, carrots, and salt; cook, stirring occasionally, until softened, 8 to 10 minutes. Add the garlic and cook until fragrant, about 1 minute. Add the flour and cook, stirring constantly, until golden, about 1 minute. Slowly whisk in the chicken broth and milk; bring to a simmer, whisking often. Stir in the rice, pepper, and cayenne; return to a simmer. Turn the heat

to medium-low, cover, and cook, stirring often, until the rice has absorbed much of the liquid and is just tender, 20 to 25 minutes.

3. Add the chicken and continue to cook uncovered over medium-low heat, stirring occasionally, until it is no longer pink, about 4 minutes. Off the heat, whisk in the cheddar and peas.

4. Pour the mixture into a 9 by 13-inch baking dish (or a shallow casserole dish of similar size) and sprinkle with the bread crumb topping. Bake until the topping is browned and the casserole is bubbling, 20 to 25 minutes. Cool for 10 minutes. Sprinkle with the parsley and serve with the lemon wedges.

➤ VARIATIONS

Chicken and Rice Casserole with Sun-Dried Tomatoes and Spinach

SERVES 6 TO 8

Oil-packed sun-dried tomatoes are superior to the dried variety in both flavor and texture. Be sure to drain them well and pat them dry.

PLANNING AHEAD: Follow the recipe through step 4, cooking the chicken through completely, about 10 minutes, before adding the sun-dried tomatoes, mozzarella, and spinach. Pour the mixture into a 9 by 13-inch baking dish (or a shallow casserole dish of similar size). Wrap the dish tightly with plastic wrap and poke several vent holes with the tip of a paring knife. Refrigerate the chicken and rice until cool, about 3 hours, then wrap tightly with another sheet of plastic wrap. Refrigerate the topping and casserole separately for up to 3 days.

TO BAKE: Allow the covered dish to sit at room temperature for 1 hour. Adjust an oven rack to the middle position and heat the oven to 400 degrees. Remove the plastic wrap and sprinkle with the bread-crumb topping. Bake, uncovered, until bubbly and heated through, about 45 minutes. Cool for 10 minutes. Sprinkle with the parsley and serve with the lemon wedges.

TOPPING

- 4 slices white sandwich bread, torn into quarters
- 1 cup pine nuts
- 2 tablespoons unsalted butter, melted
- 1/2 ounce Parmesan cheese, grated (about 1/4 cup)

FILLING

- 1 tablespoon olive oil
- 3 medium garlic cloves, minced or pressed through a garlic press
- 1 pound bag curly-leaf spinach, washed and stemmed
- 4 tablespoons unsalted butter
- 1/4 cup all-purpose flour
- 3 1/2 cups low-sodium chicken broth
- 3 1/2 cups whole milk
- 1 1/2 cups long-grain white rice
- 1 teaspoon dried oregano
- 1 teaspoon salt
- 1/8 teaspoon ground black pepper
- 2 pounds boneless, skinless chicken breasts, trimmed of excess fat and prepared according to the illustrations on page 51
- 1 cup (one 8-ounce jar) oil-packed sun-dried tomatoes, drained, patted dry, and chopped coarse
- 8 ounces mozzarella cheese, shredded (about 2 2/3 cups)
- 2 tablespoons chopped fresh parsley leaves
- 1 lemon, cut into wedges

1. FOR THE TOPPING: Process the bread, pine nuts, and butter in a food processor fitted with the steel blade until coarsely ground, about ten 1-second pulses. Transfer to a bowl and toss with the Parmesan; set aside.

2. FOR THE FILLING: Adjust an oven rack to the middle position and heat the oven to 400 degrees. Heat the oil and garlic in a Dutch oven over medium-high heat; cook until the garlic is lightly golden, stirring often, about 2 minutes. Add the spinach by handfuls and stir to coat the spinach with oil until just wilted, about 4 minutes. Transfer the spinach to a colander set over the sink and gently squeeze the spinach to release the excess moisture. Coarsely chop the spinach and set aside.

3. Wipe the pot clean with a wad of a paper towels. Add the butter and melt over medium heat. Add the flour and cook, stirring constantly, until golden, about 1 minute. Slowly whisk in the chicken broth and milk; bring to a simmer, whisking often. Stir in the rice, oregano, salt, and pepper; return to a

simmer. Reduce the heat to medium-low, cover, and cook, stirring often, until the rice has absorbed much of the liquid and is just tender, 20 to 25 minutes.

4. Add the chicken and continue to cook uncovered over medium-low heat, stirring occasionally, until it is no longer pink, about 4 minutes. Off the heat, stir in the sun-dried tomatoes, mozzarella, and chopped spinach.

5. Pour the mixture into a 9 by 13-inch baking dish (or a shallow casserole dish of similar size) and sprinkle with the bread-crumb topping. Bake until the topping is browned and the casserole is bubbling, 20 to 25 minutes. Cool for 10 minutes. Sprinkle with the parsley and serve with the lemon wedges.

Chicken and Rice Casserole with Chiles, Corn, and Black Beans

SERVES 6 TO 8

Don't skip the rinsing of the black beans or the sauce will turn gray. Be sure to thaw and drain the corn thoroughly before stirring it into the filling.

PLANNING AHEAD: Follow the recipe through step 3, cooking the chicken through completely, about 10 minutes, before adding the Pepper Jack, black beans, and corn. Pour the mixture into a 9 by 13-inch baking dish (or a shallow casserole dish of similar size). Wrap the dish tightly with plastic wrap and poke several vent holes with the tip of a paring knife. Refrigerate the chicken and rice until cool, about 3 hours, then wrap tightly with another sheet of plastic wrap. Refrigerate the topping and casserole separately for up to 3 days.

TO BAKE: Allow the covered dish to sit at room temperature for 1 hour. Adjust an oven rack to the middle position and heat the oven to 400 degrees. Remove the plastic wrap and sprinkle with the tortilla-crumb topping. Bake, uncovered, until bubbly and heated through, about 45 minutes. Cool for 10 minutes. Sprinkle with the cilantro and serve with the lime wedges.

TOPPING

8	ounces tortilla chips (about 2 cups)
2	tablespoons unsalted butter, melted

FILLING

4	tablespoons unsalted butter
1	medium onion, minced
2	medium red bell peppers, stemmed, seeded, and chopped medium
2	medium jalapeño chiles, stemmed, seeded, and minced
1	teaspoon ground cumin
1/8	teaspoon cayenne pepper
1	teaspoon salt
3	medium garlic cloves, minced or pressed through a garlic press
1/4	cup all-purpose flour
3 1/2	cups low-sodium chicken broth
3 1/2	cups whole milk
1 1/2	cups long-grain white rice
1/8	teaspoon ground black pepper
2	pounds boneless, skinless chicken breasts, trimmed of excess fat and prepared according to the illustrations on page 51
8	ounces Pepper Jack cheese, shredded (about 2 2/3 cups)
1	(15.5-ounce) can black beans, drained and rinsed
1 1/2	cups frozen corn, thawed and drained
2	tablespoons chopped fresh cilantro leaves
1	lime, cut into wedges

1. FOR THE TOPPING: Process the tortilla chips and butter in a food processor fitted with the steel blade until coarsely ground, about 15 seconds; set aside.

2. FOR THE FILLING: Adjust an oven rack to the middle position and heat the oven to 400 degrees. Melt the butter in a Dutch oven over medium heat. Add the onion, bell peppers, jalapeños, cumin, cayenne, and salt; cook, stirring occasionally, until the vegetables are softened, about 10 minutes. Add the garlic and cook until fragrant, about 1 minute. Add the flour and cook, stirring constantly, until golden, about 1 minute. Slowly whisk in the chicken broth and milk; bring to a simmer, whisking often. Stir in the rice and pepper and return to a simmer. Turn the heat to medium-low, cover, and cook, stirring often, until the rice has absorbed much of the liquid and is just tender, 20 to 25 minutes.

3. Add the chicken and continue to cook uncovered over medium-low heat, stirring occasionally, until no longer pink, about 4 minutes. Off the heat, stir in the Pepper Jack, black beans, and corn.

4. Pour the mixture into a 9 by 13-inch baking dish (or a shallow casserole dish of similar size) and sprinkle with the tortilla-crumb topping. Bake until the topping is browned and the casserole is bubbling, 20 to 25 minutes. Cool for 10 minutes. Sprinkle with the cilantro and serve with the lime wedges.

CHICKEN DIVAN CASSEROLE

CHICKEN, BROCCOLI, AND CHEDDAR cheese—beyond these three ingredients there is some debate about what constitutes an authentic chicken Divan. We're not sure exactly how the dish was first served at the Paris restaurant for which it is named, but we're willing to wager it didn't include canned cream soup or processed cheese food, nor was it spooned out of a casserole dish tableside. Nevertheless, that's what the dish has become, according to recipes we sampled. After years of decline, chicken Divan has become the epitome of "dump and bake" cooking, in which simple, fresh ingredients are replaced with processed convenience products, smothered in cheesy cream sauces, and finally destroyed by eons of oven time, all in the name of a quick Tuesday night supper. We had no desire to restore chicken Divan to its original status as fancy French restaurant fare, but we hoped to develop an easy way to let those three basic ingredients anchor a simple one-dish meal.

Since many recipes for chicken Divan suggested serving the saucy dish over rice, we decided to save time and pots (always a major concern in the test kitchen) and include rice in the casserole to make a complete meal. Our first attempts resembled other chicken and rice casseroles we had developed: bite-sized chicken pieces tossed with rice and broccoli in a creamy cheddar sauce. It was a tried-and-true technique, but this time tasters were ambivalent. A broccoli spear simply dipped in the cheddar sauce tasted great, but when the florets were completely covered with the sauce and baked, even for a relatively short period of time, the broccoli turned limp and army green, and its fresh flavor was overwhelmed by the creamy sauce. We tried first blanching the broccoli in boiling water to set its vibrant green color, but even this reliable restaurant trick couldn't keep the broccoli from turning to mush.

We went back to the drawing board. How could we protect the broccoli from both the sauce and the withering heat of the oven? We decided to try a layering approach, spreading cooked rice on the bottom of a baking dish, covering the rice with a layer of broccoli, and placing whole chicken breasts on top. The sauce was then poured over the chicken, and a bread-crumb topping was sprinkled over the sauce. The test failed, but not before we learned something. Long before the chicken breasts cooked through, the rice grains had completely overcooked. When we checked on the dish halfway through the cooking time, however, we noticed that the broccoli pieces directly under the chicken had remained bright green, while those in the spaces between the chicken breasts were drab and mushy. Clearly, the chicken had shielded the broccoli from the worst of the oven's heat.

Next we tried slicing the breasts into thin cutlets, both to increase the surface area we could cover and to reduce the necessary cooking time. This worked quite well: the chicken cooked through in about 30 minutes, and the broccoli was pleasantly green and just tender. With the

SHINGLING TECHNIQUE FOR CASSEROLES

Shingle the cutlets over the entire top of the casserole so that they overlap just slightly.

sauce confined to the top of the dish, we expected the rice to be dried out, but we found that the juices released by the chicken had kept it moist, and imparted a nice flavor to it as well.

This technique worked well, but the thinly sliced cutlets made for scant portions, and were awkward to serve out of the casserole dish. We tried slicing the cutlets in half and overlapping them to fit more into the dish. This required a few more minutes in the oven, but when we served it up, the rice and broccoli were still in good shape. The chicken, rice, and broccoli had all come out of one dish, but each element was distinct, not smothered together in a heavy sauce. We made simple pilaf-style rice, sautéing chopped onion and broccoli stalks for extra flavor, and undercooking the rice just slightly to allow for the carryover and oven cooking.

For the cheese sauce, we stayed with the traditional cheddar, but tasters found a small addition of grated Parmesan contributed a welcome

nuttiness and, along with a pinch of cayenne pepper, gave the sauce a more grown-up flavor. Our first batches tasted great, but we forgot, again, to account for all the extra moisture the chicken released when it cooked. It thinned the sauce to the point where it puddled in the bottom of the dish, rather than coating the chicken as we had planned. We compensated by reducing the amount of liquid and holding the flour constant. Once the cheese was stirred into this sauce it looked too thick, but after the chicken had contributed its moisture, it was just right: creamy and thick, but not pasty.

Chicken Divan Casserole

SERVES 6 TO 8

You may use either sliced, slivered, or whole blanched almonds in the topping. Adjust the grinding time as necessary—the nuts should be in small pieces, not ground to a powder.

PLANNING AHEAD: Follow the recipe through step 4, plunging the broccoli immediately into a bowl of ice water after cooking. Remove the broccoli from the ice water when cool, pat dry, and transfer to a bowl. Refrigerate the topping, broccoli, rice, and sauce in separate bowls, tightly wrapped with plastic wrap, for up to 1 day.

TO BAKE: Poke several vent holes in the plastic wrap covering the rice and the sauce. Microwave both, separately, on high power until hot, 3 to 5 minutes. Continue to assemble and bake the casserole as directed in step 5.

CUTTING CHICKEN CUTLETS FOR A CASSEROLE

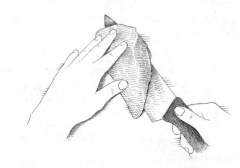

1. Slice the breasts in half horizontally into thin cutlets.

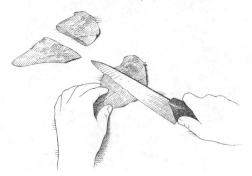

2. Cut the cutlets in half again crosswise into roughly 3 by 3-inch pieces.

TOPPING

1	cup sliced, slivered, or whole blanched almonds (see the headnote)
3	slices white sandwich bread, torn into quarters
2	tablespoons unsalted butter, melted

FILLING

	Salt
1	medium bunch broccoli (about 1½ pounds), florets trimmed to 1-inch pieces, stalks peeled and chopped medium (see page 214)
1	tablespoon olive oil
1	medium onion, minced
1½	cups long-grain white rice

3½ cups water
4   tablespoons unsalted butter
¼   cup all-purpose flour
2   cups low-sodium chicken broth
¾   cup heavy cream
6   ounces sharp cheddar, shredded (about 2 cups)
1   ounce Parmesan cheese, grated (about ½ cup)
⅛   teaspoon cayenne pepper
    Ground black pepper
2   pounds boneless, skinless chicken breasts, trimmed of excess fat and prepared according to the illustrations on page 51
1   lemon, cut into wedges

1. FOR THE TOPPING: Process the almonds in a food processor fitted with the steel blade until coarsely ground, 5 to 10 seconds. Add the bread and butter and process to a uniformly coarse crumb, about six 1-second pulses; set aside.

2. FOR THE FILLING: Adjust an oven rack to the middle position and heat the oven to 400 degrees. Bring 4 quarts of water to a boil in a Dutch oven over high heat. Season with 1 tablespoon salt and add the broccoli florets. Cook until bright green, about 1 minute. Drain thoroughly and spread out over a baking sheet to cool; set aside.

3. Wipe the Dutch oven dry, add the oil, and return to medium heat until shimmering. Add the

onion, broccoli stems, and ½ teaspoon salt; cook until softened, about 7 minutes. Add the rice and cook, stirring to coat the grains with oil, for about 1 minute. Add the water and bring to a simmer. Cover, turn the heat to low, and cook until the water is absorbed and the rice is just tender, about 16 minutes.

4. Meanwhile, melt the butter in a small saucepan over medium heat. Add the flour and cook, stirring constantly, until golden, about 1 minute. Slowly whisk in the chicken broth and cream; bring to a simmer, whisking often. Off the heat, whisk in the cheeses and cayenne until smooth. Season with salt and pepper to taste. Cover and set aside until ready to use.

5. Spread the cooked rice into a 9 by 13-inch baking dish (or a casserole dish of similar size) and arrange the broccoli florets in an even layer over the rice. Following the illustration on page 55, shingle the chicken cutlets over the broccoli so that they overlap slightly. Pour about 2 cups of the sauce over the chicken and sprinkle with the bread-crumb topping. Bake until the chicken is cooked through and the edges are bubbling, 30 to 35 minutes. Cool for 10 minutes. Serve with the lemon wedges, passing the remaining sauce separately.

➤ VARIATION
Chicken Florentine Casserole
SERVES 6 TO 8
When adding the spinach to the hot pan, toss it thoroughly to distribute the oil and garlic, otherwise the garlic will burn. Try to squeeze as much liquid as possible from the spinach after cooking to keep the rice from turning green.

PLANNING AHEAD: Follow the recipe through step 4, refrigerating the topping, spinach, rice, and sauce in separate bowls, tightly wrapped with plastic wrap, for up to 1 day.
TO BAKE: Poke several vent holes in the plastic wrap covering the rice and the sauce. Microwave both, separately, on high power until hot, 3 to 5 minutes. Assemble and bake the casserole as directed in step 5.

TOPPING
4   slices white sandwich bread, torn into quarters
2   tablespoons unsalted butter, melted

GIVE IT A SQUEEZE

Cooking can turn spinach watery, causing it to dilute other flavors. To remove excess liquid, transfer the cooked spinach to a colander in a sink. Using tongs, gently press juices from the spinach. Return the spinach to the skillet, season it, and serve.

FILLING

2	tablespoons plus 2 teaspoons olive oil
2	medium garlic cloves, minced or pressed through a garlic press
2	pounds bagged curly-leaf spinach, washed and stemmed
1	medium onion, minced
	Salt
1½	cups long-grain white rice
3½	cups water
4	tablespoons unsalted butter
¼	cup all-purpose flour
2	cups low-sodium chicken broth
¾	cup heavy cream
6	ounces Gruyère cheese, shredded (about 2 cups)
1	ounce Parmesan cheese, grated (about ½ cup)
⅛	teaspoon ground nutmeg
	Ground black pepper
2	pounds boneless, skinless chicken breasts, trimmed of excess fat and prepared according to the illustrations on page 51
2	tablespoons minced fresh parsley leaves
1	lemon, cut into wedges

1. FOR THE TOPPING: Process the bread and butter in a food processor fitted with the steel blade until coarsely ground, about six 1-second pulse; set aside.

2. FOR THE FILLING: Adjust an oven rack to the middle position and heat the oven to 400 degrees. Heat 1 tablespoon of the oil and half of the garlic in a Dutch oven over medium-high heat; cook, stirring often, until the garlic is lightly golden, about 2 minutes. Add half of the spinach by handfuls and stir to coat the spinach with the oil until just wilted, about 4 minutes. Transfer to a colander set over the sink. Add 1 more tablespoon oil and the remaining garlic; return to medium-high heat and cook, stirring often, until the garlic is lightly golden, about 1 minute. Add the remaining spinach and repeat; transfer to the colander. Gently squeeze the spinach to release excess moisture (see the illustration on page 57). Coarsely chop the spinach and set aside.

3. Wipe the pot clean with paper towels. Add the remaining 2 teaspoons oil and return to medium heat until shimmering. Add the onion and 1 teaspoon salt; cook until softened and golden, about 7 minutes. Add the rice and cook, stirring to coat the grains with oil, for 1 minute. Add the water and bring to a simmer; cover, turn the heat to low, and cook until the water is absorbed and the rice is just tender, about 16 minutes.

4. Meanwhile, melt the butter in a small saucepan over medium heat. Add the flour and cook, stirring constantly, until golden, about 1 minute. Slowly whisk in the chicken broth and cream; bring to a simmer, whisking often. Off the heat, whisk in the cheeses and nutmeg until smooth. Season with salt and pepper to taste and set aside, covered, until ready to use.

5. Spread the cooked rice into a 9 by 13-inch baking dish (or a shallow casserole dish of similar size) and spread the spinach in an even layer over the rice. Following the illustration on page 55, lay the chicken cutlets over the spinach so that they overlap slightly. Pour about 2 cups of the cheese sauce over the chicken and sprinkle with the bread-crumb topping. Bake until the chicken is cooked through and the edges are bubbling, 30 to 35 minutes. Cool for 10 minutes. Sprinkle with the parsley and serve with the lemon wedges, passing the remaining sauce separately.

CHICKEN CORDON BLEU CASSEROLE

TRADITIONAL CHICKEN CORDON BLEU IS made of chicken cutlets layered with thin slices of ham and Gruyère cheese, then breaded and sautéed—not a casserole by anyone's definition. But the layering of chicken cutlets in our Chicken Divan and Chicken Florentine recipes (see pages 56 and 57) reminded us of this dish, and made us wonder if we could adapt our new technique to incorporate some of its flavors.

We wanted to alternate slices of ham with the chicken cutlets as they were shingled across the casserole. Tasters liked the flavor of baked ham from the deli counter, but the thin slices seemed insubstantial sandwiched between the chicken cutlets. Thicker supermarket ham steaks tended to be salty and gristly, and released a tremendous amount of briny liquid into the casserole when cooked. So we went back to the deli ham but sliced it thicker—about a quarter of an inch—and were pleased with the results.

We took our existing cheese sauce and added a healthy quantity of Dijon mustard; tasters felt it paired very well with the strong flavor of the ham. This hearty dish seemed to cry out for potatoes instead of rice, so we experimented with cooking thin potato slices in the cheese sauce. Our plan was to then layer them beneath the chicken and ham, creating a built-in side dish of cheesy scalloped potatoes.

This was much easier said than done. Potatoes that were partially cooked in the sauce did not finish evenly in the oven—the ones at the center were still undercooked when the chicken was done. Next we tried cooking them on the stovetop until tender, but since potatoes are reluctant to absorb moisture from a thickened sauce, this took over 40 minutes. There were other problems as well: Since were trying to cook a large quantity of potatoes in a relatively small amount of liquid, the potatoes tended to stick to the pan. And once the potatoes were cooked, they had to be lifted out of the sauce with a mesh strainer so that we would have sauce left to pour over the chicken, a messy procedure.

This was one case where two pots were better than one. Cooking the potato slices in salted boiling water solved all of these problems in one go. We then drained them, tossed them with half of the sauce, and layered them right in the pan. As the dish baked in the oven, the chicken released flavorful juices that soaked into the potatoes and thinned the cheese sauce to the proper consistency.

Chicken Cordon Bleu Casserole

SERVES 6 TO 8

In a tasting of different styles of deli hams, tasters disliked the texture of boiled hams (notable for their molded rectangular shape and pink exterior). Choose baked or Virginia-style ham, and ask for it to be sliced ¼ inch thick.

PLANNING AHEAD: Prepare the topping and cheese sauce as directed in steps 1 and 3 of the recipe, then refrigerate in separate bowls, tightly wrapped with plastic wrap, for up to 1 day.

TO BAKE: Poke several vent holes in the plastic wrap covering the sauce and microwave on high power until hot, 3 to 5 minutes. Cook the potatoes as directed in step 2, then assemble and bake the casserole as directed in step 4.

TOPPING

4	slices white sandwich bread, torn into quarters
2	tablespoons unsalted butter, melted

FILLING

3	pounds russet potatoes (about 5 medium potatoes), peeled and sliced ⅛ inch thick
	Salt
4	tablespoons unsalted butter
I	medium onion, chopped
2	teaspoons minced fresh thyme leaves
2	medium garlic cloves, minced or pressed through a garlic press
6	tablespoons all-purpose flour
2	cups low-sodium chicken broth
¾	cup heavy cream
6	ounces Gruyère, shredded (about 2 cups)
3	tablespoons Dijon mustard
¼	teaspoons cayenne pepper
	Ground black pepper
2	pounds boneless, skinless chicken breasts, trimmed of excess fat and prepared according to the illustrations on page 51
12	ounces deli ham, sliced ¼ inch thick, rind trimmed, and halved or quartered into 3-inch pieces
2	tablespoons minced fresh parsley leaves
I	lemon, cut into wedges

1. FOR THE TOPPING: Process the bread and butter in a food processor fitted with the steel blade until coarsely ground, about six 1-second pulses; set aside.

2. FOR THE FILLING: Adjust an oven rack to the middle position and heat the oven to 400 degrees. Place the potatoes, 6 cups water, and 1 teaspoon salt in a Dutch oven. Bring to a boil over high heat, then reduce the heat to a simmer. Cook,

uncovered, until the potatoes are partially cooked, about 2 minutes. Using a slotted spoon, remove the potatoes to a bowl and set aside.

3. Meanwhile, melt the butter in a medium saucepan over medium heat. Add the onion, thyme, and ½ teaspoon salt; cook until the onions are softened, about 6 minutes. Add the garlic and cook until fragrant, about 1 minute. Add the flour and cook, stirring constantly, until golden, about 1 minute. Slowly whisk in the chicken broth and cream; bring to a simmer, whisking often. Off the heat, whisk in the Gruyère, Dijon, and cayenne until smooth. Season with salt and pepper to taste. Cover and set aside until ready to use.

4. Toss the potatoes with half of the sauce and spread into the bottom of a 9 by 13-inch baking dish (or a shallow casserole dish of similar size). Following the illustration on page 55, shingle alternating pieces of the chicken and ham over the potatoes, overlapping as needed. Pour the remaining sauce evenly over the chicken and sprinkle with the bread-crumb topping. Bake until the chicken is cooked through and the casserole is bubbling, 30 to 35 minutes. Cool for 10 minutes. Sprinkle with the parsley and serve with the lemon wedges.

Chicken Casserole with Spring Vegetables

THE TERM "SPRING VEGETABLE" SUGGESTS a light dish infused with simple, delicate flavors—hardly the way we would describe most of the chicken casserole recipes we tested after scouring cookbooks and the Internet. With mushy vegetables, tasteless chunks of overcooked chicken, and a heavy, pasty sauce, these casseroles said spring like Siberia. We set out to develop a recipe that would prove "light" and "creamy" are not mutually exclusive culinary concepts.

Because of their universal availability and mild flavor, we choose to work with boneless, skinless chicken breasts cut into bite-size pieces. Every recipe we consulted, however, called for "cooked chicken," and many went so far as to instruct us how to cook it in case we didn't have leftovers on hand. In some cases the chicken was poached, in others it was roasted, but in every case it was a completely separate step, with no connection to the rest of the recipe. This made little sense to us—the juices released by chicken during cooking are extremely flavorful, so why waste them? By the same token, the chicken's flavor would be greatly improved by cooking it in a sauce instead of plain water or stock. The sauce and the meat flavor each other in turn—it's part of the theory behind braising, and it seemed just as relevant to our casserole filling. And lastly, we didn't see how chicken that went into the oven fully cooked could come out of the oven anything less than overcooked.

Our plan to avoid overcooking, therefore, was to prepare a flour-thickened sauce on the stovetop, add the vegetables and raw chicken pieces, and then transfer the filling to a casserole dish and finish it in the oven. The trouble, as our first test showed, was uneven cooking; by the time the chicken pieces at the center were cooked through, those at the edges were seriously overdone. The efficient transfer of heat to the center of the pan was slowed further by the fact that the chicken was cold—dumping two pounds of refrigerated ingredients into the filling lowered the overall temperature of the casserole significantly. Next we ran a series of tests in which the chicken was partially cooked in the sauce before transferring the hot filling to the oven. We found that by cooking the chicken just until it lost its raw color, it retained enough heat to finish cooking quickly and evenly in the oven without drying out.

"Spring vegetable" can be an imprecise term, but the readily available choices include leeks, carrots, peas, and asparagus. Chopped leeks took the place of the usual onion—they were sautéed in butter along with the carrots before adding the flour and the remaining sauce ingredients. Tasters approved of a small amount of garlic, which provided a savory background note without overwhelming the delicate flavors of the vegetables. As the asparagus and peas were quick to overcook, we decided to add them just at the end, before transferring the dish to the oven. This worked well for the peas, which remained bright and fresh tasting, and too well for the 1-inch pieces of asparagus, which remained a bit crunchy. Trying to time the asparagus by adding it to the sauce a few minutes sooner seemed risky—the width of the spears varied from bunch to bunch, and asparagus has a notoriously narrow window for proper doneness. Another option was to quickly blanch the asparagus in boiling water, then shock it in an ice bath to stop the cooking, but this seemed like too much effort for a simple casserole. The solution was to cut the spears on a sharp bias into very thin slices. This ensured that the pieces were cooked through, but still big enough to look distinct (and more attractive than the average vegetable chunk).

For the sauce, we considered flour-thickened combinations of chicken broth, milk, and cream. In other chicken casseroles we had found success with equal amounts of milk and broth, but in this case, the milk contributed a sweetness that dulled the fresh taste of the vegetables. Tasters preferred a 2-1 ratio of broth to cream, which produced a rich sauce with a neutral flavor, allowing the more delicate-tasting vegetables to shine through. Concerned that our sauce might turn out bland, we experimented with additional ingredients like wine, sherry, and assorted cheeses, but found that the simpler, cleaner flavors of the original were much preferable. Fresh herbs were approved by tasters, specifically tarragon. Tasters also appreciated the addition of lemon juice, but its flavor tended to die in the heat of the oven, so we opted to serve lemon wedges on the side.

Chicken Casserole with Spring Vegetables and Tarragon Cream Sauce

SERVES 6 TO 8

It is important to let the casserole cool and the sauce thicken for at least 10 minutes before serving.

PLANNING AHEAD: Follow the recipe through step 2, simmering the chicken until it is completely cooked, about 10 minutes, before adding the asparagus and peas. Pour the mixture into a 9 by 13-inch baking dish (or a shallow casserole dish of similar size). Wrap the dish tightly with plastic wrap and poke several vent holes with the tip of a paring knife. Refrigerate the casserole until cool, about 3 hours, then wrap it tightly with another sheet of plastic wrap. Refrigerate the topping and casserole separately for up to 2 days.

TO BAKE: Allow the covered dish to sit at room temperature for 1 hour. Adjust an oven rack to the middle position and heat the oven to 400 degrees. Remove the plastic wrap and sprinkle with the bread-crumb topping. Cover tightly with foil and bake until bubbling, about 35 minutes. Remove the foil and continue to bake until the topping has browned, about 10 minutes longer. Cool for 10 minutes. Serve with the lemon wedges.

TOPPING

4	slices white sandwich bread, torn into quarters
2	tablespoons unsalted butter, melted

FILLING

4	tablespoons unsalted butter
3	medium leeks, white and light green parts only, halved lengthwise, sliced $1/4$ inch thick, and rinsed well
3	medium carrots, peeled, halved lengthwise, and sliced $1/4$ inch thick
$1^1/2$	teaspoons salt
3	medium garlic cloves, minced or pressed through a garlic press
6	tablespoons all-purpose flour
2	cups low-sodium chicken broth
1	cup heavy cream
2	pounds boneless, skinless chicken breasts, trimmed of excess fat and prepared according to the illustrations on page 51
1	pound asparagus, tough ends trimmed, sliced thin on the bias
1	cup frozen peas
3	tablespoons chopped fresh tarragon leaves
$1/4$	teaspoon ground black pepper
1	lemon, cut into wedges

1. FOR THE TOPPING: Process the bread and butter in a food processor fitted with the steel blade until coarsely ground, about six 1-second pulses; set aside.

2. Adjust an oven rack to the middle position and heat the oven to 400 degrees. Melt the butter in a Dutch oven over medium heat. Add the leeks, carrots, and salt; cook, stirring occasionally, until the vegetables are softened but not browned, about 10 minutes. Add the garlic and cook until fragrant,

about 1 minute. Add the flour and cook, stirring constantly, until golden, about 1 minute. Slowly whisk in the chicken broth and cream; bring to a simmer, whisking often. Add the chicken and cook, stirring occasionally, until no longer pink, about 4 minutes. Stir in the asparagus, peas, tarragon, and pepper.

3. Pour the mixture into a 9 by 13-inch baking dish (or a shallow casserole dish of similar size) and sprinkle with the bread-crumb topping. Bake until browned and very bubbly, 20 to 25 minutes. Cool for 10 minutes. Serve with the lemon wedges.

➤ VARIATIONS

Chicken Casserole with Summer Squash, Sun-Dried Tomatoes, and Basil

SERVES 6 TO 8

Half-inch slices may seem thick for squash and zucchini, but they will shrink when salted and cooked. If not sliced thick enough, they will overcook in the oven. Don't stir the squash too often when it's in the skillet, or it will not brown properly.

PLANNING AHEAD: Follow the recipe through step 4, simmering the chicken until it is completely cooked, about 10 minutes, before adding the sun-dried tomatoes and sautéed squash. Pour the mixture into a 9 by 13-inch baking dish (or a shallow casserole dish of similar size). Wrap the dish tightly with plastic wrap and poke several vent holes with the tip of a paring knife. Refrigerate the casserole until cool, about 3 hours, then wrap it tightly with another sheet of plastic wrap. Refrigerate the topping and casserole separately for up to 2 days.

TO BAKE: Allow the covered dish to sit at room temperature for 1 hour. Adjust an oven rack to the middle position and heat the oven to 400 degrees. Remove the plastic wrap and sprinkle with the bread-crumb topping. Cover tightly with foil and bake until bubbling, about 35 minutes. Remove the foil and continue to bake until the topping has browned, about 10 minutes longer. Cool for 10 minutes. Serve with the lemon wedges.

TOPPING

4   slices white sandwich bread, torn into quarters
2   tablespoons unsalted butter, melted

FILLING

1   pound zucchini, halved lengthwise, then sliced crosswise into 1/2-inch pieces

1   pound summer squash, halved lengthwise, then sliced crosswise into 1/2-inch pieces
    Kosher salt
2   tablespoons olive oil
4   tablespoons unsalted butter
1   medium onion, minced
3   medium garlic cloves, minced or pressed through a garlic press
6   tablespoons all-purpose flour
2   cups low-sodium chicken broth
1   cup heavy cream
2   pounds boneless, skinless chicken breasts, trimmed of excess fat and prepared according to the illustrations on page 51
1   cup (one 8-ounce jar) oil-packed sun-dried tomatoes, drained, patted dry, and chopped coarse
1/3 cup chopped fresh basil leaves
1/4 teaspoon ground black pepper
1   lemon, cut into wedges

1. FOR THE TOPPING: Process the bread and butter in a food processor fitted with the steel blade until coarsely ground, about six 1-second pulses; set aside.

2. FOR THE FILLING: Toss the zucchini and summer squash together with 2 tablespoons kosher salt in a large colander set over a bowl, and let stand 30 minutes.

3. Adjust an oven rack to the middle position and heat the oven to 400 degrees. Spread the salted squash evenly over a double layer of paper towels and pat dry with additional paper towels, wiping off any residual salt. Heat 1 tablespoon of the oil in a 12-inch nonstick skillet over high heat until just smoking. Add half of the squash and cook, stirring occasionally, until golden brown and slightly charred, 5 to 7 minutes. Spread the squash out on a baking sheet. Add the remaining tablespoon oil to the pan and return to high heat and until just smoking. Cook the remaining squash and transfer it to the baking sheet; set aside.

4. Melt the butter in a Dutch oven medium heat. Add the onion and 1 teaspoon kosher salt; cook, stirring occasionally, until softened, about 6 minutes. Add the garlic and cook until fragrant, about 1 minute. Add the flour and cook, stirring

constantly, until golden, about 1 minute. Slowly whisk in the chicken broth and cream; bring to a simmer, whisking often. Add the chicken and cook, stirring occasionally, until no longer pink, about 4 minutes. Stir in the sun-dried tomatoes, basil, pepper, and sautéed squash.

5. Pour mixture into a 9 by 13-inch baking dish (or a casserole dish of similar size) and sprinkle with the bread-crumb topping. Bake until the top is browned and very bubbly, 20 to 25 minutes. Cool for 10 minutes. Serve with the lemon wedges.

Chicken Curry Casserole with Cauliflower, Peas, and Potatoes

SERVES 6 TO 8

Some curry powders are milder than others; add additional cayenne or serve with Tabasco sauce if the final dish is not as spicy as desired. Unsweetened shredded coconut is available in natural-food stores as well as in grocery stores.

PLANNING AHEAD: Follow the recipe through step 2, simmering the chicken until it is completely cooked, about 10 minutes, before adding the cauliflower and peas. Pour the mixture into a 9 by 13-inch baking dish (or a shallow casserole dish of similar size). Wrap the dish with plastic wrap and poke several vent holes with the tip of a paring knife. Refrigerate the casserole until cool, about 3 hours, then wrap it tightly with another sheet of plastic wrap. Refrigerate the casserole for up to 2 days.

TO BAKE: Allow the covered dish to sit at room temperature for 1 hour. Adjust an oven rack to the middle position and heat the oven to 400 degrees. Remove the plastic wrap, cover tightly with foil, and bake until bubbling, about 40 minutes. Remove the foil, sprinkle with the almonds, and continue to bake until they are toasted, about 20 minutes longer. Cool for 10 minutes. Sprinkle with the cilantro before serving.

4	tablespoons unsalted butter
1	large onion, minced
4	teaspoons curry powder
1/8	teaspoon cayenne pepper
1/2	cup shredded unsweetened coconut
1	very ripe banana, peeled and chopped coarse
4	medium garlic cloves, minced or pressed through garlic press
1	(1½-inch) piece ginger, peeled and grated
5	tablespoons all-purpose flour
2	cups low-sodium chicken broth
1	cup heavy cream
1½	pounds red potatoes, scrubbed and cut into ³/₄-inch cubes
2	pounds boneless, skinless chicken breasts, trimmed of excess fat and prepared according to the illustrations on page 51
1	medium head cauliflower (about 2 pounds), cored and the florets cut into ³/₄-inch pieces (see page 227)

INGREDIENTS: Curry Powder

Like chili powder, curry powder is not a single spice but rather a blend of spices. Unlike chili powder, which contains about 80 percent chile pepper, there is no single dominant spice in curry powder. Instead, flavors vary greatly depending on the blend. Among the spices most commonly used are cardamom, cumin, fenugreek, turmeric (which gives curry its characteristic yellow color), fennel, nutmeg, and chiles. We chose seven mild curry powders (hot curry powder, which contains more red pepper and other hot spices, is also available) and tasted them all in a simple rice pilaf, cooking the curry powder in oil briefly to allow the flavors to bloom.

Overall, tasters leaned toward big, bolder, brighter blends that delivered a lot of color and flavor. Tone's, a darling of the discount-club stores, led the pack and was praised for its "good, heavy spice mix."

Unfortunately, some manufacturers consider their exact spice blends to be proprietary information and they would not share that information with us. Therefore, we cannot speculate on why Tone's dominated over such specialty brands as Penzey's and Kalustyan's.

THE BEST CURRY POWDER

Tone's Curry Powder ($7.39 for 16 ounces) is sold in many warehouse clubs and was praised by tasters for its "strong" curry flavor.

1 cup frozen peas
1 teaspoon salt
¼ teaspoon ground black pepper
1 cup sliced almonds
2 tablespoons chopped fresh cilantro leaves

1. Adjust an oven rack to the middle position and heat the oven to 400 degrees. Melt the butter in a Dutch oven over medium heat. Add the onion, curry, and cayenne; cook, stirring occasionally, until the onion is softened, about 6 minutes. Add the coconut and cook until fragrant, about 1 minute. Add the banana, garlic, and ginger; cook, mashing the banana into a paste with the back of a wooden spoon, until fragrant, about 1 minute. Add the flour and cook, stirring constantly, until golden, about 1 minute. Slowly whisk in the chicken broth and cream. Add the potatoes and bring to a simmer, stirring occasionally. Cover, turn the heat to low, and cook, stirring occasionally, until the potatoes are just tender, about 20 minutes.

2. Add the chicken and cook, stirring occasionally, until no longer pink, about 4 minutes. Stir in the cauliflower, peas, salt, and pepper.

3. Pour the mixture into a 9 by 13-inch baking dish (or a shallow casserole dish of similar size). Bake for 20 minutes. Sprinkle the sliced almonds over the top and continue to bake until the almonds are browned and the casserole is bubbling, about 10 minutes longer. Cool for 10 minutes. Sprinkle with the cilantro before serving.

CHICKEN ENCHILADAS WITH CHILI SAUCE

TAKE A SOFTENED TORTILLA, STUFF IT WITH A savory chicken filling, roll it, encase it in a spicy chili sauce, and serve it with an assortment of creamy and crunchy toppings, and you have quite possibly the most popular Mexican dish in the world. And for good reason. Chicken enchiladas are a complete meal that offers a rich and complex combination of flavors, textures, and ingredients. The problem with preparing enchiladas at home is that traditional cooking methods require a whole day of preparation. Could we simplify the process, yet retain the authentic flavor of the real thing?

We began by preparing five simplified recipes, hoping to uncover valuable tips and techniques. All of them produced disappointing results. Mushy tortillas, bland or bitter sauces, uninspired fillings, too much cheese, and lackluster flavor left tasters yearning for something tastier and more authentic.

A side-by-side tasting of corn and wheat flour tortillas came out clearly in favor of the corn, with its more substantial texture. Tasters also preferred the small 6-inch tortillas, with 8-inch tortillas a close second. These sizes provided the best proportion of tortilla to filling to sauce, and both sizes fit neatly into a 9-inch-wide baking pan. Although ingredients and size mattered, we were happy to discover that brand didn't. Given the big flavors from the sauce and filling, flavor differences between various brands of tortillas (which are rather bland tasting anyway) were not important in the final dish.

Our next task was to figure out how to treat the tortillas so that they would be soft and pliable to roll and toothsome to eat. The traditional approach is to dip each tortilla in hot oil (to create a moisture barrier) and then in the sauce (to add flavor) prior to assembly. Although this technique works well, it is time-consuming, tedious, and messy. We tried rolling chilled corn tortillas straight from the package, but they were tough and cracked easily. Heating a stack of tortillas in the microwave also proved disappointing. The tortillas were soft, but the resulting enchiladas were mushy. Next we tried wrapping the tortillas in foil and steaming them on a plate over boiling water. These tortillas were also easy to roll but were wet and soggy when baked.

Thinking back to the traditional first step of dipping the tortilla in oil gave us an idea. Using the modern-day convenience of oil in a spray can, we placed the tortillas in a single layer on a baking sheet, sprayed both sides lightly with vegetable oil, and warmed them in a moderate oven. This proved to be the shortcut we were hoping to find. The oil-sprayed, oven-warmed tortillas were pliable, and their texture after being filled, rolled, and baked was nearly perfect.

Because red chili sauce is the most common sauce used in enchiladas, we decided to prepare a half dozen traditional recipes. The flavors were spicy and complex, the textures smooth and somewhat thick, the colors deep orange-red. The problem was that whole dried chiles played a central role in all of these sauces. Not only are whole chiles difficult to find in some areas, but they require substantial preparation time, including toasting, seeding, stemming, rehydrating, and processing in a blender. Store-bought chili powder would have to be part of the solution.

The obvious question was how to augment the flavor of the usually bland chili powder available in the supermarket. Our first thought was to heat the chili powder in oil, a process that intensifies flavors. We began by sautéing onions and garlic and then added the chili powder to the pan. This indeed produced a fuller, deeper flavor. We enhanced the flavor by adding ground cumin, coriander, and oregano—ingredients often found in authentic red chili sauces—as well as cayenne pepper for more heat. Tasters gave this combo a thumbs-up.

Many traditional recipes incorporate tomatoes for substance and flavor. With a nod toward convenience, we explored canned tomato products first. We tried adding diced tomatoes and then pureeing the mixture. The texture was too thick and too tomatoey. Tomato sauce turned out to be a better option.

Focusing on flavor next, we prepared a batch with 2 teaspoons of sugar, which succeeded in expanding and enriching the flavor of the spices.

ASSEMBLING ENCHILADAS

1. Smear the entire bottom of a 9 by 13-inch baking dish with ¾ cup chili sauce.

2. Place the tortillas on two baking sheets. Spray both sides lightly with cooking spray. Bake until the tortillas are soft and pliable, about 4 minutes.

3. Place the warm tortillas on a work surface. Increase the oven temperature to 400 degrees. Place ⅓ cup filling down the center of each tortilla.

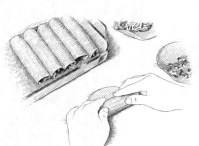

4. Roll each tortilla tightly by hand. Place them in a baking dish, side by side, seam-side down.

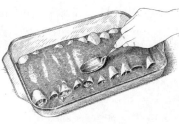

5. Pour the remaining chili sauce over the top of the enchiladas. Use the back of a spoon to spread the sauce so it coats the top of each tortilla.

6. Sprinkle ¾ cup shredded cheese down the center of the enchiladas.

Two teaspoons of lime juice constituted the final flavor adjustment, adding just enough acidity to activate the taste buds and enliven the sauce.

Next, we were on to the filling and started with how to cook the chicken. We tried the common method of poaching, but tasters said this chicken was dry and bland. We tried roasting both white and dark meat, which was extremely time-consuming, although tasters really liked the dark meat. Obsessed with speed and flavor, we had an idea. Why not use boneless, skinless thighs and cook them right in the sauce? Cutting the thighs into thin strips across the grain, we added them to the pan after the spices were fragrant. The chicken cooked in less than 10 minutes, and it was nicely seasoned. Cooking the chicken, in the sauce also lent the sauce a wonderful richness. To separate the chicken from the sauce, we poured the contents of the pot through a medium-mesh strainer.

With the chicken cooked and ready for the filling, we needed to add just a few complementary ingredients. Cheese topped our list. *Queso fresco*, the traditional choice, is a young, unripened cheese with a creamy color, mild flavor, and crumbly texture. Because it is not readily available in the United States, we tried farmers' cheese. Tasters liked this cheese for its creamy texture and mellow flavor. But it was Monterey Jack and sharp white cheddar that made the top of the list. The Jack is mellow, while the cheddar adds a sharp, distinctive flavor. (Cheese, we discovered, also helps to bind the filling ingredients.)

Looking for more heat, we taste-tested the addition of fresh jalapeños, chipotles in adobo sauce, and pickled jalapeños. The fresh jalapeños were too mild. Chipotles (smoked jalapeños stewed in a seasoned liquid) added a distinctive, warm heat and smoky flavor that some tasters enjoyed but that most found too spicy and smoky. Everyone was surprised to find that the very convenient pickled jalapeños (sold in both cans and jars) were the favorite. The vinegar pickling solution added spicy, bright, and sour notes to the filling.

Some recipes suggest filling and rolling one enchilada at a time, but we much preferred the efficiency offered by the assembly-line approach.

We spread the oil-sprayed, oven-warmed tortillas on the countertop and spread ⅓ cup of filling down the center of each. We rolled them tightly and placed them seam-side down, side by side, along the length of a 9 by 13-inch baking pan that had a little sauce in it. We then poured the rest of the sauce over the enchiladas and sprinkled them with a bit of extra cheese. We experimented with oven temperatures and times before settling on 400 degrees for 20 minutes, at which point the enchiladas were hot and ready to be served.

Enchiladas are traditionally eaten with an array of raw, salad-like garnishes. Tasters passed on chopped tomatoes, saying they did not add much flavor or texture. Raw onions were considered "too harsh." Sour cream and avocado were chosen for their cooling qualities, and romaine lettuce was favored for its "fresh, crispy crunch." Finally, there were the lime wedges.

Start to finish, our chicken enchiladas now took less than an hour and a half to make: 20 minutes for the sauce, 15 for the filling, 30 to assemble and bake, and 10 to prep the toppings. Not bad for a dish with authentic Mexican flavor.

~

Chicken Enchiladas with Red Chili Sauce

SERVES 4 TO 6

If you prefer, Monterey Jack can be used instead of cheddar or, for a mellower flavor and creamier texture, try substituting an equal amount of farmers' cheese. Be sure to cool the chicken before filling the tortillas, or the hot filling will make the enchiladas soggy.

PLANNING AHEAD: Assemble the casserole as directed through step 3, but do not bake. Wrap the dish tightly with plastic wrap and refrigerate for up to 2 days or freeze, tightly wrapped with an additional layer of foil, for up to 1 month. (If frozen, thaw in the refrigerator for at least 24 hours.)

TO BAKE: Allow the covered dish to sit at room temperature for 1 hour. Adjust an oven rack to the middle position and heat the oven to 400 degrees. Remove the plastic wrap and cover the dish tightly with foil. Bake until it is hot and the cheese melts, about 30 minutes. Uncover and serve immediately, passing the sour cream, avocado, lettuce, and lime wedges separately.

SAUCE AND FILLING

1½	tablespoons vegetable or corn oil
1	medium onion, chopped fine
3	medium garlic cloves, minced or pressed through a garlic press
3	tablespoons chili powder
2	teaspoons ground coriander
2	teaspoons ground cumin
½	teaspoon salt
2	teaspoons sugar
4	boneless, skinless chicken thighs (about 12 ounces), trimmed of excess fat and cut into ¼-inch-wide strips
2	(8-ounce) cans tomato sauce
¾	cup water
½	cup coarsely chopped fresh cilantro leaves
1	(4-ounce) can pickled jalapeños, drained and chopped (about ¼ cup)
8	ounces sharp cheddar cheese, shredded (about 2⅔ cups)

TORTILLAS AND TOPPINGS

10	(6-inch) corn tortillas
	Vegetable or corn oil cooking spray
3	ounces sharp cheddar cheese, shredded (about 1 cup)
¾	cup sour cream
1	avocado, diced medium
5	romaine lettuce leaves, washed, dried, and shredded
2	limes, quartered

1. FOR THE SAUCE AND FILLING: Heat the oil in a medium saucepan over medium-high heat until hot and shimmering but not smoking. Add the onion and cook, stirring occasionally, until softened and beginning to brown, about 5 minutes. Add the garlic, chili powder, coriander, cumin, salt, and sugar; cook, stirring constantly, until fragrant, about 30 seconds. Add the chicken and cook, stirring constantly, until coated with the spices, about 30 seconds. Add the tomato sauce and water; stir to separate the chicken pieces. Bring to a simmer, then reduce the heat to medium-low; simmer uncovered, stirring occasionally, until the chicken is cooked through and the flavors have melded, about 8 minutes. Pour the mixture through a medium-mesh strainer into a medium bowl, pressing on the chicken and onions to extract as much sauce as possible; set the sauce aside. Transfer the chicken mixture to a large plate; freeze for 10 minutes to cool, then combine with the cilantro, jalapeños, and the 8 ounces shredded cheddar in a medium bowl and set aside.

2. Adjust the oven racks to the upper- and lower-middle positions and heat the oven to 300 degrees.

3. TO ASSEMBLE: Following the illustrations on page 65, smear the entire bottom of a 9 by 13-inch baking dish with ¾ cup of the chili sauce. Place the tortillas in a single layer on two baking sheets. Spray both sides lightly with cooking spray. Bake until the tortillas are soft and pliable, about 4 minutes. Transfer the warm tortillas to a work surface. Increase the oven temperature to 400 degrees. Spread ⅓ cup filling down the center of each tortilla. Roll each tortilla tightly by hand and place, seam-side down, side by side on the sauce in the baking dish. Pour the remaining chili sauce over the top of the enchiladas. Use the back of a spoon to spread the sauce so it coats the top of each tortilla. Sprinkle the 3 ounces shredded cheddar down the center of the enchiladas.

4. TO BAKE: Cover the baking dish with foil. Bake the enchiladas on the lower-middle rack until they are heated through and the cheese is melted, 20 to 25 minutes. Uncover and serve immediately, passing the sour cream, avocado, lettuce, and lime wedges separately.

ROLLING TORTILLAS MADE EASY

COOL AND STIFF **WARM AND PLIABLE**

Straight from the refrigerator, a corn tortilla is too stiff to roll and will tear at the edges (left). Spraying the tortilla with oil and heating it for four minutes in a 300-degree oven will make the tortilla pliable and easy to manage (right).

Cheese Enchiladas

Queso fresco is a slightly salty, fresh Mexican cheese, also known as queso blanco. If unavailable, substitute 6 ounces of sharp cheddar.

Follow the recipe for Chicken Enchiladas with Red Chili Sauce, making the following changes. Omit the chicken and cheddar. Add 2 medium red bell peppers, stemmed, seeded, and chopped fine with the onion in step 1 and cook until softened, about 8 minutes. Continue to follow the recipe as directed, adding 6 ounces (about 2 cups) shredded Monterey Jack Cheese and 4 ounces (about 1 cup) crumbled queso fresco (see the headnote) with the cilantro and jalapeños at the end of step 1.

DICING AN AVOCADO

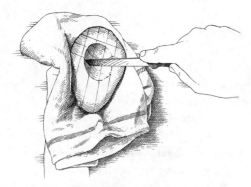

1. Use a dish towel to hold the avocado steady. Make ½ -inch cross-hatch incisions in the flesh with a dinner knife, cutting down to but not through the skin.

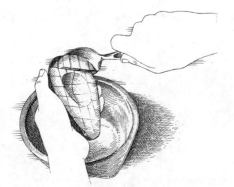

2. Separate the diced flesh from the skin using a spoon inserted between the skin and the flesh, gently scooping out the avocado cubes.

CHICKEN TORTILLA CASSEROLE

IN THEORY, CHICKEN TORTILLA CASSEROLE— sometimes called Mexican lasagna—makes for a refreshing change of pace from more traditional chicken casseroles, with the addition of chiles, beans, and layers of earthy corn tortillas. In practice, however, this dish suffers from the same problems that plague its north-of-the-border relations. Our research turned up countless recipes for this dish, most of which insisted on disguising overcooked chicken with cans of cream soup and gobs of cheese, then baking the whole mess until the flavors were as lifeless as the Mojave desert.

Our goal was to breathe some life and spice into this heavy dish. To accomplish that we would have to eliminate the creamy sauce and drastically reduce the lengthy oven time. Our plan was to create a spicy filling, then spread it between three layers of corn tortillas, the topmost of which would be covered with melted cheese.

We knew what not to put in our sauce—canned cream of chicken soup—but as for the rest of the ingredients, recipes varied widely. Tasters didn't care for Tex-Mex options such as olives, mushrooms, or green bell peppers, but did like pinto beans, red bell peppers, and chipotle peppers, in addition to the ubiquitous tomatoes, onions and garlic. They also liked cumin and chili powder, but not in the large quantities suggested by most recipes. Just a teaspoon of each contributed plenty of spice without masking the subtler flavors of the beans and vegetables. For the cheese, we determined that a mixture of cheddar and Monterey Jack delivered good flavor and still melted well, without becoming stringy or greasy. Cilantro and lime juice were the natural Southwestern choices to round out the filling.

For the chicken, bite-size pieces of boneless breasts seemed the only logical choice, given our layered approach. All of the recipes we found started with "cooked chicken," but we knew from prior testing that we could obtain much better results, with much less oven time, if the chicken was first partially cooked in the sauce, then allowed to finish cooking in the oven. (See Creamy Chicken and Rice Casserole with Peas, Carrots, and Cheddar on page 52.) This technique delivered chicken that was tender and juicy, cooked evenly throughout the casserole dish, and flavored by the sauce in which it cooked.

Our first attempt at assembling the dish was a disaster in more ways than one. The middle layers of tortillas had completely disintegrated, leaving behind a homely sort of cornmeal mush. Meanwhile, the top layers, instead of crisping up, had withered and toughened into a leathery mess. The filling was dry, as the moisture had all soaked into the tortillas. And even though the dish had been in the oven for only 30 minutes, the fresh flavors of the cilantro, chiles, and lime juice were muddy and washed out.

We tackled the tortilla problem first. They acted like a sponge in our casserole, soaking up all available liquid and turning to mush in the process. We knew from traditional enchilada recipes that a quick dunk in hot oil would create a moisture barrier, but heating up oil for deep-frying seemed like too much trouble. Our own enchilada recipe solved this problem by spraying the tortillas with cooking spray and heating them briefly in a low oven, and we were pleased to discover that this method worked in our casserole as well. The inner layers were better—distinct rows of tortillas were visible—but overall they were still mushy. The top layer, however, was dramatically improved. The tortillas were crispy like nacho chips, even buried under a layer of melted cheese.

With most of our casseroles we found that an oven temperature of 400 degrees provided the best balance between quick and even cooking. But this dish was an exception. We increased the heat to 450 degrees to maximize the crispness of the topping and to minimize the amount of time that the tortillas had to soak up liquid. At this temperature, the casserole was in and out of the oven in 15 minutes—just long enough to finish the chicken, melt the cheese, and crisp up the top layer of tortillas.

Despite these efforts, the inner layers of tortillas were still breaking down too much, absorbing all of the liquid and leaving behind a dry filling. How could we keep the liquid in the sauce, and out of the tortillas? We had not, until this point, used any flour in our recipes, as we had decided against a thick, creamy sauce. But perhaps by thickening the sauce with a small quantity of flour, we could keep the tortillas drier, because water bound up in swollen starch granules is more difficult for foods to absorb. The addition of just 2 tablespoons of flour did the trick: The filling remained saucy and the tortilla layers were soft but still intact.

One problem remained. We had worked hard to produce a casserole that did not turn into a homogenous mush when baked, but now we watched in horror as hungry tasters massacred the dish with spatulas and serving spoons. The crispy top layer of tortillas was difficult to cut through without mangling the layers beneath it. We resolved the issue by quartering the tortillas that made up the top layer so there would be no need to hack through a whole one.

Chicken Tortilla Casserole
SERVES 6 TO 8

Keep your corn tortillas wrapped in plastic or covered with a damp kitchen towel until ready to use—they will dry out quickly. Serve with additional accompaniments such as salsa, diced avocado, sour cream, or scallions if desired.

PLANNING AHEAD: Assemble the casserole as directed through step 5, making the following changes: Cook the chicken through completely in step 2, about 10 minutes. Allow the chicken mixture to cool to room temperature before stirring in the cilantro and lime. Do not bake the casserole. Wrap the dish with plastic wrap and poke several vent holes with the tip of a paring knife. Refrigerate the casserole until cool, about 3 hours, then wrap it tightly with another sheet of plastic wrap and refrigerate the casserole for up to 2 days.

TO BAKE: Allow the covered dish to sit at room temperature for 1 hour. Adjust an oven rack to the middle position and heat the oven to 400 degrees. Remove the plastic wrap and cover tightly with foil. Bake until the cheese is bubbling, about 1 hour. Remove the foil and continue to bake until the cheese has browned and the top layer of tortillas is crisp, about 10 minutes longer. Cool for 10 minutes. Sprinkle with the remaining 2 tablespoons of cilantro before serving.

2   tablespoons vegetable oil

1   large onion, chopped fine

2   red bell peppers, stemmed, seeded, and diced
        medium

1   teaspoon ground cumin

1   teaspoon chili powder

³/₄   teaspoon salt

3   medium garlic cloves, minced or pressed
        through a garlic press

2   tablespoons all-purpose flour

2   cups low-sodium chicken broth

2   canned chipotle chiles in adobo sauce,
        chopped, with 2 teaspoons sauce

2   (15.5-ounce) cans pinto beans, drained and
        rinsed

1   (14.5-ounce) can diced tomatoes, drained

2   pounds boneless, skinless chicken breasts,
        trimmed of excess fat and prepared according
        to the illustrations on page 51

¹/₄   cup plus 2 tablespoons chopped fresh cilantro
        leaves

2   tablespoons lime juice

¹/₄   teaspoon ground black pepper

18   (6-inch) round corn tortillas
        Vegetable cooking spray

6   ounces cheddar cheese, shredded (about
        2 cups)

6   ounces Monterey Jack cheese, shredded
        (about 2 cups)

1. Adjust an oven rack to the middle position and heat the oven to 300 degrees. Heat the oil in a Dutch oven over medium heat until shimmering. Add the onion, bell peppers, cumin, chili powder, and salt; cook, stirring occasionally, until the vegetables are soft and the onions are golden, about 10 minutes. Add the garlic and cook until fragrant, about 1 minute.

2. Add the flour and cook, stirring constantly, until golden, about 1 minute. Slowly whisk in the chicken broth and bring to a simmer, whisking often. Add the chipotles with adobo sauce, beans, and tomatoes; simmer until the flavors have blended, about 5 minutes. Add the chicken and cook, stirring occasionally, until no longer pink, about 4 minutes. Stir in ¼ cup of the cilantro, the lime juice, and pepper.

3. Meanwhile, spray both sides of the tortillas with cooking spray and lay on two baking sheets (some overlapping is fine). Bake until the tortillas are soft and pliable, about 5 minutes. Remove the tortillas from the oven. Increase the oven temperature to 450 degrees.

4. Toss the cheeses together in a medium bowl. Spread ⅓ of the chicken mixture in a 9 by 13-inch baking dish (or a shallow casserole dish of similar size). Layer 6 of the tortillas on top of the filling, overlapping as needed, and sprinkle with 1½ cups of the cheese. Repeat the process to form a second layer.

5. Spread the remaining filling in the baking dish. Cut the remaining 6 tortillas into quarters and spread over the top with the remaining 1 cup cheese. Bake until the cheese is golden brown and the casserole is bubbling, about 15 minutes. Cool for 10 minutes. Sprinkle with the remaining 2 tablespoons cilantro before serving.

MEDITERRANEAN CHICKEN CASSEROLE

CHICKEN WITH ARTICHOKES AND OLIVES, simmered in a sauce of tomatoes, white wine, garlic and herbs, is a classic Mediterranean recipe, but not one that lends itself well to a quick weeknight casserole. Or so we were convinced after trying out some of the halfhearted recipes we found, most of which consisted of canned artichokes and olives tossed with cubed chicken and a jarred pasta sauce.

We wanted to develop an authentic version of this dish that retained the convenience, if not the look (or taste), of the commonplace chicken casseroles that were so abundant in cookbooks, magazines, and on the Internet. In doing so we saw a chance to move away from the boneless, skinless chicken chunks that dominated casserole recipes. Traditionally this dish involves braising bone-in chicken pieces for hours—not an option on a Tuesday night. Oven roasting bone-in, skin-on chicken breasts was easy, however, and appropriate for this rustic recipe, if we could find a way to easily incorporate the sauce into the same dish.

Preparing the sauce involved sautéing garlic and reducing white wine, so we were committed to starting out on the stovetop. Bringing out the skillet meant we could also sear the chicken breasts and use the pan juices to build extra flavor into the sauce, so the decision was more than worth washing the extra dish. Fresh herbs were a must for the sauce, and tasters preferred thyme and parsley to the other likely candidates, oregano and basil. Kalamata olives were an easy choice for their mild, fruity flavor and availability in most supermarkets. Artichokes presented a problem: trimming and prepping fresh ones was well beyond the scope of a quick supper, but canned artichokes tasted tinny, and the jarred variety were briny and soft—they turned to mush when they hit the pan. We went with frozen artichokes by default: they had a firm, appealing texture, even though they were lacking in the flavor department.

Our game plan was to sear just the skin side of the chicken breasts, then set them aside while we deglazed the pan and built a quick sauce with the olives, artichokes, and canned diced tomatoes. Next we would pour the sauce into the baking dish, place the chicken on top (partially

TRIMMING SPLIT CHICKEN BREASTS

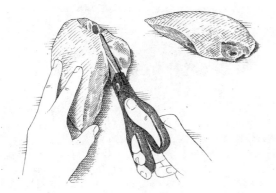

Using kitchen shears, trim off the rib sections from each breast, following the vertical line of fat from the tapered end of the breast up to the socket where the wing is attached.

submerged in the sauce but with the crispy skin high and dry), and then roast it at a high heat until cooked through, allowing the juices exuded by the chicken to add further flavor to the sauce.

The results weren't bad, but we had seriously underestimated the amount of liquid that eight chicken breasts would give off while roasting. The sauce, fairly dry to begin with, was close to bubbling over the sides of the dish, and it looked and tasted watery. We had to take steps to thicken the sauce and boost the flavors. The first task was simple: we drained off the juice from the canned tomatoes, reduced the wine further, and added a tablespoon of tomato paste to give the sauce some body. Now the sauce was so dry going into the baking dish that it resembled a chunky relish, but when it came out of the oven it was the perfect consistency for spooning over the roasted chicken. However, the flavors were still letting us down, and the artichokes were the worst offenders.

We knew that one way to boost flavor in a bland, watery vegetable was through roasting. We didn't want to tack any more time onto this supposedly quick recipe, so we altered the procedure to take advantage of the time we had. We tossed the artichokes with olive oil, salt, and pepper, spread them out in the baking dish, and roasted them for the 25 minutes or so that it took to sear the chicken breasts and make the pan sauce. Then we simply added the sauce to the baking dish with the artichokes before roasting the chicken. The roasted artichokes were noticeably improved, with a deeper flavor and sturdier texture.

The flavors were now good but very strong, and the combination of wine, olives, and garlic had left us craving something sweet. We considered adding a pinch of sugar to the sauce to balance things out, then reconsidered and tried orange juice, hoping to boost the acidity along with the sweetness. We simply substituted ½ cup of orange juice for half of the wine, then reduced them together in the pan. The resulting sauce was so flavorful and bright that we abandoned the lemon wedges we had planned to serve on the side.

Mediterranean Chicken Casserole with Tomatoes, Olives, and Artichokes

SERVES 8

To thaw the frozen artichokes quickly, microwave them on high, covered, for 3 to 5 minutes, then drain them thoroughly in a colander.

PLANNING AHEAD: This recipe cannot be made ahead or frozen.

2	(9-ounce) boxes frozen artichokes, thawed and drained (see the headnote)
2	tablespoons plus 4 teaspoons olive oil
	Salt and ground black pepper
8	split, bone-in, skin-on chicken breasts (about 10 to 12 ounces each), trimmed following the illustration on page 71
1	large onion, minced
2	teaspoons minced fresh thyme leaves
6	medium garlic cloves, minced or pressed through a garlic press
1/2	cup dry white wine
1/2	cup orange juice
2	(14.5-ounce) cans diced tomatoes
1	tablespoon tomato paste
1	cup Kalamata olives, pitted and chopped coarse
2	tablespoons chopped fresh parsley leaves

1. Adjust an oven rack to the middle position and heat the oven to 450 degrees. Toss the artichokes with 2 tablespoons of the oil, ½ teaspoon salt, and ¼ teaspoon pepper. Spread into a 9 by 13-inch baking dish (or a shallow casserole dish of similar size) and roast until browned at the edges, 20 to 25 minutes. Leave the artichokes in the dish and set aside.

2. Meanwhile, dry the chicken thoroughly with paper towels, then season liberally with salt and pepper. Heat 1 teaspoon oil in a 12-inch skillet

---

EQUIPMENT: Kitchen Shears

A pair of kitchen shears is not an essential kitchen implement. But when you need to butterfly or trim chicken, there is no tool better suited to the task than kitchen shears. To test their versatility, we also used kitchen shears to cut lengths of kitchen twine, trim pie dough, and cut out parchment paper rounds. We found two pairs to recommend.

Wüsthof Kitchen Shears ($28) made easy, smooth cuts even through small chicken bones and completed all tasks flawlessly. The size and proportion of the shears felt ideal—the blades could open wide for large jobs and to achieve more forceful cutting, but the shears were also suited to smaller, more detailed tasks such as snipping pieces of twine. These shears boasted heft, solid construction, and textured handles that were comfortable, even when wet and greasy. They were also suitable and comfortable for left-handed users.

Messermeister Take Apart Kitchen Shears ($17) were also great performers, though the blades didn't have quite the spread of those on the Wüsthof shears. These shears, too, made clean, easy cuts and accomplished all tasks without hesitation. The Messermeister shears came apart for cleaning, which we found to be neither a benefit nor a disadvantage. The soft,

rubber-like handles proved extremely comfortable but were clearly designed for right-handed users.

THE BEST KITCHEN SHEARS
Wüsthof Kitchen Shears (top) made smooth, easy cuts through bones and performed all tasks flawlessly. They were suitable and comfortable for both lefties and righties. Messermeister Take Apart Kitchen Shears (bottom) also performed well, but were clearly designed for right-handed users.

over medium-high heat until smoking. Carefully lay half of the chicken, skin-side down, in the pan and cook to a deep golden color, about 5 minutes. Transfer the chicken to a plate. Add 1 more teaspoon oil to the skillet and return to medium-high heat until smoking; brown the remaining chicken and transfer it to a plate.

3. Pour off any fat left in the skillet. Add the remaining 2 teaspoons oil to the skillet and return to medium heat until shimmering. Add the onion and thyme; cook, stirring often, until golden, about 6 minutes. Add the garlic and cook until fragrant, about 1 minute. Add the wine and orange juice; bring to a simmer and cook, scraping any browned bits off the bottom of the pan, until reduced by half, about 8 minutes. Add the tomatoes and tomato paste; simmer until the sauce is slightly thickened, about 5 minutes. Add the olives and season with salt and pepper to taste.

4. Pour the sauce over the artichokes in the baking dish and stir to combine. Nestle the chicken breasts into the sauce, skin-side up, and bake until the juices run clear when the chicken is cut with a paring knife, or the thickest part of the breast registers 160 degrees on an instant-read thermometer, about 30 minutes. Transfer the chicken to a platter or individual plates and allow to rest for 5 minutes. Spoon some of the artichokes and sauce over top of the chicken. Sprinkle with the parsley before serving.

CHICKEN VESUVIO

CHICKEN AND WEDGES OF POTATOES, BAKED in a sauce of garlic, white wine, and herbs, is known in Chicago's Italian restaurants as chicken Vesuvio. Though it is indeed a baked, one-pot supper, most cooks would not consider it an easy weeknight casserole because of the length of initial stovetop cooking it requires: both chicken and potatoes must be browned in batches before being baked. However, our success with Mediterranean Chicken Casserole with Tomatoes, Olives, and Artichokes (see page 72), which employs a similar technique, inspired us to attempt a streamlined

version of chicken Vesuvio.

The potatoes in chicken Vesuvio are what truly define the dish—they are well browned but not particularly crisp in the end, as they soak up the flavorful garlic wine sauce while cooking. Since we did not want to take the time to brown the potatoes in batches on the stovetop, we had little choice but to rely on the oven to get the job done. We would turn the oven up to 475 degrees, toss the potatoes with olive oil, and then roast them in the baking dish while we seared the chicken breasts and prepared the pan sauce. Once the wedges were browned, we would place the seared chicken breasts on the potatoes, pour the pan sauce over the top, and roast the chicken until cooked through.

Our first attempts were not encouraging. The potatoes had barely any color after nearly half an hour in the hot oven. Reasoning that the first part of the potato to brown would be the edge in contact with the pan, we tried arranging the wedges so that the cut sides were all flush against the bottom of the baking dish. The results were better: we could see through the clear glass bottom of the dish that the bottoms of the potatoes had indeed begun to brown, faintly, after 30 minutes. When we tried to toss them, however, we found they were completely fused to the bottom of the dish. Prying at them with a spatula only broke them to pieces.

We knew that the potatoes would release from the pan when they had browned sufficiently; we just had to speed up the process. So we tried preheating the oiled baking dish in the hot oven, but quickly learned the hard way that trying to arrange the wedges neatly in an oily, blisteringly hot pan was messy and painful. Our next idea was to give up. If we couldn't toss the potatoes before adding the chicken, then we would simply let them roast undisturbed for the entire time. We also tried sprinkling the oiled pan with salt and pepper, hoping the granular particles would discourage the potatoes from sticking.

This worked surprisingly well. After the chicken was cooked through (about 30 minutes more), the potatoes were reasonably brown and released cleanly from the pan with the help of a metal spatula. One final adjustment further improved the color: moving the oven rack to the lowest position. At last, the potatoes were a deep golden brown.

There was little room for variation in the traditional Vesuvio pan sauce, which consists of garlic, lemon, white wine, thyme, and oregano. We did find that tasters preferred to squeeze fresh lemon over the finished dish rather than adding juice to the sauce. When pouring the sauce over the chicken and potatoes, we noticed bits of garlic clinging to the chicken skin, which we feared would burn when they were put back into the hot oven. We were soon proven right. We decided to pour half of the sauce over just the potatoes, reserving the other half to sauce the chicken once it was cooked.

Chicken Vesuvio

SERVES 4

Don't worry if the potatoes seem stuck to the baking dish after the initial 30 minutes of roasting. After the sauce is added to the dish, the potatoes will release while the chicken is cooking. Try to buy chicken breasts that weigh 10 to 12 ounces each with the skin intact. If split breasts are of different sizes, check the smaller ones a few minutes early to see if they are cooking more quickly, and remove them from the baking dish if they are done ahead. If you would like to amend this recipe to serve six, follow the instructions below, increasing the potatoes to 2½ pounds and the chicken to 6 split, bone-in breasts. For this quantity you will need to use a 10 by 15-inch casserole dish to ensure proper browning of the chicken.

PLANNING AHEAD: This recipe cannot be made ahead or frozen.

3 tablespoons olive oil
  Salt and ground black pepper
2 pounds red potatoes, scrubbed and cut into
  ³/₄-inch wedges
4 split, bone-in, skin-on chicken breasts (about
  10 to 12 ounces each), trimmed following the
  illustration on page 71
5 medium garlic cloves, minced or pressed
  through a garlic press
2 teaspoons minced fresh thyme leaves
2 tablespoons chopped fresh oregano leaves

1 cup dry white wine
1 cup low-sodium chicken broth
1 lemon, cut into wedges

1. Adjust an oven rack to the lowest position and heat the oven to 475 degrees. Grease a 9 by 13-inch baking dish (or a shallow casserole dish of similar size) with 2 teaspoons of the oil, then sprinkle the dish evenly with ½ teaspoon salt and ¼ teaspoon pepper. Toss the potatoes with 1 tablespoon oil. Arrange the potatoes in the baking dish in a single layer, with a cut side flush against the bottom of the pan. Lean any extra potato wedges up against the sides of the pan. Roast until the potatoes are just beginning to brown, about 30 minutes. (Do not stir the potatoes.)

2. Meanwhile, heat 1 teaspoon oil in a 12-inch skillet over medium-high heat until smoking. Dry the chicken thoroughly with paper towels, then season generously with salt and pepper. Carefully lay the chicken breasts, skin-side down, in the skillet and cook to a deep golden color, about 5 minutes. Transfer the chicken to a plate.

3. Pour off any fat left in the skillet. Add the remaining 1 tablespoon oil to the skillet and return to medium heat until shimmering. Add the garlic, thyme, and oregano; cook, stirring often, until golden and fragrant, about 2 minutes. Add the wine and broth and bring to a simmer, scraping any browned bits off the bottom of the pan. Simmer until reduced by half, about 10 minutes. Season with salt and pepper to taste.

4. Pour half of the sauce evenly over the potatoes. Lay the chicken, skin-side up, on top of the potatoes. Roast until the juices run clear when the chicken is cut with a paring knife, or the thickest part of the breast registers 160 degrees on an instant-read thermometer, about 30 minutes. Transfer the chicken to a platter or individual plates and allow to rest for 5 minutes. Use a metal spatula to release and transfer the potatoes to the platter. Serve immediately, passing the extra sauce and lemon wedges separately.

THANKSGIVING TURKEY BAKE

THE CLASSIC COMBINATION OF TURKEY, gravy, stuffing, and cranberry sauce tastes much too good to have only one day a year. Yet the incredible amount of shopping, prep, and clean-up necessary for such a meal takes about a year to recover from. We wanted to replicate the flavors of this traditional meal, without all the work, in the form of a casserole. Before diving into the particulars, however, we needed to firm up our concept. Using bread stuffing for the bulk of the dish, we could either mix chunks of turkey meat into it, or layer slices of turkey breast over the top of it before baking. When we gave both ideas a whirl in the kitchen, tasters unanimously preferred the slices of turkey layered over the stuffing, and so we were on our way.

Taking a closer look at the slices of turkey, we noted that slicing cutlets from a boneless breast was fairly simple; however, using ready-made turkey cutlets was even easier. The quality of turkey cutlets can vary dramatically from brand to brand, and the best you can do is inspect packages carefully and sample local brands to identify the best product. Two pounds of cutlets shingled nicely on top of the stuffing in a standard 9 by 13-inch casserole dish served roughly eight people.

Focusing next on the stuffing, we tossed aside the idea of cutting up and drying our own bread cubes in favor of using a bag of dried stuffing mix. Following the package instructions (which rehydrate the stuffing with water and a little butter), however, didn't work. The stuffing tasted stale and bland. Treating the stuffing mix as if it were plain dried bread cubes, we then tried adding some sautéed sausage, onions, and celery, as well as some fresh thyme and sage, chicken broth, and eggs. Although the pre-packaged flavors were still somewhat evident, the stuffing was much improved. We tried several brands, styles, and flavors of bagged stuffing mix and all worked fine. Tasters did, however, prefer those that were plain or seasoned simply with herbs.

Moving on to the gravy, our goal was to achieve a good flavor despite the fact that we wouldn't have the benefit of any roast turkey drippings. What we did have, luckily, were drippings left from the sautéed sausage used in the stuffing. Using these browned bits, we built a simple gravy by adding some sautéed onions and celery, flour, and broth and allowing the mixture to simmer for roughly 20 minutes. It wasn't long before we realized that all of the vegetables used to add flavor to the gravy were also used in the stuffing. So rather than cut and sauté the same vegetables twice, we found we could build and simmer the gravy using all the sautéed vegetables, then, after straining the gravy, toss the vegetables (along with a little gravy) into the stuffing.

Now we had only a few more details to resolve. We knew we wanted a layer of cranberry sauce to go into the dish first. And while making cranberry sauce from frozen cranberries is relatively easy, we decided to give canned whole cranberry sauce a try, thinking that the difference in flavor and texture would be minimal once the dish was baked. We just want to capture that bright, tart

THE RIGHT CUTLET

TRY TO AVOID BUYING PACKAGES WITH ragged, inconsistently sized cutlets, like those on top. The even cutlets (below) will cook at the same rate and look better.

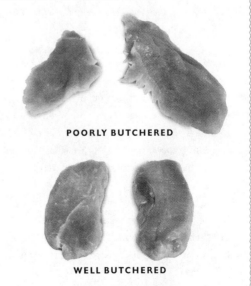

POORLY BUTCHERED

WELL BUTCHERED

taste of cranberries, and the canned variety did the job just fine.

Our final challenge was how to assemble and bake the casserole. The dish requires 30 minutes in the oven to cook the turkey and heat the stuffing; however, the edges and tops of the turkey cutlets turned dry and crisp when not covered with foil. We found that pouring some of the gravy over the cutlets before cooking added extra flavor and gave us some insurance that the turkey would not be dried out at the end of the cooking time. But we were left with a rather boring-looking casserole. Although tasty, this dish is definitely not a real looker. Some minced parsley helped matters by providing both color and a fresh flavor, and toasted pecans added a nice texture. This casserole is no replacement for Thanksgiving dinner, but it does satisfy a Thanksgiving craving and can be made in about an hour using only one pot, a large bowl, and a casserole dish.

Thanksgiving Turkey Bake

SERVES 8

Plain bags of dried bread cubes for stuffing are preferred, but if none are available, choose one that looks minimally flavored. The quality of store-bought turkey cutlets can vary dramatically from brand to brand, and the best you can do is inspect packages carefully and sample local brands to identify the best product (see the photos on page 75). Often, a butcher will cut fresh turkey cutlets from a turkey breast upon request.

PLANNING AHEAD: Follow the recipe through step 3 but do not add eggs. Refrigerate the stuffing and gravy in separate bowls, tightly wrapped with plastic wrap, for up to 2 days.

TO BAKE: Poke several vent holes in the plastic wrap covering the stuffing and the gravy and add the beaten eggs. Microwave both, separately, on high power until hot, 3 to 5 minutes. Continue to assemble and bake the casserole as directed in step 4.

I	(14-ounce) bag dried bread or cornbread cubes for stuffing (see the headnote)
3	tablespoons unsalted butter
12	ounces bulk pork sausage (such as Jimmy Dean)
2	medium onions, minced
3	celery ribs, chopped fine
	Salt
3	medium garlic cloves, minced or pressed through a garlic press
2	teaspoons fresh minced thyme leaves (or 1/2 teaspoon dried)
1/2	cup all-purpose flour
3	cups low-sodium beef broth
4	cups low-sodium chicken broth
2	bay leaves
	Ground black pepper
2	large eggs, lightly beaten
I	tablespoon minced fresh sage leaves
I	(16-ounce) can whole-berry cranberry sauce
2	pounds turkey cutlets or 2 pounds boneless turkey breast (see the illustration on page 77)
I	cup coarsely chopped pecans, toasted in a dry skillet over medium heat until fragrant, about 7 minutes
1/4	cup minced fresh parsley leaves

1. Adjust an oven rack to the middle position and heat the oven to 400 degrees. Place the bread cubes in a large mixing bowl and set aside. Melt 1 tablespoon of the butter in a Dutch oven over medium-high heat. Add the sausage and cook, breaking the meat into small pieces with a wooden spoon, until the sausage loses its raw color, about 5 minutes. Transfer to the bowl with the bread cubes.

2. Return the Dutch oven to medium-high heat and melt the remaining 2 tablespoons butter. Add the onions, celery, and 1/2 teaspoon salt; cook, scraping the browned bits off the bottom of the pot, until dry, sticky, and lightly browned, about 5 minutes. Add the garlic and thyme; cook until fragrant, about 30 seconds. Add the flour and cook, stirring constantly, until golden, about 1 minute. Slowly whisk in the broths; add the bay leaves, bring to a simmer, and cook, whisking often and scraping the browned bits off the bottom of the pot, until the gravy is thickened and you have about 5½ cups, 20 to 25 minutes. Season with salt and pepper to taste.

3. Strain the gravy through a mesh strainer (you should have about 4 cups). Add the strained vegetables, 1 cup of the gravy, the eggs, and sage to the bowl with the bread cubes; toss to coat evenly.

4. Spread the cranberry sauce evenly over the bottom of a 9 by 13-inch baking dish (or a shallow casserole dish of similar size). Press the stuffing into an even layer on top of the cranberry sauce. Shingle the turkey cutlets over the stuffing (see the illustration on page 55), and pour 2 cups strained gravy over the turkey. Cover the dish tightly with foil and bake until the turkey is fully cooked and the stuffing is hot, 20 to 30 minutes. Cool for 10 minutes. Meanwhile, heat the remaining gravy in a microwave on high power until hot, about 2 minutes. Sprinkle the toasted pecans and parsley over the casserole. Serve, passing the extra gravy separately.

CUTTING TURKEY CUTLETS

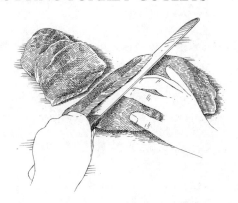

If you can't find good prepackaged turkey cutlets or a butcher to cut them for you, simply buy a small, boneless turkey breast and slice the cutlets yourself. After removing all skin and fat, use a long, nonflexible slicing knife to cut slices, on the bias starting at the tapered end, that are between ⅛ inch and ¼ inch thick.

TURKEY AND WILD RICE BAKE

TURKEY WITH WILD RICE, FRUIT, AND NUTS is a classic autumnal combination of flavors and textures. And since we had already developed a Thanksgiving Turkey Bake, we thought we could also create a similar casserole with wild rice instead of stuffing. Our goal was to create a layered casserole with a bottom layer of tender wild rice accented with dried cherries and herbs, followed by slices of fresh turkey. (This was not meant to be a casserole made from leftovers.) We envisioned a crunchy topping that would protect the turkey against the arid atmosphere of the oven, and a tasty sauce (or gravy) that would keep the filling and turkey moist. To begin the construction of our casserole, we divided our project into four components: the wild rice and dried cherry layer that would form the foundation of the casserole, the turkey, the pecan topping, and the sauce (or gravy) that we knew would be needed to add flavor and keep the turkey moist.

The wild rice that we find in the grocery store is actually the edible seed of an aquatic grass and not, botanically speaking, a variety of rice at all. Native to North America, wild rice is harvested green and then cured and dried. The grain is then hulled, removing the fibrous shell, and the shiny black seed is exposed. It is this seed that we recognize as wild rice. Often referred to as a grain, its distinctive grassy flavor and toothsome texture are the qualities that endear it to the culinary world (for more information, see page 79). Many wild rice recipes suggest using a combination of wild and white rice as a way to mitigate the cost of the wild rice. In an effort to shorten the long cooking time required to tenderize the wild rice, we tried using packaged combinations of long-grain white and wild rice. Yet, in all of our tests, overzealous quantities of white rice and artificial dried seasoning packets overwhelmed the wild rice, muting its distinct flavor.

We wanted the unusual flavor of this unique cereal grain to shine in this dish, and chose to extend it and tame its strong flavor with only a small amount of white rice. To minimize the number of pots needed, we opted for the convenience of boil-in-bag rice and were able to cook it and the wild rice in the same pot. After removing the bag of rice, we added the wild rice to the same water and cooked it until tender. In the time that the wild rice took to cook we were able to put together the rest of the filling. To the white rice we added sautéed onion and carrot, then stirred in dried cherries. The concentrated tart-sweet flavor of the cherries was just what we were looking for to flavor the rice. We tested dried cranberries as well and found that they are an acceptable substitute if dried cherries are unavailable, although their flavor is not as pronounced.

The turkey and topping commanded our attention next. We knew that we weren't about to buy a whole turkey to make this dish, and fortunately the demand for the low-fat bird has led to the popularity and availability of fresh, boneless turkey cutlets. We started by shingling thinly sliced turkey cutlets over the wild rice filling. With little fat (and no skin) to protect the cutlets from heat, we decided that in addition to a moistening sauce, a topping would be helpful in preventing the turkey from drying out. We combined fresh bread crumbs with butter and chopped parsley. To add crunch, we tried walnuts, almonds, and pecans. Tasters preferred the buttery richness of the pecans and felt they paired well with the wild rice and dried cherries.

To build the sauce, we started with a classic butter-and-flour-thickened chicken-stock sauce, or velouté. Flavored with fresh thyme and bay leaf, the sauce had good flavor and consistency, but we wondered if replacing some of the chicken broth with apple cider might add more depth to this sauce. As it turned out, the combination of the sweet cider with the tart dried cherries was perfect. After mixing a portion of the sauce into the rice, we poured the remainder over the turkey cutlets, topped the turkey with the protective bread-crumb coating, and baked the casserole

until the turkey was cooked through and the crumb topping was golden brown.

The combination of moist, tender turkey, toothsome wild rice, fruit, and buttery pecans represents American food at its finest. Perfect for a weeknight supper or holiday entertaining, this recipe lets you bring turkey to the table any time of year.

Turkey and Wild Rice Bake with Dried Cherries and Pecans

SERVES 6 TO 8

Simmer the wild rice slowly, making sure to stop the cooking process at just the right moment by checking it for doneness every couple of minutes past the 30-minute mark. Dried cranberries, although much sweeter, can be substituted for the dried cherries.

PLANNING AHEAD: Follow the recipe through step 4. Refrigerate the topping, rice mixture, and sauce in separate bowls, tightly wrapped with plastic wrap, for up to 1 day.

TO BAKE: Poke several vent holes in the plastic wrap covering the rice and the sauce. Microwave both, separately, on high power until hot, 3 to 5 minutes. Continue to assemble and bake the casserole as directed in step 5.

TOPPING
½	cup pecans
3	slices white sandwich bread, torn into quarters
2	tablespoons unsalted butter, melted
¼	cup minced fresh parsley leaves

GETTING THE TEXTURE RIGHT

Undercooked wild rice is tough and hard to chew. At the other end of the spectrum, overcooked wild rice bursts, revealing the pasty starch concealed beneath the glossy coat. Perfectly cooked wild rice is chewy but tender, the individual grains plumped but intact.

UNDERCOOKED   **PERFECTLY COOKED**   **OVERCOOKED**

FILLING

4 bay leaves

Salt

1 (1-cup) pouch boil-in-bag white rice

1½ cups wild rice

5 tablespoons unsalted butter

1 medium onion, minced

1 large carrot, peeled and chopped fine

¾ cup dried cherries

Ground black pepper

5 tablespoons all-purpose flour

2 cups apple cider

3 cups low-sodium chicken broth

4 sprigs fresh thyme

2 teaspoons cider vinegar

2 pounds turkey cutlets or 2 pounds boneless turkey breast (see the illustration on page 77)

1. FOR THE TOPPING: Process the pecans in a food processor fitted with the steel blade until coarsely ground, about 5 seconds. Add the bread and butter; process to a uniformly coarse crumb, about six 1-second pulses. Transfer to a bowl and toss with the parsley; set aside.

2. FOR THE FILLING: Bring 4 quarts of water, 2 of the bay leaves, and 1 teaspoon salt to a boil in a Dutch oven over high heat. Add the white rice pouch and wild rice; bring to a simmer. Cook, adjusting the heat as necessary to maintain a simmer, until the white rice is nearly tender, about 7 minutes. Remove the white rice pouch and allow it to drain briefly in a colander; empty the rice into a large bowl and set aside. Continue to simmer the wild rice until it is plump and completely tender, 30 to 45 minutes longer. Drain, discarding the bay leaves, and transfer the wild rice to the bowl with the white rice.

3. Meanwhile, melt 2 tablespoons of the butter in a 12-inch skillet over medium heat. Add the onion, carrot, and ¼ teaspoon salt; cook, stirring frequently, until the vegetables are softened but not browned, about 4 minutes. Add to the bowl with the rice. Stir in the dried cherries. Season with salt and pepper to taste; set aside.

4. Add the remaining 3 tablespoons butter to the skillet and return to medium-high heat until melted. Add the flour and cook, stirring constantly, until golden, about 1 minute. Gradually whisk in the cider, broth, thyme, and the remaining 2 bay leaves; bring to a simmer and cook, whisking constantly, until slightly thickened, about 5 minutes. Remove the pan from the heat and discard the thyme and bay leaves. Stir in the vinegar and season with salt and pepper to taste.

5. Adjust an oven rack to the middle position and heat the oven to 400 degrees. Add 2 cups of the sauce to the rice mixture and toss to combine. Spread the rice mixture into a 9 by 13-inch baking dish (or a shallow casserole dish of similar size). Season the turkey cutlets with salt and pepper. Following the illustration on page 55, shingle the turkey cutlets over the rice so that they overlap slightly. Pour the remaining sauce over the turkey and sprinkle with the breadcrumb topping. Bake until the turkey is fully cooked and the rice is hot, 35 to 40 minutes. Cool for 10 minutes before serving.

INGREDIENTS: Wild Rice

Wild rice is something of a misnomer. The standard offering in most supermarkets is cultivated wild rice—grown under regulated conditions in man-made paddies. True to its name, real wild rice is grown in the wild. Hand-harvested from lakes and rivers in Minnesota and Canada, true wild rice can be very expensive, as much as $9 per pound. (Cultivated wild rice costs $3 to $5 per pound.) We wondered if it was worth spending more money on "wild" wild rice. To find out, we cooked each type of rice and tasted them straight. The hand-harvested wild rice had a pale appearance, smoky flavor, and light, tender texture. So that's the rice for our pilaf, right? As it turned out, we preferred the cultivated wild rice for its deep, ebony color and resilient texture, especially when contrasted with the tender white rice used in the pilaf. Although the flavor of cultivated wild rice is slightly less robust than that of the real thing, when it comes to pilaf, we'll save our pennies and go for the cultivated rice.

CHILI MAC

SYNONYMOUS WITH SIMPLER TIMES, AND simpler food, chili mac was once a favorite childhood comfort food whose appeal, for many of us, extends well into adulthood.

Initial testing prompted reminiscing, and the test kitchen was divided about which version of chili mac (mom's, of course) was best. For some it was a macaroni-and-cheese-like version with a bit of chili stirred in. For others it was predominantly chili with a little macaroni added for heft. Others insisted (after tasting the previous examples) that there could be only one way to make the best chili mac: spicy chili, with elbows stirred in (no other pasta would do) and lots of gooey, melted cheese on top. Our goal was to come up with a recipe that was a combination of the best spicy beef chili and creamy macaroni with cheese. We wanted a simple dish that would appeal to young and old alike. It couldn't be overly seasoned, or it would lose its kid appeal. It couldn't be too cheesy, or grownups wouldn't be happy.

Our first challenges were finding the correct heat level for the chili and the ideal proportion of chili to macaroni. We focused on the chili first and started with lean ground beef, which we browned, then drained to remove the excess fat. Then we sautéed onion, red bell pepper, and a generous amount of garlic. In lieu of fresh chiles, (jalapeños added too much heat), we added chili powder and found that the best way to tame the raw flavor of the powder was to sauté it with the aromatics. This helped to bloom the flavors of the chili and reduce its harshness. Cumin was added along with the chili powder, and what we had was a "taco seasoned" ground beef mixture that was waiting for the tomato component to transform it into chili. We added diced tomato, simmered the chili for 20 minutes, and had our first taste. With 1 tablespoon of chili powder and 2 teaspoons of cumin, the chili was spicy enough without being overbearing. The thickness was ideal: spoonable and thick. Satisfied with our chili, we moved on to the macaroni that needed to be stirred in.

We started by cooking a full pound of elbows to the al dente stage. We knew that the macaroni would continue to cook in the oven, and would absorb liquid as it baked. What we didn't count on was how much liquid it would soak up. Our first try in the oven turned what seemed to be a promising casserole into bad cafeteria food. The macaroni had taken over, and the casserole was dry and bland. We decided to try increasing the amount of tomato in the chili, and added tomato puree so it would better coat the pasta. We also added a small amount of brown sugar to help tame the acidity of the tomato. We cut the amount of macaroni down to ½ pound, but the resulting dish was still too dry. We found that if we reserved some of the pasta-cooking water and added it back to the chili and macaroni mixture in the pot, we were able to control the consistency more efficiently. The tomato puree combined with the water to form a moist, flavorful coating for the pasta. To boost the chili flavor that had been diluted by the pasta, we increased the chili powder to 2 tablespoons and the cumin to 1 tablespoon.

At this point, we needed to put the cheese component into play. We tried casseroles made with cheddar and Monterey Jack cheeses separately, then together. Tasters found the cheddar to be grainy and greasy. The creaminess of the Monterey Jack was just what we were striving for, but the flavor was a bit too mild. We found a hybrid cheese called Co-Jack in our supermarket, a blend of mild colby and Monterey Jack cheeses. The flavor of the colby, combined with the creaminess of the Monterey Jack, made these cheeses ideal for topping the chili mac. After just 15 minutes in the oven, the topping turned a bubbly, golden brown. Better than most remembered from mom's kitchen, this substantial chili mac reminded us all of simpler times and the uncontrived, satisfying food of our youth. It can easily be prepared ahead without sacrificing quality, or doubled to feed a hungry crowd of any age.

Chili Mac

SERVES 6 TO 8

Reserve some of the pasta-cooking water so that it can be used to thin out the chili as needed. Ground turkey (1½ pounds) can be substituted for the ground beef. If you can't find Co-Jack cheese, just substitute equal amounts of colby and Jack cheese instead.

Planning Ahead: Follow the recipe through step 4, but do not sprinkle with cheese or bake. Wrap the chili mac tightly with plastic wrap and poke several vent holes with the tip of a paring knife. Refrigerate until cool, about 3 hours, then wrap it tightly with another sheet of plastic wrap and refrigerate for up to 2 days. This dish can also be frozen, tightly covered with foil, for two months. Thaw for 24 hours in the refrigerator before baking.

To Bake: Allow the covered dish to sit at room temperature for 1 hour. Adjust an oven rack to the middle position and heat the oven to 400 degrees. Remove the plastic wrap, sprinkle with the cheese, and cover tightly with foil. Bake until the mixture is hot and bubbling, 40 to 45 minutes. Remove the foil and continue to cook until the cheese begins to brown, 5 to 10 minutes longer. Cool for 10 minutes before serving.

	Salt
½	pound elbow macaroni (about 2 cups uncooked pasta)
3	tablespoons vegetable oil
1½	pounds 85 percent lean ground beef
2	medium onions, chopped medium
1	red bell pepper, stemmed, seeded, and chopped medium
6	medium garlic cloves, minced or pressed through a garlic press
2	tablespoons chili powder
1	tablespoon ground cumin
1	(14.5-ounce) can diced tomatoes
1	(28-ounce) can tomato puree
1	tablespoon light or dark brown sugar
8	ounces Colby Jack (Co-Jack) cheese, shredded (about 2⅔ cups)

1. Adjust an oven rack to the middle position and heat the oven to 400 degrees. Bring 4 quarts of water to a boil in a Dutch oven over high heat. Stir in 1 tablespoon salt and the macaroni; cook until al dente, about 5 minutes. Reserve ¾ cup of the pasta water and drain the pasta. Transfer the pasta to a bowl and set aside.

2. Wipe the Dutch oven dry. Add 1 tablespoon of the oil and return to medium-high heat until shimmering. Add the beef and cook, breaking up the pieces with a wooden spoon, until it is no longer pink and beginning to brown, 5 to 8 minutes. Drain the beef through a colander, discarding the drippings, and set it aside.

3. Add the remaining 2 tablespoons oil to the Dutch oven and return to medium-high heat until shimmering. Add the onions, red pepper, garlic, chili powder, and cumin; cook, stirring occasionally, until the vegetables are softened and beginning to brown, about 7 minutes. Add the diced tomatoes, tomato puree, brown sugar, the reserved pasta water, and the drained beef; bring to a simmer and cook, stirring occasionally, until the flavors have melded, about 20 minutes.

4. Stir in the cooked pasta and season with salt and pepper to taste. Pour into a 9 by 13-inch baking dish (or a shallow casserole dish of similar size) and sprinkle with the cheese. Bake until the cheese is melted and browned, about 15 minutes. Cool for 5 to 10 minutes before serving.

BEEF TERIYAKI CASSEROLE

TERIYAKI IS A TRADITIONAL JAPANESE DISH that has quickly become an American household name. Unfortunately, it usually refers to either a sickly sweet or insanely salty sauce that turns to a shellac-like varnish over tough pieces of meat underneath a broiler or on the grill. Not only did we want to make a good version of beef teriyaki, but we wanted to make enough of it to feed a crowd in the form of an easy casserole complete with a bottom layer of white rice and a middle layer of crisp vegetables. Obviously the grill and the broiler were out of the picture in terms of cooking methods (some casserole vessels crack or shatter under the intense heat of a broiler), but we wondered if we could make decent teriyaki using a hot oven.

In order for this dish to work, we needed to nail the flavor and consistency of the teriyaki sauce, the slightly charred exterior and tender interior of the meat, and find a reasonable, casserole-friendly cooking method.

Turning first to the sauce, we noted that it is traditionally a simple combination of several Asian ingredients that walk a narrow line between overly sweet and overly salty. Soy sauce and sugar are the primary flavoring agents along with sherry or mirin (sweetened Japanese rice wine meant for cooking). Attaining the proper balance was merely matter of trial and error; too much soy, and the sauce was inedible, but too little, and the sauce was bland, overly sweet, and one-dimensional. We also found it necessary to add a little garlic, ginger, and scallion to round out the sauce's flavor.

Moving on to the type of meat, we tried all the usual suspects found at the butcher counter: sirloin, steak tips, top round, flank steak, rib eye, and blade steaks. Taking into account varying prices and textures, one cut in particular shone above the rest: steak tips. They were not too expensive, their hearty flavor stood up nicely to the potent teriyaki sauce, and their texture remained tender and juicy even if slightly over cooked. To make the meat easy to eat and serve, we cut the tips into bite-size pieces. The one downside of using steak tips, however, is that they can be somewhat difficult to shop for or find (see page 83 for information on buying steak tips).

To sort out how to cook the teriyaki beef, we tried the simplest approach first: assembling the casserole with the raw meat lying on top, we poured the teriyaki sauce over the meat and baked it in a hot oven. No dice. The sauce slid off the meat, leaving it naked, pale, and bland, then proceeded to filter down through the casserole, landing in an unattractive, inky pool at the bottom of the dish. Obviously, the meat and sauce would need to be seared and thickened before being added to the casserole. Searing the meat, then tossing it with the sauce after it was thickened with some cornstarch on the stovetop created just the effect we wanted, giving the meat a slightly charred exterior that was well coated with a dark, glossy glaze.

As for the other components of the dish, we already knew we wanted a layer of colorful vegetables arranged over white rice (and then topped with the glazed and seared meat). Because the baking time of the beef teriyaki layer is relatively short, both the rice and the vegetables needed to be fully cooked before being assembled in the casserole dish. Using a single pot of boiling water, we simply blanched the vegetables, then used the same water to cook the rice. Sprinkling a few toasted sesame seeds over the assembled casserole before baking and adding some minced scallion greens before serving finished this dish, which is not only a great version of beef teriyaki, but an unusual and surprising casserole.

WILL THE REAL STEAK TIP PLEASE . . .

Steak tips can be cut from a half-dozen muscles and are sold in three basic forms: cubes, strips, and steaks. To make sure that you are buying the most flavorful cut (called flap meat sirloin tip by butchers, and pictured at right), buy whole steaks and cut them into pieces yourself.

CUBES   **STRIPS**   **STEAKS**

Beef Teriyaki Casserole

SERVES 8 TO 10

Mirin is a sweet Japanese cooking wine often found in the grocery store next to other Asian sauces. Note that the scallion whites and greens are used separately.

PLANNING AHEAD: This dish cannot be made ahead or frozen.

	Salt
1	pound green beans, trimmed and cut into 1-inch lengths
3	medium red bell peppers, stemmed, seeded, and sliced into ¼-inch-thick strips
1½	cups long-grain white rice
4	pounds sirloin steak tips, cut into 1-inch chunks
3	tablespoons vegetable oil
¾	cup soy sauce
1½	cups mirin
6	tablespoons sugar
2	tablespoons cornstarch
1	(4-inch) piece fresh ginger, peeled and grated fine
6	medium garlic cloves, minced or pressed through a garlic press
6	scallions, white and light green parts minced and dark green parts sliced thin
1	tablespoon sesame seeds, toasted in a dry skillet over medium heat until golden and fragrant, about 7 minutes

1. Adjust an oven rack to the middle position and heat the oven to 450 degrees. Bring 4 quarts of water to a boil in a large pot (with a perforated pasta insert, if available) over high heat. Add 1 tablespoon salt, the beans, and peppers; cook until the vegetables are brightly colored and slightly crunchy, about 1 minute. Remove the vegetables from the boiling water with a slotted spoon (or by lifting out the pasta insert, if using) and spread out over a paper-towel-lined baking sheet to drain and cool. Return the water to a boil and add the rice; cook until almost tender but still firm to the bite, about 12 minutes. Drain thoroughly.

2. Meanwhile, thoroughly pat the meat dry with paper towels. Heat 1 tablespoon of the oil in a 12-inch nonstick skillet over medium-high heat until just smoking. Distribute half of the meat evenly in the skillet and cook, without stirring, until well browned on one side, about 4 minutes. Transfer the meat to a clean plate; set aside. Add 1 more tablespoon oil to the skillet and return to medium-high heat until just smoking; brown the remaining meat and transfer it to the plate.

3. Whisk the soy sauce, mirin, sugar, and cornstarch together until the sugar has dissolved; set aside. Add the remaining tablespoon

BUYING STEAK TIPS

STEAK TIPS CAN COME FROM TWO AREAS of the cow. One kind comes from tender, expensive cuts in the middle of the cow, such as the tenderloin. These tips are a superior cut and not what we consider to be a true steak tip, which should be a more pedestrian cut that is magically transformed into a desirable cut through cooking. If the steak tips at your market cost $8 to $10 per pound, the meat likely comes from the tenderloin.

True steak tips come from various muscles in the sirloin and round and cost about $5 per pound. After tasting 50 pounds of cheap steak tips, tasters had a clear favorite: a single muscle that butchers call flap meat and that is typically labeled "sirloin tips." A whole piece of flap meat weighs about 2½ pounds. One piece can range in thickness from ½ inch to 1½ inches and may be sold as cubes, strips, or small steak (see page 82). It has a rich, deep, beefy flavor and a distinctive longitudinal grain.

We found that it's best to buy flap meat in steak form rather than cubes or strips, which are often cut from nearby muscles in the hip and butt that are neither as tasty nor as tender. Because meat labeling is so haphazard, you must visually identify this cut; buying it in steak form makes this easy.

oil to the skillet and return to medium heat until shimmering. Add the ginger, garlic, and minced scallions; cook until fragrant, about 30 seconds. Briefly re-whisk the soy mixture and add it to the skillet. Bring to a simmer and cook until thickened, 1 to 2 minutes. Off the heat, add the browned meat and toss to coat.

4. Spread the rice into a 9 by 13-inch baking dish (or a shallow casserole dish of similar size). Spread the cooked beans and red peppers over the rice. Spread the beef evenly over the vegetables and sprinkle with the sesame seeds. Bake until the beef looks dark and glossy, 15 to 20 minutes. Sprinkle with the sliced scallion greens. Serve immediately.

Lamb and Eggplant Moussaka

A WORKHORSE OF FINE GREEK RESTAURANTS and diners alike, moussaka is a rich casserole of roasted eggplant, meat-enriched tomato sauce, and creamy béchamel. It is similar to lasagna in that it is a layered casserole, with sheets of eggplant instead of noodles sandwiching the filling and sauce. Moussaka can be a delicate, nuanced casserole, but more often than not, it's a heavy-handed, one-dimensional mess. The eggplant is foul with grease and the filling and sauce are cloyingly rich yet disappointingly bland. We wanted to make a version worth all the effort (it can be time consuming to prepare each of the three components) and worthy of serving to a crowd.

Eggplant is the Achilles' heel of moussaka. Most of the recipes we found either pan-fry or roast the eggplant before assembling the casserole. Fried eggplant was, across the board, greasy. The porous texture of the vegetable greedily soaked up oil from the pan, and then leached it into the moussaka once baked (with the rich lamb filling, additional grease is one thing moussaka never needs). We found that roasted eggplant wasn't nearly as greasy, requiring a minimum amount of oil to brown, and had a superior texture and flavor. The high heat of the oven effectively caramelized the eggplant, magnifying its sweetness and tempering it bitterness. So roasting it was.

But before roasting the eggplant, we knew that we wanted to apply a trick common to many moussaka recipes: salting. Dusting the raw eggplant slices with a liberal coating of salt and allowing them to sit for a spell in a colander draws out much of the eggplant's moisture, which in turn partially collapses the vegetable's cell walls, making it denser, more flavorful, and less likely to "sponge up" grease. The only drawback to salting is the time required: it takes a minimum of a half hour for the salt to work its magic. Sometimes we find that salting is an unnecessary step (like in the Oven-Baked Ratatouille on page 254), but in this instance, where texture was just as important as the flavor, we thought that it was essential to the success of the moussaka.

Once salted, drained, and patted dry, the eggplant was ready for the oven. We tossed it in a small amount of olive oil to promote browning and experimented with temperatures ranging between 375 and 500 degrees. Roasted too hot, the edges of the eggplant burned before the center cooked. Too low, and the slices took an eternity to brown and consequently turned mushy. We finally settled on 450 degrees as the perfect temperature because the eggplant slices browned evenly without turning too soft in about 45 minutes—just perfect, since this gave us enough time to prepare the filling and béchamel.

But we were in for a rude surprise. We had cooked two sheet pans' worth of eggplant slices (from 4 pounds of eggplant), the most the oven could accommodate at one time. When we went to assemble the moussaka, we found that there were barely enough eggplant slices for two layers in an 8 by 8-inch baking dish, or just four dinner-sized servings. We wanted the recipe to serve double that. So, to fill a 9 by 13-inch baking dish, we would have to prepare a staggering 8 pounds of eggplant, requiring a minimum of two hours to roast it all (two baking sheets a batch, the most home ovens will cook evenly). Coupling the extensive cooking time with the effort required for the filling and sauce, this was quickly becoming a long-winded recipe.

We decided to revisit how we were preparing the moussaka and whether or not there was a way to streamline things. After a significant amount of discussion in the test kitchen, it occurred to us that we could limit the layers of the moussaka to just three thick layers—instead of the more traditional six thin layers—and thereby minimize the amount of eggplant necessary. And instead of slicing the eggplant into broad planks, we opted to cut it into chunky cubes, which allowed us to squeeze a slightly higher volume of eggplant onto each of the baking sheets. We placed these chunks of eggplant on the bottom of the casserole to be blanketed in filling, which was then capped with béchamel. Unconventional, perhaps, but it was a simple solution that minimized the work and time required.

The best lamb-and-tomato fillings we have tasted are rich, slightly sweet, and perfumed with cinnamon and oregano. Unlike ground beef that is sold with the fat content marked on the package, ground lamb is generally unmarked and almost always pretty fatty. We quickly realized that the meat needed to be browned and the excess fat drained off before we could add the filling's other ingredients. Removing the excess fat also removed much of the lamb's gaminess—a flavor with which some tasters took issue.

A good quantity of onions and garlic was a given, their sweetness and piquancy lending the filling a solid bottom end flavor. We experimented with the usual canned tomato products—whole, diced, and pureed—and preferred the latter. Both whole (chopped coarsely) and diced tomatoes failed to break down to the thick, jammy consistency characteristic of our favorite moussaka fillings. To boost the fruity sweetness of the puree, we included a couple of tablespoons of tomato paste and sugar. Slowly simmered for about half an hour, the filling's excess moisture evaporated and the flavors blended and tightened. After a couple of batches tasted flat, we realized that the filling needed some acidity—any tartness had been cooked out of the tomatoes. We easily settled on red wine as the best option because it provided a mildly acidic kick and a fruitiness that intensified the flavor of the tomatoes.

As for seasoning the filling, Greeks tend to include a fairly substantial amount of cinnamon. We found that too much cinnamon easily overpowered the dish's other flavors, so we settled on a modest ¾ teaspoon as the ideal amount. Briefly toasted in the skillet's dry heat, the spice's flavor was fuller than when left untoasted. And for herbs, oregano and parsley lent the right amount of freshness.

We had tested a variety of béchamel-style sauces for other recipes in this book and felt we had a leg up on things. The béchamel for moussaka should ideally form a thick blanket over the top, effectively sealing in the filling. We quickly realized that the béchamel for moussaka had to be significantly thicker than most of those that we had prepared for other types of recipes. We added additional flour incrementally until we attained a thick, velvety texture that sealed in the bubbling filling and browned attractively.

In classic recipes, the béchamel is often enriched with a crumbly aged cheese called Myzithra. Salty, drier, and richer-tasting than Greece's more common feta cheese, we found that Myzithra's flavor could be approximated with a healthy dose of Parmesan.

Baking the moussaka was a simple matter of watching the filling percolate beneath the béchamel. We found that a moderately hot oven—400 degrees—quickly brought the moussaka up to temperature without burning the béchamel.

Lamb and Eggplant Moussaka

SERVES 6 TO 8

Look for eggplants that are glossy, feel firm, and are heavy for their size. Dried oregano may be substituted for the fresh; reduce the amount to 1½ teaspoons.

PLANNING AHEAD: Assemble the moussaka as directed through step 6, but do not bake. Wrap the dish tightly with plastic wrap and refrigerate for up to 3 days.

TO BAKE: Allow the moussaka to sit at room temperature for about 1 hour. Adjust an oven rack to the middle position and heat the oven to 400 degrees. Remove the plastic wrap and wrap the dish tightly with foil. Bake for 20 minutes, then remove the foil. Return the moussaka to the oven and continue to bake until browned and bubbly, about 20 minutes longer. Cool for 10 minutes. Sprinkle with the parsley before serving.

EGGPLANT

4	pounds globe eggplant (about 4 medium), peeled and cut into 1-inch cubes
	Kosher salt
3	tablespoons olive oil

FILLING

2	pounds ground lamb
2	tablespoons olive oil
1	medium onion, minced
	Kosher salt
4	medium garlic cloves, minced or pressed through a garlic press
3/4	teaspoon ground cinnamon
2	tablespoons tomato paste
1/2	cup dry red wine
1	tablespoon chopped fresh oregano leaves
2	tablespoons chopped fresh parsley leaves
1	(28-ounce) can tomato puree
1	teaspoon sugar
	Ground black pepper

BÉCHAMEL

3	tablespoons unsalted butter
4	tablespoons all-purpose flour
2	cups whole milk
2	ounces Parmesan cheese, grated fine (about 1 cup)
	Pinch ground nutmeg
	Salt and ground black pepper

1. FOR THE EGGPLANT: Adjust the oven racks to the lower- and upper-middle positions and heat the oven to 450 degrees. Toss the eggplant with 2 tablespoons of kosher salt in a large colander set over a bowl and let stand for 30 minutes.

2. Working in batches, spread the eggplant between a double layer of paper towels and press firmly with your hands until the eggplant is dry and compressed; transfer to a large bowl and toss with the 3 tablespoons olive oil. Spread the eggplant into an even layer over two rimmed baking sheets and bake until light golden brown, 40 to 50 minutes, rotating the pans halfway though the roasting time. Set the baking sheets on wire racks to cool.

3. FOR THE FILLING: Adjust an oven rack to the middle position and heat the oven to 400 degrees. Cook the lamb in a large Dutch oven over medium-high heat, stirring occasionally, until well browned, about 10 minutes. Using a slotted spoon, transfer the lamb to a paper towel-lined plate; set aside.

4. Pour off all of the fat from the pot, add 2 tablespoons oil, and return to medium heat until shimmering. Add the onion and 1 teaspoon kosher salt; cook, stirring occasionally, until the onion has softened and is beginning to brown, about 5 minutes. Add the garlic and cinnamon; cook until fragrant, about 30 seconds. Stir in the tomato paste and cook, stirring constantly, for 30 seconds. Add the wine, oregano, 1 tablespoon of the parsley, tomato puree, sugar, and 1/4 teaspoon pepper; bring to a simmer. Reduce the heat to low, cover partially, and simmer, stirring occasionally, until the juices have evaporated and the sauce has thickened, 25 to 30 minutes.

5. FOR THE BÉCHAMEL: Melt the butter in a medium saucepan over medium-high heat. Add the flour and cook, stirring constantly, for about 1 minute. Gradually whisk in the milk; bring to a simmer and cook, whisking often, until the sauce thickens, about 1 minute. Remove from the heat and whisk in the Parmesan and nutmeg. Season to taste with salt and pepper.

6. TO ASSEMBLE: Spread the eggplant into an even layer across the bottom of a 9 by 13-inch baking dish (or a shallow casserole dish of similar size). Spread the meat filling evenly over the eggplant. Pour the béchamel evenly over the meat. Bake until browned and bubbly, about 20 minutes. Cool for 10 minutes. Sprinkle with the remaining tablespoon parsley before serving.

HOPPIN' JOHN

WHILE GENERALLY SERVED ON NEW Year's Day for good luck during the upcoming year, hoppin' John is good anytime as a robust casserole. Authentic hoppin' John, as made in the Carolinas, is a white rice pilaf or casserole flavored with smoked pork, black-eyed peas, herbs, and spices. There are different suggestions as to the origin of its odd name, but some researchers believe it is derived from the Creole-inflected French *pois a pigeon*, or pigeon pea—the original bean used in the dish.

Whatever the name may mean, we find that too often hoppin' John is chock-full of overcooked peas and soggy, wet rice. Often the dish is strangely bland—necessitating the use of great quantities of hot sauce. We wanted to devise a recipe that did not overcook the peas or rice and that was both highly flavored and balanced. We also wanted to cook it in the oven, like a casserole, to free up the stovetop for other uses.

Hoppin' John is usually made with black-eyed peas (more readily available than the authentic pigeon pea), although field peas are sometimes substituted. We were unable to find a source for field peas north of the Mason-Dixon line, so we stuck with black-eyed peas. We tried peas in different forms and were surprised with what we discovered. Canned peas were out of the question. They were slimy and did not hold up well to any further cooking. Dried peas cooked unevenly; sometimes the peas were tough and wrinkled (a sure sign of staleness), while other times they were tender to a fault. Luckily, we found precooked black-eyed peas in the frozen-foods aisle. These peas retained their shape and pleasing texture and need only minutes to cook, as opposed to the hours of cooking dried peas require.

We found that hoppin' John's deep flavor rested squarely on the pork. Smoked ham hock is authentic but problematic. Tasters enjoyed the flavor but disliked the texture of the meat, which we shredded and returned to the pot after the dish had simmered. Salt pork was vetoed for its overwhelmingly "chewy" texture. Diced cooked ham was the favorite for its pleasing texture, but

it lacked the smokiness of the ham hock. A small amount of bacon, in addition to the ham, added the requisite smokiness and also supplied ample fat in which to sauté the vegetables.

From the many options for vegetables we selected only aromatics, onions and garlic, which added body, sweetness, and pungency. Other vegetables, like celery and bell pepper, detracted from the simple flavors of the pork, peas, and rice. For herbs, thyme and bay leaves are traditional, and everyone in the kitchen liked them. We decided to stir in parsley at the end for color and to add a bit of freshness.

Tradition dictates that hoppin' John be fueled by a good deal of heat, most commonly from fresh chiles. We found that jalapeño chiles imparted a distinct but inappropriate flavor to the dish. Small pequín chiles had great flavor, but they can be hard to find. In the end, we found that dried red pepper flakes lent a pleasant heat that blossomed as we ate the dish but never became overwhelming. We also like to pass hot pepper sauce on the side so people can spice things up to their liking.

With the flavors settled, we were ready to cook the rice. We wanted rice that was fluffy, not sodden or sticky, as it is in too many rice casseroles. We knew that the choice of rice and the ratio of liquid to rice were crucial to success. While we generally love pilafs made with basmati rice, its flavor was too distinct in this case. Medium-grain rice cooked up too creamy. Plain long-grain white rice proved the best choice. It had a firm, pleasing texture, was not sticky, and had a neutral flavor.

After cooking numerous pots of rice, we found that 3½ cups liquid to 1½ cups rice provided the texture we desired. We also substituted chicken broth for some of the water to add a little more flavor.

As with pilafs, we found that toasting the rice in the pan with the fat and aromatic vegetables brought out its flavor. A casserole dish (covered with foil to keep the rice from drying out) in the regulated heat of the oven proved to be the best way to cook the rice. On top of the stove, a saucepan became overfilled with ingredients and the rice cooked very unevenly.

Although cooking hoppin' John in the oven mitigated this problem, it did not completely solve it. We found that the rice, when combined with the other ingredients, cooked a bit unevenly; the rice on the bottom cooked faster than that in the upper portion of the baking dish. We found it necessary to stir the casserole about halfway through baking to redistribute the rice and liquid.

Hoppin' John
SERVES 4 TO 6

Frozen black-eyed peas have a surprisingly good texture and flavor. Do not use canned peas in this recipe; they are too mushy and can't withstand baking in the oven.

PLANNING AHEAD: This dish cannot be made in advance or frozen.

1	tablespoon vegetable oil
6	ounces cooked ham, cut into $\frac{1}{2}$-inch cubes (about $1\frac{1}{4}$ cups)
4	ounces (about 4 slices) bacon, chopped medium
1	medium onion, chopped medium
3	medium garlic cloves, minced or pressed through a garlic press
$1\frac{1}{2}$	cups long-grain white rice
$1\frac{1}{2}$	teaspoons minced fresh thyme leaves
$\frac{1}{2}$	teaspoon red pepper flakes
2	bay leaves
2	cups low-sodium chicken broth
$1\frac{1}{2}$	cups water
1	teaspoon salt
	Ground black pepper
1	(10-ounce) package frozen black-eyed peas, thawed and rinsed
2	tablespoons minced fresh parsley leaves

1. Adjust an oven rack to the middle position and heat the oven to 375 degrees. Grease a 9 by 13-inch baking dish (or a shallow casserole dish of similar size) and set aside.

2. Heat the oil in a large skillet over medium-high heat until shimmering but not smoking. Add the ham and cook until the fat has rendered, about 6 minutes. Add the bacon and cook until slightly crisp, about 3 minutes. Use a slotted spoon to remove the ham and bacon from the pan and set aside on a paper-towel-lined plate.

3. Spoon off and discard all but 2 tablespoons of the fat from the pan and return to the burner. Reduce the heat to medium; add the onion and cook, stirring frequently, until softened, about 4 minutes. Add the garlic and cook until fragrant, about 30 seconds longer. Stir in the rice, thyme, and red pepper flakes and cook, stirring frequently, until the rice is coated and glistening, about 1 minute longer. Transfer the rice mixture to the baking dish and add the bay leaves.

4. Return the skillet to the heat; add the chicken broth, water, salt, and pepper to taste. Increase the heat to medium-high, scraping the browned bits off the bottom of pan with a wooden spoon. Add the black-eyed peas, ham, and bacon, bring to a boil, and pour over the rice mixture, stirring to combine.

5. Cover the baking dish tightly with foil and bake for 20 minutes. Remove from the oven, stir the rice (if the rice appears too dry, add $\frac{1}{4}$ cup more water), re-cover with foil, and cook until the rice is fully tender, 20 to 25 minutes more. Remove the dish from the oven and discard the bay leaves. Stir in the parsley, re-cover the dish, and allow it to rest for 5 to 10 minutes before serving.

MEDITERRANEAN-STYLE SHRIMP

ORZO, THE TINY RICE-SHAPED PASTA, IS usually added to Italian-style soups or made into pasta salad. However, there's a third, more novel way to prepare it that we thought would be perfect for making a casserole. Orzo can be cooked "pilaf style," or sautéed briefly in oil with flavorings before liquid is added, deepening the pasta's flavor and color. And, if diligently stirred as it simmers, the orzo will release starches into the cooking liquid and turn it creamy—not quite as creamy as risotto, perhaps, but rich and velvety nevertheless. Inspired by Mediterranean-style pilafs in which rice, fish, vegetables, and fresh herbs are baked together until the flavors meld, we envisioned a casserole of orzo pilaf studded with large, juicy shrimp and tender vegetables. The method for the orzo pilaf was simple and foolproof; choosing appropriate vegetables, broth, and a method in which to prepare the shrimp was a different matter. And then there was the baking time: How long and at what temperature would we achieve the best results?

We wanted to limit the vegetables to a select few to keep preparation brief—nothing adds to prep time like cleaning and cutting a long list of vegetables. Onions seemed like a natural for depth and body, as did the crisp, sweet crunch of red bell peppers. We tried yellow and red onions and found that we preferred the sweeter, milder flavor and brighter color of the red onions. Sautéed until just beginning to brown, the vegetables added solid flavor and a bit of bite to the otherwise tender-textured pilaf.

For flavor, color, and acidity, we also decided to add tomatoes. Canned diced tomatoes kept things easy and flavorful; skinning, seeding, and chopping fresh tomatoes took too much time, and the bland flavor and mealy texture of the fresh supermarket tomatoes simply couldn't match that of the canned. In order for the orzo to toast properly, the tomatoes needed to be added after the orzo, not sautéed with the other vegetables.

As for flavoring the pilaf, a healthy dose of garlic seemed essential to keep in the Mediterranean spirit of things. Sautéed briefly with the onions and peppers, finely minced garlic retained a potent kick through to the end. A handful of coarsely chopped fresh herbs seemed apropos as well, and after testing a slew of options, tasters favored a simple combination of oregano and scallions. The oregano lent the casserole a decidedly Greek edge while the scallions—added raw to the top—added a sharp bite to accent things.

After we had prepared a few batches of the pilaf, we realized that the straw yellow color of the toasted orzo seemed pale against the deep red of the bell pepper and tomato, so we decided to intensify the orzo's color by adding a pinch of saffron. Toasted with the orzo, it suffused the pasta with a sunny orange hue and its characteristic flavor.

Finally ready to tackle the shrimp, we knew that we had a variety of things to test. First off, we preferred larger shrimp, left whole, because they stayed moist longer than smaller shrimp, an important factor considering that they were to be baked. As for cooking them, searing the shrimp in a smoking skillet gave the shrimp a sweet, caramelized flavor that, surprisingly, tasters thought clashed with the light, bright flavors of the pilaf. A lower-temperature sauté, however, lent little flavor at all. Baking the shrimp on top of the pilaf dried them out and turned them rubbery.

Embedding the raw shrimp in the pilaf and then baking it, however, was a whole different story. Protected by the orzo, the shrimp stayed moist and tender. And it was the easiest method yet: All that was required was to season the shrimp with salt and pepper before adding them to the pilaf. The orzo shielded the shrimp from the oven's direct heat, effectively preventing them from drying out and toughening. A relatively hot oven, 400 degrees, cooked the shrimp evenly in

INGREDIENTS: Saffron

While many people know that saffron is the most expensive spice in the world, few are aware that it is grown in a variety of locations and that its price and quality can vary considerably. Though the bulk of commercially produced saffron comes from Spain and Iran, it is also harvested on a small scale in India, Greece, France, and, closer to home, in Lancaster County, Pennsylvania. We decided to toss saffron from different places purchased at different prices into a few pots and set up a test. We prepared three batches of risotto alla Milanese—the purest way to taste the subtle differences and see the different shades of orange—and flavored one with Spanish saffron, one with Indian, and one with American.

The finished risotti were similar in hue, though the Indian "Kashmir" saffron threads were darkest prior to cooking. In a blind tasting, we overwhelmingly chose the Pennsylvania-grown saffron over both the Spanish and Indian, judging it the "most potent" and "perfumed" of the three. Surprisingly, no one cared much for the Indian saffron, which is almost twice as costly as the other two and generally regarded as one of the best in the world. Greider's Saffron is exclusively available from the Pennsylvania General store (www.pageneralstore.com).

about 20 minutes—just enough time for the flavors of the pilaf and the shrimp to combine.

While we liked the overall concept and flavor of the casserole, we thought it was a little bland. It needed a splash of acid, or something sharp and pungent for accent. A healthy shot of lemon juice sprinkled over the finished dish certainly helped, especially when we added some lemon zest to the pilaf as it cooked. Capers and anchovies were both interesting additions, but tasters had mixed feelings in each case. Then we came up with a slightly oddball addition: feta cheese. The cheese's salty, briny bite perfectly pointed up the sweetness of the shrimp and the fruitiness of the tomato and bell pepper. We normally shy away from combining cheese and fish, but in this instance, it was a perfect pairing—and authentically Greek. At first, we crumbled it and scattered it over the finished dish, but found it actually tasted better if baked on top of the casserole. Feta doesn't really melt per se; instead it browns and intensifies in flavor.

Mediterranean-Style Shrimp and Orzo Casserole

SERVES 6 TO 8

Make sure that the orzo is al dente, or slightly firm to the bite; otherwise it may overcook in the oven. If you don't have saffron, ¼ teaspoon ground turmeric can add a similar orange-ish color, but not the flavor. Be careful not to add too much turmeric because its flavor is bitter when used in excessive amounts.

PLANNING AHEAD: This recipe cannot be made ahead or frozen.

1½	pounds large shrimp (31 to 40 count), peeled and deveined
	Salt and ground black pepper
3	tablespoons extra-virgin olive oil
1	medium red onion, minced
1	large red bell pepper, stemmed, seeded, and chopped fine
6	medium garlic cloves, minced or pressed through a garlic press
1	pound orzo
1	large pinch saffron
1	tablespoon lemon zest and 2 tablespoons lemon juice
4	cups low-sodium chicken broth
1	cup water
1	(28-ounce) can diced tomatoes, drained
4	teaspoons chopped fresh oregano leaves
12	ounces feta cheese, crumbled into large pieces (about 3 cups)
4	scallions, white and light green parts only, sliced thin

1. Adjust an oven rack to the middle position and heat the oven to 400 degrees. Season the shrimp generously with salt and pepper; set aside.

2. Heat the oil in a 12-inch skillet over medium heat until shimmering. Add the onion, pepper, and ½ teaspoon salt; cook, stirring occasionally, until the vegetables are softened and beginning to brown, about 6 minutes. Add the garlic and cook until fragrant, 30 seconds. Add the orzo, saffron, and lemon zest; cook, stirring frequently, until the orzo is coated with oil and lightly browned, about 4 minutes. Stir in the broth and water; cook, stirring occasionally, until the grains of orzo are mostly tender yet still slightly firm at the center, about 12 minutes. Stir in the tomatoes, oregano, and seasoned shrimp.

3. Pour into a 9 by 13-inch baking dish (or a shallow casserole dish of similar size). Sprinkle the feta over the top and bake until the shrimp are cooked through and the cheese is lightly browned, about 20 minutes. Sprinkle with the lemon juice and garnish with the scallions. Serve immediately.

CRAB IMPERIAL

CRAB IMPERIAL IS A CLASSIC SOUTHERN seafood dish. It showcases fresh, briny crabmeat lightly bound with a creamy filling, topped with buttered crumbs, and baked until golden and bubbly. Simple and unadorned by definition, a classic crab imperial recipe should showcase the fresh brininess of premium crabmeat. Unfortunately, research turned up conglomerations of greasy mayonnaise-based dishes, starchy white sauces, or leaden, stuffing-like casseroles. The results hardly did the venerable crab justice. Our goal was for the star of this dish to be the crab, with a minimum of filler. The rest of the filling needed to complement the delicate crab, without being overpowering, and we wanted a topping that was rich, buttery, golden, and crispy.

While its genesis is unclear, crab imperial is synonymous with the Chesapeake Bay region of Maryland and traditionally features the Atlantic blue crab. Atlantic blue crab is always sold cooked and is available in four grades: lump, backfin, special, and claw. Lump meat is of the highest quality and is nothing but large chunks of meat removed from the body, so consequently it's the priciest of options. Fresh crabmeat is found in plastic containers in the fish department and is often sold pasteurized to prolong its shelf life. If fresh unpasteurized crabmeat is available, it is well worth the extra money, as its flavor is far superior to the crab that has been subjected to the pasteurization process.

While this is a dish that by virtue of its title should be fit for a king, you shouldn't need the wealth of royalty to prepare it. We knew that to bring the crabmeat to the forefront, we would need at least 1½ pounds of the crustacean to work with. Given the cost of fresh crabmeat, we wondered if we could successfully augment the precious crab with fish that had similar characteristics, without sacrificing the integrity of the dish. We tried shrimp, but found that its assertive flavor and contrasting texture overshadowed the tender sweetness of the crab. We decided that a firm-fleshed white fish might be more appropriate and tested halibut, haddock, and cod. All served admirably as a subtle backdrop to the crab. Their textures were similar, and they neither overshadowed nor detracted from the inimitable crab flavor. We sautéed onion and red bell pepper, then added the white fish and cooked it until it had lost its translucency and was easy to flake and combine with the crab.

To make up the filling, we turned to cream cheese, thinned with milk. Tasters preferred it to the greasy mayonnaise-based recipes, both because of the consistency it gave the dish and for its richness, which was the perfect foil for the crabmeat. For seasoning we added Worcestershire sauce, Dijon mustard, hot pepper sauce, and Old Bay seasoning. Old Bay is a seasoning blend of more than a dozen herbs and spices, and is often paired with seafood; in the South it is a must-have when it comes to crabmeat.

We wanted a substantial bread-crumb topping that would add a textural contrast to the tender crab filling. We tested fresh bread-crumb toppings with a multitude of seasonings, and, in the end, decided that the best course of action was to keep it simple. A generous layer of freshly made bread crumbs, mixed with unsalted butter and fresh parsley, was all that was needed to form the golden crust we were seeking, without obscuring the delicate crab flavor.

In this recipe, the crabmeat reigns supreme. Decadently rich and deeply satisfying, a small portion, served with a simple green salad, is a royal feast.

Crab Imperial

SERVES 6 TO 8

We recommend buying fresh or pasteurized crabmeat sold on ice at the fish counter rather than the tuna-style cans found in the supermarket aisles.

PLANNING AHEAD: Follow the recipe through step 3. Refrigerate the crab mixture and topping in separate bowls, tightly wrapped with plastic wrap, for up to 1 day.

TO BAKE: Poke several vent holes in the plastic wrap covering the crab mixture and microwave on high until the mixture begins to bubble around the edges, 3 to 5 minutes. Stir gently to combine, and continue to assemble and bake the casserole as directed in step 4.

TOPPING

4	slices white sandwich bread, torn into quarters
2	tablespoons unsalted butter, melted
2	tablespoons minced fresh parsley leaves

FILLING

3	tablespoons unsalted butter
2	tablespoons minced onion
1	medium red pepper, stemmed, seeded, and chopped fine

½	pound firm white fish (such as cod, haddock, or halibut), skinned and cut into ½-inch chunks
12	ounces cream cheese
¼	cup whole milk
3	tablespoons lemon juice
1	tablespoon Worcestershire sauce
1	tablespoon Dijon mustard
2	teaspoons Tabasco sauce, plus more for serving
1½	teaspoons Old Bay Seasoning
1	pound fresh or pasteurized crabmeat, squeezed dry and picked over for bits of shell
1	lemon, cut into wedges

1. FOR THE TOPPING: Process the bread and butter in a food processor fitted with the steel blade until coarsely ground, about six 1-second pulses. Transfer to a bowl and toss with the parsley; set aside.

2. FOR THE FILLING: Melt 2 tablespoons of the butter in a 12-inch nonstick skillet over medium heat. Add the onion and red pepper; cook until soft and translucent, 3 to 5 minutes. Add the white fish and cook, stirring occasionally to flake the fish into small pieces, until fully opaque, about 4 minutes. Set aside to cool.

3. Microwave the cream cheese in a large bowl on high power until very soft, 20 to 40 seconds. Whisk in the milk, lemon juice, Worcestershire, Dijon, Tabasco, and Old Bay until smooth. Gently fold in the crabmeat and the cooled white fish mixture.

4. Adjust an oven rack to the middle position and heat the oven to 400 degrees. Grease the bottom and sides of a 9-inch square baking dish (or a shallow casserole dish of similar size) with the remaining tablespoon butter. Sprinkle 3 tablespoons of the bread-crumb topping evenly over the dish. Spread the crab mixture over the dish and sprinkle with the remaining bread-crumb topping. Bake until browned and bubbling, 20 to 25 minutes. Serve immediately with the lemon wedges and Tabasco.

NEW ENGLAND FISH CHOWDER CASSEROLE

DEPENDING ON WHAT REGION OF NEW England you are in and who is manning the stove, fish chowder can be brothy, punctuated with tidbits of fish and potato, or it can be stodgy enough to support a spoon upright. We tend to favor the rib-sticking nature of the latter. But what if you omit the broth almost entirely and turn the chowder into a baked casserole? Thick cubes of potato and tender pieces of flaky cod enriched with cream and flavored with bacon—it sounded pretty good to us. We imagined a casserole with all the flavors of the classic stew, just in an easy-to-transport, easy-to-serve format.

By its very nature, chowder is a simple dish, composed of onions, bacon, potatoes, fish, broth, and cream. Seasonings and herbs are kept to a bare minimum; this is a Yankee dish, after all, born out of a particularly frugal approach to cooking (and life). For a "dry" version of chowder, we wanted to keep things as simple as possible, though we weren't against fleshing things out a bit if the dish warranted it.

For our first test, we cobbled together a recipe based on our favorite fish chowder, but instead of simmering the potatoes in cream and broth, we boiled them until tender and combined them in the baking dish with the sautéed onions, rendered bacon, and cubes of raw cod. We doused everything with cream, covered the dish, and baked it until the fish was flaky. The results were blander than we expected; downright boring, in fact. Without the flavorful broth and the commingling of ingredients through simmering, the casserole's flavors were disjointed, as if nothing had blended. And too much cream virtually buried the fish's flavor. Despite the casserole's shortcomings, we still liked the concept. After our first misstep, we realized that we could cook the casserole in the same fashion as a chowder, simply with more aromatic vegetables and significantly less broth. The fish could go into the casserole raw and bake in the oven; otherwise, it was certain to turn rubbery.

We increased the amount of onion and chose to add celery to the mix for its penetrating flavor and vegetal crunch—just the right vegetable to accent the casserole's creamy flavor and smooth texture. A little garlic—downright heretical in classic chowder—also found its way into the casserole upon tasters' demands.

Once the vegetables were completely softened in the rendered bacon fat (we removed and reserved the browned bacon bits until the vegetables were tender to prevent them from burning), we added cubed russet potatoes and just enough clam juice and cream to cover. We cooked the potatoes until tender, stirred in the pieces of cod, and poured the filling into a baking dish. From there it went into the oven to simmer away until the fish was tender and flaky, the broth condensed, and the flavors blended.

For the most part, it worked beautifully. The fish was tender and flavorful, the slick of broth rich but still a little bland. A couple of bay leaves and some minced thyme rounded it out easily enough. A splash of white wine—not too uncommon in chowder—brought some welcome acidity, both cutting the richness and enlivening the cod's mild flavor.

The potatoes, however, were a problem. Although starchy-textured russets are the common choice for chowder, they came across as gummy in this instance. We opted to substitute denser-textured Yukon Golds. They better withstood simmering and baking, and also had a more assertive flavor. And their buttery-yellow color added much-needed visual appeal to the otherwise pale casserole.

Without the starches released by the russets, the broth turned out too thin. The fix, however, was simple: flour. We added a small amount to the vegetables prior to adding the broth and cream. As everything simmered, the flour effectively tightened the liquid, and by the time the casserole emerged from the oven, it was silky smooth and creamy without being cloying.

Now we were three quarters of the way there and just needed to come up with a topping—a casserole simply isn't a casserole without some sort of crispy topping. Plain old bread crumbs were acceptable, though they seemed pedestrian here. On a whim, we covered the dish with a handful of a classic chowder accompaniment: oyster crackers

and chopped parsley leaves. Somehow the casserole seemed complete now—an entire re-imagination of one of New England's classics.

New England Fish Chowder Casserole

SERVES 6 TO 8

While cod is the classic choice for fish chowder, it can be difficult to find in certain parts of the country. Any semi-firm white fish may be substituted.

PLANNING AHEAD: Follow the recipe through step 2. Transfer the filling to a large bowl or container, wrap tightly with plastic wrap, and poke several vent holes with the tip of a paring knife. Refrigerate the filling until cool, about 3 hours, then wrap tightly with another sheet of plastic wrap and refrigerate for up to 2 days.

TO BAKE: Poke several vent holes in the plastic wrap covering the filling and microwave on high power until hot, 3 to 5 minutes, before continuing with step 3.

FILLING

4	ounces (about 4 slices) bacon, chopped medium
2	medium onions, minced
2	medium celery ribs, cut into 1/2-inch pieces
2	medium garlic cloves, minced or pressed through a garlic press
1/4	cup all-purpose flour
1	(8-ounce) bottle clam juice
1	cup heavy cream
1/4	cup dry white wine
1	teaspoon minced fresh thyme leaves
2	bay leaves
2	pounds Yukon Gold potatoes, peeled and cut into 1/2-inch chunks
	Salt and ground white pepper
1 1/2	pounds skinless cod fillets, cut into 1-inch cubes
2	cups oyster crackers
2	tablespoons minced fresh parsley leaves
1	lemon, cut into wedges

1. Adjust an oven rack to the middle position and heat the oven to 400 degrees. Cook the bacon in a large saucepan over medium heat until crisp,

about 6 minutes. Using a slotted spoon, transfer the bacon to a paper-towel-lined plate; set aside.

2. Add the onions and celery to the bacon fat left in the pan; cook over medium heat, stirring occasionally, until softened, about 5 minutes. Add the garlic and cook until fragrant, about 30 seconds. Add the flour and cook, stirring constantly, until golden, about 1 minute. Gradually whisk in the clam juice, cream, and wine. Add the thyme, bay leaves, potatoes, and crisp bacon. Bring to a boil, cover, and reduce the heat to low; cook, stirring occasionally, until the potatoes are just tender, 30 to 35 minutes. Discard the bay leaves and season with salt and pepper to taste.

3. Stir in the cod and transfer to a 9 by 13-inch baking dish (or a shallow casserole dish of similar size) and wrap tightly with aluminum foil. Bake until the cream has thickened and the cod is fully cooked, about 25 minutes. Sprinkle evenly with the oyster crackers and parsley. Serve immediately with the lemon wedges.

SOY-GLAZED SALMON CASSEROLE

IT'S A SAFE BET THAT THE PROMISE OF spring played a role in the conception of this recipe. Our craving for fresh fish, crisp vibrant vegetables, and clean flavors led us to develop an Asian-inspired recipe that would combine salmon, white rice, and vegetables in a one-dish meal suitable for the oven (and a casserole dish).

Glazing salmon with soy sauce is often done on the grill or in a skillet, with great success. The soy sauce forms a lacquered exterior that is both tasty and attractive. We wondered if we could achieve this same effect from salmon that was baked in the oven along with rice and vegetables. And since we knew that a dish with all these components would need a sauce to unify them, we decided to devise a soy-based sauce that would withstand the time it took to cook both the salmon and the vegetables.

Thinking that the sauce might be the trickiest part of this recipe, we decided to tackle it first, starting with a combination of dry sherry, chicken broth, soy sauce, rice vinegar, and chili sauce. The rice vinegar balanced the saltiness of the soy sauce, and the chili sauce added spiciness and heat. To tame the harsh bite of the chili sauce, we sweetened the mix with sugar. We knew that ginger and garlic were the key flavoring components that we wanted in this dish. So we tried adding them raw to the sauce mixture and found their flavors harsh, almost medicinal. Seeking to mellow their flavors, we decided to sauté them along with shiitake mushrooms, which we had chosen over white button mushrooms for their meaty flavor and texture. Then we deglazed the skillet with the sauce mixture. The sauce now had the flavor we were seeking, but it lacked the viscosity needed to coat the salmon. A small amount of cornstarch dissolved in the glaze did the trick and provided just enough thickening to coat the salmon without reminding us of bad Chinese takeout.

The choice of additional vegetables for the casserole revolved around those that were fairly firm and could withstand the heat of the oven while still retaining their integrity. We wanted crisp vegetables, when all was said and done, and there were many good options from which to choose. We narrowed the field down to red peppers, for their sweetness and color, and bok choy. This leafy vegetable resembles Swiss chard, and its tender leaves and firm stalks make it ideal for this dish.

EQUIPMENT: Spider

More often referred to as a mesh skimmer or strainer, this piece of equipment is invaluable when it comes to working with boiling water or hot oil. Compared with a slotted spoon, which generally retrieves only a few food items from the water or oil at a time, this not so itsy-bitsy spider has a wide basket made of open webbed (hence the name) mesh that can cradle food and allow excess water or oil to drain away quickly.

Blanching the vegetables briefly brought up their flavor and diminished their raw vegetable taste, but that meant another dirty pot, and we had yet to deal with the rice. We discovered that instead of draining the water that we used to blanch the vegetables, we could recycle it and use it for the rice.

We boiled long-grain white rice until just tender in the blanching water, then drained it and combined it with the vegetables. This mixture of rice and vegetables went into our baking dish, and we laid the salmon on top of the rice. Instead of mixing the sauce with the rice to moisten it, we found that if we poured the soy mixture over the salmon, the fish became glazed with the sauce, which protected it from the drying heat of the oven. Leaving a bit of space between the pieces of salmon ensured that the sauce would make its way down to the rice and vegetables below to perfume the rice and impart its Asian flavors, without drowning the rice and vegetables in liquid.

The salmon, baked at 450 degrees, turned the caramelized color that wanted, due to the sugar and the soy in the sauce mixture. The oiliness of the salmon was tempered by the clean flavors of ginger, garlic, and rice vinegar. Here was a casserole where the salmon was the star but the vegetables remained crisp and vibrant, and the rice tender, flavorful, and moist.

Soy-Glazed Salmon with Shiitake Mushrooms and Bok Choy

SERVES 6

Asian chili sauce can be found in the international section of most supermarkets. If it is not available, 1 to 2 teaspoons of Tabasco can be substituted. You can substitute 1½ pounds of Napa cabbage, cored and shredded into ½-inch thick pieces, for the bok choy.

PLANNING AHEAD: Follow the recipe through step 3. Refrigerate the rice mixture and sauce in separate bowls, tightly wrapped with plastic wrap, for up to 1 day.

TO BAKE: Poke several vent holes in the plastic wrap covering the rice and the sauce. Microwave both, separately, on high power until hot, 3 to 5 minutes. Continue to assemble and bake the casserole as directed in step 4.

Salt
- 1 medium red bell pepper, stemmed, seeded, and sliced into ¼-inch-thick strips
- 1 small head bok choy (about 1¼ pounds), cored and sliced crosswise into ½-inch-thick shreds
- 1½ cups long-grain white rice
- 1 cup low-sodium chicken broth
- ½ cup soy sauce
- ½ cup dry sherry
- ¼ cup rice vinegar
- ¼ cup sugar
- 1 tablespoon Asian chili sauce
- 1 tablespoon cornstarch
- 3 tablespoons vegetable oil
- 12 ounces shiitake mushrooms, brushed clean, stems discarded, and sliced into ¼-inch-thick strips
- 1 (2-inch) piece fresh ginger, peeled and minced
- 6 medium garlic cloves, minced or pressed through a garlic press
- 6 (6-ounce) center-cut salmon fillets (roughly 1 to 1¼ inches thick), skin removed
- 4 scallions, white and light green parts only, sliced thin

1. Adjust an oven rack to the middle position and heat the oven to 450 degrees. Bring 4 quarts of water to a boil in a large pot (with a perforated pasta insert, if available) over high heat. Add 1 tablespoon salt, the pepper, and bok choy; cook for 10 seconds. Transfer the vegetables to a colander using a slotted spoon or mesh spider (see page 94) or by lifting out the pasta insert, if using. Pat dry with paper towels and transfer to a large bowl.

2. Return the water to a boil and add the rice; cook until almost tender but still firm to the bite, about 12 minutes. Drain through a fine mesh strainer, shaking to remove any excess water. Toss with the red pepper and bok choy and set aside.

3. Whisk the chicken broth, soy sauce, sherry, rice vinegar, sugar, chili sauce, and cornstarch together in a medium bowl; set aside. Heat the oil in a 12-inch nonstick skillet over medium-high heat until shimmering. Add the shiitakes and cook, stirring constantly, until lightly browned, about 8 minutes. Add the ginger and garlic; cook

until fragrant, about 1 minute. Briefly re-whisk the soy mixture and add it to the pan; bring to a simmer and cook, whisking often, until the sauce has thickened, about 4 minutes. Remove from the heat.

4. Spread the rice and cabbage mixture into a 9 by 13-inch baking dish (or a shallow casserole dish of similar size). Lay the salmon fillets, skinned-side down, about ¼ inch apart on top of the rice. Pour the shiitake sauce evenly over the salmon. Bake until the salmon is cooked through and the rice is steaming, about 20 minutes. Sprinkle with the scallions and serve immediately.

BAKED BOUILLABAISSE

BOUILLABAISSE IS A CLASSIC PROVENÇAL dish with humble origins. But what may have begun as a fisherman's cost-effective family meal has evolved into a renowned and fashionable fish stew.

Authentic bouillabaisse relies on a deeply flavored fish stock (or fumet) made from scratch with fish frames and shells. After simmering for hours, the briny sweet broth is strained and the supporting flavors are added—tomato, wine, fennel, olive oil, and the most expensive spice on the planet: saffron. When the broth portion of the stew is fully assembled, a variety of fish and crustaceans are added and poached in the complex broth. It is always served with thick slices of French bread or garlic croutons to sop up the flavorful broth, and with *rouille*, a luxuriant roasted red pepper and garlic mayonnaise. Our goal was to create an oven-friendly adaptation of this classic that was authentic in spirit, without being overly time consuming. We wanted it to feature widely available fish that would be conducive to consistent oven poaching, and a broth that was redolent of classic Mediterranean flavors.

Our plan was to arrange fish and shellfish in a shallow baking dish and pour an intensely flavored broth over the top. The dish would then be covered, and as it baked, the fish would steam in the aromatic broth. Large garlic croutons would be served on the side, as well as a shortcut rouille.

First, we focused on the medley of seafood that would be the heart of the stew. Nearly all bouillabaisse recipes emphasize that a variety of fish and shellfish are essential to bringing character to the stew. They caution against using fish that are too delicate in constitution or too strong in flavor. Certain fish have no place in bouillabaisse, among them bluefish and mackerel, which are too oily and intrusive. Others, like lobster and squid, aren't worth the trouble or expense. In our tests, other fish fell out of play early on for the simple reason that their cooking times were too dissimilar. Sole was so thin that it overcooked in a flash. Mussels and clams opened up and turned to rubber before the other fish had cooked. In a traditional stovetop bouillabaisse, upward of six different aquatic species are layered into the pot, with longer-cooking varieties going in first, while the more delicate varieties top the stack. Our oven version did not afford us that luxury. We needed seafood of similar size and density, as they would all be cooked together, and we wanted to limit the variety to three diverse but widely available species. Shrimp and scallops fit the bill for our first two choices. We chose large shrimp and sea scallops, which average 1½ inches in diameter, for their uniform cooking times. To round out our trio, we tested a variety of fish that we were fortunate enough to be able to

REMOVING TENDONS FROM SCALLOPS

The small, rough-textured, crescent-shaped muscle that attaches the scallop to the shell will toughen when cooked. Remove the tendons before cooking the scallops, using your fingertips to peel each one away from the side of the scallop. (Some scallops may come with tendons removed.)

locate, given our proximity to the coast. While there were myriad obscure varieties from which to choose, haddock, cod, sea bass, and halibut were our favorites. We preferred the halibut for its sweet, firm flesh that retained its shape during cooking. We used a total of 4 pounds of seafood, which will easily serve 6 to 8 hungry people.

Next we focused on the broth. We sautéed fresh fennel, carrot, onion, and lots of garlic in olive oil. Our next ingredients were white wine and a stand-in for fish fumet: bottled clam juice. We started with 2 cups of wine and 2 bottles of clam juice. The wine was sour and acidic, and the clam juice imparted a salty, fishy flavor that was overpowering. We pulled back on the wine, opting to simmer it briefly to eliminate the raw alcohol aftertaste. One bottle of clam juice proved to be the perfect amount to lend an ocean-like brininess without being obtrusive. Perfumed with undertones of licorice from the fresh fennel, the white wine, and the generous amount of garlic, this broth gave us a solid foundation on which to build the rest of our dish. Next we added diced tomatoes with their juice and the illustrious saffron.

Saffron threads are the yellow-orange stigmas from the crocus plant. It takes over 14,000 of these tiny threads, hand-picked and dried, to make one ounce of saffron. Fortunately, a little bit of this costly crocus goes a long way. (Saffron has a pungent flavor that can taste medicinal if used in excess.) Another of saffron's distinguishing characteristics is the vibrant yellow-gold color that it imparts to a dish. We found that a mere ¼ teaspoon of the precious filament was enough to perfume the broth with its distinctive flavor, color, and aroma.

We added fresh thyme and bay leaf, and briefly simmered the mixture down to what we thought was the proper amount to pour over the fish. It turned out that the fish exuded such a copious quantity of liquid during baking that our base became diluted and thin. It did, however, pick up great natural flavors from the fish. We tried reducing the sauce until almost all of the liquid had disappeared, which took about 15 minutes. At this point, the sauce seemed to have neither broth

nor stew potential, but when poured over the fish and baked it proved to be the ideal amount. The unique flavors of the shrimp, scallop, and haddock juices combined with the saffron-infused tomato base to produce the ideal amount of flavorful liquid. The generous quantity was ideal for steaming the fish to perfection, with plenty left to serve in a soup plate. A sprinkling of fresh tarragon added a clean anise-like flavor and a brightness that gave the stew distinction.

All that remained were the finishing touches: the croutons and rouille. For the croutons, we sliced a French baguette and brushed the slices with garlic-infused olive oil, then toasted them until golden and crisp. For the rouille, we started with garlic and roasted red pepper, then combined them in the food processor with cayenne, lemon juice, and prepared mayonnaise. To thicken the rouille, we added 2 ounces of bread we had reserved from the baguette, and drizzled in good-quality extra-virgin olive oil to round out the flavor.

We finally had a richly scented broth with complex flavors, the right combination of perfectly cooked fish, and a garlicky rouille. This upscale seafood chowder is easy to shop for, quick to prepare, and will bring the flavors and aromas of the French seaside into your kitchen.

Baked Bouillabaisse
SERVES 6 TO 8

Be sure to buy sea scallops, which are large, as opposed to bay scallops, which can be tiny—they will cook more evenly in the oven alongside the other fish. If fresh fennel is unavailable, substitute ¼ teaspoon fennel seed. Choose saffron threads, as opposed to ground saffron, for best flavor; see page 89 for more information about buying this spice.

PLANNING AHEAD: Follow the recipe through step 3. Wrap the garlic toasts tightly with plastic wrap and store them at room temperature. Refrigerate the rouille and the tomato mixture in separate bowls, tightly wrapped with plastic wrap, for up to 1 day.

TO BAKE: Adjust an oven rack to the middle position and heat the oven to 400 degrees. Continue to assemble and bake the bouillabaisse as directed in step 4.

GARLIC TOASTS

6	medium garlic cloves, minced or pressed through a garlic press
1/4	cup extra-virgin olive oil
1	baguette (about 10 ounces), sliced 1/2 inch thick, two slices reserved for the rouille
	Salt and ground black pepper

ROUILLE

2	large jarred roasted red peppers, rinsed and patted dry with paper towels
1	cup mayonnaise
2	slices baguette, torn into small pieces
3	medium garlic cloves, minced or pressed through a garlic press
1/8	teaspoon cayenne pepper
1	tablespoon lemon juice
1/4	cup extra-virgin olive oil
	Salt and ground black pepper

BOUILLABAISSE

1/4	cup olive oil
1	small fennel bulb, stalks and fronds discarded, bulb cored, and chopped fine (see the illustrations on page 220)
1	large carrot, peeled and chopped fine
2	medium onions, chopped fine
8	medium garlic cloves, minced or pressed through a garlic press
3/4	cup vermouth or dry white wine
1	(8-ounce) bottle clam juice
1	(14.5-ounce) can diced tomatoes
1/2	teaspoon red pepper flakes
1/4	teaspoon saffron threads
5	sprigs fresh thyme
2	bay leaves
2	pounds firm white fish (such as halibut or haddock), skin removed and cut into 2-inch chunks
1	pound large sea scallops, tendons removed (see the illustration on page 96)
1	pound extra-large shrimp (21 to 25 count), peeled and deveined
	Salt and ground black pepper
1/4	cup chopped fresh tarragon leaves
1	lemon, cut into wedges

1. FOR THE GARLIC TOASTS: Adjust an oven rack to the middle position and heat the oven to 400 degrees. Heat the garlic with 1/4 cup of the olive oil in a medium saucepan over medium heat until the garlic begins to brown, about 2 minutes, then remove it from the heat. Using a pastry brush, brush the oil onto one side of each piece of bread. Arrange the bread, oiled side facing up, in a single layer on a rimmed baking sheet. Sprinkle generously with salt and pepper. Bake until golden, 7 to 10 minutes; set aside and leave the oven on.

2. FOR THE ROUILLE: Process the peppers, mayonnaise, bread, garlic, cayenne, and lemon juice in a food processor fitted with the steel blade until smooth, about 30 seconds. With the machine running, slowly drizzle 1/4 cup olive oil through the feed tube and continue to process to a thick, mayonnaise-like consistency. Season to taste with salt and pepper; set aside.

3. FOR THE BOUILLABAISSE: Heat 1/4 cup oil in a Dutch oven over medium heat until shimmering. Add the fennel, carrot, and onions; cook, stirring occasionally, until vegetables have softened, about 5 minutes. Add the garlic and cook until fragrant, about 1 minute. Add the vermouth, increase the heat to medium-high, and simmer until reduced to 1/2 cup, about 4 minutes. Add the clam juice, tomatoes, red pepper flakes, saffron, thyme, and bay leaves; continue to simmer until most of the liquid has evaporated, 15 to 18 minutes. Remove from the heat and discard the thyme sprigs and bay leaves.

4. Arrange the white fish in a single layer in a 9 by 13-inch baking dish (or a shallow casserole dish of similar size). Tuck the shrimp and scallops in between the pieces of fish. Sprinkle generously with salt and pepper. Spoon the tomato mixture evenly over the seafood and cover with foil. Bake until the fish is thoroughly cooked, 40 to 45 minutes. Arrange the garlic toast around the edges of the dish. Sprinkle with the fresh tarragon and serve immediately, passing the rouille and lemon wedges separately.

BAKED PENNE WITH SUMMER SQUASH, TOMATOES, AND BASIL **PAGE 28**

EASY MEAT LASAGNA WITH HEARTY TOMATO-MEAT SAUCE **PAGE 37**

POLENTA CASSEROLE WITH SAUTÉED BELL PEPPERS AND SAUSAGE **PAGE 43**

CHICKEN ENCHILADAS WITH RED CHILI SAUCE **PAGE 66**

CHILI MAC **PAGE 81**

103

BEEF POT PIE **PAGE 127**

SALMON AND LEEK POT PIE WITH PUFF-PASTRY TOPPING **PAGE 136**

SKILLET THAI CURRY WITH SWEET POTATOES AND TOFU **PAGE 240**

CHICKEN TAGINE WITH OLIVES AND LEMON **PAGE 202**

HEARTY BEEF STEW **PAGE 149**

SKILLET CHICKEN AND RICE WITH CARROTS, PEAS, AND PARMESAN **PAGE 216**

BROCCOLI AND CHEESE CASSEROLE **PAGE 250**

BAKED RISOTTO WITH BUTTERNUT SQUASH AND ALMONDS **PAGE 265**

CHEESE SOUFFLÉ WITH SPINACH **PAGE 291**

112

FRENCH TOAST CASSEROLE **PAGE 296**

SLOW-COOKER ASIAN SPICED PORK RIBS WITH NOODLES **PAGE 317**

2

POT PIES AND MORE

WITH ITS FLAKY CRUST AND TENDER CHUNKS of meat and vegetables, a pot pie just might be the ultimate comfort food. In this chapter, we have included all-American classics, like chicken, beef, and vegetable pot pies, as well as celebrated savory pies from farther afield, like shepherd's pie and tamale pie. There are also a few new recipes here that we invented ourselves and hope will soon become just as popular, like Pork Tinga and Sweet Potato Pot Pie—a Mexican spin on shepherd's pie (see page 143).

The challenges to making a great pot pie are many. If the sauce is too thin, the topping will turn soggy; if the filling is overcooked by even a moment before assembly, the meat will turn tough and sinewy and the vegetables mushy and flavorless while they're in the oven. Never mind the toppings—it took us days in the kitchen to identify and solve the myriad problems they pose. For example, we discovered that a solid sheet of pastry stretched across the spring vegetable pot pie caused the delicate vegetables in the filling to overcook and turn unappetizing colors. The open network of a biscuit topping proved a better option.

Then there's the time issue. Some pot pies we have tried are so complicated that they can take all day to prepare. As we developed the recipes in this chapter, we sought ways to streamline the process without succumbing to convenience foods like canned soup or pre-cut frozen vegetables—an all too common path in this age of prefab cuisine. To save time when making the Beef Pot Pie (page 127), we trimmed flavorful chuck roast into tiny, quick-cooking pieces. In our Spring Vegetable Pot Pie (page 133), we found that the asparagus could be added raw to the filling. We think the little extra effort it takes to use fresh ingredients is well worth it in the long run.

Since most pot pies, excluding delicate fish and vegetable pot pies, can be successfully prepared well in advance, they are a lifesaver when it comes to weeknight dinners (see each recipe for specific make-ahead instructions). For the best results, we found that the filling and topping should be stored separately. The filling can be kept in an airtight container or well wrapped in its baking dish in either the refrigerator or the freezer. Just make sure to reheat it to a simmer in either a saucepan or the microwave before adding the topping.

Toppings must be added at the last minute to the hot filling, but many of the toppings in this chapter can also be made ahead, sparing you lots of tedious last-minute work. Unless otherwise specified in the recipe (some recipes simply do not work with particular toppings), feel free to mix and match fillings and toppings. Top a chicken pot pie with biscuits one week, pastry the next. And when you're short on time, try the puff pastry topping—it takes minutes to prepare and generates a minimal amount of dishes to wash.

Pot-Pie Toppings

WHETHER IT'S FLAKY PIE DOUGH, PUFFY biscuits, crisp puff pastry, or simple toast points, a pot pie's topping is what makes it so alluring. While each topping has its own unique texture and flavor, all are fairly interchangeable and most of the pot pies in this chapter can be prepared with any of them. We have made recommendations for each pie, but feel free to choose whichever seems most appealing—or the topping for which you happen to have all the ingredients on hand. That said, there are some limitations when matching fillings and toppings. For example, very wet or delicate fillings, like the filling for Spring Vegetable Pot Pie (page 133) or Salmon and Leek Pot Pie (page 136), do not pair well with a solid sheet of puff pastry or pastry dough because the sealed top prevents the evaporation of excess moisture and the topping turns gummy. Individual, pre-baked squares of puff pastry or toast points are the best options for this type of pie.

SAVORY PIE DOUGH
The perfect pastry dough shatters into flaky shards at the lightest touch of a fork. Most home cooks, however, assume that preparing dough of this caliber is easier said than done. After exhaustively testing pie dough for a variety of pies—both savory and sweet—we've learned a few things that can take the challenges out of pastry preparation. As with much cooking, the secret is in the details.

Pastry dough is a simple combination of all-purpose flour, salt, water, and fat. The first three ingredients are standard; the fat, however, is controversial. After testing the usual suspects—shortening, butter, oil, and lard—we believe that a combination of shortening and butter make the richest-flavored and flakiest pie crust. Oil made for a dense, cardboard-like crust; as for lard, it had a rich flavor and yielded a flaky crust, but its artery-clogging nature put us off. Shortening and butter each make for a good crust, but for different reasons: shortening creates the flakiest texture and butter the best flavor. Vegetable shortening is hydrogenated, a process in which hydrogen gas is pumped into vegetable oil to incorporate air and to raise its melting point above room temperature. Translated into cooking terms, this means that it doesn't melt as easily as butter and makes for a very flaky, tender crust. The downside is that shortening is flavorless—the whole reason we add the butter.

Where things can go most wrong with pastry dough is the temperature of the fat and the mixing method. Pastry dough is flaky because small bits of fat melt in the oven and produce steam that, in turn, creates flaky layers in the dough. If the fat melts beforehand or the dough is under- or over-mixed, these pockets fail to form and the dough is dense, tough, or crumbly.

Prior to mixing, it is imperative that the fat be well chilled. If it softens, it will melt into the dough and make it tough. We cut both the shortening and butter into cubes and keep them refrigerated until we are ready to use them. On hot days, we go as far as to chill the equipment and flour to prevent the fat from melting upon contact.

To further ensure that the fat stays cool, we have come up with a two-step mixing method: We cut the cold shortening and butter into the flour in a food processor fitted with the steel blade, and then add the liquid by hand with a rubber spatula in a mixing bowl. The food processor efficiently cuts the fat into the flour without heating it, as mixing by hand can do. But when water is added to the dough in the food processor, the dough can easily overwork and thereby toughen. By hand with a rubber spatula, it's easy to *just* combine the dough with the minimum amount of water required. In a food processor, it's all too easy to add too much water, which causes gluten formation and a tough crust.

We realize not everyone has a food processor, so we've come up with a substitute: a standard box grater. The butter—left as a whole stick—can be frozen and grated into the flour on the large holes of a standard box grater (see illustration 2 on page 121).

Many home cooks find rolling the dough the most challenging task, but it's easy with well-made dough. The dough should be chilled prior to rolling to keep the butter from melting and the dough from sticking (easily one of the most common problems). For absolutely failsafe rolling, we recommend sandwiching the dough between sheets of parchment paper or plastic wrap. This method minimizes the need for additional flour, too much of which will toughen the dough. Follow the illustrations on page 120 for rolling out the dough and fitting it to the baking dish.

BISCUITS

Like pastry dough, biscuit dough is a simple combination of ingredients that, for the best results, takes some finesse to prepare. Improperly made biscuits are tough and dense—more hockey puck than comestible. Temperature and handling once again play a pivotal role in success.

Steam produced by chunks of melting butter—in conjunction with baking powder and baking soda—is responsible for a biscuit's fluffy, tender texture. If the butter melts when it's mixed into the flour, it will turn pasty and the resulting biscuits will be squat and dense. As with pastry dough, we recommend cutting the butter into the flour with a food processor fitted with the steel blade, then transferring the mixture to a mixing bowl to stir in the liquid—buttermilk in this case. Follow the instructions on page 121 for a step-by-step look at preparing biscuit dough.

The flour used in biscuits plays an important role in the texture and rise of the biscuit. Low-protein or "soft" flour (such as cake flour or White Lily, a favored brand in the South) encourages a moist, tender, cake-like crumb. Higher-protein or "strong" flour promotes a crispier crust and a drier, denser crumb. We've found that mixing the two yields a biscuit with the best of both worlds: a crispy top and a light, tender crumb. If you don't happen to have both in the pantry, straight all-purpose flour works fine too. (If you make biscuits frequently and want to stock just one type of flour, we recommend that you choose a low-protein all-purpose flour like Gold Medal.)

For the highest-rising biscuits, a sharp biscuit cutter is imperative. A dull edge (such as the rim of a juice glass) will smear rather than cut the biscuit edges, prohibiting proper lift. We strongly recommend investing in an inexpensive set of biscuit cutters.

PUFF-PASTRY TOPPING

Frozen puff pastry is the easiest and fastest topping with which to cover a pot pie. We're not talking homemade stuff here: the commercially prepared dough from Pepperidge Farm tastes great and is fuss-free. (Dufour, another commercial brand, is even better tasting because it is made with butter: Pepperidge Farm is made with vegetable shortening. Unfortunately, Dufour puff pastry can only be found at specialty stores.) To use frozen puff pastry, it must first be defrosted enough to unfold it without the seams cracking. (It comes folded in thirds.) Our favorite (foolproof) method for defrosting the dough is to leave it in the refrigerator overnight. The next day the dough will be the perfect texture to roll and trim. But we don't always have that much forethought, so more often than not, we thaw it on the countertop. Depending on the ambient temperature of your kitchen, this can take anywhere from 30 minutes to one hour. Test the dough every few minutes by trying to unfold it. If it opens up without the seams cracking, it's good to go. If the dough does crack a little, refold it and wait until it softens: cracks can be rerolled together.

Puff pastry can either be used as a full sheet or cut into individual rectangles. Using the full sheet of pastry dough simply requires rolling the dough to fit the casserole dish and tucking the sides in, as with conventional pastry dough. This crust, however, does not work well with all the pies: very wet fillings, like the Spring Vegetable Pot Pie (page 133) will turn the puff pastry gummy.

For very wet fillings, or in instances where presentation is important, we recommend cutting the puff pastry into individual rectangles. We cut a single sheet of dough (there are two sheets per 1.1 pound box) along the folds and three times crosswise to form 12 even rectangles, the perfect amount to top a 9 by 13-inch baking dish. Then we partially bake the rectangles on a baking sheet placed on the bottom rack of the oven, to ensure even cooking and proper browning. (They get baked again on top of the pot pie.) Using these individual rectangles allows you to serve the pot pie neatly, so that each person gets an attractive and perfectly portioned serving with its own topping.

For the best results, puff pastry should be kept chilled until baked. Warm dough gets sticky and doesn't rise as well in the oven. Also, puff pastry attains the best lift when cooked at a relatively high temperature. For casseroles topped with whole sheets of puff pastry, 400 degrees works fine; for individual rectangles (which are baked twice, once alone and once on top of a casserole), 425 degrees is a better option.

If the pastry warms up as you work with it, simply slide it into the freezer on a baking sheet for a few minutes to firm up. Well-chilled puff pastry should require a minimal amount of flour on the work surface to prevent it from sticking. Sandwiching the pastry sheets between parchment paper guarantees that it won't stick.

TOAST-POINT TOPPING

This simple topping variation is the traditional accompaniment to numerous creamy seafood dishes. Slices of bread are trimmed of their crusts, cut into triangles, and brushed with butter before toasting in the oven. Points "par-toasted" to a light golden brown darkened to a rich caramel brown when shingled atop casseroles. After testing a variety of different types of bread, we found that a hearty, dense-crumbed white sandwich bread, like Pepperidge Farm, is the best choice (unless you have a local bakery producing the equivalent).

Savory Pie-Dough Topping

MAKES ENOUGH FOR I POT-PIE RECIPE

For a double-crust effect, simply tuck the overhanging dough down into the pan side. This tucked crust will become soft in the oven, like the bottom crust on a pie.

PLANNING AHEAD: You can prepare the dough through step 2 up to 2 days ahead of time and store it wrapped in plastic in the refrigerator until ready to use. Let stand at room temperature until malleable. The dough can also be frozen, well wrapped in plastic, for up to 2 months.

1½	cups (7½ ounces) all-purpose flour, plus more for dusting the work surface
½	teaspoon salt
4	tablespoons vegetable shortening, chilled
8	tablespoons unsalted butter, chilled and cut into ¼-inch cubes
3–5	tablespoons ice water

1. Process the flour and salt in a food processor fitted with the steel blade until combined. Add the shortening and process until the mixture has the texture of coarse sand, about 10 seconds. Scatter the butter cubes over the flour mixture; cut the butter into the flour until the mixture is pale yellow and resembles coarse crumbs, with butter bits no larger than small peas, about ten 1-second pulses. Turn the mixture into a medium bowl.

2. Sprinkle 3 tablespoons ice water over the mixture. With a rubber spatula, use a folding motion to mix. Press down on the dough with the broad side of the spatula until the dough sticks together, adding up to 2 tablespoons more ice water if necessary. Press the dough into a 5 by 4-inch rectangle (see illustration 1 on page 120) and wrap tightly with plastic wrap. Refrigerate until chilled, at least 30 minutes.

3. When the pot-pie filling is ready, following illustrations 2 through 7 on page 120, roll the dough on a floured surface to a 15 by 11-inch rectangle, about ⅛ inch thick. (If making individual pies, roll the dough ⅛ inch thick and cut 6 dough rounds about 1 inch larger than the dish circumference.) Place the dough over the pot-pie filling. Trim the dough to within ½ inch of the pan lip. Tuck the overhanging dough back under itself so the folded edge is flush with the pan lip. Flute the edges all around. Alternatively, don't trim the dough and simply tuck the overhanging dough down into the pan side. Cut at least four 1-inch vent holes in a large pot pie or one 1-inch vent hole in each smaller pie. Proceed with pot-pie recipe.

MAKING PIE DOUGH

1. Cut the butter into the flour mixture until the mixture is pale yellow and resembles coarse crumbs, with butter bits no larger than small peas, about ten 1-second pulses.

2. Transfer the mixture to a bowl and add the ice water bit by bit, tossing and pressing the dry ingredients against the sides of the bowl.

3. Too much water is better than too little—a dry dough cannot be rolled out, but you can flour the work surface if the dough is wet. Ideally, the dough will clear the sides of the bowl and be wet to the touch.

ROLLING OUT AND ARRANGING PIE DOUGH ON A POT PIE

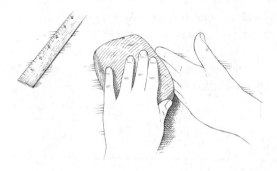

1. Press the dough into a 5 by 4-inch rectangle and wrap tightly with plastic wrap. Refrigerate until chilled, at least 30 minutes.

2. When the pot-pie filling is ready, roll the dough on a floured surface to a 15 by 11-inch rectangle, about ⅛ inch thick.

3. Roll the dough loosely over the rolling pin and unroll it evenly over the baking dish.

4. Lay the rectangle of dough for a large pie or dough rounds for individual pies over the pot-pie filling, trimming the dough to within ½ inch of the pan lip.

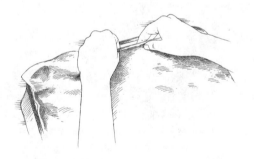

5. For a fluted edge, tuck the overhanging dough back under itself so the folded edge is flush with the lip of the pan.

6. Holding the dough with the thumb and index finger of one hand, push the dough with the index finger of your other hand to form a pleated edge. Repeat all around the edge to flute the dough.

7. For a double-crust effect, simply tuck the overhanging dough down into the pan side. This tucked crust will become soft in the oven, like the bottom crust on a pie.

Fluffy Buttermilk-Biscuit Topping

MAKES ENOUGH FOR 1 POT-PIE RECIPE

Mixing the butter and dry ingredients quickly so the butter remains cold and firm is crucial to producing light, tender biscuits. Make sure that your butter is well chilled before mixing it into the dry ingredients. If your kitchen is exceptionally warm, you may want to chill the flour along with the butter.

PLANNING AHEAD: After you have made the dough and cut out the biscuits, they can be refrigerated on a lightly floured baking sheet covered with plastic wrap for up to 2 hours.

1	cup (5 ounces) all-purpose flour, plus more for dusting the work surface
1	cup (4 ounces) plain cake flour
2	teaspoons baking powder
1/4	teaspoon baking soda
1	teaspoon sugar
1/2	teaspoon salt
8	tablespoons unsalted butter, chilled and cut into 1/4-inch cubes
3/4	cup cold buttermilk, plus 1 to 2 tablespoons if needed

1. Pulse the flours, baking powder, baking soda, sugar, and salt in a food processor fitted with the steel blade. Add the butter pieces; pulse until the mixture resembles coarse cornmeal with a few slightly larger butter lumps, about ten 1-second pulses.

2. Transfer the mixture to a medium bowl; add the buttermilk and stir with a fork until the dough gathers into moist clumps. Following illustrations 1 through 3 on page 122, transfer the dough to a floured work surface and form into a rough ball. Using a rolling pin, gently roll the dough out to 1/2 inch thick. Using a 2½- to 3-inch biscuit cutter, stamp out 8 to 12 rounds of dough. Space the biscuits evenly over the filling in the baking dish. If making individual pies, cut the dough slightly smaller than the circumference of each dish.

➤ VARIATIONS

Parmesan Biscuits

Follow the recipe for Fluffy Buttermilk Biscuit Topping, decreasing the butter to 5 tablespoons. After the fat has been processed into the flour and transferred to the bowl, add 4 ounces grated Parmesan cheese (about 2 cups); toss lightly, then stir in the buttermilk.

MIXING BUTTERMILK BISCUIT DOUGH

1. Cut a chilled stick of butter into 1/4-inch cubes. Place the butter cubes on a plate and chill briefly in the freezer. With a spatula, add the butter cubes to the dry ingredients in a food processor fitted with the steel blade, and pulse until the mixture resembles coarse cornmeal with a few slightly larger butter lumps.

2. If you don't have a food processor, combine the dry ingredients in a bowl. Rub a frozen stick of butter against the large holes of a regular box grater over the bowl with the dry ingredients.

3. With two butter knives, work the grated butter into the dry ingredients. By not using your fingertips, you will reduce the chance that the butter will melt.

Herb Biscuits

Follow the recipe for Fluffy Buttermilk Biscuit Topping, adding 3 tablespoons minced fresh parsley leaves or 2 tablespoons minced fresh parsley leaves and 1 tablespoon minced fresh tarragon leaves or dill leaves after the fat has been processed into the flour.

Cornmeal Biscuits

Follow the recipe for Fluffy Buttermilk Biscuit Topping, replacing the cake flour with 1 cup fine-ground cornmeal.

ROLLING OUT AND CUTTING THE BISCUITS

1. Transfer the dough to a floured work surface and form into a rough ball. Using a rolling pin, gently roll the dough out to ½ inch thick.

2. Using a 2½- to 3-inch biscuit cutter, stamp out 8 to 12 rounds of dough. If making individual pies, cut the dough slightly smaller than the circumference of each dish.

3. Arrange the dough rounds over the warm filling before baking.

Individual Puff-Pastry Rectangles

MAKES ENOUGH FOR I POT-PIE RECIPE

This topping is partially baked and finished on top of the pot pie. If you prefer puff-pastry circles to rectangles, use a very sharp biscuit cutter and a quick, forceful cutting motion; otherwise the thin layers of dough may stick to each other and not rise fully in the oven.

PLANNING AHEAD: The rectangles may be prepared and stored at room temperature, well wrapped in plastic, for up to 5 days.

> Flour for dusting work surface
> I sheet (9½ by 9 inches) frozen commercial puff pastry, thawed at room temperature for 30 minutes
> I large egg, lightly beaten

Adjust an oven rack to the lowest position and heat the oven to 425 degrees. Dust a work surface lightly with flour and unfold the sheet of puff pastry. Following the illustration below, use a pizza cutter or sharp paring knife to cut the dough into 3 pieces along the seams, then crosswise in fourths to make 12 rectangles. Brush each square with beaten egg and transfer to a baking sheet lined with parchment paper. Chill the dough on the baking sheet in the freezer for 10 minutes. Remove the pan from the freezer and place it

MAKING PUFF PASTRY RECTANGLES

Use a pizza cutter or sharp paring knife to cut the sheet of puff pastry into three pieces along the seams, then crosswise in fourths to make 12 rectangles. Brush each square with beaten egg and transfer to a baking sheet lined with parchment paper.

directly in the oven. Bake for 10 minutes or until the rectangles are puffed and lightly browned. Remove from the oven and place the baking sheet on a wire rack to cool.

EASY PUFF-PASTRY TOPPING

If you're in a hurry, a sheet of frozen puff pastry will make a quick and easy topping for most pot pies (don't use it for pies with more delicate fillings like salmon or spring vegetables as they will cook too quickly beneath a sealed topping). Just thaw one full sheet of pastry until soft enough to bend (about 30 minutes at room temperature). Gently unfold the dough and roll it out on a floured work surface to a 15 by 11-inch rectangle that is ⅛ inch thick. Drape the pastry over the filling and trim and finish following the techniques used with pie dough (see the illustrations on page 120).

Toast-Point Topping

MAKES ENOUGH FOR 1 POT-PIE RECIPE

A dense sandwich loaf, like Pepperidge Farm, delivers the best results.

PLANNING AHEAD: The toast points may be prepared and stored in aluminum foil at room temperature for up to 1 day.

10	slices good-quality white sandwich bread, crusts trimmed and cut in half diagonally into triangles
4	tablespoons unsalted butter, melted
	Salt and ground white or black pepper

Adjust an oven rack to the lowest position and heat the oven to 425 degrees. Brush each side of the bread slices with melted butter, season with salt and pepper, and arrange in a single layer on a baking sheet. Bake until light golden brown, about 10 minutes. Transfer the baking sheet to a wire rack to cool.

CHICKEN POT PIE

MOST EVERYONE LOVES A GOOD CHICKEN POT pie, though few seem to have the time or energy to make one. Not surprising. Like a lot of satisfying dishes, traditional pot pie takes time. Before the pie even makes it to the oven, the cook must poach a chicken, take the meat off the bone and cut it up, strain the stock, prepare and blanch vegetables, make a sauce, and mix and roll out biscuit or pie dough. Given the many time-consuming steps it can take to make a pot pie, our goal was to make the best one we could as quickly as possible. Pot pie, after all, was intended as weeknight supper food.

Our experiences with making pot pie also made us aware of two other difficulties. First, the vegetables tend to overcook. A filling that is chock-full of bright, fresh vegetables going into the oven looks completely different after 40 minutes of high-heat baking under a blanket of dough. Carrots become mushy and pumpkin-colored, while peas and fresh herbs fade from spring green to drab olive. We wanted to preserve the vegetables' color as long as it didn't require any unnatural acts to do so.

We began by determining the best way to cook the chicken, using chicken parts for this initial round of tests. Steaming the chicken was time consuming, requiring about one hour, and the steaming liquid didn't make a strong enough stock for the pot-pie sauce. Roast chicken also required an hour in the oven, and by the time we took off the skin and mixed the meat in with the sauce and vegetables, the roasted flavor was lost. We had similar results with braised chicken. It lost its delicious flavor once the browned skin was removed.

Next we tried poaching, the most traditional cooking method. Of the two poaching liquids we tried, we preferred the chicken poached in wine and stock to the one poached in stock alone. The wine infused the meat and made for a richer, more full-flavored sauce. To our disappointment, however, the acidity of the wine sauce caused the peas and fresh herbs to lose their bright green color in the oven. Vegetables baked in the stock-only sauce kept their bright color, though the bland sauce needed perking up—a problem we'd have to deal with later. Now we were ready to test poached chicken parts against quicker-cooking boneless, skinless chicken breasts.

Because boneless, skinless breasts cook so quickly, sautéing is generally a good cooking method for them. So before comparing our preference for poached parts versus poached breasts, we tried cooking the breasts three different ways. We cut raw breast meat into bite-size pieces and sautéed them; we sautéed whole breasts, shredding the breast meat once it was cool enough to handle; and we poached whole breasts in stock, also shredding the meat.

For simplicity's sake, we had hoped to like the sautéed whole breasts but once again, poaching was our favorite method. Sautéing caused the outer layer of meat to turn crusty, a texture we did not like in the pie. The sautéed chicken pieces also floated independently in the sauce, their surfaces too smooth for the sauce to adhere to. By contrast, the tender, irregularly shaped poached chicken pieces mixed well with the vegetables and, much like textured pasta, caused the sauce to cling.

Our only concern with the poached boneless, skinless breasts was the quality of the stock. In earlier tests, we found that bone-in parts could be poached in canned broth (rather than home-made stock) without much sacrifice in flavor. We surmised that the bones and skin improved the flavor of the broth during the long cooking time. But we wondered how quick-cooking boneless, skinless breasts would fare in canned broth. The answer? Not as bad as we feared. In our comparison of the pies made with boneless breasts poached in homemade stock and canned broth, we found little difference in quality. Evidently, it's not the cooking time of the chicken but the abundance of ingredients in a pot pie that makes it possible to use canned broth with no ill consequences. Ultimately, we were able to shave half an hour off the cooking time (10 minutes to cook the breasts compared with 40 minutes to cook the parts). For those who like either dark or a mix of dark and white meat in their pie, boneless, skinless chicken thighs can be used as well.

A good pot pie with fresh vegetables, warm pastry, and a full-flavored sauce tastes satisfying. One with overcooked vegetables tastes stodgy and old-fashioned. So we made pies with raw vegetables, sautéed vegetables, and parboiled vegetables. After comparing the pies, we found that the vegetables sautéed before baking held their color and flavor best, the parboiled ones less so. The raw vegetables were not fully cooked at the end of the baking time and gave off too much liquid, watering down the flavor and thickness of the sauce.

Our final task was to develop a sauce that was flavorful, creamy, and of the proper consistency. Chicken-pot-pie sauce is traditionally based on a roux (a mixture of butter and flour sautéed together briefly), which is thinned with chicken broth and often enriched with cream.

Because of the dish's inherent richness, we wanted to see how little cream we could get away with using. We tried three different pot-pie fillings, using ¼ cup cream, ¼ cup half-and-half,

INGREDIENTS: Frozen Peas

In the test kitchen, we've come to depend on frozen peas. Not only are they more convenient than their fresh comrades in the pod but also they taste better. In test after test, we've found that frozen peas are tender and sweet, while fresh peas are starchy and bland. To understand this curious finding, which defies common sense, we did some research.

Green peas are one of the oldest vegetables known to humankind. Despite this long history, however, they are relatively delicate and have little stamina. They lose a substantial portion of their nutrients within 24 hours of being picked, which explains the starchy, bland flavor of most peas found in supermarket produce departments. These not-so-fresh peas might be several days old (or more). Frozen peas, on the other hand, are picked, cleaned, sorted, and frozen within several hours of harvest, thus helping to preserve their delicate sugars and flavors. When commercially frozen vegetables began to appear in the 1920s, green peas were among the first.

Finding good frozen peas is not hard. After tasting peas from the two major national frozen-food purveyors, Birdseye and Green Giant, along with organically grown peas from Cascadian Farm, our panel found little difference among them. All of the peas were sweet and fresh, with a bright green color. Unless you grow your own or stop by a local farm stand for fresh-picked peas, you're best off buying frozen.

and 1½ cups milk. Going into the oven, all of the fillings seemed to have the right consistency and creaminess; when they came out, however, it was a different story. Vegetable and meat juices diluted the consistency and creaminess of the cream and half-and-half sauces. To achieve a creamy-looking sauce, we would have needed to increase the cream dramatically. Fortunately, we didn't have to try it, because we actually liked the milk-enriched sauce. The larger quantity of milk kept the sauce creamy and it tasted delicious.

To keep the sauce from becoming too liquidy, we simply added more flour. A sauce that looks a little thick before baking will become the perfect consistency after taking on the chicken and vegetable juices released during baking.

We had worked out the right consistency, but because we had been forced to abandon the wine for the vegetables' sake, the sauce tasted a little bland. Lemon juice, a flavor heightener we had seen in a number of recipes, had the same dulling effect on the color of the vegetables as the wine. We tried sherry, and it worked perfectly. Because sherry is more intensely flavored and less acidic than wine, it gave us the flavor we were seeking without harming the peas and carrots.

Chicken Pot Pie

SERVES 6 TO 8

Mushrooms can be sautéed along with the celery and carrots, and blanched pearl onions can stand in for the onion.

PLANNING AHEAD: You can make the filling up to 3 days ahead of time and store it in an airtight container in the refrigerator. It may also be frozen for up to 3 months. Before topping the filling, it must be reheated to a simmer in a saucepan or in the microwave, as a cold filling will turn the topping gummy.

1	recipe Savory Pie-Dough Topping (page 119) or Fluffy Buttermilk-Biscuit Topping (page 121)
1½	pounds boneless, skinless chicken breasts and/or thighs
2	cups low-sodium chicken broth
1½	tablespoons vegetable oil
1	medium-large onion, chopped fine
3	medium carrots, peeled and cut crosswise ¼ inch thick
2	small celery ribs, cut crosswise ¼ inch thick
	Salt and ground black pepper
4	tablespoons unsalted butter
½	cup all-purpose flour
1½	cups whole milk
½	teaspoon dried thyme
3	tablespoons dry sherry
1	cup frozen green peas
3	tablespoons minced fresh parsley leaves

1. Make the pie-dough or biscuit topping and refrigerate it until ready to use.

2. Adjust an oven rack to the lower-middle position and heat the oven to 400 degrees. Put the chicken and broth in a small Dutch oven or stockpot over medium heat. Cover and bring to a simmer; simmer until the chicken is just done, 8 to 10 minutes. Transfer the chicken to a large bowl, reserving the broth in a measuring cup.

3. Increase the heat to medium-high; heat the oil in the now-empty pan. Add the onion, carrots, and celery; sauté until just tender, about 5 minutes. Season to taste with salt and pepper. While the vegetables are sautéing, shred the meat into bite-size pieces. Transfer the cooked vegetables to a bowl with the chicken; set aside.

4. Melt the butter over medium heat in the again-empty pan; add the flour and cook until golden, about 1 minute. Whisk in the reserved chicken broth, the milk, any accumulated chicken juices, and thyme. Bring to a simmer, then continue to simmer until the sauce fully thickens, about 1 minute. Season to taste with salt and pepper; stir in the sherry.

5. Pour the sauce over the chicken mixture; stir to combine. Stir in the peas and parsley. Adjust the seasonings. Pour the mixture into a 9 by 13-inch baking dish (or a shallow casserole dish of similar size) or six 12-ounce ovenproof dishes. Top with the pie-dough or biscuit topping; bake until the topping is golden brown and the filling is bubbly, 30 minutes for a large pie and 20 to 25 minutes for smaller pies. Allow to cool for 5 to 10 minutes before serving.

Chicken Pot Pie with Spring Vegetables

Follow the recipe for Chicken Pot Pie, replacing the celery with 1 pound thin asparagus stalks that have been trimmed and cut into 1-inch pieces. Add the asparagus with the peas in step 5.

Chicken Pot Pie with Wild Mushrooms

The soaking liquid used to rehydrate dried porcini mushrooms replaces some of the broth used to poach the chicken and then to enrich the sauce. (See page 41 for more information on rehydrating porcini mushrooms.)

Follow the recipe for Chicken Pot Pie, soaking 1 ounce dried porcini mushrooms in 2 cups warm tap water until softened, about 20 minutes. Lift the mushrooms from the liquid, strain the liquid, and reserve 1 cup. Use the soaking liquid in place of 1 cup of the chicken broth. Proceed with the recipe, cooking the rehydrated porcini and 12 ounces sliced white button mushrooms with the vegetables in step 2. Finish as directed.

Chicken Pot Pie with Corn and Bacon

This southern variation with corn and bacon works especially well with the biscuit topping.

Follow the recipe for Chicken Pot Pie, replacing the oil with ¼ pound (about 4 slices) bacon, cut crosswise into ½-inch-wide strips. Cook the bacon over medium heat until the fat is rendered and the bacon is crisp, about 6 minutes. Remove the bacon from the pan with a slotted spoon and drain it on paper towels. Cook the vegetables in the bacon fat. Add the drained bacon to the bowl with the chicken and cooked vegetables. Proceed with the recipe, replacing the peas with 2 cups fresh or frozen corn.

BEEF POT PIE

PLAINLY STATED, BEEF POT PIE IS BEEF STEW baked under a crusty topping. After hours of slow simmering, the stew is ladled into a baking dish, topped with biscuits or a pastry crust, and cooked even longer. It is an all-day affair, requiring hours of diligent attention. To us, it begs the question: Why? Certainly there's nothing wrong with such a labor of love, but we wanted a simpler, faster alternative. Could a richly flavored beef pot pie—with all the nuance of a slow-simmered beef stew—be made in a fraction of the time?

We commenced the testing process with our primary concern: the choice of meat. Beef stew develops its rich flavor through the slow, deliberate simmering of inexpensive yet flavorful cuts of beef. Our favorite cut happens to be chuck roast, a marbled, collagen-rich roast that contains a good deal of flavor, as long as it is cooked slowly over low heat. Cooked quickly and over high heat, it's as tough and bland as a tire. Clearly, if we wanted a quick-cooking cut of meat, we had to look elsewhere. Tender steaks were an obvious choice. Our first choice was blade steak, an underutilized, reasonably priced steak we have used for beef teriyaki and kebabs. Trimmed into small cubes, browned, and simmered in the oven underneath a biscuit crust, it toughened and tasted like liver. Pricey sirloin steaks treated in the same fashion yielded nearly identical results. Without a doubt, tender cuts were best left to the high heat of the grill or skillet. And tenderloin and other exorbitantly priced cuts were out of the question on principle alone; this was meant to be a homey pot pie, after all.

Frustrated, we decided to revisit chuck roast. How could we hasten its cooking and turn the tough meat tender? Trimming the meat into smaller cubes than our stew specified—petite ½-inch as opposed to 1½-inch pieces—seemed like a logical next step. After browning the meat and simmering it slowly on the stovetop, we found that it was both tender and flavorful within 45 minutes—a far cry from the multi-hour simmer required for the stew. Now this was in the ballpark for pot pie.

With the meat chosen, we could now work on finessing the pie's flavor. Sticking closely to our beef stew recipe, we chose to include onions and carrots, as well as a hint of garlic and a substantial splash of red wine. To extract as much flavor as possible from the vegetables, we diced them small and browned them well. Consequently, the vegetables weren't prime players in the finished dish (as they are in chicken pot pie), but tasters didn't seem to mind; they thought it was all about the meat and sauce. For broth, we tried both chicken and beef broth. Chicken broth yielded a weakly flavored stew, while beef broth made the stew taste tinny. We reached consensus through compromise: a can of each.

To further enrich the flavor, we borrowed a trick from Cajun cooking and lightly toasted the flour that is used for a thickener. Subjected to dry heat (with or without oil or butter), flour browns and develops a nutty, malty flavor. Cajun cooks brown the flour to a dark mahogany when making gumbo; we took it to a light chestnut for our pot pie filling. As with our stew, we rounded out the filling's flavor with a spoonful of tomato paste—fruity yet densely flavored—and a heaping teaspoon of fresh thyme leaves. The flavor was a surprisingly close approximation to the slow-cooked stew, ready in just a third of the time.

INGREDIENTS: Canned Beef Broth

As a general rule, we favor canned chicken broth over canned beef broth because of its stronger, cleaner flavor. Most brands of beef broth we have tasted have been either extremely salty, extremely bland, or both. Canned beef broth also possesses a tinny flavor that we have found carries over to the soup or stew to which it is added. A little research proved that the regulations regarding the contents of beef broth are lax at best, allowing for an absolute minimum of meat to be used by manufacturers. (Current U.S. Department of Agriculture regulations stipulate that as little as an ounce of beef to a gallon of water may be used and the product may still be labeled "broth").

That said, beef broth adds a much-needed kick to certain beef-based dishes in which straight chicken broth contributes too mild a flavor, like the filling for Beef Pot Pie (this page). To mitigate the tinny flavor, we temper the beef broth with an equal part chicken broth. The resulting flavor is not unlike mild veal broth. While we cannot recommend a particular brand of canned beef broth, we do recommend purchasing low-sodium varieties.

Beef Pot Pie

SERVES 6 TO 8

For the best flavor, buy a chuck roast and trim and cut it yourself rather than purchasing prepackaged stew meat. Dried thyme (1 teaspoon) can be successfully substituted for fresh.

PLANNING AHEAD: You can make the filling up to 3 days ahead of time and store it in an airtight container in the refrigerator. It may also be frozen for up to 3 months. Before topping the filling, it must be reheated to a simmer in a saucepan or in the microwave, as a cold filling will turn the topping gummy.

1	recipe Savory Pie-Dough Topping (page 119) or Fluffy Buttermilk-Biscuit Topping (page 121)
3	pounds chuck roast, trimmed and cut into ½-inch cubes
	Salt and ground black pepper
1	tablespoon vegetable oil
1	large onion, chopped fine
2	large carrots, peeled and chopped medium
4	medium garlic cloves, minced or pressed through a garlic press
5	tablespoons all-purpose flour
¾	cup dry red wine
1¾	cups low-sodium chicken broth
1¾	cups low-sodium beef broth
1	tablespoon tomato paste
2	teaspoons minced fresh thyme leaves
1	cup frozen peas

1. Make the pie-dough or biscuit topping and refrigerate it until ready to use.

2. Dry the beef thoroughly on paper towels, then season it generously with salt and pepper. Heat the oil in a large Dutch oven over medium-high heat until shimmering but not smoking. Sprinkle half the meat into the pot (the pieces should be close but not touching) and cook, without stirring, until well browned on one side, about 4 minutes. Stir the meat and continue to cook, stirring occasionally, until the meat is completely browned, about 5 minutes longer. Transfer it to a medium bowl. Return the pot to high heat, brown the remaining beef as before, and transfer it to the bowl.

3. Return the pot to medium heat and add the onion, carrots, and ½ teaspoon salt (add a tablespoon of water if necessary to prevent the browned bits on the pan bottom from burning). Cook, stirring frequently, until the onion has browned lightly and softened, 4 to 6 minutes. Add the garlic and cook until fragrant, about 30 seconds. Add the flour and cook, stirring constantly, until lightly browned, about 1 minute. Gradually whisk in the wine, scraping the browned bits off the bottom of the pan. Whisk in the broths, tomato paste, and thyme. Add the browned meat, including any accumulated juices, and bring to a simmer. Reduce the heat to low, partially cover, and continue to simmer, stirring occasionally, until the meat is tender, about 45 minutes

4. Meanwhile, adjust an oven rack to the middle position and heat the oven to 400 degrees. When the meat is tender, stir in the peas and transfer the filling to a 9 by 13-inch baking dish (or a shallow casserole dish of similar size) or six 12-ounce ovenproof dishes. Top with the pie-dough or biscuit topping; bake until the topping is golden brown and the filling is bubbly, 30 minutes for a large pie and 20 to 25 minutes for smaller pies. Allow to cool for 5 to 10 minutes before serving.

CLEANING A GARLIC PRESS

Garlic presses make quick work of garlic but are notoriously hard to clean. Recycle an old toothbrush with a worn brush for this job. The bristles will clear bits of garlic from the press and are easy to rinse clean.

> ↣ VARIATIONS

Beef Pot Pie with Portobello Mushrooms, Sherry, and Rosemary

Follow the recipe for Beef Pot Pie, adding one sprig fresh rosemary to the filling during the final 15 minutes of simmering in step 3. While the filling simmers, melt 2 tablespoons unsalted butter in a large skillet over medium-high heat. Add 1 pound portobello mushroom caps (about 6 medium caps), brushed clean and cut into ½-inch pieces, and ¼ teaspoon salt; cook, stirring occasionally, until well browned, about 8 minutes. Stir in ¼ cup dry sherry and scrape the browned bits off the skillet, then remove from the heat. Stir the mushroom mixture into the filling with the peas in step 4, and discard the rosemary sprig.

Beef Pot Pie with Guinness, Glazed Pearl Onions, and Bacon

Follow the recipe for Beef Pot Pie, replacing the chicken broth and red wine with a 12-ounce bottle (1½ cups) of Guinness Extra Stout (or other stout beer) and ½ cup of water. While the filling simmers, cook 6 ounces (about 6 slices) bacon, chopped, in a large nonstick skillet until brown and crisp, 8 to 9 minutes. Remove the bacon from the pan using a slotted spoon and drain on a paper towel–lined plate, leaving the rendered fat in the skillet. Increase the heat to medium-high, add 8 ounces frozen (not thawed) pearl onions and ½ teaspoon sugar, and cook until well browned, 9 to 10 minutes. Transfer the onions to the paper towel–lined plate with the bacon. Stir the bacon and onions into the filling in step 4, omitting the peas.

ROOT VEGETABLE POT PIE

A THICK, HEARTY ROOT VEGETABLE POT PIE seems like just the thing for the darkening days of fall. And most markets are packed with a broad range of choices to include in a filling, from vibrantly colored winter squashes like acorn, butternut, and kabocha to sugar-rich carrots and pale ivory parsnips and turnips. But a good root vegetable pot pie is easier said than done. Vegetable pot pies face hurdles that neither chicken or beef pot pies do, the biggest being how to develop a full-flavored filling without tender chunks of beef or succulent chicken. To keep this pie appropriate for vegetarians, we wanted to use vegetable broth as the base for the sauce. We wondered if we could develop a vegetable-based pot pie that tasted as good as our meat-filled pies.

After assessing a wide range of recipes for vegetable pot pie, we realized we were up against a stiff challenge. Boiled or steamed vegetables buried in a bland sauce and topped with a cardboard-like crust? No thanks, that wasn't what we wanted. Gravely disappointed in most of the recipes we tested, we opted to use our own chicken pot-pie recipe as a jumping-off point. We would omit the chicken and add a variety of vegetables and seasonings to flesh out the filling. The basic vegetables—onions, carrot, and celery—would remain, of course; without them, the filling was doomed to blandness.

We quickly decided that potatoes were an essential addition to lend some heft. Small Red Bliss potatoes won tasters over with their creamy texture and subtle flavor. Winter squash was found agreeable and became a definite contender, despite its labor-intensive preparation. We favored butternut squash because it is the easiest to peel and dice. Parsnips and turnips both seemed fair game but tasters favored the former; the latter was too strong. Rutabaga, kohlrabi, chayote? Too esoteric. Peas, however, were a must for their bright color and sweet flavor. No pot pie seems complete without them.

To extract as much flavor as possible from the onions, carrots, and celery, we chopped them all fine and cooked them slowly until very soft (like a sofrito for soup). The flavor was great, but the vegetables' uniformly mushy texture was all wrong for pot pie. We compromised and chopped the onions small, but left the celery and carrots large enough that they would not turn too soft once baked.

Cooking the potatoes, parsnips, and squash, however, proved problematic. Mixed raw into the sauce before the pie was topped and baked, they failed to fully cook before the biscuits browned. Parboiling each vegetable independently until tender worked well, but seemed fussy for such a homey dish. A third option proved the best. We tossed the potatoes, carrots, and parsnips with the onions once they were browned and put the lid on the pot so that the vegetables would "sweat" in their own moisture. The method worked, albeit with one small problem: As the potatoes began to soften, they released starch that adhered

CUTTING BUTTERNUT SQUASH WITH A CLEAVER AND MALLET

Winter squash are notoriously difficult to cut. Even the best chef's knives can struggle with their thick skins and odd shapes. We prefer to use a cleaver and mallet when trying to open a winter squash.

1. Set the squash on a damp kitchen towel to hold it in place. Position the cleaver on the skin of the squash.

2. Strike the back of the cleaver with a mallet to drive the cleaver deep into the squash. Continue to hit the cleaver with the mallet until the cleaver cuts through the squash and opens it up.

to the bottom of the pan and scorched. We found that an occasional splash of broth loosened the starches and thereby prevented the problem. Within 10 to 15 minutes, the vegetables were tender but still al dente at the core; they would finish in the sauce. To flavor the filling, a healthy dose of garlic seemed appropriate, as did fresh herbs. Parsley added color but little flavor, and rosemary was simply too much, running roughshod over the other flavors. Woodsy thyme won the most votes.

Now that we'd settled on the ingredients, we could finally tackle the sauce. As we feared, vegetable broth alone proved an unworthy substitute for chicken broth, and the pot pie we prepared with vegetable broth was much too bland. We added a bit of cream to the vegetable broth to add richness, but to no avail—the cream's high fat content muted the filling's flavor. Milk proved a better option, especially when we included cheddar cheese in the mix. A splash of cider vinegar heightened the tang of the sauce and brought out the flavor of the vegetables.

Winter Root-Vegetable Pot Pie

SERVES 6 TO 8

While the buttermilk biscuits (page 121) and flaky pie dough (page 119) used for our other pot pies both work well topping this pie, we prefer cornmeal biscuits (page 122). The sweet, grainy flavor of the corn pairs well with both the root vegetables and the tangy cheese of the filling. If you don't have fresh thyme leaves, substitute 1½ teaspoons dried thyme and add it with the broth to the roux.

PLANNING AHEAD: The filling may be made up to 1 day ahead of time and stored in an airtight container in the refrigerator. It must be reheated to a simmer before assembly to prevent the topping from turning gummy. Because of the potato in the filling, we do not recommend freezing it.

1	recipe Fluffy Buttermilk-Biscuit Topping, cornmeal variation (page 122)
6	tablespoons unsalted butter
1	large onion, minced
2	small celery ribs, sliced ½ inch thick

	Salt
2	large carrots, peeled, halved lengthwise, and sliced ½ inch thick
2	medium parsnips (about 8 to 10 ounces), peeled, halved lengthwise, and sliced ½ inch thick
1	pound small Red Bliss potatoes, scrubbed and cut into ½-inch pieces
1	pound butternut squash, peeled and cut into ½-inch pieces (about 3½ cups) (see the illustrations on page 129)
4	medium garlic cloves, minced or pressed through a garlic press
1	cup frozen peas
5	tablespoons all-purpose flour
1¾	cups low-sodium vegetable broth, plus up to ¼ cup additional broth as needed when cooking the potatoes
2¼	cups whole milk
4	ounces sharp cheddar cheese, shredded (about 1⅓ cups)
2	teaspoons cider vinegar
1	teaspoon minced fresh thyme leaves
2	tablespoons chopped fresh parsley leaves
	Pinch cayenne pepper
	Ground black pepper

1. Make the biscuit topping and refrigerate it until ready to use.

2. Adjust an oven rack to the middle position and heat the oven to 400 degrees. Melt 2 tablespoons of the butter in a Dutch oven over medium heat. Add the onion, celery, and ¾ teaspoon salt and cook, stirring occasionally, until softened and beginning to brown, about 10 minutes. Add the carrots, parsnips, potatoes, and squash; cover and cook, stirring occasionally, until the vegetables soften around the edges, about 13 minutes (if the potatoes begin to stick to the bottom of the pot, add vegetable broth, a tablespoon at a time, as needed to loosen). Stir in the garlic and cook until fragrant, about 30 seconds. Transfer the filling to a 9 by 13-inch baking dish (or a shallow casserole dish of similar size) or six 12-ounce ovenproof dishes. Sprinkle the peas evenly over the top and set aside.

3. Melt the remaining 4 tablespoons butter in a medium saucepan over medium-high heat. Once

foaming subsides, add the flour and cook, stirring constantly, for about 1 minute. Gradually whisk in the 1¾ cups vegetable broth and the milk, bring to a simmer, and cook until the sauce thickens, about 1 minute. Remove from the heat and whisk in the cheddar. Stir in the vinegar, thyme, parsley, and cayenne pepper and season with salt and pepper to taste.

4. Pour the sauce over the filling and stir with a wooden spoon to distribute evenly. Arrange the biscuits on top and bake until the biscuits are golden brown and the filling is bubbly, 30 minutes for a large pie and about 20 minutes for smaller pies. Allow to cool for 5 to 10 minutes before serving.

SPRING VEGETABLE POT PIE

RIDING HIGH ON THE SUCCESS OF THE WINTER Root-Vegetable Pot Pie (page 130), we decided to gamble on a vegetable pot pie filled with the lighter, brighter flavors of spring. Given the innately milder flavors of spring vegetables, was this raising the bar too high? Could we develop a recipe just as flavorful as the root vegetable pie?

"Spring vegetables" is one of those generic descriptions chefs throw about to refer to any number of early season vegetables. As a general rule, they are mild and herbaceous in flavor, requiring a light hand with seasoning as well as

---

EQUIPMENT: Vegetable Peelers

You might imagine that all vegetable peelers are pretty much the same. Not so. In our research, we turned up more than 25 peelers, many with quite novel features. The major differences were the fixture of the blade (either stationary or swiveling), the material of the blade (carbon steel, stainless steel, or ceramic), and the orientation of the blade to the handle (either straight in line with the body or perpendicular to it). The last arrangement, with the blade perpendicular to the handle, is called a harp or Y peeler because the frame looks like the body of a harp or the letter Y. This type of peeler, which is popular in Europe, works with a pulling motion rather than the shucking motion of most American peelers.

To test the peelers, we recruited several cooks and asked them to peel carrots, potatoes, lemons, butternut squash, and celery root. In most cases, testers preferred Oxo's new I-Series model and their Good Grips peeler. Our favorite peeler in the test kitchen for many years, the Good Grips was recently revamped, creating a new favorite: the I-Series peeler. This new model has a more slender grip than the original, comes outfitted with replaceable blades, and is weighted so that peeling requires less effort on the part of the cook. Overall, cooks preferred both models for their sharp stainless steel blades that swivel. Peelers with stationary blades are fine for peeling carrots, but they have trouble hugging the curves on potatoes. As for blade material, we found that peelers made from stainless steel, carbon steel, and ceramic could be either sharp or dull. We concluded that sharpness is a factor of quality control during the manufacturing process and not blade material.

Testers did, however, find the Messermeister peeler, with its serrated blade, to be a unique take on creating a sharper peeler. We found its performance exceptional in that it peels peaches, other ripe stone fruit, and tomatoes—a difficult task for even the sharpest of non-serrated peelers. The only drawback to the Messermeister is that many of the testers with larger-than-average hands felt the handle to be too small.

The Y-shaped peelers tested well, although they removed more flesh along with the skin on potatoes, lemons, and carrots and therefore did not rate as well as the Oxo swivel blade peelers. The one case where this liability turned into an asset was with butternut squash, where these Y-shaped peelers took off the skin as well as the greenish-tinged flesh right below the skin in one pass. With the Oxo peelers, it was necessary to go over the peeled flesh once the skin had been removed. Among Y-shaped peelers, testers preferred the Kuhn Rikon.

OUR FAVORITE PEELERS

OXO I-SERIES   MESSERMEISTER   KUHN RIKON

The sleek-handled Oxo I-Series peeler is our new favorite (left). The Messermeister peeler (middle) works great on delicate fruit, but the handle is less than ideal. The Kuhn Rikon peeler (right) takes off very wide, thick strips of peel, making it especially good for peeling winter squash or celery root.

careful cooking because they overcook easily, losing both their color and flavor. Leeks, peas, and asparagus all fit the bill, as do spinach, artichokes, and fiddleheads. Identifying the best mix for a pot-pie filling was the crux of our testing.

Working with the root vegetable pot pie as our starting point, we began altering the recipe. We chose to replace the onions in the winter root-vegetable pot pie with leeks and omit the celery altogether because of its pervasive flavor. The carrots, however, remained, lending sweetness and some much-needed color to the filling. We also decided to keep the Red Bliss potatoes in the mix for their heft and flavor. But because we wanted this pot pie to have a lightness to it, we decided to reduce the quantity by half a pound.

Artichokes sounded appealing, but in practice were just too much trouble. It didn't make sense to peel and prepare fresh artichokes only to have their delicate flavor masked by the filling. As for canned or jarred artichokes, we found that they contributed an artificial flavor to the filling.

So with artichokes ruled out, it looked like asparagus could be the star of the show. Asparagus can be fussy to cook and we worried how it would fare submerged in the filling. When undercooked, asparagus tastes grassy and bland; overcooked, it is close to cabbage in both smell and flavor. There's a small window in which asparagus is crisp yet tender, and still vibrantly colored. For our first attempt at cooking the stalks, we sautéed them with the rest of the vegetables, but they overcooked by the

INGREDIENTS: Vegetable Broth

With the ranks of vegetarians growing yearly and more people subscribing to healthier diets, vegetable broth is now vying for shelf space with chicken broth. There are a slew of options available, but how do they all taste? We gathered nine popular brands of packaged vegetable broth and tasted them in three different applications: warmed broth (tasted neat), in a hearty vegetable-enriched stock, and in asparagus risotto.

The winner of the straight broth tasting, Swanson, was praised for its "nice sweet-sour-salty balance," though some tasters noted the "barely perceptible vegetable flavor." Second-place Better than Bouillon was deemed "good, nicely flavored," and "very tasty," but many found it "very sour" with "strong metallic flavors." Coming in at the bottom of the tasting was Kitchen Basics, which lost points for a sweet molasses flavor that one taster described as "honey tea." It's no surprise that top-ranked Swanson had the highest sodium level, with 970 milligrams per cup, compared with 330 milligrams per cup of Kitchen Basics, which had the lowest sodium level. Salt was perceived as flavor, whereas the less salty broths were deemed bland and flavorless.

For the second test, we enriched the canned vegetable broth with roasted vegetables and garlic to see how it would taste when combined with hearty flavors. We pitted the winner, Swanson, and the loser, Kitchen Basics, from the previous test against each other. Swanson eked out a win, with a saltier flavor that most tasters preferred. Kitchen Basics was praised by some as "flowery," "earthy," and "more vegetal," though it was those same qualities that some tasters listed as negatives in the plain

broth tasting. Neither broth was bad; each had different flavor characteristics that worked in this application.

In the asparagus risotto, the results were surprising. We threw in what we thought would be a ringer—Swanson reduced-sodium chicken broth, the winner of our canned chicken broth tasting—to compete against the Swanson and Kitchen Basics vegetable broths. Swanson vegetable broth was the tasters' favorite, praised as "well-balanced" with "round, full flavors." Kitchen Basics was liked by some for its "rich and hearty" flavor, though most tasters found its "muddy" color distracting, resulting in a last-place finish. The chicken broth finished a strong second.

The long and short of it? Tasted straight, the differences between the nine broths were dramatic, but once mixed into a soup, risotto, or sauce, the flavors were less distinct than we would have expected. If you are using canned vegetable broth in a recipe with lots of other strong flavors, it probably doesn't matter which broth you use. If the flavors of the broth are going to be more up front, you should probably use Swanson. And if you are sensitive to salt, you may want to check the sodium level before you buy.

THE BEST VEGETABLE BROTH

Swanson Vegetable Broth had the most flavor of the nine brands we tested. It also contains the most sodium, which partly explains its strong showing in our tasting.

time the pot pie finished. We then tried blanching them (boiling in rapid water until tender and then "shocking" in ice water to stop the cooking and set the color) before adding them to the finished filling, but they overcooked with this method as well. Surprisingly, the easiest method yielded the best flavor. Simply tossing the raw sliced asparagus over the hot filling just before topping it yielded perfectly cooked, tender pieces.

As for the sauce, the heavy milk-enriched sauce we used for the winter root vegetables simply didn't work with the lighter flavors of this dish. Replacing the milk with additional broth lightened things a good deal, but the cheddar overpowered the spring vegetables. A switch to nutty Parmesan proved successful, especially since its flavor has long been a classic match for asparagus. For brightness, we added lemon juice. A small splash helped; a full tablespoon galvanized the flavor of the vegetables. A little lemon zest added with the juice effectively rounded out the lemon flavor. With a pinch of cayenne pepper to clarify things, the sauce was finished.

As for the topping, we tried them all: pie dough, biscuits, puff pastry, and toast points. The best option proved to be the traditional buttermilk biscuits. We found that pot pies prepared with a solid crust topping yielded overcooked, drab green

CUTTING ASPARAGUS ON THE BIAS

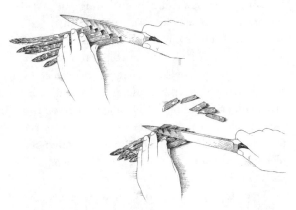

To cut the asparagus quickly and evenly, arrange the stalks in staggered groups of five on a cutting board and then cut them into ½-inch pieces on the bias.

asparagus. We suspected that the topping trapped escaping steam and thereby prompted rapid boiling of the filling. When we pulled the pie from the oven, we could see—through the baking dish's glass side—the filling feverishly boiling away. With its openings from which steam could escape, the biscuit topping was the obvious way to prevent this problem.

Spring Vegetable Pot Pie

SERVES 6 TO 8

While we prefer vegetable broth in this recipe, chicken broth may be substituted. To cut multiple asparagus stalks on the bias at the same time, line up several in a row parallel to you and cut at a 45-degree angle.

PLANNING AHEAD: Because of the delicate nature of the filling, this pie is best consumed the same day that it is prepared. The potato and leek mixture may be prepared through step 2 and the sauce may be prepared through step 3 and stored separately for up to 8 hours in airtight containers in the refrigerator. The asparagus and peas should be stored separately from the other vegetables. After you combine the sauce and filling, be sure to reheat it to a simmer, before putting on the topping, or the topping will be gummy.

I	recipe Fluffy Buttermilk-Biscuit Topping, regular or herb variation (page 121)
6	tablespoons unsalted butter
3	medium leeks, white and light green parts only, halved lengthwise, sliced ¼ inch thick, and rinsed well
I	large carrot, peeled and cut into ½-inch pieces
	Salt
I	pound small Red Bliss potatoes, scrubbed and cut into ½-inch pieces
3	medium garlic cloves, minced or pressed through a garlic press
I	pound asparagus, trimmed and cut on the bias into ½-inch pieces
I	cup frozen peas
7	tablespoons all-purpose flour
4	cups low-sodium vegetable broth, plus up to ¼ cup additional broth as needed when cooking the potatoes

2   ounces Parmesan cheese, grated fine
    (about 1 cup)
1   tablespoon lemon juice, plus ½ teaspoon
    finely grated lemon zest
4   teaspoons chopped fresh tarragon leaves
    Ground black pepper

1. Make the biscuit topping and refrigerate it until ready to use.

2. Adjust an oven rack to the middle position and heat the oven to 400 degrees. Melt 2 tablespoons of the butter in a Dutch oven over medium heat. Add the leeks, carrot, and ¾ teaspoon salt; cook, stirring occasionally, until the leeks have softened but are still bright green, about 7 minutes. Add the potatoes, cover, and cook, stirring occasionally, until the potatoes begin to soften around the edges, about 10 minutes (if the potatoes stick, add vegetable broth, 1 tablespoon at a time, as needed). Stir in the garlic and cook until fragrant, about 30 seconds. Transfer to a 9 by 13-inch baking dish (or a shallow casserole dish of similar size) or six 12-ounce ovenproof dishes. Sprinkle the asparagus and peas evenly over the top and set aside.

3. Melt the remaining 4 tablespoons butter in a medium saucepan over medium-high heat. Add the flour and cook, stirring constantly, for about 1 minute. Gradually whisk in the 4 cups of vegetable broth, bring to a simmer, and cook until the sauce thickens, about 1 minute. Remove from the heat and whisk in the Parmesan. Stir in the lemon juice, zest, and tarragon and season with salt and pepper to taste.

4. Pour the sauce over the filling and stir with a wooden spoon to distribute evenly. Arrange the biscuits on top and bake until the biscuits are golden brown and the filling is bubbly, about 30 minutes for a large pie and about 25 minutes for smaller pies. Allow to cool for 5 to 10 minutes before serving.

HOW TO CLEAN LEEKS

A. Hold the leek under running water and shuffle the cut layers like a deck of cards.

B. Or, slosh the cut end of the leek up and down in fresh, still water. Repeat as necessary.

SALMON POT PIE

AS THE BREADTH OF THIS CHAPTER INDICATES, pot pies come in all stripes—some classic, some not so classic. Fish pies fall into the former category, and we found recipes dating back hundreds of years. Some of the earliest English cookbooks contain recipes for fish pies, including one called "stargazey" pie, where small whole fish or eels were baked into a pie with their heads "gazing" upward from the pie's perimeter. More modern recipes tend to be less imaginative, generally resembling a convenient use for leftovers from Friday night's fish dinner. The most common fish pies use either a flaky white fish like cod, or the firm-fleshed salmon. Since salmon is wildly popular and reasonably priced, we decided it would be just the thing for our first tests.

We collected a variety of salmon pie recipes and prepared those that seemed most promising. The best out of the collection were reasonably light and simple, highlighting the fish's distinct flavor. Our favorites bound the fish and a complementary vegetable or two in a fairly light, milk-based sauce. As for toppings, flaky pastry and mashed-potato crusts were common, as was puff pastry—an option we were most attracted to, given how easy it is to use. Readily available in most supermarkets, frozen puff pastry is a cinch to prepare: just defrost, roll out to size, and bake.

We learned a couple of important lessons from our initial tests. First, the salmon was overcooked in all the recipes we tried. The recipes required precooking the fish before mixing it into the sauce; this resulted in chalky-textured and flavorless fish. It was pretty obvious to us that the fish could be added raw to the hot filling and sauce and then cook through by the time the topping browned. Second, for the most part, the sauces were thin and bland, or thick and spicy; none were quite right. And finally, as for the vegetables, they were mostly invisible. We wanted to find vegetables that complemented the salmon but held their own ground in the sauce. Based on previous testings, we chose a simple combination of leeks and peas—both classic accompaniments to salmon because of their mild, sweet flavor. We included a large volume of leeks, cooking them in butter until they were soft and supple but still vibrantly colored. As for the peas, we knew that frozen peas require little cooking—they (like the salmon) would cook through in the oven.

Next, we tackled the sauce. We wanted something relatively light that would allow the flavors of the salmon and leeks to shine through yet was flavorful in its own right. Following the lead of our other pot pies, we made a sauce in between a béchamel (a milk-based sauce) and a velouté (a broth-based sauce) by blending milk and bottled clam juice and then thickening it with a flour and butter roux. The brininess of the clam juice paired well with the salmon's sweet flesh; chicken broth, our usual choice, had an off taste in this sauce because it clashed with the flavor of the salmon. After a few tests, we settled on equal parts clam juice and milk for the sauce.

Balanced but rather bland, our sauce needed some seasoning to add spark. Since nutmeg is traditionally used in classic French cream-based sauces, it seemed worth a try here. A scant pinch was all that was necessary; any more was too overpowering. A little cayenne pepper brought clarity to the sauce by cutting through the richness, as did a substantial splash of lemon juice. For herbs, we looked no further than dill; its light, almost tangy flavor is without parallel as a complement to salmon. With a few tweaks here and there—seasoning and thickening—we attained the perfect replacement for the canned soup that so many other recipes relied upon.

Sauce and filling under our belt, we finally tackled the salmon. We cut fillet into small (½-inch) cubes and tossed them in the sauce with the filling. Shielded from direct heat by the sauce and topping (yet to come), the salmon stayed moist and flavorful. After a couple of tests, we found that the fish had the best flavor if seasoned with salt and

REMOVING PINBONES FROM SALMON

1. Using the tips of your fingers, gently rub the surface of the salmon to locate any pinbones.

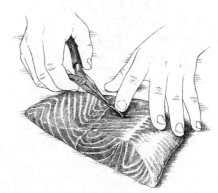

2. If you feel any bones, use a pair of needle-nose pliers or tweezers to pull them out.

pepper prior to mixing it into the pie filling.

Now on to the topping. Crisp, buttery, and ultra-convenient, frozen puff pastry seemed the perfect choice. We just had to find the best method for preparing it. In our first attempt, we rolled out sheets of the defrosted dough and trimmed them to snugly fit the top of the baking dish, sealing the filling beneath. Unfortunately, the tight seal of the pastry across the top of the filling caused the salmon to quickly overcook. Clearly, a solid sheet would not do.

We shifted gears and experimented with cutting the pastry into discrete pieces, prebaking them to ensure that they'd be crisp once nestled on top of the pie. First, we cut the pastry using cookie cutters and biscuit cutters, but the pieces puffed only slightly once baked. It appeared that the cut edges had stuck together, preventing the pastry from rising effectively. For the best rise, puff pastry must be cut with a very sharp edge. We decided that the best way to ensure a good rise was to cut the puff pastry with a sharp paring knife into simple rectangles, the size of which was dictated by the existing creases in the puff pastry (frozen puff pastry comes folded in thirds, like a business letter). We first cut the pastry sheet into three long rectangles, then cut each rectangle crosswise into fourths, giving us a total of 12 rectangles, just perfect for covering a pot pie.

Salmon and Leek Pot Pie

SERVES 6 TO 8

A solid topping does not work well with this dish because it will cause the fish to overcook. Our favorite topping choice is puff pastry rectangles (page 122), with toast points (page 123) being a very close second. In the filling, black pepper works fine, though we prefer the milder flavor and pale appearance of white pepper. Do not try substituting dried dill for the fresh; the flavor is a pale imitation.

PLANNING AHEAD: The filling may be prepared up to a day ahead of time and stored in an airtight container in the refrigerator. Reheat the filling to a simmer in a saucepan or the microwave before adding the salmon to prevent the fish from overcooking and the topping from turning gummy.

1	recipe Individual Puff-Pastry Rectangles (page 122) or Toast-Point Topping (page 123)
6	tablespoons unsalted butter
3	medium leeks, white and light green parts only, halved lengthwise, sliced 1/4 inch thick, and rinsed well
2	medium garlic cloves, minced or pressed through a garlic press
1	cup frozen peas
2	pounds salmon fillets, pinbones and skin removed, cut into 1/2-inch pieces
	Salt and ground white pepper
7	tablespoons all-purpose flour
2	(8-ounce) bottles clam juice
2	cups whole milk
2	tablespoons lemon juice
1/4	cup chopped fresh dill leaves
	Pinch ground nutmeg
	Pinch cayenne pepper
1	lemon, cut into wedges

1. Make the puff-pastry rectangles or toast points.

2. Adjust an oven rack to the lower-middle position and heat the oven to 400 degrees.

3. Melt 2 tablespoons of the butter in a large skillet over medium heat. Add the leeks and 1/2 teaspoon salt and cook, stirring occasionally, until softened, about 6 minutes. Stir in the garlic and cook until fragrant, about 30 seconds. Transfer to a 9 by 13-inch baking dish (or a shallow casserole dish of similar size) or six 12-ounce ovenproof dishes and sprinkle with the peas; set aside.

4. Season the salmon with salt and ground white pepper and set aside at room temperature. Melt the remaining 4 tablespoons butter in a medium saucepan over medium-high heat. Add the flour and cook, stirring constantly, for about 1 minute. Gradually whisk in the clam juice and then the milk, bring to a simmer, and cook until the sauce thickens, about 1 minute. Remove from the heat, stir in the lemon juice, dill, nutmeg, and cayenne and season with salt and white pepper to taste.

5. Add the salmon to the casserole dish with the rest of the filling. Pour the sauce over the top and stir gently with a wooden spoon to distribute it evenly. Place the partially baked puff-pastry

rectangles on top of the filling and bake until the topping is a deep golden brown, the sauce is bubbly, and the salmon is fully cooked, 13 to 15 minutes. Allow to cool for 5 to 10 minutes before serving. Pass lemon wedges separately.

➤ VARIATION

Shrimp and Halibut Pot Pie

Follow the recipe for Salmon and Leek Pot Pie, replacing the salmon with 1 pound medium shrimp (40 to 50 count), peeled and deveined, and 1 pound halibut, cut into ½-inch cubes. Monkfish may be substituted for the halibut. We prefer this pie with Toast-Point Topping (see page 123).

SHEPHERD'S PIE

NOTHING MORE THAN A RICH LAMB STEW blanketed under a mashed-potato crust, shepherd's pie is a hearty casserole originally from the cool climes of sheep-centric northern Britain. Today, it is as much a part of American cookery as British, best eaten on a blustery winter day while sidled up to a roaring fire with a frothy pint of stout. It's arguably America's favorite lamb dish.

Like numerous other dishes in this book, shepherd's pie was a meal made on Monday with Sunday night's leftovers—the remnants of the roast, vegetables, and mashed potatoes. In this day and age, few of us have such delicious Sunday dinners, much less leftovers, so we aimed to create an assertively flavored shepherd's pie from scratch.

Our first step was to figure out what cut of lamb worked best. To save on prep time, we hoped to use ground lamb. Shepherd's pie made with ground lamb tasted OK, but it was somewhat bland. If you're pinched for time, ground lamb is a decent choice, but we prefer our favorite cut of lamb for stewing, shoulder chops. It is easy to cut the meat off the bone and into cubes and, after searing, the meat delivers a rich lamb flavor without tasting gamy or greasy, as lamb often does. While many of the recipes we gathered required minced lamb, we preferred larger, more toothsome chunks.

Choosing vegetables to flavor the lamb proved easy. Sautéed carrots and onions added sweetness and depth. A touch of garlic added a little zest, and sweet frozen peas—characteristic of many British-style meat stews—brought bright color to an otherwise drab-looking dish.

For herbs, we wanted big flavors strong enough to stand up to the lamb's richness. Rosemary and thyme are traditional lamb flavorings, and they tasted great in this instance. Fresh, not dried, herbs provided the best flavor.

As for the liquid in the stew, we settled on chicken broth enriched with red wine. Beef broth clashed with lamb's earthy flavors, while chicken broth was neutral. After testing a variety of red wines, we liked a medium-bodied Côtes du Rhone best because it is well rounded, low in tannins, and not oaky, traits that allowed it to marry well with all the flavors in the dish. In addition to the broth and wine, we added a little Worcestershire sauce for its sweetness and savory tang.

With the stew assembled and cooked, we were ready to top it off with a mashed-potato crust. We quickly found out that simple mashed potatoes would not do; they crumbled and broke down while baking. We started our adjustments by reducing the amount of butter and dairy we usually add to mashed potatoes. To give the potatoes some structure, we then added egg yolks to the potatoes, turning the mashed potatoes into what the French call duchess potatoes. The yolks did the trick; the potatoes retained their shape and texture and picked up a little more richness in the bargain. (Given the added richness of the yolks, we felt that whole milk, rather than half-and-half, was the better dairy choice.) The yolks also gave the potatoes a slight golden hue that complemented the deep brown of the stew beneath.

We tried a variety of methods for assembling the casserole and were most pleased with the simplest route. The stew fit into either a 9 by 13-inch baking dish or, more snugly, into a 10-inch pie plate, which made for a more attractive presentation than the rectangular dish. A large rubber spatula was the best tool for spreading the potatoes evenly across the top of the stew. We found that it was important to completely cover the stew and seal the edges of the pan with the potato topping; otherwise the stew sometimes bubbled out of the pan.

Because the lamb is already tender when it goes into the casserole, the baking time is short. Once the potato crust turns golden brown, the shepherd's pie is ready to come out of the oven.

Shepherd's Pie

SERVES 6 TO 8

Diced lamb shoulder chops give the filling a much richer flavor than ground lamb. If you prefer to use ground lamb, see the variation that follows. This recipe includes basic assembly instructions for a 9 by 13-inch baking dish. For a fancier presentation in a 10-inch pie plate, see the illustrations below. See page 228 for information about buying lamb shoulder chops.

PLANNING AHEAD: You can make the filling up to 3 days ahead of time and store it in an airtight container in the refrigerator. It may also be frozen for up to 3 months. The topping, however, is best made on the day the pot pie is prepared. The filling must be brought to a simmer before topping it.

FILLING

3	pounds lamb shoulder chops, trimmed of bones and excess fat and cut into 1-inch pieces (about 1½ pounds meat)
1½	teaspoons salt
1	teaspoon ground black pepper
3	tablespoons vegetable oil
2	medium onions, chopped coarse
2	medium carrots, peeled and cut into ¼-inch slices
1	medium garlic clove, minced or pressed through a garlic press
2	tablespoons all-purpose flour
1	tablespoon tomato paste
2¼	cups low-sodium chicken broth
¼	cup full-bodied red wine
1	teaspoon Worcestershire sauce
1	teaspoon chopped fresh thyme leaves
1	teaspoon chopped fresh rosemary leaves
1	cup frozen peas, thawed

TOPPING

2	pounds large russet potatoes, peeled and cut into 2-inch cubes
1	teaspoon salt
6	tablespoons unsalted butter, softened
¾	cup whole milk, warmed
2	large egg yolks
	Ground black pepper

MAKING PIE-SHAPED SHEPHERD'S PIE

The filling and potato topping for our shepherd's pie fit nicely in a standard 9 by 13-inch baking dish. But for a fancier presentation, we like to bake the pie in a 10-inch pie plate. The mashed potato topping rises high above the filling, much like a lemon meringue pie or baked Alaska. If you want to try this presentation, follow the steps below.

1. Place the filling in a 10-inch pie plate and then drop spoonfuls of mashed potatoes around the perimeter of the pie plate.

2. Use a rubber spatula to attach the potatoes to the rim of the pie plate. It's important to seal the edges this way to prevent the filling from bubbling out of the pie plate in the oven.

3. Drop the remaining mashed potatoes in the center of the pie plate and then smooth the top with a spatula. Because the topping rises so high, we recommend baking the pie on a rimmed baking sheet to catch any leaks.

1. FOR THE FILLING: Season the lamb with the salt and pepper. Heat 2 tablespoons of the oil in a 12-inch skillet over medium-high heat until shimmering. Add half of the lamb and cook, stirring occasionally, until well browned on all sides, 5 to 6 minutes. Remove the lamb from the pan and set aside in a medium bowl. Heat the remaining tablespoon oil in the pan. Add the remaining lamb and cook, stirring occasionally, until well browned on all sides, 5 to 6 minutes. Transfer the lamb to the bowl.

2. Reduce the heat to medium and add the onions and carrots to the fat in the now-empty pan. Cook until softened, about 4 minutes. Add the garlic, flour, and tomato paste and cook until the garlic is fragrant, about 1 minute. Whisk in the broth, wine, and Worcestershire sauce. Stir in the thyme, rosemary, and browned lamb. Bring to a boil, reduce the heat to low, cover, and simmer until the lamb is just tender, 25 to 30 minutes.

3. FOR THE TOPPING: Meanwhile, put the potatoes in a large saucepan; add water to cover and ½ teaspoon of the salt. Bring to a boil and continue to cook over medium heat until the potatoes are tender when pierced with a knife, 15 to 20 minutes. Drain the potatoes well, return them to the pan, and set the pan over low heat. Mash the potatoes, adding the butter as you mash. Stir in the warm milk and then the egg yolks. Season with the remaining ½ teaspoon salt and pepper to taste.

4. TO ASSEMBLE AND BAKE: Adjust an oven rack to the middle position and heat the oven to 400 degrees. Stir the peas into the lamb mixture and check the seasonings. Pour the lamb mixture evenly into a 9 by 13-inch baking dish (or a shallow casserole dish of similar size). With a large spoon, spread the mashed potatoes over the entire filling. Starting at the sides to ensure a tight seal, use a rubber spatula to smooth out the potatoes and anchor them to the sides of the baking dish. (You should not see any filling.) Bake until the top turns golden brown, 20 to 25 minutes. Allow to cool for 5 to 10 minutes and then serve.

➤ VARIATION

Shepherd's Pie with Ground Lamb

Follow the recipe for Shepherd's Pie, substituting 1½ pounds ground lamb for the shoulder chops. Cook, one half at a time, until well browned, about 3 minutes for each batch of lamb. Proceed as directed, reducing the simmering time in step 2 to 15 minutes.

TAMALE PIE

TAMALE PIE HAS ITS ROOTS IN SOUTHWESTERN cooking. A mildly spicy ground meat filling is topped with a cornmeal crust and baked. Although time and fashion have altered the recipe from decade to decade, the basic idea remains the same. A good pie contains a juicy, spicy mixture of meat and vegetables encased in or topped with a cornmeal crust that is neither too stiff nor too loose. Bad tamale pies, however, are dry and bland and usually have too much or too little filling.

We did have a number of questions about how to prepare the cornmeal topping. For starters, we tested fine-ground cornmeal (such as Quaker, which is sold in most supermarkets) against coarser meals. As expected, the crust made with fine-ground cornmeal was slightly smoother, but it was also bland in comparison with the toothsome crust made with coarse-ground cornmeal. We made the topping with water and stock as well as with and without butter. Tasters preferred the clean, simple flavor of mush made with just water, salt, and cornmeal. The stock and butter added more flavor and fat to the crust than was necessary. We found that 4 cups of water to 1½ cups cornmeal yielded a spoonable texture with enough structure to contain the meat filling.

Authentic and modern recipes use a variety of techniques to make the mush; some cook it slowly over low heat to keep it from burning, while others use the microwave. We found it difficult to keep an eye on the mush in the microwave, and cooking it low and slow was unnecessary. Using medium-high heat and a heavy-duty whisk, the mush took only 3 minutes to thicken to the right consistency.

With the cornmeal-mush topping in place, we moved on to the filling. Most recipes use either ground beef or ground pork as the base, but we liked the flavor of both mixed together. An all-beef pie turned out boring and tough, while an all-pork pie was light and mealy. A pie made with equal amounts of beef and pork turned out flavorful and nicely textured.

Most tamale pie fillings call for tomatoes, corn, and black beans. We found that this simple recipe easily accommodates canned and frozen vegetables with no ill effect on the final flavor. Seasoned with onion, garlic, jalapeño, and a little fresh oregano, the tamale filling tasted fresh and spicy.

Putting together filling and topping was simple. We piled the meat filling into a large baking dish and topped it with cheese and the cornmeal mush, which, as loose as it was, was easy to spread in an even layer to the edges of the dish. A moderately high oven temperature heat did the best job setting the crust and heating the filling. The cheese, trapped beneath the cornmeal and above the filling, melted into an appealingly smooth layer.

Tamale Pie

SERVES 6 TO 8

We like coarse-ground cornmeal (about the texture of kosher salt) for the topping. We had good results with Goya Coarse Yellow Cornmeal. To keep the cornmeal mush at a spreadable consistency, cover it while assembling the pie. If the mush does get too dry, simply loosen it with a little hot water. Dried oregano is a suitable replacement for fresh, but the amount should be reduced to 1½ teaspoons and it should be added in step 2 with the tomatoes. Spiciness varies from jalapeño to jalapeño, and since much of the heat resides in the seeds, we suggest mincing the seeds separately from the flesh, then adding minced seeds to suit your taste for heat.

Planning Ahead: The filling may be prepared up to 3 days ahead of time and stored in an airtight container in the refrigerator. It may also be frozen for up to 3 months. The topping, however, must be prepared just before assembly. The filling should be brought to a simmer before topping it.

FILLING

	Butter for greasing the casserole dish
1	tablespoon vegetable oil
¾	pound 90 percent lean ground beef
¾	pound ground pork
1	large onion, chopped fine
1	medium jalapeño chile, stemmed, seeded, and minced
2	medium garlic cloves, minced or pressed through a garlic press
1	teaspoon ground cumin
¼	teaspoon cayenne pepper
1	tablespoon chili powder
1	teaspoon salt
1	(14.5-ounce) can diced tomatoes
1	(15.5-ounce) can black beans, drained and rinsed
1	cup fresh or frozen corn
1	tablespoon minced fresh oregano leaves
	Ground black pepper
4	ounces Monterey Jack cheese, shredded (about 1⅓ cups)

TOPPING

4	cups water
¾	teaspoon salt
1½	cups coarse cornmeal
¼	teaspoon ground black pepper

1. FOR THE FILLING: Butter a 9 by 13-inch baking dish (or a shallow casserole dish of similar size) or 6 individual 12-ounce dishes and set aside. Adjust an oven rack to the middle position and heat the oven to 375 degrees.

2. Heat the oil in a large skillet over high heat until shimmering. Add the ground beef and pork and cook, breaking up large clumps of meat with a wooden spoon, until it is no longer pink and beginning to brown, about 4 minutes. Add the onion and jalapeño and cook until just softened, about 3 minutes. Add the garlic, cumin, cayenne, chili powder, and salt and cook until aromatic, about 30 seconds. Add the tomatoes and their juice, the black beans, and corn. Simmer until most of the liquid has evaporated, about 3 minutes. Remove the pan from the heat and stir in the oregano and pepper to taste. Set aside.

3. FOR THE TOPPING: Bring the water to a boil in a large, heavy-bottomed saucepan over high heat. Add the salt and then slowly pour in the cornmeal while whisking vigorously to prevent lumps from forming. Reduce the heat to medium-high and cook, whisking constantly, until the cornmeal begins to soften and the mixture thickens, about 3 minutes. Remove the pan from the heat and stir in the pepper.

4. TO ASSEMBLE AND BAKE: Spoon the beef mixture evenly into dish and sprinkle the Monterey Jack evenly over the top of the casserole. Gently spread the cornmeal mixture over the cheese using a flexible rubber spatula, pushing the mixture to the very edges of the baking dish. Wrap tightly with aluminum foil and bake for 30 minutes. Remove the foil and continue to bake until the crust is beginning to brown and the filling is bubbly, 15 to 20 minutes. Allow to cool for 10 minutes before serving.

VEGETABLE AND BEAN TAMALE PIE

LOADED WITH BEANS, VEGETABLES, AND CHEESE and topped with a cornmeal crust, tamale pie seemed ripe for a strictly vegetable (meat-free) variation. With so much going on in the filling, we wondered whether we would even miss the meat. For our first attempt, we took the simplest route possible by omitting the beef and adding additional beans to make up the difference in volume. The pie lacked the full flavor and satisfying richness of the meat version and tasted like a bad potluck-dinner casserole—a dish thrown together to appease the token vegetarian in the crowd. The beans were tinny, the vegetables bland, and the sauce nothing but tomato sauce seasoned with chili powder. Clearly, we needed to take a different route if we wanted a successful meatless tamale pie.

There was little we could do to improve the flavor of the canned beans: they are what they are. And the vegetables themselves could never make up for the meat's full flavor. More cheese would make it richer and thereby better, but that

seemed too easy a route to pursue: more fat makes anything taste better (the dirty secret of many vegetarian recipes). We sensed that the sauce itself was the key to rescuing this variation.

Sauces in Mexican cooking, which inspired this dish, are prepared in a manner very different than European-style sauces. The base ingredients—tomatoes, onions, garlic, chilies, etc.—are roasted over high heat until darkly browned, even burned in spots, and then pureed. The resulting sauce is "fried" or cooked in hot oil until the flavors have fully blended and intensified. We didn't pursue this route in the original meat pie because of all the ingredients that required cooking before the pie was assembled: roasting unnecessarily complicated matters. In this case, where the filling could be prepared without cooking, roasting made a good deal of sense.

We combined the basic ingredients in the sauce from the meat version—tomatoes, onions, and garlic (coarsely chopped and moistened with a little oil)—on a baking sheet and roasted them in a very hot oven until the edges of the onions were lightly browned and the tomatoes were charred in spots. After a quick spin in the blender with the same roster of spices from the meat version, we had a sauce that was dramatically different in flavor. The tomato's fruitiness was intensified and the garlic tasted sweeter and fuller. To further sharpen the flavors, we added a pinch of brown sugar and a splash of lime juice. The sauce at this stage tasted good enough that we opted to skip the

INGREDIENTS: Chipotle Chiles

Smoky, sweet, and moderately spicy, chipotle chiles are jalapeno chiles that have been smoked over aromatic wood and dried. They are sold as is—wrinkly, reddish brown, and leathery—or canned in "adobo," a tangy, oily, tomato-and-herb-based sauce. We recommend purchasing canned chipotles because they are already reconstituted by the adobo and, consequently, are easier to prepare. Most recipes call for just a chile or two as they are so potent, but the remaining chiles keep indefinitely if stored in an airtight container in the refrigerator, or they may be frozen. Cans of chipotles in adobo are readily available in the Mexican food section of most supermarkets.

"frying" altogether; the flavor was solid enough without the extra effort.

Not wanting to reinvent the wheel, we assembled the vegetable pie as we had the meat version, topping the filling with a layer of cheese followed by the cornmeal crust. Simmered in the sauce beneath the crust, the beans absorbed the sauce's flavor. For a bit of vegetal crunch and color, we added raw zucchini, which softened to a pleasingly tender, yet firm texture. With such a rich and full-bodied filling, nobody missed the meat at all.

Vegetable and Bean Tamale Pie

SERVES 6 TO 8

For a spicier version of the pie, try adding an additional chipotle chile to the sauce and substituting Pepper Jack cheese for the Monterey Jack.

PLANNING AHEAD: The roasted tomato sauce and the bean and vegetable mixture may be prepared up to 3 days ahead of time and stored separately in airtight containers in the refrigerator. The sauce may also be frozen in an airtight container for up to 3 months; the filling cannot be frozen. The sauce should be reheated before being mixed with the bean and vegetable filling in step 2. The topping must be prepared just before assembly.

FILLING

2	(28-ounce) cans diced tomatoes, well drained, with 2 cups juice reserved
1	medium onion, chopped coarse
4	medium garlic cloves, chopped coarse
1/2	teaspoon salt
1	tablespoon vegetable oil
2	canned chipotle chiles in adobo sauce, minced
1	teaspoon ground cumin
1	tablespoon chili powder
4	teaspoons lime juice
2	(15.5-ounce) cans black beans, drained and rinsed
1	(15.5-ounce) can kidney or pinto beans, drained and rinsed
1 1/2	cups fresh or frozen corn
1	medium zucchini (about 12 ounces), cut into 1/2-inch cubes
2	teaspoons minced fresh oregano leaves
1/4	cup chopped fresh cilantro leaves
8	ounces Monterey Jack cheese, shredded (about 2 2/3 cups)

TOPPING

4	cups water
3/4	teaspoon salt
1 1/2	cups coarse cornmeal
1/4	teaspoon ground black pepper

1. FOR THE FILLING: Adjust an oven rack to the middle position and heat the oven to 475 degrees. Toss the tomatoes, onion, garlic, ½ teaspoon salt, and oil together in a mixing bowl and spread out onto a foil-lined, rimmed baking sheet. Roast, stirring occasionally, until the vegetables begin to brown darkly about the edges, 35 to 40 minutes. Transfer to a blender; add the chiles, cumin, chili powder, lime juice, and 2 cups of reserved tomato juice. Puree until the mixture is slightly chunky, 8 to 10 seconds. Season with salt and pepper to taste.

2. Reduce the oven temperature to 375 degrees. Mix together the beans, corn, zucchini, and herbs in a 9 by 13-inch baking dish (or a shallow casserole dish of similar size). Pour the pureed tomato sauce over the filling and stir with a wooden spoon to distribute evenly.

3. FOR THE TOPPING: Bring the water to a boil in a large, heavy-bottomed saucepan over high heat. Add the salt and then slowly pour in the cornmeal while whisking vigorously to prevent lumps from forming. Reduce the heat to medium-high and cook, whisking constantly, until the cornmeal begins to soften and the mixture thickens, about 3 minutes. Remove the pan from the heat and stir in the pepper.

4. TO ASSEMBLE AND BAKE: Sprinkle the Monterey Jack evenly over the top of the casserole. Gently spread the cornmeal mixture over the cheese using a flexible rubber spatula, pushing the mixture to the very edges of the baking dish. Wrap tightly with aluminum foil and bake for 30 minutes. Remove the foil and continue to bake until the crust is beginning to brown and the filling is bubbly, 30 to 35 minutes. Allow to cool for 10 minutes before serving.

Pork Tinga and Sweet Potato Pot Pie

NEVER HEARD OF IT? YOU'RE NOT ALONE; WE hadn't either, until we invented it. Well, truth be told, tinga is a classic Mexican pork and sausage stew; the topping, however, came in a flash of inspiration. Thinking of shepherd's pie—the British pie in which meat stew (beef or lamb) is encased in a mashed potato crust—we thought about topping tinga with mashed sweet potatoes, since pork and sweet potatoes are such a felicitous combination. Our Mexican-style "shepherd's pie" is unconventional, perhaps, but delicious nonetheless.

So what exactly is pork tinga? Classically defined, it is a long-simmered stew of pork shoulder and chorizo sausage that is liberally seasoned with garlic, chiles, and a variety of herbs and spices. Considering how quickly our other pot pies pull together, we were loath to prepare a classic (read multi-hour) tinga. We decided to try a faster route by choosing a cut of meat that would cook faster than the pork shoulder. After trying a few different options, we found that thinly sliced pork loin fit the bill. A quick sear before simmering added deep flavor to the meat—rich enough to fill the void left by the long-simmered shoulder. And it was ready in a quarter of the total cooking time of the classic rendition.

Now that we had changed the cut of meat, we also decided to take a few liberties with other ingredients. Because Mexican-style chorizo sausage is seasoned so assertively with garlic, hot pepper, paprika, and herbs, we found many of the spices normally added to tinga were somewhat redundant and could be excluded without affecting the stew's overall flavor. The fundamental flavors, however, remained untouched: lots of sautéed onion and garlic, smoky chipotle chiles, and tomatoes—canned diced tomatoes in this case.

As for the topping, we prepared mashed sweet potatoes in a dozen-odd fashions, all yielding pretty poor results. Mushy and fibrous, or just plain waterlogged, none delivered the flavorful "mash" we wanted. Most recipes simmered the sweet potatoes in seasoned water until tender prior to mashing. But sweet potatoes are not regular potatoes; they have a significantly higher moisture content. Simmering them like a regular potato only dilutes their flavor.

After a little experimentation, we found that sweet potatoes contain enough moisture that they can be cut into rough chunks and steamed with the scantest amount of additional liquid. Water diluted the flavor, and milk was little better, though on the right track. Heavy cream proved the best bet, lending both flavor and richness. A little butter added to the mashed sweet potatoes rounded out the richness, and brown sugar intensified their natural flavor. In our quest for a smooth, lump-free topping, we turned to a ricer for processing the cooked potato. In a pinch, a potato masher does the trick, though consistency will be a little on the "rustic" side.

But there is more to a pot-pie topping than flavor alone. While flavorful, the mashed sweet potatoes weren't stiff enough to form an adequate crust atop the stew. In the oven's high heat, the "mash" ran into a smooth layer and sunk a bit into the tinga. To add structure, the answer was as simple as adding a beaten egg to the mixture; once heated, the egg firmed up the potatoes and gave the topping a crustiness we liked. For a bit of crunch, we sprinkled a handful of toasted pumpkin seeds over the top. Definitely unconventional, our pork tinga pot pie might nevertheless become a classic someday.

Pork Tinga and Sweet Potato Pot Pie

SERVES 6 TO 8

If you can't find chorizo sausage, substitute kielbasa or andouille, though the filling's flavor won't be quite as intense. If you don't have a food mill or ricer, use a potato masher and try to attain a smooth texture (a few chunks are fine).

PLANNING AHEAD: The topping cannot be made ahead, but the filling may be prepared up to 3 days in advance and stored in an airtight container in the refrigerator. It may also be frozen in an airtight container for up to 3 months. The filling should be brought to a simmer before topping it; otherwise the topping will be overcooked by the time the filling is heated through.

TOPPING

4 tablespoons unsalted butter, cut
   into 4 pieces
3 tablespoons heavy cream
1 teaspoon salt
2 teaspoons dark brown sugar
3 pounds sweet potatoes (about 3 large or
   4 medium potatoes), peeled, quartered
   lengthwise, and cut crosswise
   into $1/4$-inch slices
1 large egg, lightly beaten
   Ground black pepper

FILLING

2 pounds boneless pork loin (preferably blade
   end), cut into thin strips
   Salt and ground black pepper
6 teaspoons vegetable oil
1 pound chorizo, quartered lengthwise and then
   cut crosswise into $1/4$-inch-thick pieces
2 medium onions, minced
2 tablespoons water
8 medium garlic cloves, minced or pressed
   through a garlic press
3 canned chipotle chiles in adobo sauce, minced
1 (28-ounce) can diced tomatoes, drained
$31/2$ cups low-sodium chicken broth
2 tablespoons brown sugar
1 tablespoon coarsely chopped fresh oregano
   leaves
$1/2$ cup toasted pumpkin seeds (optional)

1. FOR THE TOPPING: Combine the butter, cream, salt, sugar, and sweet potatoes in a large Dutch oven. Cover and cook over low heat, stirring occasionally, until the potatoes fall apart when poked with a fork, 50 to 55 minutes. Remove from the heat and transfer the mixture to the hopper of a food mill or ricer and process into a large bowl. Quickly stir in the egg and pepper and cover with aluminum foil to keep warm.

2. FOR THE FILLING: Meanwhile, adjust an oven rack to the middle position and heat the oven to 400 degrees. Season the pork liberally with salt and pepper. Heat 2 teaspoons of the oil in a large Dutch oven over medium-high heat until smoking. Add half the pork in a single layer and cook, without stirring, until browned, $1\frac{1}{2}$ to 2 minutes. Flip the pork strips and continue to cook until brown on the second side, $1\frac{1}{2}$ to 2 minutes longer. Transfer to a 9 by 13-inch baking dish (or a shallow casserole dish of similar size). Add 1 teaspoon oil to the Dutch oven and repeat with the remaining pork.

3. Return the Dutch oven to medium-high heat and add the remaining 3 teaspoons oil. Add the chorizo and cook, stirring frequently, until lightly browned, about 2 minutes. Add the onions, $\frac{1}{4}$ teaspoon salt, and the water, scraping the browned bits off the bottom of the pan. Cook, stirring frequently, until the onions soften, about 3 minutes. Stir in the garlic and chipotles and cook until fragrant, about 30 seconds. Add the tomatoes, broth, brown sugar, and oregano and bring to a simmer. Reduce the heat to medium-low and continue to simmer until the liquid is reduced by half and the flavors have blended, about 15 minutes. Pour the mixture over the pork in the baking dish and stir to combine.

4. Place large dollops of the mashed sweet potatoes evenly over the top of the filling and spread into an even, smooth layer using a flexible rubber spatula, pushing it to the very edges of the baking dish. Sprinkle the pumpkin seeds (if using) over the top and bake until the topping is firm and the filling is bubbly, about 30 minutes. Allow to cool for 5 to 10 minutes before serving.

3

OVEN BRAISES AND STEWS

SIMMERED SLOWLY IN THE OVEN IN A HEAVY, lidded pot, braised dishes and oven-cooked stews are the original "cover-and-bake" dinners. The slow cooking tenderizes tough meats, ensures creamy, toothsome beans, and marries varied flavors into a robust, deeply satisfying meal. Every dish in this chapter cooks for a minimum of 45 minutes (and up to three hours) unsupervised in the oven, and few require more than a minute's effort once out of the oven. We have included a wide range of recipes in this chapter, from weeknight-oriented one-pot meals to more complicated classics best suited to relaxed weekend cooking. There are American standards like pot roast and country captain chicken, as well as more wide-ranging favorites like Indian pork vindaloo and Italian osso buco.

Virtually all of the recipes in this chapter are prepared in a similar fashion. Meat—be it chicken, beef, pork, or lamb—is browned, then aromatic vegetables are sautéed, after which broth is added. The pot is then transferred to a moderate oven to simmer until the flavors have unified and the meat is tender. The flavor of each dish is built incrementally and thus, for the best results, it is important to cook both carefully and patiently. Make sure to follow the visual clues offered in each recipe. For example, the meat should be darkly browned on all sides. If not, the flavor of the braise or stew is liable to be mild and the color of the broth will be anemic. Vegetables, too, should be softened and lightly browned so that they release their flavor. Undercooked, crunchy vegetables will soften while in the oven, but the flavor they contribute to the broth will not be as potent. A minute or two of patient attention is well worth it in the end.

As for equipment necessary in this chapter, a heavyweight Dutch oven is the best cooking vessel because it retains heat well and cooks evenly. Lightweight pots are subject to temperature fluctuations that will negatively affect stovetop cooking and oven simmering. The Dutch oven must also be ovenproof—no plastic handles or lids that may melt. That said, it's important to be mindful of hot handles and always grasp the pots carefully with oven mitts.

Most of the recipes in this chapter store well and even improve after a few days in the refrigerator as the flavors continue to develop. Check the notes that accompany each recipe for pertinent storage information.

BEEF STEW

BEEF STEW SHOULD BE RICH AND SATISFYING. Our goal in developing a recipe for it was to keep the cooking process simple without compromising the stew's deep, complex flavor. We focused on the following issues: What cut or cuts of beef respond best to stewing? How much and what kind of liquid should you use? When and with what do you thicken the stew?

Experts tout different cuts as being ideal for stewing. We browned 12 different cuts of beef, marked them for identification, and stewed them in the same pot. (For more information on various beef cuts, see the illustration below.) Chuck proved to be the most flavorful, tender, and juicy. Most other cuts were too stringy, too chewy, too dry, or just plain bland. The exception was rib-eye steak, which made good stew meat but is too

POSSIBLE CUTS FOR BEEF STEW

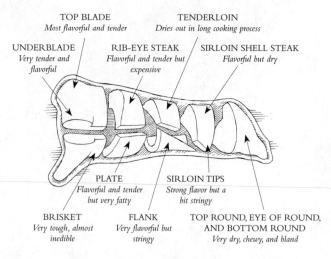

TOP BLADE
Most flavorful and tender

TENDERLOIN
Dries out in long cooking process

UNDERBLADE
Very tender and flavorful

RIB-EYE STEAK
Flavorful and tender but expensive

SIRLOIN SHELL STEAK
Flavorful but dry

PLATE
Flavorful and tender but very fatty

SIRLOIN TIPS
Strong flavor but a bit stringy

BRISKET
Very tough, almost inedible

FLANK
Very flavorful but stringy

TOP ROUND, EYE OF ROUND, AND BOTTOM ROUND
Very dry, chewy, and bland

We stewed 12 different cuts of beef from every part of the cow. Chuck, which consists of the underblade and the top blade, was the most flavorful and cooked up quite tender.

expensive a cut to use for this purpose.

Our advice is to buy a steak or roast from the chuck and cube it yourself. Precut stewing beef is often made up of irregularly shaped end pieces from different muscles that cannot be sold at retail as steaks or roasts because of their uneven appearance. Because of the differences in origin, precut stewing cubes in the same package may not be consistent in the way they cook or taste. If you cut your own cubes from a piece of chuck, you are assured that all the cubes will cook in the same way and have the flavor and richness of chuck.

The names given to different cuts of chuck vary, but the most commonly used names for retail chuck cuts include boneless chuck-eye roasts, cross-rib roasts, blade steaks and roasts, shoulder steaks and roasts, and arm steaks and roasts. We particularly like chuck-eye roast, but all chuck cuts are delicious when cubed and stewed.

Having settled on our cut of beef, we started to explore how and when to thicken the stew. Dredging meat cubes in flour is a roundabout way of thickening stew. The floured beef is browned, then stewed. During the stewing process, some of the flour from the beef dissolves into the liquid, causing it to thicken. Although the stew we cooked this way thickened up nicely, the beef cubes had a "smothered steak" look.

We also tried two thickening methods at the end of cooking—a *beurre manié* (softened butter

---

EQUIPMENT: Dutch Ovens

A large Dutch oven is one of the most useful pieces of cookware you can own, and it's virtually essential to preparing the braised dishes and stews in this chapter. By definition, a Dutch oven is nothing more than a wide, deep pot with a cover. Originally, they were constructed of heavyweight cast iron and designed to be set directly in an open fire and buried beneath coals. An entire meal could be cooked in this fashion, from soup to roast and even dessert. We have come far from those early days, and now that every household has an oven, Dutch ovens are primarily used for dishes that start on the stovetop and finish in moderate heat in the oven. As for the curious name, it traces back hundreds of years to a time when the highest-quality cast iron came from Holland. While you can still find a cast-iron Dutch oven close to the original style (which held its own in testing), we wanted to find the very best and put a dozen models of varying prices and construction through their paces.

First off, we found that a Dutch oven should have a capacity of at least 6 quarts to be useful. Eight quarts is even better. As we cooked in the pots, we came to prefer wider, shallower Dutch ovens because it's easier to see and reach inside them, and they offer more bottom surface area to accommodate larger batches of meat for browning. This reduces the number of batches required to brown a given quantity of meat and therefore reduces the chances of burning the flavorful pan drippings. Ideally, the diameter of a Dutch oven is twice as great as its height.

We also preferred pots with a light-colored interior finish, such as stainless steel or enameled cast iron. It is easier to judge the caramelization of the drippings at a glance in these pots. Dark finishes can mask the color of the drippings, which may burn before you realize it. Our favorite pot is the 8-quart All-Clad Stainless Stockpot (despite the name, this pot is a Dutch oven). The 7-quart Le Creuset Round French Oven, which is made of enameled cast iron, also tested well. These pots are quite expensive, costing at least $150 even on sale. A less expensive alternative is the old school–style 7-quart Lodge Dutch Oven, which is made from cast iron. This pot is extremely heavy (a whopping 17 pounds), making it a bit hard to maneuver. It must be seasoned (wiped with oil) regularly, and the dark interior finish is not ideal, but it does brown food quite well and costs just $45.

THE BEST DUTCH OVENS
Our favorite pot is the 8-quart All-Clad Stainless Stockpot (left). Despite the name, this pot is a Dutch oven. Expect to spend nearly $200 for this piece of cookware. A less expensive alternative is the 7-quart Lodge Dutch Oven (right), which costs about $45. However, since this pot is made from cast iron, it may react with acidic sauces and is not appropriate for all recipes, especially those that contain significant amounts of tomatoes or wine.

mixed with flour) and cornstarch mixed with water. Both methods are acceptable, but the beurre manié lightened the stew's color, making it look more like pale gravy than rich stew juices. Also, the extra fat did not improve the stew's flavor enough to justify its addition. For those who prefer thickening at the end of cooking, we found that cornstarch dissolved in water did the job without compromising the stew's dark, rich color.

Pureeing the cooked vegetables is another thickening method. Once the stew is fully cooked, the meat is pulled from the pot and the juices and vegetables are pureed to create a thick sauce. Tasters felt this thickening method made the vegetable flavor too prominent.

Ultimately, we opted for thickening the stew with flour at the beginning—stirring it into the sautéing onions and garlic, right before adding the liquid. Stew thickened this way was not any better than stew thickened at the end with cornstarch, but it was easier. There's no last-minute work; once the liquid starts to simmer, you're free to do something else.

We next focused on stewing liquids. We tried water, wine, canned beef broth, canned chicken broth, combinations of these liquids, and beef stock. Stews made with water were bland and greasy, while those made entirely with wine were too strong. The stew made from beef stock was delicious, but we decided that beef stew, which has many hearty ingredients contributing to its flavor profile, does not absolutely need beef stock, which is quite time-consuming to make. When we turned to canned broths, the chicken outscored the beef broth. (For more information about the problems with canned beef broth, see page 127.) The stew made entirely with chicken broth was good, but we missed the acidity and flavor provided by the wine. In the end, we preferred a combination of chicken broth and red wine.

We tested various amounts of liquid and found that we preferred stews with a minimum of liquid, which helps to preserve a strong meat flavor. With too little liquid, however, the stew may not cook evenly, and there may not be enough sauce to spoon over starchy accompaniments. A cup of liquid per pound of meat gave us sufficient sauce to moisten a mound of mashed potatoes or polenta without drowning them.

We tested various kinds of wine and found that fairly inexpensive fruity, full-bodied young wines, such as Chianti or Zinfandel, were best. (See page 149 for more information on the best options for cooking wines.)

To determine when to add the vegetables, we made three different stews, adding carrots, potatoes, and onions to one stew at the beginning of cooking and to another stew halfway through the cooking process. For the third stew, we cooked

CUTTING STEW MEAT

To get stew meat pieces that are cut from the right part of the animal and regularly shaped, we suggest buying a boneless roast and cutting the meat into cubes yourself. A 3-pound roast, once trimmed, should yield 2 ¾ pounds of beef, the maximum amount that can be easily browned in a Dutch oven in two batches.

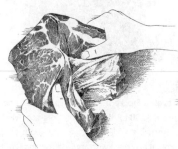 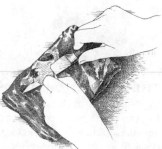 

1. Pull apart the roast at its major seams (delineated by lines of fat and silver skin). Use a knife as necessary.

2. With a paring knife, trim off excess fat and silver skin.

3. Cut the meat into cubes or chunks as directed in specific recipes.

the onions with the meat but added steamed carrots and potatoes when the stew was fully cooked. The stew with vegetables added at the beginning was thin and watery. The vegetables had fallen apart and given up their flavor and liquid to the stew. The beef stew with the cooked vegetables added at the last minute was delicious, and the vegetables were the freshest and most intensely flavored. However, it is more work to steam the vegetables separately. Also, vegetables cooked separately from the stew don't really meld all that well with the other flavors and ingredients. We prefer to add the vegetables partway through the cooking process. They don't fall apart this way and they still have enough time to meld with the other stew ingredients. There is one exception to this rule. Peas should be added just before serving the stew, to preserve their fresh color and texture.

One final note: The meat passes from tough to tender fairly quickly. Often, at the 1¾-hour mark, we found that the meat would still be chewy. Fifteen minutes later, it would be tender.

INGREDIENTS: Red Wine for Stew

When making a dish that uses red wine, our tendency is to grab whichever inexpensive dry red is on hand, usually the leftover contents of a recently opened bottle. But we began to wonder what difference particular wines would make in the final dish and decided to investigate.

We called on the advice of several local wine experts, who gave us some parameters to work with when selecting red wines to use in a braise such as hearty beef stew or cacciatore. (The rules are slightly different when making some dishes, such as beef burgundy, that traditionally rely on a particular kind of wine.)

When choosing a red wine for a basic stew, look for one that is dry (to avoid a sweet sauce) and has good acidity (to aid in breaking down the fibers of the meat). Keep in mind that any characteristic found in the uncooked wine will be concentrated when cooked.

From tests we ran in the test kitchen, we found that soft, fruity wines such as Merlot yielded a "grape jelly" flavor, which most tasters thought was too sweet for beef stew or cacciatore. Also watch out for wines that have been "oaked," usually older wines; the oak flavor tends to become harsh and bitter as it is cooked.

In another 15 minutes, the meat would start to dry out. Taste the meat often as the stew nears completion to prevent this problem.

❧

Hearty Beef Stew
SERVES 6 TO 8

An 8-quart Dutch oven is the best choice for this dish because it allows you to brown the meat in just two batches. See the information at left about choosing a red wine for this dish.

PLANNING AHEAD: This beef stew can be prepared through step 3, stored in an airtight container, and refrigerated for up to 5 days. Spoon off any hardened fat from the top, bring the stew back to a simmer over medium-low heat in a covered saucepan or Dutch oven, and proceed with step 4. Add broth or water to adjust the consistency, if necessary. Because of the potatoes, we do not recommend freezing it.

3	pounds chuck roast, trimmed and cut into 1½-inch cubes (see the illustrations on page 148)
	Salt and ground black pepper
3	tablespoons vegetable oil
2	medium onions, chopped coarse
3	medium garlic cloves, minced or pressed through a garlic press
3	tablespoons all-purpose flour
1	cup dry red wine
2	cups low-sodium chicken broth
2	bay leaves
1	teaspoon dried thyme
1	pound red potatoes (about 3 medium), scrubbed and cut into 1-inch cubes
4	large carrots, peeled and sliced ¼ inch thick
1	cup frozen peas
¼	cup minced fresh parsley leaves

1. Adjust an oven rack to the lower-middle position and heat the oven to 300 degrees. Dry the meat thoroughly with paper towels, then season it generously with salt and pepper. Heat 1 tablespoon of the oil in a large ovenproof Dutch oven over medium-high heat until shimmering. Add half of the meat to the pot so that the individual pieces are

close together but not touching. Cook, not moving the pieces until the sides touching the pot are well browned, about 3 minutes. Turn each piece and continue cooking until most sides are well browned, about 5 minutes longer. Transfer the beef to a medium bowl, add another tablespoon oil to the pot, and swirl to coat the pan bottom. Brown the remaining beef; transfer to the bowl and set aside.

2. Reduce the heat to medium, add the remaining tablespoon oil to the empty Dutch oven, swirling to coat the pan bottom. Add the onions and ¼ teaspoon salt. Cook, stirring frequently and vigorously, scraping the bottom and edges of the pot with a wooden spoon to loosen any browned bits, until the onions have softened, about 5 minutes. Add the garlic and continue to cook for 30 seconds. Stir in the flour and cook until lightly colored, about 2 minutes. Add the wine, scraping up the remaining browned bits from the bottom and edges of the pot and stirring until the liquid is thick. Gradually add the broth, stirring constantly and scraping the pan bottom and edges to dissolve the flour. Add the bay leaves and thyme and bring to a simmer. Add the meat and return to a simmer. Cover and place the pot in the oven. Cook for 1 hour.

3. Remove the pot from the oven and add the potatoes and carrots. Cover and return the pot to the oven. Cook just until the meat is tender, about 1 hour. Remove the pot from the oven.

4. Add the peas, cover, and allow to stand for 5 minutes. Stir in the parsley, discard the bay leaves, adjust the seasonings, and serve immediately.

BEEF CARBONNADE

A BASIC BEEF STEW CAN BE ALTERED IN DOZENS of ways, usually by adding more ingredients to the pot. But you can also go the other way and strip beef stew down to its bare bones (the beef). If you also trade the carrots and potatoes in for an abundance of onions and add a good dose of beer, you've created a Belgian beef stew called *carbonnade à la flammande*.

Beef, beer, and onions have an affinity—they're an ensemble with great appeal (think burger, onion rings, and a beer). In a carbonnade, the heartiness of beef melds with the soft sweetness of sliced onions in a broth that is deep and rich with the malty flavor of dark beer.

We made several versions of carbonnade and found that despite the simple and few ingredients, making a poor one is quite easy. We wound up with several batches of tough, tasteless beef and onions in a pale, insipid broth. Not quite what we had in mind.

We used the framework of our recipe for hearty beef stew to arrive at an improved carbonnade. The procedure for that recipe is as follows: The beef is browned in batches and set aside, the onions are sautéed in the empty pot, flour is sprinkled over the onions, and liquid is added. Then the beef is returned to the pot, and the covered pot goes into the oven, where it simmers until the beef is fork-tender.

In developing a recipe for carbonnade, the first departure from our beef stew recipe came with the selection of beef. For a basic beef stew, we prefer a chuck roast cut into 1½-inch chunks. A chuck roast comprises a number of different muscles interwoven with intramuscular fat and connective tissue. The fat and tissue make for good texture and flavor, and the different muscles make for pieces of meat with differing textures, even when cooked.

The substance of carbonnade is purely beef and onion—there are no chunks of potatoes or carrots to compete with the beef. Consequently, we wanted smaller pieces of beef of a uniform texture that would be a better match for the soft, thinly sliced onions. Enter 1-inch-thick blade steaks (also called top blade or flatiron steaks), which are small, long, narrow steaks cut from the shoulder area of the animal (see the illustration on page 146). Most blade steaks have a decent amount of fat marbling, which gives them a good flavor as well as a tender texture. One taster described the blade steak in carbonnade as "buttery," a quality that is well suited to this stew. The trade-off is that these smaller steaks are a bit more time-consuming to trim of silver skin and gristle, but they are well worth it.

Onions—and a good deal of them—go into a carbonnade. Two pounds was the right amount in relation to the amount of beef. We tried white and red onions, but both were cloyingly sweet. Yellow onions tasted the best. After browning the beef, the bottom of the pot was crusty with *fond*, or browned bits. Do not underestimate the importance of the fond—it furnishes the stew with color and flavor. As we had done with our hearty beef stew, we added ¼ teaspoon salt along with the thinly sliced onions to help release their moisture. This helps to keep the fond from burning and to loosen it from the pot when deglazing. Garlic is not an ingredient in all carbonnade recipes, but we liked its heady essence; a small amount is added to the onions only after the onions are cooked so that it does not burn.

The right beer is key to achieving a full, robust carbonnade. Beers of the light, lager persuasion, those commonly favored in America, lack guts— they result in light-colored, watery-tasting stews. We tried a number of different beers and found that reasonably dark ales, very dark ales, and stouts made the richest and best-tasting carbonnades. A few of our favorites were Chimay (a Trappist ale from Belgium), Newcastle Brown Ale, Anchor Steam (this beer cannot technically be classified as an ale), Samuel Smith Taddy Porter, and Guinness Extra Stout.

We tried making carbonnades with beer as the only liquid, but they lacked backbone and sometimes had an overwhelming bitterness, depending on the type of beer used. Equal parts chicken broth and beer made a deeper, more solid-tasting stew. The addition of dried thyme and a bay leaf provided herbal notes that complemented the other flavors. Just a bit of cider vinegar perked things up, and a bit of dark brown sugar rounded out the flavors.

Carbonnade à la Flammande
SERVES 6 TO 8

To make sure the beef browns well, dry the pieces thoroughly with paper towels. Don't bother making this stew with a light-colored beer—both the color and the flavor will be insipid. We particularly liked Newcastle Ale, Anchor Steam, and Chimay. For those who like a heavier beer with a slightly bitter flavor, porter and stout are good as well.

PLANNING AHEAD: Carbonnade can be stored in an airtight container and refrigerated for up to 5 days. Spoon off any hardened fat from the top and bring the stew back to a simmer over medium-low heat in a covered saucepan or Dutch oven. Add broth or water to adjust the consistency, if necessary. It may also be frozen for up to 3 months.

3–3½	pounds top-blade steaks, gristle removed, cut into 1-inch pieces (see the illustrations below)
	Salt and ground black pepper
3	tablespoons vegetable oil
4	medium onions, halved and sliced thin
2	medium garlic cloves, minced or pressed through a garlic press
3	tablespoons all-purpose flour
1½	cups low-sodium chicken broth

TRIMMING BLADE STEAKS

1. Each steak has a line of gristle running down the center that should be removed. To remove the gristle, halve each steak lengthwise, leaving the gristle on one half.

2. Cut away the gristle from the half to which it is still attached.

3. Cut the trimmed meat crosswise into 1-inch pieces.

1½	cups dark beer
¾	teaspoon dried thyme
1	bay leaf
1	tablespoon dark brown sugar
1	tablespoon cider vinegar

1. Adjust an oven rack to the lower-middle position and heat the oven to 300 degrees. Dry the meat thoroughly with paper towels, then season it generously with salt and pepper. Heat 1 tablespoon of the oil in a large ovenproof Dutch oven over medium-high heat until shimmering. Add half of the meat to the pot so that the individual pieces are close together but not touching. Cook, not moving the pieces until the sides touching the pot are well browned, about 3 minutes. Turn each piece and continue cooking until most sides are well browned, about 5 minutes longer. Transfer the beef to a medium bowl, add another tablespoon oil to the pot, and swirl to coat the pan bottom. Brown the remaining beef; transfer the meat to the bowl and set aside.

2. Reduce the heat to medium-low, add the remaining tablespoon oil to the empty Dutch oven, and swirl to coat the pan bottom. Add the onions and ¼ teaspoon salt and cook, stirring occasionally and vigorously, scraping the bottom and edges of the pot with a wooden spoon to loosen the browned bits, until the onions have released some moisture, about 5 minutes. Increase the heat to medium and cook, stirring occasionally and scraping the bottom and edges of the pot, until the onions are limp, softened, and lightly browned, about 15 minutes. Stir in the garlic and cook until fragrant, about 30 seconds. Add the flour and stir until the onions are evenly coated.

3. Stir in the broth, scraping the pan bottom and edges with a wooden spoon to loosen the browned bits. Gradually add the beer, stirring constantly and scraping the pan edges to dissolve the flour. Add the thyme, bay leaf, brown sugar, and cider vinegar as well as the browned beef and accumulated juices, pushing down the beef to submerge the pieces; sprinkle with salt and pepper, bring to a simmer, cover, and place in the oven. Cook until the beef is fork-tender, 1½ to 2 hours. Discard the bay leaf, season with salt and pepper to taste, and serve.

BEEF GOULASH

THIS SIMPLE EASTERN EUROPEAN STEW HAS been around for centuries. The word *goulash* comes from the Hungarian *gulyas,* which means "herd of cattle." Originally, cattlemen seared and stewed beef until the liquid evaporated and then dried the meat in the sun. When needed, the meat was rehydrated with water to create either stew or soup, depending on how much liquid was added. Goulash stew—without the drying step—is the more popular version in the United States.

There are several versions of modern goulash. Beef, onions, garlic, and paprika are constants. Other possible ingredients include potatoes, tomatoes, and bell peppers. Our goal was to create a very simple stew with tender, flavorful beef and browned onions in a rich, intensely flavored sauce. The sauce would be thick and brownish red in color, both from the paprika and from the good browning that the meat and onions would receive.

As with our Hearty Beef Stew, we found that chuck roast is the best choice because it cooks up tender and flavorful. Traditional recipes brown the beef in lard, and we found that the gentle pork flavor of good lard does add something to this dish. Given the fact that most cooks don't have lard on hand, we tried bacon fat as a substitute. Tasters reacted negatively to goulash made with bacon fat. They said the smoky flavor imparted by the bacon was at odds with this stew. Vegetable oil turned out to be a better choice. Although not as flavorful as lard, oil will suffice.

On a related subject, we found that leaving a little fat attached to the pieces of meat boosts flavor and is especially important if lard is not used. You will need to defat the stew before serving, but this is easily done with a spoon.

In these early tests, we found that browning the meat well was essential to flavor development in goulash. The hearty, rich flavor and color of goulash is dependent on browning the meat and onions and then deglazing the crusty, deep-brown bits stuck to the bottom of the Dutch oven.

We found that adding a little salt with the onions caused them to release moisture and kept them from scorching. The moisture from the onions also helps to loosen the browned bits, a process that is completed once the liquid is added to the pan. Although onions are a must, the recipes we looked at were divided on the question of garlic. Tasters, however, were not. Everyone in the test kitchen liked garlic in this stew. Six cloves added depth and also balanced the sweetness of the paprika and onions.

Once the garlic is fragrant, it's time for the paprika to go into the pot. We used 5 tablespoons of sweet Hungarian paprika in our goulash (see page 190 for more details). We added flour at the same time, to thicken the stew.

Recipes uncovered in our research use an assortment of liquids, including water, beef broth, and chicken broth. We found that water created a bland stew, and canned beef broth, in conjunction with the large volume of paprika, contributed a bitter edge to the goulash. Chicken broth proved to be the best option, lending the stew solid body and just enough richness without competing with the other flavorings.

Some recipes also include wine in the mix, although authentic recipes do not. We tried varying amounts of red wine, and tasters felt that its flavor was overpowering. Goulash should be soft and mellow; while red wine added complexity, it also made the stew acidic and a bit harsh. A few sources suggested white wine, but tasters were again unimpressed.

Our recipe was coming together: browned beef and onions, garlic and paprika for flavor, and chicken broth as the liquid. But we still had two major issues to resolve—tomatoes and vegetables. We started with the tomatoes.

Many goulash recipes contain tomato, although the original dish (which dates back several centuries before the arrival of tomatoes from the New World) certainly did not. We decided to make four batches of goulash: one with canned diced tomatoes, one with plain tomato sauce, one with tomato paste, and one with no tomato product. The diced tomatoes and tomato sauce proved to be too dominant and made the stew reminiscent of beef cacciatore. Tomato paste, however, blended into the background and enhanced other flavors in the dish. Compared with the stew made with no tomato product, the version with tomato paste was more complex and appealing. In fact, the tomato paste functioned a bit like wine in terms of adding depth, but it was also much more subtle than wine and thus more in tune with the spirit of goulash.

Vegetables were easy to incorporate into the dish. Tasters liked large chunks of red and green bell peppers, especially when added to the stew near the end of the cooking time. When added earlier (just after the onions are browned is a common choice), the peppers became mushy and fell apart. We found that if they are added to the stew while it is in the oven, the peppers soften without turning mushy.

We tested carrots, cabbage, celery, and green beans (ingredients used in some of the recipes we had collected), but did not like any of them in goulash. Potatoes were a different story. Several recipes add them to the stew pot with the liquid so that they fall apart and thicken the stew. Although we did not like this approach, we did like potatoes simmered in the stew until tender. Adding the potatoes partway through the oven cooking time yielded this result, and so we decided to use the potatoes in a variation.

Many Hungarian goulash recipes do not include sour cream, which seems more popular in German and Austrian versions. But our tasters all felt that sour cream mellows and enriches this stew. To prevent the sour cream from curdling, we combined it with a little hot stewing liquid to temper it and then stirred the mixture back into the stew pot.

Goulash is traditionally served over buttered egg noodles or spätzle. Egg noodles require almost no effort to cook and are our first choice. Mashed potatoes are not traditional, but they make an excellent accompaniment, too.

Beef Goulash

SERVES 6 TO 8

If you like things spicy, feel free to add a pinch of cayenne or hot paprika. We found that the flavor from the beef fat adds something to this stew, so don't trim the meat too closely. We recommend removing external fat from the chuck roast but leaving the internal fat alone unless it is excessively thick. Serve the stew over 1 pound of buttered egg noodles. Try tossing the noodles with 1 tablespoon of toasted caraway seeds for a distinctive and delicious flavor combination. The caraway is an unusual and authentic touch.

PLANNING AHEAD: Beef Goulash can be prepared through step 4, stored in an airtight container, and refrigerated for up to 5 days. Spoon off any hardened fat from the top and bring the stew back to a simmer over medium-low heat in a covered saucepan or Dutch oven. Add broth or water to adjust the consistency, if necessary, and continue with step 5. It may also be frozen for up to 3 months. (The potato and caraway version, however, does not freeze well.)

3	pounds chuck roast, trimmed and cut into 1½-inch cubes (see the illustrations on page 148)
	Salt and ground black pepper
3	tablespoons vegetable oil or lard
3	medium onions, chopped coarse
6	medium garlic cloves, minced or pressed through a garlic press
5	tablespoons sweet paprika
¼	cup all-purpose flour
3	cups low-sodium chicken broth
2	tablespoons tomato paste
2	bay leaves
1	teaspoon dried marjoram
1	large red bell pepper, stemmed, seeded, and chopped coarse
1	large green bell pepper, stemmed, seeded, and chopped coarse
½	cup sour cream
¼	cup minced fresh parsley leaves

1. Adjust an oven rack to the lower-middle position and heat the oven to 300 degrees. Dry the beef thoroughly with paper towels, then season it generously with salt and pepper. Heat 1 tablespoon of the oil in a large ovenproof Dutch oven over medium-high heat until shimmering. Add half of the meat to the pot so that the individual pieces are close together but not touching. Cook, not moving the pieces until the sides touching the pot are well browned, about 3 minutes. Turn each piece and continue cooking until most sides are well browned, about 5 minutes longer. Transfer the beef to a medium bowl, add another tablespoon oil to the pot, and swirl to coat the pan bottom. Brown the remaining beef; transfer the meat to the bowl and set aside.

2. Reduce the heat to medium, add the remaining tablespoon oil to the empty Dutch oven, and swirl to coat the pan bottom. Add the onions and ¼ teaspoon salt. Cook, stirring frequently and vigorously, scraping the bottom and edges of the pot with a wooden spoon to loosen the browned bits, until the onions have softened and browned, about 8 minutes. Stir in the garlic and cook until fragrant, about 30 seconds. Add the paprika and flour and stir until the onions are evenly coated and fragrant, about 2 minutes.

3. Stir in 1½ cups of the broth, scraping the pan bottom and edges with a wooden spoon to loosen the remaining browned bits, and continue stirring until the flour is dissolved and the liquid thickened. Gradually add the remaining broth, stirring constantly and scraping the pan bottom and edges to dissolve the flour. Stir in the tomato paste, bay leaves, marjoram, and ¾ teaspoon salt. Add the browned beef and accumulated juices, stir to blend, and submerge the meat under the liquid. Bring to a simmer, cover the pot, and place it in the oven. Cook for 1 hour and 20 minutes.

4. Remove the pot from the oven and stir in the red and green peppers. Cover and return the pot to the oven. Cook just until the meat is tender, about 40 minutes. Remove the pot from the oven. If serving immediately, spoon off the fat that rises to the top.

5. Place the sour cream in a medium bowl and stir about ½ cup of the hot stewing liquid into it. Stir the sour cream mixture back into the stew. Stir in the parsley and season to taste with salt and pepper. Serve immediately.

> VARIATION

Beef Goulash with Potatoes and Caraway

With potatoes added, there's no need to serve this stew over noodles. Caraway is a traditional addition to Hungarian goulash.

Follow the recipe for Beef Goulash, reducing the amount of beef to 2½ pounds, adding 1 teaspoon caraway seeds with the paprika and flour, and adding ¾ pound red potatoes, peeled and cut into 1-inch dice, after the stew has cooked in the oven for 1 hour. Proceed as directed.

BRAISED BRISKET

BRAISED BRISKET IS A WORKHORSE MEAL. IT'S cheap, can serve many people (or just a few, with great leftovers), and is usually cooked with straightforward, universally appealing ingredients. The all-too-common problem with brisket, however, is that the meat turns out extraordinarily dry and chewy.

Briskets are available in two styles: "first" or "flat" cut and "second" or "point" cut. Each is technically half a brisket or less: a whole brisket, hewn from the primal cut, is upward of a dozen pounds. We prefer pieces from the second (point) cut because they tend to be thicker, more tender, and more flavorful. A 3-pound point cut brisket perfectly fits the bottom of a large Dutch oven and easily feeds six to eight, a convenient cut of meat indeed.

The method for braising brisket is the same as for other stews and braises. The meat is first browned, then set aside while the browned bits left behind in the pot are used to make a flavorful sauce. The browned beef is nestled back into the pot with the sauce, the liquid is brought to a gentle simmer, and the meat is cooked until tender.

Using this basic method as our starting point, we noted that there are three keys to cooking brisket so that it doesn't taste dry or chewy. First, oven temperatures higher than 300 degrees turn the simmer into a boil (which dries out the meat), while oven temperatures lower than 300 degrees simply add unnecessary hours to the cooking time.

Second, we found it takes several hours of constant simmering for the brisket to turn tender. A 3-pound piece of brisket requires 2½ to three hours in the oven, at which point a dinner fork should slide in and out of its center with little resistance. Third, it is necessary to slice the brisket thin across the grain when serving.

Core to the universal appeal of brisket is the flavorful sauce that accompanies it. Noting that many recipes use caramelized onions as the base for the sauce, we used the drippings left over from browning the meat to lightly caramelize a large quantity of onions. We added brown sugar and tomato paste to bring out the sweetness of the onions and round out the flavor of the sauce. We used both beef and chicken broth, along with red wine, for the liquid component, and completed the flavor profile with garlic, bay leaves, and fresh thyme. The brisket was submerged in this flavorful liquid so that the meat was almost smothered by the onions as it cooked. The final touch was a

LOCATING THE BRISKET

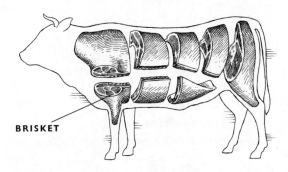

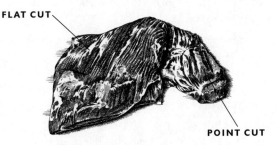

Butchers often separate the whole brisket into two parts, the flat cut (left portion) and the point cut (right portion). The point cut is a bit thicker and contains more fat. It is more tender than the flat cut and is our first choice.

dash of cider vinegar, added just before serving, to brighten the flavor of the well-simmered sauce. Far from chewy or dry, our version of brisket has plenty of sauce to pour over the fork-tender slices of beef.

Braised Beef Brisket

SERVES 6 TO 8

Make sure to use an ovenproof pot, like an 8-quart Dutch oven, that is large enough so that the brisket lies flat.

PLANNING AHEAD: Braised Beef Brisket can be prepared through step 2, stored in an airtight container, and refrigerated for up to 5 days. Store the meat in the sauce, spoon off any hardened fat from the top, and bring it back to a simmer over medium-low heat in a covered saucepan or Dutch oven. Add broth or water to adjust the consistency, if necessary, and continue with step 3. It may also be frozen for up to 3 months.

1	beef brisket (about 3 pounds), preferably point cut (see the illustration on page 155), trimmed of excess fat
	Salt and ground black pepper
2	tablespoons vegetable oil
6	large onions (about 3 pounds), halved and sliced thin
2	tablespoons brown sugar
6	medium garlic cloves, minced or pressed through a garlic press
1	teaspoon tomato paste
1/4	cup all-purpose flour
1/2	cup dry red wine
1	cup low-sodium beef broth
1	cup low-sodium chicken broth
4	bay leaves
4	sprigs fresh thyme
1	tablespoon cider vinegar

1. Adjust an oven rack to the middle position and heat the oven to 300 degrees. Dry the brisket thoroughly with paper towels, then season generously with salt and pepper. Heat the oil in a large ovenproof Dutch oven over high heat until smoking. Cook the brisket until dark brown on the first side, about 5 minutes. Flip the brisket and cook until well browned on the second side,

about 5 minutes longer. Transfer the brisket to a large plate; set aside.

2. Reduce the heat to medium. Add the onions, sugar, and 1/4 teaspoon salt. Using a wooden spoon, scrape the browned bits from the pan bottom and edges. Cook, stirring frequently, until the onions are softened and lightly browned, about 10 minutes. Stir in the garlic and tomato paste and cook until fragrant, about 30 seconds. Stir in the flour and cook for 1 minute. Slowly stir in the wine to dissolve the flour and cook until almost dry, about 1 minute. Stir in the beef broth, chicken broth, bay leaves, and thyme. Return the brisket to the pot, nestling it in the liquid, and bring to a simmer. Cover the pot, transfer it to the oven, and cook until a fork slides easily in and out of the center of the roast, 2½ to 3 hours.

3. Transfer the brisket to a cutting board, tent with foil, and let rest for 15 minutes. Remove and discard the bay leaves and thyme from the sauce, stir in the vinegar, and season with salt and pepper to taste. Slice the brisket thin across the grain. Arrange the meat on a warmed platter and spoon some of the sauce over it. Serve, passing the remaining sauce at the table.

➤ VARIATION

Braised Brisket with Sauerkraut and Prunes

This traditional German recipe offers a good balance between sweet and sour.

Follow the recipe for Braised Beef Brisket, reducing the amount of onions to 1½ pounds (about 3 large onions). Stir in 2 pounds packaged sauerkraut, well rinsed and drained (about 3 cups), and 1 cup pitted prunes along with the broths in step 2. Proceed with the recipe as directed.

SIMPLE POT ROAST

POT ROAST, A SLOW-FOOD SURVIVOR OF GEN-erations past, has stubbornly remained in the repertoire of Sunday-night cookery, but with few good reasons. The meat is often tough, stringy, and so dry that it must be drowned with the sauce that, mercifully, accompanies the dish.

A good pot roast by definition entails the transformation of a tough (read cheap), nearly unpalatable cut of meat into a tender, rich, flavorful main course by means of a slow, moist cooking process called braising. It should not have to be sliced; rather, the tension of a stern gaze should be enough to break it apart. Nor should it be pink in the middle—save that for prime rib or steak.

The meat for pot roast should be well marbled with fat and connective tissue to provide the dish with the necessary flavor and moisture. Recipes typically call for roasts from the sirloin (rump), round (leg), or chuck (shoulder). When all was said and done, we cooked a dozen cuts of meat to find the right one.

The sirloin roasts we tested—the bottom rump roast and top sirloin—were the leanest of the cuts and needed a longer cooking time to be broken down to a palatable texture. The round cuts—top round, bottom round, and eye of round—had more fat running through them than the sirloin cuts, but the meat was chewy. The chuck cuts—shoulder roast, boneless chuck roast, cross rib, chuck mock tender, seven-bone roast, top-blade roast, and chuck-eye roast—cooked up the most tender, although we gave preference to three of these cuts (see below for more information). The high proportion of fat and connective tissue in these chuck cuts gave the meat much-needed

moisture and superior flavor.

Tough meat, such as brisket, can benefit from the low, dry heat of oven roasting, or it can be boiled. With pot roast, however, the introduction of moisture by means of a braising liquid is thought to be integral to the breakdown of the tough muscle fibers. We wanted to find out how much liquid, and what kind, was needed to best cook the roast and supply a good sauce.

Before we began the testing, however, we needed to deal with the aesthetics of the dish. Because pot roast is traditionally cooked with liquid at a low temperature, the exterior of the meat will not brown sufficiently unless it is first sautéed in a Dutch oven on the stovetop. High heat and a little oil were all that were needed to caramelize the exterior of the beef and boost both the flavor and the appearance of the dish.

Using water as the braising medium, we started with a modest ¼ cup, as suggested in a few recipes. This produced a roast that was unacceptably fibrous, even after hours of cooking. After increasing the amount of liquid incrementally, we found that the moistest meat was produced when we added liquid halfway up the sides of the roast (depending on the cut, this amount could be between two and four cups). The greater amount of liquid also accelerated the cooking process, shaving off nearly one hour from the cooking time needed for a roast cooked in

CHUCK ROASTS

The seven-bone pot roast (left) is a well-marbled cut with an incredibly beefy flavor. It gets its name from the bone found in the roast, which is shaped like the number seven. Because it is only 2 inches thick, this roast needs less liquid and less time to braise. Do not buy a seven-bone pot roast that weighs more than 3½ pounds, as it will not fit into a Dutch oven. This roast is also sometimes referred to as a seven-bone steak.

The top-blade pot roast (middle) is also well marbled with fat and connective tissue, which make this roast very juicy and flavorful. Even after thorough braising, this roast retains a distinctive strip of connective tissue, which is not unpleasant to eat. This roast may also be sold as a blade roast.

The chuck-eye pot roast (right) is the fattiest of the three roasts and the most commonly available. Its high proportion of fat gives pot roast great flavor and tenderness. Because of its thicker size, this roast takes the longest to cook.

SEVEN-BONE POT ROAST **TOP-BLADE POT ROAST** **CHUCK-EYE POT ROAST**

just ¼ cup of liquid. Naively assuming that more is always better, we continued to increase the amount of water, but to no better effect.

Next we tested different liquids, hoping to add flavor to the roast and sauce. Along with our old standby, water, we tested red wine, low-sodium canned chicken broth, and low-sodium canned beef broth. Red wine had the most startling effect on the meat, penetrating it with a potent flavor that most tasters agreed was "good, but not traditional pot roast." However, tasters did like the flavor of a little red wine added to the sauce after the pot roast was removed from the pan. Each broth on its own failed to win tasters over completely—the chicken broth was rich but gave the dish a characteristic poultry flavor, while the beef broth tasted sour when added solo. In the end, we found that an equal amount of each did the job, with the beef broth boosting the depth of flavor and the chicken broth tempering any sourness.

Because different amounts of liquid would have to be added to the pot depending on the size and shape of each individual roast, we chose to use 1 cup each of chicken and beef broth, and to add enough water to bring the liquid level halfway up the sides of the roast.

Trying to boost the flavor of the sauce even more, we added the basic vegetables—carrot, celery, onion, and garlic—to the pot as the meat braised. Unfortunately, the addition of raw vegetables made the pot roast taste more like a vegetable stew. We then tried sautéing them until golden brown and found that the caramelized flavor of the vegetables added another layer of flavor to the sauce. Tomato paste, an ingredient found in several recipes, was not a welcome addition. Tasters appreciated the sweetness it added but not the "tinny" flavor. A little sugar (2 teaspoons) added to the vegetables as they cooked gave the sauce the sweetness tasters were looking for.

HOW TO TIE A TOP-BLADE ROAST

1. Slip a 6-foot piece of twine under the roast and tie a double knot.

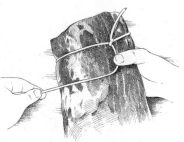

2. Hold the twine against the meat and loop the long end of the twine under and around the roast.

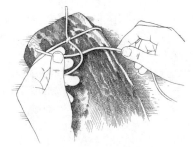

3. Run the long end through the loop.

4. Repeat this procedure down the length of the roast.

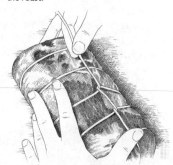

5. Roll the roast over and run the twine under and around each loop.

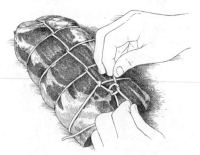

6. Wrap the twine around the end of the roast, flip over the roast, and tie to the original knot.

Some recipes thicken the sauce with a mixture of equal parts butter and flour (*beurre manié*); others use a slurry of cornstarch mixed with a little braising liquid. Both techniques made the sauce more gravy-like than we preferred, and we didn't care for the dilution of flavor. We chose to remove the roast from the pot, then reduce the liquid over high heat until the flavors were well concentrated and the texture more substantial.

As for the best cooking method for pot roast, there are two schools of thought: on the stove or in the oven. After a few rounds of stovetop cooking,

SCIENCE: The Mystery of Braising

Braising—searing meat, partially submerging it in liquid in a sealed pot, and then cooking it until fork-tender—is a classic technique used for tough cuts of meat. Pot roast is the most familiar of these dishes, but this category also includes braised brisket (both plain and corned) as well as other boiled dinners, braised ribs, and shanks.

A variety of cooks have put forward theories about why and how braising (as opposed to roasting or boiling) works. We set out to devise a series of experiments that would explain the mystery of braising.

Before kitchen testing began, we researched the meat itself to better understand how it cooks. Meat (muscle) is made up of two major components: muscle fibers, the long thin strands visible as the "grain" of meat, and connective tissue, the membranous, translucent film that covers the bundles of muscle fiber and gives them structure and support. Muscle fiber is tender because of its high water content (up to 78 percent). Once meat is heated beyond about 120 degrees, the long strands of muscle fiber contract and coil, expelling moisture in much the same way that it's wrung out of a towel. In contrast, connective tissue is tough because it is composed primarily of collagen, a sturdy protein that is in everything from the cow's muscle tendons to its hooves. When collagen is cooked until its temperature exceeds 140 degrees, it starts to break down to gelatin, the protein responsible for the tender, rich meat and thick sauces of braised dishes such as pot roast.

In essence, then, as meat cooks, it both dries out (the meat fibers lose moisture) and becomes softer (the collagen melts). That is why, depending on the cut, meat is best either when cooked rare or when pot-roasted—cooked to the point at which the collagen dissolves completely. Anything in between is dry and tough, the worst of both worlds.

This brings us to why braising is an effective cooking technique for tough cuts of meat. To determine the relative advantages of roasting, braising, and boiling, we constructed a simple test. One roast was cooked in a 250-degree oven, one was braised, and one was simmered in enough liquid to cover it. The results were startling. The dry-cooked roast never reached an internal temperature of more than 175 degrees, even after four hours, and the meat was tough and dry (see "Roasting versus Braising," below). To our great surprise, both the braised and boiled roasts cooked in about the same amount of time, and the results were almost identical. Cutting the roasts in half revealed little difference—both exhibited nearly full melting of the thick bands of connective tissue. As for the taste and texture of the meat, tasters were hard-pressed to find any substantial differences between the two. Both roasts yielded meat that was exceedingly tender, moist, and infused with rich gelatin.

The conclusion? Dry heat (roasting) is ineffective because the meat never gets hot enough to fully melt the collagen. It does not appear that steam heat (braising) enjoys any special ability to soften meat, compared with boiling. Braising has one advantage over simmering or boiling, however—half a pot of liquid reduces to a sauce much faster than a full pot.

ROASTING VERSUS BRAISING

A distinctive pattern of fat and connective tissue runs through the meat of a chuck roast (left). When cooked in dry heat, or roasted (middle), the fat and sinew do not break down sufficiently, even after many hours in the oven. Cooking the meat in moist heat, or braising (right), promotes a more complete breakdown of the fat and connective tissue, yielding very tender meat.

we felt that it was too difficult to maintain a steady, low temperature, so we began oven cooking, starting out at 250 degrees. This method required no supervision, just a turn of the meat every 30 to 40 minutes to ensure even cooking. We then tested higher temperatures to reduce the cooking time. Heat levels above 350 degrees boiled the meat to a stringy, dry texture because the exterior of the roast overcooked before the interior was cooked and tender. The magic temperature turned out to be 300 degrees—low enough to keep the meat at a low simmer, and high enough to shave a few more minutes off the cooking time.

As noted above, pot roast is well-done meat—meat cooked to an internal temperature above 165 degrees. Up to this point, we were bringing the meat to an internal temperature of 200 to 210 degrees, the point at which the fat and connective tissue begin to melt. In a 300-degree oven, the roast came to that temperature in a neat 2½ hours, by no means a quick meal but still a relatively short time in which to cook a pot roast. But we still had not achieved our goal of fall-apart tenderness. We went back and reviewed our prior testing to see what we might have missed.

Once in a great while in the test kitchen we happen upon a true "Eureka!" moment, when a chance test result leads to a breakthrough cooking technique. Some days before, we had forgotten to remove one of the roasts from the oven, allowing it to cook one hour longer than intended. Racing to the kitchen with our instant-read thermometer, we found the internal temperature of the roast was still 210 degrees, but the meat had a substantially different appearance and texture. The roast was so tender that it was starting to separate along its muscle lines. A fork poked into the meat met with no resistance and nearly disappeared into the flesh. We took the roast out of the pot and sliced into it. Nearly all the fat and connective tissue had dissolved into the meat, giving each bite a soft, silky texture and rich, succulent flavor. We "overcooked" several more roasts. Each roast had the same great texture. The conclusion? Not only do you have to cook pot roast until it reaches 210 degrees internally, but the meat has to remain at that temperature for a full hour. In other words, cook the pot roast until it's done—and then keep on cooking!

Simple Pot Roast
SERVES 6 TO 8

Our favorite cut for pot roast is a chuck-eye roast. Most markets sell this roast with twine tied around the center (see the photo on page 157); if necessary, do this yourself. Seven-bone and top-blade roasts are also good choices for this recipe. Remember to add only enough water to come halfway up the sides of these thinner roasts, and begin checking for doneness after two hours. If using a top-blade roast, tie it before cooking (see the illustrations on page 158) to keep it from falling apart.

PLANNING AHEAD: Simple Pot Roast can be prepared through step 3, stored in an airtight container, and refrigerated for up to 5 days. Spoon off any hardened fat from the top and bring the pot roast back to a simmer over medium-low heat in a covered Dutch oven. Add broth or water to adjust the consistency, if necessary, and continue with step 4. It may also be frozen for up to 3 months. (The root vegetable variation, however, does not freeze well.)

1	boneless chuck-eye roast (about 3½ pounds), trimmed of excess fat
	Salt and ground black pepper
2	tablespoons vegetable oil
1	medium onion, chopped medium
1	small carrot, peeled and chopped medium
1	small celery rib, chopped medium
2	medium garlic cloves, minced or pressed through a garlic press
2	teaspoons sugar
1	cup low-sodium chicken broth
1	cup low-sodium beef broth
1	sprig fresh thyme
1–1½	cups water
¼	cup dry red wine

1. Adjust an oven rack to the middle position and heat the oven to 300 degrees. Dry the roast thoroughly with paper towels, then season it generously with salt and pepper.

2. Heat the oil in a large ovenproof Dutch oven over medium-high heat until shimmering

but not smoking. Brown the roast thoroughly on all sides, about 10 minutes, reducing the heat if the fat begins to smoke. Transfer the roast to a large plate; set aside.

3. Reduce the heat to medium; add the onion, carrot, and celery to the pot and cook, stirring occasionally, until they begin to brown, about 8 minutes. Add the garlic and sugar; cook until fragrant, about 30 seconds. Add the chicken and beef broths and thyme, scraping the pan bottom and edges with a wooden spoon to loosen the browned bits. Return the roast and any accumulated juices to the pot; add enough water to come halfway up the sides of the roast. Cover, bring the liquid to a simmer over medium heat, and then transfer the pot to the oven. Cook, turning the roast every 30 minutes, until fully tender (a meat fork or sharp knife slips easily in and out of the meat), 3½ to 4 hours.

4. Transfer the roast to a carving board; tent with foil to keep warm. Allow the liquid in the pot to settle about 5 minutes, then use a wide spoon to skim the fat off the surface; discard the thyme sprig. Boil over high heat until reduced to about 1½ cups, about 8 minutes. Add the wine and reduce to 1½ cups, about 2 minutes. Season with salt and pepper to taste.

5. Using a chef's knife or carving knife, cut the meat into ½-inch-thick slices, or pull apart into large pieces; transfer the meat to a warmed serving platter and pour about ½ cup of the sauce over the meat. Serve, passing the remaining sauce separately.

➤ VARIATIONS
Pot Roast with Root Vegetables
In this variation, carrots, potatoes, and parsnips are added near the end of cooking to make a complete meal.

1. Follow the recipe for Simple Pot Roast. In step 2, when the roast is almost tender (a sharp knife should meet little resistance), transfer the roast to a cutting board. Pour the braising liquid through a mesh strainer and discard the solids. Return the liquid to the empty pot and let it settle for 5 minutes; use a wide spoon to skim the fat off the surface. Return the roast to the liquid and add 8 medium carrots, peeled and sliced ½ inch thick

(about 3 cups), 1½ pounds small red potatoes, halved if larger than 1½ inches in diameter (about 5 cups), and 5 large parsnips, peeled and sliced ½ inch thick (about 3 cups), submerging them in the liquid. Continue to cook until the vegetables are almost tender, 20 to 30 minutes.

2. Transfer the roast to a carving board; tent with foil to keep warm. Add the wine and salt and pepper to taste; boil over high heat until the vegetables are fully tender, 5 to 10 minutes. Using a slotted spoon, transfer the vegetables to a warmed serving bowl or platter; using a chef's or carving knife, cut the meat into ½-inch-thick slices or pull apart into large pieces; transfer to the bowl or platter and pour about ½ cup of the sauce over the meat and vegetables. Serve, passing the remaining sauce separately.

Stracotto (Pot Roast with Mushrooms, Tomatoes, and Red Wine)
This is the Italian version of pot roast.

1	boneless chuck-eye roast (about 3½ pounds), trimmed of excess fat
	Salt and ground black pepper
2	tablespoons vegetable oil
1	medium onion, chopped medium
1	small carrot, peeled and chopped medium
1	small celery rib, chopped medium
10	ounces white button mushrooms, stems trimmed, brushed clean, and quartered
2	medium garlic cloves, minced or pressed through a garlic press
2	teaspoons sugar
½	cup low-sodium chicken broth
½	cup low-sodium beef broth
½	cup dry red wine
1	(14.5-ounce) can diced tomatoes
1	sprig fresh thyme
1 –1½	cups water
1	sprig fresh rosemary

1. Adjust an oven rack to the middle position and heat the oven to 300 degrees. Dry the roast thoroughly with paper towels, then season it generously with salt and pepper.

2. Heat the oil in a large ovenproof Dutch oven over medium-high heat until shimmering but not smoking. Brown the roast thoroughly on all sides, about 10 minutes, reducing the heat if the fat begins to smoke. Transfer the roast to a large plate; set aside.

3. Reduce the heat to medium, add the onion, carrot, celery, and mushrooms to the pot, and cook, stirring occasionally, until the vegetables begin to brown, about 8 minutes. Add the garlic and sugar and cook until fragrant, about 30 seconds. Add the chicken and beef broths, wine, tomatoes and their juices, and thyme, scraping the pan bottom and edges with a wooden spoon to loosen the browned bits. Return the roast and any accumulated juices to the pot. Add enough water to come halfway up the sides of the roast. Bring the liquid to a simmer over medium heat, then cover the pot tightly with the lid. Transfer the pot to the oven. Cook, turning the roast every 30 minutes, until fully tender (a meat fork or sharp knife slips easily in and out), 3½ to 4 hours.

4. Transfer the roast to a carving board and tent with foil to keep warm. Allow the liquid in the pot to settle for about 5 minutes, then use a wide spoon to skim the fat off the surface. Add the rosemary and boil over high heat until the liquid is reduced to about 1½ cups, about 8 minutes. Discard the thyme and rosemary sprigs. Season with salt and pepper to taste.

5. Using a chef's knife or carving knife, cut the meat into ½-inch-thick slices or pull it apart into large pieces. Transfer the meat to a warmed serving platter and pour the sauce and vegetables over it. Serve immediately.

BRAISED SHORT RIBS

IN THE SUPERMARKET MEAT CASE, SHORT RIBS are little understood, rather intimidating hunks of meat and bone that are frequently shunned. But braise them, and they become tender and succulent. Then douse them with a velvety sauce containing all the rich, bold flavors from the braise, and they are as satisfying as beef stew, but with much more panache. All of this, however, comes at a price: short ribs are outrageously fatty. The challenge is to get them to give up their fat.

The first step in most braises is browning the meat. Browning adds color and flavor, but in the case of short ribs it also presents an opportunity to render some of the fat. We tried browning both on the stovetop and in the oven and quickly became proponents of oven browning. As long as you own a roasting pan large enough to hold all of the ribs in a single layer, you can use the oven to brown them in just one batch. This eliminates the need to brown in multiple batches on the stove, which can create a greasy, splattery mess and result in burnt drippings in the bottom of the pot. In the oven, the ribs can brown for a good long time to maximize rendering. (Because they brown unattended, you can use that time to prepare the other ingredients for the braise.) The single inconvenience of oven browning is deglazing the roasting pan on the stovetop, which makes a burner-worthy roasting pan a prerequisite.

Like a beef stew, short ribs need aromatic vegetables. After having made a couple of batches with onions only, we chose to use a combination of onions, carrots, celery, and garlic for full, round flavor.

Braising liquids required only a cursory investigation. Homemade beef stock was out of the question because just about no one makes it. Based on previous tastings in the test kitchen, we also discounted canned beef broth. Canned chicken broth, however, offered sufficient backbone and, when enriched by the flavor and body contributed by the short ribs themselves, made for a rich, robust sauce. We began using a combination of red wine, chicken broth, and water. We eventually eliminated the water, but the sauce, despite the abundance of aromatics and herbs, remained strangely hollow and lacking. All along we had been using a cheap, hardly potable wine. After stepping up to a good, solid one worthy of drinking, the sauce improved dramatically; it had the complexity and resonance that we were seeking.

To transform the braising liquid into the sauce we were after, we needed to thicken it. After various experiments, we found that adding flour to the sautéed vegetables before pouring in the liquid resulted in a sauce that was lustrous and had the perfect consistency.

~

Short Ribs Braised in Red Wine with Bacon, Parsnips, and Pearl Onions

SERVES 6

Even well browned short ribs can release a lot of fat when braised, so it is important to thoroughly skim the braising liquid before serving. Though this recipe and the one that follows call for widely available English-style short ribs, both recipes will also work with flanken-style short ribs (see page 164 for more information about short ribs). We like to serve these short ribs with mashed potatoes, but they also taste good over egg noodles.

PLANNING AHEAD: Short ribs can be stored in an airtight container and refrigerated for up to 5 days, though the garnish should not be made ahead of time. Store the meat in the broth, spoon off any hardened fat from the top, and bring the meat and broth back to a simmer over medium-low heat in a covered saucepan or Dutch oven. Add broth or water to adjust the consistency, if necessary. This dish may also be frozen for up to 3 months.

SHORT RIBS

6	pounds bone-in English-style short ribs, trimmed of excess fat and silver skin, or bone-in flanken-style short ribs (see page 164)
	Salt and ground black pepper
3	cups dry red wine
3	large onions, chopped medium
2	medium carrots, peeled and chopped medium
1	large celery rib, chopped medium
9	medium garlic cloves, chopped
1/4	cup all-purpose flour
4	cups low-sodium chicken broth
1	(14.5-ounce) can diced tomatoes
1 1/2	tablespoons minced fresh rosemary leaves
1	tablespoon minced fresh thyme leaves
3	bay leaves
1	teaspoon tomato paste

BACON, PARSNIP, AND PEARL ONION GARNISH

6	ounces (about 6 slices) bacon, cut into 1/2-inch pieces
4	medium parsnips, peeled and cut diagonally into 1/2-inch pieces
8	ounces frozen pearl onions (do not thaw)
1/4	teaspoon sugar
1/4	teaspoon salt
6	tablespoons minced fresh parsley leaves

1. FOR THE RIBS: Adjust an oven rack to the lower-middle position and heat the oven to 450 degrees. Arrange the short ribs, bone-side down, in a single layer in a large flameproof roasting pan; season with salt and pepper to taste. Roast until the meat begins to brown, about 45 minutes; drain off all liquid and fat with a bulb baster. Return the pan to the oven and continue to cook until the meat is well browned, 15 to 20 minutes longer. (For flanken-style short ribs, arrange the ribs in a single layer in a large flameproof roasting pan; season with salt and pepper. Roast until the meat begins to brown, about 45 minutes; drain off all liquid and fat with a bulb baster. Return the pan to the oven and continue to cook until the meat is browned, about 8 minutes; flip each piece and cook until the second side is browned, about 8 minutes longer.) Transfer the ribs to a large plate; set aside. Drain the fat into a small bowl and reserve. Reduce the oven temperature to 300 degrees. Place the roasting pan on two stovetop burners set at medium heat; add the wine and bring to a simmer, scraping up the browned bits on the pan bottom with a wooden spoon. Set the roasting pan with the wine aside.

2. Heat 2 tablespoons of the reserved fat in a large ovenproof Dutch oven over medium-high heat; add the onions, carrots, and celery. Cook, stirring occasionally, until the vegetables soften, about 12 minutes. Add the garlic and cook until fragrant, about 30 seconds. Stir in the flour until combined, about 45 seconds. Stir in the wine from the roasting pan, the chicken broth, tomatoes, rosemary, thyme, bay leaves, tomato paste, and salt and pepper to taste. Bring to a boil and add the short ribs, completely submerging the meat in the liquid; return the liquid

to a boil, cover the pot, place it in the oven, and simmer until the ribs are tender, about 2 to 2½ hours.

3. Transfer the ribs from the pot to a large plate, removing the excess vegetables that may cling to the meat; discard any loose bones that have fallen away from the meat. Tent the meat with aluminum foil and set aside. Strain the braising liquid into a medium bowl, pressing out the liquid from the solids; discard the solids; set aside.

4. TO PREPARE THE GARNISH AND FINISH THE DISH: Cook the bacon in a Dutch oven over medium heat until just crisp, about 10 minutes; remove with a slotted spoon to a plate lined with paper towels. Add the parsnips, pearl onions, sugar, and salt to the Dutch oven; increase the heat to high and sauté, stirring occasionally, until browned, about 5 minutes. Meanwhile, spoon off and discard the solidified fat from the reserved braising liquid. Add the defatted liquid to the Dutch oven and bring to a simmer, stirring occasionally; season with salt and pepper to taste. Submerge the ribs in the liquid and return to a simmer. Reduce the heat to medium and cook, partially covered, until the ribs are heated through and the onions and parsnips are tender, about 5 minutes longer; gently stir in the bacon. Divide the ribs, vegetables, and sauce among individual bowls, sprinkle each with 1 tablespoon of the parsley, and serve.

➤ VARIATION

Porter-Braised Short Ribs with Prunes, Brandy, and Lemon Essence

Brandy-soaked prunes take the place of vegetables here, so this version is particularly suited to a mashed root vegetable or potato accompaniment. Use a dark, mildly assertive beer, not a light lager.

PRUNE, BRANDY, AND LEMON ESSENCE GARNISH

½	cup brandy
8	ounces pitted prunes, each prune halved
2	teaspoons brown sugar
	Salt and ground black pepper
2	teaspoons grated lemon zest
6	tablespoons minced fresh parsley leaves

1. Follow the recipe for Short Ribs Braised in Red Wine with Bacon, Parsnips, and Pearl Onions, substituting 3 cups porter beer for the red wine, eliminating the rosemary, and substituting 2 tablespoons Dijon mustard and 2 teaspoons Worcestershire sauce for the tomato paste. Continue with the recipe through step 3.

2. TO PREPARE THE GARNISH AND FINISH THE DISH: Bring the brandy to a boil in a small saucepan; off the heat, add the prunes and let stand until they are plump and softened, about 15 minutes. Meanwhile, spoon off and discard the solidified fat

---

INGREDIENTS: Short Ribs

Short ribs are just what their name says they are, "short ribs," cut from any part along the length of the cow's ribs. They can come from the lower belly section or higher up toward the back, from the shoulder (or chuck) area, or from the forward midsection.

When we started testing short ribs, we went to the local grocery store and bought out their supply. What we brought back to the test kitchen were 2-to-4-inch lengths of wide, flat rib bone, to which a rectangular plate of fatty meat was attached (see the photo below left). We also ordered short ribs from the butcher. Imagine our confusion when these turned out to be long, continuous pieces of meat, about ¾ inch thick, that had been cut across the ribs and grain and that included two or three segments of rib bone (see the photo below right). The former, we learned, are sometimes called English-style short ribs, and the latter are called flanken-style short ribs.

We braised both types of ribs. The ones from the butcher were favored by most tasters because the relatively thin, across-the-grain cut made the meat more pleasant to eat; the supermarket ribs were a bit stringier because they contained longer segments of grain. Both types were equally tender and good, but considering the cost ($5.99 versus $2.99 per pound) and effort (special order) required to procure the butcher-cut specimens, we decided to go with the supermarket variety.

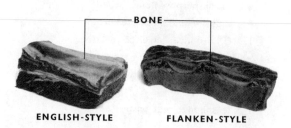

BONE

ENGLISH-STYLE   FLANKEN-STYLE

from the braising liquid. Bring the braising liquid to a boil in a Dutch oven over medium-high heat, stirring occasionally. Add the brandy, prunes, and brown sugar; season with salt and pepper to taste. Submerge the ribs in the liquid and return to a simmer. Reduce the heat to medium-low and cook, partially covered, until the ribs are heated through, about 5 minutes longer; gently stir in the lemon zest. Divide the ribs, vegetables, and sauce among individual bowls, sprinkle each with 1 tablespoon of the parsley, and serve.

GROUND BEEF CHILI

LIKE POLITICS, CHILI PROVOKES HEATED debate. Some purists insist that a chili that contains beans or tomatoes is just not chili. Others claim that homemade chili powder is essential or that ground meat is taboo. But there is one kind of chili that almost every American has eaten (or made) at one time or another. It's the kind of chili you liked as a kid and still see being served at Super Bowl parties. Made with ground meat, tomatoes, and store-bought chili powder, this thick, fairly smooth chili is spiced but not spicy. It is basic grub (and it can be great grub) that's not intended to fuel impassioned exchanges over the merits of ancho versus New Mexico chiles.

Although this simple chili should come together easily, it shouldn't taste as if it did. The flavors should be rich and balanced, the texture thick and lush. Unfortunately, many "basic" recipes yield a pot of underspiced, underflavored chili reminiscent of Sloppy Joes. We set out to develop a no-fuss chili that tasted far better than the sum of its common parts and could be thrown into the oven to simmer away until done—without an iota of attention.

Most of the recipes for this plain-spoken chili begin by sautéing onions and garlic. Tasters liked red bell peppers added to these aromatics but rejected other options, including green bell peppers, celery, and carrots. After this first step, things became less clear. The most pressing concerns were the spices (how much and what kind) and the meat (how much ground beef and whether or not

to add another meat). There were also the cooking liquid (what kind, if any) and the proportions of tomatoes and beans to consider.

Our first experiments with these ingredients followed a formula we had seen in lots of recipes: 2 pounds ground beef, 3 tablespoons chili powder, 2 teaspoons ground cumin, and 1 teaspoon each red pepper flakes and dried oregano. Many recipes add the spices after the beef has been browned, but we knew from experience with curry that ground spices taste better when they get direct contact with hot cooking oil.

To see if this was true for chili, we set up a test with three pots of chili: one with the ground spices added before the beef, one with the spices added after the beef, and a third in which the spices were toasted in a separate skillet and added to the pot after the beef. The batch made with the spices added after the beef tasted weak. The batch made with the spices toasted in a separate pan was better, but the clear favorite was the batch made with spices added directly to the pot before the beef. In fact, subsequent tests revealed that the spices should be added at the outset—along with the aromatics—to develop their flavors fully.

Although we didn't want a chili with killer heat, we did want real warmth and depth of flavor. Commercial chili powder is typically 80 percent ground dried red chiles mixed with garlic powder, onion powder, oregano, ground cumin, and salt. To boost flavor, we increased the amount of chili powder from 3 to 4 tablespoons, added more cumin and oregano, and tossed in some cayenne for heat. We tried some more exotic spices, including cinnamon (which was deemed "awful"), allspice (which seemed "out of place"), and coriander (which "added some gentle warmth"). Only the coriander became part of our working recipe.

It was now time to consider the meat. The quantity (2 pounds) seemed ideal when paired with two 15.5-ounce cans of beans. Tests using 90 percent, 85 percent, and 80 percent lean ground beef showed that there is such a thing as too much fat. Pools of orange oil floated to the top of the chili made with ground chuck (80 percent lean beef). At the other end of the spectrum, the chili made with 90 percent lean beef was a tad bland—not bad, but not as full flavored as the chili made with 85 percent lean beef, which was our final choice.

We wondered if another type of meat should be used in place of some of the ground beef. After trying batches of chili made with ground pork, diced pork loin, sliced sausage, and sausage removed from its casing and crumbled, tasters preferred the hearty flavor and creamy texture of an all-beef chili. (The exception was one batch to which we added bacon; many tasters liked its smoky flavor, so we made a version with bacon and black beans as a variation on the master recipe.)

Some of us have always made chili with beer and been satisfied with the results. Nodding to the expertise of others, we tried batches made with water (too watery), chicken broth (too "chickeny" and dull), beef broth (too tinny), wine (too acidic), and no liquid at all except for that in the tomatoes (beefy tasting and by far the best). When we tried beer, we were surprised to find that it subdued that great beefy flavor. We decided to keep the beer cold for dinnertime.

Tomatoes were definitely going into the pot, but we had yet to decide on the type and amount. We first tried two small (14.5-ounce) cans of diced tomatoes. This amount was clearly not enough. What's more, the tomatoes were too chunky, and they were floating in a thin sauce. We tried two 28-ounce cans of diced tomatoes, pureeing the contents of one can in the blender to thicken the sauce. Although the chunkiness was reduced, the sauce was still watery. Next we paired one can of tomato puree with one can of diced tomatoes, and, without exception, tasters preferred the thicker consistency. We generally don't like the slightly cooked flavor of tomato puree, but this recipe needed the body it provided. In any case, after the long simmering time, any such flavor was hard to detect.

With all of the stovetop cooking out of the way, we slid the chili into the oven to percolate. We tried a variety of temperatures until we found that 300 degrees kept the chili at a slow, occasionally bubbling simmer. At the one-hour mark, the chili still tasted a little raw; at two hours, it tasted great—sweet, rich, and fully blended, though a

little watery. We found that removing the Dutch oven's lid halfway through the cooking time allowed excess moisture to evaporate. This also proved a good juncture to give the chili a quick stir, which prevented the ground beef from settling to the bottom of the pot and possibly scorching.

Most recipes add the beans toward the end of cooking, the idea being to let them heat through without causing them to fall apart. But this method often makes for beans that are bland islands floating in a sea of highly flavorful chili. After testing several options, we found it best to add the beans with the tomatoes. The more time the beans spent in the pot, the better they tasted. In the end, we preferred dark red kidney beans or black beans because both keep their shape better than light red kidney beans, the other common choice.

With our recipe basically complete, it was time to try some of those offbeat additions to the pot that other cooks swear by, including cocoa powder, ground coffee beans, raisins, chickpeas, mushrooms, olives, and lima beans. Our conclusion? Each of these ingredients was either weird tasting or too subtle to make much difference. Lime wedges, passed separately at the table, both brightened the flavor of the chili and accentuated the heat of the spices. Our chili was now done. Although simple, it is, we hope, good enough to silence any debate.

~

Simple Beef Chili with Kidney Beans

SERVES 8 TO 10

Good choices for condiments include diced fresh tomatoes, diced avocado, sliced scallions, chopped red onion, chopped cilantro leaves, sour cream, and shredded Monterey Jack or cheddar cheese. If you are a fan of spicy food, consider using a little more of the red pepper flakes or cayenne, or both.

PLANNING AHEAD: Beef chili can be stored in an airtight container and refrigerated for up to 5 days (the flavor actually improves after sitting for at least a day). Spoon off any hardened fat from the top and bring the chili back to a simmer over medium-low heat in a covered saucepan or Dutch oven. Add broth or water to adjust the consistency, if necessary. It may also be frozen for up to 3 months.

2   tablespoons vegetable oil

2   medium onions, minced

I   red bell pepper, stemmed, seeded, and
    chopped medium

6   medium garlic cloves, minced or pressed
    through a garlic press

1/4 cup chili powder

I   tablespoon ground cumin

2   teaspoons ground coriander

I   teaspoon red pepper flakes

I   teaspoon dried oregano

1/2 teaspoon cayenne pepper

2   pounds 85 percent lean ground beef

2   (15.5-ounce) cans dark red kidney beans,
    drained and rinsed

I   (28-ounce) can diced tomatoes

I   (28-ounce) can tomato puree
    Salt

2   limes, cut into wedges

1. Adjust an oven rack to the lower-middle position and heat the oven to 300 degrees. Heat the oil in a large ovenproof Dutch oven over medium heat until shimmering but not smoking. Add the onions, bell pepper, garlic, chili powder, cumin, coriander, pepper flakes, oregano, and cayenne; cook, stirring occasionally, until the vegetables are softened and beginning to brown, about 10 minutes. Increase the heat to medium-high and add half of the beef; cook, breaking up the pieces with a wooden spoon, until no longer pink and just beginning to brown, about 4 minutes. Add the remaining beef and cook, breaking up the pieces with a wooden spoon, until no longer pink, about 4 minutes. Add the beans, tomatoes with their juice, tomato puree, and 1/2 teaspoon salt and bring to a boil.

2. Cover the pot and transfer to the oven. Cook for 1 hour, then remove the lid and stir to redistribute the meat and beans. Cook, uncovered, until the beef is tender and the chili is dark, rich, and slightly thickened, about 1 hour. Season with additional salt to taste. Serve with the lime wedges and condiments (see the headnote), if desired.

➤ VARIATION

Beef Chili with Bacon and Black Beans

Cut 8 ounces (about 8 slices) bacon into 1/2-inch pieces. Fry the bacon in a large ovenproof Dutch oven over medium heat, stirring frequently, until browned, about 8 minutes. Pour off all but 2 tablespoons fat, leaving the bacon in the pot. Follow the recipe for Simple Beef Chili with Kidney Beans, substituting the bacon fat in the Dutch oven for the vegetable oil and two 15.5-ounce cans of black beans for the kidney beans.

OSSO BUCO

OSSO BUCO, OR ITALIAN BRAISED VEAL SHANKS, is too venerable a dish to be fiddled with. When developing this recipe, we entered the kitchen with a bit of humility. We decided the best way to approach the dish was to perfect (and simplify, if possible) the cooking technique and to extract the most flavor from the simple ingredients: veal shanks (which are browned), aromatics (onions, carrots, and celery, all sautéed), and liquids (a blend of wine, stock, and tomatoes).

To start, we gathered three classic recipes and prepared each in the test kitchen. At the tasting, there was little consensus about these recipes, although white wine was clearly preferred to red wine. Tasters did, however, offer similar ideas as to what constitutes the perfect osso buco: it should be rich in flavor and color and somewhat brothy, but not stewy. This first goal is the reason why we prefer osso buco to veal stews made with boneless shoulder meat. While shoulder meat can be a bit wan, veal shanks are robust and the bone adds tremendous flavor to the stewing liquid. With these traits in mind, we created a rough working recipe and set out to explore the two main components in this dish—the veal shanks and the braising liquid.

Most recipes we reviewed call for shanks from the upper portion of the hind leg cut into pieces between 1 and 1½ inches thick. We found that purchasing shanks is tricky, even when we special-ordered them. From one market, we received stunning shanks with a lovely pinkish blush that were ideal except for the weight. Each shank weighed between 12 and 16 ounces—too large for individual servings. Part of the charm of osso buco is receiving an individual shank as a portion. We concluded that shanks should weigh 8 to 10 ounces (with the bone) and no more. At another market, the shanks were generally in the ideal weight range, but the butchering job was less than perfect. In the same package, shank widths varied from 1 to 2½ inches and were occasionally cut on an extreme bias, making it difficult to tie them (we'll explain tying shortly) and sear them evenly.

The first step, then, is to shop carefully. We found a thickness of 1½ inches and a weight of 8 ounces to be ideal. Make sure all the shanks you buy are close to these specifications. Each shank should have two nicely cut, flat sides to facilitate browning.

Preparing the meat for braising was the first step. Most recipes call for tying the shanks and dredging them in flour before searing. We found that tying a piece of butcher's twine around the equator of each shank does prevent the meat from falling apart and makes for a more attractive presentation. When we skipped this step, the meat fell off the bone and floated about the pot.

Although we do not generally dredge meat in flour before browning, we felt we should at least try it, considering that the majority of osso buco recipes include this step. Tasters felt that the meat floured before searing was gummy and lacked depth. The flour on the meat browns instead of the meat itself, and the flour coating may peel off during the long braising time.

To develop the best flavor in the shanks, we seasoned them heavily with salt and pepper and seared them until a thick, golden brown crust formed. We seared the shanks in two batches (even if they could all fit in the pan at the same time) so that we could deglaze the pan twice with wine, thereby enriching the braising liquid doubly.

The most difficult part of developing this recipe was attaining an ideal braising liquid and sauce. Braising, by design, is a relatively inexact cooking method because the rates at which the liquid reduces can vary greatly. Some of the initial recipes we tried yielded far too much liquid, which was thin in both flavor and texture. In other cases, the liquid nearly evaporated by the time the meat was tender. We needed to create a foolproof, flavorful braising liquid and cooking technique that would produce a suitable volume of rich sauce and would not need a lot of last-minute finessing.

We experimented with numerous techniques to attain our ideal liquid, including reductions before braising and after braising (with the aromatics and without) and a reduction of the wine to a syrup during the deglazing process. In the end, we settled on the easiest method—natural reduction in the oven. The seal on most Dutch ovens is not perfectly tight, so the liquid reduces as the osso buco cooks. We found further simmering on the stovetop to be unnecessary as long as we started out with the right amount of liquid in the pot.

The braising liquid traditionally starts with veal stock. Since few cooks have homemade veal stock on hand and it cannot be found canned, we knew that chicken broth would be our likely starting point. Two cups seemed liked the right amount, and further tests confirmed this. To enrich the flavor of the broth, we used a hefty amount of chopped onions, carrots, and celery. Tasters liked the large amount of garlic in one recipe, so we finely chopped about five cloves and added them to the pot prior to the stock. We rounded out the flavors with two bay leaves.

Early in our tests, we hoped to write the recipe in even amounts, using whole vegetables, one can of stock, one bottle of wine, etc. But an entire bottle of wine proved overwhelming. The resulting sauce was dominated by acidity. Some testers also felt that the meat was tougher than in previous batches with less wine. We scaled the wine back to 2½ cups, about two thirds of a bottle, and were happy with the results. More than half of the wine is used to deglaze the pot between searing batches of veal shanks and thus the final dish is not as alcoholic or liquidy as it might seem.

With the wine and broth amounts settled, we needed to figure out how to best incorporate the tomatoes. Most tasters did not like too much tomato because they felt it easily overwhelmed the other flavors. Fresh tomatoes are always a gamble outside of the summer months, so we chose canned, diced tomatoes, thoroughly strained of their juice. This approach worked out well, and the tomatoes did not overwhelm the sauce.

We still needed to figure out the ideal braising time. Several sources suggested cooking osso buco to an almost "pulled-pork" consistency. Tasters loved the meat cooked this way, but it was less than attractive—broken down and pot-roast-like. We wanted compact meat firmly attached to the bone, so we cooked the meat just until it was fork-tender but still clinging to the bone. Two hours in the oven produced veal that was meltingly soft but still affixed to the bone. With some of the larger shanks, the cooking time extended to about 2½ hours.

We experimented with oven temperature and found that 325 degrees reduced the braising liquid to the right consistency and did not harm the texture of the meat. While beef stews are best cooked at 300 degrees, veal shanks have so much collagen and connective tissue that they can be braised at a slightly higher temperature.

Just before serving, osso buco is sprinkled with gremolata—a mixture of minced garlic, parsley, and lemon zest. We were surprised to find variations on this classic trio. A number of recipes include orange zest, mixed with lemon zest or on its own. Other recipes include anchovies. We tested three gremolatas: one traditional, one with orange zest mixed equally with lemon zest, and one with anchovies. Tasters liked all three but favored the traditional version.

In some recipes the gremolata is used as a garnish, and in others it is added to the pot just before serving. We chose a compromise approach, stirring half the gremolata into the pot and letting it stand for five minutes so that the flavors of the garlic, lemon, and parsley would permeate the dish. We sprinkled the remaining gremolata on individual servings for a hit of freshness.

EQUIPMENT: Kitchen Tongs

Tongs are one of our favorite tools in the kitchen, perfect for a variety of tasks, from grilling to stirring pasta. Sometimes the more thought you give something the better, but sometimes good enough is best left alone. The latter seems to be the case with tongs. We found that the simplest design—your basic, lightweight, agile-yet-sturdy restaurant tongs—easily bested all the new, "improved" tongs we tried. Testers dismissed tricky self-locking mechanisms, curved handles, nylon pincers, tight springs, and excess heft.

Oversized tweezers, for example, are not a good substitute for tongs, and the heft you value in a saucepan or stockpot is not a good quality when it comes to tongs. Heavy tongs (one pair weighed 10 ounces, twice as heavy as our top-rated models)

became tiresome to use, as did tongs with too much tension built into their springs. Tongs that respond to a light touch are the easiest and most comfortable to use as well as the most effective. We also liked tongs with the widest span between the pincers (6 inches or more was ideal) since they could hold big items, such as a roast.

To test the effectiveness of the tongs (and the one pair of tweezers), we used them to pick up slim asparagus spears, retrieve corn on the cob from boiling water, sauté slippery scallops, pan-fry breaded chicken cutlets, move ramekins filled with water and chocolate mousse from one spot to another, and turn a 3-pound pot roast. One lightweight pair of restaurant-style stainless steel tongs passed every test, and another, similar pair came very close.

THE BEST KITCHEN TONGS

EDLUND LOCKING 12-INCH TONGS
These stainless steel tongs turned in a perfect score, excelling in each and every test. They're light, agile, and easy to use.

OXO GOOD GRIPS LOCKING 12-INCH TONGS
These stainless steel tongs with rubber handles merited a perfect score in all tests but one—grasping a filled ramekin. Since most cooks are unlikely to use tongs for this purpose, we gave these tongs high marks anyway.

Osso Buco

SERVES 6

To keep the meat attached to the shank bone during the long simmering process, tie a piece of twine around the thickest portion of each shank before it is browned. Use a zester, vegetable peeler, or paring knife to remove the zest from a single lemon and then mince it with a chef's knife. Osso buco is traditionally served with risotto alla Milanese (saffron-flavored risotto made with meat stock). We have an oven-baked version of risotto alla Milanese on page 264.

PLANNING AHEAD: Osso buco may be prepared through step 3 up to 3 days ahead of time and stored in an airtight container in the refrigerator. The meat should be stored and reheated in the braising liquid to prevent it from drying out. Scrape the chilled fat off the top and bring the osso buco to a simmer over medium-low heat in a covered Dutch oven, adding broth or water to adjust the consistency, if necessary. The gremolata should be prepared just before serving.

OSSO BUCO

6	veal shanks (8 to 10 ounces and 1½ inches thick each), tied around the equator with butcher's twine
	Salt and ground black pepper
6	tablespoons vegetable oil
2½	cups dry white wine
2	medium onions, chopped medium
2	medium carrots, peeled and chopped medium
2	medium celery ribs, chopped medium
6	medium garlic cloves, minced or pressed through a garlic press
2	cups low-sodium chicken broth
2	bay leaves
1	(14.5-ounce) can diced tomatoes, drained

GREMOLATA

3	medium garlic cloves, minced or pressed through a garlic press
2	teaspoons minced lemon zest
¼	cup minced fresh parsley leaves

1. FOR THE OSSO BUCO: Adjust an oven rack to the lower-middle position and heat the oven to 325 degrees.

2. Heat a large ovenproof Dutch oven over medium-high heat until it is very hot. Meanwhile, dry the shanks thoroughly with paper towels, then season generously with salt and pepper. Add 2 tablespoons of the oil to the Dutch oven and swirl to coat the pan bottom. Place three shanks in a single layer in the Dutch oven and cook until they are golden brown on one side, about 5 minutes. Flip the shanks and cook on the second side until golden brown, about 5 minutes longer. Transfer the shanks to a bowl and set aside. Off the heat, add ½ cup of the wine to the Dutch oven, scraping the bottom with a wooden spoon to loosen any browned bits. Pour the liquid into the bowl with the browned shanks. Return the pot to medium-high heat, add 2 more tablespoons oil, and heat until shimmering. Brown the remaining shanks, about 5 minutes for each side. Transfer the shanks to the bowl with the other shanks. Off the heat, add 1 cup wine to the pot, scraping the bottom to loosen the browned bits. Pour the liquid into the bowl with the shanks.

3. Set the pot over medium heat. Add the remaining 2 tablespoons oil and heat until the oil is shimmering. Add the onions, carrots, and celery and cook, stirring occasionally, until soft and lightly browned, about 9 minutes. Add the garlic and cook until lightly browned, about 1 minute longer. Increase the heat to high and stir in the chicken broth, remaining 1 cup wine, juices from the veal shanks, and bay leaves. Add the tomatoes and veal shanks to the pot (the liquid should just cover the shanks). Cover the pot, bring to a simmer with the lid slightly ajar, and place the pot in the oven. Cook the shanks until the meat is easily pierced with a fork, but not falling off bone, about 2 hours.

4. FOR THE GREMOLATA: Combine the garlic, lemon zest, and parsley in a small bowl. Stir half of the gremolata into the pot, reserving the rest for garnish. Season with salt and pepper to taste. Let the osso buco stand, uncovered, for 5 minutes.

5. Remove the shanks from the Dutch oven, cut off and discard the butcher's twine, and place 1 veal shank in each bowl. Ladle some braising liquid over each shank and sprinkle with a portion of the remaining gremolata. Serve immediately.

BRAISED LAMB SHANKS

ONE OF THE GREAT PLEASURES OF COOKING is turning relatively tough cuts of meat into meltingly tender dishes. Among the most richly flavored of these tougher cuts is the lamb shank, which is simply the bottom portion of the fore or hind leg of a lamb.

Like other cuts of meat that come from the joints of animals, such as oxtails or short ribs, lamb shanks are extremely flavorful when properly cooked. This is because they contain a high proportion of connective tissue and fat, which break down during cooking and add flavor to the meat.

However, the presence of all this connective tissue and fat means that shanks can only be cooked using a long, slow, moist cooking method that will cause the connective tissue to disintegrate and render the fat without drying out the meat. The only practical cooking method for achieving this goal is braising, which means cooking the meat partially covered in liquid, usually in a closed container. Braising keeps the temperature of the meat relatively low—around the boiling point of water—for a long period, which is exactly what is needed to convert the tough collagen to tender gelatin.

While we obtained satisfactory results by braising shanks on top of the stove, we prefer braising in an oven because of its unique heating properties. With the heat coming from all directions, the meat cooks more evenly. This is a particular advantage, given that many pans have hot spots that cause them to heat unevenly on a burner.

Because of the high fat content of this cut, several straightforward precautions are necessary to keep the level of fat in the final product to a minimum. First, if your butcher has not already done so, take the time to trim the lamb shanks of the excess fat that encases the meat. Even a long, slow braise will not successfully render all of the exterior fat on a lamb shank. Trimming it helps you avoid that potential problem.

Browning the shanks well before braising them also helps render some of the exterior fat. The other advantage of browning is that it provides a great deal of flavor for the dish. Be sure to drain the fat from the pan after browning.

The third important step is to remove the fat from the braising liquid after the shanks have been cooked. To do this, take the shanks out of the braising liquid, strain out the vegetables, and allow the sauce to rest undisturbed for a short while. Then, using a ladle, carefully skim the fat that has risen to the surface and discard it. This process can be facilitated by transferring the sauce to a tall, narrow container before setting it aside to rest. If, after skimming the liquid, you find that it still has too much fat, you may repeat this step after 10 more minutes, although with most shanks this will not be necessary. Further, if the braise is prepared well in advance of serving, you may refrigerate the braising liquid, then remove the solidified fat from the top of the liquid.

The braising liquid, along with the aromatics you add to it, will greatly enhance the flavor of the entire dish. Stock is the traditional braising liquid because it adds textural richness as well as depth of flavor. As we have said before in these pages, making homemade stock is not practical. We recommend, therefore, using canned chicken broth, not beef broth, for this braise. The chicken broth complements the flavor of the lamb shanks.

Wine is a particularly good addition to the braising liquid, giving it both complexity and acid. The acid is especially important because of the richness of the lamb. Too little acid creates a dull, rather flat-tasting dish. On the other hand, too much acid results in a harsh, off-putting flavor. After trying different ratios, we found that 2 parts wine to 3 parts broth gives the best flavor. We found that either white wine or red works well, the difference being that red wine will give you a richer, deeper finish.

Whatever liquid you use for braising, we discovered, it should cover all but the top inch of the shanks. This is a departure from classic braising, where less liquid is used. We adopted this method after leaving shanks to braise in the oven, then returning some time later to find that the liquid had boiled away and the shanks were burned. Unless you are using a true braising pan with an extremely tight-fitting lid, a fair amount of liquid will escape during the cooking process. Using more liquid prevents the pan from drying out, no matter how loose the seal is.

Lamb shanks need not be served whole, though we prefer them this way for their dramatic appeal. Once the shanks are cooked and cooled, you may remove the meat from the bone before reincorporating it with the vegetables and sauce. The resulting stew-type dish will be less impressive in presentation but equally delicious. You may also vary the choice of herbs and spices according to your taste; we've included suggestions in the following recipes.

Lamb Shanks Braised in Red Wine

SERVES 6

If you're using smaller shanks than the ones called for in this recipe, reduce the initial braising time in step 3 from 1½ hours to 1 hour. Serve these braised shanks over mashed potatoes or polenta.

PLANNING AHEAD: Lamb shanks may be prepared through step 3 up to 3 days ahead of time. The meat should be stored and reheated in the braising liquid. When ready to serve, remove the solidified fat on the surface, then warm the dish over medium heat.

I	tablespoon olive oil
6	lamb shanks (³/₄ to I pound each), trimmed of excess fat
	Salt and ground black pepper
2	medium onions, sliced thick
3	medium carrots, peeled and cut crosswise into 2-inch pieces
2	celery ribs, cut crosswise into 2-inch pieces
4	medium garlic cloves, peeled
2	tablespoons tomato paste
2	teaspoons minced fresh thyme leaves
2	teaspoons minced fresh rosemary leaves
2	cups dry red wine
3	cups low-sodium chicken broth

1. Adjust an oven rack to the lower-middle position and heat the oven to 350 degrees. Heat the oil in a large ovenproof Dutch oven over medium-high heat until shimmering. Meanwhile, season both sides of the shanks generously with salt and pepper. Swirl to coat the pan bottom with the oil. Place 3 shanks in a single layer in the pan and cook, turning once, until nicely browned all over, about 7 minutes. Transfer the shanks to a plate and set aside. Brown the remaining shanks and transfer them to the plate.

2. Drain all but 2 tablespoons of fat from the pot. Add the onions, carrots, celery, garlic, tomato paste, herbs, and a light sprinkling of salt. Cook until the vegetables soften slightly, 3 to 4 minutes. Add the wine, then the broth, stirring with a wooden spoon to loosen the browned bits on the pan bottom. Bring the liquid to a simmer. Add the shanks and season with salt and pepper to taste.

3. Cover the pot and transfer it to the oven. Braise the shanks for 1½ hours. Uncover and continue braising until the shank tops are browned, about 30 minutes. Turn the shanks and braise until the other side is browned and the meat is fall-off-the-bone tender, 15 to 30 minutes longer.

4. Remove the pot from the oven and let the shanks rest in the sauce for at least 15 minutes. Carefully transfer the shanks to individual plates. Arrange a portion of the vegetables around each shank. With a large spoon or ladle, skim the excess fat from the braising liquid and adjust the seasonings. Spoon some of the braising liquid over each shank and serve immediately.

➤ VARIATION

Braised Lamb Shanks with Lemon and Mint

Grate the zest from 1 lemon, then cut the lemon into quarters. Follow the recipe for Lamb Shanks Braised in Red Wine, replacing the thyme and rosemary leaves with 1 tablespoon minced fresh mint leaves and replacing the red wine with dry white wine. Add the quartered lemon to the braising liquid in step 2. Proceed as directed, stirring the lemon zest and an additional 1 tablespoon minced fresh mint leaves into the sauce just before serving.

POZOLE

POZOLE IS THE MEXICAN NAME FOR BOTH
hominy (dried field corn kernels treated with
lime and boiled until tender but still chewy) and
a stew made with hominy and pork. The stew is
made throughout Mexico in several quite distinct
incarnations. *Pozole blanco* (white pozole) is prepared without any chiles. *Pozole rojo* (red pozole) is
made with dried red chiles, and *pozole verde* (green
pozole) is made with tomatillos, fresh green chiles,
and cilantro. Pozole blanco seems fairly bland
compared with the red and green versions, so we
decided to focus on the latter two styles.

Whether red or green, pozole should have a
complex, richly flavored broth with lots of body.
The meat, which is shredded, must be exceedingly
tender, while the hominy should be toothsome
and sweet. A garnish of chopped raw vegetables
(lettuce, radishes, and herbs) is added at the table.

Although pozole has become popular in the
United States, especially in the Southwest, most
American cooks balk at preparing traditional
recipes, many of which take 12 hours or more to
execute. One of the culprits here is the hominy.
If you begin with dried field corn, you must boil
it with slaked lime to loosen the hulls. You must
then wash the corn to remove the hulls, and pinch
the germ from each kernel by hand. Preparing
hominy can take an entire afternoon. We wanted
to figure out how to use canned, or precooked,
hominy to save time.

Another concern when making pozole is the
meat. In Mexico, pozole is traditionally made
with cuts rarely sold in American supermarkets
(unsmoked pig's feet and pig's head, for example).
We would have to find an acceptable substitute.

With these goals in mind, we started work on
a red pozole recipe. (We figured that green pozole
could be a variation of our red pozole.) The meat
issue seemed like the first one to tackle.

Authentic pozole is made with bones from the
head, neck, shank, and feet of the pig, supple-
mented with some boneless meat from the shoulder or loin. We wondered how important bones
were to this dish. We prepared one batch with
boneless shoulder meat only and another with a
bone-in shoulder roast. (We chose the shoulder

not only because of availability but because it has
consistently proven to be the best cut for stewing.)
The liquid of the pozole prepared without bones
was weak in flavor and thin in texture. The version made with the bone-in shoulder roast had a
distinctive, satisfying pork flavor. It was obvious
to tasters that bones are key to developing rich,
full-bodied pork flavor. In addition, the bones
released a large amount of gelatin that gave the
pozole a voluptuous body.

There are two cuts from the shoulder, Boston
butt and picnic roast (see the illustration on page
174). Since Boston butt is typically sold without
the bone, we decided to use the picnic roast. We
found that a 5-pound roast, once trimmed of its
thick skin and fat, yielded just under 3 pounds of
boneless meat—enough for the stew.

Pozole differs from other meat stews in that the
meat is shredded rather than cubed. The meat is
usually stewed in large chunks until it is tender
enough to pull apart by hand. Just to make sure
that tradition is best, we tried cutting the meat into
cubes before cooking it, but shredding the cubed
meat proved quite tedious. We then tried cooking
the roast whole, but this increased the cooking time
dramatically. Finally, we tried cutting the meat
into large chunks, following the natural lines of
the muscles as we removed the meat from the
bone. This approach worked best—the stewing
time was not excessive (two hours did the trick)
and the meat was easy to shred. The sizes and
shapes of these chunks varied from 3 by 1-inch
strips to 4-inch cubes. From a 5-pound roast we
obtained eight or nine randomly shaped chunks
plus the bone, which had some pieces of meat
tightly attached.

Pozole differs from most stews in another
regard. Stew meat is typically browned to enhance
the flavor of both the meat and the stewing liquid. In many pozole recipes, the meat is simply
added raw to the simmering liquid. The reason
is simple: Browning inhibits the shredding process and creates a firmer, crustier texture on the
outside of each piece of meat. Another choice is
to sweat the meat with some onions. We tried
both simmering and sweating and found that the
latter method developed more flavor in the liquid

without firming up the texture of the meat. Just make sure to cook the onions first so that they will release some liquid and thus prevent the meat from burning or scorching on the outside.

In addition to onions, garlic is the other aromatic ingredient typically added at the outset when making pozole. Once the onions are soft, the garlic goes into the pot and cooks just until fragrant. We found that gentle sweating, rather than browning, works best for both alliums.

Once the meat has been sweated, it's time to add the liquid and other seasonings. We tested water and canned chicken broth (figuring that homemade stock, while always good, wouldn't be necessary in such a highly flavored dish). Although the water was fine, the broth was superior, adding not only depth of flavor but body to the stewing liquid. Tomatoes also add moisture to this dish. Although some versions of red pozole reserve the tomatoes as part of the garnish, our tasters liked the tomatoes cooked right into the stew. The acidity of the tomatoes created a more lively dish. (Note that for green pozole, the tomatoes should be used as a garnish.)

Oregano is a signature ingredient in pozole. Several varieties are grown in Mexico, all of which differ from the Mediterranean oregano popular in this country. Mexican oregano does not have the anise compounds found in Mediterranean varieties. Its flavor is earthier and more potent. We tested pozole with dried Mexican, dried Mediterranean, and fresh Mediterranean oregano. (We were unable to purchase fresh Mexican oregano.) The dried Mediterranean oregano had a strong pizza-parlor flavor that was out of place in pozole. The fresh Mediterranean oregano was a better substitute for the dried Mexican oregano, which we prefer but which can be difficult to find.

The final component of the pozole to examine was the chiles. The red color comes from dried chiles, so we tested several possibilities; anchos, New Mexico reds, and pasillas. We removed stems and seeds from the dried chiles, soaked them in boiling water, and then pureed the chiles and soaking liquid to create a thick paste. (We tested toasting the chiles before soaking but found this step added little to this dish.) The paste was added to the pot once the meat was tender. We liked all three chiles but preferred the deep reddish brown color and rich, sweet, raisiny flavor of the anchos.

We also tested chili powder, sprinkling some into the pot once the onions, garlic, and meat had been sweated. Although the results weren't terrible, everyone in the test kitchen agreed that the pozole made with powder instead of a puree of whole chiles was less complex tasting and less appealing. It's worth spending the extra few minutes soaking and pureeing the anchos as directed in our recipe.

We found that it can be difficult to create a stew that pleases all tasters, especially when it comes to heat. For this reason, we think it makes sense to mix three quarters of the ancho chile puree into the pozole and serve the rest at the table with the other garnishes. Individuals who like spicy food can swirl extra chile puree into their bowls.

It was time to deal with the hominy. We started by preparing one batch of pozole with freshly rehydrated hominy (which took hours to prepare) and another batch with canned hominy (which took seconds to drain and rinse). The pozole with freshly cooked hominy was superb, but the pozole with canned hominy was pretty good. It was chewy (as hominy should be) and relatively sweet.

After a few more tests, we found that cooking the canned hominy in the stew for 40 to 45 minutes allows the hominy to soak up some of the flavorful broth. Don't try to cook canned hominy

BEST CUTS FOR PORK STEWS

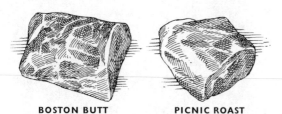

BOSTON BUTT   **PICNIC ROAST**

We found that cuts from the shoulder of the pig are the best for stewing. These cuts have enough fat to keep the meat moist as it cooks. (Loin cuts, on the other hand, are much too lean for stewing.) We recommend buying a boneless Boston butt (also called a pork shoulder blade Boston roast) for vindaloo and buying a picnic roast (also called a pork shoulder arm picnic roast) for pozole.

any longer. We found that the texture will suffer and the hominy will become soggy if simmered for an hour or more.

Canned hominy comes in white and yellow varieties, depending on the type of field corn used. We tested white and yellow hominy and found that both types are fine. Flavor isn't much of an issue; white and yellow hominy are both sweet and "corny" tasting. In terms of appearance, yellow hominy looks a bit better in green pozole, but the difference is slight. (The chile puree used to make red pozole makes it impossible to tell the difference between white and yellow hominy in this version.)

Our pozole recipe turned out to be remarkably simple—no more than an hour of hands-on work and a start-to-finish time of about three hours. Do take the 10 minutes needed to prepare all the suggested garnishes. The lettuce, radishes, cilantro, oregano, and lime juice all brighten this stew and turn it into a one-dish meal.

Pozole Rojo
SERVES 8 TO 10

This earthy-tasting, full-flavored pork and hominy stew originated in Mexico, although it is now just as popular in the American Southwest. This stew is typically accompanied by an assortment of crunchy toppings (each in a small bowl) and warm tortillas. Ancho chiles—dried, mild-flavored, brick-red chiles—are used to create a rich flavor and color in this dish. Mexicans use oregano liberally but their varieties are different from Mediterranean oregano. If available, use dried Mexican oregano; fresh Mediterranean oregano is a better substitute than dried.

PLANNING AHEAD: Pozole can be stored in an airtight container and refrigerated for up to 5 days. Spoon off any hardened fat from the top and bring the stew back to a simmer over medium-low heat in a covered saucepan or Dutch oven. Add broth or water to adjust the consistency, if necessary. The pozole may also be frozen for up to 3 months. Prepare the garnishes just before serving.

1	bone-in picnic roast (about 5 pounds)
	Salt and ground black pepper
2	tablespoons vegetable oil

2	medium-large onions, chopped coarse
5	medium garlic cloves, minced or pressed through a garlic press
1	(14.5-ounce) can diced tomatoes
1	tablespoon chopped fresh oregano leaves or 1 teaspoon dried Mexican oregano
6	cups low-sodium chicken broth
1½	cups water
2	ounces dried ancho chiles (about 3 large)
3	(15-ounce) cans white or yellow hominy, drained and rinsed

GARNISHES

2	limes, cut into quarters
½	head romaine lettuce, sliced crosswise into thin strips
6	medium radishes, sliced thin
1	small onion, minced
	Roughly chopped fresh cilantro leaves
	Chopped fresh oregano or dried Mexican oregano
¼	cup pureed ancho chiles (prepared with stew)
	Flour or corn tortillas, warmed

1. Adjust an oven rack to the lower-middle position and heat the oven to 300 degrees. Trim the thick skin and excess fat from the meat and cut along the muscles to divide the roast into large pieces of various sizes. Dry the meat thoroughly with paper towels, then season it generously with salt and pepper.

2. Heat the oil in a large ovenproof Dutch oven over medium heat until shimmering but not smoking. Add the onions and ¼ teaspoon salt. Cook, stirring frequently, until the onions have softened, about 4 minutes. Stir in the garlic and cook until fragrant, about 30 seconds.

3. Add the meat and stir often until the meat is no longer pink on the outside, about 8 minutes. Add the tomatoes, oregano, broth, and ½ teaspoon salt. Increase the heat to medium-high and bring to a simmer. With a large spoon, skim off any scum. Cover, place in the oven, and cook until the meat is very tender, about 2 hours.

4. Meanwhile, bring the water to a boil. Remove the stems and seeds from the ancho chiles and soak in a medium bowl with the boiling water

until soft, about 20 minutes. Puree the chiles and soaking liquid in a blender until smooth. Pour the mixture through a strainer and reserve ¼ cup of the pureed anchos for a garnish.

5. Remove the pot from the oven and remove the meat and bones from the stew. Stir in the hominy and the remaining ¾ cup pureed anchos. Cover and return the pot to the oven and cook until the hominy is hot and the flavors meld, about 45 minutes.

6. Meanwhile, when the meat is cool, shred it using your fingers or the tines of two forks; discard the bones. Stir the shredded meat into the stew. If serving immediately, spoon off any fat that rises to the top and then simmer until the meat is hot, about 10 minutes. Taste to adjust seasonings. Ladle the stew into individual bowls and serve immediately with the garnishes.

➤ VARIATION

Pozole Verde

Green pozole is lighter and more refreshing than its red cousin. It is prepared with cilantro, jalapeños, and tomatillos. These ingredients are cooked for a very short time; the flavors are bigger, brighter, and fresher tasting. A slightly different cast of characters accompanies this pozole as garnishes.

Follow the recipe for Pozole Rojo, eliminating the tomatoes and ancho chiles. While the pozole is simmering, puree 1 pound tomatillos, husked, washed, and quartered; 3 medium jalapeños, stemmed, seeded, and chopped coarse; ½ small onion, chopped coarse; and ½ cup water in a blender until smooth, 2 to 3 minutes. Add 2 bunches (about 5 cups) fresh cilantro leaves and stems and puree until smooth, about 2 minutes more. When the pozole comes out of the oven in step 5, remove the meat and stir in the hominy. Simmer as directed. Stir the tomatillo mixture into the stew along with the shredded meat and simmer until hot, 10 to 15 minutes. For the garnishes, add chopped tomato, chopped avocado, and minced jalapeño and eliminate the cilantro, oregano, and ancho chile puree.

PORK VINDALOO

VINDALOO IS A COMPLEX, SPICY DISH THAT originated in Goa, a region on India's western coast. Because Goa was once a Portuguese colony, much of the local cuisine incorporates Indian and Portuguese ingredients and techniques. In fact, the word *vindaloo* comes from the Portuguese words for wine vinegar (*vinho*) and garlic (*alhos*). In addition to these two ingredients, vindaloo gets its warm, pungent flavor from a mixture of spices (such as cumin and cardamom), chiles (usually in the form of cayenne and paprika), tomatoes, and mustard seeds. As for the main ingredient, although there are versions made with chicken, beef, or lamb (see Lamb Vindaloo, page 312), vindaloo is most often made with pork.

A well prepared vindaloo features tender meat in a thick, reddish-orange sauce with a delicately balanced flavor. The heat of the chiles is tamed by the sweetness of the aromatic spices and the acidity of the tomatoes and vinegar. Onions and garlic add pungency, while the mustard seeds lend their unique flavor and crunch.

Most vindaloo recipes we tested were pretty good but we noticed two recurring problems—tough and/or dry meat and muddled flavors. We decided to start with the meat component in this dish and then test the flavoring options.

Given our experience stewing beef, we figured that pork shoulder would make the best stew. To test this proposition, we stewed various cuts of pork from the shoulder and loin, including several kinds of chops. The shoulder cuts were far superior to the loin. Like beef chuck, pork shoulder has enough fat to keep the meat tender and juicy during the long cooking process.

Pork shoulder is often called Boston butt or Boston shoulder in markets. The picnic roast also comes from the shoulder. For vindaloo, a boneless Boston butt is your best option because there is less waste. (You can use a picnic roast, but the bone, skin, and thick layer of fat will need to be discarded.) As with beef, we recommend buying a boneless roast and cutting it into cubes yourself. When we purchased precut pork labeled "stew meat," the results were disappointing. The pieces were irregularly sized and seemed to have come from several parts of the animal. The resulting stew had some pieces that were dry and others that were overcooked.

We browned the pork to enhance its flavor and that of the stewing liquid. Make sure to leave a little room in the pot between the pieces of meat and plan on a total of at least seven minutes to get each pork cube well browned. We found that 2¾ pounds of pork cubes could be browned in two batches in a large Dutch oven and decided to limit the meat to this amount.

Spices are the cornerstones of this stew. We used a classic combination of sweet and hot spices, and found that we got the best flavor from small amounts of many spices, rather than larger amounts of fewer spices. For chile flavor, we used sweet paprika and cayenne. To give the stew its characteristic earthy qualities, we added cumin, along with sweet, aromatic cardamom and cloves. Mustard seeds, a spice used frequently in the cooking of South India, added pungency. Bay leaves rounded out the flavor of this stew and a sprinkling of cilantro just before serving lent the final fresh note.

Our next area of concern was the stewing liquid. Most traditional recipes simply use water. The theory is that water is a neutral medium that allows the flavors of the meat and spices to come through as clearly as possible. We wondered, though, if chicken broth would add richness and body to the stewing liquid. We prepared two batches—one with water, the other with chicken broth. Tasters felt that the chicken broth added complexity and fullness without calling attention to itself.

A hallmark of pork vindaloo is its interplay of sweet and sour flavors. Two tablespoons of red wine vinegar and 1 teaspoon of sugar provided the right balance. In order to give it time to soften and mix with the other flavors, we added the vinegar at the beginning of cooking. For further acidity, diced canned tomatoes, with their juices, were far less work than fresh tomatoes (which needed to be peeled and seeded) and performed admirably in taste tests.

Pork Vindaloo

SERVES 6 TO 8

If Boston butt proves difficult to find, a bone-in picnic roast will also work nicely in this recipe. In addition to the bone, a picnic roast typically is covered with skin and a thick layer of fat. When trimmed, a 5-pound picnic roast will yield the same amount of meat (about 2¾ pounds) as a 3-pound Boston butt. Premeasure the flour with the spices to add them easily. Serve with basmati rice.

PLANNING AHEAD: Pork Vindaloo can be stored in an airtight container and refrigerated for up to 5 days. Spoon off any hardened fat from the top and bring the stew back to a simmer over medium-low heat in a covered saucepan or Dutch oven. Add broth or water to adjust the consistency, if necessary. It may also be frozen for up to 3 months.

3	pounds boneless Boston butt roast (see page 174), trimmed and cut into 1½-inch cubes
	Salt and ground black pepper
3	tablespoons vegetable oil
3	medium onions, chopped coarse
8	medium garlic cloves, minced or pressed through a garlic press
3	tablespoons all-purpose flour
1	tablespoon sweet paprika
¾	teaspoon ground cumin
½	teaspoon ground cardamom
¼	teaspoon cayenne pepper
¼	teaspoon ground cloves
1½	cups low-sodium chicken broth
1	(14.5-ounce) can diced tomatoes
2	bay leaves
1	teaspoon sugar
2	tablespoons red wine vinegar
1	tablespoon mustard seeds
¼	cup minced fresh cilantro leaves

1. Adjust an oven rack to the lower-middle position and heat the oven to 300 degrees. Dry the meat thoroughly with paper towels, then season it generously with salt and pepper. Heat 1 tablespoon of the oil in a large ovenproof Dutch oven over medium-high heat until shimmering but not smoking. Add half of the meat to

the pot so that the individual pieces are close together but not touching. Cook, not moving the pieces until the sides touching the pot are well browned, 2 to 3 minutes. Turn each piece and continue cooking until most sides are well browned, about 5 minutes longer. Transfer the meat to a medium bowl, add another tablespoon oil to the pot, and swirl to coat the pan bottom. Brown the remaining meat; transfer the meat to the bowl and set aside.

2. Reduce the heat to medium, add the remaining tablespoon oil to the empty Dutch oven, and swirl to coat the pan bottom. Add the onions and ¼ teaspoon salt and cook, stirring frequently and vigorously, scraping the bottom and edges of the pot with a wooden spoon to loosen any browned bits, until the onions have softened, about 5 minutes. Stir in the garlic and cook until fragrant, about 30 seconds. Add the flour, paprika, cumin, cardamom, cayenne, and cloves. Stir until the onions are evenly coated and fragrant, about 2 minutes.

3. Gradually add the broth, scraping the pan bottom and edges with a wooden spoon to loosen the remaining browned bits and dissolve the flour. Add the tomatoes, bay leaves, sugar, vinegar, and mustard seeds and bring to a simmer. Add the browned pork and accumulated juices, submerging the meat in the liquid. Return to a simmer, cover, and place in the oven. Cook for 2 hours.

4. Remove the pot from the oven. If serving immediately, spoon off any fat that rises to the top. Remove the bay leaves, stir in the cilantro, and adjust the seasonings. Serve immediately.

PORK BRAISED IN MILK

MAIALE AL LATTE (PORK LOIN BRAISED IN MILK), a humble and intriguing dish, is considered one of the best illustrations of regional northern Italian cooking—and yet, there are those in Naples who claim it as their own, while still others say it's a Tuscan classic. Most of the recipes we found originated with women who gave them to neighbors who gave them to their daughters who have continued to pass them on. Regardless of geographic origin, all recipe writers profess that "my mother's version is best."

The basic recipe remains the same: A pork loin is slow-cooked in milk long enough for the milk to coagulate into delicious (if inelegant) little clumps of browned milk protein. The simplest recipe we tried was really just that—a pork loin browned in olive oil, then covered and slowly simmered in milk. Although the pork itself was tender and sweet, our tasters found the sauce bland. We wanted a meatier flavor in the sauce and thought that salt pork (suggested in several recipes) rather than olive oil might fit the bill. Sure enough, browning the pork in salt pork (which had first been chopped and rendered) yielded a much more flavorful dish.

Next, we tried rubbing the pork with garlic and herbs. This added much-needed flavor but produced little burnt bits on the crust, so instead we added the same ingredients to the salt pork along with carrots, celery, and onion. Once the roast was done, we strained out these aromatic vegetables and the salt pork, and the resulting sauce was more complex and better tasting. In our research, we had seen several versions of this recipe with nutmeg, cinnamon, and Parmesan cheese. However, tasters found the sweet spices almost cloying, and the Parmesan was, well, too cheesy for the pork. We decided to pass on all three of these embellishments.

Most recipes call for cooking the dish on the stovetop, but we found that the meat cooked somewhat unevenly. Once the meat is browned and the braising liquid brought to a simmer, we generally like to braise meat in the oven. As we expected, the even heat of the oven yielded a more evenly cooked roast.

Rosy-colored pork struck several tasters as odd in this dish, where the pork is usually cooked until well done. We found that because the pork braises in so much liquid, the meat will not dry out if cooked to a slightly higher than usual (at least by our custom) internal temperature of 150 degrees. At this temperature, the pork was still juicy, and its pale gray color was deemed more traditional.

This is a dish that experienced eaters love, whether they have fond memories of sitting down to their grandmother's table or have braved their guests' doubtful stares and made it themselves time after time. If you are new to this recipe, you must suspend your aesthetic ideals; as the milk cooks down, it turns into little pale brownish clumps that, frankly, look like a broken mess of unappetizing curds. If you want a less rustic look, we discovered that the sauce can be smoothed out by blending it or straining it (for less quantity and thickness).

In the end, we found that pork braised in milk is especially moist, juicy, and flavorful. Both main ingredients, even the skeptics agreed, are transformed by this exceptional cooking method.

Pork Loin Braised in Milk

SERVES 6

Although the sauce is traditionally served as is (with the unattractive milk clumps floating in it), it can be pureed in a blender or poured through a fine-mesh strainer for a more refined look. Use leftover meat in sandwiches.

PLANNING AHEAD: The pork may be prepared through step 3 and stored in an airtight container in the refrigerator for up to 3 days. The meat should be stored in the finished sauce and gently reheated in a covered Dutch oven over medium-low heat. We do not recommend freezing it.

1/4	pound salt pork (see page 268), cut into 1/2-inch chunks
1	boneless center-cut pork loin (2 1/4 to 2 1/2 pounds), tied at even intervals along the length with 5 pieces of butcher's twine
1/2	teaspoon salt
1	teaspoon ground black pepper
1	medium onion, halved
8	medium garlic cloves, peeled and left whole
1	medium carrot, peeled and halved lengthwise
1	medium celery rib, halved lengthwise
1	bay leaf
1	sprig fresh rosemary or fresh thyme
3 1/2	cups whole milk
1/3	cup white wine

1. Adjust an oven rack to the middle position and heat the oven to 325 degrees. Place the salt pork in a large, ovenproof Dutch oven over medium-high heat and cook until some of the fat is rendered, about 4 minutes. Dry the roast thoroughly with paper towels, then season it generously with salt and pepper and place it in the pot, fat-side down. Cook, turning occasionally, until the roast begins to brown, about 6 minutes. Add the onion, garlic, carrot, celery, bay leaf, and rosemary and continue cooking until the pork is well browned on all sides, about 6 minutes longer. Add the milk and bring to a simmer.

2. Transfer the pot to the oven, partially cover with the lid, and cook, turning occasionally, until the pork is tender and registers 150 degrees on an instant-read thermometer, the milk is reduced by half, and light brown clumps of milk solids appear, about 1 hour.

3. Transfer the pork loin to a platter and tent with aluminum foil. Using a slotted spoon, remove and discard the salt pork, onion, carrot, celery, bay leaf, and rosemary. Set the pot over high heat, add the wine, and cook, scraping up any browned bits with a wooden spoon, until the sauce reduces to about 2 cups, 7 to 10 minutes. If you are straining the sauce, pour it through a fine-mesh strainer into a serving bowl. If you are pureeing it, transfer it to a blender and puree until smooth, then transfer to a serving bowl. If you are leaving it chunky, simply transfer it to a serving bowl.

4. Cut the pork crosswise into 1/2-inch-thick slices and arrange them on the platter. Drizzle 1/2 cup of the sauce over the sliced pork and serve immediately, with more sauce passed separately.

PORK LOIN WITH RED CABBAGE AND APPLES

PORK, CABBAGE, AND APPLES ARE BY NO MEANS a new combination. We've come across dozens of recipes that combine these three ingredients in myriad ways, from homey fry-ups to fussy restaurant-style compositions. There's a good reason for the popularity of these ingredients: the trio balance each other perfectly in both flavor and texture. But, despite all the recipes we found in which they starred, we failed to come across a simple braised dish that featured them. What would it take to develop a no-fuss, one-pot pork, cabbage, and apple dinner?

For this recipe, we decided that the best approach would be a braise (modeled loosely on Alsace's *choucroute garni*, pork and sauerkraut braised in white wine with juniper berries, allspice, and apples). We chose a pork loin for its convenience (little trimming required and easy to truss up), vibrant red cabbage for color, and Granny Smith apples for their tartness. We seared the meat, then sautéed the cabbage and apples with onions until soft. We added a shot of broth, slid the Dutch oven into the oven, and simmered everything until the meat was fork-tender. But what had sounded good in theory failed to come together in practice: the meat was tough and bland, and the cabbage was pale and mushy, though highly flavored from the meat juices. The flavors were promising; the textures were not.

We needed to alter either the cut of meat or the cooking method. The low heat and moisture—so beneficial to tougher cuts of meat—was turning the lean pork loin rubbery and bland. Evidently, pork loin was not the ideal cut for this dish, lacking both the collagen-rich connective tissue and the fat to keep the meat moist. A large pork butt

or shoulder would be the better choice, but would require the kind of serious trimming and labor we were trying to avoid.

To achieve the best results, we now knew that the loin needed to be cooked in a drier environment. Simply reducing the amount of broth we added to the braise yielded slightly better meat without adversely affecting the cabbage; bathed by the juices released by the roast, it still tasted good. We reduced the liquid incrementally in subsequent batches and found, somewhat surprisingly, that the less liquid we used, the better both the pork and cabbage became. After starting our tests with 2 cups, we had whittled it down to just ½ cup. The pork didn't dry out and the flavor of the cabbage and apples was more concentrated. Within 45 minutes, the pork had reached an internal temperature of 135 degrees—it would finish cooking through with residual heat as it rested. Drier than a braise, but moister than a roast, this hybrid method seemed to work.

With a basic method in hand, we could start tackling the auxiliary flavors Borrowing from the classic seasonings of choucroute, we chose to flavor the cabbage with a blend of juniper and allspice berries and bay leaves and thyme. Juniper berries lent the woodsy, penetrating bite of pine—a perfect foil to the sweet-tart flavor of the apples. And the thyme and bay leaves rounded out the juniper's bite. Added early on as the vegetables sautéed, the whole juniper and allspice berries softened enough in flavor and texture to become perfectly edible—no hunting and pecking through the cabbage to remove them.

As the apples broke down, they lost much of their fruity tartness. Looking to pump up the flavor, we decided to replace the chicken broth with apple cider, which added a fruity base we couldn't achieve using only fresh fruit.

There was one nagging issue that we needed to solve. During the slow simmer, the once vibrant red cabbage turned an anemic bluish hue. It tasted fine, but the color was less than appetizing. With a little research, we found the answer to our problem. Red cabbage is high in anthocyanins, the pigment responsible for the vibrant reds of vegetables like cabbage, beets,

THE IMPORTANCE OF TYING

UNTIED AND UNEVEN   **TIED AND TIDY**

Straight from their supermarket packaging, most pork loins will lie flat in the pan and cook unevenly (left). Tying the roast not only yields more attractive slices but ensures that the roast will have the same thickness from end to end so that it cooks evenly (right).

and radishes. Anthocyanins are water-soluble and will leach from food into the liquid in which it is cooked; hence the cabbage's sickly shade. But there's a quick fix: acid. Adding a splash of vinegar brought the red right back.

Pork with Red Cabbage, Apples, and Juniper

SERVES 4

A blade-end pork loin is the best choice for this dish, though the cut might be hard to find. (See below for more information on blade-end pork loins.) Whole allspice and juniper berries are available in the spice aisle of the supermarket. Although the juniper berries are soft and perfectly edible by the time the meat is done, they can be removed if you prefer. If you can't find juniper berries, a tablespoon of gin, stirred into the cabbage in step 2, is a suitable substitution. Make sure to add the gin off the heat so that it does not ignite. In a pinch, apple juice may be substituted for the cider.

PLANNING AHEAD: This dish is best eaten the day it is prepared. Reheating can toughen the pork. We recommend serving the leftovers in sandwiches.

I	boneless center-cut pork loin (2¼ to 2½ pounds), tied at even intervals along the length with 5 pieces of butcher's twine Salt and ground black pepper
I	tablespoon vegetable oil
I	large onion, halved and sliced thin
2	bay leaves
4	sprigs fresh thyme
10	juniper berries
10	allspice berries
2	medium Granny Smith apples (about ¾ pound), peeled, cored, and chopped coarse
I	small head red cabbage (about 1¼ pounds) quartered, cored, and sliced ¼ inch thick
½	cup apple cider
I	teaspoon light or dark brown sugar
2	teaspoons apple cider vinegar

1. Adjust an oven rack to the lower-middle position and heat the oven to 300 degrees. Dry the roast thoroughly with paper towels, then season generously with salt and pepper. Heat the oil in a large ovenproof Dutch oven over medium-high heat until just smoking. Brown the roast thoroughly on all sides, reducing the heat if the fat begins to smoke, about 10 minutes. Transfer the roast to a large plate.

2. Reduce the heat to medium and heat until the fat remaining in the pot is shimmering. Add the onion, bay leaves, thyme sprigs, juniper berries, allspice berries, and ¾ teaspoon salt; cook, scraping the browned bits off the bottom of the pan, until the onions are soft and beginning to brown, about 6 minutes. Add the apples and cabbage; cook until the cabbage has softened and reduced in volume, about 8 minutes. Stir in the cider and sugar. Lay the roast, fat-side down, on top of the cabbage. Cover, transfer to the oven, and cook until an instant-read thermometer inserted into the center of the roast reads 135 degrees, 45 to 50 minutes (the temperature of the roast will rise to 145 degrees while it rests).

3. Transfer the roast to a carving board and tent loosely with foil. Continue to cook the cabbage mixture over medium-high heat, stirring frequently, until the excess liquid has evaporated, 5 to 10 minutes. Add the vinegar and season with salt and pepper to taste. Remove and discard the bay leaves and thyme, as well as the juniper and allspice berries, if desired. Slice the pork into ½-inch-thick pieces and serve immediately with the cabbage.

BLADE VERSUS CENTER LOIN PORK

BLADE

CENTER LOIN

The blade-end roast is closest to the shoulder and tends to have a higher fat content and more connective tissue than the center loin, which is a little more tender.

COUNTRY-STYLE RIBS AND BEANS

THERE'S A SIMPLE SOUTHERN SIDE DISH IN which black-eyed peas, collard greens, and a smoked ham hock are stewed together for hours until the beans are creamy, the greens are velvety soft, and the broth is suffused with the smoky sweetness of the ham. Slow simmering over low heat transforms this trio of modest ingredients into something profoundly different: rich, earthy, and surprisingly complex. The dish is kitchen alchemy at its best—and in our eyes, worthy of main course status.

Part of the charm of the dish to us was the mechanics. As the beans and greens stew, the beans absorb the "pot liquor" (or "likker"), the rich broth shed by the greens and ham hock. The broth is so flavorful that, in some instances, it is served on its own as a soup course, or ladled over dry, coarse cornbread. Our goal was to capitalize on the flavors and basic technique of the recipe, but expand the dish into a full-blown meal with the addition of a heftier cut of meat. Ham hocks may be flavorful, but they yield a scant amount of edible meat (the bulk of a ham hock is skin and gelatinous fat—hence the great flavor).

Our basic concept for the recipe was to brown the meat, sauté aromatics including onions and garlic, and then simmer the beans, collards, meat, and aromatics in the oven until tender. In other words, we were going to treat it like a classic braise. Our first choice for a more substantive cut of meat to replace the hock was center-cut pork chops; we thought that the meat would become fork-tender as it simmered and the bones would add flavor to the broth.

Unfortunately, we found that the chops didn't fare well through the long spell in the oven. Clearly too lean, the chop meat toughened and the broth sapped the meat of its flavor. Looking for a cut that could better withstand the oven time, we selected country-style ribs. Taken from the backbone, at the juncture of the shoulder and loin, country-style ribs are very flavorful and resilient because of the relatively high amount of fat and connective tissue between the bones. A long, slow simmer at a moderate temperature breaks down the connective tissue, turning it into rich gelatin, which in turn keeps the meat moist. These ribs proved perfect for the dish, and their flavor, in fact, improved the longer they simmered.

As for the black-eyed peas, we followed our standard dried bean protocol and soaked them overnight before preparing the dish. Unfortunately, the beans turned mushy within 45 minutes, well before the ribs were tender. Unsoaked beans proved to be a better option, requiring about an hour to become tender—just enough time for the ribs to cook.

Stewed from the start with the beans and ribs, the collard greens became soggy and soft, and took on an unappealing drab green color. While this seemed to be the standard according to Southern tradition, we much prefer collard greens with a little bite and a brighter color. In previous recipes, we found that they can be sliced thin and cooked in a few minutes, like any other hearty green. So we added them to the brothy beans once the meat was tender and simmered them on the stovetop to the desired texture, which took just a few minutes. They retained a bright, glossy green color and a fresher, livelier flavor than the long-cooked greens. Not quite traditional perhaps, but the greens had a flavor, texture, and color that tasters liked best (with only minor dissent from one Southern-born test cook).

The ribs lent a rich pork flavor to the beans and

MEASURING SPICES NEATLY

Measuring spices can be tricky, especially if measuring spoons won't fit into narrow bottles. We recommend working over a sheet of parchment paper, wax paper, or paper towel. Fill the measuring spoon, mounding excess spice over the spoon, and with a flat spatula, sweep off the excess onto the paper below. To return excess spice to the bottle, just fold the paper and slide in the spice.

greens, but tasters missed the smoky backbeat laid down by the hock in the original recipe. The solution proved simple: bacon. Rendered after the ribs were browned, a quarter pound of bacon yielded enough fat in which to cook the onions and garlic, and enough meat to deliver the same smoky flavor that the ham hock had provided.

Between the ribs, beans, bacon, and greens, the dish had a solid, rich flavor that tasters were pleased with, but everyone agreed that it needed *something* to perk it up. Southerners typically add a pepper-spiked vinegar to stewed collard greens, which sounded like just the thing to accent the sweet earthiness of this dish. Following a traditional recipe, we steeped a few small hot chile peppers in vinegar and then sprinkled the vinegar over the beans and greens. The acidity and heat were both welcome, but not quite the answer we were looking for. Tasters wanted something with a bit more body—something crunchy, spicy, and tart that they could bite into. Italian-style pickled hot peppers were suggested, but then a better idea arose: pickled red onions. They have all the flavor and texture we sought, and a vibrant color to offset the dull beige of the beans and pork. We steeped thinly sliced red onions in red wine vinegar with red pepper flakes and bay leaves for a rounder flavor. The onions were spicy (but not incendiary), crunchy,

and vibrantly magenta—just the accent we wanted. We may have broken with tradition, but this was Southern-inspired cooking through and through.

≈

Braised Country-Style Ribs with Black-Eyed Peas, Collard Greens, and Pickled Onions
SERVES 6 TO 8

Because of the long time in the oven, canned or frozen black-eyed peas are not suitable in this dish. Leftover pickled onions can be used in sandwiches and salads.

PLANNING AHEAD: The recipe can be made through step 3 and refrigerated (storing the pickled onions and stew separately) for up to 2 days. Bring the stew to a simmer in a covered saucepan or Dutch oven over medium-low heat before proceeding with step 4.

RIBS, PEAS, AND COLLARD GREENS

2	pounds country-style pork ribs (see the illustration at left), trimmed of excess fat
	Salt and ground black pepper
1	teaspoon vegetable oil
4	ounces (about 4 slices) bacon, sliced crosswise into 1/4-inch strips
1	medium red onion, chopped medium
1	large celery rib, chopped fine
6	medium garlic cloves, minced or pressed through a garlic press
1	pound dried black-eyed peas, sorted through and rinsed (see the illustration on page 184)
3 1/2	cups low-sodium chicken broth
1	cup water
2	bay leaves
1	bunch collard greens (about 1 pound), stems removed and sliced thin crosswise (see the illustration on page 233)

PICKLED ONIONS

3/4	cup red wine vinegar
2	tablespoons sugar
1/2	teaspoon salt
1/4	teaspoon red pepper flakes
2	bay leaves
1	medium red onion, halved and sliced thin

COUNTRY-STYLE PORK RIBS

THESE MEATY, TENDER RIBS ARE CUT from the upper side of the rib cage from the fatty blade end of the loin. Butchers usually cut them into individual ribs and package several together.

183

1. FOR THE RIBS: Adjust an oven rack to the lower-middle position and heat the oven to 300 degrees. Dry the ribs thoroughly with paper towels, then season generously with salt and pepper. Heat the oil in a large ovenproof Dutch oven over medium-high heat until just smoking. Place the ribs in a single layer and cook, without moving, until well browned, about 5 minutes. Flip the ribs over and continue to cook until brown on the second side, about 4 minutes longer. Transfer the ribs to a plate.

2. Pour off any fat remaining in the pot and return to medium heat. Add the bacon and cook, stirring frequently, until most of the fat is rendered, about 3 minutes. Add the onion and celery; cook, stirring occasionally, until softened and beginning to brown, about 6 minutes. Add the garlic and cook until fragrant, about 30 seconds. Add the beans, broth, water, bay leaves, and browned ribs; bring to a simmer. Cover, transfer to the oven, cook until the beans are tender and a sharp knife easily slips in and out of the meat, about 1 hour.

3. FOR THE PICKLED ONIONS: Meanwhile, bring the vinegar, sugar, salt, red pepper flakes, and bay leaves to a boil over medium-high heat in a small saucepan. Add the onion, return to a boil, and cook for 1 minute. Transfer to a shallow bowl and refrigerate until cooled.

SORTING DRIED BEANS WITH EASE

It is important to pick over and rinse dried beans to remove any stones or debris before cooking. To make this easier, sort dried beans on a white plate or cutting board. The neutral background makes any unwanted matter easy to spot and remove.

4. Transfer the ribs to a carving board and tent loosely with foil to keep warm. Return the pot to medium-high heat and stir in the collards; cook until wilted and tender, 4 to 8 minutes. Remove and discard the bay leaves and season with salt and pepper to taste. Serve immediately with the ribs and pickled onions.

CHICKEN PROVENÇAL

CHICKEN PROVENÇAL MAY REPRESENT THE best of French peasant cooking—chicken pieces on the bone simmered in a liquid flavored with tomatoes, garlic, herbs, and olives—but it is not well known here in the United States. We soon discovered why. The handful of recipes we tested produced rubbery, dry chicken, dull and muddy flavors, and a sauce that was too thick or too thin, too sweet or too greasy. (One recipe included a half cup of mayonnaise!)

The chicken was our starting point. Most recipes we reviewed begin with browning a cut-up whole chicken, removing the parts from the pot, sautéing some aromatic vegetables, deglazing the pot with white wine or dry vermouth, adding stock, tomatoes, olives, and herbs, and then simmering the chicken in the liquid until it is cooked. When we used a whole cut-up chicken, we encountered several problems. First, the breast pieces always dried out and lacked flavor after cooking. Second, the skin, although crisp after browning, turned soggy and unappealing after braising. Finally, the wings contained mostly inedible skin and very little meat. We tried again, using only dark meat, which, with its extra fat and connective tissue, was better suited to braising. The meat turned out tender, moist, and flavorful—far more appealing than either the breasts or the wings. We had used whole legs for this first test with dark meat, but because tasters preferred the meatier thighs to the drumsticks, we decided to make the dish with thighs only.

Next we addressed the skin. Its flabby texture after cooking made it virtually inedible. When we began with skinless thighs, however, they stuck to the pan, the outer layer of meat becoming tough and dry with browning. The skin, it turns out, acts as a necessary cushion between the meat and the pan, so we left it on for browning and then discarded it. We also wondered if the amount of browning mattered. A side-by-side taste test—one batch made with lightly browned thighs, the other with deeply browned thighs—revealed that more browning renders more fat and results in more chicken flavor. The dish prepared with deeply browned thighs had a rich flavor that was far superior to the blander taste of the other.

We assumed that olive oil was essential to this dish (it is ostensibly from Provence, after all), but most recipes (which use about three tablespoons) were too greasy. We browned a batch of thighs in a meager 1 tablespoon of oil and found that the skin quickly rendered a couple of additional tablespoons of fat. But even with this reduced amount of fat, tasters found the final dish to be greasy. Pouring off all but 1 tablespoon of fat after browning the chicken eliminated the greasiness, but now the flavor of the sauce was lacking. We were throwing flavor out with the rendered fat. We tried another test using just 1 teaspoon of oil. Sure enough, using less olive oil at the beginning allowed for a stronger chicken flavor in the final dish because we were discarding less chicken fat.

PITTING NIÇOISE OLIVES

Removing the pits from tiny niçoise olives by hand is not an easy job. We found the following method to be the most expedient. Cover a cutting board with a clean kitchen towel and spread the olives on top, about 1 inch apart from each other. Place a second clean towel over the olives. Using a mallet, pound all of the olives firmly for 10 to 15 seconds, being careful not to split the pits. Remove the top towel, and, using your fingers, press the pit out of each olive.

We had one more test in mind—drizzling 2 teaspoons of extra-virgin olive oil over the finished dish just before serving. Tasters approved of the additional fruity olive flavor.

Our final tests with the chicken focused on the cooking method. Almost by definition, chicken Provençal is braised (browned and then cooked in a tightly covered pot in a small amount of liquid in a low-temperature oven for a lengthy period of time). We tried temperatures upward of 350 degrees, but found that 300 degrees did the best job. Much higher and the chicken toughened, much lower and it simply took forever for the chicken to become tender. Technically, thighs are considered done when they reach an internal temperature of 170 degrees, or after 30 minutes of braising. Unfortunately, 30 minutes of braising produced thighs that were not as meltingly tender as desired, and the chicken did not have enough flavor. What if we were to cook them longer? Would they dry out?

To our great surprise, after trying longer and longer cooking times, we ended up keeping the dish in the oven for a whopping 1½ hours. At this point, the meat simply fell off the bone; it was exceedingly tender and flavorful, and the thighs did not seem overcooked. Additional tests, however, revealed that slightly less time—1¼ hours, wherein the meat reaches an internal temperature of 210 degrees—was perfect, as the meat stayed on the bone. Why this long cooking time? The long stay in the oven breaks down the connective tissue in the thighs, much as it does in a pot roast, yielding more tender meat. (White meat contains little connective tissue, so there's no benefit to cooking it longer.) In addition, thighs have plenty of fat that keeps them moist as they braise away.

Many recipes call for browning onions after the chicken is browned and taken out of the pot. Tasters approved of some onion, but not a lot, commenting that a modest amount of its pungent flavor was enough to balance the sweetness of the tomatoes. Garlic is most often added next and sautéed briefly to bring forth its flavor. Preliminary tests showed that both dry white wine and dry vermouth work well for deglazing the pan, but the wine turned out to be the favorite among tasters. The vermouth seemed to exaggerate the acidity of the tomatoes.

Crushed and pureed canned tomatoes each produced a thick, sweet, overbearing sauce reminiscent of bad Italian restaurant fare. Canned diced tomatoes, though more promising, presented the opposite problem: Even when drained they contain a fair amount of liquid, and the resulting sauce was too thin. We added a few tablespoons of tomato paste to the diced tomatoes, and the texture improved dramatically—now the sauce coated the chicken without overwhelming it. Chicken broth rounded out the flavors while providing a bit more volume. For a more intense flavor and better consistency, we ended up reducing the braising liquid after removing the braised chicken from the pot.

Whole niçoise olives appear in just about every recipe, but tasters complained about the pits. Niçoise are so small that pitting by hand with a knife is unreasonable. We tried substituting kalamatas, gaetas, and oil-cured olives, but none of them sufficed. The flavors of their brine or oil were too strong and inappropriate. While discussing this predicament with colleagues, we came up with a method for pitting niçoise olives that involves a mallet and clean kitchen towels (see the illustration on page 185). The pitted olives are best stirred in at the end of cooking, just prior to serving.

As for seasonings, the combination of dried herbs referred to as *herbes de Provence* (lavender, marjoram, basil, fennel seed, rosemary, sage, summer savory, and thyme) seemed like a shoo-in. But tasters said that when used alone, these dried herbs were too strong, giving the sauce a flavor that bordered on medicinal. Fresh thyme, oregano, and parsley with a bay leaf were preferred, and a teaspoon of the dried blend became an optional item. A pinch of cayenne balanced the sweet tomatoes.

Inspired by one of the better initial recipes tested, we tried adding a teaspoon of minced anchovies before deglazing. Although tasters could not identify the ingredient, everyone agreed the sauce tasted richer and fuller. The final item on our list was lemon zest, a common and, as it turned out, welcome addition. We found that the zest is best added at two points: first to the braising liquid while it is being reduced (just before

serving) and second to the finished dish itself, sprinkled on top along with the parsley.

These last, light, fresh touches of lemon zest and parsley reminded us of how far we'd come from even the thought of adding mayonnaise to this classic country dish. We felt we had restored it to the status it deserves.

Chicken Provençal
SERVES 4

This dish is often served with rice or slices of crusty bread, but soft polenta is also a good accompaniment. Niçoise olives are the preferred olives here; the flavor of kalamatas and other types of brined or oil-cured olives is too potent.

PLANNING AHEAD: Chicken Provençal may be stored in an airtight container in the refrigerator for up to 3 days. It may also be frozen for up to 3 months. The chicken should be stored and reheated in the cooking liquid. Reheat the dish in a covered saucepan or Dutch oven over medium-low heat, adding broth or water as needed to adjust the consistency. The parsley and lemon zest garnish should be prepared just before serving.

8	bone-in, skin-on chicken thighs (about 3 pounds), trimmed of excess skin and fat
	Salt and ground black pepper
1	tablespoon extra-virgin olive oil
1	small onion, minced
6	medium garlic cloves, minced or pressed through a garlic press
1	anchovy fillet, minced (about 1 teaspoon)
$1/8$	teaspoon cayenne pepper
1	cup dry white wine
1	cup low-sodium chicken broth
1	(14.5-ounce) can diced tomatoes, drained
$2^1/2$	tablespoons tomato paste
$1^1/2$	tablespoons chopped fresh thyme leaves
1	teaspoon chopped fresh oregano leaves
1	bay leaf
1	teaspoon herbes de Provence (optional)
$1^1/2$	teaspoons grated lemon zest
$1/2$	cup niçoise olives, pitted (see the illustration on page 185)
1	tablespoon chopped fresh parsley leaves

1. Adjust an oven rack to the lower-middle position; heat the oven to 300 degrees. Dry the chicken thighs thoroughly with paper towels, then season generously with salt and pepper. Heat 1 teaspoon of the oil in a large ovenproof Dutch oven over medium-high heat until shimmering but not smoking. Add 4 of the chicken thighs, skin-side down, and cook without moving them until the skin is crisp and well browned, about 5 minutes. Turn the chicken pieces and brown on the second side, about 5 minutes longer; transfer to a large plate. Add the remaining chicken thighs to the pot and repeat, then transfer them to a plate and set aside. Discard all but 1 tablespoon of fat from the pot; when the chicken has cooled, remove and discard the skin (see the illustration on page 201).

2. Add the onion to the fat in the Dutch oven and cook, stirring occasionally, over medium heat until softened and browned, about 4 minutes. Add the garlic, anchovy, and cayenne; cook, stirring constantly, until fragrant, about 1 minute. Add the wine and scrape up the browned bits from the pan bottom and edges with a wooden spoon. Stir in the chicken broth, tomatoes, tomato paste, thyme, oregano, bay leaf, and herbes de Provence (if using). Submerge the chicken pieces in the liquid and add the accumulated chicken juices to the pot. Increase the heat to high, bring to a simmer, cover, then set the pot in the oven; cook until the chicken offers no resistance when poked with the tip of a paring knife but is still clinging to the bones, about 1¼ hours.

3. Using a slotted spoon, transfer the chicken to a serving platter and tent with foil. Discard the bay leaf. Set the Dutch oven over high heat, stir in 1 teaspoon of the lemon zest, bring to a boil, and cook, stirring occasionally, until slightly thickened and reduced to 2 cups, about 5 minutes. Stir in the olives and cook until heated through, about 1 minute. Meanwhile, mix the remaining ½ teaspoon zest with the parsley. Spoon the sauce over the chicken, drizzle the chicken with the remaining 2 teaspoons olive oil, sprinkle with the parsley mixture, and serve.

➤ VARIATION
Chicken Provençal with Saffron, Orange, and Basil
Follow the recipe for Chicken Provençal, adding ⅛ teaspoon saffron threads along with the wine, and substituting orange zest for the lemon zest and 2 tablespoons chopped fresh basil leaves for the parsley.

CACCIATORE

CACCIATORE, WHICH MEANS "HUNTER-STYLE" in Italian, originally referred to a simple method of cooking fresh-killed game. Game hen or rabbit would be sautéed along with wild mushrooms, onions, and other foraged vegetables and then braised with wine or stock. Unfortunately, when applied to chicken and translated by American cooks, cacciatore mutated into a generic pasty "red sauce" dish, often featuring sauces that were greasy and overly sweet along with dry, overcooked chicken. We thought it was time for a resurrection. We knew there was a really good version of this dish to be found, and that it was an easy, one-pot meal sort of dish.

From the beginning we knew that we wanted a sauce that was just substantial enough to cling to the chicken; we didn't want the chicken to be swimming in broth, nor did we want a sauce reminiscent of Spackle. Another thing we wanted was a streamlined cooking method. After developing Chicken Provençal (page 186), we thought cacciatore could be prepared in a similar fashion, with some stovetop preparation but with most of the cooking time happening in the oven.

We began our work, as we often do, with a blind taste test. We gathered an abundance of recipes (every "Italian" cookbook seems to include some form of cacciatore), then selected what seemed to be the more "authentic" versions (no boneless, skinless chicken breasts, no jarred tomato sauces) written by prominent Italian cooks. All four of these recipes started with the same basic preparation, one that we would also use for our working recipe. Chicken (a whole chicken cut up, in all but one of the recipes) is dredged in flour and sautéed in olive oil, then removed from the pan. Next, the pan is deglazed—a process in which a liquid is used to lift the browned bits from the pan bottom—with either wine or stock. Vegetables—most often tomatoes, onions, and mushrooms—are added to the braise, and the dish is then cooked until the meat is fall-apart tender.

As we reviewed the tasters' notes from this trial run, we noticed two problems common to all the recipes. First, tasters found the dishes to be too greasy (nearly an inch of oil floated at the top of one dish); second, they disliked the presence of chicken skin in the final product. The skin, which was crisp after the initial sauté, had become soggy and unappealing.

All of the recipes except one had other serious problems as well. One was too vegetal, another included black olives that proved too dominant a flavor, and a third had no tomatoes, an omission that tasters thought took the dish too far from what Americans consider to be a classic cacciatore. The fourth recipe was much more promising. It started off with chicken thighs rather than a whole, cut-up chicken and used a mixture known as *beurre manié*, made from equal parts flour and softened butter, to thicken the sauce. The dark thigh meat remained much more moist and plump than the fibrous, flavorless breast meat we had ended up with in the other recipes. (It was also much easier to simply buy a package of thighs than to cut up a whole chicken.) The thighs also gave the braising liquid a more intense flavor. Unfortunately, the beurre manié overthickened the sauce, giving it a gravy-like consistency.

From the test results we were able to come to a few conclusions and devise a working recipe. Chicken thighs were in, but the flabby skin was out, and this, we hoped, would reduce the over-abundance of grease in the dish. Wine was our liquid of choice for braising, although we had yet to determine whether to use red or white. Finally, we wanted to keep the additional vegetables to a minimum—a combination of onions, mushrooms, and tomatoes was all that would be needed.

We assumed that the flabby skin issue could be solved by using skinless chicken thighs. But that assumption proved to be untrue. A batch made with skinless thighs, while good, lacked the intense flavor of the batches made with skin-on chicken. The rendered fat and juice from the chicken skin caramelized on the pan bottom, which, when deglazed, made a big contribution to the flavor of the sauce. In addition, the skin protected the flesh of the chicken from direct contact with the high heat, thereby preventing the meat from forming a fibrous crust.

We found that pulling the skin off the thighs after the initial browning cost the dish none of its flavor while allowing us to serve the dish sans skin. Removing the skin before braising also eliminated the problem of excess grease. The fat from the skin is first rendered over high heat, which helps to keep the skin from sticking to the pan bottom. The extra fat is then disposed of, but the caramelized bits are left behind for deglazing.

Next came the braising medium. Preliminary testing suggested that red wine would prevail. Most tasters liked its bold presence, although some thought the hearty flavor of the wine was a bit too harsh. We tried cutting the wine with small amounts of water, dry vermouth, and chicken broth and found that the latter buffered the strong presence of the wine and rounded out the flavors. (Since some tasters preferred the lighter, brothier taste of the version made with white wine, we decided to offer that as a variation on the master recipe.)

At this point the sauce was rich in flavor but lacking in substance. Truthfully, it was more like a broth; the vegetables and chicken were lost in the liquid. We remembered that the flour used to dredge the chicken thighs had been thrown away with the skin. We would have to introduce it somewhere else. A beurre manié was too complicated for this streamlined dish, so we ended up adding a little flour directly to the vegetables as they were finishing their sauté. The sauce was now silky and robust. On a whim we threw in a piece of Parmesan cheese rind, an option we had noticed in one of the recipes tested earlier. The sauce, very good before, now surpassed all of our expectations. It was substantial, lavish, and amply flavored.

We were finally down to the finishing details. Portobello mushrooms, bursting with the essence of red wine, added an earthy flavor and meaty chew. We also found that just about any herb would complement the recipe; we chose sage for its mellow, woodsy flavor.

Chicken Cacciatore with Portobellos and Sage
SERVES 4

The Parmesan cheese rind is optional, but we highly recommend it for the robust, savory flavor it adds to the dish. An equal amount of minced fresh rosemary can be substituted for the sage. See page 149 for information about choosing a red wine for this dish.

PLANNING AHEAD: Chicken cacciatore may be stored in an airtight container in the refrigerator for up to 3 days. It may also be frozen for up to 3 months. The chicken should be stored and reheated in the braising liquid. Reheat the dish in a covered saucepan or Dutch oven over medium-low heat, adding broth or water as needed to adjust the consistency.

8	bone-in, skin-on chicken thighs (about 3 pounds), trimmed of excess skin and fat
	Salt and ground black pepper
I	teaspoon olive oil
I	medium onion, chopped medium
8	ounces portobello mushroom caps (about 3 medium), brushed clean and cut into 3/4-inch chunks
4	medium garlic cloves, minced or pressed through a garlic press
I1/2	tablespoons all-purpose flour
I1/2	cups dry red wine
1/2	cup low-sodium chicken broth
I	(14.5-ounce) can diced tomatoes, drained
2	teaspoons minced fresh thyme leaves
I	Parmesan cheese rind, about 4 by 2 inches (optional)
2	teaspoons minced fresh sage leaves

1. Adjust an oven rack to the lower-middle position; heat the oven to 300 degrees. Dry the chicken thighs thoroughly with paper towels, then season generously with salt and pepper. Heat the oil in a large ovenproof Dutch oven over medium-high heat until shimmering but not smoking. Add 4 of the chicken thighs, skin-side down, and cook without moving them until the skin is crisp and well browned, about 5 minutes. Turn the chicken pieces and brown on the second side, about 5 minutes longer; transfer to a large plate. Add the remaining chicken thighs to the pot and repeat, then transfer them to a plate and set aside. Discard all but 1 tablespoon of fat from the pot; when the chicken has cooled, remove and discard the skin (see the illustration on page 201).

2. Add the onion, mushrooms, and 1/2 teaspoon salt to the empty Dutch oven. Cook over medium-high heat, stirring occasionally, until moisture evaporates and the vegetables begin to brown, 6 to 8 minutes. Add the garlic and cook until fragrant, about 30 seconds. Stir in the flour and cook, stirring constantly, for about 1 minute. Add the wine, scraping the pot bottom and edges with a wooden spoon to loosen the brown bits. Stir in the broth, tomatoes, thyme, Parmesan rind (if using), 1/2 teaspoon salt (omit salt if using cheese rind), and pepper to taste. Add the chicken pieces and accumulated juices, submerging the chicken in the liquid. Bring to a simmer and place the pot in the oven. Cook until the chicken offers no resistance when poked with the tip of a paring knife but is still clinging to the bones, about 1 1/4 hours. Remove the pot from the oven.

3. Discard the cheese rind, stir in the sage, and adjust the seasonings. Serve immediately.

VARIATION

Chicken Cacciatore with White Wine and Tarragon
This variation is based on chicken chasseur, the French version of cacciatore.

Mince 3 large shallots; wipe clean 10 ounces white button mushrooms and quarter if large, halve if medium, or leave whole if small. Follow the recipe for Chicken Cacciatore with Portobellos and Sage, substituting the shallots for the onions, the white button mushrooms for the portobellos, dry white wine for the red wine, and 2 teaspoons minced fresh tarragon leaves for the sage.

CHICKEN PAPRIKASH

THIS HUNGARIAN SPECIALTY HAS BEEN POPULAR in this country for decades, and with good reason. The chicken is succulent, the flavors mellow and a bit sweet, and the color a vibrant red. Sour cream makes the sauce comforting but not overly rich, while paprika gives the stew its characteristic appearance and flavor.

Paprikash is a simple stew, but you wouldn't know it from all the recipes out there. Too many recipes have lengthy ingredient lists, and the resulting stews taste muddled. We wanted to keep the focus on the main flavors—the chicken, the sour cream, and the paprika, with vegetables in the background. Another common problem with this dish is the sauce. In many versions, the sauce is thick and gluey. Ideally, the sauce will have the right consistency to coat egg noodles. A sauce that is too thick can't do this.

We began our tests by examining the chicken component. After several tests, we concluded that paprikash (like other chicken stews) is best made

---

INGREDIENTS: Paprika

The brilliant red powder we call paprika comes from the dried pods (fruit) of the plant species *Capsicum annuum L.*, the clan of peppers that ranges from sweet bells to the very hottest chiles. Several varieties of *Capsicum annuum L.* are used to produce paprika; there is no one specific "paprika pepper." Pods differ in shape and size and vary in degree of potency. Some are round, others are elongated. Some show no pungency, others are fairly hot.

The best paprika is thought to come from Hungary and Spain. In the United States, California and Texas are the main producers. Most European paprika pods are set out to dry naturally in the sun, a process that takes up to 25 days. Domestically grown paprika pods are oven-dried in about 30 hours.

Paprikas can be hot, sweet, or somewhere in between. The differences in pungency, color, and flavor relate to the proportion of mesocarp (fruit wall), placenta (the white veins), and seeds that are ground together. Sweet paprika is made mostly from the peppers' mesocarp, while hot paprika is a product of the placenta and seeds. The latter are ground to yield a spicy powder with an orange-brown color and, some spice experts say, poor flavor. It is almost as pungent as common chile powders and cayenne pepper.

The problem with all of this information is that except for allowing you to choose intelligently between sweet and hot paprika, it does you little practical good at the supermarket. In stores and catalogs we uncovered six choices: McCormick's (from California), Whole Foods Organic (also California), Penzeys Hungary Sweet, Szeged Hungarian Hot, Pendery's Spanish, and Igo Basque Piment d'Espelette (also from Spain). The Pendery's Spanish paprika had the deepest red color. Tasters likened the color of the rest to "Crayola-orange," "saffron," or "brick."

Once the paprikas were in the stews, there were equally diverse comments on flavor. Penzeys Hungary Sweet emerged as the overall favorite, hailed for its "roasty," "bold," and "balanced" flavor. The spice did not overpower the stew, but it had plenty of depth. Pendery's Spanish was the runner-up. It had an "earthy" quality and very rich flavor (though not as rich as our winner), with fruity notes. McCormick's finished in third place and was touted for its "lush," "big red pepper" flavor. Stews made with the other three paprikas received less favorable comments. Szeged Hungarian Hot was deemed intense and slightly bitter, the Whole Foods paprika was judged bland and uninteresting, and the Basque Piment d'Espelette was so hot that it was hard to detect any flavor (tasters liked this paprika the least).

Our conclusion? Chicken paprikash is best flavored with Hungarian sweet paprika. Other sweet paprikas (from Spain or California) can deliver good results, but don't use hot paprika in this dish.

Tasters enjoyed the robust but balanced flavor of Penzeys Hungary Sweet (left) and gave this paprika top scores. Pendery's Spanish (center) took second place—hailed for its deep color and rich flavor. McCormick's (right) earned third place in the tasting and is widely available in supermarkets.

with bone-in thighs. White meat dried out in our tests and drumsticks were not terribly meaty. We decided to replace the whole cut-up chicken called for in most recipes with eight thighs.

We focused on the paprika next (see page 190 for more details). Many recipes suggest seasoning the chicken with salt and paprika before browning it. We tried this approach and were disappointed with the results. Although the kitchen initially filled with that wonderful paprika aroma, the smell soon turned to singed peppers. The flavor of the finished dish was bitter, and the color had morphed from bright red to burnt sienna. We decided to season the chicken with salt and black pepper and add the paprika later.

With our chicken browned and reserved, we started to test various vegetable options, including onions, peppers, carrots, mushrooms, and tomatoes. Onions were a must—their pungent flavor balanced the sweetness of the paprika. Tasters found both red and green peppers to be welcome additions to the pot. They enhanced the natural sweetness of the paprika and worked well with the onions and chicken. Long strips of pepper felt out of place in this dish, so we cut each pepper in half widthwise before slicing it thin. These shorter strips softened a bit more in the pot and proved easier to eat.

Tasters rejected carrots and mushrooms. Although tasty additions, neither seemed essential and so both were vetoed. Tomatoes, however, were deemed crucial to achieving a proper balance between the sweet and acidic components in this dish. Tomato paste muddied the colors and flavors, but tasters responded favorably to the addition of diced canned tomatoes. We found it best to drain the tomatoes so that their juice did not overwhelm the flavors of the other vegetables.

With the vegetables in place, we focused on the seasonings. We found it best to add the paprika to the pot once the onions and peppers had softened. A quick sauté in oil brought out the full flavor of this spice. We tried adding some garlic with the paprika but found its flavor oddly out of place with the mellow sweet flavors in paprikash. Tasters felt that a little dried marjoram was a worthy addition. We also added some flour to the pot at this point

to help thicken the stew. A tablespoon of flour provided just enough thickening power.

Although the drained tomatoes provide a little moisture, most paprikash recipes call for some wine to deglaze the pan. We found red wine too harsh. White wine worked better with the other flavors.

Sour cream is the final component, added only when the chicken has completely stewed. It gives the sauce body and tang has a thickening effect as well. Some sources suggest using both heavy cream and sour cream. Although we liked the effect that the heavy cream had on the consistency of the sauce (it was velvety and smooth), we missed the tang of recipes made with just sour cream. In the end, we decided to finish the stew with ⅓ cup of sour cream.

If sour cream is added directly to the pot, it can curdle. Tempering the sour cream (stirring some of the hot liquid from the stew pot into the sour cream, then adding the warmed sour cream mixture to the pot) will prevent curdling. Once the sour cream goes into the pot, the stew should be served promptly.

Chicken Paprikash

SERVES 4

In this rendition of the Hungarian classic, the natural juices of chicken, bell peppers, onions, and tomatoes are released while stewing and then enriched with sour cream to create a comforting winter dish. Use sweet, genuine Hungarian paprika for the best flavor and most vibrant color. Buttered egg noodles are our favorite accompaniment, but rice or mashed potatoes are also good options.

PLANNING AHEAD: Chicken Paprikash may be prepared through step 2 and stored in an airtight container in the refrigerator for up to 3 days. It cannot be frozen. The chicken should be stored and reheated in the cooking liquid. Reheat the dish in a covered saucepan or Dutch oven over medium-low heat, adding broth or water as needed to adjust the consistency, and continue with step 3.

8   bone-in, skin-on chicken thighs (about 3 pounds), trimmed of excess skin and fat
     Salt and ground black pepper

I	teaspoon vegetable oil
I	large onion, halved and sliced thin
I	large red bell pepper, stemmed, seeded, halved widthwise, and cut into thin strips
I	large green bell pepper, stemmed, seeded, halved widthwise, and cut into thin strips
3½	tablespoons sweet paprika
¼	teaspoon dried marjoram
I	tablespoon all-purpose flour
½	cup dry white wine
I	(14.5-ounce) can diced tomatoes, drained
⅓	cup sour cream
2	tablespoons chopped fresh parsley leaves
	Tabasco sauce to taste

1. Adjust an oven rack to the lower-middle position; heat the oven to 300 degrees. Dry the chicken thighs thoroughly with paper towels, then season generously with salt and pepper. Heat the oil in a large ovenproof Dutch oven over medium-high heat until shimmering but not smoking. Add 4 of the chicken thighs, skin-side down, and cook without moving them until the skin is crisp and well browned, about 5 minutes. Turn the chicken pieces and brown on the second side, about 5 minutes longer; transfer to a large plate. Add the remaining chicken thighs to the pot and repeat, then transfer them to a plate and set aside. Discard all but 1 tablespoon of fat from the pot; when the chicken has cooled, remove and discard the skin (see the illustration on page 201).

2. Add the onion to the empty Dutch oven and cook over medium heat until softened, about 5 minutes. Add the red and green peppers and cook until the onions are browned and the peppers softened, about 3 minutes. Stir in 3 tablespoons of the paprika, the marjoram, and flour and cook, stirring constantly, until fragrant, about 1 minute. Add the wine, scraping the pot bottom with a wooden spoon to loosen the browned bits. Stir in the tomatoes and 1 teaspoon salt. Add the chicken pieces and accumulated juices, nestling the chicken under the onion and peppers. Bring the liquid to a simmer, cover, then set the pot in the oven; cook until the chicken offers no resistance when poked with the tip of a paring knife but is still clinging to the bones, about 1¼ hours.

3. Place the sour cream in a small bowl and combine with the remaining ½ tablespoon paprika. Remove the chicken from the pot and place a portion on each plate. Stir a few tablespoons of the hot stewing liquid into the sour cream, and then stir the mixture back into the remaining peppers and sauce. Ladle the peppers and enriched sauce over the chicken, sprinkle with parsley, and serve immediately, passing the Tabasco at the table.

COUNTRY CAPTAIN CHICKEN

FOLKLORE ABOUT COUNTRY CAPTAIN CHICKEN abounds. Some claim that a sea captain toting spices brought the recipe from India to Georgia in the early 1800s. The captain is said to have introduced the recipe (and the necessary spices) to the residents of Savannah, which was then an important shipping port for the spice trade. Others say it is named for the captain of Indian troops (called country troops) who served the dish to British soldiers, also in the 1800s.

Whatever its origin, it is universally recognized that the dish was a favorite of President Franklin D. Roosevelt. In the 1940s, he enjoyed the stew at the Little White House at Warm Springs, Georgia, where he underwent treatment for paralysis. He liked it so much that he instructed his chef to serve it to General George Patton when he visited the Little White House.

It is understandable that the comforting, curried flavor of country captain was such a favorite of F.D.R. The chicken stew is at once spicy, sweet, and fragrant, but not overpoweringly so. Almost all recipes call for tomatoes, garlic, onions, green peppers, curry powder, and raisins or currants, and cooks vary the dish with additional spices. With its playful name, colorful look, and bright flavors, it has become a well-known dish in Georgia and other parts of the South.

Before beginning our tests, we narrowed the field a bit by choosing to make the stew with chicken thighs. While some recipes call for cut-up whole chickens, we opted to use thighs only, since their dark, rich meat is flavorful and well suited to stewing. After making this decision, we prepared three different versions of this recipe. The differences among them were significant.

The first recipe intrigued us with its unusual additions of bacon and orange juice, but tasters found it unbalanced in flavor. The bacon took over, and the orange juice was lost behind the curry powder. The stewing liquid reduced during cooking but was still quite thin—not very stew-like. In this recipe, raisins appeared as a garnish, but we agreed that they would be more pleasant if plumped while stewing rather than added at the table.

The second recipe was the simplest of the three, made with the most basic of ingredients, but it left tasters wanting more flavor, more sweetness, and more spice. Several tasters also noted that it was greasy.

We liked the appearance, texture, and taste of the third recipe: the tender bites of stewed chicken, raisins, mango, and tomato with a final sprinkling of parsley won us over. The addition of flour made for a nicely thickened sauce. Another advantage of this recipe was that it removed the chicken skin after browning, while both of the other recipes left the skin on. Tasters unanimously disliked chicken skin in the stew. They left the soft, flabby skin behind on their plates and described the stew as greasy. Our technique of quickly cooking the thighs with the skin on and later removing it proved best.

Many of the recipes that we looked at do not specify a certain type of curry powder, though varieties of curry are infinite. We tested standard yellow curry powder (the kind most frequently spotted on supermarket shelves) against hotter Madras-style curry powder as well as a homemade curry powder, ground just before cooking. Tasters

HANDLING A MANGO

1. Mangoes are notoriously hard to peel, owing to their odd shape and slippery texture. We start by removing a thin slice from one end of the mango so that it sits flat on the work surface.

2. Hold the mango cut-side down and remove the skin with a sharp paring knife or serrated knife in thin strips, working from top to bottom.

3. Once the peel has been removed, cut down along one side of the flat pit to remove the flesh from one side of the mango. Do the same thing on the other side of the pit.

4. Trim around the pit to remove any remaining flesh. The flesh can now be sliced or chopped as desired.

preferred the Madras-style curry powder for the heat it offered up in contrast with the sweet, round flavors of the stew. The stew made with standard curry powder was bland in comparison. The one made with homemade curry powder was good, but it didn't seem worth the effort, given how much we liked the version made with the pre-mixed Madras-style curry.

During testing, tasters always enjoyed the traditional garnish of toasted almonds. Since this stew looks and tastes like party food, we also tested a host of traditional curry garnishes to serve along with it. Mango chutney is suggested as a garnish in many country captain recipes, but we found it too strong in flavor. Bananas, shredded coconut, green apples, and scallions complemented the sweet/hot flavors of the stew perfectly.

GARNISHES FOR COUNTRY CAPTAIN CHICKEN

THESE GARNISHES ARE OPTIONAL, BUT they are an easy way to dress up this stew. Use them singly or in combination.

- ➤ 1/2 cup sliced almonds, toasted
- ➤ 1 banana, peeled and cut into 1/4-inch dice
- ➤ 1/2 cup sweetened shredded coconut
- ➤ 1 Granny Smith apple, cored and cut into 1/4-inch dice
- ➤ 4 scallions, sliced thin

Country Captain Chicken
SERVES 4

For this recipe, we like to use Madras-style curry powder, which is hotter than standard curry powder. Toasted almonds are a traditional garnish for this stew, but it's fun to pass a variety of garnishes at the table (see above for other ideas). Serve with long-grain rice or basmati rice.

PLANNING AHEAD: Country Captain Chicken may be stored in an airtight container in the refrigerator for up to 3 days. It may also be frozen for up to 3 months. The chicken should be stored and reheated in the cooking liquid. Reheat the dish in a covered saucepan or Dutch oven over medium-low heat, adding broth or water as needed to adjust the consistency. The garnishes should be prepared the day the dish is served.

8	bone-in, skin-on chicken thighs (about 3 pounds), trimmed of excess skin and fat
	Salt and ground black pepper
1	teaspoon vegetable oil
2	large onions, chopped coarse
1	medium green bell pepper, stemmed, seeded, and chopped coarse
2	medium garlic cloves, minced or pressed through a garlic press
1 1/2	tablespoons sweet paprika
1	tablespoon Madras-style curry powder
1/4	teaspoon cayenne pepper
3	tablespoons all-purpose flour
1 1/2	cups low-sodium chicken broth
1	(14.5-ounce) can diced tomatoes
1	bay leaf
1/2	teaspoon dried thyme
1/2	cup raisins
1	ripe mango, peeled, pitted, and cut into 1/4-inch dice (see the illustrations on page 193)
1/4	cup minced fresh parsley leaves

1. Adjust an oven rack to the lower-middle position; heat the oven to 300 degrees. Dry the chicken thighs thoroughly with paper towels, then season generously with salt and pepper. Heat the oil in a large ovenproof Dutch oven over medium-high heat until shimmering but not smoking. Add 4 of the chicken thighs, skin-side down, and cook without moving them until the skin is crisp and well browned, about 5 minutes. Turn the chicken pieces and brown on the second side, about 5 minutes longer; transfer to a large plate. Add the remaining chicken thighs to the pot and repeat, then transfer them to a plate and set aside. Discard all but 1 tablespoon of fat from the pot; when the chicken has cooled, remove and discard the skin (see the illustration on page 201).

2. Add the onions and bell pepper to the empty Dutch oven and reduce the heat to medium. Cook, stirring occasionally, until softened, about 5 minutes. Stir in the garlic, paprika, curry powder, and cayenne and cook until the spices are fragrant, about 30 seconds. Stir in the flour and cook for about 2 minutes. Add the broth, scraping up any browned bits that may have stuck to the pot. Add the tomatoes, bay leaf, thyme, raisins, and mango, and bring to a boil. Reduce the heat and simmer for 10 minutes. Add the chicken pieces and accumulated juices, submerging the chicken in the liquid. Return to a simmer, cover, and place the pot in the oven; cook until the chicken offers no resistance when poked with the tip of a paring knife but is still clinging to the bones, about 1¼ hours. Remove the pot from the oven.

3. Stir in the parsley, discard the bay leaf, and adjust the seasonings. Serve immediately, with garnishes if desired.

CHICKEN AND SAUSAGE GUMBO

GUMBO IS AS MUCH A PART OF NEW Orleans culture as Dixieland jazz, Mardi Gras, and beignets. It is a thick one-pot-meal sort of stew that usually includes some combination of seafood, poultry, or small game along with sausage or some other highly seasoned, cured smoked pork. Also present is the Creole and Cajun "holy trinity" of onion, bell pepper, and celery. Quite often, gumbos are thickened with okra or ground dried sassafras leaves, known as filé (pronounced fee-LAY) powder. Last, but very important, most gumbos are flavored with a dark brown roux. The roux, in our opinion, is the heart and soul of gumbo, elevating it from simple stew to culinary masterpiece. But the roux is not without its issues: a chocolate-brown roux can take upward of an hour to prepare, requiring constant stirring and frequent adjustment of heat to prevent it from burning. We wanted to find a simpler, less hands-on technique. We also wanted to do what we could to streamline both the ingredient list and the method. For the predominant flavors, we settled on a simple combination of chicken and sausage. Shrimp, a common ingredient, requires a fair amount of preparatory effort that we wanted to avoid.

In classic French cooking, a roux is nothing more than flour cooked gently in some type of fat to form a paste that is used to thicken sauces. Creole and Cajun cooks use roux as much for flavor as thickening by deeply browning the flour, which gives it a complex, toasty, smoky flavor and a deep, rich brown color (flour this deeply browned, in fact, provides little thickening power). The problem is that the flour can burn very easily, and the only safeguards against that are relatively low heat and constant stirring. In other words, it's a real pain to prepare.

We aren't the first cooks to try to shorten the cooking time. Some cooks recommend heating the oil until it smokes and then cooking the roux over high heat. Though this method produced a very dark roux, about the color of bittersweet chocolate, in less than 10 minutes there was too much sizzle and smoke. The process felt out of control, and the specter of burnt roux loomed large.

We accepted that our solution didn't lie in traditional stovetop cooking. Coming across a recipe for a microwaved roux, we gave it a whirl. We learned the hard way that microwaves and roux do not mix. We had cooked the roux in what we thought was a microwave-safe Pyrex bowl, but the moment we rested the bowl and its smoking hot contents on the countertop, it shattered into a thousand pieces. A quick call to the test kitchens at Corning Consumer Products confirmed that they do not recommend heating oil in any Pyrex product for 10 minutes on high in the microwave.

We took a safer approach next and tried the oven. We've come across oven-toasted flour before, so we thought we might be able to brown the flour darkly and simply stir it into hot oil to form the roux. Our instincts proved correct, as we were able to toast the flour to a rich peanut butter color within a half an hour. Stirred into hot fat, it worked as well as the traditional method with a fraction of the work.

To finesse the flavor of the roux, we experimented with a number of fats and oils and ended up preferring a blend. Chicken fat—rendered from the chicken thighs to be included in the gumbo—lent a richness to the dish that none of the other fats provided. There was simply not enough rendered fat to make a strictly chicken-fat roux, so we made up the difference with neutral-tasting vegetable oil. We also tried different ratios of fat to flour and found that the classic 1-1 ratio was hard to beat.

With the roux under our belts, the rest of the recipe development process focused on how best to cook and prepare the primary flavors and aromatic vegetables. We had already browned the chicken to render its fat for the roux; it simply needed to simmer in the broth to finish cooking. Chicken thighs were our top choice because of their full flavor and resiliency: it's hard to overcook them. As for the broth, chicken broth made a good deal of sense as the liquid in the gumbo. Many gumbos include wine or beer with the broth, but we found that their addition only served to complicate the flavors.

When it comes to the sausage in gumbo, andouille is the only acceptable choice (see more details at right). Heavily smoked and laced with cayenne pepper, garlic, and herbs, andouille packs a punch, and it contributed great depth to the gumbo. When simmered too long, however, the sausage turned tough and bland. We found the best option was to add it for the second half of cooking.

Two big flavoring questions concerned tomatoes—some say that gumbo just isn't gumbo without them—and garlic. Well, our tasters said that gumbo was just fine without tomatoes, but they gave the thumbs up to garlic, six cloves of it, in fact. Other seasonings in gumbo range from elaborate mixtures of herbs, spices, and sauces down to nothing more than salt. We tried what seemed like a hundred seasoning variations and finally settled on a simple combination of dried thyme and bay leaves. Our experiments with different proportions of onion, bell pepper, and celery in the holy trinity notwithstanding, the classic ratio of 1 part celery to 2 parts pepper to 4 parts onion tasted best. We did, however, switch from the traditional green bell pepper to red peppers, preferring their sweeter, fuller flavor.

Next we considered the level of spicy heat,

usually provided by cayenne pepper either alone or in combination with a hot pepper sauce, such as Tabasco. The gumbos that some of us have tasted in Louisiana were only subtly spicy, with the pepper heat very much in the background. A mere ½ teaspoon of cayenne did the trick for our tasters, all of whom favored the powder over the vinegary taste of bottled hot sauce.

Last, we considered whether to thicken the gumbo with okra or filé powder. We think both are probably acquired tastes. Thus far, everyone had been satisfied without either, and because both added distinct—and to some, unwelcome—flavors, we decided to reserve them for the variations on the master recipe.

Up to this point, we had been cooking our

INGREDIENTS: Andouille Sausage

Andouille, a highly seasoned smoked sausage, is the most authentic choice for Cajun dishes like gumbos and jambalayas. Unfortunately, authentic andouille can be tricky to find outside of the Bayou or specialty stores. To find a convenient, suitable alternative, we tasted a few styles of more widely available smoked sausages: linguiça, chorizo, and kielbasa. While definitely different in flavor than andouille, smoky, garlic-laced kielbasa was deemed the best alternative.

For the cook dead set on authenticity, Cajun-made andouille can be found via mail order. We tasted five popular brands, all found on the Internet or through catalogs, and discovered that they varied greatly in flavor and texture. Some were bland and gristly, while others were explosively spiced. Our favorite of the bunch was Chef Paul's regular (or mild) andouille, Chef Paul, of course, being Paul Prudhomme, the godfather of contemporary Cajun cooking. The andouille was deemed "rich" and earthy" with a "balanced heat level." (We also tasted Chef Paul's spicy "hot" andouille, and found its heat overpowering.) To purchase Chef Paul's andouille, check www.chefpaul.com.

gumbo on the stovetop and realized that shifting it to the oven was not much of a stretch. An oven set at 300 degrees—the temperature at which we do most of our braising—cooked the gumbo in the same time as on the stovetop. Not much of a change, but it freed up burner space for other tasks. Within an hour and a half (adding the sausage for the last half hour), the flavors had fully unified and the chicken was fork-tender. Definitely simplified, but far from compromised, our gumbo took a minimum of effort (compared to the classic method) and was certainly worthy of the bayou.

Chicken and Sausage Gumbo

SERVES 6 TO 8

Make sure the broth is tepid (100 to 110 degrees) before adding it to the roux; otherwise it may not combine properly. If you cannot find andouille sausage, an equal amount of kielbasa or other smoked sausage may be substituted. If you would like to add okra to the gumbo, add 10 ounces thawed frozen okra with the vegetables in step 4. If you can find it, fresh okra can be used in place of the frozen, though it tends to be more slippery. If you want to use filé powder, add 1½ teaspoons with the parsley and scallions in step 5. Serve this dish with a generous amount of rice.

PLANNING AHEAD: Chicken and Sausage Gumbo may be stored in an airtight container in the refrigerator for up to 3 days. It may also be frozen for up to 3 months. The chicken should be stored and reheated in the cooking liquid. Reheat the dish in a covered saucepan or Dutch oven over medium-low heat, adding broth or water as needed to adjust the consistency.

½	cup all-purpose flour
10	bone-in, skin-on chicken thighs (about 3¾ pounds), trimmed of excess skin and fat Salt and ground black pepper
¼	cup plus 1 teaspoon vegetable oil, or more as needed
2	medium onions, chopped fine
1	medium red bell pepper, stemmed, seeded, and chopped fine
1	medium celery rib, chopped fine
6	medium garlic cloves, minced or pressed through a garlic press
1	teaspoon dried thyme
¼	teaspoon cayenne pepper
6	cups low-sodium chicken broth, warmed
2	bay leaves
1	pound smoked sausage, such as andouille or kielbasa, sliced ¼ inch thick
½	cup minced fresh parsley leaves
4	medium scallions, white and green parts, sliced thin

1. Adjust an oven rack to the middle position and heat the oven to 400 degrees. Spread the flour in an even layer on a parchment paper–lined baking sheet. Bake, stirring occasionally, until uniformly browned to the color of peanut butter, about 25 minutes. Cool on a wire rack. Reduce the oven temperature to 300 degrees.

2. Dry the chicken thighs thoroughly with paper towels, then season generously with salt and pepper. Heat 1 teaspoon of the oil in a large ovenproof Dutch oven over medium-high heat until shimmering but not smoking. Add 5 of the chicken thighs, skin-side down, and cook without moving them until the skin is crisp and well browned, about 5 minutes. Turn the chicken pieces and brown on the second side, about 5 minutes longer; transfer to a large plate. Add the remaining chicken thighs to the pot and repeat the browning process, then transfer them to a plate and set aside. When the chicken has cooled, remove and discard the skin (see the illustration on page 201). Drain the fat from the pan into a measuring cup. Add enough vegetable oil (about ¼ cup) to yield ½ cup total fat.

3. Heat the fat-and-oil mixture in a clean Dutch oven over medium-high heat until it registers 200 degrees on an instant-read thermometer, 1½ to 2 minutes. Reduce the heat to medium and gradually stir in the browned flour with a wooden spoon or spatula, working out any lumps that form. Continue stirring constantly, reaching into the corners of the pan, until the mixture is smooth, about 2 minutes.

4. Add the onions, bell pepper, celery, garlic, thyme, cayenne, and 1 teaspoon salt to the roux and cook, stirring frequently, until the vegetables soften, 8 to 10 minutes. Add the chicken broth in a

slow, steady stream while vigorously stirring. Stir in the bay leaves and place the browned chicken thighs and any accumulated juices in a single layer in the pot; bring to a boil.

5. Cover the pot, transfer to the oven, and cook until the chicken is cooked through, about 1 hour. Stir the sausage into the Dutch oven and cook until the flavors have blended and the sausage is tender, about 30 minutes longer. Off the heat, stir in the parsley and scallions and season with salt, ground black pepper, and cayenne to taste. Serve.

INGREDIENTS: Okra and Filé Powder

In a Creole or Cajun dark roux, most of the starch in the flour breaks down in the cooking, so the roux does more to flavor the stew than to thicken it. That leaves the task to one of two other traditional Southern ingredients, okra and filé powder. (It's also possible, as we do in our master recipe, to go without either one for a slightly thinner stew.)

Okra pods, said to have been brought to the southern United States from Africa by the slave trade, are slender, green, usually about 3 inches in length, ridged in texture, tapered in shape, and often slightly fuzzy. The interior of the pods is sticky and mucilaginous, so once they are cut open, they thicken any liquid in which they are cooked. Okra's flavor is subtle, with hints of eggplant, green bean, and chestnut. In our gumbo testing, we could detect no taste difference between fresh and frozen okra.

The other possible thickener, filé powder, is made of ground dried sassafras leaves. It is said to have been introduced to the settlers of southern Louisiana by the native Choctaw Indians. Filé, also referred to in Louisiana as gumbo filé, adds both a gelatinous thickness and a subtle, singular flavor to gumbo. Though difficult to describe precisely, the flavor is distinctly earthy, with notes of straw, bay, marjoram, and oregano. Filé is as much a hallmark of authentic Louisiana cooking as dark roux and the holy trinity of onion, bell pepper, and celery. Filé is used in one of two ways. Diners can sprinkle a little bit onto their portion of gumbo right at the table, or the cook can stir some into the pot at the very last moment of cooking or even once the pot has come off the heat. In our recipe variation, we prefer to add it to the pot, which mellows its flavor somewhat. In stores that carry it, pale green filé powder is generally sold in tall, slender, 1-ounce jars.

One thing on which most Creole and Cajun cooks agree is that you should never use okra and filé together because the gumbo will get too thick, even gummy.

CHICKEN WITH 40 CLOVES OF GARLIC

FEW DISHES EXEMPLIFY FRENCH COUNTRY cooking better than chicken with 40 cloves of garlic. In this classic Provençal dish, humble ingredients—chicken, a few heads of garlic, and a bit of cheap wine or vermouth—undergo a dramatic transformation when subjected to a long, gentle simmer. The chicken becomes fork-tender and the seemingly absurd amount of garlic mellows, giving the dish a sweet, creamy backdrop. This is one of those classic recipes that, when prepared properly, becomes much more than the sum of its parts. But, more often than not, the chicken tends to be tough and stringy, the sauce sharp instead of mellow, the garlic overwhelming. So what's the secret to turning out a great version of this (supposedly) easy classic?

For testing purposes, we started with the two main elements of the recipe: the chicken and the garlic. Most traditional recipes use a whole, cut-up chicken, but considering that the chicken is braised, it takes very careful timing to keep the finicky white meat from overcooking. We decided to take a safer, more convenient route and use chicken thighs instead. They are easier to prepare and serve, and they are more forgiving with respect to cooking time because of their high proportion of connective tissue and collagen. As with our other braised chicken dishes, we browned the chicken with the skin on, and then removed the skin before simmering. The skin serves two purposes: it yields flavorful fat to aid in browning and protects the meat from the pan's heat.

Attaining the perfect garlic flavor was our next goal. In classic recipes, two or three heads of garlic (40 cloves, give or take a few) are separated into individual cloves and braised with the chicken. Some recipes squeeze a portion of the garlic into the braising liquid at the very end of the cooking process as a thickener, a trick we liked and wanted to incorporate into our recipe. Once the chicken was tender, we removed it from the pot and kept it warm while we strained the garlic cloves from the broth and pushed some through a strainer to rid them of their papery skins. Briefly simmered to concentrate it, the garlic puree–enriched braising liquid was quickly thick (and flavorful) enough to serve as the basis for the sauce. The whole garlic cloves were saved to serve alongside the chicken. Because the liquid is strained, it meant we could easily add whole sprigs of herbs and simply strain them with the skins—we were happy to save labor anywhere we could.

Forty cloves of braised garlic tasted like, well, mellow cooked garlic: mild and sweet, but one-dimensional. Some recipes include a little onion, an option that we found we liked, as it added flavor to the broth. Substituting shallot for the onion improved the flavor even more.

Unencumbered by herbs and wine, the braise currently tasted of nothing but pure chicken with garlic and shallots—not a bad start, but it needed more flavor to round out the dish. White wine lent some much-needed acidity to the dish, serving to intensify the sweetness of the chicken and lend definition to the pervasive garlic flavor. After testing a couple of batches, we found that a fairly substantial amount, ¾ cup, provided the best flavor. We also tried replacing the wine with dry vermouth; with its herbaceous and slightly sweet flavor, it proved a better choice than most white wines in the same price range. As for the herbs, we tried the usual suspects: thyme, rosemary, sage, parsley, and bay leaves. All but sage and parsley were deemed positive additions; sage muddied the flavors, and parsley lent little but color.

Chicken with 40 Cloves of Garlic

SERVES 4

Avoid heads of garlic that contain enormous cloves (their flavor may be too mild) as well as heads that have begun to sprout (the green shoots will make the sauce taste bitter). Serve with slices of crusty baguette onto which the garlic cloves can be spread.

PLANNING AHEAD: Chicken with 40 Cloves of Garlic may be prepared up to three days ahead of time and stored in an airtight container in the refrigerator. It cannot be frozen. The chicken should be stored in the sauce to protect it from drying out. Reheat it in a covered saucepan or Dutch oven, adding additional broth or water as necessary to adjust the consistency.

8	bone-in, skin-on chicken thighs (about 3 pounds), trimmed of excess fat and skin
	Salt and ground black pepper
1	teaspoon olive oil
1⅓	cups low-sodium chicken broth
3	medium heads garlic (about 8 ounces), outer papery skins removed, cloves separated and unpeeled
2	medium shallots, peeled and quartered pole to pole
¾	cup dry vermouth or dry white wine
2	sprigs fresh thyme
1	sprig fresh rosemary
1	bay leaf
2	tablespoons unsalted butter, cut into 4 pieces

1. Adjust an oven rack to the lower-middle position; heat the oven to 300 degrees. Dry the chicken thighs thoroughly with paper towels, then season generously with salt and pepper. Heat the oil in a large ovenproof Dutch oven over medium-high heat until shimmering but not smoking. Add 4 of the chicken thighs, skin-side down, and cook without moving them until the skin is crisp and well browned, about 5 minutes. Turn the chicken pieces and brown on the second side, about 5 minutes longer; transfer to a large plate. Add the remaining chicken thighs to the pot and repeat the browning process, then transfer them to a plate and set aside. Discard all but 1 tablespoon of fat from the pot; when the chicken has cooled, remove and discard the skin (see the illustration on page 201).

2. Off the heat, add ⅓ cup of the chicken broth and vigorously scrape the pot bottom to release any browned bits. Return the pot to medium heat and add the garlic and shallots. Cook, stirring occasionally, until the garlic is lightly browned, about 4 minutes. Add the vermouth, remaining chicken broth, thyme, rosemary, and bay leaf. Submerge the chicken in the liquid and add any accumulated chicken juices to the pot. Increase the heat to high and bring to a simmer, cover, then set the pot in the oven. Cook until the chicken offers no resistance when poked with the tip of a paring knife but still clings to the bones, about 1¼ hours.

3. Using a slotted spoon, transfer the chicken to a serving platter and tent with foil. Strain the broth through a fine-mesh strainer into a medium bowl. Remove and discard the herbs and reserve the garlic cloves and shallots, scattering half of the garlic cloves around the chicken. With a rubber spatula, push the remaining garlic cloves and the shallots through the fine-mesh strainer and into the bowl with the braising liquid; discard the skins. Return the liquid to the Dutch oven and bring to a simmer over medium-high heat, whisking occasionally to incorporate the garlic; whisk in the butter piece by piece until fully incorporated, and season with salt and pepper to taste. Drizzle a

INGREDIENTS: Dry Vermouth

Though it's often used in cooking, and even more often in martinis, dry vermouth is a potable that is paid very little attention. Imagine our surprise, then, when we did some research and turned up nearly a dozen different brands. We pared them down to eight and tasted the vermouths straight (chilled) and in simple pan sauces for chicken (containing only shallots, chicken broth, and butter in addition to the vermouth).

First, a quick description of what dry vermouth is. Its base is a white wine, presumably not of particularly high quality, as evidenced by the relatively low prices of most vermouths. The wine is fortified with neutral grape spirits that hike the alcohol level up a few percentage points to 16 to 18 percent, and it is "aromatized," or infused with, "botanicals" such as herbs, spices, and fruits. In this country, dry vermouth, also called extra-dry vermouth, is imported from France and Italy (Italian vermouths being most common here) or made domestically in California.

Two vermouths found their way into the top three in both tastings: Gallo Extra Dry and Noilly Prat Original French Dry. Gallo (left) is the fruitier of the two and made the favorite pan sauce, which tasters called balanced, complex, smooth, and round. Noilly Prat (right) is more woodsy and herbaceous and made a pan sauce that tasted fresh and balanced.

portion of the sauce over the chicken and pour the rest into a sauceboat to pass at the table.

CHICKEN TAGINE

TAGINES ARE THE MOST BASIC OF MOROCCAN dishes and probably one of the few that might be familiar to home cooks. To put it simply, tagines are the North African counterpart of what we know here as stew. There are hundreds of different tagines, from beef, poultry, and lamb to seafood, vegetable, and even fruit tagines. The most iconic version is chicken tagine with olives and lemon. The olive and lemon combination is a hallmark of Moroccan food, and when matched with earthy, aromatic spices and tender chicken, it's hard to beat. Could we replicate the exotic flavors of Fez in a home-cook-friendly recipe?

The manner in which tagines are prepared is a good bit different than western-style stews with respect to both equipment and method. Instead of a saucepan or Dutch oven, North African cooks typically use an earthenware vessel called a *tagine slaoui*. The base is relatively shallow and the lid is a steep-sided cone terminating in a narrow chimney. Some steam escapes through the opening, thus allowing the liquids within the vessel to concentrate. Thankfully, a traditional tagine slaoui is not essential for preparing tagine; a Dutch oven works fine because the stewing liquid may be reduced once the dish is done.

For chicken tagines, the chicken is first rubbed with garlic and salt or a spice rub, and left to marinate overnight so that the flavors fully permeate the meat. The chicken is then placed on the bottom of a pot, and the vegetables and herbs are layered on top. Water or broth is added and the mélange is simmered or baked until the chicken is falling-off-the-bone tender.

We made a couple of decisions from the start. First of all, we wanted to treat the dish more like a classic braise and thereby, perhaps, make it less intimidating to home cooks. We would brown the chicken, sauté the aromatic vegetables, add the broth, and simmer it in the oven until the chicken was tender. And we wanted to avoid marinating the chicken; this was simply too time consuming.

But before we could tackle the chicken, we needed to pick a basic spice blend with which to flavor the chicken and tagine. Moroccan cooking is characterized by intricate combinations of spices. Warm spices typically reserved for the sweet side of the menu in western cooking, such as cinnamon, nutmeg, cloves, cardamom, are applied with a heavy hand in Moroccan cuisine. Turmeric, paprika, and saffron are also used frequently, as much for color as for flavor. After comparing a stack of chicken tagine recipes, we chose a simple blend of the most common spices we saw listed: cumin, coriander, ginger (ground, not fresh), and paprika. Earthy, sweet, sharp, and peppery, the blend covered all the bases. And each spice is a pantry staple—no running to specialty stores for exotic ingredients.

In our first attempt at flavoring the chicken, we rubbed the spices on the chicken as we would if we were going to grill it, then browned it on the stovetop in a Dutch oven. The dry spices fell off and burned while the chicken was browning. It appeared as if the spices had difficulty adhering to the flabby chicken skin. So in the next test, we removed the chicken skin and rubbed the spices directly onto the flesh. The spices stayed on the meat, but without the fat in the skin shielding the meat from the pan's heat, the exterior of the chicken dried out and turned leathery. Mixing the spices with oil before applying them to the chicken added a layer of protection that prevented the chicken from drying out. Reducing the heat and only gently browning the meat further helped keep the spices from burning.

This spice rub method appeared to work. The chicken meat tasted of the spices—similar in flavor and intensity to chicken that had been marinated overnight. Each spice complemented the chicken's flavor and the paprika lent it a ruddy, brick-red exterior.

As for the aromatics, we knew that a substantial amount of onion was imperative to the overall flavor of the tagine. In this case, we added thinly sliced onions to the Dutch oven once the chicken was browned. As the onions softened, they exuded juices, which in turn loosened the flavorful *fond* (browned bits) left behind by the chicken. Within minutes, the onions were fully softened and tinted red by the paprika remaining in the pan. A few cloves of minced garlic and a couple of bay leaves rounded out the flavorings.

Tagines often include a surprising amount of sweetener, be it granulated sugar, honey, or a heaping handful of dried fruit. At first, it felt weird adding sugar to a savory dish (a pinch perhaps to adjust acidity, but tablespoons were a different story), but we realized the sweetness improved the flavor of both the spices and the chicken. It brought out the warm flavors of the spices and mitigated their bitterness. We quickly eliminated granulated sugar and brown sugar as boring, but deciding between honey and golden raisins proved more difficult. Tasters liked both well enough that we turned one into a variation.

We were finally ready to tackle the defining flavors of the dish: olives and lemon. Some recipes simmer the olives with the chicken from the start, but we found this rendered the broth bitter and the olives flavorless. We chose to leave the olives out until the chicken was tender, and then simmer the olives in the sauce as it reduced. The fruity flavor of the olives permeated the broth, but didn't dominate it.

The lemon flavor proved problematic. Moroccans typically use preserved lemons (lemons that have

REMOVING THE SKIN FROM BROWNED CHICKEN

Once the chicken thighs have been browned and cooled, grasp the skin from one end and pull to separate it from the meat. Discard the skin.

been cured in salt), which are as ubiquitous as pickles in American cooking. Simultaneously tart and salty, the flavor of preserved lemons is wholly unique. The problem is that preserved lemons can be virtually impossible to find outside of specialty stores (though easy to make at home if you have the months it requires for the lemons to cure). How could we replace the flavor? Fresh lemon juice didn't provide much lemony depth to the dish when added at the beginning, nor did grated lemon zest added to the finished sauce. Both were too fresh and one-dimensional tasting. A swath of lemon peel simmered in the broth was a better option, especially when combined with a substantial splash of lemon juice in the finished broth. Admittedly ersatz, our quick substitute provides the sense, if not the authentic flavor, of preserved lemon.

Chicken Tagine with Olives and Lemon

SERVES 4

This dish can also be prepared with a whole chicken (about 3½ to 4 pounds) cut into eight pieces (wings reserved for another purpose) and skinned. Tagine prepared with a whole chicken should be cooked for ½ hour less than the recipe with chicken thighs to prevent the breast meat from drying out. Feel free to experiment with different types of olives, but avoid bland Mission olives or those stuffed with pimentos. If you can find preserved lemons, omit the lemon peel and add one tablespoon of minced preserved lemon rind along with the olives in step 3. Serve this dish with couscous or rice.

PLANNING AHEAD: The recipe can be made through step 2 and stored in an airtight container in the refrigerator for up to 3 days or frozen for up to 3 months. Bring the stew to a simmer over medium-low heat before continuing with step 3.

I	teaspoon ground ginger
1½	teaspoons ground cumin
I	teaspoon ground coriander
2	teaspoons sweet paprika
	Salt and ground black pepper
3	tablespoons olive oil

8	bone-in, skin-on chicken thighs (about 3 pounds), skinned and trimmed of excess fat
I	large onion, halved and sliced thin
2	tablespoons water
4	medium garlic cloves, minced or pressed through a garlic press
2	bay leaves
1¾	cups low-sodium chicken broth
½	cup golden raisins
I	(2-inch) strip of lemon peel
3	tablespoons lemon juice
½	cup kalamata olives, pitted and chopped coarse
2	tablespoons chopped fresh parsley or cilantro leaves

1. Adjust an oven rack to the lower-middle position and heat the oven to 300 degrees. Combine the ginger, cumin, coriander, paprika, 1 teaspoon salt, ¼ teaspoon black pepper, and 2 tablespoons of the olive oil in a large bowl. Dry the chicken thoroughly with paper towels, then add to the bowl with the spices and toss to coat. Heat the remaining tablespoon oil in a large ovenproof Dutch oven over medium heat until shimmering. Add 4 of the chicken thighs, skin-side down, and cook without moving them until lightly browned, about 4 minutes. Flip the chicken over and continue to cook until the second side is golden, about 4 minutes longer. Transfer to a plate. Add the remaining chicken thighs to the pot and repeat, then transfer them to a plate and set aside.

2. Add the onion and water to the pot with the drippings and return to medium-high heat. Cook, scraping the browned bits off the bottom and edges of the pot, until the onion has softened and is beginning to brown, 5 to 6 minutes. Add the garlic and cook until fragrant, about 30 seconds. Add the bay leaves, chicken broth, raisins, lemon peel, and browned chicken with any accumulated juices; bring to a simmer. Cover, transfer to the oven, and cook until the chicken is easily pierced with a knife, about 1¼ hours.

3. Transfer the chicken to a serving platter and cover with foil to keep warm. Add the lemon juice and olives to the sauce; bring to a simmer

over medium-high heat and cook, stirring occasionally, until the sauce has reduced by half, 8 to 10 minutes. Season with salt and pepper to taste. Pour the sauce over the chicken and sprinkle with the parsley. Serve.

➤ VARIATION

Chicken Tagine with Olives, Zucchini, and Honey

Follow the recipe for Chicken Tagine with Olives and Lemon, replacing the raisins with 2 tablespoons honey. Add 1 medium zucchini (about 12 ounces), cut into ½-inch pieces, with the lemon juice and olives in step 3.

BRUNSWICK STEW

IF YOU BELIEVE THE MYTHOLOGY, BRUNSWICK stew originated as a squirrel meat and vegetable stew first prepared close to two centuries ago during a hunting expedition near Brunswick, Virginia. From these humble origins it has grown into a regional classic of some renown, replete with Southern cooks who are fiercely protective of their own "secret" recipes. Nowadays, chicken has largely replaced squirrel as the star of the stew (proof that the adage "tastes like chicken" is true), but the supporting cast of flavors appears less defined. An extremely broad range of ingredients finds its way into Brunswick stew. We found recipes that include such ingredients as ham hocks, ham, pork shoulder, venison, rabbit, ground beef, tomatoes, onions, celery, potatoes, corn, okra, cabbage, bell peppers, green beans, and lima beans. And for seasonings, the list is just as long: garlic, bay leaves, thyme, parsley, chiles, sherry, and the seemingly eccentric addition of Worcestershire sauce. Many of the recipes take an "everything but the kitchen sink" approach, leading to a muddy-flavored stew. Others take a minimalist approach, resulting in a bland and boring stew. We needed to find a happy medium.

To limit the scope of testing (which could go on for months with a recipe this loosely defined), we made some decisions from the start regarding ingredients. For meats, we wanted to exclude anything not easily found in the local supermarket, which meant both venison and rabbit had to go. For chicken, we chose thighs for their full flavor and because we knew there'd be little chance of the dark meat drying out if overcooked. We also wanted to keep the ham hock for its smoky country charm, but that's more about flavor than meat; hocks, in fact, contain little meat at all. Ground beef and pork shoulder are both supermarket staples, but they seemed like overkill to us when included in the stew; in our opinion, restraint is sometimes the key to a successful recipe. As for vegetables, we limited our choices to those we found most commonly represented in recipes: tomatoes, onions, potatoes, corn, okra, and lima beans. The last three are all widely available frozen (and taste good frozen), minimizing prep work.

As for preparation, Brunswick stew is traditionally simmered on the stovetop or over an open fire, but we wanted to move it to the oven for the sake of convenience. At a moderate temperature, we knew it could simmer unattended. A little stovetop cooking, however, was required to get the stew started. We treated the dish as we do other braises in this chapter: we browned the meat (chicken here), then cooked the aromatic vegetables—onion, celery, and garlic—in the rendered chicken fat for flavor.

We knew the chicken would take roughly one hour to become fork-tender simmered in broth at 300 degrees, but the rest of the ingredients were less predictable. Sturdy Red Bliss potatoes held up well during the hour-long cooking time if they were cut into ½-inch chunks. Any smaller and they turned mushy and unappealing. The okra, lima beans, and corn, however, overcooked within the hour. Clearly, they needed to be added later in the cooking process. A convenient juncture proved to be at the one-hour mark, when we removed the chicken and ham hock from the pot; while we stripped the meat from the bones, the vegetables could be added and simmered until tender without worrying about the chicken. Within 20 minutes, the corn and lima beans were cooked through and the okra was still a little crisp and vibrantly green—much more attractive than the dull army green of overcooked okra. Another benefit to this method is that the okra did not become particularly slimy, as it is prone to do if overcooked.

Tasters loved the smoky flavor of the ham hock, but wanted more meat than that cut could deliver. Adding another hock doubled the smoky flavor, making it too strong—and there still wasn't enough meat between the two hocks. Looking for options, we turned to ham steak. Fully cooked and easily available, it seemed the best option. When we cubed it and simmered it in the stew from the start, its flavor dissipated and became spent, like vegetables cooked too long in stock. Added at the end with the vegetables, the ham retained its flavor.

The stew was now getting close, but the overall flavor needed some finessing. A couple of bay leaves worked their magic on the broth, lending a much-needed herb flavor. It was further improved with the addition of thyme sprigs.

And as for that Worcestershire sauce that seemed so odd to us when we started out, it provided the crucial finishing touch to the stew. Sweet and tangy, it unified the flavors in a surprising fashion.

Brunswick Stew

SERVES 6 TO 8

Fresh okra can be difficult to find, but frozen okra is widely available. After tasting the two side by side, we have found frozen okra to be an acceptable substitute for fresh. If overcooked, okra turns slimy, so be mindful of the time once the okra is added to the stew. We liked a hefty jolt of hot sauce with our stew, but we leave that decision to you.

PLANNING AHEAD: The stew can be prepared through step 2 and stored in an airtight container in the refrigerator for up to 4 days, or frozen for up to 4 months. Bring the stew to a simmer over medium-low heat before continuing with step 3.

6	bone-in, skin-on chicken thighs, (about 2¼ pounds), trimmed of excess fat
	Salt and ground black pepper
1	teaspoon vegetable oil
1	medium onion, minced
1	large celery rib, chopped fine
6	medium garlic cloves, minced or pressed through a garlic press
4	cups low-sodium chicken broth
1	(28-ounce) can diced tomatoes, drained
1¼	pounds red potatoes (about 3 medium), scrubbed and cut into ½-inch cubes
1	medium smoked ham hock
2	bay leaves
4	sprigs fresh thyme
½	pound ham steak, cut into ½-inch pieces
1	cup frozen lima beans
1	cup frozen corn
1	cup fresh or frozen okra, cut crosswise into ½-inch-thick rings
	Worcestershire sauce
	Tabasco sauce

1. Adjust an oven rack to the lower-middle position; heat the oven to 300 degrees. Dry the chicken thighs thoroughly with paper towels, then season generously with salt and pepper. Heat the oil in a large ovenproof Dutch oven over medium-high heat until shimmering but not smoking. Add the chicken thighs, skin-side down, and cook without moving them until the skin is crisp and well browned, about 5 minutes. Turn the chicken pieces and brown the second side, about 5 minutes longer; transfer to a large plate. Discard all but 1 tablespoon of fat from the pot; when the chicken has cooled, remove and discard the skin (see the illustration on page 201).

2. Add the onion, celery, and ¾ teaspoon salt to the pot and cook, stirring occasionally, until softened and beginning to brown, about 6 minutes. Stir in the garlic and cook until fragrant, about 30 seconds. Add the broth, tomatoes, potatoes, ham hock, bay leaves, thyme sprigs, and chicken, with any accumulated juices; bring to a simmer. Cover, transfer to the oven, and cook until the chicken offers no resistance when poked with the tip of a paring knife but still clings to the bone, about 1¼ hours.

3. Using a slotted spoon, transfer the chicken and ham hock to a large plate. Discard the bay leaves and thyme sprigs. Add the ham steak, lima beans, corn, and okra; continue to cook

in the oven, covered, until the lima beans and okra are tender, 15 to 20 minutes. Meanwhile, following the illustration on page 217, shred the chicken meat. When the ham hock is cool enough to handle, remove the meat and discard the skin, fat, and bones. Stir the shredded chicken and ham meat back into the stew. Season with Worcestershire, Tabasco, and salt and pepper to taste. Serve immediately.

CUBAN BLACK BEAN STEW

FRANKLY, IT'S HARD TO BELIEVE THAT CUBAN black beans are traditionally relegated to side-dish status. We like them as much as a main dish—ladled onto a pillow of fluffy white rice—as we do served on the side. And we're always keen on low-maintenance dishes, especially those that cook unattended for hours, like a pot of beans. Using authentic flavors and techniques, we set out to give Cuban black beans main-dish status, aiming to transform them into a full-flavored hearty stew.

From our experience with beans, there are a few things that strike us as absolutes, the first being that dried beans are optimal for long-cooked stews and that overnight soaking is the best method to prepare them. The "quick-soak" method (see the note that accompanies the recipe) works well in a pinch for time, while not soaking at all yields unevenly cooked beans, often with chalky centers and chewy skins. And from testing our Boston baked bean recipe (see page 267), we concluded that cooking the beans slowly in a low temperature oven consistently yields the best results for creamy-fleshed beans with tender skins. Also, we knew we needed to be cautious about adding ingredients with high levels of acid, since they can adversely affect a bean's texture. High acidity can interfere with the softening of the cellulose-based bean cells, causing them to remain hard no matter how long they cook. With these concerns resolved, we were able to concentrate on building flavor and bulking up the consistency of the stew.

The first layer of flavor to work on was the *sofrito;* this is the classic Cuban aromatic flavor base that typically consists of finely chopped onion, green bell pepper, and garlic slowly cooked in olive oil. Cuban cooks traditionally add the sofrito near the end of cooking their beans, creating distinct strata of flavor as a result. Although this is a tasty and authentic way of boosting the flavors in a humble pot of beans, we wanted a deeper, more unifying effect from our sofrito. We achieved this by adding the sofrito first, allowing the aromatics to break down and meld with the beans as they simmered. This method also saves on extra dirty dishes, which is always a plus. However, the long cooking of the sofrito rendered the garlic too mild for our tastes. We easily solved the problem by adding a portion of the minced garlic to the finished stew. Sharp and pungent, the raw garlic was just the punch the stew needed.

Despite tradition, tasters disliked the vegetal bitterness of the green bell pepper added to the sofrito. So we decided to alter the sofrito even more by replacing the green bell pepper with a red one, and this partly worked. The red bell pepper added a sweetness we preferred, which also rounded out the salty and acid flavors of the stew.

With the basics in hand, we turned to the meat component of the dish. In our initial test we used ham hocks, both for their meaty, smoky flavor and because they are often paired with beans. The ham hocks we tested differed greatly; all had a consistently smoky flavor, but the amount of meat on the hock varied anywhere from ¼ cup to almost 1 cup. Looking for something a bit meatier, we turned to other options, like smoky chorizo, loaded with garlic and chiles.

By replacing the hock with chorizo, we were able to maintain the classic smoky flavor and have a consistent yield of meat. In the past we have found that chorizo, because it is a leaner sausage, does not fare well if cooked for long periods. If cooked too long, it turns rubbery and ultimately flavorless. Sure, the sausage flavor becomes one with the stew, but the meat itself is just too spent by the end of the cooking time. We needed a way to harness the smokiness and spice from the chorizo in our long simmer. We found it by sautéing the chorizo first, removing it, and then sautéing the sofrito in the rendered sausage fat. And, by reserving the chorizo and stirring it in at the end, the pieces of sausage stayed succulent and tender.

We had been using water as our cooking liquid and decided to try a combination of water and low-sodium chicken broth for our next tests, cutting down the water to 1 cup and adding 4 cups of the broth. We hoped that the chicken flavor would not overwhelm the dish. It did not. Instead, it added the heartiness we were seeking. By this point in our testing, the beans had great flavor, but they lacked cohesion—they still had a soup-like consistency when coming out of the oven. We decided to try a traditional thickening technique: mashing a small portion of the cooked beans and then stirring them back into the pot. Once stirred into the beans, the starchy pureed mixture thickened the loose broth to a more stew-like consistency.

We now had a hearty main-course stew packed with layers of flavor. It still needed contrast though, something to give it more spark. To round out the stew and brighten its flavors, we added lime juice and cilantro, which proved to be just the right finishing touches.

Cuban Black Bean Stew
SERVES 6 TO 8

If chorizo proves difficult to find, you may substitute andouille sausage. Bacon will also suffice, but use only 6 ounces and remove all but 2 tablespoons of fat from the pot once the bacon is browned. Beans should be soaked for a minimum of 8 hours and can be soaked for up to 24 hours (though for this length of time they should be stored in the refrigerator). But if time is an issue, the "quick-soak" method will work here. Simmer the beans in water for 2 minutes, then take the pot off the heat, covered, and allow to sit in the water for 1 hour. For a heartier meal, this stew may be served over steamed white rice.

PLANNING AHEAD: The stew may be prepared then refrigerated for up to 4 days, or frozen for up to 3 months. (Allow the frozen stew to thaw completely in the refrigerator before reheating, to preserve the texture of the beans.) Bring the stew to a simmer over medium-low heat before continuing with step 3.

1	tablespoon olive oil
1/2	pound chorizo sausage, quartered lengthwise and sliced 1/2 inch thick
1	large onion, minced
1	large red pepper, stemmed, seeded, and chopped fine
	Salt
8	medium garlic cloves, minced or pressed through a garlic press
2	teaspoons dried oregano
1 1/2	teaspoons ground cumin
4	cups low-sodium chicken broth
1	cup water
1	pound black beans, sorted (see the illustration on page 184), soaked overnight, and drained
2	bay leaves
2	tablespoons lime juice
1/2	cup chopped fresh cilantro leaves
	Ground black pepper
	Tabasco sauce

1. Adjust an oven rack to the lower-middle position and heat the oven to 300 degrees. Heat the oil in a large Dutch oven over medium heat until shimmering. Add the chorizo and cook, stirring frequently, until well browned, about 6 minutes. Transfer to a small bowl using a slotted spoon and set aside in the refrigerator.

2. Return the Dutch oven with the drippings to medium heat until shimmering. Add the onion, red pepper, and 3/4 teaspoon salt; cook, stirring occasionally, until softened and lightly browned, 10 to 12 minutes. Add half of the minced garlic, the oregano, and cumin; cook until fragrant, about 1 minute. Add the broth, water, beans, and bay leaves; bring to a simmer, skimming any foam from the surface. Cover, transfer to the oven, and cook until the beans are tender but not splitting, 1 1/2 to 2 hours.

3. Transfer 2 cups of the beans to a mixing bowl and mash with a potato masher or fork. Stir the mashed beans back into the stew. Add the remaining garlic, the lime juice, cilantro, and the reserved chorizo. Season with salt, pepper, and Tabasco and serve immediately.

Tuscan White Bean Stew

ALL TOO OFTEN WHITE BEAN STEW COMES TO the table in poor form, either as a mushy pulp of exploded beans or crunchy pebbles swimming in an insipid liquid. But when made right—as is usually the case in Italy and always the case in Tuscany—white bean stew can be transcendentally delicious. Knowing that this classic recipe derives its rich body and flavor from a long, undisturbed simmer, we planned on using an oven cooking method, the same one used to make our Cuban Black Bean Stew (page 206). The pot of beans cooks slowly at a low temperature, creating what the Italians call a *minestra*, or stew. The result produces uniformly tender, creamy beans and a broth with deep flavor.

After testing a number of recipes, we discovered that we really needed to focus on the two major elements of the dish: the beans and the broth. We wanted to know what type of white beans were best for the recipe and what mix of ingredients would make for a rich, flavorful broth.

We based our initial research on recipes that used navy, great northern, or cannellini (white kidney) beans. After cooking a few batches, we found that we preferred the appearance and larger size of the cannellini beans—the bean of choice in Tuscany. (However, the navy and great northern beans proved to be totally acceptable substitutes.) And after cooking numerous pots of cannellini beans, we discovered it's important that the beans be fresh (see the headnote on page 208 for more information about beans). Stale beans cook unevenly, often yielding a mix of exploded mush and crunchy beans. We found a way around this problem by seeking out a reputable source for dried beans with high turnover.

Building deep flavor in the broth was our next big concern. Italian cooks add flavor to basic chicken broth using a *soffrito*, traditionally an aromatic foundation blended from diced pancetta and finely chopped onion, celery, carrot, and garlic. Usually cooked first, the soffrito imparts a deep, subtle, cohesive flavor to the beans. The mixture, slowly cooked in olive oil until lightly browned, softens and reduces greatly in volume.

In an effort to streamline the recipe, we tried the soffrito without carrot and celery. The pancetta, onion, and garlic in the pared-down soffrito gave the stew a layer of rich flavor, but the broth tasted too one-dimensional. So we reintroduced the carrot and celery. Tasters liked the addition of vegetal and earthy sweet flavors, plus the extra bulk of the carrot and celery made our recipe heartier and more stew-like.

Yet there was still something missing in the broth's flavor balance—an acidic element. We wanted something to contrast with the creaminess of the beans and the richness of the broth, and thought canned diced tomatoes might be an appropriate candidate.

We were cautious about adding ingredients with high levels of acid, because they can prevent the beans from softening properly as they cook. In our testing, though, we found that it takes a lot of acid to completely spoil a pot of beans. So then we had to ask, when do we add the tomatoes? At the beginning, or at the end when the beans are almost fully cooked?

We cooked two batches side by side, and discovered that tasters didn't like the tomatoes stirred in at the end; the broth had a tinny flavor and the bites of tomato were acrid and overpowered the beans. The only drawback to adding the tomatoes at the beginning was that we had to cook the stew longer, but not by much. The payoff was worth it, though, because the slowly stewed tomatoes added a rich complexity and roundness to the dish that wasn't present before.

Adding the rosemary at the right time is an important factor in this dish. When left in too long, the rosemary gives the stew a medicinal taste. We found that adding a sprig during the last 15 minutes of cooking gave the rosemary enough time to steep and yielded a perfectly perfumed stew.

And by pulling out a small portion of the cooked beans, mashing them, and then re-incorporating them into the stew, we able to achieve the hearty consistency we were after. A meal in itself, the finished product is a steamy bowl of creamy beans in a rich pork-flavored broth. And for the true Tuscan experience, we recommend serving this stew with a splash of fruity extra-virgin olive oil and warm, garlicky crostini.

Tuscan White Bean Stew

SERVES 6 TO 8

If pancetta is too difficult to find, bacon may be substituted, though the flavor will not be quite the same. It should be sliced crosswise into ¼-inch-thick slices. When purchasing dried beans, look for packages with whole, clean-looking beans; split beans and dust can be indicative of old age. Beans should be soaked for a minimum of eight hours and can be soaked for up to 24 hours (but for this length of time they should be stored in the refrigerator). Serve with a crusty loaf of bread or bruschetta and a leafy green salad.

PLANNING AHEAD: The stew may be prepared through step 1, then refrigerated for up to 4 days, or frozen for up to 4 months. (Allow the frozen stew to thaw completely in the refrigerator before reheating, to preserve the texture of the beans.) Bring the stew to a simmer over medium-low heat before continuing with step 2.

1	tablespoon extra-virgin olive oil, plus more for drizzling
6	ounces pancetta, chopped fine
1	large onion, minced
2	medium celery ribs, chopped fine
1	medium carrot, peeled and chopped fine
7	medium garlic cloves, minced or pressed through a garlic press
1	pound dried cannellini, great northern, or navy beans, sorted (see the illustration on page 184), soaked overnight, and drained
4	cups low-sodium chicken broth
1	cup water
1	(28-ounce) can diced tomatoes, drained
2	bay leaves
1	sprig fresh rosemary
	Salt and ground black pepper

1. Adjust an oven rack to the lower-middle position and heat the oven to 300 degrees. Heat the oil in a large Dutch oven over medium heat until shimmering. Add the pancetta and cook, stirring occasionally, until golden brown, 4 to 5 minutes. Add the onion, celery, and carrot; cook, stirring occasionally, until very soft and lightly browned, 10 to 12 minutes. Add the garlic and cook until fragrant, about 30 seconds. Add the beans, broth, water, tomatoes, and bay leaves; bring to a simmer, skimming any foam from the surface. Cover the pot, transfer to the oven, and cook until the beans are tender but not splitting, 1½ to 2 hours.

2. Remove the pot from the oven, and submerge the rosemary sprig in the stew. Cover and let stand until fragrant, about 15 minutes.

3. Discard the bay leaves and rosemary sprig. Transfer 2 cups of the beans into a mixing bowl and mash with a potato masher or fork. Stir the mashed beans back into the stew and season with salt and pepper to taste. Serve, drizzling each portion lightly with olive oil.

➤ VARIATION

Ribollita

Leftover white bean stew is traditionally turned into *ribollita*, a stew with a thick, porridge-like consistency. To turn this recipe into ribollita, add a slice of cubed Italian-style bread to each bowl of stew and mash with a potato masher or fork until incorporated. Drizzle liberally with olive oil.

4

SKILLET CASSEROLES

WHEN MOST PEOPLE THINK OF A CASSEROLE, they think of a big, bubbling dish emerging from the oven topped with cheese or savory bread crumbs. In this chapter, however, we traded in our baking dish for a 12-inch skillet (see pages 211–212 for information on skillets) and decided to use the stovetop instead of the oven. If you don't have a 12-inch skillet with a cover (a smaller skillet will not work for these recipes), you can use a Dutch oven (also called a lidded casserole) with a capacity of at least six quarts (see page 147 for more information on Dutch ovens).

For the most part, the recipes in this chapter work fine in traditional skillets. A few, however, require a nonstick skillet, like Skillet Chicken and Potatoes with Garlic and Rosemary (page 219), Cincinnati Skillet Chili with Spaghetti (page 224), and Skillet Thai Curry with Sweet Potatoes and Tofu (page 240). In each case, because of the particular cooking method, certain ingredients (like potatoes, ground beef, and tofu), would stick to the bottom of a traditional skillet early in the cooking process and easily ruin the recipe.

While we adapted some unmistakable classics for the skillet, like Skillet Lasagna (page 238), we found that using a skillet, which allowed us to rotate ingredients in and out of the pan, freed us to be more inventive when developing recipes. This flexibility enabled us to create dishes like Skillet Chicken and Couscous with Fennel and Orange (page 221) and Skillet Beef Stroganoff (page 223), casserole-like dishes that make use of more delicate ingredients or techniques that weren't suitable for casseroles baked in the oven.

One of the most alluring qualities of casseroles is that they can be put in the oven and forgotten about for awhile, leaving you time to walk the dog, fold the laundry, or relax after a long day at work. And while using a skillet to make a casserole didn't, at first glance, seem to offer this advantage, we found that by selecting our ingredients carefully we could build at least a 20- to 30-minute "walk away" time into each of these recipes, eliminating the stress of last-minute preparation.

But skillet casseroles certainly have their challenges. Since they are meant to be a one-dish meal complete with a protein, a starch, and vegetables, we were faced with ingredients that often have very different cooking times. Orchestrating these different ingredients in and out of the skillet so that they were hot and properly cooked all at the same time proved to be quite a challenge. For example, when developing the recipe for chicken and rice, we had to figure out how to cook the rice, chicken, and broccoli (ingredients with very disparate cooking times) in the same skillet, avoiding starchy rice, dry chicken, and mushy broccoli. After much trial and error (and many a bland and overcooked dish), we learned not only how to pair the ingredients in these recipes but also the order in which they should be added to the skillet. For instance, we often started our chicken and rice dishes by first browning the chicken, then removing it while the sauce or other ingredients were prepared. Then the chicken was returned to the skillet, where it had time to finish cooking and absorb the flavors of the aromatics and other ingredients. The recipes in this chapter aim to choreograph these sorts of issues while delivering delicious one-dish meals.

Unlike many of the other recipes in this book, these skillet meals cannot be made in advance. However, by limiting the ingredient lists and keeping preparation to a minimum, we found that most of these dishes could be on the table within an hour—perfect for a busy weeknight.

STUCK-ON FOODS

If potentially sticky ingredients like potatoes adhere to the bottom of the skillet during cooking, try this tip to free them. Dip a flexible metal spatula into cold water and slide the inverted spatula blade underneath the foodstuff. The cool, wet spatula breaks the bond between the foodstuff and the skillet and makes release easy. Do not try this tip with nonstick skillets because it may damage the surface.

EQUIPMENT: Traditional Skillets

A skillet's material and construction style can make all the difference between a perfectly seared steak and a charred piece of beef fit only for the dog's dinner. Metals vary in conductivity, the speed at which heat travels through them. A highly conductive metal, then, in theory should make for a responsive, even-cooking pan, and vice versa. Gold and silver have the highest conductivity, but for obvious reasons are not practical for cooking purposes. Copper and aluminum are next in line and are commonly used for cookware, though copper pans are prohibitively expensive for most cooks (and require a lot of upkeep) and aluminum can react with acidic ingredients (affecting color and flavor) and damages easily. Lastly, stainless steel is a poor conductor of heat, but is incredibly durable and nonreactive—making it a popular choice for pans. As for construction, most pans are built in one of three styles: cast, disk bottom, and clad. In the casting construction style, molten iron is molded to form the pan, body, and handle alike. Cast-iron pans are heavy, heat up slowly, and retain their heat well (making quick, delicate adjustments of pan temperature all but impossible). Some cast-iron pots (like the Le Creuset line we tested) are also enameled, which makes them nonreactive inside and out. In the disk-bottom construction style, a relatively thin, generally stainless steel pan is covered on the bottom with a thick disk of conductive metal, like copper or aluminum. The bottom disk disperses heat well, in theory making up for the thin sides. Disk-bottom pans tend to be moderately priced.

Clad construction means that the entire pan is constructed of multiple layers of metal—usually stainless steel—bonded under intense pressure and heat. These layers often sandwich a filling made of highly conductive aluminum, thereby combining the best of both worlds: the durability of stainless steel and the conductivity of aluminum. Because clad construction is labor intensive,

skillets of this style tend to be expensive.

We tested eight 12-inch skillets of varying materials, construction, and prices, ranging from $10 to $140. Twelve-inch skillets are the most practical size, accommodating a whole (3 ½ pound) cut-up chicken, three split chicken breasts (perfect for the chicken skillet dinners in this chapter), four pork chops (as for Smothered Pork Chops, page 230), or enough potatoes to serve a crowd. It is important to note that 12 inches is the measurement of the outside perimeter; the actual cooking surface is significantly smaller because the pan walls slope inward from the edges. This is valuable real estate because the smallest difference in cooking surface will affect a recipe's outcome. For instance, the All-Clad skillet, with a 9¼-inch cooking surface, accommodated a whole chicken's worth of pieces without the pieces touching, whereas the chicken was overly crowded in the 9-inch cooking surface of the other skillets.

Did we uncover any significant differences in performance based on construction styles? Although some manufacturers tout cladding and its benefits, our kitchen testing did not support this. The two skillets we tested with disk bottoms, the Farberware and the Emerilware, did heat up a little faster than the rest of the field, but it was easy to accommodate this difference by adjusting the stovetop burner. Both of these pans also performed well in cooking tests.

The weight of the pans turned out to be more important than construction. Because you cook on the bottom of a skillet (not the sides), cladding is not that important. We concluded that a weight of three to four pounds is ideal in a 12-inch skillet. These medium-weight pans (especially those from All-Clad and Calphalon) brown foods beautifully, and most testers handled them comfortably.

THE BEST TRADITIONAL SKILLETS

We tested eight traditional skillets with 12-inch diameters (or as close as we could find in that manufacturer's line) in six applications (cooking crêpes, searing steaks, simmering a pan sauce, browning stew meat, pan-roasting chicken, and sautéing onions). The skillets are listed in order of preference based on their performance in these tests, as well as design factors.

The All-Clad Stainless 12-inch Frypan (left: $125) took top honors in our testing. The Calphalon Tri-Ply Stainless 12-inch Omelette Pan (middle: $65) and the Farberware Millennium 18/10 Stainless 12-inch Covered Skillet (right: $70) were rated best buys, costing about half as much as the winning pan.

EQUIPMENT: Nonstick Skillets

The unfortunate truth about nonstick pans is that they don't last forever. It's all too easy to inadvertently damage the coating during cooking or cleanup, rendering the pan pretty useless. While All-Clad and Calphalon both make exceptional nonstick versions of their high-end skillets, their stiff price tags give us pause. Do we really want to spend over one hundred dollars on a pan that may only last a couple of years? We were curious to see how more budget-minded nonstick skillets fared. We conducted a full set of cooking tests on eight inexpensive nonstick skillets, all purchased at hardware or discount stores for no more than $50 apiece.

Statistics reported by the Cookware Manufacturers Association indicate that 90 percent of all the aluminum cookware sold in the United States in 2001 was nonstick. The reasons to use nonstick are clear: Little or no fat is required to lubricate the food (and thereby prevent sticking), and cleanup is easy. Nonstick pans are terrific for extremely delicate, quick-cooking foods like flaky white fish and omelets.

The material used for nonstick coating, polytetrafluoroethylene—or PTFE—was developed by chemists at Dupont in the late 1930s. Trademarked originally as Teflon, the formula has evolved over the years, and now several companies in addition to Dupont sell PTFE to cookware manufacturers (many of which use individualized, proprietary, multicoat application processes to bond the coating to their pans). It is our understanding, however, that the majority of nonstick coatings today are made from the same basic substance.

The nonstick, nonreactive magic of PTFE is due, in large part, to one of the two types of atoms it contains—namely, fluorine. Every PTFE molecule contains two carbon atoms and four fluorine atoms. In the atomic world, fluorine is very highly resistant to bonding with other substances. That's why PTFE is so slippery.

And slippery it was. Every pan in our group received a good score in release ability and cleaning tests, the raisons d'être for nonstick. We tested both traits in a purposefully abusive manner by burning oatmeal into the pans over high heat for 45 minutes. That kind of treatment would trash a traditional pan, but the scorched cereal slid out of our nonstick pans with no fuss, and the pans practically wiped clean.

In their new, off-the-shelf condition, all of our pans turned in a reasonable-to-good performance cooking the foods best suited to nonstick cooking: eggs and fish. In fact, every pan but a Revere produced evenly cooked omelets and released them with ease. The omelet made in the Farberware pan was especially impressive. The Farberware also did a particularly nice job searing salmon fillets to an even, crusty, medium brown. (Salmon is much higher in fat than skinless chicken cutlets and therefore browns more easily,

even in a nonstick pan.) Overall, however, our tests indicate that any of these pans could easily handle such light-duty tasks as cooking eggs. Low cost does not mean a big trade-off here.

Sauté speed is also an important measure of a pan's performance. We tested this by sautéing 1½ cups of chopped onions over medium heat for 10 minutes in the hope of ending up with pale gold onions that bore no trace of burning. And you know what? For the most part, we did. Wearever, T-Fal, Innova, and Revere pans, which were all on the light side in terms of weight, turned out the darkest onions, but they were still well within an acceptable color range. Onions sautéed in Farberware, Meyer, Calphalon, and Bialetti pans were a shade lighter, indicating a slightly slower sauté speed. The Farberware onions, however, took top honors based on how evenly all the pieces colored.

Of course, construction quality is a concern with any piece of cookware, but especially with inexpensive models. Will the thing hold up, or will you have to replace it in six months? Based on our experience, you may well sacrifice a measure of construction quality with a budget pan. Pans with handles that were welded or riveted onto the pan body, including the Farberware, Innova, Meyer, and Calphalon, all felt solid and permanent. But the heat-resistant plastic (called phenolic) handles on the T-Fal, Revere, Bialetti, and Wearever pans were not riveted in place, and all three of them came loose during testing. That did not bode well for their future.

Of the pans we tested, the $30 Farberware Millennium offered the best combination of good nonstick performance (in suitable applications), pleasing heft (at almost 3½ pounds), and solid construction. It even beat out the priciest pan in the test, the Calphalon.

One word of caution: To maintain the pan's integrity, most manufacturers recommend using plastic, rubber, coated, or wooden utensils while cooking. Farberware, however, says that metal utensils may be used.

THE BEST NONSTICK SKILLET

The Farberware Millennium 18/10 Stainless 12-inch Nonstick Skillet costs around $30, and it delivered superior results in our tests. It was heavier than the other inexpensive pans we tested and had the most solid construction, which contributed greatly to its success.

SKILLET CHICKEN AND RICE

FROM THE PAELLA OF SPAIN AND THE SPICY *arroz con pollo* of Mexico to the Creole-inspired jambalaya, many cultures seem to have their own version of a one-pot chicken and rice dish. While there is no traditional American chicken and rice counterpart, its versatility lends itself to many flavor and texture variations. We found the allure of juicy chicken and crisp vegetables, all nestled among tender grains of rice and cooked under one lid, to be irresistible. But as we soon discovered, the ubiquity of these dishes belies the difficulty of executing them; it was no small feat to end up with properly cooked ingredients, all in one pan, all ready at the same time.

With this challenge before us, we started our testing. Indeed, we learned right away that achieving consistently cooked chicken and rice was a daunting undertaking. Our desire to add a third variable—vegetables—made the task even more difficult. With every recipe we tried, invariably one element of the dish was perfectly cooked while the others would either be undercooked or overdone. Looking for a way to perfect the three variables, we figured it was easier to start with the chicken and the rice; we hoped that once we determined how to cook them in concert, the vegetables would fall into place without much trouble.

First we needed to decide which cut of chicken to use in the recipe. We tried boneless skinless breasts, but found them to be relatively flavorless; also, by the time they were cooked through, the rice still needed another 20 to 25 minutes of cooking time. Moving on, we overlooked the next obvious choice, chicken thighs (since we knew that most people would prefer white meat for this dish), and tried split chicken breasts. The fact that the split breasts still contained the bone suggested to us that they might be protected from drying out. This was, in fact, the case. After 15 minutes they were perfectly cooked and moist. While the cooking time of the chicken breasts was slightly different than that of the rice, we found this time difference provided us a perfect opportunity to cook the vegetables.

With the choice of chicken solved, we moved on to test the cooking techniques. In our initial tests, we used a standard method for cooking the chicken with the rice. First, we browned chicken in a skillet and removed it, then softened some onions in the same pan. We added the rice to the onions, toasting it briefly. We then stirred in chicken broth, placed the chicken over the rice, covered the pan, and let it simmer over low heat for 30 minutes. Our results, however, were lackluster. The rice was unevenly cooked and the chicken was overdone and dry. We thought we could easily rectify these problems by removing the chicken from the skillet as soon it was done (about 15 minutes), while the rice continued to cook. Although this technique solved the problem of dry chicken, the rice continued to be underdone and crunchy in places, especially in the spots where the chicken had rested. Thinking that perhaps we needed to go against all convention and stir the rice while it was cooking, in our next test we gave the rice a good stir right after we removed the chicken. To our surprise, the rice was evenly cooked and tender after another 10 minutes. At this point, we were happy with the texture of the rice but felt that the dish was a little flat. In order to rectify this, we replaced one-half cup of the chicken broth with white wine, which gave acidity and brightness to the dish.

Adding the vegetables was the next hurdle to clear. With our current cooking method, we saw several promising options. The first was to add vegetables to the pan along with the onions. As our tests confirmed, this turned out to be particularly good for vegetables that could withstand long cooking times, such as carrots and mushrooms. The second option was to add the vegetables halfway through the cooking time, after we had removed the chicken. At this point, we found we could successfully add green vegetables, such as broccoli or green beans.

In addition to the vegetables, we learned that a cup of cheese stirred into the rice at the end of cooking provided a creamy richness that put the finishing touch on our version of this chicken and rice dish.

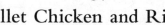

Skillet Chicken and Rice with Broccoli and Cheddar

SERVES 4 TO 6

It is important to stir the rice well when adding the broccoli florets. If not stirred thoroughly, the rice will cook unevenly.

3	bone-in, skin-on split chicken breasts (10 to 12 ounces each), cut in half crosswise
	Salt and ground black pepper
2	tablespoons vegetable oil
1	medium onion, chopped
1	pound broccoli, florets cut into 1/2-inch pieces, stems trimmed, peeled, and cut crosswise into 1/4-inch slices
4	medium garlic cloves, minced or pressed through a garlic press
1/4	teaspoon red pepper flakes
1 1/2	cups long-grain white rice
1/2	cup white wine
3 1/2	cups low-sodium chicken broth
4	ounces cheddar cheese, shredded (about 1 1/3 cups)

1. Dry the chicken thoroughly with paper towels, then season liberally with salt and pepper. Heat the oil in a 12-inch skillet over medium-high heat until just smoking. Carefully lay the chicken in the skillet, skin-side down, and cook until well browned on the first side, about 4 minutes. Flip the chicken and continue to cook until the second side is well browned, about 3 minutes. Remove the skillet from the heat, transfer the chicken to a plate, and remove all but 2 tablespoons of fat from the pan.

2. Return the pan to medium heat. Add the onion, broccoli stems, garlic, red pepper flakes, and 1/2 teaspoon salt and cook, scraping the browned bits off the bottom and edges of the pan, until the onions begin to soften, about 3 minutes. Add the rice and continue to cook until the edges turn translucent, about 3 minutes. Add the wine and chicken broth and bring to a simmer. Add the chicken to the pan skin-side up. Cover, reduce the heat to low, and cook until the chicken is no longer pink in the center and registers 160 degrees on an instant-read thermometer, about 15 minutes.

3. Transfer the chicken to a plate and cover with foil to keep warm. Add the broccoli florets, stir the rice well, cover the pan, and continue to cook until the broccoli and rice are tender, about 10 minutes. Stir in the cheddar and season to taste with salt and pepper. Serve immediately.

PREPARING BROCCOLI

1. Place the head of broccoli upside down on a cutting board and trim off the florets very close to their heads with a large knife. Cut the florets into 1/2-inch pieces.

2. Stand each stalk up on the cutting board and square it off with a large knife. This will remove the tough outer 1/8-inch layer from the stalk. Now cut the stalk into 1/4-inch pieces crosswise.

Skillet Chicken and Rice with Mushrooms and Green Beans

SERVES 4 TO 6

Due to this particular cooking method, the green beans won't retain their vibrant green color, but they will remain crisp and tender. If you don't like Havarti, any semi-soft cheese, like Gouda or Swiss, can be substituted. To ensure even cooking, stir the rice well when adding the green beans.

3	bone-in, skin-on split chicken breasts (10 to 12 ounces each), cut in half crosswise
	Salt and ground black pepper
2	tablespoons vegetable oil
1	medium onion, chopped
10	ounces white button mushrooms, brushed clean and quartered
4	medium garlic cloves, minced or pressed through a garlic press
1½	cups long-grain white rice
½	cup white wine
3½	cups low-sodium chicken broth
½	pound green beans, ends trimmed and cut into 2-inch lengths
4	ounces Havarti cheese, shredded (about 1⅓ cups)

1. Dry the chicken thoroughly with paper towels, then season liberally with salt and pepper. Heat the oil in a 12-inch skillet over medium-high heat until just smoking. Carefully lay the chicken in the skillet, skin-side down, and cook until well browned on the first side, about 4 minutes. Flip the chicken and continue to cook until the second side is well browned, about 3 minutes. Remove the skillet from the heat, transfer the chicken to a plate, and remove all but 2 tablespoons of fat from the pan.

2. Return the pan to medium heat. Add the onion, mushrooms, garlic, and ½ teaspoon salt and cook, scraping the browned bits off the bottom and edges of the pan, until the mushrooms begin to soften and start to brown, about 8 minutes. Add the rice and continue to cook until the edges

---

INGREDIENTS: Long-Grain White Rice

The beauty of white rice is its neutral flavor and ability to carry other flavors. But is all long-grain white rice created equally? We rounded up a converted rice (Uncle Ben's Converted Enriched Long Grain Rice), three standard supermarket options (Canilla Extra Long Grain Enriched Rice, Carolina Extra Long Grain Enriched Rice, and Stop & Shop Long Grain Enriched Rice), and an organic white rice (Sem-Chi Organically Grown Florida Long Grain Rice) available in bulk from a natural foods market.

When tasted plain, all of the rice brands were noted as having a "clean" flavor and being "like rice should be," with the exception of Uncle Ben's. This converted rice—processed in a way that ensures separate grains, a firm texture, and a more pronounced flavor—failed to meet our standards. The "round" and "rubbery" grains of Uncle Ben's (with its telltale yellowish tint) immediately brought back not-so-fond memories of "dining hall rice." Tasters agreed that some "stickiness" and minor "clumping"—found in the non-converted rice brands—makes for more natural looking and better tasting rice. All of the rices shown below are recommended.

CANILLA
Extra Long Grain Enriched Rice
The "distinct flavor" was likened to Jasmine rice.

CAROLINA
Extra Long Grain Enriched Rice
"Not many nuances" made for a good, clean slate.

SEM-CHI
Organically Grown Florida Long Grain Rice
This rice was rated the "chewiest" with "roasted" and "nutty" flavors.

STOP & SHOP
Long Grain Enriched Rice
This rice was preferred for its neutrality and "chewy" texture.

turn translucent, about 3 minutes. Add the wine and broth and bring to a simmer. Add the chicken to the pan skin-side up. Cover, reduce the heat to low, and cook until the chicken is no longer pink in the center and registers 160 degrees on an instant-read thermometer, about 15 minutes.

3. Transfer the chicken to a plate and cover with foil to keep warm. Stir in the green beans, stir the rice well, cover, and continue to cook until the beans and rice are tender, about 10 minutes. Stir in the cheese and season to taste with salt and pepper. Serve immediately.

Skillet Chicken and Rice with Carrots, Peas, and Parmesan

SERVES 4 TO 6

For the best results, use a high-quality Parmesan cheese.

3	bone-in, skin-on split chicken breasts (10 to 12 ounces each), cut in half crosswise
	Salt and ground black pepper
2	tablespoons vegetable oil
1	medium onion, chopped medium
3	medium carrots, peeled and chopped medium (about 1¼ cups)
4	medium garlic cloves, minced or pressed through a garlic press
½	teaspoon chopped fresh thyme leaves
1½	cups long-grain white rice
½	cup white wine
3½	cups low-sodium chicken broth
1	cup frozen peas
2	ounces Parmesan cheese, grated (about 1 cup)

1. Dry the chicken thoroughly with paper towels, then season liberally with salt and pepper. Heat the oil in a 12-inch skillet over medium-high heat until just smoking. Carefully lay the chicken in the skillet, skin-side down, and cook until well browned on the first side, about 4 minutes. Flip the chicken and continue to cook until the second side is well browned, about 3 minutes. Remove the pan from the heat, transfer the chicken to a plate, and remove all but 2 tablespoons of fat from the pan.

2. Return the pan to medium heat. Add the onion, carrots, garlic, thyme, and ½ teaspoon salt and cook, scraping the browned bits off the bottom and edges of the pan, until the onion begins to soften, about 3 minutes. Add the rice and continue to cook until the edges turn translucent, about 3 minutes. Add the wine and broth and bring to a simmer. Add the chicken to the pan skin-side up. Cover, reduce the heat to low, and cook until the chicken is no longer pink in the center and registers 160 degrees on an instant-read thermometer, about 15 minutes.

3. Transfer the chicken to a plate and cover with foil to keep warm. Add the peas, stir the rice well, cover, and continue to cook until the peas and rice are tender, about 10 minutes. Stir in the cheese and season to taste with salt and pepper. Serve immediately.

SKILLET JAMBALAYA

ORIGINATING IN THE BAYOUS OF LOUISIANA, jambalaya has become synonymous with Creole cooking. A hearty mix of shredded chicken, spicy andouille sausage, and plump shrimp all cooked together with rice and vegetables, it seemed like a natural for this chapter. Considering that jambalaya could be easily prepared in a skillet, and having already developed a reliable recipe and technique for skillet chicken and rice, we hoped to simply incorporate the ingredients that make jambalaya so distinct and develop a pretty good rendition of this Creole classic.

While some jambalaya recipes use a whole chicken, we felt using packaged chicken pieces would be a sure timesaver. We found bone-in, skin-on chicken thighs to be the best choice. Their robust flavor didn't get lost in the other flavors in the dish, and their tender meat was easy to shred and remained moist.

Next we tackled the andouille sausage, a key ingredient in any jambalaya. In order to extract the most flavor from the sausage, we found that a quick browning in the pan, after we had browned and removed the chicken, was essential. Once we browned the sausage and removed it from the pan, we then used some of the rendered fat to cook the vegetables, which further enhanced the flavor of the dish.

To re-create the flavors of jambalaya, we added a chopped red pepper to the pan along with chopped onion and a significant amount of garlic. We also added a can of diced tomatoes, and their acidity helped brighten the dish, contrasting nicely with the spicy andouille. We assumed we'd need both wine and chicken broth to cook the rice, but we discovered that the liquid and acidity of the tomatoes made the wine superfluous. We also found that using clam juice in addition to the chicken broth helped to heighten the flavor of the shrimp and give the dish its classic briny overtones. We added the browned chicken thighs back to the pan along with the rice, cooking them together for about 25 minutes before adding the shrimp.

We learned it was best to remove the chicken from the skillet at this point and add the shrimp and browned sausage to the pan last. We cooked the shrimp (and warmed the sausage) very briefly over direct heat, and then removed the pan from the heat. The residual heat of the rice and vegetables cooked the shrimp through gently without the risk of overcooking. While the shrimp was cooking, we removed the meat from the chicken thighs, shredding it easily using two forks (see the illustration below). After five minutes, the shrimp were cooked and the chicken was ready to be stirred back in. A couple of tablespoons of chopped parsley provided the finishing touch to our Creole casserole.

Skillet Jambalaya

SERVES 4 TO 6

If you cannot find andouille sausage, either chorizo or linguiça can be substituted. For a spicier jambalaya, you can add ¼ teaspoon of cayenne along with the vegetables, and/or serve it with Tabasco.

4	bone-in, skin-on chicken thighs (about 1½ pounds), trimmed of excess skin and fat
	Salt and ground black pepper
5	teaspoons vegetable oil
½	pound andouille sausage, halved lengthwise and sliced into ¼-inch pieces
1	medium onion, chopped medium
1	medium red bell pepper, stemmed, seeded, and chopped medium
5	medium garlic cloves, minced or pressed through a garlic press
1½	cups long-grain white rice
1	(14.5-ounce) can diced tomatoes, drained
1	(8-ounce) bottle clam juice
2½	cups low-sodium chicken broth
1	pound large shrimp (31 to 40 count), peeled, deveined, and rinsed
2	tablespoons chopped fresh parsley leaves

SHREDDING CHICKEN

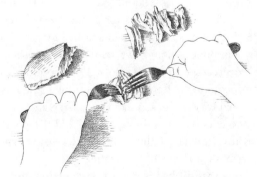

Hold one fork in each hand, with the tines facing down. Insert the tines into the chicken meat and gently pull the forks away from each other, breaking the meat apart and into long, thin strands.

1. Dry the chicken thoroughly with paper towels, then season generously with salt and pepper. Heat 2 teaspoons of the oil in a 12-inch skillet over medium-high heat until just smoking. Carefully lay the chicken thighs in the skillet, skin-side down, and cook until golden, 4 to 6 minutes. Flip the chicken over and continue to cook until the second side is golden, about 3 minutes. Remove the pan from the heat and transfer the chicken to a plate. Using paper towels, remove and discard the browned chicken skin.

2. Pour off all but 2 teaspoons of the fat left in the skillet and return to medium-high heat until shimmering. Add the andouille and cook until

lightly browned, about 3 minutes; transfer the sausage to a small bowl and set aside.

3. Add the remaining 3 teaspoons oil to the skillet and return to medium heat until shimmering. Add the onion, pepper, garlic, and ½ teaspoon salt; cook, scraping the browned bits off the bottom of the skillet, until the onion is softened, about 5 minutes. Add the rice and cook until the edges turn translucent, about 3 minutes. Stir in the tomatoes, clam juice, and chicken broth; bring to a simmer. Gently nestle the chicken into the rice. Cover, reduce the heat to low, and cook until the chicken is tender and cooked through, 30 to 35 minutes.

4. Transfer the chicken to a plate and cover with foil to keep warm. Stir the shrimp and sausage into the rice and continue to cook, covered, over low heat for 2 more minutes. Remove the skillet from the heat and let stand, covered, until the shrimp are fully cooked and the rice is tender, about 5 minutes. Meanwhile, following the illustration on page 217, shred the chicken using two forks. Stir the parsley and shredded chicken into the rice and season with salt and pepper to taste. Serve immediately.

SKILLET CHICKEN AND POTATOES WITH GARLIC AND ROSEMARY

IF YOU WALK THE STREETS OF PARIS BEFORE the noontime meal, you'll notice that in front of every butcher's store there is a vertical roaster about the size of a refrigerator filled with whole chickens. At the bottom of these roasters are piles of small potatoes basting in the juices of the skewered chickens. The end result of this symbiotic cooking method is the simplest of food combinations but also one of the most flavorful. It was these flavors that inspired us to develop a recipe for skillet chicken and potatoes.

The first challenge was to figure out what kind of chicken would be best suited for a dry-heat cooking method, the environment we thought would get us closest to that roasted flavor of rotisserie chicken. Our original thought was to use a whole chicken cut into individual components. But the disparate cooking times of the breasts and thighs, coupled with the extra effort to butcher a whole chicken, led us to rethink our choice. So we sought to develop this dish using packaged chicken parts. Considering our cooking method, we chose breasts over thighs, feeling they were better suited for dry-heat cooking and would achieve a superior roasted flavor. We also opted for bone-in chicken breasts over boneless, hypothesizing that the bone would protect the meat from drying out and that the cooking time would be more compatible with the potatoes.

Determining the best way to cook the potatoes and the chicken together was the most puzzling part of the recipe. We started by browning the chicken over medium-high heat. We then removed the chicken, added the potatoes to the pan, and let them begin to caramelize, which gave them an appealing roasted flavor. Thinking that everything would need a little moisture to cook through, we added a bit of chicken broth, placed the chicken over the potatoes, covered the skillet, and let it all cook until the potatoes were tender. This technique, however, did not work. By the time the potatoes were done, the chicken was too dry. And to make matters worse, the potatoes tasted steamed, not roasted, due to the added chicken broth. In fact, there was more liquid in the pan at the end of our cooking than there had been before we put the lid on. Thinking that the chicken had shed some moisture while it was cooking, we tried the same technique as before, but didn't add any liquid. We were surprised how well this worked. After about 15 minutes, the chicken was fully cooked and had given off a small amount of liquid. We removed the chicken, re-covered the pan, and allowed the potatoes to finish cooking. After another 15 minutes, the liquid shed by the chicken had either been absorbed by the potatoes or had evaporated, and the potatoes had browned beautifully and developed that deep-roasted flavor we were after.

Now that we had perfected the cooking of the chicken and potatoes, we could focus on the flavor of the dish. Up to this point, we had tried a series of spices, flavorings, and herbs and had settled on the classic combination of rosemary and garlic. But we found it difficult to infuse the dish with potent flavor using this particular cooking method. Since the pan was quite dry throughout the cooking process, there was no medium to extract and distribute the garlic and rosemary flavor throughout the dish. Abandoning the idea of adding the flavor during cooking, we tried adding it after cooking by building a simple pan sauce. By the time the potatoes and chicken had finished cooking, the pan had built up a decent fond, which allowed us to make a simple rosemary-and-garlic-infused sauce to serve with the chicken. A squeeze of fresh lemon juice heightened the flavor of the sauce and provided the finishing touch to our skillet chicken and potatoes.

Skillet Chicken and Potatoes with Garlic and Rosemary

SERVES 4 TO 6

This recipe works best with small Red Bliss potatoes, roughly the size of golf balls. If your potatoes are much larger, cut them into ¾-inch pieces. For this recipe, use a nonstick skillet, which will keep the potatoes from sticking to the bottom of the pan.

3	bone-in, skin-on split chicken breasts (about 10 to 12 ounces each), cut in half crosswise
	Salt and ground black pepper
2	teaspoons plus 2 tablespoons vegetable oil
1½	pounds small Red Bliss potatoes, scrubbed and cut into quarters
1	teaspoon chopped fresh rosemary leaves
2	medium garlic cloves, minced or pressed through a garlic press
2	teaspoons all-purpose flour
¾	cup low-sodium chicken broth
1	lemon, cut into wedges

1. Adjust an oven rack to the middle position and heat the oven to 200 degrees. Dry the chicken thoroughly with paper towels, then season generously with salt and pepper. Heat 2 teaspoons of the oil in a 12-inch nonstick skillet over medium-high heat until just smoking. Carefully lay the chicken breasts in the skillet, skin-side down, and cook until golden, 4 to 6 minutes. Flip the chicken over and continue to cook until the second side is golden, about 3 minutes. Remove the skillet from the heat and transfer the chicken to a plate.

2. Toss the potatoes with ¼ teaspoon salt and ¼ teaspoon pepper in a medium bowl. Add the remaining 2 tablespoons oil to the skillet and return to medium-low heat. Arrange the potatoes in the skillet, cut-side down. Lay the chicken on top of the potatoes, skin-side up, cover, and cook until the chicken is no longer pink in the center and registers 160 degrees on an instant-read thermometer, about 15 minutes.

3. Transfer the chicken to an ovenproof platter or serving dish, cover with foil, and place in the oven to keep warm. Continue to cook the potatoes, covered over medium-low heat, until they are browned and cooked through, about 15 minutes.

4. Transfer the potatoes to the platter with the chicken and cover to keep warm. Add the rosemary, garlic, and flour to the skillet and return to medium heat until fragrant and the garlic is lightly toasted, about 2 minutes. Slowly whisk in the broth and cook until the sauce is lightly thickened, about 2 minutes. Season with salt and pepper to taste. Pour the sauce over the chicken and potatoes. Serve immediately with lemon wedges.

SKILLET CHICKEN AND COUSCOUS WITH FENNEL AND ORANGE

OVER THE YEARS WE'VE DEVELOPED SEVERAL versions of the classic Moroccan tagine, a hearty, earthy stew with meat or chicken that is gently simmered with a variety of tender vegetables and aromatic spices. It's usually served with couscous, which is a must with almost every meal in Morocco but especially with a tagine. Thinking about this savory tagine inspired us to create a skillet version, one that might not be as refined as an authentic Moroccan tagine, but still an exotic and flavorful one-dish meal that could be easily prepared for dinner on a busy weeknight.

We imagined a dish that would marry tender chicken, plump couscous, and a mixture of aromatic vegetables, and that could be easily made in one skillet. Testing the chicken was our first priority. For our first tests we used bone-in chicken breasts. While the chicken came out moist and flavorful, its 15-minute cooking time didn't allow us enough of a window of opportunity to properly incorporate the other ingredients. Knowing that extending the cooking time would dry out the meat, we tried using bone-in chicken thighs instead, which proved to be just the right choice. With a cooking time of around 30 minutes (a perfect "walk away" time), the meat came out tender and juicy without the slightest hint of overcooking. However, we did find that it was necessary to remove the skin from the thighs after they were browned, since the skin added too much fat to the dish. And unlike chicken breasts, thighs contain a high amount of fat and don't need the skin's protective layer to keep them from drying out during cooking.

We wanted to keep the flavors of this dish fresh and light while limiting the ingredient list. So red onions and carrots formed the base of the dish, providing body, texture, and a clean vegetal sweetness, while a substantial amount of garlic provided a zesty undertone. We thought fennel would pair well with the other vegetables and would give the dish a crisp and refreshing anise flavor as well as a slight crunch. To punch up the flavor of the fennel even further, we added ground fennel seed along with some cayenne pepper, which gave the dish some bite. We were surprised, though, that the dish still tasted flat and boring. We initially tried adding lemon juice, but found that its sharpness conflicted with the flavor of the fennel. Thinking that orange juice, which is sweeter and less acidic, might be a good compromise, we added a cup of juice and several strips of peel, which helped pull the fennel flavor to the fore and brighten the entire dish.

Our final step was finding the best way to

PREPARING FENNEL

1. Cut off the stems and feathery fronds. (The fronds can be minced and used for a garnish.)

2. Trim a very thin slice from the base and remove any tough or blemished outer layers from the bulb.

3. Cut the bulb in half through the base. Use a small, sharp knife to remove the pyramid-shaped core.

4. Slice each half into ½-inch strips.

5. Turn the strips 90 degrees and cut crosswise into ½-inch pieces.

introduce the couscous into the broth. In our initial test, we removed the pieces of chicken after they were cooked, sprinkled a cup of couscous over the remaining vegetables and broth, and removed the skillet from the heat. After letting the couscous sit for 10 minutes, we found that it was still a little under-done in places. Thinking we had added too much couscous, we tried reducing the amount to ¾ cup, but found that it was still inconsistently cooked. It then occurred to us that the vegetables might be interfering with the cooking of the couscous. In our next test, we removed the vegetables along with the chicken and then added a cup of couscous to the skillet. Our hunch proved right. Without the vegetables in the way, the couscous easily absorbed the broth and was evenly plump and tender.

Skillet Chicken and Couscous with Fennel and Orange

SERVES 4 TO 6

Use a sharp vegetable peeler to remove the strips of peel from the orange.

8	bone-in, skin-on chicken thighs (about 3 pounds), trimmed of excess skin and fat
	Salt and ground black pepper
2	teaspoons vegetable oil
I	medium red onion, sliced thin
I	medium fennel bulb, fronds and stems removed, halved, cored, and cut into $1/2$-inch pieces (see the illustrations on page 220)
2	medium carrots, peeled and sliced $1/4$ inch thick
4	medium garlic cloves, minced or pressed through a garlic press
$1/2$	teaspoon ground fennel seed
$1/4$	teaspoon cayenne pepper
I	cup orange juice
3	(4-inch) strips of orange peel (from 2 oranges)
$1\frac{1}{2}$	cups low-sodium chicken broth
I	cup couscous
2	tablespoons chopped fresh cilantro leaves

1. Dry the chicken thoroughly with paper towels, then season generously with salt and pepper.

Heat the oil in a 12-inch skillet over medium-high heat until just smoking. Carefully lay the chicken thighs in the skillet, skin-side down, and cook until golden, 4 to 6 minutes. Flip the chicken over and continue to cook until the second side is golden, about 3 minutes. Remove the skillet from the heat and transfer the chicken to a plate. Using paper towels, remove and discard the browned chicken skin.

2. Pour off all but 2 tablespoons of the fat left in the skillet and return to medium-high heat until shimmering. Add the onion, fennel, carrots, and ½ teaspoon salt; cook, scraping the browned bits off the bottom and edges of the skillet, until the onion has softened, about 5 minutes. Add the garlic, fennel seed, and cayenne; cook until fragrant, about 1 minute. Stir in the orange juice, peel, and broth. Return the chicken to the skillet and bring to a simmer. Cover, reduce the heat to low, and cook until the chicken is tender and cooked through, 30 to 35 minutes.

3. Remove the skillet from the heat. Using a slotted spoon, transfer the chicken and vegetables to a large plate and cover with foil to keep warm. Stir the couscous into the remaining cooking liquid, cover, and let stand off the heat until tender, about 10 minutes.

4. Fluff the couscous with a fork and portion it onto individual plates. Arrange the chicken and vegetables over the couscous and sprinkle with the cilantro. Serve immediately.

SKILLET BEEF STROGANOFF

BEEF STROGANOFF IS A DECEPTIVE DISH. WHILE most people think of it as a long-simmering braise, like beef stew or beef burgundy, it is in fact a simple sauté of beef and mushrooms finished with a creamy pan sauce. But no matter how it's cooked, stroganoff is invariably overseasoned, leaden from too much sour cream, and muddled in flavor from too many ingredients. With an eye toward avoiding these pitfalls, we set out to develop a skillet version of beef stroganoff. In addition to developing a flavorful stroganoff, we wanted a recipe that would incorporate the cooking of the egg noodles in the same pan that we used for the mushrooms, beef, and sauce.

Since true beef stroganoff is a combination of a simple sauté and pan sauce, most recipes start with a tender cut of beef such as filet mignon or top loin. But using these cuts of beef didn't afford us much of a "walk away" time, and they were expensive. Searching for a cut of beef that would accommodate at least a 30-minute cooking time, but wouldn't require hours of slow simmering to become tender, we first tried shell sirloin, which was neither particularly flavorful or tender. So we next tried flank steak, which we found to be quite flavorful but also stringy. We moved on to blade steak, which comes from the shoulder, or chuck area, of the cow. These steaks, once we had cut out the thin line of gristle that ran down the center, cooked beautifully. After about 30 minutes of simmering, the beef was tender and packed with meaty flavor.

Mushrooms are another essential ingredient in stroganoff. We were after a strong mushroom presence, and we found that quartered chunks of mushrooms brought their flavor to the fore better than slices. But just simmering the mushrooms in the sauce, like many recipes suggested, gave the mushrooms a slimy exterior and did nothing to improve the dish's mushroom flavor. Instead, we

tried sautéing the mushrooms first, before cooking the meat, until their edges had browned. This made them silky and intensified their earthy flavor—a vast improvement over the mushrooms that were left to cook in the sauce. After setting aside the browned beef and mushrooms, we discovered that the pan had developed a rich fond. After building our sauce using this flavorful fond, we returned the beef and mushrooms to the pan and gently simmered the sauce until the beef was cooked through.

As for flavoring the dish, a little restraint helped. The sweet pungency of an onion provided the base notes of the sauce. We abandoned seasonings like prepared mustard, paprika, and Worcestershire, feeling that they did nothing but cover up the flavor of the beef and mushrooms. We also tried making the dish using spirits such as brandy, sherry, and red wine. Brandy and sherry were too overpowering, but the red wine gave the stroganoff some brightness and depth. A small amount of tomato paste and brown sugar improved the sauce's appearance and balanced the other flavors. To finish, we used just ¼ cup of sour cream, which provided just enough of that tangy richness we were after. To prevent the sour cream from curdling, we whisked it with a little of the hot sauce to temper it, and then whisked the mixture back into the skillet.

With the flavors settled, we turned our attention to figuring out how to incorporate the noodles into the dish. In addition to the red wine, we had been using a little bit of chicken broth as the liquid base for the dish. After the beef had simmered for 30 minutes, we added ½ pound of noodles and re-covered the skillet to let them cook. But there wasn't enough liquid for the pasta to absorb, leaving us with one big starchy disk. So we had to increase the chicken broth in half-cup increments until we found an amount that would adequately cook the noodles. At over 3 cups, however, the dish started to resemble chicken noodle soup rather than beef stroganoff. So we decreased the amount of noodles to just ⅓ pound, which we could cook with 2½ cups of broth, an amount that left the beef and mushroom flavors intact and gave the finished dish the right texture and sauciness.

INGREDIENTS: Tomato Paste

We reserve the use of tomato paste for recipes that require a deep tomato flavor, such as beef stroganoff or a tomato-flavored meat sauce. There is a vast array of tomato pastes out there, and we wondered if it mattered which one we used. To find out, we gathered seven brands for a tasting.

All delivered a big tomato punch, but Amoré is the only tomato paste that contains fat, which could account for its bigger flavor. The Amoré brand also scored points because of its tube packaging. Just squeeze out what you need and store the rest in the fridge. No fuss, no waste.

Skillet Beef Stroganoff

SERVES 4 TO 6

Top-blade steak, also known as flatiron steak, can be found in most supermarkets. If you cannot locate it, top sirloin is a suitable substitute. When buying egg noodles, peek through the bag and pick the brand with the thinnest noodles, since wider noodles make the finished dish too heavy.

3	tablespoons vegetable oil
10	ounces white button mushrooms, brushed clean, trimmed, and quartered
1½	pounds top-blade steak, gristle removed, cut into ½-inch cubes (see the illustrations on page 151)
	Salt and ground black pepper
1	medium onion, chopped medium
1	teaspoon tomato paste
1½	teaspoons dark brown sugar
1	tablespoon all-purpose flour
¾	cup dry red wine
2½	cups low-sodium chicken broth
⅓	pound thin egg noodles (about 3 cups)
¼	cup sour cream

1. Heat 1 tablespoon of the oil in a 12-inch skillet over medium-high heat until just smoking. Add the mushrooms and cook, stirring occasionally, until lightly browned, 6 to 8 minutes. Transfer to a medium bowl.

2. Dry the beef thoroughly with paper towels, then season generously with salt and pepper. Add 1 more tablespoon oil to the skillet and return to medium-high heat until just smoking. Sprinkle the beef into the skillet and cook, without stirring, until well browned on one side, about 4 minutes. Stir the meat and continue to cook, stirring occasionally, until well browned, about 2 minutes longer. Transfer the beef to the bowl with the mushrooms.

3. Add the remaining tablespoon oil to the skillet and return to medium heat until shimmering. Add the onion and ½ teaspoon salt; cook, stirring frequently, scraping the browned bits off the bottom and edges of the skillet, until the onion has softened, about 3 minutes. Stir in the tomato paste,

sugar, and flour. Whisk in the wine and chicken broth until smooth. Return the mushrooms and browned beef, along with any accumulated juices, back to the skillet; bring to a simmer. Cover, reduce the heat to low, and cook until the beef is tender, about 30 minutes.

4. Stir in the noodles and continue to cook, covered, over low heat, stirring occasionally, until the pasta is tender, 12 to 15 minutes. Whisk ½ cup of the sauce with the sour cream in a small bowl, then whisk the mixture back into the skillet. Season with salt and pepper to taste. Serve immediately.

SKILLET CINCINNATI CHILI WITH SPAGHETTI

FEW PEOPLE OUTSIDE THE MIDWEST HAVE HEARD of Cincinnati chili. Redolent of cinnamon and other warm spices, this chili is very different from its more familiar Texas brethren. One taste reveals layers of spices you expect from Middle Eastern or North African cuisine, not food from the American heartland.

Cincinnati chili is as much about the garnishes or "ways" as the chili itself. The chili alone is "one-way." With the addition of spaghetti, it's called "two-way." Adding shredded cheddar, minced onion, and kidney beans quickly brings it up to "five-way." When it came to developing our own version of a Cincinnati chili skillet casserole, we sought to build a flavorful chili in a skillet and then cook spaghetti in it, thus making our own unique "two-way" Cincinnati chili in one pan.

In our initial experiences with Cincinnati chili, we noted a couple of common problems. One was that the dish was overly greasy. The second was that it was overwhelmingly flavored, with a panoply of exotic spices, often resembling bad Middle Eastern cuisine.

While traditional chili recipes brown the meat to build flavor, most Cincinnati chili recipes boil the ground beef. This method may sound strange, but it's the hallmark of the dish, and it gives the beef a soft texture that pairs well with the other accompaniments. Boiling the beef in a shallow skillet proved to be a messy and somewhat dangerous undertaking during our first test. Searching for a safer technique, we placed the beef and a small amount of water in a covered skillet, essentially steaming the beef. While the beef had the right texture, this technique didn't allow the meat to shed enough of its fat, making the chili greasy and unappealing. We then tried a technique similar to rendering the fat from bacon but over a lower heat. Placing the beef in a cold pan, over medium heat, we cooked it gently until it was no longer pink. In addition to yielding a texture similar to that of the boiled beef, this method successfully encouraged the beef to gently shed most of its fat, allowing us to drain it off and produce a less greasy chili.

Recipes for Cincinnati chili vary greatly in the spices they use. Some use them rather sparingly, while others empty out the entire spice rack. Wanting to keep the spices to a minimum, we started with those that most recipes agreed upon: chili powder, cinnamon, allspice, and cayenne. A Texas chili is seasoned predominantly with chili powder, but we found with Cincinnati chili that a tablespoon was enough to provide background flavors and not overpower the other spices. A generous portion of cinnamon and a small amount of allspice were used to provide the chili's distinctive flavor, and a little cayenne added some heat. Unsweetened chocolate was another ingredient many recipes called for, and we liked its bittersweet, earthy undertones. However, we found that cocoa powder provided the same flavor and was much easier to incorporate into the chili.

The liquid in most Cincinnati chili recipes consists of tomato sauce and water. We tried to replace the tomato sauce with diced tomatoes, but found that the chili tasted rather thin and watery. We also considered replacing the water in our recipe, feeling that water helped little in adding flavor. Replacing the water with chicken broth gave the chili a richer, fuller flavor. Also, adding a couple tablespoons of cider vinegar made the chili brighter, and a small amount of brown sugar balanced the spices and finished off the dish.

With the chili just right, we turned our attention to the "two-way"—the addition of spaghetti. From our previous experience with other skillet-cooked pastas, we knew that we would have to increase the amount of broth in the dish to cook the spaghetti. But adding too much chicken broth gave the chili a dominant chicken flavor. Instead we tried a mix of water and broth, which gave us the proper amount of liquid to cook the pasta and didn't mask the unique and distinct flavors of the dish.

Skillet Cincinnati Chili with Spaghetti
SERVES 4 TO 6

Serve this American classic with finely chopped raw onion, shredded cheddar cheese, and Tabasco sauce. Stir the pasta well during cooking to ensure that the strands cook evenly and don't stick together. Use a nonstick skillet to keep the beef from sticking to the pan.

2	tablespoons vegetable oil
1	pound 90 percent lean ground beef
2	medium onions, minced
	Salt
2	medium garlic cloves, minced or pressed through a garlic press
1	tablespoon chili powder
1½	teaspoons cocoa powder
1	teaspoon ground cinnamon
¼	teaspoon cayenne pepper
¼	teaspoon ground allspice
3	cups low-sodium chicken broth
2	tablespoons cider vinegar
2	teaspoons dark brown sugar
1	(15-ounce) can tomato sauce
1	cup water
½	pound spaghetti, broken in half
	Ground black pepper

ACCOMPANIMENTS

1	medium onion, minced
4	ounces sharp cheddar cheese, shredded (about 1⅓ cups)
	Tabasco sauce

1. Heat 1 tablespoon of the oil and the ground beef in a 12-inch nonstick skillet over medium heat, breaking up the beef with the side of a spoon,

until no longer pink, about 6 minutes. Drain the beef in a colander and set aside.

2. Wipe the skillet clean with a wad of paper towels. Add the remaining tablespoon oil and return to medium heat until shimmering. Add the onions and ½ teaspoon salt; cook, stirring frequently, until the onions turn soft and begin to brown around the edges, about 5 minutes. Add the garlic, chili powder, cocoa, cinnamon, cayenne, and allspice; cook, stirring constantly, until fragrant, about 1 minute. Stir in the broth, vinegar, brown sugar, tomato sauce, and water. Return the beef to the skillet and bring to a simmer. Cover, reduce heat to low, and cook until the chili is deep red and the beef is tender, about 1 hour.

3. Stir in the spaghetti and continue to cook, covered, over low heat, stirring occasionally, until the pasta is tender, about 20 minutes. Season with salt and pepper to taste. Serve immediately with the accompaniments.

SKILLET AMERICAN CHOP SUEY

DESPITE ITS CHINESE NAME, CHOP SUEY IS NOT a Chinese dish. In fact, it's probably the furthest thing from it. A combination of ground beef, vegetables, and macaroni all cooked in a tomato sauce, chop suey conjures up images of grade-school cafeteria food, not the food of the Orient. Unfortunately, many of the existing chop suey recipes we found did nothing to dispel the negative associations many of us have with American chop suey. Looking past these dreadful recipes—often nothing more than ground beef mixed with canned spaghetti—we could imagine a really good chop suey, one with plenty of beefy flavor, fresh vegetables, and a bright tomato sauce. Chop suey was also appealing to us because it could neatly be prepared from start to finish in one pan with a significant amount of "walk away" time, making it a shoe-in for a skillet casserole.

As with a lot of dishes, we found it difficult to nail down just what constitutes chop suey. All recipes did agree on the central ingredient: ground beef. While a lot of recipes simply sauté the vegetables and beef together, we found that the flavor of the beef was better if we browned it before adding the other ingredients. Not only did the beef have a better texture and flavor, but the fond provided the sauce with a depth of flavor that far surpassed that of other recipes. We also took the time to brown the beef in two batches, thus eliminating the potential for overcrowding the pan, which would lead to simmering instead of browning the beef (a common mistake, which makes the dish more bland). Another complaint we had about chop suey was that it tended to be overly greasy, a problem we rectified by using 90 percent lean ground beef.

Considering the simplicity of chop suey, when it came to testing vegetables, we limited ourselves to simple pantry staples, namely onions, celery, peppers, and carrots. Onions, which provided the sauce with deep flavor, were a must. Celery gave the dish much-needed texture, while a red pepper lent both texture and a touch of sweetness. We ultimately rejected the carrots, as their earthiness conflicted with the acidity of the tomato sauce. We also found that several cloves of garlic rounded out the dish, and gave it a depth of flavor that most other recipes lacked.

When it came to the sauce, we wanted to avoid one that was too thick and pasty. In our effort to keep the sauce fresh and light, we tried using two cans of diced tomatoes and their juice. But the resulting sauce was very thin and the tomato flavor fleeting. We next tried using a combination of diced tomatoes and tomato sauce. A can of each struck a good balance. The tomato sauce gave the dish some body and distributed the tomato flavor throughout the dish, while the diced tomatoes and their juices kept the dish tasting fresh. However, with just the tomato, the dish tasted a little too much like an Italian meat sauce served over pasta. To provide the sauce with a meatier flavor and to balance the acidity of the tomatoes, we added ½ cup of chicken broth.

The chicken broth also played a key role when we added the pasta. After we had simmered the meat, vegetables, and tomato sauce for 20 minutes, enabling the flavors to develop and meld, we stirred in a half pound of macaroni. But we found that there wasn't enough liquid for the pasta to absorb, and we soon had a mass of uncooked pasta on our hands. We steadily increased the chicken broth until we had added a total of 1½ cups. While this looked really soupy initially, once the pasta had fully cooked and released its starches into the sauce, it was the perfect consistency.

Skillet American Chop Suey

SERVES 4 TO 6

Using lean ground beef will keep this dish from becoming too greasy.

5	teaspoons vegetable oil
1½	pounds 90 percent lean ground beef
1	medium onion, chopped medium
1	medium red bell pepper, stemmed, seeded, and chopped medium
1	large celery rib, chopped medium
2	medium garlic cloves, minced or pressed through a garlic press
	Salt
1	(14.5-ounce) can diced tomatoes
1	(15-ounce) can tomato sauce
1½	cups low-sodium chicken broth
½	pound elbow macaroni (about 2 cups)
	Ground black pepper

1. Heat 1 teaspoon of the oil in a 12-inch skillet over medium-high heat until just smoking. Add half of the beef and cook, breaking up the pieces with a wooden spoon, until lightly browned, about 4 minutes. Transfer the beef to a medium bowl and set aside. Add 1 more teaspoon oil to the skillet and return to medium-high heat until just smoking; brown the remaining beef and transfer to the bowl.

2. Add the remaining 3 teaspoons oil to the skillet and return to medium heat until shimmering. Add the onion, pepper, celery, garlic, and 1 teaspoon salt; cook, stirring frequently, scraping the browned bits off the bottom and edges of the skillet, until the vegetables begin to soften, about 4 minutes. Stir in the tomatoes, tomato sauce, chicken broth, and the browned beef and bring to a simmer. Cover, reduce the heat to low, and cook

until the beef and vegetables are tender, about 20 minutes.

3. Stir in the macaroni and continue to cook, covered, over low heat, stirring occasionally, until the macaroni is tender, about 20 minutes. Season with salt and pepper to taste. Serve immediately.

Skillet Lamb Curry with Cauliflower and Peas

LAMB CURRY IS A TRADITIONAL INDIAN DISH that combines the flavors of lamb and vegetables with curry spices. It can often be a complicated dish with an extended braising time. We sought to adapt this dish to maintain its potent flavors without making it an all-day affair. This meant using accessible spices and cutting the cooking time, without sacrificing the curry's full flavor.

First, we had to decide which cut of lamb to use. Boneless leg of lamb, which is the meat typically called for in stew recipes, was our initial choice. After simmering several batches, we found that the leg of lamb performed admirably, but it lacked the intense flavor and moist texture we were seeking. We tried using loin and rib chops instead, but their fine texture did not fare well in this recipe. And since these chops were more than $15 a pound, we decided to move on to our next choice: shoulder chops. These chops, which were significantly less expensive, were rendered juicy and flavorful in the dish. While removing the meat from the bone took time, it allowed us to cut the meat into cubes small enough that they only required about 40 minutes of cooking time to become tender.

Next we focused on the aromatics. Onion was essential, providing the dish with depth and body. We also used a substantial amount of garlic and ginger to lend an overall piquancy. Along with the garlic and ginger, we added jalapeño, surmising that its fresh spiciness would complement the sweetness of the lamb and round out the other flavors in dish. Carrots were also added here to supplement the curry's sweetness, as well as provide color and texture.

When it came to spices for the dish, many recipes suggest creating a curry from a blend of different herbs and spices. Although we liked this idea, the flavor difference between a homemade curry mix made with individual ground spices and a premixed curry powder from the grocery store turned out to be very small. The barely perceptible improvement in flavor was certainly not worth searching out the five or six different spices required for the homemade mix.

Next we looked for additional vegetables to add to the dish that were authentic to Indian cooking. Cauliflower was our first choice, and when added in the last 10 minutes of cooking, it emerged tender, flavorful, and tinted an attractive saffron color. We included peas for their sweetness and vibrant color, finding that if they were still frozen, we could add them with the cauliflower without risk of overcooking them, thus saving the extra step of cooking the vegetables in two stages. To the cauliflower and peas, we added Red Bliss potatoes, the requisite starch, to make the dish a more complete one-skillet dinner.

To finish, we added a dollop of plain yogurt and a sprinkling of chopped cilantro. The yogurt's tanginess was a perfect foil to the highly spiced curry, and the cilantro added a cool freshness to the dish.

CUTTING CAULIFLOWER INTO FLORETS

1. Trim the stem near the base of the head. Cut around and then pull out and discard the core.

2. Using a chef's knife, cut the individual florets from the inner stem.

3. Cut the florets in halves or quarters to yield ¾-inch pieces.

Skillet Lamb Curry with Cauliflower and Peas

SERVES 4 TO 6

While not as flavorful, leg of lamb can be substituted for the shoulder chops in this recipe (use 1 pound of boneless meat).

2	pounds lamb shoulder chops, trimmed of bones and excess fat and cut into 1-inch cubes
	Salt and ground black pepper
2	tablespoons vegetable oil
2	small onions, halved and sliced thin
2	medium carrots, peeled and chopped medium
1	jalapeño chile, stemmed, seeded, and minced
4	medium garlic cloves, minced or pressed through a garlic press
1	(1½-inch) piece ginger, peeled and grated
4	teaspoons curry powder
2	cups low-sodium chicken broth
1	pound Red Bliss potatoes (about 3 medium), scrubbed and cut into 1-inch cubes
1	head cauliflower (about 2 pounds), trimmed and cut into ¾-inch florets (about 6 cups)
1	cup frozen peas
¼	cup chopped fresh cilantro leaves
¾	cup plain yogurt (optional)

1. Dry the lamb thoroughly with paper towels, then season generously with salt and pepper. Heat 1 tablespoon of the oil in a 12-inch skillet over medium-high heat until just smoking. Add the lamb to the skillet and cook, without stirring, until well browned on one side, 3 to 5 minutes. Stir the meat and continue to cook, stirring occasionally, until well browned, 3 to 5 minutes longer. Transfer to a medium bowl.

2. Add the remaining tablespoon oil to the skillet and return to medium heat until shimmering.

INGREDIENTS:
Lamb Shoulder Chops

Lamb shoulder is sliced into two different cuts, blade chops and round bone chops. You'll find them sold in a range of thicknesses (from about ½ inch to more than 1 inch thick), depending on who's doing the butchering. (In our experience, supermarkets tend to cut them thinner, while independent butchers cut them thicker.) Blade chops are roughly rectangular in shape, and some are thickly striated with fat. Each blade chop includes a piece of the chine bone (the backbone of the animal) and a thin piece of the blade bone (the shoulder blade of the animal).

Round bone chops, also called arm chops, are more oval in shape and as a rule are substantially leaner than blade chops. Each contains a round cross-section of the arm bone so that the chop looks a bit like a small ham steak. In addition to the arm bone, there's a tiny line of riblets on the side of each chop.

As to which chop is better, we found that it is easier to remove the meat in large chunks from round bone chops. The blade chops often contain a lot of intramuscular fat and, once trimmed, will yield irregularly shaped pieces of meat. That said, our lamb curry will still be delicious if made with blade chops.

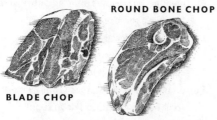

ROUND BONE CHOP

BLADE CHOP

There are two kinds of shoulder chops. The blade chop is roughly rectangular in shape and contains a piece of the chine bone and a thin piece of the blade bone. The arm or round bone contains a round cross-section of the arm bone so that the chop looks like a small ham steak. The round bone chop contains less fat and few muscles, making it easier to cut into meat for stews.

Add the onions, carrots, and ½ teaspoon salt; cook, stirring frequently, scraping the browned bits off the bottom and edges of the skillet, until the onions are lightly browned, about 6 minutes. Stir in the jalapeño, garlic, ginger, and curry powder; cook until fragrant, about 1 minute. Add the broth, potatoes, and browned lamb; bring to a simmer. Cover, reduce heat to low, and cook until the lamb is almost tender, 30 to 35 minutes.

3. Stir in the cauliflower and peas, increase the heat to medium-low, and continue to cook, covered, stirring occasionally, until the lamb and cauliflower are tender, about 7 to 10 minutes. Stir in the cilantro and season with salt and pepper to taste. Add a dollop of yogurt to each serving, if desired, and serve immediately.

SMOTHERED PORK CHOPS

MANY OF US IN THE TEST KITCHEN HAVE FOND memories from our youth of pork chops swimming in a hearty sauce packed with big onion flavor. Our mothers gave the dish different names, but it was clearly a variation on smothered pork chops. Southern at heart, authentic smothered pork chops are browned pork chops simmered under a blanket of onions (and hence "smothered") and a thick brown gravy. The pork chops share equal billing with the sauce, which should be thick and heady with sweet onions. In addition to flavoring and moistening the chops, the sauce is made in sufficient quantity to moisten egg noodles, mashed potatoes, or rice.

In our fuzzy nostalgia, we forget that the chops were probably tough and bland and the sauce gelatinous or floury. No doubt some of our harried mothers relied on canned soup to get dinner to the table quickly. Could we make smothered chops without Campbell's prepackaged help?

The most obvious first test was what type of pork chop worked best. We tend to favor thick-cut rib loin chops because they have a higher fat content than other chops, which is important to the chop's flavor. We also usually brine our chops (soak them in a solution of water, salt, and, often, sugar) to ensure moist and tender meat. For our first batch of smothered chops, we brined 1½-inch-thick rib loin chops in our standard brine, and then browned and braised the chops for half an hour (the standard braising time for all the smothered chop recipes we culled). Surprisingly, the meat was tough, dry, and flavorless. In a subsequent test, we doubled our braising time to one hour, and the chops were still bland and dry. The braising liquid, moreover, was almost intolerably saline from the brine that leached out of the meat. We figured that brining was unnecessary for braised meat because braising is a moist cooking method, and so the meat does not undergo the kind of moisture loss that is associated with grilling or sautéing. So we switched tactics completely and tried unbrined chops from ½ inch to over an inch thick. Tasters were all impressed by the substantial pork flavor and the tenderness of the meat. Tasters all favored the skinnier, ½-inch-thick chops, which were more tender than the inch-thick chops.

Because we were using thin chops, we tried shortening the braising time, but with little success. After 15 minutes, they were cooked through, but tough. After 30 minutes, they were more tender and flavorful. Extending the braise for another 15 minutes did little for either texture or flavor, so we left it at half an hour.

We found that adequately browning the chops was essential to developing richness and depth in the meat and the sauce. We were surprised by how quickly the chops browned; about two minutes per side in a very hot pan gave the chops a thick golden crust. A thorough drying of each chop with paper towels and a generous coating of salt and black pepper prior to browning helped promote a thick crust. While the crust was partially washed away during the slow braise, it enriched the flavor and color of the sauce.

A hefty amount of onions is crucial to the sauce's richness. To add a little sweetness and more color to the sauce, we cooked the onions until they browned a bit and started to soften, about five minutes. We knew adding a little salt to the onions while they cooked would help break them down faster, but we were amazed at how efficiently the salt worked. The onions released enough liquid to deglaze (or lift) the fond from the pan. We tried a variety of liquids for braising, including water, beef broth, chicken broth, and wine blended with chicken broth. Water tasted thin and flavorless. Beef broth overwhelmed the other flavors and tasted tinny and salty. Wine and chicken broth combined in equal parts toughened the meat and tasted sour. All chicken broth was the winner. It provided a supportive background for the onion and pork flavors.

To thicken the sauce, we embraced tradition and used a roux made of flour cooked in oil. Many of the recipes we found avoided using roux as a thickener, probably to keep the dish to one pan, but we were displeased with the options. Flour sprinkled into the onions while they cooked made the gravy taste of raw flour, and cornstarch turned the sauce gelatinous and translucent, making it visually unappealing. Dusting the pork chops with flour turned the exterior of the meat gummy, and the sauce again tasted of raw flour. Roux, on the other hand, did not taste of flour, adequately thickened the sauce, and added a mildly nutty flavor to the dish. Yes, it involved another pot, but the nominal hassle was well worth it. We cooked the roux for about five minutes, or just long enough to turn it light brown. We found adding room-temperature stock to the hot roux and stirring constantly helped prevent lumps from forming.

Borrowing a southern technique, we tried making the roux with rendered bacon fat instead of bland vegetable oil. The sauce tasted fantastic; the smokiness accented the sweet onions, and the meatiness reemphasized that of the pork chops. And the crisp bacon bits served well as a crunchy, visually appealing garnish.

After a half hour of braising, we were surprised by how much liquid the onions released. We did not want to use fewer onions, so we tried reducing the sauce after braising to concentrate it. A mere four to five minutes of cooking over medium-high heat, after removing the chops from the pan, thickened the sauce to a velvety gravy. A little minced parsley perked up the deep flavors.

Our mothers would be proud. We had an easy, richly flavored dish perfect for a weeknight meal, and there wasn't a can of soup in sight.

Smothered Pork Chops

SERVES 4

Make sure the chops are quite dry before browning them, to prevent sticking and to promote the best crust. The pork chops pair well with a variety of starches, which you will want to soak up the rich gravy. We liked them best with simple egg noodles, but rice or mashed potatoes also taste great.

- 4 ounces (about 4 slices) bacon, chopped
- 3 tablespoons all-purpose flour
- 1¾ cups low-sodium chicken broth
- 1 tablespoon vegetable oil
- 4 bone-in rib loin pork chops, ½ to ¾ inch thick
  Salt and ground black pepper
- 2 medium onions, halved and sliced thin
- 2 medium garlic cloves, minced or pressed through a garlic press
- 1 teaspoon minced fresh thyme leaves
- 2 bay leaves
- 1 tablespoon minced fresh parsley leaves

1. Fry the bacon in a medium saucepan over medium heat until it is lightly browned and the fat is rendered, 6 to 8 minutes. Remove the browned bacon from the pan with a slotted spoon and set aside on a small plate. Reduce the heat to medium-low and gradually stir in the flour with a wooden spoon, making sure to work out any lumps that may form. Continue stirring constantly, reaching into the edges of the pan, until the mixture is light brown, 4 to 6 minutes. Add the chicken broth in a slow, steady stream while vigorously stirring. Reduce the heat to low and keep the sauce warm.

2. Heat the oil in a 12-inch skillet over high heat until shimmering. Meanwhile, pat the chops dry with paper towels and season generously with salt and pepper. Place the chops in the pan in a single layer and cook until a deep-brown crust forms, about 2 minutes. Turn the chops over and cook for another 2 minutes. Remove the chops from the pan and set aside on a plate.

3. Reduce the heat to medium and add the onions and ½ teaspoon salt. Cook, stirring frequently and scraping any browned bits from the bottom and edges of the pan, until the onions soften and begin to brown around the edges, about 5 minutes. Stir in the garlic and thyme and cook until fragrant, about 30 seconds longer. Return the chops to the pan in a single layer and cover each chop with onions. Pour in the warm sauce, add the bay leaves, and cover with a tight-fitting lid. Reduce the heat to low and cook until the meat is tender, about 30 minutes.

4. Transfer the chops to a warmed plate and cover with foil. Increase the heat to medium high and cook, stirring frequently, until the sauce thickens to a gravy-like consistency, 4 to 6 minutes. Stir in the parsley and season with salt and pepper to taste. Cover each chop with a portion of the sauce, sprinkle with the reserved bacon, and serve immediately.

➤ VARIATIONS

Smothered Pork Chops Braised in Cider with Apples

Follow the recipe for Smothered Pork Chops, replacing the chicken broth with an equal amount of apple cider and replacing one of the onions with 1 large or 2 small Granny Smith apples, peeled, cored, and cut into ⅓-inch slices. Proceed as directed.

Smothered Pork Chops with Spicy Collard Greens

Follow the recipe for Smothered Pork Chops, increasing the oil to 2 tablespoons, reducing the onions to 1, and increasing the garlic to 4 cloves. Once the onion and garlic are cooked, add 4 cups thinly sliced collard greens and ½ teaspoon crushed red pepper flakes. Return the browned chops to the pan and proceed as directed.

SKILLET BRATWURST AND SAUERKRAUT

SOME MIGHT CALL THE DISTINCT FLAVOR OF sauerkraut an "acquired" taste, but it is a healthy and traditional foundation for several classic German and Alsatian meals. Bratwurst and sauerkraut may be the best known of these. Well-browned, flavorful sausage nestled into meltingly soft sauerkraut—what's not to love? Unfortunately, the dish traditionally relies on a long list of ingredients and a slow simmer in the oven for its full flavor. Despite these hurdles, we sensed the dish was a perfect candidate for a skillet casserole.

Browning the sausages was the first step, just a minute or two per side to intensify flavor and develop a fond, which would in turn flavor the sauerkraut. Bratwurst is the classic choice, though knockwurst is a close second; feel free to combine them if you like. Authentic bratwurst is made from a combination of pork and veal seasoned with a variety of spices, including ginger, nutmeg, and caraway. Knockwurst (or knackwurst) is a combination of beef and pork flavored with cumin and garlic. Both are fresh sausages and must be thoroughly cooked—browning gets things started, and steaming in the sauerkraut finishes the task. While we recommend a trip to your local German butcher for the best-quality sausages, your local market should carry them, if not in the meat section, then in the deli department—sometimes side-by-side with bags of sauerkraut.

With recipes dating to the early Middle Ages, sauerkraut has a long heritage. At its very simplest, sauerkraut is nothing but thinly sliced cabbage tightly packed with salt and slowly fermented. Depending on the temperature at which the cabbage is stored, fermentation may take up to a year before the sauerkraut is ready. Rarely does it go this long—one to two months is more conventional. Clearly our aim was not to make our own; store-bought would have to do. And, luckily, all the brands we tested were perfectly acceptable, especially when well rinsed to remove the potent brine.

To boost the flavor of the sauerkraut, we stuck to conventional flavorings like apple, carrot, and onion. Apples and carrots, coarsely grated on a box grater, cooked the fastest, breaking down to enrich the sauerkraut. We tried grating the onions but found they did not brown as well as when sliced, and the sauerkraut suffered, lacking depth. Despite the sweetness provided by the onions, carrots, and apples, tasters agreed that the sauerkraut needed more. While white sugar worked adequately, brown sugar lent a new dimension to this dish. A scant tablespoon was all that was necessary.

For liquid, everything from cider and beer to chicken broth and water was common in our researched recipes. Cider made the cabbage too sweet and fruity for most tasters, even when partially diluted with water. Beer added a malty note that some tasters enjoyed, but the majority felt it clashed with the sauerkraut's tang, so we skipped it. Water contributed little, so chicken broth (for convenience) was our choice, adding richness and depth without altering the dish's balanced flavors.

In the recipes we consulted, traditional seasonings included sage, caraway seeds, garlic, cloves, bay leaves, and juniper berries. We tried most of them—solo and in combination—but tasters most enjoyed the woodsy, almost camphor-like flavor of the juniper, which added complexity without competing with the assertive spiciness of the sausage.

One final though crucial lesson we learned was the importance of pricking the sausages prior to cooking. Without a liberal pricking, the sausages were prone to exploding—an unsightly mess, to say the least. A skewer or the tip of a thin paring knife worked perfectly.

One-Skillet Bratwurst and Sauerkraut

SERVES 4

Don't be alarmed when the grated apple rapidly oxidizes; the brown color won't affect the finished dish. The dish may be prepared ahead of time and reheated, but add water or chicken broth to keep the sauerkraut moist. An ideal accompaniment would be potatoes, either mashed or boiled.

I	tablespoon unsalted butter
4	bratwursts or knockwursts, punctured liberally with a small skewer
I	small onion, halved and sliced thin
10	juniper berries
I	medium carrot, peeled and grated on the large holes of a box grater
	Salt
2	pounds packaged sauerkraut, well rinsed and drained

1   **medium Granny Smith apple, peeled and grated on the large holes of a box grater**
1   **tablespoon brown sugar**
1¾   **cups low-sodium chicken broth**
      Ground black pepper

1. Melt the butter in a 12-inch skillet over medium-high heat. Add the sausages, reduce the heat to medium, and cook until well browned, about 1 minute. Roll each sausage one-quarter turn and brown the next side, about 1 minute. Repeat two more times until browned on all sides (about 4 minutes total.) Transfer the sausages to a plate.

2. Add the onion, juniper berries, carrot, and ¼ teaspoon salt to the empty skillet. Cook, stirring frequently, until the onion softens, about 3 minutes. Stir in the sauerkraut, apple, sugar, and broth, increase the heat to medium-high, and bring to a simmer. Nestle the sausages into the sauerkraut, evenly spacing them around the skillet. Cover, reduce the heat to low, and simmer until the liquid is almost evaporated, about 30 minutes. Remove the juniper berries and season with salt and pepper to taste. Transfer to a platter, arranging the sausages on the sauerkraut, and serve.

SPANISH-STYLE BRAISED LENTILS WITH SAUSAGE

THE PAIRING OF BEANS WITH CURED MEAT IS common in many cuisines. Think Cuban black beans, split pea soup, even Boston baked beans— all have rich ham, bacon, or sausage as a prime ingredient. The beans absorb the robust flavor and stretch the meat so a small amount can feed more people. For a quick skillet casserole, the pairing makes perfect sense. Fast-cooking legumes like lentils cook within the hour and are a perfect foil to hearty sausage. Because of the meat's assertive flavor, the dish requires few additional ingredients, thus limiting both preparation and shopping time. Inspired by a classic Spanish dish of green lentils flavored with paprika and *morcilla*, or blood sausage, we wanted to develop a recipe that would cook in the confines of a 12-inch skillet

and taste authentic. Morcilla is rarely available in the United States, so a less exotic sausage would have to do.

Glossy green lentils du Puy were our bean choice for this dish. Their firm texture—they retain their shape better than other lentils—and hearty flavor are ideal with sausage. For the fullest flavor, we simmered them in diluted chicken broth flavored with a bundle of fresh thyme leaves; the whole herbs imparted a great deal of flavor, with no preparation required.

We knew the lentils needed flavor help from aromatics like onion and garlic. The traditional recipes included these as well as tomato and, after tasting, we saw no reason to alter the ingredient list. The onions and garlic gave the lentils sweetness and depth, while the tomato provided fruitiness and acidity. Our only change was to toast the garlic in olive oil to a light golden color for the roundest flavor.

As for spices, paprika—smoked paprika, in particular—gave the dish all the punch it needed. Produced only in the Vera region of Spain, smoked paprika is made from pimiento peppers that are slowly smoked over oak prior to crushing. The flavor is intensely smoky and comes in three grades: sweet, hot, and bittersweet. Despite its localized Spanish production, smoked paprika is widely available in specialty stores and large markets. For this dish, we favored bittersweet paprika, because sweet was too mild and hot numbed the palate. For the best flavor, we toasted the smoked paprika briefly in the skillet before adding liquid—the heat activates the volatile oils.

Replacing morcilla sausage was a tall order. We opted for convenience rather than authenticity and tried a wide range of readily available sausages, including chorizo, linguiça, hot and sweet Italian sausage, and kielbasa. The latter won out for its smoky, sweet flavor and compact texture. In addition, kielbasa is sold ready to eat, which meant it just needed to heat through and brown a little for flavor.

Our final touch, though nontraditional, was to scatter thinly sliced scallions across the lentils. Tasters enjoyed the piquant scallion punch and the added visual appeal.

Spanish-Style Braised Lentils with Sausage

SERVES 4

Search the lentils carefully for small pebbles and other detritus; lentils almost always have hidden grit. A white plate or bowl makes foreign objects easy to see. Smoked paprika is available at many specialty stores. Be sure to choose the bittersweet variety unless you have a penchant for very spicy food; hot smoked paprika is exactly that. You can use regular paprika if you can't find smoked; the difference is, of course, that regular paprika lacks smokiness. If you like your lentils on the mushy side, cook them for an additional 5 minutes. This dish reheats well or may even be eaten at room temperature with a drizzle of lemon juice or sherry vinegar.

I	teaspoon vegetable oil
I	pound kielbasa, cut into 4 equal lengths, then split lengthwise to yield 8 pieces
I	medium onion, minced
	Salt
2	medium garlic cloves, minced or pressed through a garlic press
I¼	teaspoon smoked bittersweet paprika or regular sweet paprika
I	(14.5-ounce) can diced tomatoes, drained
5	sprigs fresh thyme, tied together with kitchen twine
I	cup lentils du Puy, picked over and rinsed (see the headnote)
I½	cups low-sodium chicken broth
I½	cups water
	Ground black pepper
2	medium scallions, sliced thin on the bias

1. Heat the oil in a 12-inch skillet over medium-high heat until shimmering. Carefully lay the sausage in the skillet, cut-side down, and cook until browned, about 2 minutes. Transfer to a plate.

2. Return the skillet with all the remaining fat to medium-high heat until shimmering. Add the onion and ½ teaspoon salt; cook, scraping the browned bits off the bottom and edges of the skillet, until the onion is softened, about 5 minutes. Add the garlic and paprika; cook until fragrant, about 1 minute. Add the tomatoes and thyme; cook for 1 minute. Stir in the lentils, broth, and water; bring to a simmer. Cover, reduce the heat to low, and cook until the lentils are almost tender but still a little crunchy, about 35 minutes.

3. Nestle the kielbasa into the lentils and continue to cook, covered, over low heat until the lentils are completely tender, about 10 minutes. Off the heat, discard the thyme bundle and season with salt and pepper to taste. Sprinkle with scallions and serve immediately.

WIPING A SKILLET CLEAN

A quick wipe of the skillet with paper towels allows you to prepare the chard, sausage, and lentils in a single pan. After the chard is removed from the pan, crumple a wad of paper towels, grab it with tongs, and use it to swab the extra oil from the pan before cooking the sausage.

SEPARATING CHARD STEMS AND LEAVES

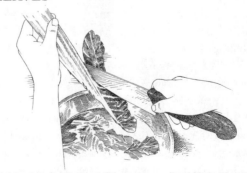

Hold each leaf at the base of the stem over a bowl filled with water. Use a sharp knife to slash the leafy portion from both sides of the thick stem. The cutting motion is the same as you would use with a machete.

➤ VARIATION

Spanish-Style Braised Lentils with Sausage and Chard

Wash and dry 1 bunch chard (10 to 12 ounces) thoroughly. Separate the stems from the leaves (see the illustration on page 233) and chop both into medium-sized pieces; reserve in separate bowls. Heat 1 teaspoon of oil in a 12-inch skillet over medium-high heat until shimmering. Add the chard greens and stir, using tongs, until just wilted, about 2 minutes. Transfer to a small bowl and set aside. Wipe pan clean with a wad of paper towels following the illustration on page 233. Follow the recipe for Spanish-Style Braised Lentils with Sausage, adding the chopped stems to the pan with the onions in step 2. Stir the wilted chard leaves into the cooked lentils before adding the sausage in step 3, and continue to follow the recipe as directed.

SKILLET SHRIMP PAELLA

IN THE PANTHEON OF RICE DISHES, PAELLA IS near the top. Packed with meat and seafood—from chicken and snails to rabbit and shrimp—myriad vegetables, and plump yet discrete grains of rice, this dish is rightly famous around the world. As is true of many classic dishes, however, it can take hours of preparation and arduous stoveside attendance (or grillside, for truly authentic paella). But when deconstructed, paella is a one-pan main dish that, with some adjustments to technique and ingredients, can easily be made within an hour. To keep our version simple, we decided to employ shrimp as our prime flavor, leaving the snails and rabbit for another day.

Paella is traditionally cooked on a stovetop or over the dying embers of a wood fire. The flavorings are sautéed and then the rice and liquid are added and simmered, uncovered, until the rice grains are tender and the liquid has evaporated. The authentic cooking vessel, called a paellera, is a large, shallow round pan made from thin steel. We found that a large skillet is a perfect substitute, as the sides gently slope and the pan itself is shallow, which allows for quick evaporation of the cooking liquid.

The heart of paella is the rice. Paella rice must be medium grain and starchy. The traditional choices are Valencian and Calasparra rice, which can be tricky to find. We found that Arborio rice (typically used in risotto) is a suitable substitute, as it possesses the same ability to absorb a lot of liquid.

Sautéed aromatics form the foundation on which paella is built. For our simplified version, we favored a simple combination of onion and garlic sautéed in olive oil. For seasonings, we included thyme sprigs, left whole to save preparation time, and sweet paprika. Saffron is another common ingredient, but tasters felt that in this case it added little. Once the paprika was toasted in the dry skillet, thus intensifying its flavor, we added well-drained canned diced tomatoes for sweetness and color.

Water as the cooking liquid made the dish taste bland, and chicken broth tasted out of place. As shrimp was to be the primary flavor in the dish, clam juice proved the best choice.

Cooking paella takes a leap of faith, as the method is different from most rice cookery. Once the liquid is added, the pan is left uncovered and the rice simmers rapidly (and unstirred) until tender. We had the best luck with medium-low heat; the grains were uniformly tender and discrete in 18 to 20 minutes. At lower temperatures, the rice turned starchy, and at higher heat, it cooked unevenly.

Tasters unanimously favored extra-large shrimp for their full flavor, tenderness, and visual appeal. To cook the shrimp, we first followed conventional recipes and added them to the rice during the final minutes of cooking. While the result was acceptable, the shrimp tasted bland, so we searched for another method. Seared shrimp packed the most flavor, so we cooked them alongside the paella in a second skillet and added them at the last minute. In a moment of clarity, we realized we could sear the shrimp in the skillet beforehand and incorporate the fond from the shrimp into the paella, thereby improving the overall flavor. Before cooking them, we tossed the shrimp with olive oil, salt, and paprika to improve their flavor and color; the paprika darkened and intensified their red hue. The seared shrimp held well in a bowl, and a brief warming before serving brought them back to temperature. Finishing touches included a scattering of scallions over the top and a spritz of lemon.

Skillet Shrimp Paella
SERVES 4 TO 6

If you want a little heat, add a pinch of cayenne pepper with the paprika or mix sweet and hot paprika.

1	teaspoon vegetable oil
1½	pounds extra-large shrimp (21 to 25 count), peeled and deveined
3	tablespoons extra-virgin olive oil
3	teaspoons sweet paprika
	Salt
1	medium onion, chopped fine
6	medium garlic cloves, sliced thin
6	sprigs fresh thyme
1	(14.5-ounce) can diced tomatoes, drained well
1½	cups Arborio rice
2	(8-ounce) bottles clam juice
2	cups water
	Ground black pepper
3	medium scallions, sliced thin on the bias
1	lemon, cut into wedges

1. Heat the vegetable oil in a large skillet over medium-high heat until smoking. Meanwhile, toss the shrimp with 1 tablespoon of the olive oil, 1 teaspoon of the paprika, and ½ teaspoon salt in a large bowl. Add half of the shrimp to the skillet in a single layer and cook until speckled brown, 30 to 45 seconds. Flip the shrimp and cook until speckled brown on the second side, about 30 seconds longer. Transfer the shrimp to a bowl. Repeat the process with the remaining shrimp. Cover the bowl with aluminum foil to keep the shrimp warm.

2. Reduce the heat to medium and add the remaining 2 tablespoons olive oil, the onion, garlic, thyme sprigs, and 1 teaspoon salt to the empty skillet. Cook, stirring frequently, until softened and beginning to brown, 3 to 5 minutes.

Stir in the remaining 2 teaspoons paprika and cook until fragrant, about 30 seconds. Stir in the tomatoes, rice, clam juice, and water. Once the liquid comes to a boil, reduce the heat to medium-low and cook, without covering or stirring, until the rice is tender and the liquid is absorbed, about 18 minutes.

3. Spread the shrimp over the rice and cover until the shrimp are heated through, about 2 minutes. Remove and discard the thyme sprigs. Season with salt and pepper to taste and sprinkle the scallions over the top. Serve immediately, bringing the skillet to the table along with the lemon wedges.

SKILLET SALMON WITH POTATOES

FLAVORFUL, HEALTHY, AND VERSATILE, SALMON has become one of the most popular and widely available fish today. So when we set out to develop a hearty skillet version of salmon with potatoes, we were surprised to find a sparse number of decent one-dish salmon recipes. Our goal, given the way salmon pairs so well with other vegetables, was to see if we could come up with a skillet dinner with salmon and potatoes as the star ingredients. Not only did we think that the two together would be a sure crowd pleaser, but we thought they would likely have compatible cooking times.

During our research, we found several recipes that poached the salmon in a flavorful broth studded with vegetables. Unlike a court bouillon, the classic medium for poaching fish, these broths contained a minimal amount of liquid, which was later served along with the fish. And while none of the recipes included potatoes, we felt that we could easily adapt this method to our skillet version of salmon and potatoes.

We focused first on the vegetables used to flavor the broth. Considering that this poaching liquid would later be served along with the fish, we found that it was necessary to first sauté the vegetables in butter in order to extract their full vegetal sweetness into the broth. While most of these poaching liquids use onion, we found that the less pungent flavor of leeks paired better with the other ingredients. In addition to leeks, we favored the earthy sweetness of carrots and the subtle anise flavor of fennel as the base of our broth.

When it came to the potatoes, we tested russet, Yukon Gold, white boiling, and Red Bliss potatoes. The russets, which were dry and flavorless, broke apart while cooking, so they were quickly ruled out. The Yukon Gold and white boiling potatoes both held their shape well, but their texture was slightly grainy. The Red Bliss were the clear choice all the way around. Their creamy texture and simple flavor complemented the other vegetables perfectly.

With the vegetables chosen, we turned our attention to the broth itself. Many recipes used either straight white wine, or a combination of wine and fish stock. Since we didn't have the time or the inclination to make fish stock, we ruled it out immediately. However, using only wine created a dish that was too acidic and gave the vegetables a slightly metallic taste. We tried using half wine and half water, but the resulting dish tasted very thin. We then tested a combination of white wine and bottled clam juice. This proved to be the best mix: The wine provided just the right level of acidity, while the briny clam juice accentuated the flavor of the fresh fish.

We could now focus on how to put the dish together. Up to this point, we had been making the broth, adding the potatoes, and covering the pan. After 15 minutes, we laid the salmon over the partially cooked potatoes, re-covered the pan, and let the two cook till done, which took another 15 minutes. While this technique worked well, we felt the flavors of the vegetables and fish could be made a little deeper. We first tried searing the fish in the skillet before we built the broth, hoping the browned exterior would accentuate its flavor. This didn't work. The flavor was only marginally better, and after the final poaching, the fish's crisp exterior was lost. We also tried reducing the amount of broth in which we were cooking the vegetables and the fish. We had been using 2½ cups of broth, which covered the potatoes, but we felt this amount

might be diluting the overall flavor. Reducing the amount of liquid by a cup, we found the flavors in the dish much deeper. In order to round out the flavor of this satisfying skillet casserole, we added a light sprinkling of chives and a squeeze of lemon.

Skillet Salmon with Potatoes
SERVES 4

Cod or other sturdy white fish can be substituted for the salmon. If the fish fillets are much thinner than 1 inch, simply fold the fish over to make it thicker. (See page 135 for directions on removing pinbones from salmon).

2	tablespoons unsalted butter
I	small fennel bulb, fronds and stems removed, halved, cored, and cut into ¹/₂-inch pieces (see the illustrations on page 220)
2	medium carrots, peeled and chopped fine
	Salt
I	(8-ounce) bottle clam juice
¹/₂	cup dry white wine
2	medium leeks, white and light green parts only, sliced into ¹/₄-inch rounds, thoroughly rinsed and dried (about I¹/₂ cups)
³/₄	pound small Red Bliss potatoes, scrubbed and cut into I-inch chunks
4	center-cut salmon filets (6 ounces each, about I to I¹/₄ inches thick), pinbones and skin removed
	Ground black pepper
I	tablespoon chopped fresh chives
I	lemon, cut into wedges

1. Melt the butter in a 12-inch skillet over medium-high heat. Add the fennel, carrots, and ½ teaspoon salt; cook, stirring occasionally, until the fennel begins to soften, 3 to 5 minutes. Add the clam juice, white wine, leeks, and potatoes; bring to a simmer. Cover, reduce the heat to low, and cook until the potatoes are almost tender, about 15 minutes.

2. Season the salmon generously with salt and pepper and lay it on top of the vegetables; continue to cook, covered, over low heat until the salmon is opaque and just firm, about 15 minutes. Season

the broth with salt and pepper to taste. To serve, arrange the salmon and vegetables on individual plates or shallow bowls, and pour broth over each serving. Sprinkle with the chives and serve with the lemon wedges.

SKILLET LASAGNA

LASAGNA IS A CROWD-PLEASING DISH THAT never goes out of style. With layers of chewy pasta, rich, gooey cheese, and creamy ricotta, it is so good that second helpings are nearly always mandatory. But lasagna is not a dish you throw together at the last minute. Even with the advent of no-boil noodles, it still takes a good chunk of time to make the components and assemble and bake the casserole.

While lasagna is traditionally made with fully or partially cooked components that are melded together during baking, we wondered if it would possible to take the same flavors and components of lasagna and cook them stovetop in a skillet instead of in the oven. Our plan was simple. We would first brown the meat and remove it from the pan, then build a thin but flavorful sauce. Then we'd add the pasta (mafalda, a narrow, ripple-edged pasta that resembles lasagna noodles), which we figured could be slowly simmered while the pan was covered, fulfilling the "walk away" time we were aiming for. We would finish the dish by adding mozzarella, ricotta, and any other flavors we deemed necessary.

Most lasagna sauces simmer for hours, which allows the ingredients to meld and their flavors to develop. But in this skillet version, we wanted to forgo a long-simmered sauce, so we limited the time that it took to simmer the sauce to the time that it took to cook the pasta. Aiming to keep our ingredient list to a minimum, we started with onions and garlic, which gave the sauce its depth. We also added a chopped red pepper, which appealed to us both for its sweetness and for the texture it lent the sauce. Since this recipe was meant to be a one-dish meal, we felt it necessary to add some protein to the dish. We tried ground beef, but thought that it made the dish bland and uninteresting. We instead opted to use crumbled sweet Italian sausage, which added much more flavor than the ground beef.

With the aromatics and meat under control, we next turned to the type of tomatoes we would use in the sauce. We started our tests with two cans of tomato puree, but found that the sauce was a tad too heavy and the pasta tended to sit on top of the sauce, making it cook unevenly. We tried adding a little water to give the pasta a better medium in which to cook, but the resulting lasagna was too bland. Abandoning tomato puree, we switched to diced tomatoes with their juices. This sauce was much thinner, which meant that the pasta would cook more evenly. We needed to add a third can of diced tomatoes, however, to make up for the tomato flavor we lost when eliminating the puree.

INGREDIENTS:
Supermarket Mozzarella Cheese

We selected five widely available brands of supermarket, or low-moisture, mozzarella cheese and sampled those made with part-skim or whole milk. Because the most common use for this type of cheese is quick and convenient melting, we decided to include both preshredded and block forms. Fifteen *Cook's Illustrated* staff members tasted these cheeses both raw (all block cheeses were tasted shredded) and melted on pizza. Separate tests were performed in this manner, one for the category of preshredded cheeses and the other for block cheeses. We found the block cheese to be better than the preshredded cheese (though this cheese was pretty good). Based on our testing, here are the two that came out on top:

THE BEST PRESHREDDED MOZZARELLA CHEESE
Kraft Shredded Low-Moisture Part-Skim Mozzarella was described by tasters as "rich," "tangy," and "fresh."

THE BEST BLOCK MOZZARELLA CHEESE
Dragone Low-Moisture Mozzarella Cheese (whole milk) was described by tasters as "rich and creamy" and "tangy and briny."

The extra can of diced tomatoes (with their juices) added just the right amount of liquid, allowing a half pound of pasta to cook fully while giving the finished lasagna enough moisture to keep it from being too dry.

To replicate the cheesiness of a traditional lasagna, we stirred in a cup of shredded mozzarella after the pasta had finished cooking. Stirring in the ricotta in a similar fashion didn't give us the results we were looking for, however. Once mixed in, the sweet creaminess of the ricotta became lost and only succeeded in making the sauce appear grainy and shockingly pink. Instead we placed dollops of ricotta on top of the lasagna and then re-covered the pan, allowing the added cheese to heat through. This way, the ricotta remained distinct from the other ingredients. The ricotta also created an attractive pattern over the top of the lasagna, while a sprinkling of freshly chopped basil gave it the flavor of authentic, oven-baked lasagna.

Skillet Lasagna

SERVES 4 TO 6

If you prefer a spicier lasagna, use hot Italian sausage.

1	tablespoon olive oil
1	pound sweet Italian sausage, removed from its casing
1	medium onion, chopped medium
1	medium red bell pepper, stemmed, seeded, and chopped medium
2	medium garlic cloves, minced or pressed through a garlic press
	Salt and ground black pepper
3	(14.5-ounce) cans diced tomatoes, drained (reserve the juice and add enough water to measure 2½ cups)
½	pound mafalda pasta, broken into 2-inch lengths
4	ounces whole-milk mozzarella cheese, shredded (about 1⅓ cup)
8	ounces whole-milk ricotta cheese (about 1 cup)
3	tablespoons chopped fresh basil leaves

INGREDIENTS: Mafalda

Mafalda, or mafaldini, is a narrow, ripple-edged pasta that resembles lasagna noodles and is widely available in supermarkets.

1. Heat the oil in a 12-inch skillet over medium-high heat until shimmering. Add the sausage, breaking the meat into small pieces with a wooden spoon, and cook until it loses its raw color but has not browned, about 5 minutes. Using a slotted spoon, transfer the sausage to a paper towel–lined plate.

2. Pour off all but 1 tablespoon of fat from the skillet and return to medium heat until shimmering. Add the onion, bell pepper, garlic, 1 teaspoon salt, and ¼ teaspoon black pepper; cook until the bell pepper begins to soften, about 4 minutes. Add the tomatoes, reserved tomato juice, and pasta; bring to a simmer. Cover, reduce heat to low, and cook, stirring occasionally, until the pasta is tender, about 20 minutes.

3. Remove the skillet from the heat and stir in the mozzarella and sausage. Dot with heaping tablespoons of ricotta, cover, and let stand off the heat for 3 minutes. Sprinkle with the basil. Serve immediately.

SKILLET THAI CURRY WITH TOFU

THAI FOOD, WITH ITS STRIKING BLEND OF tastes, textures, and colors, is enjoying a growing popularity across the country. There is no dish that exemplifies this blend of flavors and textures better than a Thai curry. Crunchy vegetables and tender meats are bathed in a sauce made with creamy coconut milk, salty fish sauce, lime juice, and aromatic curry paste. And since Thai curries are basically stews, we figured they would be a perfect option for a one-dish skillet dinner.

Considering that many recipes for Thai curry contain numerous esoteric ingredients and can employ some intricate techniques, we sought to develop a recipe that would simplify and streamline the process of making Thai curry at home.

Before we tested the particular ingredients in the curry, we first sought to determine what should form the base of the dish. Although coconut milk traditionally anchors a Thai curry, it is red curry paste that gives this dish its distinct flavor. Curry paste, not to be confused with yellow curry powder, is a mixture of potent aromatics, including chiles, garlic, ginger, lemon grass, and lime leaves. While it is possible to make these pastes at home, we considered the process too involved and the ingredients too esoteric to justify doing so. Thankfully, we found that decent red curry pastes were available in most supermarkets.

We also questioned how to coax the most flavor out of the curry paste. Most traditional recipes call for frying the curry paste in the thick coconut cream taken from the top of the can of coconut milk. But this proved to be time consuming, laborious, and messy. Simply mixing the curry paste and coconut milk together and bringing the two to a simmer did not extract sufficient flavor,

however, and left the overall dish tasting thin. We attributed the lack of flavor to the fact that the curry paste wasn't fried in hot oil. So in our next test we tried sautéing the curry paste in a little oil and then adding the coconut milk. This gave us the deep flavor we were looking for without the need to invest a lot of effort. To finish the base, we added fish sauce, which provided the dish with its trademark saltiness. We also added brown sugar to temper the spiciness of the curry paste.

With a flavorful base developed, we next focused on the protein and vegetables that went into the dish. Considering the trend toward lighter eating, we chose tofu to play the starring role. We had hoped to simply add cubes of tofu to a simmering base, but found that the tofu became slightly slimy when cooked this way. Browning the tofu on several sides was a vast improvement. Wondering if we could take the browning a step further, perhaps by making the tofu crispy, we tried dusting the tofu with cornstarch. This only succeeded in making the dish thick and pasty. To the tofu, we also added snow peas and strips of red pepper. These two vegetables provided a crispiness that complemented the texture of the tofu, as well as providing the dish with vibrant color.

INGREDIENTS: Fish Sauce

Fish sauce is a very potent Asian condiment based on the liquid from salted, fermented fish—and it smells as such. Fish sauce, like anchovy paste, has a very concentrated flavor and, when used in appropriately small amounts, lends foods a salty complexity that is impossible to replicate.

We gathered six brands of fish sauce—one from Vietnam (where it is known as *nuoc mam*), one from Philippines (*patis*), and the rest from Thailand (*nam pla*) from our local supermarket, natural food store, and Asian market. Tasters had the option of tasting the fish sauce straight up (which few could stomach) or in a dipping sauce.

There were differences noted immediately among the sauces. Color correlated with flavor; the lighter the sauce, the lighter the flavor. Tasters had preferences among the sauces, but those preferences varied greatly from taster to taster. In the end, all of the sauces were recommended. In fact, there was only one point (out of 10) separating all six sauces.

With such a limited ingredient list—most of the brands contained some combination of fish extract, water, salt, and sugar—the differences among sauces were minimal. And because fish sauce is used in such small amounts, minute flavor differences get lost among the other flavors of a dish. If you are a fan of fish sauce and use it often, you might want to make a special trip to an Asian market to buy a rich, dark sauce that is suitably pungent. But for most applications, we found that the differences were negligible. Because most supermarkets don't carry a wide selection of fish sauce, we recommend buying whatever is available. That will most likely be Thai Kitchen, an Americanized brand found in most grocery stores that was the lightest-colored (and flavored) sauce we tasted.

But our curry still seemed to lack substance. The addition of rice seemed logical, but trying to incorporate rice into the existing dish was a daunting task, so we searched for an alternative that might be easier. We hit upon the idea of using sweet potatoes. While they seemed unusual, they provided an excellent foil for the aggressive flavors of the curry. In addition to giving the dish some heft, the potatoes gave us about 20 minutes of "walk away" time, which was just right. This simmering time also meant that the flavors of the dish had more time to develop, creating an even more flavorful curry. After adding a squeeze of lime juice and a healthy dose of fresh basil, we found that we had an exotic and satisfying one-pan meal.

Skillet Thai Curry with Sweet Potatoes and Tofu

SERVES 4 TO 6

The heat of red curry paste can vary from brand to brand, so unless you are familiar with the particular brand you are using, or you really like spicy food, it's better to start off with the lesser amount indicated. In the test kitchen, we use Thai Kitchen brand, which is widely available in supermarkets. This curry is a satisfying meal on its own or can be served with rice. Light coconut milk can be substituted for the regular coconut milk; however, the sauce will be slightly thinner. Use a nonstick skillet to keep the tofu from sticking to the pan.

14	ounces extra-firm tofu
2	tablespoons vegetable oil
1–1½	tablespoons red curry paste
1	(14-ounce) can coconut milk
2	tablespoons fish sauce
4	teaspoons light brown sugar
¼	cup water
2	medium sweet potatoes (about 1½ pounds), peeled and cut into ¾-inch cubes
1	medium red bell pepper, stemmed, seeded, and cut into ¼-inch strips
½	pound snow peas, strings removed
½	cup coarsely chopped fresh basil leaves
1	tablespoon fresh lime juice
	Salt

1. Slice the tofu into ¾-inch planks. Lay the planks on a clean kitchen towel and cover with a second kitchen towel. Lightly press the tofu until its surface is dry. Unwrap and cut it into ¾-inch cubes.

2. Heat 1 tablespoon of the oil in a 12-inch nonstick skillet over medium-high heat until shimmering. Add the tofu in a single layer and cook until golden brown on one side, about 2 minutes. Gently stir the tofu and cook until a second side is golden brown, about 2 minutes. Transfer to a plate and set aside.

3. Add the remaining tablespoon oil to the skillet and return to medium heat until shimmering. Add the curry paste and cook, stirring constantly, until very fragrant, about 1 minute. Whisk in the coconut milk, fish sauce, light brown sugar, and water. Add the sweet potatoes and tofu; bring to a simmer. Turn heat to low, cover, and cook until the potatoes are tender, 15 to 20 minutes.

4. Add the red bell pepper and snow peas, increase the heat to medium-low, and continue to cook, covered, until the peas are crisp-tender, about 4 minutes. Remove the skillet from the heat and stir in the basil and lime juice. Season with salt to taste. Serve immediately.

INGREDIENTS:
Store-Bought Curry Paste

In Thailand, many cooks rely on curry pastes purchased at food markets or in small shops. In the United States, supermarket shoppers may see small jars of Thai curry paste. How do store-bought pastes compare with homemade? We purchased Thai Kitchen red curry paste at the supermarket and several other brands at a local Asian market. All of these store-bought curry pastes were more potent than our homemade versions, so you must use far less. We found that all of the brands tested, including Thai Kitchen, which is nationally available, made good curries. The flavors were not as full as the recipes made with our homemade pastes, but the time saved is significant. So if you see Thai Kitchen curry paste in the supermarket, don't hesitate to buy and use this product.

5

SAVORY SIDE DISHES

MORE OFTEN THAN NOT, THE MAIN COURSE CAN command all of a cook's attention, which leaves the side dishes to fend for themselves. Consequently, the beans may burn, the vegetables can turn mushy, and the rice inevitably sticks. There's a reason supermarket shelves are packed with heat-and-serve potatoes and the freezer section has dozens of microwaveable vegetable "medleys." These convenience foods may be quick and easy, but by no means are they palatable.

We wanted to develop a collection of side dishes that, once assembled, require a minimum of attention while they cook. All of the recipes in this chapter slide into the oven and bake, for the most part, unattended. There are supper standards like Weekday Scalloped Potatoes (page 255), Broccoli and Cheese Casserole (page 250), and Boston Baked Beans (page 267), as well as time-saving creations we developed, like Baked Rice Casserole (page 261) and Italian White Bean Casserole with Rustic Crouton Crust (page 269). In certain cases, we altered a dish's existing cooking method to make it easier. Baked risotto without a single stir? We've got three versions. Ratatouille without four pans? A mixing bowl and casserole dish is all that is needed for our version.

Many of these side dishes can be assembled a day or two ahead of time and heated; others can be frozen for months and pulled from the freezer as needed. Many of the vegetables can be blanched a day or two ahead of time and stored in the refrigerator until necessary. Sauces, too, can be whipped up in advance and stored separately. Most need to be reheated before being added. As far as reheating goes, a microwave is often the best bet because it doesn't affect the texture or consistency of sauces, starches, or vegetables the way stovetop or oven reheating can. Check the headnote of each recipe for the particulars on each recipe.

For those dishes that do not store or reheat well, like Quick Green Bean Casserole (page 245) and Winter Root-Vegetable Gratin (page 258), you can certainly get a leg up on some of the preparation. Ingredients can be measured out, bread-crumbs ground, and in some cases, the vegetables may be trimmed, cut, and stored for a few hours wrapped in damp paper towels.

SLOW-ROASTED TOMATOES

ROASTING FLAWLESS, VINE-RIPENED TOMATOES with garlic and olive oil takes them to a new level of perfection; the tomatoes' juices are concentrated by the steady heat and become one with the garlic and herb-scented olive oil. As a relish for grilled or roasted meats or a topping for toasted bread, this dish is hard to beat. It is the distillation of summer in one easy-to-assemble and foolproof dish.

There are only five ingredients in this dish and, for the best results, each must be flawless. In other words, this is not a place to use pale, cardboard-like supermarket tomatoes and cheap oil, as roasting merely magnifies their flaws. The tomatoes must be the best you can find, preferably from your local farmers market—or your garden, if you are so lucky. In the heart of a New England winter, we used "vine-ripened" tomatoes from our gourmet market with some success, but we longed for the beauties of August, still warm from the sun's touch.

The oil should be good quality, extra-virgin olive oil. We tried batches with varying oils and the differences were profound: the best-quality oil was in a league of its own, heady, with an herbaceous, peppery aroma and a taste that elevated the tomatoes beyond comparison. (For recommendations about brands of olive oil, see page 243.)

For flavoring the tomatoes, garlic and basil were the only choices, according to our tasters. Oregano, mint, thyme, and rosemary all seemed inappropriate in this circumstance. Slivered garlic fared better than minced, and looked much more attractive, too. The fine slivers practically melted during the slow bake, reduced to sweet and slightly chewy tidbits.

As this is a rustic dish, hand-torn basil leaves were the logical choice. Because they shrivel to mere shadows of themselves in the oven, we tore the leaves in large pieces and left small leaves whole. Layering the leaves both on top and underneath the tomatoes guaranteed potent flavor.

For seasoning, a coarse salt, such as kosher or sea salt, was the unanimous choice of tasters for its crunchy texture and intense bursts of salinity.

Regular table salt will do in a pinch, of course.

Preparation takes mere moments, but the roasting takes some time. These are not oven-dried tomatoes, which can take upwards of eight hours in a tepid oven, but they are also not classic oven-roasted tomatoes, heat-shriveled to a near candy-like sweetness and intensity. Aiming for something in between, we set the baking temperature parameters between 300 and 400 degrees and began testing.

INGREDIENTS: Supermarket Extra-Virgin Olive Oils

When you purchase an artisanal olive oil in a high-end shop, certain informational perks are expected (and paid for). These typically include written explanations of the character and nuances of the particular oil as well as the assistance of knowledgeable staff. But in a supermarket, it's just you and a price tag (usually $8 to $10 per liter). How do you know which supermarket extra-virgin olive oil best suits your needs? To provide some guidance, we decided to hold a blind tasting of the nine best-selling extra-virgin oils typically available in American supermarkets.

The label "extra-virgin" denotes the highest quality of olive oil, with the most delicate and prized flavor. (The three other grades are virgin, pure, and olive pomace. Pure oil, often labeled simply olive oil, is the most commonly available.) To be tagged as extra-virgin, an oil must meet three basic criteria. First, it must contain less than 1 percent oleic free fatty acids per 100 grams of oil. Second, the oil must not have been treated with any solvents or heat. (Heat is used to reduce strong acidity in some nonvirgin olive oils to make them palatable. This is where the term "cold pressed" comes into play, meaning that the olives are pressed into a paste using mechanical wheels or hammers and are then kneaded to separate the oil from the fruit.) Third, it must pass taste and aroma standards as defined by groups such as the International Olive Oil Council (IOOC), a Madrid-based intergovernmental olive oil regulatory committee that sets the bar for its member countries.

Tasting extra-virgin olive oil is much like tasting wine. The flavors of these oils range from citrusy to herbal, musty to floral, with every possibility in between. And what one taster finds particularly attractive—a slight briny flavor, for example—another might find unappealing. Also like wine, the flavor of a particular brand of olive oil can change from year to year, depending on the quality of the harvest and the olives' place of origin.

We chose to taste extra-virgin olive oil in its most pure and unadulterated state: raw. Tasters were given the option of sampling the oil from a spoon or on neutral-flavored French bread and were asked to eat a slice of green apple—for its acidity—to cleanse the palate between oils. The olive oils were evaluated for color, clarity, viscosity, bouquet, depth of flavor, and lingering of flavor.

Whereas in a typical tasting we are able to identify a clear winner and loser, in this case we could not. In fact, the panel seemed to quickly divide itself into those who liked a gutsy olive oil with bold flavor and those who preferred a milder, more mellow approach. Nonetheless, in both camps, one oil clearly had more of a following than any other—the all-Italian-olive Da Vinci brand. Praised for its rounded and buttery flavor, it was the only olive oil we tasted that garnered across-the-board approval with olive oil experts and staff members alike. Tasters in the mild-and-delicate camp gave high scores to Pompeian and Whole Foods oils. Among tasters who preferred full-bodied, bold oils, Colavita and Filippo Berio earned high marks.

THE BEST ALL-PURPOSE EXTRA VIRGIN OLIVE OIL

Da Vinci Extra Virgin Olive Oil (left) was the favorite in our tasting of leading supermarket brands. It was described as "very ripe," "buttery," and "complex."

THE BEST MILD OIL

Pompeian Extra Virgin Olive Oil (center) was the favorite among tasters who preferred a milder, more delicate oil. It was described as "clean," "round," and "sunny."

THE BEST FULL-BODIED OIL

Colavita Extra Virgin Olive Oil (right) was the favorite among tasters who preferred a bolder, more full-bodied oil. It was described as "heavy," "complex," and "briny."

In a 400-degree oven, the garlic browned too quickly and turned acrid, ruining the dish. Erring on the side of caution, we lowered the temperature to 325 degrees and were pleased with the results. Within 1½ hours, the tomatoes were slightly wrinkled and touched with brown but, more importantly, their juices had largely evaporated and been replaced by the olive oil. A lower temperature yielded no better-tasting results and took longer, so we stuck with 325 degrees.

Slow-Roasted Tomatoes

SERVES 4 TO 6

For flavor and color contrast, feel free to mix and match varieties of tomatoes. Use whatever tomatoes you can find, as long as they are flawlessly ripe. If you are left with a pool of olive oil in the pan, save it for flavoring a vinaigrette or brushing on bruschetta. Serve these tomatoes with roast chicken or fish.

PLANNING AHEAD: This dish tastes best prepared and served on the same day. It can be served slightly warm or at room temperature.

    ½   cup extra-virgin olive oil
    4   medium garlic cloves, sliced thin
    I   cup lightly packed fresh basil leaves, torn into
         large pieces
    2   pounds vine-ripened tomatoes, cored and
         sliced ½ inch thick
    I   teaspoon kosher salt

1. Adjust an oven rack to the lower-middle position and heat the oven to 325 degrees. Grease the bottom of a 9 by 13-inch nonreactive glass or ceramic baking dish (or shallow casserole dish of similar size) with 2 tablespoons of the oil. Sprinkle half of the garlic and half of the basil leaves across the bottom of the dish. Lay the tomato slices in the dish, overlapping the edges if necessary to fit. Sprinkle with the salt and the remaining garlic, basil, and oil.

2. Roast until the tomatoes are slightly shriveled and their juices have been replaced with oil, about 1½ hours. Cool at least 20 minutes or up to 1 hour before serving. Serve warm or at room temperature.

GREEN BEAN CASSEROLE

IN CERTAIN REGIONS OF THE COUNTRY, NO holiday table is complete without a green bean casserole. Steamed green beans are topped off with lashings of creamy mushroom sauce and fried onion rings. It sounds great in theory, but in reality, it's generally pretty dismal, since it is prepared from convenience products like frozen beans, canned soup, and commercially fried onion rings (from those little cardboard cans). The truth is that the casserole is a real pain to make from scratch because each component—green beans, sauce, mushrooms, onion rings—requires separate preparation in its own pot or pan. We wanted to find way to simplify the casserole and make it easier to prepare from scratch—no more cans.

We started our testing with the green beans. The conventional rigmarole for cooking green beans—boiling in salted water, then shocking in ice water, drying with paper towels, and, finally, reheating—takes a lot of work. Could we keep it to just one pan and cook the beans in the sauce? We began by using a stovetop steaming technique originally developed in the test kitchen for stir-frying tough vegetables. The plan was to steam the beans in a covered skillet with a little water, remove the lid partway through to evaporate the water, then build a quick pan sauce around the beans as they finished cooking. The beans, however, steamed in only eight minutes, leaving little time to make a decent sauce after the water had evaporated. Switching the cooking order, we then tried making the sauce first. Building good flavor and texture by sautéing aromatics (such as garlic and onion) and a little flour, we next stirred in cream, a little broth to lighten things, and fresh thyme leaves. Adding the beans right to the sauce, we covered the skillet and cooked them until almost tender (omitting the water altogether), then removed the lid to thicken the sauce. Not only did these beans turn out more flavorful, but by removing the lid near the end of cooking, we were able to closely monitor the doneness of the beans. The beans and sauce were ready to go into the oven.

We still had the mushrooms and the onion

topping to deal with. Sautéing the mushrooms in a separate skillet and then tossing them with the green beans was easy enough, but it added another pan to the equation. Would the mushrooms hold if we cooked them prior to the green beans in the same skillet? Absolutely—since they were being reheated in the sauce, it wasn't an issue. Basic white mushrooms tasted pretty bland, so we chose meatier cremini mushrooms, and sliced them thin to cook and brown quickly.

We wanted a way to streamline the standard fried onion topping. Looking for a crispy texture with a tasty fried onion flavor, we developed a topping that combined breadcrumbs with sautéed onions. Tasters thought the onions were too bland in our new topping, and so, on a whim, we tried sharper-flavored shallots and found their flavor much more preferable. Tasters felt the shallots, with their potent flavor, balanced the richness of the casserole. And combined with the bread-crumbs, the mixture crisped to a golden brown in the oven, giving us a topping that turned out just as tasty, if not tastier, than the original

--&>--

Quick Green Bean Casserole

SERVES 8

The key to cooking all of the casserole components in a single skillet is wiping the skillet out periodically with paper towels. A half teaspoon of dried thyme may be substituted for the fresh thyme.

PLANNING AHEAD: This dish is best eaten immediately after being baked.

TOPPING

2   slices white sandwich bread, torn into quarters
1   tablespoon unsalted butter, melted
1   tablespoon vegetable oil
2   large shallots, minced

FILLING

2   tablespoons vegetable oil
10   ounces cremini mushrooms, stems discarded, caps brushed clean, and sliced 1/4 inch thick
    Salt
2   tablespoons unsalted butter

1   medium onion, minced
2   medium garlic cloves, minced or pressed through a garlic press
1   tablespoon all-purpose flour
2   pounds green beans, stem ends trimmed and cut into 2-inch lengths
3   sprigs fresh thyme
2   bay leaves
3/4   cup heavy cream
3/4   cup low-sodium chicken broth
    Ground black pepper

1. FOR THE TOPPING: Process the bread and butter in a food processor fitted with the steel blade until coarsely ground, about six 1-second pulses. Transfer to a small bowl. Heat the oil in a 12-inch nonstick skillet over medium heat until shimmering. Add the shallots and cook, stirring frequently, until soft and translucent, about 6 minutes. Add to the bowl with the breadcrumbs; toss to combine and set aside.

2. FOR THE FILLING: Adjust an oven rack to the middle position and heat the oven to 400 degrees. Wipe the skillet clean with a wad of paper towels (see page 233). Add the oil and heat over medium-high heat until shimmering. Add the mushrooms and 1/4 teaspoon salt; cook, stirring occasionally, until the moisture released by the mushrooms has evaporated and the mushrooms are well browned, about 8 minutes. Transfer to a plate and set aside.

3. Wipe the skillet clean with a wad of paper towels. Add the butter and melt over medium heat. Add the onion and cook until softened and beginning to brown, about 8 minutes. Stir in the garlic and flour; cook, stirring often, until fragrant, about 30 seconds. Add the beans, thyme, bay leaves, cream, and broth; increase the heat to medium-high, cover, and cook until the beans are partly tender but still crisp at the center, about 4 minutes.

4. Discard the bay leaves and thyme. Stir in the sautéed mushrooms. Season the sauce to taste with salt and pepper. Transfer to a 9 by 13-inch baking dish (or shallow casserole dish of similar size) and sprinkle with the breadcrumb topping. Bake until the filling is bubbling and the topping is golden, about 20 minutes. Serve immediately.

CREAMY CORN PUDDING

CORN PUDDING IS A COMBINATION OF CORN, eggs, milk, and cream; basically, a savory corn custard graced with a generous helping of freshly cut kernels. It seemed like the perfect summer-time no-fuss, no-muss oven-baked casserole. We set out to develop a recipe for a tender, creamy custard with lots of corn flavor.

Many American cookbooks include recipes for corn pudding, and while some call for cheese and herbs and others add chiles, the recipes invariably boil down to a combination of milk, cream, eggs, and corn. Given the consistency of the recipes, we were quite surprised to find that our first batch of puddings was a complete failure: each and every one curdled and wept, producing an unwanted pool of watery liquid. The pudding cooked in a water bath—a large roasting pan filled with hot water—was better than those exposed directly to the oven heat. As with other oven-baked puddings, the water bath tempered the heat and protected the eggs from overcooking. But the water bath alone was not enough to produce a smooth, tender custard. It seemed obvious that the corn in the pudding was the source of the escaping liquid found in every pudding. The question was how to get rid of the moisture in the corn without losing the fresh corn flavor that is essential to the dish.

After experimenting with various options, we settled on a simple two-step approach. First we cooked the corn kernels in a little butter, just until the moisture in the pan had almost evaporated. Then we eliminated a bit more of the corn's liquid by simmering the kernels in heavy cream. Because heavy cream, unlike milk or even light cream, can be cooked at a boil without curdling, we reasoned that it would be safe to simmer the corn together with the cream that was already part of the recipe. When we tried this method, we were very happy with the results (we added whole milk later, along with the eggs). When we made the pudding with corn that had been briefly sautéed and then simmered with heavy cream to make a thick mixture, we had a dish with great flavor and without any seeping liquid.

Now we were ready to move on to balancing the flavors. The first thing we noticed about our now smooth and creamy custard was the corn—there was too much of it. To reduce the corn-to-custard ratio, we cut back from 4 cups of corn to 3 cups. This helped, but there still seemed to be too many large kernels intruding on the tender custard. Perhaps pureeing some of the corn, we thought, would smooth out the texture without sacrificing any of the intense corn flavor. But pureeing did the job too well; we wanted the pudding to have some chew, and now it didn't have enough. Next we tried grating the corn directly off one ear of corn on the coarse side of a box grater. This method gave us just what we were looking for in terms of flavor as well as texture.

Now that we had solved the problem of

REMOVING KERNELS FROM CORN COBS

Hold the cob on its end inside a large, wide bowl and cut off the kernels using a paring knife.

MILKING CORN

Once you have cut off the kernels, scrape the remaining pulp off the cob and squeeze out the milk by pressing firmly on the cob with the back of a butter knife.

weeping and developed a satisfying texture for the pudding, we thought it was just a bit too rich. We decided to try using whole eggs alone instead of the two whole eggs plus two yolks we had been using. We tried three whole eggs first and liked the pudding better. Next we tried four whole eggs, and this version was even better. The two extra whites seemed to lighten the dish, while the custard remained smooth and tender—just what we wanted.

Creamy Corn Pudding

SERVES 6

For the best flavor, this dish should only be made with the freshest corn. Cooking the pudding in a water bath is necessary for an even and creamy texture throughout. The recipe can be doubled and baked in a 9 by 13-inch baking dish (or casserole dish of similar size) for 30 to 35 minutes.

PLANNING AHEAD: Corn pudding must be served hot and cannot be reheated, so plan accordingly.

6	medium ears fresh corn, husks and silk removed
3	tablespoons unsalted butter, plus more for greasing the baking dish
2/3	cup heavy cream
1 1/2	teaspoons salt
1	teaspoon sugar
1/4	teaspoon cayenne pepper
1 1/3	cups whole milk
4	large eggs, beaten lightly
1	tablespoon cornstarch

1. Following the illustrations on page 246, cut the kernels from 5 of the ears of corn into a medium bowl. Scrape the cobs with the back of a butter knife to collect the milk in the same bowl (you should have about 2½ cups kernels). Grate the remaining ear of corn on the coarse side of a box grater set in the bowl with the cut kernels and milk (you should have about ½ cup grated kernels). Firmly scrape this cob with the back of a butter knife to collect the pulp and milk in the same bowl.

2. Adjust an oven rack to the lower-middle position, place a large empty roasting pan on the rack, and heat the oven to 350 degrees. Bring 2 quarts water to a boil in a kettle or saucepan. Generously grease an 8-inch square baking dish (or shallow casserole dish of similar size) with butter; set aside.

3. Melt the 3 tablespoons butter in a Dutch oven over medium-high heat. Add the corn kernels and milk from the cobs; cook, stirring occasionally, until the corn is bright yellow and the liquid has almost evaporated, about 5 minutes. Add the cream, salt, sugar, and cayenne; cook, stirring occasionally, until the mixture has thickened and a spoon leaves a trail when the pan bottom is scraped, about 5 minutes. Transfer the corn mixture to a large bowl. Stir in the milk, then whisk in the eggs and cornstarch. Pour the mixture into the prepared baking dish.

4. Set the baking dish in the roasting pan that is already in the oven. Fill the roasting pan with boiling water to reach halfway up the baking dish. Bake until the center jiggles slightly when shaken and the pudding has browned lightly in spots, 20 to 25 minutes. Remove the baking dish from the water bath. Cool 10 minutes before serving.

PROVENÇAL SUMMER SQUASH CASSEROLE

IN PROVENCE, THE ABUNDANCE OF SUMMER vegetables is often dealt with in simple vegetable dishes called *tians* or gratins. One of the most classic versions includes nothing but summer squash and zucchini. The squashes are thinly sliced, shingled out in an alternating pattern, and showered with herbs and broth. Baked until the vegetables are tender and the flavors blend, this dish is both visually pleasing and simple to prepare—just the thing to use up the never-ending surplus of squash that always seems to arise by midsummer.

Provence-grown squash must taste better than our local squash, because the dishes we prepared from authentic recipes were pretty uninspiring. Bland and boring, they failed to capture the clean flavors and crisp texture of the squash in the way we assumed they would. The squash was either dried out and leathery, or waterlogged and mushy. It was pretty obvious to us that baking temperature had a major impact on both the flavor and texture of the casserole.

Recipes we had tried ranged over 100 degrees in cooking temperature—350 to 450 degrees—and yielded very different results. On the lower end of the scale, the squash shed torrents of liquid and turned mushy; the casserole looked like vegetable soup. At the higher end of the cooking time, the squash slices shriveled up to a dried, leathery consistency, even when doused liberally with broth. We baked casseroles at varying temperatures for different lengths of time until we reached the best compromise of flavor and texture at 400 degrees. The top half of the squash slices withered a bit and intensified in flavor, and the bottom half stayed moist and tender.

At the lower temperatures, broth was superfluous because the squash itself exuded so much liquid; at the higher temperatures, it was essential to prevent the squash from completely drying out. We experimented with adding varying amounts of broth and settled on 1 cup. By the time the squash was tender, most of the broth had evaporated, leaving a few spoonfuls, or just enough to dribble over top of the squash after serving. We had initially been using chicken broth, but we found that we much preferred the cleaner, more complementary flavor of vegetable broth. The chicken broth imparted its distinctive flavor to the mild-flavored squash, while the vegetable broth merely reinforced the vegetal qualities of the squash.

We experimented with spiking the broth with various acids—vinegar, lemon, and wine—to brighten the casserole's flavor, and liked the results. Our top choice was wine because it packed more flavor than either of the other two. Lemon juice and vinegar added sharpness, but no depth. A substantial ½ cup of dry, fruity (not oaky) white wine contributed the best flavor (we left out ½ cup of the broth to accommodate the difference in volume).

We knew we wanted to add aromatic onions to the dish in some fashion. Minced raw onion,

tossed in between the layers of squash, lent little but a sharp bite and slightly crunchy texture because the onion barely cooked, sandwiched as it was between the layers. Sautéing the onion first in olive oil proved a more successful tack to take; its sharpness was tempered and the natural sweetness of the onion intensified the squash's own mild sweetness. We favored red onions over yellow because of their inherent sweetness. We also chose to spread the onion slices in a layer across the bottom of the pan to simplify the assembly process. The bubbling broth percolated up from the bottom, diffusing the onion's flavor through the squash. As an added bonus, the onion slices provided some traction for the squash slices, preventing them from sliding on the slippery bottom of the casserole dish during assembly. For a hint of fire, we added a pinch of crushed red pepper flakes along with the onions.

Some of the recipes we tried were heavily laced with garlic, a kick from which we knew our version could benefit. We sprinkled raw, finely minced garlic among the sliced squash, as we had the onion in the first tests, but the flavor proved too assertive—the garlic, like the onion, required cooking first. In our next version, we sautéed the garlic with the onion, which tempered its sharpness and pungency, but the flavor was too localized: the bottom portion of squash had a potent garlicky flavor, but the top had none (mysteriously, the onion's flavor spread better than

ASSEMBLING THE CASSEROLE

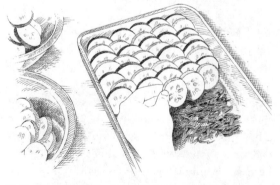

Tightly shingle the slices of squash and zucchini in alternating rows over the top of the onions (the slices will be nearly vertical).

248

the garlic's). Then it finally occurred to us that we should just add the garlic to the broth and wine we sprinkled over the shingled squash. Evenly dispersed throughout the casserole, the sautéed garlic added just the edge the squash needed. We also decided to add herbs to the broth. Basil, marjoram, oregano, savory, and parsley are all common choices, but woodsy thyme proved to be the favorite among tasters because they felt its flavor paired especially well with the squash and onions.

Provençal Summer Squash Casserole

SERVES 6 TO 8

While we like the flavor and colors of this dish when made with a combination of summer squash and zucchini, it tastes just as good when made only with one or the other.

PLANNING AHEAD: This dish is best served right away, so plan accordingly.

3	tablespoons extra-virgin olive oil
I	large red onion, halved and sliced thin
	Pinch red pepper flakes
	Salt
4	medium garlic cloves, minced or pressed through a garlic press
1/2	cup dry white wine
1/2	cup low-sodium vegetable broth
I	teaspoon minced fresh thyme leaves
	Ground black pepper
I	pound summer squash, sliced 1/4 inch thick
I	pound zucchini, sliced 1/4 inch thick

1. Adjust an oven rack to the middle position and heat the oven to 400 degrees. Heat 2 tablespoons of the oil in a 12-inch skillet over medium-high heat until shimmering. Add the onion, pepper flakes, and 1/2 teaspoon salt; cook, stirring frequently, until the onion has softened and browned around the edges, about 10 minutes. Spread evenly over the bottom of a 9 by 13-inch baking dish (or shallow casserole dish of similar size); set aside.

2. Add the remaining tablespoon oil and the garlic to the skillet and return to medium heat until fragrant, about 30 seconds. Stir in the wine, broth, and thyme, scraping the bottom of the pan to loosen any browned bits. Season to taste with salt and pepper; remove the skillet from the heat and set aside.

3. Following the illustration on page 248, shingle the slices of squash and zucchini in alternating rows over the onions. Pour the broth mixture evenly over the squash. Bake until the squash has softened and is just beginning to brown, 40 to 45 minutes. Serve hot.

> VARIATION

Squash Casserole with Feta, Lemon, and Oregano

Follow the recipe for Provençal Summer Squash Casserole, making the following changes: Substitute 1 teaspoon minced fresh oregano leaves and 1 teaspoon grated lemon zest for the thyme in step 2. Sprinkle 2 ounces of feta, crumbled (about 1/2 cup), over the squash before baking in step 3.

BROCCOLI AND CHEESE CASSEROLE

IT'S OUR STRONG BELIEF IN THE TEST KITCHEN that smothering broccoli with cheese sauce is more than just a sneaky way to get kids to eat their vegetables. Adults love it too, with the exception, perhaps, of George Bush, Sr. Shamefully, and all too often, this classic dish comes to the table with overcooked and washed-out-looking broccoli swimming in a gloppy, greasy, broken cheese sauce. We wanted to create an attractive broccoli and cheese casserole with character and dimension—one you could serve to company, and that would entice even the pickiest eaters. Our challenge, then, was to construct a casserole with bright green broccoli—tender, not mushy—with an elegant cheese sauce and a golden bread-crumb topping.

In our initial tests we tried a variety of methods to cook the broccoli. Sautéing the broccoli before assembling the casserole brought out the strong sulfur compounds found in this member of the cabbage family: this batch had a faint but distinct odor of rotten eggs. And the final product was unevenly colored, exhibiting alternating splotches of olive drab and bright emerald green. Thinking we could save some time and effort, we tried throwing the broccoli into the casserole raw. The results were abysmal: by the time the broccoli was tender, it was army green, the sauce was curdled and broken, and the bread crumbs were overly browned.

The tests confirmed what we knew to be true, namely that broccoli requires a moist-heat cooking method to keep the florets tender and cook the tough stalks through. Ordinarily our test-kitchen recommendation is to steam broccoli, as it tends to absorb too much moisture when boiled. However, for this casserole, we didn't mind the extra moisture and thought boiling would be quick and easy.

Also, partially cooking the broccoli in salted boiling water (a common method referred to as blanching) would ensure that the broccoli would be fully seasoned to its core, not unlike pasta boiled in salted water. Most importantly, we favored blanching as a fast way to set that fresh green color we wanted. The test kitchen's food scientist explained to us that as broccoli cooks, some of the air between its cells expands and bubbles off, bringing the cell walls closer together. As the cell walls become closer, the amount of chlorophyll per square inch is concentrated, making the vegetable appear to be a brighter green. However, the success of this technique is contingent on cooking time. If broccoli is overcooked, the bright green chlorophyll converts to pheophytin, turning the broccoli an ugly olive drab.

With the broccoli cooked, we could now focus on the cheese sauce. Recipes we found included a variety of styles, though most of them were implausibly rich. Yolks and cream just seemed too heavy to us; this was a vegetable dish, after all. We looked to some classic French recipes for inspiration and saw flour-thickened, milk-based sauces (béchamels) ladled over a variety of blanched vegetables (proving that camouflaging vegetables for finicky eaters is nothing new). The

lighter consistency and flavor of the béchamel better allowed the taste of the vegetables to come through. The sauce also didn't separate into a curdled mess while in the oven the way some of the richer sauces did.

But the béchamel alone didn't give this dish enough punch, so we added sharp cheddar cheese—the customary accompaniment to broccoli—to our working béchamel. Now closer to a Mornay sauce, our sauce tasted good, but it seemed somewhat heavy and cloying to most of the tasters. Cutting the milk with a portion of chicken broth lightened the sauce, and lent a rounder, savory edge tasters enjoyed.

But the sauce still required some help. Sharp cheddar imparted a grainy texture to the otherwise supple sauce. We experimented with other styles of cheddar and found that cutting the sharp cheese with mild-tasting, creamy colby cheese yielded the best-textured sauce. For a little nuance, we added a pinch of cayenne pepper, minced garlic, and dried mustard, flavorings we borrowed from our macaroni and cheese sauce. Far from its French roots, perhaps, this casserole with its creamy "Mornay" sauce is delicious nonetheless.

Broccoli and Cheese Casserole
SERVES 6 TO 8

If you cannot find colby cheese, longhorn will work just as well.

PLANNING AHEAD: Complete step 1 (the topping) and step 3 (the sauce) of the recipe and refrigerate them in separate bowls, tightly wrapped with plastic wrap, for up to 2 days. The prepped, uncooked broccoli can be wrapped loosely in damp paper towels and stored in a zipper-lock plastic bag for up to 2 days.

TO BAKE: Cook the broccoli as directed in step 2. Poke several vent holes in the plastic wrap covering the sauce and microwave on medium-high power, whisking occasionally, until hot, 4 to 6 minutes. Continue to assemble the casserole and bake as directed in step 4.

TOPPING

2   slices white sandwich bread, torn into quarters
1   tablespoon unsalted butter, melted

FILLING

Salt

1   large bunch broccoli (about 2 pounds), florets trimmed to 1-inch pieces, stalks peeled and chopped medium (about 8 cups) (following the illustrations on page 214)

3   tablespoons unsalted butter

1   medium garlic clove, minced or pressed through a garlic press

1/2   teaspoon dry mustard

Pinch cayenne pepper

3   tablespoons all-purpose flour

1   cup low-sodium chicken broth

1 1/2   cups whole milk

8   ounces colby cheese, shredded (about 2 2/3 cups)

4   ounces sharp cheddar cheese, shredded (about 1 1/3 cups)

Ground black pepper

1. FOR THE TOPPING: Process the bread and butter in a food processor fitted with the steel blade until coarsely ground, about six 1-second pulses; set aside.

2. FOR THE FILLING: Adjust an oven rack to the middle position and heat the oven to 400 degrees. Bring 4 quarts of water to a boil in a large pot. Add 1 tablespoon salt and the broccoli to the boiling water; cover and cook until bright green and crisp-tender, about 3 minutes. Drain the broccoli and leave it in the colander; set aside.

3. Meanwhile, melt the butter in a medium saucepan over medium heat. Stir in the garlic, mustard, and cayenne; cook until fragrant, about 30 seconds. Add the flour and cook, stirring constantly, until the flour turns golden, about 1 minute. Slowly whisk in the broth and milk; bring to a simmer and cook, whisking often, until large bubbles erupt at the surface and the mixture is slightly thickened, about 5 minutes. Off the heat, whisk in the colby and cheddar. Season to taste with salt and pepper.

4. Spread the broccoli in a 9 by 13-inch baking dish (or shallow casserole dish of similar size). Re-whisk the cheese sauce briefly and pour over the broccoli. Sprinkle with the bread-crumb topping. Bake until golden brown and

bubbling around the edges, about 15 minutes. Cool for 5 minutes before serving.

➤ VARIATION

Broccoli and Cheese Casserole with Roasted Red Peppers

Follow the recipe for Broccoli and Cheese Casserole, adding a 13-ounce jar of roasted red peppers, drained, rinsed, patted dry, and chopped medium, to the seasoned sauce in step 3.

CAULIFLOWER CASSEROLE

ONCE WE HAD DEVELOPED OUR BROCCOLI AND Cheese Casserole (see page 250), we thought that we could simply substitute cauliflower for broccoli for a simple variation. But we were wrong: the cooking times didn't quite match up, and the flavor and texture of the sauce weren't as complementary as we hoped. With a few alterations, however, we thought it could work.

Blanching, or quickly simmering in rapidly boiling, seasoned water, worked as well with cauliflower as it did with the broccoli, with one major exception: the denser cauliflower absorbed a good deal of the cooking liquid. Subsequently, when we baked the casserole, a fair amount of water pooled in the bottom of the casserole, thus diluting the sauce. To remedy the situation, we blotted the cauliflower dry on paper towels after blanching, and effectively absorbed the excess moisture.

As for the sauce, we much preferred a richer Mornay prepared exclusively with cream, not the leaner whole milk and broth combination we used in the sauce for the broccoli. The richer flavor better matched the stronger flavor and denser texture of the cauliflower. Because the cream was so much thicker, we found that we had to reduce the amount of flour from the original sauce by two thirds. Just 1 tablespoon lent all the thickening power the cream needed.

To match the cauliflower's stronger flavor, we slightly altered the sauce's components. With the garlic, we added minced shallot for a fuller allium flavor, and we substituted minced fresh thyme for the mustard (cauliflower can have a slight mustardy flavor all on its own). And with these simple changes, we were able to develop a few variations—variations on a variation.

Cauliflower Casserole

SERVES 6 TO 8

Gruyère or cheddar can be used in place of the Parmesan. See the illustrations on page 227 for information about cutting up cauliflower.

PLANNING AHEAD: Complete the recipe through step 3 and refrigerate the topping, sauce, and cauliflower in separate bowls, tightly wrapped with plastic wrap, for up to 2 days. Poke several vent holes in the plastic wrap covering the sauce and microwave on medium-high power, whisking occasionally, until hot, 3 to 4 minutes. Continue to assemble the casserole and bake as directed in step 4.

TOPPING
2   slices white sandwich bread, torn into quarters
1   tablespoon unsalted butter, melted

FILLING
    Salt
1   large head cauliflower (about 3 pounds), trimmed and cut into 3/4-inch florets (about 8 cups)
2   tablespoons unsalted butter
1   medium shallot, minced
1   medium garlic clove, minced or pressed through a garlic press
1   tablespoon all-purpose flour
1½   cups heavy cream
    Pinch ground nutmeg
    Pinch cayenne pepper
    Ground black pepper
1   teaspoon minced fresh thyme leaves
2   ounces Parmesan cheese, grated fine (about 1 cup)

1. FOR THE TOPPING: Process the bread and butter in a food processor fitted with the steel blade until coarsely ground, about six 1-second pulses; set aside.

2. FOR THE FILLING: Adjust an oven rack to the middle position and heat the oven to 450 degrees. Bring 4 quarts water to a boil in a large pot and add 1 tablespoon salt. Add the cauliflower and cook until tender on the outside but slightly crunchy inside, about 3 minutes. Drain the cauliflower in a colander and rinse with cold water to cool. Place the blanched cauliflower on a rimmed baking sheet lined with paper towels.

3. Melt the butter in a large skillet over medium heat. Add the shallot and cook, stirring frequently, until softened, about 2 minutes. Add the garlic and cook until fragrant, about 30 seconds. Stir in the flour until well combined, about 1 minute. Whisk in the cream and bring to a boil. Stir in the nutmeg, cayenne, ¼ teaspoon salt, ⅛ teaspoon pepper, thyme, and ⅔ cup of the Parmesan until well combined, about 1 minute. Remove the pan from the heat.

4. Arrange the cauliflower in a 9 by 13-inch baking dish (or shallow casserole dish of similar size). Pour the cream mixture over the cauliflower and mix gently to coat the cauliflower evenly. Sprinkle with the remaining ⅓ cup Parmesan. Sprinkle the breadcrumb topping evenly over the cheese. Bake until the top is golden brown and the sauce is bubbling around the edges, about 10 minutes. Serve immediately.

➤ VARIATIONS

Cauliflower Gratin with Leeks and Gruyère

Halve 3 small leeks lengthwise, using the white and light green parts only, and rinse well (see page 134 for information on cleaning leeks); slice crosswise into ¼-inch pieces (you should have about 1 cup). Follow the recipe for Cauliflower Casserole, adding the leeks along with the shallot and substituting 1 cup shredded Gruyère for the Parmesan.

Cauliflower Gratin with Ham and Cheddar

Cut 6 ounces ham steak into ½-inch cubes (you should have about 1 cup). Follow the recipe for Cauliflower Casserole, adding the ham steak along with the shallot and substituting 1 cup shredded cheddar for the Parmesan.

OVEN-BAKED RATATOUILLE

A CLASSIC DISH IN SOUTHERN FRANCE, ratatouille is the embodiment of all things summer captured in a humble side dish. Eggplant, squash, tomato, onion, garlic, and herbs are all perfectly cooked, drenched with extra-virgin olive oil, and seasoned with herbs and garlic. The flavors are light and multi-layered; each vegetable can be tasted independently, heightened by the presence of the others. But what sounds like an easy dish is actually far from it. Each of the vegetables is cooked separately before combining to maximize its flavor and texture, but this requires multiple pans and a lot of supervision. Ratatouille is derived from *touiller*, the French verb "to stir," pointing—for French speakers at least—to the amount of work involved. We love the flavors of ratatouille, but we don't love the work required to prepare it; side dishes shouldn't require a full *batterie* of pans. We wanted to develop a simpler, less hands-on approach to preparing ratatouille, one in which the vegetables could be blended and cooked in unison—all in the oven.

Intuition led us to believe that roasting would be the best approach. The high heat could concentrate the flavors of the vegetables and evaporate those exuded juices that turn most of the "one-pot" versions of ratatouille we have tried soupy and one-dimensional. The oven-cooked vegetables may not be cooked as perfectly as they are in stovetop recipes, but our hopes were high.

Our intuition proved only partially correct: while the vegetables retained their distinct flavors and discrete shapes at temperatures above 400 degrees, they tended to cook unevenly and burn around the edges. Reducing the temperature 25 degrees at a time, we found the results more consistent with each batch. We found the best compromise between flavor and texture at 375 degrees; the vegetables cooked evenly and appeared to retain their shape. None were too mushy, aside from the tomatoes, but they are supposed to be that way.

With a basic method in hand, we could return to the fundamentals: the specific choice and preparation of the vegetables. Eggplant is usually the 800-pound gorilla of ratatouille, but we weren't having any problems with it in our oven-roasted version. Many recipes salt the eggplant prior to cooking to drain off its excess moisture, but the oven's high heat made this step (thankfully) unnecessary. We simply peeled it and cut it into largish cubes. Within the hour the ratatouille cooked, the eggplant shrunk dramatically in size as the moisture evaporated, and its flavor intensified. We tried the three commonly available types of eggplant—globe, Italian, and Japanese—and found that they all tasted similar in the end. We stuck with the widely available globe variety.

Like eggplant, summer squash is often salted before cooking to draw off excess moisture, and once again, we found this step unnecessary. We preferred the flavor and texture of the squash "as is," unpeeled and cut into fairly large cubes. Summer squash and zucchini are interchangeable here, since their flavor is nearly identical.

As for the onion, yellow onions tasted fine, but we preferred the sweetness and color of red onions. The onion caramelized in the high heat, even lightly charring in spots to add an occasional (pleasantly) bitter bite to the dish. Minced and chopped onion both disappeared among the mix of vegetables; thinly sliced, the onion added textural and visual contrast.

Fresh tomatoes made little sense in this instance because we knew that, outside of the peak summer months, they would have little flavor and a poor texture. Picked at the height of the season, canned tomatoes are guaranteed to be ripe and sweet. And easy, too: canned diced tomatoes require no preparation outside of draining. At first, we thought it would be imperative to thoroughly drain the tomatoes to prevent the ratatouille from becoming soggy, but the resulting ratatouille was too dry and the vegetables burned around the edges. A less thorough draining left enough juice in the tomatoes to moisten the other vegetables and prevent burning.

As for the seasonings, ratatouille is all about the vegetables, and any auxiliary flavorings should be kept to a minimum. A hint of garlic, a spray of herbs, and a shot of acidity are the norm. Minced garlic lent a harsh flavor that was too dominant. Thinly slivered garlic proved a better option because it added a milder, sweeter flavor as it melted into the vegetables. As for herbs, a little went a long way. Thyme, parsley, oregano, marjoram, and basil are all common options, but we chose to let the woodsy flavor of thyme fly solo.

Once the vegetables were roasted, we added a sprinkle of vinegar to brighten the ratatouille's flavors, and the casserole was good to go; a near perfect rendition with a minimum of fuss. To gild the lily, we added a handful of pine nuts, a not uncommon addition in classic recipes. The oily nuts lent just the right richness and a pleasing crunch.

Oven-Baked Ratatouille

SERVES 6 TO 8

This dish can be served either hot or at room temperature as a side dish, a topping for rice or pasta, or even a chunky sauce to accompany roasted chicken. If serving at room temperature, you may want to season with additional vinegar and salt to perk up the flavor.

PLANNING AHEAD: This dish tastes best when prepared and served on the same day; however, it can be refrigerated for up to 2 days. Allow the ratatouille to come to room temperature (see the note above) before serving.

I	medium eggplant (about I pound), peeled and cut into ³/₄-inch cubes
I	medium red onion, halved and sliced ¹/₄ inch thick
2	medium zucchini or summer squash, cut into ¹/₂-inch cubes
I	(28-ounce) can diced tomatoes, drained and ¹/₃ cup juice reserved
5	medium garlic cloves, sliced thin
¹/₄	cup extra-virgin olive oil
I	teaspoon fresh thyme leaves
I	teaspoon salt
¹/₈	teaspoon ground black pepper
I¹/₂	tablespoons red wine vinegar
¹/₄	cup pine nuts, toasted in a small dry skillet over medium heat until fragrant and golden, about 7 minutes

1. Adjust an oven rack to the middle position and heat the oven to 375 degrees. Combine the eggplant, onion, zucchini, tomatoes and reserved juice, garlic, olive oil, thyme, salt, and pepper in a large bowl and mix well. Transfer to a 9 by 13-inch baking dish (or shallow casserole dish of similar size). Roast until the vegetables have softened and have browned in spots, about 1 hour, stirring thoroughly halfway through the cooking time.

2. Stir the vinegar into the vegetables and sprinkle the pine nuts over the top. Serve hot or cooled to room temperature.

WEEKDAY SCALLOPED POTATOES

TRADITIONALLY RESERVED FOR HOLIDAYS AND special events, scalloped potatoes are luxuriously diet-defying. Cooked in fantastic amounts of heavy cream, butter, and cheese, their richness is hardly suitable for your average supper (or diet). But more and more versions of both frozen and boxed scalloped potatoes have been showing up in the supermarket, claiming to be easy additions to the weekday dinner. Although these quick products taste horrible, they are more convenient and lighter than traditional scalloped potatoes, which makes them more suitable for weeknight cooking. We wanted a lighter, more convenient recipe, but we also wanted a recipe that would taste good.

To begin, we made several standard scalloped potato recipes. We rubbed shallow dishes with garlic, sliced potatoes and laid them in rows, topped them with heavy cream and cheese, and baked them. The ingredient lists were similar in their inclusion of garlic, cream, and sliced russets, but some also called for half-and-half or milk while others called for butter and flour. All of the recipes were unabashedly rich and took as long as 1½ hours to make from start to finish. Several tasted pasty from the flour (used as a thickener for the sauce), and nearly all were a bit dull from the sheer lack of aromatics beyond garlic. Not only did these stodgy potato dishes need to be lightened up considerably, but they begged for more flavor, as well as a realistic midweek cooking time.

Starting with the potatoes, we cooked russet, all-purpose, and Yukon Gold potatoes side by side in basic scalloped fashion. While Yukon Gold and all-purpose potatoes weren't bad, tasters found them a bit waxy. The traditional russets, with their tender bite and earthy flavor, were the unanimous favorite. The russets also formed tighter, more cohesive layers owing to their higher starch content.

Heavy cream is the obvious diet-defying ingredient in traditional scalloped potatoes, so we figured it was probably to blame for their characteristic heft. To relieve some of the heaviness, we tried replacing the heavy cream with a number of less fatty liquids. We tried half-and-half, but the sauce curdled as it bubbled away in the oven. Half-and-half, as it turns out, doesn't have enough fat to keep the dairy proteins from coagulating under high heat. Supplementing some of the heavy cream with whole milk worked well (no curdling), but the potatoes still tasted a bit heavy and dairy-rich for an everyday meal. Next we tried replacing some of the heavy cream with canned chicken broth and found that the broth mitigated some of the cream's heaviness. After trying a variety of broth-to-cream ratios, we landed on a 50-50 split.

With the sauce lightened up, it was time to tweak its flavor. While the delicate flavor of shallots was easily overpowered, a little sautéed onion and garlic worked wonders. Fresh thyme and dried bay leaves also helped to spruce up the sauce with an herbaceous flavor that was neither showy nor distracting.

Up until now, we had been using the tiresome technique of layering the raw potatoes and sauce in a shallow dish and baking them in the oven for 1½ hours. To speed things up, we tried parboiling the potatoes in water first, then combining them with a sauce (thickened with flour to achieve the proper consistency in less time), and finishing them in the oven. Although this did shave nearly 45 minutes off the cooking time, the potatoes

had a hollow flavor, the sauce tasted gummy and flat, and we spent much of the time we had saved washing dirty pots.

Next, we tried parcooking the sliced potatoes in the chicken broth and cream in a covered pot on top of the stove before dumping it all into a shallow casserole dish and finishing it in the oven. Here was our solution. This technique gave the potatoes a head start on the stovetop, where they released some of their starch into the sauce. The potato starch, a natural thickening agent, transformed the consistency of the cooking liquid into a true sauce, negating the need for flour.

When simmered slowly on the stovetop for 10 minutes, at which time the potatoes were about halfway cooked, the casserole required only about 20 minutes in a 425-degree oven to finish. We sprinkled a handful of cheddar over the top, and the potatoes emerged from the oven as a bubbling inferno with a golden crown. Although the ripping hot potatoes and sauce make for a sloppy casserole straight out of the oven, a rest of 10 minutes is all that's needed for them to cool off a bit and cohere.

Weekday Scalloped Potatoes

SERVES 8 TO 10

Slicing the potatoes ⅛ inch thick is crucial for the success of this dish. Use a mandoline, V-slicer (see page 257 for more information), or food processor fitted with a ⅛-inch slicing blade, or slice the potatoes carefully by hand using a very sharp knife. If the potato slices discolor as they sit, put them in a bowl and cover with the cream and chicken broth.

PLANNING AHEAD: Follow the recipe through step 1. Cover the dish with plastic wrap and poke several vent holes with the tip of a paring knife. Refrigerate for up to 24 hours.

TO BAKE: Let the casserole sit at room temperature for about 1 hour. Adjust an oven rack to the middle position and heat the oven to 400 degrees. Remove the plastic wrap and sprinkle with the cheddar. Cover the dish tightly with foil and bake until the mixture is hot and bubbling, about 45 minutes. Remove the foil and continue to cook until the cheese begins to brown, about 30 minutes longer. Allow the casserole to cool for 10 minutes before serving.

4 tablespoons unsalted butter

2 medium onions, minced

4 medium garlic cloves, minced or pressed
through a garlic press

2 tablespoons chopped fresh thyme leaves

2½ teaspoons salt

½ teaspoon ground black pepper

5 pounds russet potatoes (about 9 medium),
peeled and sliced ⅛ inch thick

2 cups low-sodium chicken broth

2 cups heavy cream

3 bay leaves

8 ounces cheddar cheese, shredded (about
2⅔ cups)

1. Adjust an oven rack to the middle position and heat the oven to 425 degrees. Melt the butter in a large Dutch oven over medium-high heat. Add the onions and cook until softened and beginning to brown, about 8 minutes. Add the garlic, thyme, salt, and pepper; cook until fragrant, about 30 seconds. Add the potatoes, broth, cream, and bay leaves; bring to a simmer. Cover, reduce the heat to medium-low, and continue to simmer until the potatoes are almost tender (a paring knife can be slipped into and out of a potato slice with some resistance), about 10 minutes. Discard the bay leaves. Pour the potato mixture into a 9 by 13-inch baking dish (or shallow casserole dish of similar size) and press gently into an even layer.

2. Sprinkle the cheddar over the top of the potatoes. Bake until the cream is bubbling around the edges and the top is golden brown, 20 to 30 minutes. Cool for 10 minutes before serving.

➤ VARIATIONS

Weekday Scalloped Potatoes with Chipotle Chiles and Smoked Cheddar Cheese
Follow the recipe for Weekday Scalloped Potatoes, making the following changes: Add 2 canned chipotle chiles in adobo sauce, minced (about 3 tablespoons), to the pot with the garlic in step 1. Substitute an equal amount of smoked cheddar cheese, shredded, for the regular cheddar.

Weekday Scalloped Potatoes with Mushrooms
Brush 1 pound cremini mushrooms clean and slice ¼ inch thick. Brush 8 ounces of shiitake mushrooms clean, remove and discard the stems, and slice the caps ¼ inch thick. Follow the recipe for Weekday Scalloped Potatoes, adding the mushrooms to the butter along with the onions in step 1; cook until the moisture released by the mushrooms has evaporated, about 15 minutes. Continue with the recipe as directed.

WINTER ROOT-VEGETABLE GRATIN

SOMETIMES RECIPE DEVELOPMENT TAKES US so far afield from the recipe being tested that it leads to an entirely different dish. When we developed Weekday Scalloped Potatoes (page 255), we wanted to include a variation that included the sweet flavor and bright color of root vegetables like carrots and parsnips. We thought it would be a simple substitution of ingredients—equal parts carrots and parsnips for a portion of the potatoes—but we were wrong. Our first attempts proved disastrous; the carrots and parsnips were mushy, the potatoes hard, and the gratin soupy. Clearly, this wasn't going to work out as a simple variation: Carrots and parsnips have less starch and more moisture than potatoes, and when substituted for a portion of the potatoes, the root vegetables didn't work with the potato-starch-thickened gratin sauce. Not to mention the cooking times, which didn't quite jibe. Despite the problems, we liked the flavors and wanted to turn this into a successful root vegetable and potato casserole.

Because of the different starch content and cooking times of the root vegetables, the sauce and cooking method we used in the Weekday Scalloped Potatoes simply wouldn't work. But luckily we had our testing notes from that dish, from which we thought we could extrapolate a workable method. We had disliked flour-thickened sauces in the potato gratins we tried (too starchy), but with the diminished starch content in this version, they seemed to make sense.

EQUIPMENT: Mandolines and V-Slicers

What's cheaper than a food processor and faster than a chef's knife? A mandoline. This hand-operated slicing machine comes in two basic styles: the classic stainless steel model, supported by legs, and the plastic hand-held model, often called a V-slicer. We put both types of machines—ranging in price from $8.99 to $169—to the test. To determine the winners, we sliced melons, cut carrots into julienne (matchstick pieces), cut potatoes into batonnet (long, skinny French fry pieces), and sliced potatoes into thin rounds. Then we evaluated three aspects of the mandolines: ease of use, including degree of effort, adjustment ease, grip/handle comfort, and safety; quality, including sturdiness and uniformity/cleanliness of slices; and cleanup.

The Progressive Mandoline Multi Slicer ($8.99) and the Target Mandoline Slicer ($9.99) are plastic V-slicers with similar designs. Testers gave these models high marks for safety, handle comfort, and blade sharpness, which helped them whip through melon and potato slices. Interchangeable blade platforms cut respectable julienne and batonnet, though these cuts required more effort on the part of testers.

The two other V-slicers tested were the Börner V-Slicer Plus ($34.95) and the Joyce Chen Asian Mandoline Plus ($49.95). The latter produced flawless melon slices, carrot julienne, and potato batonnet but got low marks for its small, ineffective safety mechanism and tricky blade adjustment. Testers also downgraded the poorly designed and not very sturdy base. The Börner unit sliced melons and carrots with little effort, but the potato slices were inconsistent and required more effort to produce. The Börner's well-designed safety guard, however, kept hands away from blades, and its adjustments were quick and easy to make. In the end, testers preferred the cheaper V-slicers made by Progressive and Target to either of these more expensive options.

We also tested two classic stainless steel mandolines. The deBuyer mandoline from Williams-Sonoma ($169) was controversial. Shorter testers had difficulty gaining leverage to cut consistently; some melon slices were ⅛ inch thicker on one side. However, the safety mechanism, sturdiness, and adjustment mechanism were lauded by taller testers. With some practice, all testers were able to produce perfect slices, julienne, and batonnet with the Bron Coucke mandoline ($99). This machine has fewer parts to clean and switch out than its plastic counterparts and requires less effort to operate, once the user becomes familiar with it. Still, the quality comes at an awfully high price.

THE BEST V-SLICERS
Plastic mandolines (also called V-slicers) may not be as sturdy as stainless steel versions, but their quality far exceeds the minimal dollar investment. Among the four models tested, we liked the Progressive (left) and Target (right) slicers, which are similar in design.

THE BEST CLASSIC MANDOLINE
Of the two stainless steel mandolines tested, we preferred this model made by Bron Coucke. Note, however, that it costs 10 times more than a good V-slicer.

Once again, however, the moisture content of the carrots and parsnips came into play. A standard béchamel (a flour-thickened, milk-based sauce) turned into a watery soup in the oven.

Making the béchamel stiffer by adding more flour was clearly part of the equation, but we also thought that cheese might tighten it without making the texture too gummy. We added the cheese that had been scattered across the top of the potato casserole to the béchamel. The results were as successful as we hoped: The sauce was creamy and, more importantly, pretty smooth—there was little graininess from the flour. It took us a few more attempts of fussing with amounts of flour and cheese until we reached a consistency that was stiff enough and rich enough to absorb the moisture exuded by the carrots and parsnips. What looked as stiff as wallpaper paste in the pan thinned in the oven to a creamy, velvety consistency.

We had hoped to cook the vegetables in the sauce on the stovetop, as we did with the Weekday Scalloped Potatoes. But the potatoes and root vegetables required different lengths of time, and the carrots tinted the sauce a slightly muddy orange. Making matters even worse, the longer the béchamel cooked, the thicker and gummier it got. Instead, we followed a more classical method and baked the raw vegetables in the sauce until they were tender. For the most even results, we found that the gratin needed a fairly substantial time in the oven at a moderate temperature. Baked at a high temperature, the vegetables cooked irregularly; the parsnips were done long before the potatoes. Baking at lower temperatures evened out the cooking, but took an eternity. Wrapping the gratin tightly in aluminum foil expedited matters, though the foil prevented the top of the casserole from browning. Removing the foil for the last few minutes of baking was an easy fix.

Although we now had a basic cooking method in hand, the gratin still needed work. Despite the sharp cheddar in the sauce, it tasted a little thin and needed to be richer. Augmenting the milk with cream improved matters, and after tasting different ratios, we found that we liked equal parts of each. To simplify things, we switched to half-and-half. Aromatics like garlic and onions

adversely affected the clean flavor of the potatoes and carrots, so we opted to leave them out. Minced thyme leaves, however, lent a complementary touch that tasters liked.

Winter Root-Vegetable Gratin
SERVES 8 TO 10

Slicing the vegetables ⅛ inch thick is crucial for the success of this dish. Use a mandoline, V-slicer, or food processor fitted with a ⅛-inch slicing blade, or slice the vegetables carefully by hand using a very sharp knife.

PLANNING AHEAD: This dish is best served right away, though it can be successfully reheated in the microwave.

4	tablespoons unsalted butter
6	tablespoons all-purpose flour
3	cups half-and-half
12	ounces sharp cheddar cheese, shredded (about 4 cups)
1	teaspoon minced fresh thyme leaves
2	teaspoons salt
½	teaspoon ground black pepper
3	pounds russet potatoes (about 4 large), peeled and sliced ⅛ inch thick
1	pound carrots (about 4 medium), peeled and sliced ⅛ inch thick
1	pound parsnips (about 4 medium), peeled and sliced ⅛-inch thick
1	tablespoon chopped fresh parsley leaves

1. Adjust an oven rack to the middle position and heat the oven to 350 degrees. Melt the butter over medium-high heat in a large Dutch oven. Add the flour and cook, stirring constantly, until the flour turns golden, about 1 minute. Slowly whisk in the half-and-half; bring to a simmer and cook, whisking often, until the sauce thickens, about 1 minute. Off the heat, whisk in the cheddar, thyme, salt, and pepper. Add the potatoes, carrots, and parsnips; stir gently, using a rubber spatula, until combined.

2. Pour the vegetable mixture into a 9 by 13-inch baking dish (or shallow casserole dish of similar size) and press gently into an even layer. Cover the pan tightly with aluminum

foil and bake until the vegetables are tender (a paring knife can be slipped into them with very little resistance), about 1 hour and 20 minutes. Remove the foil and continue to cook until the top is lightly browned, about 10 minutes. Cool for 10 minutes. Sprinkle with the parsley before serving.

CANDIED SWEET POTATO CASSEROLE

CANDIED SWEET POTATOES ARE A TRADITIONAL side dish served alongside a roast ham or Thanksgiving turkey. All too often, however, they turn out watery, overseasoned, and overly sweet, tasting more like a loose, crustless pumpkin pie than a savory side dish. We wanted lightly seasoned and perfectly cooked sweet potatoes soft enough to slice with a fork, yet resilient enough not to fall through the fork tines while being eaten. And we wanted a topping that adds another dimension to the dish, instead of one that just weighs it down with sweetness.

To start, we followed the method touted in many cookbooks, and boiled peeled pieces of sweet potato before tossing them with a brown sugar–and-butter sauce. Despite the popularity of this method, we found these sweet potatoes to be watery and lacking in flavor. Boiling the sweet potatoes washed away vital flavors and added moisture that was difficult to get rid of. We tried partially cooking the sweet potatoes in the microwave before mixing them with the sauce but found that they overcooked easily, while the sauce still lacked substantial flavor. Next we tossed raw, peeled pieces of sweet potato with brown sugar and butter and baked them in a covered casserole dish. This method also produced a watery sauce as well as unevenly cooked sweet potatoes. As the brown sugar and butter began to melt, the potatoes leached some of their liquid, making a watery cooking solution in which the potatoes began to float. It was difficult to keep these floating sweet potatoes completely submerged, and any unsubmerged parts of the potatoes dried out.

We had better luck once we tried cooking the sweet potatoes on the stovetop. When we cooked the potatoes in a Dutch oven with butter and brown sugar, the flavors of the potatoes and the sauce melded. Moistened with a little water and covered, the sweet potatoes cooked perfectly in about 50 minutes, resulting in the ultimate candied sweet potatoes, with a rich and complex sauce. Although the sauce was still a bit watery when we removed the lid, it was easy to crank up the heat and reduce it quickly to a thicker consistency.

We then tested adding chicken broth, wine, and cider, but tasters preferred the clean taste of the sweet potatoes on their own, seasoned with only a little salt and pepper. While a few tasters preferred the flavor of dark brown sugar to light brown, most found it overpowering. White sugar, on the other hand, was unanimously deemed too bland. We also tried all sorts of spices and herbs, but tasters once again preferred the simple flavors of sweet potatoes seasoned only with salt and pepper.

Now that the potatoes were done, we could focus on the topping. Pecans are a natural with sweet potatoes. We decided to leave them whole instead of chopping them, and this made for a nice presentation. Mixed with a beaten egg white, brown sugar, and some cayenne and cumin, this was a topping that could hold its own against the robust sweet potatoes. After just 15 minutes in a hot oven, this casserole was cooked through and the flavors had melded.

Candied Sweet Potato Casserole

SERVES 10 TO 12

For a more intense molasses flavor, use dark brown sugar in place of light brown sugar.

PLANNING AHEAD: Follow the recipe through step 2. Refrigerate the sweet potato mixture in a large bowl tightly wrapped with plastic wrap for up to 1 day.

TO BAKE: Poke several vent holes in the plastic wrap covering the potatoes and microwave on medium-high power until hot, 3 to 5 minutes. Continue to assemble and bake the casserole as directed in steps 3 and 4.

SWEET POTATOES

8	tablespoons unsalted butter, cut into 1-inch chunks
5	pounds sweet potatoes (about 8 medium), peeled and cut into 1-inch cubes
1	cup packed light brown sugar
1½	teaspoons salt
½	teaspoon ground black pepper
½	cup water

PECAN TOPPING

1	egg white, lightly beaten
½	cup packed light brown sugar
⅛	teaspoon salt
	Pinch cayenne pepper
	Pinch ground cumin
2	cups pecan halves

1. FOR THE SWEET POTATOES: Melt the butter in a large Dutch oven over medium-high heat. Add the sweet potatoes, brown sugar, salt, pepper, and water; bring to a simmer. Reduce the heat to medium-low, cover, and cook, stirring often, until the sweet potatoes are tender (a paring knife can be slipped into and out of the center of the potatoes with very little resistance), 45 to 60 minutes.

2. When the sweet potatoes are tender, remove the lid and bring the sauce to a rapid simmer over medium-high heat. Continue to simmer until the sauce has reduced to a glaze, 7 to 10 minutes.

3. FOR THE TOPPING: Meanwhile, mix all the ingredients for the topping together in a medium bowl; set aside.

4. Adjust an oven rack to the middle position and heat the oven to 450 degrees. Pour the potato mixture into a 9 by 13-inch baking dish (or shallow casserole dish of similar size). Spread the topping over the potatoes. Bake until the pecans are toasted and crisp, 10 to 15 minutes. Serve immediately.

➤ VARIATION

Candied Sweet Potato Casserole with Toasted Marshmallow Topping

Follow the recipe for Candied Sweet Potato Casserole, substituting 4 cups mini marshmallows for the pecan topping. Bake until the marshmallows are crisp and golden, about 5 minutes.

BAKED RICE CASSEROLE

BAKED RICE CASSEROLES PROMISE A SOLUTION to the vexing problem of how to serve rice for a crowd. Unlike rice cooked on a stovetop, a rice casserole baked in a serving dish is ready for the table or buffet, and it retains its heat much longer than regular rice, thanks to a protective topping and a creamy sauce. With these advantages come numerous challenges, however, as we discovered when we tested several of the dozens of recipes we found in cookbooks and on the Internet. A dry, pasty texture plagued some recipes; others were overloaded with cheese and other fatty ingredients—either way, swallowing more than a mouthful was a trial. The texture of the rice never failed to disappoint: "blown out" grains were commonplace, as were pockets of crunchy, undercooked rice.

The flavor combinations we encountered in these recipes were too numerous to mention, but all the recipes were sorely in need of a fundamental technique for cooking the rice thoroughly and evenly. We set out to develop a basic recipe for a rice casserole with a simple cheese sauce that could be easily varied by adding or substituting any number of ingredients.

We considered our options for cooking the rice. Many recipes call for "cooked rice," which we found unhelpful: the amount of rice needed to fill a casserole dish precluded using leftovers, and in any event, starting with fully cooked rice guaranteed that the grains would overcook in the oven, at least around the edges. Others suggest the compromise of parboiling the rice in salted water, then draining and adding it to a sauce made separately. We objected for two reasons: the extra pot, and the wasted opportunity to flavor the rice by cooking it together with aromatics and the sauce.

With this in mind, we began testing recipes in which the rice is cooked in the flour-thickened liquid that becomes the sauce. Our plan was to build the entire dish in a Dutch oven on the stovetop, then pour it into a baking dish, add a breadcrumb topping, and finish it in the oven. This would allow us to boost flavor by sautéing aromatics in butter (tasters liked onion and garlic) before adding the flour, liquids, and rice. The chief question became how long to cook the rice on the stovetop before transferring the mixture to the oven. We tried a variety of cooking times and were surprised to learn that the best results were obtained by cooking the rice for a full 20 minutes before pouring the mixture into the baking dish. Any less and the rice came out of the oven chalky and underdone, especially at the center. Increasing the oven time only worsened the discrepancy in doneness between edges and center, and dried out the dish as well. Under normal circumstances, 20 minutes in boiling water would be enough to overcook rice, yet ours was just tender. The reason, we discovered, was the flour—rice cooks more slowly in a flour-bound sauce because much of the water is trapped by swollen starch granules so that the rice grains are unable to absorb it. This same principle helped with the problem of uneven doneness: once in the oven the rice cooked more slowly, and thus more evenly, because of the limited quantity of readily available moisture to absorb.

Next we tested the type and quantity of liquid to use when cooking the rice. Our options were water, milk, chicken broth, and cream, but tasters found the latter, in addition to the butter and cheese, made the dish too rich. Even whole milk, in the volume necessary to cook the three cups of raw rice needed to fill a casserole dish, made for a heavy sauce. The casserole made entirely with broth was, not surprisingly, too "chickeny" for what was otherwise a vegetarian dish. Tasters found the right balance of flavor and richness with an even mixture of milk and chicken broth, diluted with a few cups of water.

Even with only ¼ cup of flour to thicken 10 cups of liquid, our casseroles were turning out a little pasty, thanks to all the extra starch released from the rice grains as they cooked. We tried rinsing the rice to remove some of it, but this was only marginally effective. Much better results were obtained by reducing the flour even further, down to a mere 2 tablespoons. With all that liquid, the sauce started out very thin—perfect for cooking rice—then thickened as the rice absorbed water and leached starch.

We had only to adjust the flavors in our basic cheese sauce. Tasters favored sharp cheddar over milder cheeses, as it contrasted with the rich starchiness of the dish; a dash of cayenne pepper was approved for the same reason. The fresh flavors of lemon and parsley contributed a welcome brightness, but only when sprinkled on the finished dish: even a relatively short spell in the oven left them washed out and muted.

Baked Rice Casserole
SERVES 8

Stir the sauce frequently for the first few minutes after adding the rice, as this is when the rice is most likely to clump and stick to the bottom of the pan.

PLANNING AHEAD: Follow the recipe through step 2. Pour the rice mixture into a 9 by 13-inch baking dish (or shallow casserole dish of similar size). Cover the dish with plastic wrap and poke several vent holes using the tip of a paring knife. Refrigerate until cool, about 3 hours, then wrap tightly with another sheet of plastic wrap. Refrigerate the topping and casserole separately for up to 3 days.

TO BAKE: Allow the covered dish to sit at room temperature for 1 hour. Adjust an oven rack to the middle position and heat the oven to 400 degrees. Remove the plastic wrap and sprinkle with the breadcrumb topping. Bake, uncovered, until bubbly and heated through, about 45 minutes. Cool for 10 minutes. Sprinkle with the parsley and serve with the lemon wedges.

TOPPING
- 4 slices white sandwich bread, torn into quarters
- 2 tablespoons unsalted butter, melted

RICE
- 4 tablespoons unsalted butter
- 1 medium onion, minced
- 3 medium garlic cloves, minced or pressed through a garlic press
- 2 tablespoons all-purpose flour
- 4 cups low-sodium chicken broth
- 4 cups whole milk
- 2 cups water
- 3 cups long-grain white rice
- 1 teaspoon salt
- ¼ teaspoon ground black pepper

1/8 teaspoon cayenne pepper

8 ounces sharp cheddar cheese, shredded
(about 2²/₃ cups)

2 tablespoons chopped fresh parsley leaves

I lemon, cut into wedges

1. FOR THE TOPPING: Process the bread and butter in a food processor fitted with the steel blade until coarsely ground, about six 1-second pulses; set aside.

2. FOR THE RICE: Adjust an oven rack to the middle position and heat the oven to 400 degrees. Melt the butter in a Dutch oven over medium heat. Add the onion and cook until softened and beginning to brown, about 8 minutes. Add the garlic and cook until fragrant, about 30 seconds. Add the flour and cook, stirring constantly, until the flour turns golden, about 1 minute. Slowly whisk in the broth, milk, and water; bring to a simmer, whisking often. Stir in the rice, salt, pepper, and cayenne; return to a simmer. Reduce the heat to medium-low, cover, and cook, stirring often, until the rice has absorbed much of the liquid and is just tender, 20 to 25 minutes. Off the heat, stir in the cheddar.

3. Pour the rice mixture into a 9 by 13-inch baking dish (or shallow casserole dish of similar size) and sprinkle with the breadcrumb topping. Bake until the topping is browned and the casserole is bubbling, 20 to 25 minutes. Cool for 10 minutes. Sprinkle with the parsley and serve with the lemon wedges.

➤ VARIATIONS

Coconut Cardamom Rice Casserole

SERVES 8

If you would like to make this dish spicier, leave in some or all of the jalapeño seeds. If jasmine rice is unavailable, substitute conventional long-grain white rice.

PLANNING AHEAD: Follow the recipe through step 2. Pour the rice mixture into a 9 by 13-inch baking dish (or shallow casserole dish of similar size). Cover the dish with plastic wrap and poke several vent holes using the tip of a paring knife. Refrigerate until cool, about 3 hours, then wrap tightly with another sheet of plastic wrap. Refrigerate the topping and casserole separately for up to 3 days.

TO BAKE: Allow the covered dish to sit at room temperature for 1 hour. Adjust an oven rack to the middle position and heat the oven to 400 degrees. Remove the plastic wrap and sprinkle with the breadcrumb topping. Bake, uncovered, until bubbly and heated through, about 45 minutes. Cool for 10 minutes. Sprinkle with the cilantro and serve with the lime wedges.

TOPPING

I cup roasted, unsalted cashews

4 slices white sandwich bread, torn into quarters

2 tablespoons unsalted butter, melted

RICE

2 tablespoons unsalted butter

I medium onion, minced

2 jalapeño chiles, stemmed, seeded, and chopped fine (see the headnote)

I tablespoon minced fresh ginger

2 medium garlic cloves, minced or pressed through a garlic press

I teaspoon ground cardamom

4 cups low-sodium chicken broth

4 cups coconut milk

2 cups water

3 cups jasmine rice

I teaspoon salt

1/4 teaspoon ground black pepper

2 tablespoons chopped fresh cilantro leaves

I lime, cut into wedges

1. FOR THE TOPPING: Process the cashews in a food processor fitted with the steel blade until coarsely ground, 5 to 10 seconds. Add the bread and butter and process to a uniformly coarse crumb, about six 1-second pulses; set aside.

2. FOR THE RICE: Adjust an oven rack to the middle position and heat the oven to 400 degrees. Melt the butter in a Dutch oven over medium heat. Add the onion and jalapeños; cook until the vegetables have softened, about 8 minutes. Add the ginger, garlic, and cardamom; cook until fragrant, about 1 minute. Add the broth, coconut milk, and water; bring to a simmer. Add the rice, salt, and pepper; return to a simmer. Turn the heat to medium-low, cover, and cook, stirring often, until the rice has absorbed much of the liquid and

is just tender, 20 to 25 minutes.

3. Pour the rice mixture into a 9 by 13-inch baking dish (or shallow casserole dish of similar size) and sprinkle with the breadcrumb topping. Bake until the topping is browned and the casserole is bubbling, 20 to 25 minutes. Cool for 10 minutes. Sprinkle with the cilantro and serve with the lime wedges.

Butternut Squash Rice Casserole

SERVES 8

Ricotta adds a particularly creamy flavor and texture to this casserole. If the ricotta you purchase is very grainy or if you prefer a smoother texture, pulse it in a food processor fitted with the steel blade until smooth.

PLANNING AHEAD: Follow the recipe through step 2. Pour the rice mixture into a 9 by 13-inch baking dish (or shallow casserole dish of similar size). Cover the dish with plastic wrap and poke several vent holes using the tip of a paring knife. Refrigerate, storing the breadcrumb topping separately, for up to 2 days. Refrigerate until cool, about 3 hours, then wrap tightly with another sheet of plastic wrap. Refrigerate the topping and casserole separately for up to 3 days.

TO BAKE: Allow the covered dish to sit at room temperature for 1 hour. Adjust an oven rack to the middle position and heat the oven to 400 degrees. Remove the plastic wrap and sprinkle with the breadcrumb topping. Bake, uncovered, until bubbly and heated through, about 45 minutes. Cool for 10 minutes. Serve with the lemon wedges.

TOPPING

1	cup pecans
4	slices white sandwich bread, torn into quarters
2	tablespoons unsalted butter, melted

RICE

2	tablespoons unsalted butter
1	pound butternut squash, peeled and cut into 1-inch cubes
1	medium onion, minced
2	medium garlic cloves, minced or pressed through a garlic press
3	tablespoons chopped fresh sage leaves
2	tablespoons all-purpose flour
4	cups low-sodium chicken broth
4	cups whole milk
2	cups long-grain white rice
1/8	teaspoon ground nutmeg
1	teaspoon salt
1/4	teaspoon ground black pepper
12	ounces ricotta cheese (about 1 1/2 cups)
1	ounce Parmesan cheese, grated (about 1/2 cup)
1	lemon, cut into wedges

1. FOR THE TOPPING: Process the pecans in a food processor fitted with the steel blade until coarsely ground, 5 to 10 seconds. Add the bread and butter and pulse to a uniformly coarse crumb, about six 1-second pulses; set aside.

2. FOR THE RICE: Adjust an oven rack to the middle position and heat the oven to 400 degrees. Melt the butter in a Dutch oven over medium heat. Add the squash and cook, stirring occasionally, until just beginning to soften, about 5 minutes. Add the onion and cook until softened and beginning to brown, about 8 minutes. Add the garlic and sage; cook until fragrant, about 1 minute. Add the flour and cook, stirring constantly, until the flour turns golden, about 1 minute. Slowly whisk in the broth and milk; bring to a simmer, whisking often. Stir in the rice, nutmeg, salt, and pepper; return to a simmer. Turn the heat to medium-low, cover, and cook, stirring often, until the rice has absorbed much of the liquid and is just tender, about 20 to 25 minutes. Off the heat, stir in the ricotta and Parmesan.

3. Pour the rice mixture into a 9 by 13-inch baking dish (or shallow casserole dish of similar size) and sprinkle with the breadcrumb topping. Bake until the topping is browned and the casserole is bubbling, 20 to 25 minutes. Cool for 10 minutes. Serve with the lemon wedges.

BAKED RISOTTO

RISOTTO MAY BE ONE OF THE HALLMARKS OF northern Italian cooking, but nobody ever said it was easy. Vigilant attention is essential for success, but that's something not all of us have the time or patience for. There's a time and place for traditional risotto, but there's also room for a faster, less demanding version: oven-baked risotto. Baked risotto has been widely popularized by noted cookbook author Patricia Wells, and we found a solid dozen recipes in different cookbooks, all of which tipped their hat to her. Her method is simple: Onions are sautéed in butter, Arborio rice is stirred in and briefly toasted, hot broth and flavorings are added, and the rice is baked in the oven until tender. The first half of the recipe mirrors traditional risotto; the second half is downright heretical. Isn't risotto defined by its intensive stirring? After preparing several batches, our opinion was swayed. While not quite as creamy as the original, it was a close second—and without a single stir. Clearly, this likeable technique was worth expanding upon to develop our own renditions of this simple side dish.

Our big concerns heading into testing were oven temperature and liquid volume. On the stovetop, risotto is cooked at a reasonable clip, simmering rapidly, but not quite boiling. How could we replicate this in the oven? Baked at too high a temperature, the rice would boil rapidly and cook unevenly; too low, and the rice would stew. We tried temperatures ranging from 300 degrees to 450 degrees and found that 400 degrees yielded the best results. The temperature kept the rice at a steady simmer, but below a full-blown boil.

We also realized that the liquid volume was just as important to the texture as the oven temperature. In classic risotto, liquid is added in minute increments just as the rice absorbs it, but for oven baking, it must be added all at once. There's no room for last-minute adjustments of volume, so the amount must be perfect. In our first batches, we added too much liquid and the grains of rice blew out and turned mushy. We decreased the volume of liquid in subsequent tests until we reached the ideal consistency.

While our baked risotto would not be mistaken for the more classically made risotto (it was drier and firmer textured), we decided that we could amplify its flavor to make up for any textural discrepancies. A few cloves of garlic, thinly slivered and sautéed with the onions, added an extra dimension that tasters liked. Minced garlic had proved too assertive, infusing the risotto with an unpleasant, almost plastic flavor. A couple of bay leaves, briefly simmered with the broth and then baked in the risotto, added herb flavor and aroma (without washing or mincing). And to make up for the missing creaminess, we folded in twice as much Parmesan as is traditional. It was a different sort of unctuous texture than the velvety sauce of a true risotto, but it certainly sufficed.

Baked Risotto

SERVES 6 TO 8

Avoid buying Arborio rice from bulk bins or in old-looking packages. Old or stale rice does not cook as well as fresher rice and may require substantial amounts of additional liquid—a real problem with this recipe because it is baked out of sight in the oven. If you cannot find Arborio rice, standard medium-grain or short-grain rice will do in a pinch, though the texture will not be as creamy. Vegetable broth may be substituted for the chicken broth. For a classic match, use the optional saffron and serve the risotto with Osso Buco (page 170).

PLANNING AHEAD: This dish is best served right away, though it can be successfully reheated in the microwave. Stovetop or oven reheating can dry out the rice.

3½	cups low-sodium chicken broth
2	bay leaves
4	tablespoons unsalted butter
I	medium onion, minced
3	medium garlic cloves, sliced thin
	Salt
2	cups Arborio rice (see the headnote)
	Large pinch saffron (optional)
½	cup dry white wine
2	ounces Parmesan cheese, grated fine (about I cup)
	Ground black pepper

1. Adjust an oven rack to the middle position and heat the oven to 400 degrees. Bring the broth and bay leaves to a simmer in a medium saucepan over medium heat. Cover the pot and reduce the heat to the lowest setting to keep the broth warm until needed.

2. Melt the butter in a 12-inch skillet over medium heat. Add the onion, garlic, and ½ teaspoon salt and cook, stirring occasionally, until the onions are soft and translucent, about 10 minutes. Add the rice and saffron (if using); cook, stirring frequently, until the grain edges are transparent, about 4 minutes. Add the wine and cook until the wine is completely absorbed by the rice, about 1 minute. Transfer the mixture to a 9 by 13-inch baking dish (or shallow casserole dish of similar size) and pour the warm broth over the top. Bake until the rice is tender and all the liquid is absorbed, 25 to 30 minutes. Stir in the Parmesan and season with salt and pepper to taste. Serve immediately.

➤ VARIATIONS

Baked Risotto with Butternut Squash and Almonds

Follow the recipe for Baked Risotto, making the following changes: Add a pinch ground nutmeg to the broth in step 1. Stir 1½ pounds butternut squash, peeled, seeded, and cut into ½-inch cubes, and 1½ teaspoons minced fresh sage leaves into the rice in the baking dish before adding the broth in step 2. (Depending on the age of squash, the risotto may require an additional 5 to 7 minutes of baking time.) Before serving, sprinkle the risotto with ¾ cup skin-on sliced almonds that have been toasted in a small dry skillet over medium heat until fragrant and golden, about 7 minutes.

Baked Risotto with Mushrooms and Red Wine

Melt 2 tablespoons butter in a 12-inch nonstick skillet over medium-high heat. Add 1 pound cremini mushrooms, brushed clean and each one cut into 4 to 6 wedges, 1 small onion, sliced thin, ½ teaspoon minced fresh thyme leaves, and ½ teaspoon salt; cook until the mushrooms have shed their liquid and are browned, about 10 minutes; set aside. Follow the recipe for Baked Risotto, substituting ½ cup of dry red wine for the white wine. Stir the sautéed mushrooms into the rice in the baking dish before adding the broth in step 2. Continue with the recipe as directed.

BOSTON BAKED BEANS

HEADY WITH SMOKY PORK AND BITTERSWEET molasses, authentic Boston baked beans are both sweet and savory, a unique combination of the simplest ingredients, unified and refined during a long simmer—a fine example of the whole being greater than the sum of its parts.

A close reading of recipes—and there are thousands out there—made it clear that authentic Boston baked beans are not about fancy seasonings. They are about developing intense flavor by means of the judicious employment of canonical ingredients (beans, pork, molasses, mustard, and sometimes onion) and slow cooking. Tasters quickly rejected recipes with lengthy lists of nontraditional ingredients and short cooking times.

The most important item on the shopping list is, of course, the beans, the classic choice being standard dried white beans in one of three sizes: small white beans, midsize navy or pea beans, or large great northern beans. While the latter two choices were adequate, tasters preferred the small white beans for their dense, creamy texture and their ability to remain firm and intact over the course of a long simmer. (The two larger sizes tended to split.) Consistent with the test kitchen's previous findings, we found that there is no need to soak beans before cooking, so we gladly skipped that step. We did test canned white beans and were not impressed by their lackluster performance. Within two hours of baking, they turned to mush and lacked the full flavor of the dried beans.

Next came the meat. Some type of cured pork is essential for depth of flavor and lush texture, though its flavor should never dominate. Although traditionalists swear by salt pork, we first tried pork brisket, which is a meatier version of salt pork. Its flavor was enjoyable, but tasters felt the beans lacked richness—the brisket was too lean. Not surprisingly, salt pork scored high with tasters, although some felt the flavor was too mild. Bacon, a more modern choice, was deemed "too smoky and overwhelming" for most, though the heartier pork flavor was appreciated. On a whim, we put both salt pork and bacon into the pot and found the perfect solution. The bacon brought the desired depth to the beans, and the salt pork muted the bacon's hickory tang. Twice as much salt pork as bacon proved the right balance.

In traditional recipes, the salt pork is cast raw into the beans (often as a large piece) and melts into the sauce, but during tests it failed to render completely. Gelatinous chunks of fatty pork bobbing among the beans left even the most carnivorous taster cold. We first diced the pork into smaller bits, but this was only a partial success; unmelted fat remained. Next, we browned it in the Dutch oven prior to adding the beans, and the results were surprising: this simple step (not recommended in any of the recipes we'd found) made the flavor of the beans significantly fuller and better than anything we had yet tasted. Apparently, the melted fat more readily flavored the cooking liquid, and the browned bits of meat tasted richer.

While yellow onion is a controversial ingredient in classic recipes, we sensed its flavor could be important, and our intuition proved right. Tasters loved its sweetness and the full flavor it lent the beans, especially once sautéed in the rendered pork fat. Tasters favored a fine dice so that the onion all but disappeared by the time the beans were ready.

Next, we tackled the final two ingredients: mustard and molasses. Dried mustard, the standard choice, had worked fine up until now, but we felt home cooks were more likely to have prepared mustard on hand. And it provides a perk—vinegar—to cut the beans' sweetness. We tested several varieties, including Dijon, German whole grain, yellow, and brown. They all brought a unique angle to the beans, but brown mustard—Gulden's brown mustard, in particular—was best, imparting a pleasant sharpness without calling attention to itself. Even with the mustard's tang, though, we found it necessary to add vinegar for acidity. Most classic recipes that include cider vinegar add it at the start of the cooking time, but we found the acidity stayed sharper when added to the beans once finished. A scant teaspoon proved enough to cut the molasses' sweetness and accent the other flavors.

The molasses, we discovered, would take some finessing, as its brutish flavor and intense sweetness dominated the beans when added carelessly. After tasting batches made with mild, full-flavored (also known as "robust"), and blackstrap varieties, most tasters preferred the subtler tones of the mild variety. We settled on just ½ cup baked with the beans for a balance of moderate sweetness and palate-cleansing bitterness. A tablespoon added after cooking gently reemphasized its character.

All that was left to do now was tweak the cooking time. For testing purposes, we had cooked the beans at 250 degrees for six to seven hours. While pleased with the results, we were curious to see what other temperatures might accomplish. We knew that, to a certain extent, flavor and texture were in opposition. The longer the beans cooked, the better the sauce's flavor, but past a certain crucial moment of equilibrium, time worked against the beans, turning them to mush.

We tested cooking temperatures in increments of 25 degrees between 200 and 350 degrees and met with interesting results. At 200 degrees, the beans took upward of eight hours to cook and were still on the crunchy side. At 350 degrees, the beans percolated vigorously and exploded. Midpoints of 275 and 300 degrees were more successful. The beans were creamy textured and the sauce full flavored. With little difference in the outcome when either temperature was used, we chose 300 degrees, which made the beans cook faster, finishing in just about five hours—less time than we had thought possible.

While pleased with the texture and flavor, we still wanted a thicker sauce—soupy beans were not acceptable. We discovered that it was not simply a matter of reducing the volume of water, however, as this led to unevenly cooked beans. We had been cooking the beans from start to finish covered with a lid, which had prevented the cooking liquid from reducing effectively. When we removed the lid for the last hour in the oven, we got the results we were seeking—the sauce had reduced to a syrupy, intensified state that perfectly coated the beans.

Boston Baked Beans
SERVES 4 TO 6

If you prefer a stronger molasses flavor, substitute dark or "robust" molasses for the mild. For the richest flavor, look for chunks of salt pork with a high fat-to-meat ratio.

PLANNING AHEAD: The cooked beans can be stored in an airtight container in the refrigerator for up to 4 days.

TO REHEAT: Heat the beans in a covered saucepan or Dutch oven over medium-low heat. Add additional water as needed to adjust the consistency.

4	ounces salt pork, trimmed of rind and cut into $\frac{1}{2}$-inch cubes
2	ounces (about 2 slices) bacon, chopped fine
I	medium onion, minced
$\frac{1}{2}$	cup plus I tablespoon mild molasses
I$\frac{1}{2}$	tablespoons prepared brown mustard, such as Gulden's
I	pound (about 2$\frac{1}{2}$ cups) dried small white beans, rinsed and picked over (see the illustration on page 184)
	Salt
9	cups water
I	teaspoon cider vinegar
	Ground black pepper

Adjust an oven rack to the lower-middle position and heat the oven to 300 degrees. Cook the salt pork and bacon in a large Dutch oven over medium heat, stirring occasionally, until it is lightly browned and most of the fat is rendered, about 7 minutes. Add the onion and cook until softened and beginning to brown, about 8 minutes. Add ½ cup of the molasses, the mustard, beans, 1¼ teaspoons salt, and the water; increase the heat to medium-high and bring to a boil. Cover the pot and set in the oven. Bake until the beans are tender, about 4 hours, stirring once after 2 hours. Remove the lid and continue to bake until the liquid has thickened to a syrupy

consistency, 1 to 1½ hours longer. Remove the beans from the oven; stir in the remaining tablespoon of molasses and the vinegar. Season to taste with salt and pepper. Serve.

➤ VARIATION
Barbecued Baked Beans

Barbecued baked beans are slow-simmered, oven-cooked beans that are similar to Boston baked beans. Barbecued baked beans are a bit brasher in flavor, however, so they stand up better to the big flavors of grilled and barbecued foods. Black coffee is not such a strange companion to beans. It often appears in chili recipes, "cowboy" cooking, and barbecue sauce recipes. If you do not have time to make freshly brewed coffee, instant will do.

PLANNING AHEAD: The cooked beans can be stored in an airtight container in the refrigerator for up to 4 days.

TO REHEAT: Heat the beans in a covered saucepan or Dutch oven over medium-low heat. Add additional water as needed to adjust the consistency.

4	ounces (about 4 slices) bacon, chopped fine
I	medium onion, minced
4	medium garlic cloves, minced or pressed through a garlic press
I	pound (about 2$\frac{1}{2}$ cups) dried small white beans, rinsed and picked over (see the illustration on page 184
I	cup strong black coffee
$\frac{1}{4}$	cup packed dark brown sugar
I	tablespoon mild molasses
I$\frac{1}{2}$	tablespoons prepared brown mustard, such as Gulden's
$\frac{1}{2}$	cup plus I tablespoon barbecue sauce
$\frac{1}{2}$	teaspoon Tabasco sauce
	Salt
8	cups water
	Ground black pepper

Adjust an oven rack to the lower-middle position and heat the oven to 300 degrees. Cook the bacon in a large Dutch oven over medium heat, stirring occasionally, until it is lightly browned and most of the fat is rendered, about 7 minutes. Add the onion and cook until softened and beginning to brown, about 8 minutes. Add the garlic and cook

BUYING SALT PORK

FATTY

LEAN

The salt pork shown at top has a high ratio of fat to meat and is preferable in this recipe to leaner, meatier salt pork, like the piece shown below.

until fragrant, about 30 seconds. Add the beans, coffee, brown sugar, molasses, mustard, ½ cup of the barbecue sauce, Tabasco, 2 teaspoons salt, and water; increase the heat to medium-high and bring to a boil. Cover the pot and set in the oven. Bake until the beans are tender, about 4 hours, stirring once after 2 hours. Remove the lid and continue to bake until the liquid has thickened to a syrupy consistency, 1 to 1½ hours longer. Remove from the oven and stir in the remaining tablespoon of barbecue sauce. Season to taste with salt and pepper.

ITALIAN WHITE BEAN CASSEROLE

CANNELLINI ALL'UCCELLETTO, OR "BEANS cooked like a little bird," is a traditional Tuscan dish as ubiquitous to the region as baked beans are to Boston and cheese steaks are to Philadelphia. So what exactly are "beans cooked like little birds"? Essentially, they are white beans stewed for hours with tomatoes, garlic, and sage—a common Italian method for preparing small game birds like quail. The flavors blend and sweeten, the beans turn creamy, and the piercing sage flavor mellows to a tame undertone. Accompanied with a crusty loaf of bread and a few curls of Parmesan cheese, the dish serves as a light meal or side dish. We liked the concept and flavors of the dish, but not the time required to prepare it. We sought to rework the classic into a faster-to-the-table side dish, complete with a crisp, rustic bread topping. The flavor was classic; the method we developed was anything but.

Traditionally, the dish is prepared with dried cannellini beans, which easily account for much of the long cooking time. While we generally prefer the superior flavor and texture of dried beans, milder-tasting, softer-textured canned beans can be an acceptable substitution when time is tight. The trick, however, is infusing them with flavor without turning them to mush. Canned beans simply cannot withstand extended cooking.

That said, we knew we had to develop much of the flavor of the dish prior to the beans' introduction. Following the lead of traditional recipes, we prepared a *soffrito* (a slow-cooked mélange of vegetables) using sautéed onion, carrot, and celery. Cooked slowly over moderate heat, the vegetables shrunk to a fraction of their raw volume and developed a sweet, vegetal flavor base for the beans. Once we added the beans, however, we found the sharp flavor of the celery was too pronounced, so we left it out. We also favored red onion over yellow for the way its sweet flavor intensified the inherent sweetness of the beans.

As for the garlic, northern Italian cooks are much more reserved than southern Italian cooks. In other words, a little goes a long way. When we added minced garlic to the beans, its flavor was deemed too assertive by most tasters, even when we reduced the volume. A milder, subtler hint of garlic seemed more fitting. We borrowed a traditional technique and lightly toasted slivered cloves in the oil before adding the vegetables for the soffrito. Started in the cold oil, the garlic slowly cooked and developed a sweet, nutty flavor and golden color. But it's a fine line between toasted and burnt: any hue darker than light golden, and the garlic can taste bitter and acrid. The addition of the vegetables effectively prevented the garlic from browning any further. A pinch of crushed red pepper flakes, toasted with the garlic, added a hint of smoky heat.

Following tradition, we were adding the tomatoes to the soffrito once it had cooked down, just before adding the beans. Surprisingly, the flavor of canned tomatoes contributed little. Yes, they were fruity and acidic, but most tasters thought they required a good deal of cooking to develop the fullness that this dish required. Breaking with the original concept, we substituted jarred roasted

INGREDIENTS: Canned White Beans

While it is hard to beat the full flavor and firm texture of dried beans cooked from scratch, canned beans can be perfectly acceptable in certain applications, like our Italian White Bean Casserole with Rustic Crouton Crust (this page). The dish is so richly flavored that the stronger flavor of the dried beans isn't missed, and the cooking time is short enough that the softer canned beans do not have a chance to overcook and turn mushy.

But are all canned cannellini beans of equal caliber? We looked for multiple brands of nationally distributed cannellini beans to taste against one another, and found so few that we decided to include both great northern and navy beans in the tasting as well. From sweet to bland and chalky to mushy, the different brands ran the gamut in quality. Our favorite of the bunch tasted straight from the can were Westbrae Organic great northern beans, which won accolades for their "earthy" flavor and "creamy" texture. In second place, tasters liked Progresso cannellini beans for their "plump shape" and "sweet, slightly salty" flavor. While the "weird" grayish hue of the cannellini beans from Goya was off-putting to many tasters, the beans possessed a solid flavor and scored well enough to come in third.

BEST CANNED WHITE BEANS

WESTBRAE	**PROGRESSO**	**GOYA**
ORGANIC GREAT NORTHERN BEANS	CANNELLINI BEANS	CANNELLINI BEANS
"Earthy flavor" and "creamy texture"	"Plump and sweet"	"Weird" gray color but solid flavor

red peppers for the tomatoes. Sweeter, slightly smoky, and richer, they were more densely packed with flavor than the tomatoes and required less cooking.

Without the tomatoes and the liquid in which the beans were cooked, the dish needed some liquid to keep things moist. Neutral-tasting chicken broth filled the role well. To replace the tomatoes' acidity, we added a splash of white wine.

As the original dish is typically served with a crusty loaf of hearty bread, we sought a topping that contributed a similar flavor and texture. Finely ground crumbs didn't quite cut it: the bread crumbs were too sandy in texture and "wheaty" in flavor. We wanted more texture and flavor—the crunchy crust and tough pull of a rustic loaf, and the flavor variation between crumb and crust. We opted to leave the bread in large chunks and toss them in a garlic-flavored olive oil (so they would taste like bruschetta) before scattering them over the beans. Dusted with Parmesan, the croutons browned attractively while in the hot oven and had a flavorful distribution of crisp crust and tender, sweet crumb.

Italian White Bean Casserole with Rustic Crouton Crust

SERVES 8 TO 10

If canned cannellini beans prove hard to find, substitute canned navy or great northern beans. Serve this dish alongside roasted chicken or pork.

PLANNING AHEAD: Prepare the beans as directed in step 2, transfer to a medium bowl, and cover tightly with plastic wrap. They can be refrigerated for up to 3 days.

TO BAKE: Prepare the topping as directed in step 1. Assemble and bake the casserole as directed in step 3.

TOPPING

2	medium garlic cloves, minced or pressed through a garlic press
3	tablespoons extra-virgin olive oil
1	ounce Parmesan cheese, grated fine (¹/₂ cup)
¹/₄	teaspoon black pepper
1	loaf (about 12 ounces) rustic Italian bread, cut into 1-inch chunks (about 6 cups)

BEANS

¹/₄	cup extra-virgin olive oil
6	medium garlic cloves, sliced thin
¹/₄	teaspoon red pepper flakes
1	medium red onion, minced
1	medium carrot, peeled and chopped fine
¹/₂	teaspoon salt
¹/₂	cup dry white wine
4	(15.5-ounce) cans cannellini beans, drained and rinsed
1	(13-ounce) jar roasted peppers, drained and chopped medium (about 1¹/₂ cups)
¹/₄	cup chopped fresh sage leaves
1	cup low-sodium chicken broth
2	tablespoons minced fresh parsley leaves

1. FOR THE TOPPING: Combine the garlic, oil, Parmesan, and pepper in a large bowl. Add the bread and toss until evenly coated; set aside.

2. FOR THE BEANS: Adjust an oven rack to the middle position and heat the oven to 400 degrees. Heat the oil, garlic, and red pepper flakes in a large skillet or Dutch oven over medium heat. As the oil begins to sizzle, shake the pan back and forth so that the garlic does not stick (stirring with a wooden spoon may cause the garlic to clump). Cook until the garlic turns very pale gold, about 4 minutes. Add the onion, carrot, and salt; cook, stirring occasionally, until softened and beginning to brown, about 10 minutes. Stir in the wine and cook until partially evaporated, about 30 seconds. Stir in the beans, roasted peppers, sage, and broth; bring to a simmer.

3. Pour the bean mixture into a 9 by 13-inch baking dish (or shallow casserole dish of similar size). Arrange the bread-crumb topping in an even layer over the beans. Bake until the bread has browned and the filling is bubbly, 25 to 30 minutes. Cool for 10 minutes. Sprinkle with the parsley before serving.

INGREDIENTS: Jarred Roasted Red Peppers

Jarred peppers are convenient, but are all brands created equal? To find out, we collected five brands from local supermarkets. The contenders were Divina Roasted Sweet Peppers, Greek Gourmet Roasted Sweet Red Peppers, Lapas Sweet Roasted Peppers, Gaea Flame Roasted Red Peppers, and Peloponnese Roasted Florina Whole Sweet Peppers. Three of these brands identified the type of pepper used (Divina, Gaea, and Peloponnese all use Florina peppers), and we wondered if a company's willingness to identify the variety of pepper it was selling would be an indicator of the quality of the pepper. In other words, would tasters prefer the clearly identified Florina peppers over the generics (whose main ingredient was identified only as "peppers")? To more easily identify their preferences, tasters tried the peppers straight from the jar.

What we found was that tasters did not necessarily prefer the peppers labeled Florina. What counted was the flavor and texture of the pepper itself, as well as the flavor of the brine. The top two brands, Divina (roasted Florina pimento red peppers) and Greek Gourmet (fire-roasted peppers), were preferred for their "soft and tender texture" (the Divinas) and "refreshing," "piquant," "smoky" flavor (the Greek Gourmets). The other brands were marked down for their lack of "roasty" flavor and for the unpleasantly overpowering flavor of the brines. These peppers were described as having a "pepperoncini-like sourness" or a "sweet and acidic aftertaste"; one person said they tasted as if they'd been "buried under brine and acid."

The conclusion? Tasters preferred peppers with a full, smoky, roasted flavor, a spicy but not too sweet brine, and a tender-to-the-tooth texture.

BEST JARRED ROASTED RED PEPPERS
Divina peppers (left) were the top choice of tasters. Greek Gourmet peppers (right) were a close second.

SWEET NOODLE KUGEL

IN JEWISH CUISINE THE TERM "KUGEL" DEFINES a broad category of eggy baked puddings traditionally served alongside main course savory items. Such is the case with sweet noodle kugel; however, it's also sweet enough to pass for a dessert. Typically, sweet noodle kugel is a mixture of egg noodles, butter, raisins, cinnamon, and, often, nuts, all bound with an egg–cottage cheese mixture. This Jewish comfort food often gets a bad rap for being a tasteless, starchy nest of noodles weighed down by goopy dairy products. We aimed to create a rich, full-flavored kugel that wasn't overly dense—one that would have dinner guests reaching for extra helpings during the main course and for even more during dessert.

In our research we learned that noodle kugels are most likely based on a dish called *schalet*, a fruit-filled noodle dough brought to America by Jewish immigrants. Over time, with the influx of immigrants from all over Europe, an American version of sweet noodle kugel developed with more standard characteristics, like the inclusion of cottage cheese, raisins, and cinnamon.

We chose a number of recipes fitting the American sweet noodle kugel description, plus some that went outside of the cottage cheese–raisins-cinnamon parameters (one featured cinnamon-flavored applesauce, another apricot preserves). After testing a batch, we decided to stay with the classic recipe. We preferred the lightness and curdy consistency of the cottage cheese, the raisins' small bursts of sweetness, and the cinnamon's addition of depth and warmth. Our tests, however, revealed we would need to fix the dairy element of the dish, as well as come up with a way to make the kugel more flavorful.

Following tradition, we decided to try different combinations of sour cream, cottage cheese, and cream cheese. Tasters commented that the mix of sour cream and cottage cheese proved to be watery, overly tangy, and not rich enough. Sour cream and cream cheese together created a very dense, overly rich kugel, and still too tangy. Taking the sour cream out of the equation left us with a mix of just cottage cheese and cream cheese, which created a bland disaster.

A mix of all three, however, helped us achieve our goal, giving us a balanced mix of tangy sour cream, cottage cheese, and rich-textured cream cheese. Combining the three with fresh lemon zest, we succeeded in creating a rich dairy filling with a touch of lightness. But the flavor of our kugel was still on the boring side of the fence; tasters also felt that it needed some textural contrast.

Looking back over our test results, we noticed that tasters liked kugels that had toppings. They preferred a sweet, crunchy nut topping very similar to a streusel without the flour. In testing different types of sugar in our topping, we discovered that white sugar was cloying and plain; light brown sugar was good, but lacked a deep enough flavor; and dark brown sugar was the winner, with its deep molasses flavor. When we added crunchy walnuts, we found the topping that would provide the extra boost of flavor we wanted.

❦

Sweet Noodle Kugel with Golden Raisins and Walnuts

SERVES 10 TO 12

We liked the clean, sweet flavor of golden raisins in this kugel; however, regular raisins will work just fine. Serve this sweet noodle kugel as a side dish or save it for dessert. It is good hot, warm, or chilled.

PLANNING AHEAD: Assemble the kugel as directed through step 5. Cover tightly with plastic wrap and refrigerate for up to 24 hours.

TO BAKE: Allow the kugel to sit at room temperature for about 1 hour. Adjust an oven rack to the middle position and heat the oven to 350 degrees. Remove the plastic wrap and cover tightly with foil. Bake until the kugel is hot throughout, about 20 minutes. Remove the foil and continue to bake until the top is golden, about 25 minutes longer.

TOPPING

4	tablespoons unsalted butter, softened
1/2	cup dark brown sugar
1/2	cup chopped walnuts
1	teaspoon ground cinnamon

FILLING

3	tablespoons unsalted butter
	Salt
I	pound extra-wide egg noodles
2	cups sour cream
2	cups cottage cheese
I	pound cream cheese
2	large eggs, plus 2 large yolks
½	cup sugar
2	teaspoons vanilla extract
2	teaspoons grated lemon zest
I	cup golden raisins

1. FOR THE TOPPING: Mash the butter, sugar, walnuts, and cinnamon together in a small bowl, using a rubber spatula; set aside.

2. FOR THE FILLING: Adjust an oven rack to the middle position and heat the oven to 350 degrees. Grease a 9 by 13-inch baking dish (or shallow casserole dish of similar size) with 1 tablespoon of the butter; set aside.

3. Bring 4 quarts of water to a boil in a large pot. Add 1 tablespoon salt and the noodles. Cook until almost tender but still a little firm to the bite, about 6 minutes. Drain the noodles, transfer them to a large bowl, and toss with the remaining 2 tablespoons butter. Allow the noodles to cool.

4. Meanwhile, combine the sour cream, cottage cheese, and cream cheese in the bowl of an electric mixer fitted with the paddle attachment. Beat until smooth, about 1 minute. Add the eggs and yolks, sugar, vanilla, and lemon zest; continue to beat until combined, stopping the mixer and scraping down the sides of the bowl with a rubber spatula, as needed.

5. Add the cream cheese mixture and raisins to the cooled noodles; toss to combine. Transfer the mixture to the prepared baking dish. Dot the walnut topping evenly over the noodles.

6. Bake until the noodles on the surface are golden and crispy, 40 to 45 minutes. Allow the kugel to cool for 5 minutes. Serve hot or warm, or refrigerate and serve cold.

INGREDIENTS: Egg Noodles

Egg noodles are not the stars of the pasta world. They lack the panache of penne, the sultriness of spaghetti, the rotundity of rotini. Yet in their role as trusty sidekick to dishes like beef stroganoff and chicken paprikash, egg noodles can make or break a meal. Noodles that are mealy, pasty, or fishy have no place in your cupboard.

Classic egg noodles are thick, wide ribbons of pasta that have a slightly higher fat content than other kinds of pasta because of their high percentage (up to 20 percent) of eggs. Their firm, sturdy texture is what makes them so appealing with casseroles or heavy soups and stews.

We chose eight widely available brands, cooked them in salted water, and tasted them plain (tossed in a small amount of canola oil to prevent clumping). We were looking for a clean, slightly buttery flavor and firm yet yielding texture. The top two finished within one point of each other and were clearly superior to the rest of the pack. Problems with the rest of the field included excessive thickness, gumminess, off flavors, or no flavors (the only no-yolk brand in the test fell victim to the last problem).

The top choice, Light 'n Fluffy, was praised for its "clean, neutral" flavor and superior texture. Close behind was Black Forest Girl, a German brand found in the international aisle of some supermarkets (or by mail order from www.germandeli.com), and described by fans as "yummy" with a "wheaty" flavor and "firm" texture. Either brand will make an excellent partner to your next stew.

THE BEST EGG NOODLES
Light 'n Fluffy Extra Wide Egg Noodles won fans with their "buttery flavor" and "firm, delicate" texture.

SAVORY NOODLE KUGEL

SAVORY NOODLE KUGELS AREN'T REALLY ALL that common. Of the few recipes we found, most feature everyday vegetables in a bland, dry, and forgettable side dish. We knew we needed to go back to the drawing board if we were going to create a kugel with chutzpah. Our desire was for a side dish creation that would pair as well with juicy roast beef as it would with crispy-skinned chicken. The perfect candidate would have a custardy bottom with a slightly crunchy top, and be driven by an intense vegetable flavor.

We wanted to keep the flavors of our kugel simple. After trying several different types of savory kugels, including those built around onions, cabbage, and carrots, tasters preferred the onion version, believing that it would be the most neutral complement to a wide range of main courses. While the onions were only lightly browned in the recipe we had prepared, we knew that the dish would benefit if the onions were more deeply caramelized.

From experience, we knew there are a variety of techniques for caramelizing onions, most of which take a good deal of burner time. Starting with gentle heat, we cooked the onions in vegetable oil over a medium-low flame. This produced well-browned onions, but required nearly an hour. Aiming to trim time, we increased the heat to medium and found that it only took half as much time as before. Over medium heat, the onions developed a complexity and multilayered flavor that tasters preferred, but the final product made for a messy clean-up and left a lot of flavor stuck in the pan.

When it came to choosing between regular and nonstick pans, we decided on the slippery, nonstick surface. This pan was easier to clean, and the flavorful juices did not cling to the pan but were instead forced to mingle with the onions, giving us the intensity we were after.

One last opportunity for developing as much flavor as possible from the onions was the choice of fat. We had been using vegetable oil for all of our testing and liked it because it allowed for a clean onion flavor. In one test we used olive oil, which was overpowering with a bitter edge, and when using butter we found that it tasted extremely round and muted. The combination of vegetable oil and butter was the winner, releasing a clean, well-defined onion flavor lightly tempered with the rich taste of butter.

There was no doubt that the caramelized onions increased the flavor intensity of the kugel; however, tasters wanted more flavor dimension. Liking the clean subtle flavors of cauliflower, we thought it would be a good vegetable for rounding out the intense onion flavor. How to incorporate it into the dish became our next challenge.

Wanting to draw out some sweet nuttiness from the cauliflower, we tried to come up with an efficient way to brown it. Our best idea was to test cooking it in the same pan as the onion; this gave us decent results, but the moisture from the cauliflower caused the onions to caramelize more slowly. And in the end, the cauliflower broke down too much and never really got the color we were looking for. However, it did soak up the succulent caramelized onion flavor, which brought out more of the nutty cauliflower flavor and gave us a new idea.

For our next set of tests, we considered the following: if partially cooked before assembling the casserole, the cauliflower might absorb the caramelized onion flavor during the baking time. (We cooked it in boiling water for about 5 minutes until mostly tender but still crunchy.) We were right—the cauliflower came out perfectly tender, not mushy, like in our initial tests. Still, though, we had one last element to finesse, and that was striking the balance between a rich custard bottom, a moist cross-section of noodles, and a golden, crunchy top.

Our test kugels came out dry in places, creating a patchy custard bottom. Our savory kugel recipe lacked the moist richness of dairy, which is present in our sweet noodle version. So, to ensure we had an even layer of custard on the bottom, we decided to add extra eggs, which worked. However, after 40 minutes in a hot, dry oven, the noodles above the custard were still drying out.

Adding ½ cup chicken broth to the kugel

before baking, plus covering the casserole with foil, helped to solve our moisture problems. And to get our golden top, we added small dots of butter to the kugel before baking. In addition, we found it best to remove the foil halfway through the baking to achieve a crunchy top.

Savory Noodle Kugel with Caramelized Onions and Cauliflower

SERVES 8 TO 10

We recommend serving this kugel hot, when the custard, cauliflower, and noodles are soft and steamy (unlike sweet kugel, which can be served either hot or cold). This makes a good side dish for pot roast or brisket.

PLANNING AHEAD: Follow the recipe through step 4. Toss the cooled noodles, onions, and cauliflower together in a large bowl. Cover the bowl tightly with plastic wrap and refrigerate for up to 24 hours.

TO BAKE: Allow the noodle mixture to sit at room temperature for about 1 hour. Adjust an oven rack to the middle position and heat the oven to 350 degrees. Add the eggs to the noodle mixture and continue to assemble and bake the kugel as directed in step 5.

8	tablespoons unsalted butter
2	tablespoons vegetable oil
2	large onions, minced
	Salt and ground black pepper
1	medium head cauliflower (about 2 pounds), cored and cut into 3/4-inch florets (about 6 cups) (see page 227)
1	pound extra-wide egg noodles
6	large eggs, lightly beaten
1/2	cup low-sodium chicken broth

1. Adjust an oven rack to the middle position and heat the oven to 350 degrees. Grease a 9 by 13-inch baking dish (or shallow casserole dish of similar size) with 1 tablespoon of the butter; set aside.

2. Melt 3 more tablespoons butter with the oil over high heat in a 12-inch nonstick skillet. Add the onions and 1/2 teaspoon salt; cook until the onions begin to soften, about 5 minutes. Reduce the heat to medium and continue to cook the onions, stirring frequently, until they are golden brown and sweet, about 25 minutes longer. Remove from the heat and season with salt and pepper to taste.

3. Meanwhile, bring 4 quarts of water to boil in a large pot (with a perforated pasta insert, if available) over high heat. Add 1 tablespoon salt and the cauliflower; cook until the cauliflower is mostly tender but still slightly crunchy at the core, about 5 minutes. Transfer the cauliflower to a paper towel–lined baking sheet using a slotted spoon (or by lifting out the pasta insert, if using).

4. Return the water to a boil and add the noodles; cook until almost tender but still firm to the bite, about 6 minutes. Drain the noodles, transfer them to a large bowl, and toss with 2 more tablespoons butter. Allow the noodles to cool to room temperature.

5. Add the onions, cauliflower, and eggs to the cooled noodles; toss to combine. Transfer the mixture to the prepared baking dish. Pour the chicken broth evenly over the noodles and dot with the remaining 2 tablespoons butter. Cover the dish tightly with foil and bake until the kugel is warm, about 20 minutes. Remove the foil and continue to bake until the noodles on the surface are golden and the center is hot, about 20 minutes longer. Cool for 5 minutes before serving.

6

BREAKFAST AND BRUNCH

VERSATILE, NUTRITIOUS, AND FLAVORFUL, EGGS are probably one of the most perfect foods. And while eggs are used in a wide range of dishes, from sweet to savory, most people associate eggs with breakfast. In this chapter we've reached beyond run-of-the-mill scrambled egg and bacon dishes and developed casseroles that focus on the multi-faceted egg meal.

Ranging from American classics such as baked grits and corned beef hash to a Spanish-inspired egg and potato casserole and a classic French cheese soufflé, the recipes here were developed with simplicity in mind. Many of the casseroles in this chapter can be prepared in advance, refrigerated overnight, and baked the next morning, making them perfect for a relaxed Sunday brunch with friends or even a busy weeknight dinner at home. There are also dishes like the frittata and the corned beef hash that are more like our skillet casseroles in chapter 4, and these require a little more hands-on cooking. To make up for this extra care, however, we tried to keep the preparation and cooking times to a minimum.

All of these casseroles, while easy, require that you pay attention to the details. The most common problem we encountered was overbaking, which often led to curdled and grainy custards and dry, deflated soufflés. Since all ovens vary in temperature, it is important to pay close attention to the visual clues provided in each recipe and check on the casserole before the prescribed time. For added insurance against an unpredictable oven and ruined casseroles, we suggest using an oven thermometer (see page 284 for recommendations).

As for egg size, we developed all these recipes using large eggs. While using larger or smaller eggs won't have an adverse effect on recipes such as the baked grits or the frittata, it will harm the soufflé as well as custard-based dishes like the breakfast strata, the potato and egg casserole, 24-Hour "Omelet," and Baked French Toast.

FRITTATAS

FRITTATAS HAVE ALL THE GOOD CHARACTER-istics of omelets without the finicky cooking technique. Italian in origin, frittatas incorporate more filling than omelets, making them more substantial. They are also more forgiving than omelets when it comes to cooking. In the time it takes to make two omelets, you can make a frittata that feeds four. However, frittatas are not foolproof. It took some testing to avoid the common pitfalls—typically, toughness and dryness—and create a recipe that yielded a moist yet firm frittata every time.

The first issue we dealt with was pan size. Starting with a dozen eggs, we made frittatas in skillets measuring 10 inches and 12 inches. We found that the 12-inch pan was optimal. The frittata made with the 10-inch pan was a little too thick and there were too many eggs in the pan, which made cooking the frittata cumbersome. We then tried making the same frittata in both a traditional pan and a nonstick pan. While we found we could produce satisfactory frittatas in both pans, we had to use a lot more oil in the traditional pan to prevent sticking, making the resulting frittata slightly greasy. The 12-inch nonstick pan was the winner.

After several tests, we determined that about two cups of filling was enough for a dozen eggs. Any more than that amount created problems with the frittata cooking evenly; any less, and the frittata lacked substance. To keep the procedure simple,

MAKING A FRITTATA

Once the bottom of the frittata is firm, use a thin spatula to lift the edge closest to you. Tilt the skillet slightly toward you so the uncooked egg runs underneath. Return the skillet to a level position and swirl gently to distribute the uncooked egg.

we wanted to sauté most of our fillings in the same pan as the frittata. Doing so would enable us, after sautéing, to simply pour the beaten eggs over the filling and proceed with shaping the frittata.

The methods for cooking the frittata fell into three camps: cooking the frittata fully on the stovetop, cooking the frittata fully in the oven, and starting the frittata on the stovetop and then finishing it in the oven. We first tried cooking the frittata fully on the stovetop, but no matter what we did, the underside always ended up tough and overcooked. Cooking the frittata fully on the oven proved problematic as well. We tried cooking at different temperatures and for different lengths of time, but the results were either too dry or unevenly cooked. A combination of the two turned out to work the best. Using this method, we cooked the frittata almost fully on the stovetop and then placed it in the oven and allowed the top to finish cooking. The resulting frittata was evenly cooked and firm without being too dry—exactly what we had been looking for.

These frittatas don't have to be eaten hot. They can be served at room temperature or even cold, so timing isn't an issue, as it is with omelets. Serve frittatas with potatoes, a vegetable side dish, and/or a leafy salad.

Goat Cheese Frittata with Fresh Herbs

SERVES 6

Feel free to mix and match herbs to suit your taste. To avoid a tough, dry frittata, pay close attention to the visual clues provided in the recipe.

2	tablespoons unsalted butter
1	small onion, minced
3	tablespoons minced fresh herb leaves, such as parsley, basil, dill, tarragon, or mint
4	ounces goat cheese, crumbled (about 1 cup)
1/2	teaspoon salt
1/2	teaspoon ground black pepper
12	large eggs, lightly beaten

1. Adjust an oven rack to the upper-middle position and heat the oven to 350 degrees.

2. Heat the butter in a 12-inch nonstick, ovenproof skillet over medium heat. Swirl the skillet to distribute the butter evenly over the bottom and the sides. Add the onion and cook until softened, about 4 minutes. Stir in the herbs. Spread in a single layer.

3. Meanwhile, stir the goat cheese, salt, and pepper into the eggs.

4. Pour the egg mixture into the skillet; stir lightly with a fork until the eggs start to set. Once the bottom is firm, use a thin, nonmetallic spatula to lift the frittata edge closest to you (see the illustration on page 276). Tilt the skillet slightly toward you so that the uncooked egg runs underneath. Return the skillet to a level position and swirl gently to evenly distribute the egg. Continue cooking for about 40 seconds then lift the edge again, repeating the process until the egg on top is no longer runny.

5. Transfer the skillet to the oven; bake until the frittata top is set and dry to the touch, 2 to 4 minutes, making sure to remove the frittata as soon as the top is just set.

6. Run the spatula around the skillet edge to loosen the frittata; invert onto a serving plate. Serve warm, at room temperature, or chilled.

Asparagus Frittata with Mint and Parmesan

SERVES 6

Choose asparagus spears that are about 1/2 inch in diameter. The asparagus can be parcooked in advance and refrigerated until needed. If doing so, plunge the asparagus into ice water after blanching to stop the cooking process and then drain.

	Salt
1/2	pound asparagus, tough ends snapped off, cut into 1-inch pieces
2	tablespoons unsalted butter
1	small onion, minced
1	tablespoon minced fresh mint leaves
2	tablespoons minced fresh parsley leaves
1	ounce Parmesan cheese, grated fine (about 1/2 cup)
1/2	teaspoon ground black pepper
12	large eggs, lightly beaten

1. Adjust an oven rack to the upper-middle position and heat the oven to 350 degrees.

2. Bring 4 quarts of water to a boil in a large pot. Add 1 tablespoon salt and the asparagus, cover, and cook until bright green and crisp-tender, about 2 minutes. Drain the asparagus and set it aside in the colander.

3. Heat the butter in a 12-inch nonstick skillet over medium heat. Swirl the skillet to distribute the butter evenly over the bottom and the sides. Add the onion; cook until softened, about 4 minutes. Add the mint, parsley, and asparagus; toss to coat with the butter. Spread in a single layer.

4. Meanwhile, stir the Parmesan, ½ teaspoon salt, and the pepper into the eggs.

5. Pour the egg mixture into the skillet; stir lightly with a fork until the eggs start to set. Once the bottom is firm, use a thin, nonmetallic spatula to lift the frittata edge closest to you (see the illustration on page 276). Tilt the skillet slightly toward you so that the uncooked egg runs underneath. Return the skillet to a level position and swirl gently to evenly distribute the egg. Continue cooking for about 40 seconds then lift the edge again, repeating the process until the egg on top is no longer runny.

6. Transfer the skillet to the oven; bake until the frittata top is set and dry to the touch, 2 to 4 minutes, making sure to remove the frittata as soon as the top is just set.

7. Run the spatula around the skillet edge to loosen the frittata; invert onto a serving plate. Serve warm, at room temperature, or chilled.

BUYING EGGS

Freshness Egg cartons are marked with both a sell-by date and a pack date (the latter is also known as the Julian date). The sell-by date is the legal limit for when the eggs may be sold and is within 30 days of the pack date. The pack date is the day the eggs were graded and packed, which is generally within a week of being laid but, legally, may be as much as 30 days. In short, a carton of eggs may be up to two months old by the end of the sell-by date. Even so, according to the U.S. Department of Agriculture, they are still fit for consumption for an additional three to five weeks past the sell-by date. Sell-by and pack dates are thus by no means an exact measure of an egg's fitness; they provide vague guidance at best.

How old is too old? We tasted two- and three-month old eggs that were perfectly palatable. At four months the white was very loose and the yolk "tasted faintly of the refrigerator," though it was still edible. Our advice? Use your discretion. If the egg smells odd or displays discoloration, pitch it. Older eggs also lack the structure-lending properties of fresh eggs, so beware when baking. Both the white and yolk become looser. We whipped four-month old eggs and found that they deflated rapidly.

Color The shell's hue depends on the breed of the chicken. The run-of-the-mill Leghorn chicken produces the typical white egg. Larger brown-feathered birds, such as Rhode Island Reds, produce the ecru- to coffee-colored eggs common to New England. Despite marketing hype to the contrary, a kitchen taste test proved that shell color has no effect on flavor.

Grade Although eggs are theoretically sold in three grades—AA, A, and B—we found only grade A eggs for sale in nearly a dozen markets in Massachusetts and New York. Grade AA eggs are the cream of the crop, possessing the thickest whites and shells, according to the American Egg Board. Grade B eggs are used commercially.

The Pack Date is the three-number code stamped above or below the sell-by date. The numbers run consecutively, starting at 001 for January 1 and ending with 365 for December 31. These eggs were packed on March 19 (078). The number next to the pack date (P1970) is an internal code for egg packers.

Feta Cheese Frittata with Olives and Sun-Dried Tomatoes

SERVES 6

Blot the tomatoes on paper towels to absorb the excess oil. Since the feta cheese and olives are salty, this frittata needs no additional seasoning.

2	tablespoons unsalted butter
1	small onion, minced
1	small garlic clove, minced or pressed through a garlic press
2	tablespoons minced fresh basil leaves
1/2	cup oil-packed sun-dried tomatoes, drained, patted dry, and chopped coarse
1/4	cup oil-cured olives, pitted and minced
2	ounces feta cheese, crumbled (about 1/2 cup)
1/2	teaspoon ground black pepper
12	large eggs, lightly beaten

1. Adjust an oven rack to the upper-middle position and heat the oven to 350 degrees.

2. Heat the butter in a 12-inch nonstick skillet over medium heat. Swirl the skillet to distribute the butter evenly over the bottom and the sides. Add the onion and garlic; cook until softened, about 4 minutes. Add the basil, tomatoes, and olives; stir to coat with the butter. Spread in a single layer.

3. Meanwhile, stir the feta and pepper into the eggs.

4. Pour the egg mixture into the skillet; stir lightly with a fork until the eggs start to set. Once the bottom is firm, use a thin, nonmetallic spatula to lift the frittata edge closest to you (see the illustration on page 276). Tilt the skillet slightly toward you so that the uncooked egg runs underneath. Return the skillet to a level position and swirl gently to evenly distribute the egg. Continue cooking for about 40 seconds then lift the edge again, repeating the process until the egg on top is no longer runny.

5. Transfer the skillet to the oven; bake until the frittata top is set and dry to the touch, 2 to 4 minutes, making sure to remove the frittata as soon as the top is just set.

6. Run the spatula around the skillet edge to loosen the frittata; invert onto a serving plate. Serve warm, at room temperature, or chilled.

BREAKFAST STRATA

WHAT'S QUICKER THAN QUICHE, STURDIER than soufflé, and combines the best qualities of both? The answer is strata, a layered casserole that in its most basic form comprises bread, eggs, cheese, and milk or cream. Layered among them are flavorful fillings that provide both substance and character, and the result is, in essence, a golden brown, puffed, hearty, savory bread pudding. Strata is easy to prepare, can be made ahead, and feeds a crowd for a holiday brunch or a garden-variety weekend breakfast.

But strata is not without its pitfalls. In our experience, strata often suffers from largesse. Many of the recipes we sampled were too rich for breakfast, with a belly-busting overabundance of custard. And then there were the fillings, where an everything-but-the-kitchen-sink approach led to wet, sagging, overwrought stratas. One we sampled early on included mustard, garlic, nutmeg, marinated artichoke hearts, raw green peppers, cherry tomatoes, ham, Parmesan, fontina, and goat cheese. Such overindulgence not only sends unlucky diners scrambling for Maalox but turns a simple, workhorse dish into a self-parody. Our goal was to scale back strata, keeping it just rich enough while choosing flavorings and fillings that would blend into the chorus, not hog the spotlight.

Bread is the foundation of strata. Although sliced white sandwich bread is the most common choice, recipes also call for Italian, French, sourdough, multigrain, rye, pumpernickel, challah, focaccia, and even hamburger and hot dog buns. We tried them all and preferred supermarket Italian and French breads for their strong crumb and neutral flavor. Since no one objected to the crust, we left it in place. While many recipes specify cubes of bread, we preferred slices because they added to the layered effect of the casserole. Half-inch-thick slices were best; anything thicker was too chewy, and thin slices just melted away. We also preferred the texture of stale bread (or fresh bread dried in the oven) and found that buttering the slices added richness and flavor.

Our next consideration was the custard that binds the bread. In a battery of tests, tasters were divided between mixtures with equal parts dairy and egg and those with twice as much dairy as egg. The solution was to meet in the middle, adding a little extra dairy to the 50/50 mixture. As for the dairy, we tested low-fat milk, whole milk, half-and-half, and heavy cream, both alone and in combinations. The half-and-half was the clear winner.

As a basic flavoring, sautéed shallots won over onions and garlic. We had a surprise in store when we tested another flavoring common to a few strata recipes: white wine. It showed promise, lightening the flavor of the whole dish. But it also imparted an unwelcome boozy flavor. We corrected this problem by applying a technique used in sauce making, reduction, which cooked off the alcohol and concentrated the flavor. The reduced wine brightened the flavor of the whole dish considerably.

One last observation about the most basic seasonings, salt and pepper: Strata requires a generous dose of each, and seasoning both the custard and the filling individually and liberally is the most effective way to bring all the flavors into focus.

Even with the right basic ingredients in the right proportions, test after test proved that high-moisture fillings such as sausage and raw vegetables ruined the strata's texture. Moisture leached into the casserole, leaving it wet enough to literally slosh and ooze when cut. To correct this problem, we took to sautéing all filling ingredients until they looked dry in the pan, evaporating moisture that would otherwise end up in the strata. Whatever your filling choice, this critical step will make the difference between a moist, tender dish and one that resembles a wet sponge.

One of strata's charms, especially during the busy holiday season, is that it can—in fact, most recipes claim it should—be assembled well ahead of time. We rested assembled stratas overnight, for four hours, for one hour, and not at all. Only the fresh-made strata, which was noticeably less cohesive than the rested versions, failed to make the cut. Once assembled, strata can be rested anywhere from one hour to overnight.

A test-kitchen colleague suggested weighing down the assembled strata during its rest, and this step had a dramatic effect. Without exception, the weighted stratas had a perfectly even, custardy texture throughout. In stratas rested without the weight, it was not unusual to encounter a bite of bread that had not been fully penetrated with custard.

Once in the oven, the strata cooked much more evenly in a wide, shallow baking dish than in the deep soufflé dish called for in many recipes. Lowering the baking temperature from the widely recommended 350 degrees to 325 was

ASSEMBLING THE STRATA

1. Layer the bread and the filling in the baking dish.

2. Pour the custard mixture evenly over the assembled layers.

3. Cover the surface flush with plastic wrap and weight the strata.

an additional tactic we adopted to even out the cooking. Baking the strata until the top was crisp and golden brown was another common recommendation, but we found that this often produced an overcooked, overly firm, and even rubbery interior. We found it best to remove the strata from the oven when the top was just beginning to brown, and the center was barely puffed and still slightly loose when the pan was gently jiggled. With just a five-minute rest, the center finished cooking from residual heat, reaching the perfectly set, supple texture we prized.

Breakfast Strata with Spinach and Gruyère

SERVES 6 TO 8

Three 1-pound boxes of brown or powdered sugar, laid side by side over the plastic-covered surface, make ideal weights for the assembled strata (see the illustration on page 280). A gallon-size zipper-lock bag filled with about 2 pounds of sugar or rice also works. Though each strata calls for a certain type of cheese, feel free to substitute any good melting cheese, such as Havarti, sharp cheddar, or colby.

16–20	(½-inch-thick) slices supermarket French or Italian bread
8½	tablespoons unsalted butter, softened
1	small onion, minced
2	(10-ounce) packages frozen chopped spinach, thawed and squeezed dry
	Salt and ground black pepper
1	cup medium-dry white wine, such as Sauvignon Blanc
12	ounces Gruyère cheese, shredded (about 4 cups)
12	large eggs
3½	cups half-and-half

1. Adjust an oven rack to the middle position and heat the oven to 225 degrees. Arrange the bread in a single layer on a large baking sheet and bake until dry and crisp, about 40 minutes, turning over the slices halfway through the drying time. (Alternatively, leave the slices out overnight to dry.) When cooled, butter the slices on one side with 4 tablespoons of the butter; set aside.

2. Heat 3 tablespoons butter in a medium non-stick skillet over medium heat. Cook the onion until fragrant and translucent, about 3 minutes; add the spinach and salt and pepper to taste and cook, stirring occasionally, until the spinach and onion are combined, about 2 minutes. Transfer to a medium bowl; set aside. Add the wine to the skillet, increase the heat to medium-high, and simmer until reduced to ¼ cup, about 5 minutes; set aside.

3. Butter a 9 by 13-inch baking dish (or shallow casserole dish of similar size) with the remaining 1½ tablespoons butter and arrange half the bread slices, buttered-side up, in a single layer in the dish. Sprinkle half of the spinach mixture, then 1⅓ cups of the Gruyère evenly over the bread slices. Arrange the remaining bread slices in a single layer over the cheese; sprinkle the remaining spinach mixture and another 1⅓ cups cheese evenly over the bread. Whisk the eggs in a medium bowl until combined; whisk in the reduced wine, half-and-half, 1 teaspoon salt, and pepper to taste. Pour the egg mixture evenly over the bread layers; cover the surface flush with plastic wrap, weigh it down (see the illustration on page 280), and refrigerate for at least 1 hour or up to overnight.

4. Remove the dish from the refrigerator and let it stand at room temperature for 20 minutes. Meanwhile, adjust an oven rack to the middle position and heat the oven to 325 degrees. Uncover the strata and sprinkle the remaining 1⅓ cups cheese evenly over the surface; bake until both the edges and the center are puffed and the edges have pulled away slightly from the sides of the dish, about 60 minutes. Cool on a wire rack for 5 minutes; serve.

Breakfast Strata with Sausage, Mushrooms, and Monterey Jack

SERVES 6 TO 8

Mushrooms contain a lot of water that must be cooked out before they are added to the strata. The mildness of Monterey Jack works well in this dish. Other possible choices are cheddar and Havarti.

16–20   (¹/₂-inch-thick) slices supermarket French or
        Italian bread

5¹/₂   tablespoons unsalted butter, softened

  1   pound bulk breakfast sausage, crumbled

  1   small onion, minced

  1   pound white button mushrooms, brushed
        clean and quartered
        Salt and ground black pepper

  1   cup medium-dry white wine, such as
        Sauvignon Blanc

 12   ounces Monterey Jack cheese, shredded
        (about 4 cups)

 12   large eggs

3¹/₂   cups half-and-half

  3   tablespoons minced fresh parsley leaves

1. Adjust an oven rack to the middle position and heat the oven to 225 degrees. Arrange the bread in a single layer on a large baking sheet and bake until dry and crisp, about 40 minutes, turning over the slices halfway through the drying time. (Alternatively, leave the slices out overnight to dry.) When cooled, butter the slices on one side with 4 tablespoons of the butter; set aside.

2. Heat the sausage in a medium nonstick skillet over medium heat. Cook, breaking the meat into small pieces with a wooden spoon, until it loses its raw color and begins to brown, about 7 minutes; add the onion and cook, stirring frequently, until fragrant and translucent, about 3 minutes longer. Add the mushrooms to the skillet and cook until the mushrooms no longer release liquid, about 10 minutes; transfer the mixture to a medium bowl and season to taste with salt and pepper. Add the wine to the skillet, increase the heat to medium-high, and simmer until reduced to ¼ cup, about 5 minutes; set aside.

3. Butter a 9 by 13-inch baking dish (or shallow casserole dish of similar size) with the remaining 1½ tablespoons butter and arrange half the bread slices, buttered-side up, in a single layer in the dish. Sprinkle half of the sausage mixture, then 1⅓ cups of the Monterey Jack evenly over the bread slices. Arrange the remaining bread slices in a single layer over the cheese; sprinkle the remaining sausage mixture and another 1⅓ cups cheese evenly over the bread. Whisk the eggs in a medium bowl until combined; whisk in the reduced wine, half-and-half, parsley, 1 teaspoon salt, and pepper to taste. Pour the egg mixture evenly over the bread layers; cover the surface flush with plastic wrap, weigh it down (see the illustration on page 280), and refrigerate for at least 1 hour or up to overnight.

4. Remove the dish from the refrigerator and let it stand at room temperature for 20 minutes. Meanwhile, adjust an oven rack to the middle position and heat the oven to 325 degrees. Uncover the strata and sprinkle the remaining 1⅓ cups cheese evenly over the surface; bake until both the edges and the center are puffed and the edges have pulled away slightly from the sides of the dish, about 1 hour and 20 minutes. Cool on a wire rack for 5 minutes; serve.

~·~

Breakfast Strata with Potatoes, Rosemary, and Fontina

SERVES 6 TO 8

If you have leftover potatoes, simply skip the second step and add 3 cups of diced cooked potatoes in step 3.

16–20   (¹/₂-inch-thick) slices supermarket French or
        Italian bread

8¹/₂   tablespoons unsalted butter, softened

1¹/₂   pounds Red Bliss potatoes, scrubbed and cut
        into ¹/₂-inch cubes
        Salt

  1   small onion, minced

  4   medium garlic cloves, minced or pressed
        through a garlic press

  1   tablespoon minced fresh rosemary leaves
        Ground black pepper

  1   cup medium-dry white wine, such as
        Sauvignon Blanc

 12   ounces fontina cheese, shredded (about 4 cups)

 12   large eggs

3¹/₂   cups half-and-half

  3   tablespoons minced fresh parsley leaves

1. Adjust an oven rack to the middle position and heat the oven to 225 degrees. Arrange the bread in a single layer on a large baking sheet and bake until dry and crisp, about 40 minutes,

turning over the slices halfway through the drying time. (Alternatively, leave the slices out overnight to dry.) When cooled, butter the slices on one side with 4 tablespoons of the butter; set aside.

2. Place the potatoes, 1 quart of water, and ½ teaspoon salt in a large saucepan. Bring to a boil over high heat; reduce the heat to a simmer and cook until the potatoes are just tender, about 4 minutes. Drain the potatoes.

3. Heat 3 tablespoons butter in a medium non-stick skillet over medium heat, add the potatoes, and cook until just beginning to brown, about 10 minutes. Add the onion and cook, stirring frequently, until softened and translucent, about 3 minutes longer; add the garlic and rosemary and cook until fragrant, about 2 minutes longer. Transfer the mixture to a medium bowl; season to

SHREDDING SOFT CHEESE

Semisoft cheeses such as Monterey Jack, cheddar, or mozzarella can stick to a box grater and cause a real mess. Here's how to keep the holes on the grater from becoming clogged.

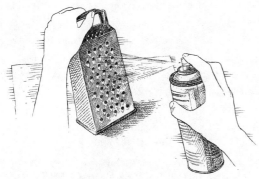

1. Use nonstick cooking spray to lightly coat the side of the box grater with the large holes.

2. Shred the cheese as usual. The cooking spray will keep the cheese from sticking to the surface of the grater.

taste with salt and pepper and set aside. Add the wine to the skillet, increase the heat to medium-high, and simmer until reduced to ¼ cup, about 5 minutes; set aside.

4. Butter a 9 by 13-inch baking dish (or shallow casserole dish of similar size) with the remaining 1½ tablespoons butter; arrange half the bread slices, buttered-side up, in a single layer in the dish. Sprinkle half of the potato mixture, then 1⅓ cups of the fontina evenly over the bread slices. Arrange the remaining bread slices in a single layer over the cheese; sprinkle the remaining potato mixture and another 1⅓ cups cheese evenly over the bread. Whisk the eggs in a medium bowl until combined; whisk in the reduced wine, half-and-half, parsley, 1 teaspoon salt, and pepper to taste. Pour the egg mixture evenly over the bread layers; cover the surface flush with plastic wrap, weigh it down (see the illustration on page 280), and refrigerate for at least 1 hour or up to overnight.

5. Remove the dish from the refrigerator and let it stand at room temperature for 20 minutes. Meanwhile, adjust an oven rack to the middle position and heat the oven to 325 degrees. Uncover the strata and sprinkle the remaining 1⅓ cups cheese evenly over the surface; bake until both the edges and the center are puffed and the edges have pulled away slightly from the sides of the dish, about 1 hour and 10 minutes. Cool on a wire rack for 5 minutes; serve.

24-HOUR "OMELET"

THE NAME OF THIS EGG DISH IS RATHER MIS-leading, but it's a recipe that has been handed down for generations, particularly, it seems, in the Midwest. This homey casserole is nothing like the omelet that you order at your favorite breakfast joint. Nor does it take a day to bake. It's meant to be assembled in the evening, often the night before a hectic holiday morning like Christmas, and then popped into the oven to bake while the coffee brews and the children and houseguests wake up. Cheesy and golden, it puffs up impressively above the rim of the baking dish. While similar to breakfast strata, a 24-hour omelet focuses more on the eggs and less on the bread, and usually forgoes the meats and vegetables that often star in a strata. Consisting of an eggy custard, bread, and cheese, the 24-hour omelet is lighter than the fluffiest scrambled egg and practically melts in your mouth. Invariably, however, most recipes we found for 24-hour omelets suffer the fate of normal omelets; they are often overstuffed with myriad ingredients, losing their eggy richness in the confusion of vegetables and spices. With the intent of keeping the ingredients and preparation simple, we set out to develop the tastiest 24-hour omelet possible.

We decided to start our tests with the bread, since it plays such an important role in the texture of this dish. Unlike a strata, where the bread remains a distinct component of the dish, with this recipe we wanted the bread to "melt" into the custard (a simple mixture of eggs and milk or cream). As such, we ruled out rustic loaves with heavy crusts or any bread that was overly chewy. Trying a number of loaves of white bread, we found that a firm, dense loaf provided the best texture (we liked Pepperidge Farm Hearty White). We also learned it was best to avoid really soft loaves as they had a tendency to break down too much, lending the dish an unpleasant raw, yeasty flavor. In the course of testing, we also discovered that buttering the bread added a richness and flavor to the omelet that was favored among tasters.

The custard was the next component to examine. In past experiences, we had found that a custard with two parts of dairy to one part egg provided the best texture and flavor. Bearing in mind the name of the dish, we felt it should have a pronounced egg flavor. We therefore reduced the amount of dairy called for in most recipes, encouraging the egg flavor to dominate. In the end, we settled on a custard consisting of eight whole eggs (about 2 cups) and 3 cups of dairy. When it came to the type of dairy, we tested the recipe with milk, half-and-half, and heavy cream (both on their own and in combinations). Wanting to keep the emphasis on the eggs in the dish, we chose the milk, as both the half-and-half and the cream masked the egg flavor and made the dish too heavy.

With the strata recipe, we found it necessary to weigh down the assembled dish while it rested overnight in order to evenly distribute the custard. Curious as to whether we would have to employ this technique with the assembled 24-hour omelet, we tried a weighted and an unweighted casserole side by side. We found that, because there was more custard in relation to bread in the 24-hour omelet, weighting the dish was an unnecessary step.

The final crucial ingredient to address was the cheese. In the recipes we consulted, the amount of cheese ranged from a scant cup to a whopping 1½ pounds. After several tests, we settled on an amount in between these two figures, ¾ pound. This proportion added a rich flavor but didn't have an adverse effect on the consistency of the omelet. As for the type of cheese, we found it better to use cheeses that are high in moisture and melt well,

EQUIPMENT: Oven Thermometers

Unless you have your oven routinely calibrated, there is a good chance that its temperature reading may be off. We tested the home ovens of 16 friends and colleagues and found that many varied as much as 50 degrees in either direction. Since improper temperatures can and will affect the outcome of these casseroles, we recommend purchasing an inexpensive oven thermometer and checking it once the oven is heated. After testing a slew of models and rating them for readability, stability, and accuracy, we found that we preferred two models, both priced under $15—a small investment for such insurance.

THE BEST OVEN THERMOMETERS

The most stable thermometer in the group, in part because of its 4-inch length, the Taylor Classic Oven Guide Thermometer (left) was also very accurate. The uncluttered dial design of the Component Design Magnet Mounted Oven Thermometer (right) and its magnet-mounted stability earned it a second-place rating.

such as cheddar, Monterey Jack, and Havarti. It proved wise to stay away from firmer cheeses, such as Parmesan and Asiago, which gave the omelet a dry texture.

For other flavors, we concluded that simpler was better. A small amount of onion provided a little pungency, but didn't overwhelm the cheese and eggs. To finish, we experimented with a little dry mustard and Tabasco, which together gave the dish a hint of spiciness and accentuated the creaminess of the eggs.

24-Hour "Omelet"

SERVES 6 TO 8

We prefer Pepperidge Farm Hearty White bread, but any firm, dense loaf of white bread will do. The omelet needs to sit in the refrigerator, well covered, for at least 8 hours in order to achieve the desired consistency, and it can be made up to 36 hours in advance.

4	tablespoons unsalted butter, softened
10	slices high-quality white sandwich bread
12	ounces cheddar cheese, shredded (about 4 cups)
8	large eggs
3	cups whole milk
1	small onion, grated
1	teaspoon salt
1/2	teaspoon ground black pepper
1	teaspoon dry mustard
1/2	teaspoon Tabasco sauce

1. Grease the bottom and sides of a 9 by 13-inch baking dish (or shallow casserole dish of similar size) with 1 tablespoon of the butter. Spread the remaining 3 tablespoons butter evenly over one side of each bread slice. Cut the bread into 1-inch pieces. Scatter half of the bread evenly in the prepared dish, and sprinkle with half of the cheddar. Repeat with the remaining bread and cheese.

2. Whisk the eggs, milk, onion, salt, pepper, mustard, and Tabasco together in a medium bowl. Pour evenly over the bread and press lightly to submerge. Cover tightly with plastic wrap and refrigerate for at least 8 hours or up to 36 hours.

3. Adjust an oven rack to the middle position and heat the oven to 350 degrees. Remove the dish from the refrigerator and discard the plastic wrap. Bake until puffed and golden brown, about 60 minutes. Serve immediately.

> VARIATIONS

24-Hour "Omelet" with Pepper Jack and Chipotle Chiles

Follow the recipe for 24-Hour "Omelet," making the following changes: substitute an equal amount of shredded Pepper Jack cheese for the cheddar. Whisk 1 minced canned chipotle chile and 1 tablespoon adobo sauce with the eggs in step 2. Sprinkle 1/4 cup minced fresh cilantro leaves over the top before baking.

24-Hour "Omelet" with Sun-Dried Tomatoes and Mozzarella

Follow the recipe for 24-Hour "Omelet," making the following changes: substitute an equal amount of shredded mozzarella for the cheddar. Sprinkle 1/2 cup grated Parmesan (about 1 ounce) and 4 ounces oil-packed sun-dried tomatoes (about 1/2 cup), drained, patted dry, and chopped coarse, between the two layers of bread in step 1.

POTATO AND EGG CASSEROLE

WHETHER SERVED AS HOME FRIES OR HASH browns, the dense texture and earthy flavor of potatoes is a perfect complement to rich, creamy eggs. Capitalizing on the affinity that potatoes and eggs have for one another, we had the idea of developing a hearty casserole that would feature both and would be suitable for serving a crowd at brunch or dinner. A review of cookbooks yielded several recipes matching our requirements, but all of them, once executed, fell far below our expectations. It was clear that we would have to start from scratch and build our own potato and egg casserole from the ground up.

Our first task was to determine the best type of potatoes to use, and russet potatoes were our first choice. The ensuing casserole was certainly passable, but we felt that the russet's high starch content and low moisture made the dish a little too dry. Thinking that a potato with low starch and high moisture would be a perfect fit, we switched to Red Bliss potatoes. But these potatoes lacked the texture and flavor presence we were looking for. In our next test we used Yukon Gold potatoes. The Yukon Golds had an ideal balance of moisture and starch. With a creamy texture and faintly nutty flavor, they were in perfect harmony with the eggy custard. The question now was how to prepare the potatoes.

Up to this point we had been using parboiled ¼-inch slices of potato, but we wondered if this was the best choice. We tried several casseroles that started with raw potatoes, both sliced thin and grated, but found them to be starchy and grainy, with a distinct raw flavor. It was clear to us that the potatoes needed to cook before being added, in order to remove some of their starch and soften their texture. We also tried cutting the potatoes several different ways to see the effect it had on the casserole. We tried slicing the potatoes in the food processor, but this made them so thin that they overcooked and became mushy before the custard

was set. We also tried large chunks of potatoes, but when prepared this way, the custard and potatoes seemed discordant. In the end, we returned to using the ¼-inch slices, as they resulted in the best taste overall.

While testing the potatoes, we had been using a custard that consisted of eight eggs to a quart of dairy. While this was suitable, we wanted to bring the egg flavor to the fore. Trying the casserole again with half the amount of dairy (eight eggs and 2 cups dairy), we found that the dish was rather dry and a little rubbery. Compromising, we tried using 3 cups of dairy, which turned out to be the perfect balance. The casserole had an eggy flavor, but there was enough moisture to keep the ingredients from becoming too dry. When it came to the type of dairy, we tried using milk, half-and-half, and heavy cream. Milk, it turned out, was too thin and left the dish bereft of flavor. Both half-and-half and heavy cream provided plenty of flavor, but the heavy cream was too cloying, so we opted to go with the half-and-half.

Since many tasters felt that the potatoes and egg, on their own, were a little bland, we looked for ways to increase the overall flavor of the dish. In our initial tests, we used one medium onion, but we decided that the dish needed a more "oniony" presence. We tried doubling the amount to two onions, which worked perfectly. We also felt that the casserole could benefit from more richness, so we increased the amount of olive oil in which we sautéed the onions. While it seemed excessive, ¼ cup olive oil lent a fruity richness, which the potatoes thirstily absorbed. Bacon also contributed some richness to the potatoes and egg. Rendering the bacon in the olive oil, along with the onions, added a smoky meatiness to the casserole that tasters overwhelmingly approved. Cheddar cheese was another ingredient that was warmly received by tasters. Adding a bit of sharpness and complementing the smokiness of the bacon, the cheddar also aided in the browning of the exterior. To further the browning, we sprinkled a small amount of Parmesan over the top of the dish, and found that its nuttiness provided the finishing touch to our potato and egg casserole.

STORING EGGS

WE HAVE FOUND THAT EGGS SUFFER MORE from the vagaries of improper storage than from age. The egg tray inside the refrigerator door is not the ideal location, for two reasons: temperature and protection. The American Egg Board recommends 40 degrees for storage, but we have found the average door temperature in our six test-kitchen refrigerators to be closer to 45 degrees. The interior top shelf is a better bet—ours register between 38 and 40 degrees. Eggs are also better stored in their protective cardboard carton; when removed, they may absorb flavors from other foods. We've made "oniony" cakes and cookies with improperly stored eggs. The carton also helps to maintain humidity, which is ideally 70 to 80 percent, according to the Egg Board.

EQUIPMENT: Garlic Presses

Most cooks dislike the chore of mincing garlic, and many turn to garlic presses. We know that many professional cooks sneer at this tool, but we have a different opinion. In hundreds of hours of use in our test kitchens, we have found that this little tool delivers speed, ease, and a comfortable separation of garlic from fingers.

The garlic press offers other advantages. First is flavor, which changes perceptibly depending on how the cloves are broken down. The finer a clove of garlic is cut, the more flavor is released from its broken cells. Fine mincing or pureeing, therefore, results in a fuller, more pungent garlic flavor. A good garlic press breaks down the cloves more than the average cook would with a knife. Second, a good garlic press ensures a consistently fine texture, which in turn means better distribution of the garlic throughout the dish.

The question for us, then, was not whether garlic presses work but which of the many available presses work best. Armed with 10 popular models, we pressed our way through a mountain of garlic cloves to find out.

Garlic press prices can vary by as much as a shocking 700 percent, from about $3 up to $25. Some are made from metal and others from plastic. Some offer devices to ease cleaning, and most show subtle differences in handle and hopper design.

Most garlic presses share a common design consisting of two handles connected by a hinge. At the end of one handle is a small, perforated hopper; at the end of the other is a plunger that fits snugly inside the hopper. The garlic cloves in the hopper get crushed by the descending plunger when the handles are squeezed together, and the puree is extruded through the perforations in the bottom of the hopper.

Some presses employ a completely different design—a relatively large cylindrical container with a tight-fitting screw-down plunger. These presses are designed for large capacity, but the unusual design failed to impress us. The screw-type plungers required both pressure and significant repetitive motion, which contributed to hand fatigue. This seemed like a lot of work just to press garlic. Matters did not improve when the hoppers were loaded with multiple garlic cloves. Even greater effort was required to twist down the plungers, and the texture of the garlic puree produced was coarse and uneven.

A good garlic press should not only produce a smooth, evenly textured puree but also be easy to use. To us, this meant that different users should be able to operate it without straining their hands. With several notable exceptions, all of our presses performed reasonably well in this regard.

Several of our test cooks wondered if we could make an easy task even easier by putting the garlic cloves through the presses without first removing their skins. Instructions on the packaging of Zyliss and Bodum presses specified that it was OK to press unpeeled cloves, and our tests bore out this assertion. Though the directions for several other presses did not address this issue specifically, we found that Oxo and Endurance presses also handled unpeeled garlic with ease. We did note, however, that the yield of garlic puree was greater across the board when we pressed peeled cloves. While we were at it, we also tried pressing chunks of peeled fresh ginger. The Zyliss, Kuhn Rikon, and Oxo presses were the only three to excel in this department, and we found that smaller chunks, about 1/2 inch, were crushed much more easily than larger, 1-inch pieces.

When all was said and pressed, the traditionally designed, moderately priced Zyliss turned out to be comfortable and consistent, and it produced the finest, most even garlic puree. In addition, it handled unpeeled garlic and small chunks of fresh ginger without incident. While other presses got the job done, the Zyliss just edged out the field in terms of both performance and design.

THE BEST GARLIC PRESS

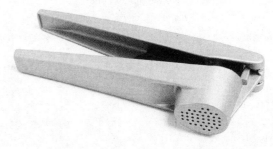

We found that this Zyliss press can handle two cloves at once, producing very finely pureed garlic in a flash.

Potato and Egg Casserole with Bacon and Cheddar

SERVES 6 TO 8

We prefer the buttery flavor and creamy texture of Yukon Gold potatoes in this recipe; however, russet potatoes will also work. Handle the sliced potatoes gently after they are boiled—they can break apart quite easily. This casserole is best when assembled, baked, and eaten the same day. However, both the potatoes and the onion mixture can be prepared in advance and stored separately in airtight containers in the refrigerator.

1	tablespoon unsalted butter, softened
2	pounds Yukon Gold potatoes (about 3 large), peeled and sliced 1/4 inch thick
	Salt
1/4	cup extra-virgin olive oil
6	ounces (about 6 slices) bacon, cut crosswise into 1/4-inch-thick strips
2	medium onions, chopped medium
6	medium garlic cloves, minced or pressed through a garlic press
2	teaspoons minced fresh thyme leaves
8	large eggs
3	cups half-and-half
8	ounces cheddar cheese, shredded (about 2 2/3 cups)
1/8	teaspoon cayenne pepper
1	teaspoon ground black pepper
1	ounce Parmesan cheese, grated fine (about 1/2 cup)
	Tabasco sauce

1. Adjust an oven rack to the middle position and heat the oven to 375 degrees. Grease the bottom and sides of a 9 by 13-inch baking dish (or shallow casserole dish of similar size) with the butter; set aside.

2. Place the potatoes, 1 quart of water, and 1/2 teaspoon salt in a large saucepan. Bring to a boil over high heat; reduce the heat to a simmer and cook until the potatoes are just tender, about 4 minutes. Drain and transfer to a large mixing bowl.

3. Meanwhile, heat the oil in a 12-inch nonstick skillet over medium heat until shimmering.

Add the bacon, onions, and 1/2 teaspoon salt; cook, stirring frequently, until the onions have browned and the bacon is crisp, 20 to 25 minutes. Add the garlic and thyme; cook until fragrant, about 1 minute. Remove from the heat and add to the bowl with the potatoes; fold gently, using a rubber spatula to combine. Cool for 10 minutes.

4. Whisk the eggs, half-and-half, cheddar, cayenne, black pepper, and 1 teaspoon salt together in a large bowl. Add the cooled potatoes and fold gently, using the rubber spatula. Pour the mixture into the prepared baking dish and press gently into an even layer. Sprinkle with the Parmesan. Bake until the eggs have set and the top is lightly browned, about 40 minutes. Cool for 10 minutes. Serve with Tabasco.

➤ VARIATION

Potato and Egg Casserole with Chorizo and Red Peppers

Follow the recipe for Potato and Egg Casserole with Bacon and Cheddar, making the following changes: Substitute 6 ounces chorizo sausage, each sausage halved lengthwise then sliced 1/4 inch thick, for the bacon, and 2 teaspoons minced fresh oregano leaves for the thyme. Add 1 large red bell pepper, stemmed, seeded, and chopped medium, with the onions in step 3. Mix 1/2 teaspoon ground coriander, 1/2 teaspoon ground cumin, and 1/2 teaspoon chili powder with the eggs in step 4.

CHEESE SOUFFLÉ

SOUFFLÉS HAVE ALWAYS HAD A BAD REPUTA-tion as elaborate haute-cuisine dinosaurs that you'd only see served with white gloves and silver trays in overpriced restaurants. Or, if you were brave enough to make one at home, it would take hours to prepare and would require tiptoeing around the oven lest you deflate your handiwork. But soufflés are actually incredibly easy to put together and, when made properly, are unlikely to fall even at the heaviest of stomping. When most people think of soufflés, they usually think of sweet desserts. But a well-made cheese soufflé is a thing of beauty. When made properly, soufflés are meltingly rich with the subtle flavor of egg and cheese. However, when made poorly, they become foamy and flavorless, like pieces of styrofoam.

The first challenge in developing a recipe for a well-made soufflé was to decide what type of base to use. Our research had turned up two options. The first was a béchamel, the classic French sauce made with flour, butter, and milk. The second was a *bouillie*, which is a simple paste made from flour and milk. Preparing two soufflés, one with each type of base, we found that the soufflé made with the béchamel was preferred over the bouillie-based soufflé. Tasters commented that the béchamel-based soufflé had more body and a richer flavor, while the bouillie-based soufflé tasted slightly bland and starchy. It appeared that butter made all the difference.

We next focused on the ratio of eggs yolks to egg whites in our soufflé. In most recipes, we found a ratio of 5 whites to 3 yolks. But in using this ratio, we found that the soufflé was too foamy and lacked the velvety texture we were seeking. Decreasing the egg whites until we reached an equal ratio of 3 whites to 3 yolks, we found a soufflé with a rich and creamy mouthfeel and

BEATING EGG WHITES

CURDLED EGG WHITES   **SMOOTH EGG WHITES**

Whipped egg whites can be finicky and require a keen eye and close attention for the best results. If improperly handled, they won't have the structure to properly support the soufflé. The batch of whites on the left is overwhipped and has curdled. For perfect whipped whites every time, start with slightly warmed egg whites and a low mixer speed. Only add the cream of tartar once the egg whites have developed some structure. A soft peak will droop slightly downward from the tip of the whisk; a stiff peak, as seen on the right, will stand tall.

without a hint of foaminess.

When it came to the cheese for our soufflé, we tried Gruyère, Parmesan, cheddar, and Monterey Jack. Gruyère and Parmesan were the most popular choices. Tasters found cheddar to be too sharp and Jack to be too mild. As for the amount of cheese, we learned that if we added too much to the dish, the structure of the soufflé would be heavy and the soufflé would collapse. With 4 ounces of cheese, the soufflé had plenty of flavor and still puffed beautifully.

While the cheese and egg provided the soufflé with ample flavor, we felt that we needed to provide some depth to the soufflé. Onions were a logical choice, but even small amounts turned out to be too intrusive. We instead looked to the milder shallot. One finely minced shallot added to the béchamel base provided just a hint of pungency and complemented the dominant flavor of the cheese. In addition to the shallot, ground mustard added a hint of spiciness and helped to draw out the nuttiness of the Gruyère.

Happy with the flavor of our soufflé, we had one item left to examine: the baking dish. Up to this point, we had been using a traditional round ceramic soufflé dish. Concerned that very few people would actually have one of these in their kitchen, we looked for an alternative. Looking around the test kitchen, we finally settled on a glass loaf pan. Following the exact technique we had used with the soufflé dish, we tried it out. Surprisingly, it worked just as well, although it did lack the visual appeal of the round soufflé dish. Considering the success of the glass loaf pan, we tried making the soufflé in a metal loaf pan. But we found that the slippery metal surface didn't allow the soufflé to achieve the height that it did in the glass pan and that the exterior became too dark before the inside was fully cooked. We also wondered if it would be possible to double the recipe and bake it in a 9 by 13-inch baking dish. Again we had success. Although it took slightly longer to cook, and didn't quite reach the heights of the smaller soufflés, the large soufflé had the same great taste and melt-in-your-mouth texture.

FOLDING EGG WHITES

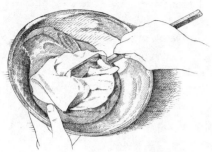

1. Using a rubber spatula, gently stir a quarter of the whites into the base to lighten it. Scrape the remaining whites onto the lightened base. Cut through the center of the two mixtures down to the bottom of the bowl.

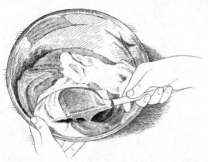

2. Pull the spatula toward you, scraping along the bottom and up the side of the bowl.

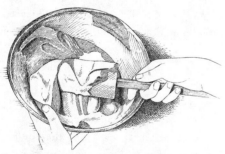

3. Once the spatula is out of the mixture, rotate the spatula so that any mixture clinging to it falls back onto the surface of the batter.

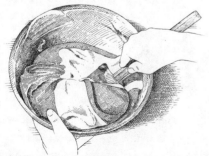

4. Spin the bowl a quarter of a turn and repeat this process until the beaten whites are just incorporated and no large streaks of whites remain visible.

Cheese Soufflé

SERVES 3 TO 4

A 1½-quart soufflé dish can be substituted for the loaf pan. This recipe can also be doubled and baked in either two glass loaf pans or one 9 by 13-inch baking dish. If using a 9 by 13-inch baking dish, extend the cooking time 5 to 10 minutes.

3½	tablespoons unsalted butter
½	ounce Parmesan cheese, grated (about ¼ cup)
1	medium shallot, minced
3	tablespoons all-purpose flour
1	cup whole milk
4	ounces Gruyère cheese, shredded (about 1⅓ cups)
½	teaspoon salt
¼	teaspoon dry mustard
¼	teaspoon ground black pepper
	Pinch nutmeg
3	large eggs, yolks and whites separated
¼	teaspoon cream of tartar

1. Adjust an oven rack to the middle position and heat the oven to 350 degrees. Grease the bottom and sides of an 8½ by 4½-inch glass loaf pan with ½ tablespoon of the butter. Sprinkle half of the Parmesan into the pan and shake to coat evenly; set aside.

2. Melt the remaining 3 tablespoons butter in a medium saucepan over medium heat. Add the shallot and cook until softened, about 2 minutes. Stir in the flour and cook, stirring constantly, until golden, about 1 minute. Slowly whisk in the milk; bring to a simmer and cook, whisking constantly, until thickened and smooth, about 1 minute. Off the heat, whisk in the Gruyère, salt, mustard, pepper, and nutmeg. Transfer the mixture to a large bowl. Whisk in the egg yolks until completely incorporated; set aside.

3. In the bowl of a standing mixer fitted with the whisk, or with a handheld electric mixer, beat the egg whites at low speed until combined, about 10 seconds. Add the cream of tartar, increase the speed to medium-high, and beat until stiff peaks form, about 2 minutes (see the photograph on page 289).

4. Using a rubber spatula, stir one quarter of the whipped egg whites into the yolk mixture until almost no white streaks remain. Gently add the remaining whites and fold with the spatula until just combined and some white streaks remain (see the illustrations on page 290). Gently pour the mixture into the prepared pan and sprinkle with the remaining Parmesan. Bake until the top is nicely browned, the center jiggles slightly, and an instant-read thermometer inserted through the side reads 170 degrees, 25 to 30 minutes. Serve immediately.

➤ VARIATIONS

Cheese Soufflé with Fines Herbes

Follow the recipe for Cheese Soufflé, stirring 1 tablespoon chopped fresh chives, 1 tablespoon chopped fresh parsley leaves, and 1½ teaspoons chopped fresh tarragon leaves into the yolk mixture in step 4, before folding in the egg whites.

Cheese Soufflé with Spinach

Place 4 ounces frozen spinach and 1 tablespoon water in a small microwave-proof bowl, cover tightly with plastic wrap, and microwave on high until thawed, 2 to 4 minutes. Drain the spinach and transfer to a clean kitchen towel; wring until dry. Chop the spinach coarsely and set aside. Follow the recipe for Cheese Soufflé, stirring the cooked chopped spinach and ½ teaspoon chopped fresh thyme leaves into the yolk mixture in step 4, before folding in the egg whites.

WHAT IS CREAM OF TARTAR?

CREAM OF TARTAR, AN ACID, ACTS AS A stabilizer when beating egg whites. It does this by adding hydrogen ions, creating a more stable molecular structure. The added hydrogen also lowers the pH slightly (from about 9 to 8), which makes the foam less prone to coagulation. In addition to stabilizing the egg whites during beating, cream of tartar acts as a bleaching agent, enhancing the whiteness of the foam, which is why it's used in angel food cake.

CORNED BEEF HASH

CORNED BEEF HASH IS NOT A BREAKFAST FOR those who fear fat or like to start the day with yogurt and wheat germ. By its very nature, hash is a hearty, stick-to-your-ribs meal. Legends abound as to the origins of fried meat and potato hash. "Hash house" was a colloquial term in the late 19th century for any cheap eating establishment, hash being a fry-up of questionable meat.

Corned beef hash, in particular, can be traced back to New England ingenuity and frugality. What was served as boiled dinner the night before was recycled as hash the next morning. All the leftovers—meat, potatoes, carrots, and sometimes cabbage—would be fried up in a skillet and capped with an egg. Perhaps because this is a dish of leftovers, we found traditional recipes to be few and far between, as if corned beef hash were a common-sense dish, unworthy of a recipe. And the recipes we did find produced starchy, one-dimensional hash that was light on flavor. Knowing that most people do not have leftovers from a boiled dinner sitting in their refrigerator, we set out to create a flavorful hash with fresh ingredients that was easy to prepare.

Meat and potatoes are the heart and soul of this dish—everything else is just seasoning. While leftover beef from a boiled dinner is ideal, we found that deli-style corned beef can be just as satisfying. At first, we diced the meat into pieces equivalent in size to the potatoes, but this led to tough and chewy meat that sharply contrasted with the potatoes' velvety softness. Mincing the beef kept it tender and imparted a meatier flavor to the hash. There is no need for a uniform mince; we chopped the meat coarse and then worked our knife back and forth across it until the meat was reduced to ¼-inch or smaller pieces.

Potatoes were an easy choice. Texture being foremost, we knew we wanted starchy potatoes that would retain some character but would soften and crumble about the edges to bind the hash together. We quickly ruled out anything waxy, such as red potatoes, because they remained too firm. Russets were our top choice.

Before they are combined with the beef, the potatoes must be parboiled. While we generally boil our potatoes whole and unpeeled so they don't absorb too much liquid, we discovered that peeling and dicing the potatoes prior to cooking worked fine in this instance. And they cooked more quickly, too. To echo the flavors of the corned beef, we added a couple of bay leaves and a bit of salt to the cooking water. After about four minutes of cooking, just after the potatoes had come to a boil, we had perfect potatoes—soft but not falling apart.

As for other vegetables, tasters quickly ruled out anything but onions. Carrots may be traditional, but tasters agreed that their sweetness compromised the simplicity of the hash. Onions, on the other hand, added a characteristic body and roundness that supported the meat and potatoes rather than detracting from them. We liked the onions best when they were cooked slow and steady, until lightly browned and meltingly soft. Along with the onions, we chose garlic and thyme to flavor the hash. Garlic sharpened the dish and a modicum of thyme added an earthiness that paired well with the beef.

Although the potatoes loosely bind this mixture together, most recipes call for either stock or cream to hold the ingredients more firmly in place. We tested both and preferred the richness of the cream. A little hot pepper sauce added with the cream brought some spice to the dish.

After cooking several batches of hash at varying temperatures and with differing techniques, we realized that a fairly lengthy cooking time was crucial to the flavor. The golden crust of browned meat and potatoes deepened the flavor of the hash. The recipes we tried deal with the crust in various ways. Some preserve the crust in one piece, cooking both sides by flipping the hash or sliding it onto a plate and inverting it back into the skillet; other recipes suggest breaking up the crust and folding it back into the hash. After trying both styles, tasters preferred the latter for its better overall flavor. And it's a lot easier than trying to flip the heavy, unwieldy hash. We lightly packed the hash into the skillet with the back of a wooden spoon, allowed the bottom to crisp up, and then folded the bottom over the top and repeated the process several times. In this way, the crisp browned bits

get evenly distributed throughout the hash.

Tasters agreed that the eggs served with hash need to be just barely set, so that the yolks break and moisten the potatoes. While poaching is the best technique for preserving a lightly cooked yolk, it can be something of a hassle. We found that we could "poach" the eggs in the same pan as the hash by nestling the eggs into indentations in the hash, covering the pan, and cooking them over low heat. The results were perfect: runny yolks with the eggs conveniently set in the hash and ready to be served.

Corned Beef Hash

SERVES 6

A well-seasoned cast-iron skillet is traditional for this recipe, but we prefer a 12-inch nonstick skillet. The nonstick surface leaves little chance of anything sticking and burning. Our favorite tool for flipping the hash is a flat wooden spatula, although a stiff plastic spatula will suffice. We like our hash served with ketchup.

2	pounds russet potatoes (about 4 medium), peeled and cut into $1/2$-inch dice
	Salt
2	bay leaves
4	ounces (about 4 slices) bacon, chopped
I	medium onion, diced
2	medium garlic cloves, minced or pressed through a garlic press
$1/2$	teaspoon minced fresh thyme leaves
I	pound corned beef, minced (pieces should be $1/4$ inch or smaller)
$1/2$	cup heavy cream
$1/4$	teaspoon Tabasco sauce
6	large eggs
	Ground black pepper

1. Bring the potatoes, 5 cups of water, ½ teaspoon salt, and the bay leaves to a boil in a medium saucepan over medium-high heat. Once boiling, cook the potatoes for 4 minutes, then drain and set the potatoes aside.

2. Cook the bacon in a 12-inch nonstick skillet over medium-high heat until it is crisp and the fat is partially rendered, about 4 minutes.

Add the onion and cook, stirring occasionally, until softened and browned at the edges, about 5 minutes. Add the garlic and thyme and cook until fragrant, about 30 seconds. Add the corned beef and stir until thoroughly combined with the onion mixture. Mix in the potatoes and lightly pack the mixture into the pan with a spatula. Pour the heavy cream and Tabasco sauce evenly over the hash. Cook undisturbed for 4 minutes, then, with the spatula, invert the hash, a portion at a time, and fold the browned bits back into the hash. Lightly repack the hash into the pan. Repeat the process every minute or two until the potatoes are thoroughly cooked, about 8 minutes longer.

3. Make six indentations (each measuring about 2 inches across) equally spaced on the surface of the hash. Crack one egg into each indentation and sprinkle the eggs with salt and pepper to taste. Reduce the heat to medium-low, cover the pan, and cook until the eggs are just set, 4 to 6 minutes. Divide the hash into six wedges, each wedge containing one egg, and serve immediately.

BAKED CHEESE GRITS

A STAPLE OF THE SOUTHERN BREAKFAST TABLE, grits are a nutritious and substantial start to the day. They appear in many guises, including simmered and sweetened with maple syrup or molasses; cooked to a thick consistency, cooled, and fried in slices; and, our favorite, enriched with cheese and spices and baked until brown on the top and creamy in the middle. From experience, however, we have found that baked cheese grits are often far from perfect. They are either bland and watery or too thick and pasty. For our recipe, we wanted a compromise—hearty, robust flavor that did not overwhelm the subtlety of the grits.

We started by cooking the grits. There are two kinds of grits: instant, which cook in five minutes; and old-fashioned, which cook in 15 minutes. In a side-by-side tasting, most tasters thought the instant grits were too creamy and tasted overprocessed. The old-fashioned grits were creamy yet retained a slightly coarse texture that tasters liked. They are called grits for a reason.

To add richness without relying solely on butter, as many recipes do, we cooked the grits in milk rather than water. The grits tasted good, but more in a hot-breakfast-cereal way—not the flavor we were hoping for. And the flavor of the grits disappeared behind the lactose-heavy milk flavor. Even when we diluted the milk significantly, the grits tasted too heavily of cooked milk. We then tried a small amount of heavy cream and water mixed together. Everyone liked this batch—the grits were rich, but without an overwhelming dairy flavor. We were surprised to find that cooked cream does not develop the same strong "cooked" flavor as milk. This is because the extra fat in cream keeps the milk proteins from breaking down when heated. After a few more batches of varying proportions, we found that 1 part cream to 3 parts water provided the best flavor.

To improve on things, we tried a few simple additions that would deepen the flavor of the grits without being overpowering. A small diced onion cooked in the saucepan before adding the liquid brought depth and a touch of sweetness. Many tasters liked a little garlic as well, but others thought the garlic overwhelmed the other flavors, so we left it out. Hot pepper sauce added a piquancy that cut through the richness.

With the grits cooked, we needed a cheese to fold in before baking. Recipes we found included everything from pasteurized cheese slices to a Spanish cheese called Manchego. A Spanish cheese seemed too far afield for such a humble dish, but we were ready to try just about anything. Monterey Jack and Pepper Jack cheeses made the grits taste sour, although the jalapeños in the cheese were appreciated and led us to increase our amount of hot sauce. Regular cheddar was bland, but the flavor was getting there. Extra-sharp cheddar proved to be the winner. The flavor was assertive and complemented the subtle corn flavor. Everyone in the test kitchen also liked smoked cheddar, but thought that it might be a little strong for the breakfast table.

Now it was time to bake our grits. We knew we wanted a dense texture, more akin to baked polenta than custardy spoon bread. We started off by adding two lightly beaten eggs to the grits before baking, but this provided an airy, almost soufflé-like texture that most tasters found unpleasant. We needed more eggs (and their coagulating proteins) to bind the grits and give the dish the dense texture we desired. Four eggs made the grits too heavy, and the egg flavor predominated. Three eggs, on the other hand, provided just enough structure without making the grits taste too eggy.

Forty-five minutes in a 350-degree oven (with a little more cheese sprinkled on to help brown the top) finished off the grits perfectly. We had attained our ideal baked grits: rich and flavorful, with a clear corn flavor.

Baked Cheese Grits

SERVES 6 TO 8

Old-fashioned grits are well worth the extra 10 minutes of cooking; instant grits will bake up too smooth and have an overprocessed flavor. Grits are ready when they are creamy and smooth but retain a slight coarseness. We prefer a very sharp aged cheddar, but feel free to use whatever extra-sharp cheddar you like. Or, for a heartier flavor, substitute smoked cheddar or smoked Gouda.

3	tablespoons unsalted butter
1	medium onion, chopped fine
4½	cups water
1½	cups heavy cream
¾	teaspoon Tabasco sauce
1	teaspoon salt
1½	cups old-fashioned grits (see the headnote)
8	ounces extra-sharp cheddar cheese, shredded (about 2⅔ cups)
4	large eggs, lightly beaten
¼	teaspoon ground black pepper

1. Adjust an oven rack to the lower-middle position and heat the oven to 350 degrees. Grease the bottom and sides of a 9 by 13-inch baking dish (or shallow casserole dish of similar size) with 1 tablespoon of the butter; set aside.

2. Melt the remaining 2 tablespoons butter in a large saucepan over medium heat. Add the onion and cook until softened but not browned, about 4 minutes. Stir in the water, cream, Tabasco, and salt; bring to a boil. Slowly whisk in the grits; reduce the heat to low and cook, stirring frequently, until the grits are thick and creamy, about 15 minutes.

3. Off the heat, whisk in 1⅔ cups of the cheese, the eggs, and pepper. Pour the mixture into the prepared baking dish and smooth the top with a rubber spatula. Sprinkle the remaining 1 cup cheese over the top. Bake until the top is browned and the grits are hot, 35 to 45 minutes. Cool for 10 minutes before serving.

➤ VARIATIONS

Baked Grits with Sausage and Red Pepper

This version of baked grits is a complete meal. Any type of sausage can be substituted for the breakfast sausage; just make sure to break it into ½-inch pieces.

Heat 1 teaspoon vegetable oil in a 10-inch, nonstick skillet over medium heat until shimmering. Add 1 pound breakfast sausage links, cut into ½-inch pieces, and cook until lightly browned, about 6 minutes. Transfer the sausage to a paper towel–lined plate and set aside. Pour off all but 1 teaspoon of the fat from the skillet and return to medium heat until shimmering. Add 1 medium red pepper, stemmed, seeded, and chopped fine, and cook until slightly softened, about 1½ minutes. Transfer the peppers to the plate with the sausage. Follow the recipe for Baked Cheese Grits, stirring the cooked sausage and peppers into the grits with the cheese and eggs in step 3.

Baked Grits with Shrimp and Chipotle Peppers

Nestling the shrimp into the grits protects them from overcooking and becoming tough while the grits are baking.

Follow the recipe for Baked Cheese Grits, making the following changes: Add 3 cloves minced garlic to the pan with the onion in step 2 and omit the Tabasco. Stir 3 minced canned chipotle chiles and 1 tablespoon adobo sauce into the grits with the cheese and eggs in step 3. After pouring the grits into the baking dish, nestle 1½ pounds extra-large (21 to 25 count) shrimp, peeled and deveined, into the grits so that they are no longer visible. Proceed as directed.

BAKED FRENCH TOAST CASSEROLE

FRENCH TOAST IS A DISH THAT NATURALLY ADAPTS to being cooked as a casserole. Baked French toast is simply a bread pudding, in which bread is soaked in an egg and dairy custard and then gently baked. And while baked French toast can be made many ways, after several taste tests, we favored a casserole-like French toast that is presented as layers of rich, creamy custard and toothsome pieces of bread, all covered by a sweet, candy-like topping of brown sugar, butter, and pecans. As such, this dish was much more than French toast or casserole—it was breakfast heaven. Hoping for a recipe that could be prepared the night before and then baked the following morning, we set out to closely examine each component of the dish and develop a casserole that would meet the parameters of our best recipes.

We first dealt with the choice of bread. Initially, we tried using tender, butter-enriched loaves of challah and brioche, but found that their soft, spongy crumb disintegrated and left the dish with little texture. Moving on to supermarket loaves, we tried using several different varieties of sliced white bread. The results from these tests, while improved, still left us yearning for something with a denser, heartier texture. Next up were loaves of Italian and French bread, both of which we purchased at the supermarket. The dense texture and chewy crust of these loaves was exactly what we were looking for. In the end, we preferred the slender loaves of the French bread since their smaller slices fit together easily without large gaps between them.

We next examined whether the crust should be removed from the bread. Trying two casseroles, one with the crust and one without, we found that we far preferred the one that was prepared with the crust. The French toast made with the crustless bread was too soft and lacked a caramelized flavor. We also found during our tests that the pudding was better if we dried the bread in a moderately hot oven, allowing it to toast slightly, before assembling the dish. The casserole made with the dried toasted bread had a firmer texture

and deeper flavor, while the dish made with the fresh bread was too soft and tasted flat.

For the custard, we tried using milk, half-and-half, heavy cream, and combinations of the three, and concluded that an equal proportion of milk and half-and-half provided us with a rich, silky liquid base that was neither too cloying nor too bland and watery. We made custards both with whole eggs and with a combination of whole eggs and yolks. Although we liked the richness of the whole egg–and–yolk combination, we preferred the firm consistency and eggy flavor that eight whole eggs gave the custard. We added a healthy dose of cinnamon to give the dish its familiar French toast flavor. In addition to cinnamon, nutmeg gave the dish a warm, nutty flavor and vanilla contributed an aromatic, floral sweetness. When it came to baking the custard, a relatively low oven temperature of 350 degrees was best. Going above 350 degrees, in order to shorten the baking time, only left us with curdled and grainy custards.

The topping of the French toast was the last component to address. In our initial test, tasters had preferred a topping that called for creaming brown sugar and butter with a little bit of corn syrup, into which we folded pecans. While we were happy with the flavor and texture this topping brought to the dish, there were two items that we wanted to address: the corn syrup and the nuts. Considering that the topping was mostly brown sugar, we wondered if the corn syrup might be redundant. Removing the corn syrup, we tried the French toast again, and were quite surprised by the result. We found that the corn syrup wasn't there necessarily for sweetness but to keep the sugar and butter from separating during baking. Without the corn syrup, the French toast turned into a greasy mess. We also considered using different types of nuts in the topping. We knew that pecans were certainly a good option, but we wanted to try some alternatives. Trying walnuts, almonds, and hazelnuts in the topping, we were surprised to find that only the walnuts were a suitable substitute. The almonds and hazelnuts, with their higher oil content, became overbrowned and bitter by the time the custard had cooked through. During our tests, we also discovered that creaming the butter and sugar was a superfluous step. Simply stirring all the ingredients together in a bowl until well blended worked just as well and didn't require the use of a mixer.

French Toast Casserole

SERVES 6 TO 8

The dish needs to be refrigerated at least 8 hours to attain the correct texture. Do not refrigerate for longer than 24 hours, or the bread will disintegrate. Assemble the topping just before baking. Walnuts can be substituted for the pecans.

I	(16-ounce) loaf French bread, sliced 1/2 inch thick
I	tablespoon unsalted butter, softened
8	large eggs
2	cups whole milk
2	cups half-and-half
I	tablespoon sugar
2	teaspoons vanilla extract
1/2	teaspoon ground cinnamon
1/2	teaspoon ground nutmeg

TOPPING

12	tablespoons unsalted butter, softened
3	tablespoons corn syrup
1 1/3	cups packed (9 1/3 ounces) light brown sugar
1 1/2	cups coarsely chopped pecans

1. Adjust the oven racks to the upper- and lower-middle positions and heat the oven to 325 degrees. Arrange the bread in a single layer on two baking sheets. Bake until dry and light golden brown, about 25 minutes, rotating the baking sheets front to back and top to bottom halfway

through the baking time. Transfer to a wire rack and cool completely.

2. Grease the bottom and sides of a 9 by 13-inch baking dish (or shallow casserole dish of similar size) with the butter. Layer the dried bread tightly in the prepared dish (you should have two layers).

3. Whisk the eggs, milk, half-and-half, sugar, vanilla, cinnamon, and nutmeg together in a large bowl. Pour evenly over the bread and press lightly to submerge. Cover tightly with plastic wrap and refrigerate for at least 8 hours or up to 24 hours.

4. FOR THE TOPPING: When ready to bake, adjust an oven rack to the middle position and heat the oven to 350 degrees. Mix the butter, corn syrup, and brown sugar together in a medium bowl with a rubber spatula until smooth and incorporated. Stir in the pecans.

5. Remove the casserole from the refrigerator and discard the plastic wrap. Spoon the topping over the casserole, then spread it into an even layer using the rubber spatula. Place the baking dish on a rimmed baking sheet and bake until puffed and golden, about 60 minutes. Cool for 10 minutes before serving.

➤ VARIATION

Baked Rum-Raisin French Toast Casserole

Combine 1½ cups raisins and 1 cup rum in a microwave-safe bowl, cover with plastic wrap, and poke several vent holes with the tip of a paring knife. Microwave on high until the rum comes to a boil, 1 to 2 minutes. Set aside, covered, until the raisins are plump, about 15 minutes. Drain thoroughly, discarding the rum (or save it for another use). Follow the recipe for French Toast Casserole, sprinkling the plumped raisins in between the two layers of bread in step 2.

7

SLOW-COOKER FAVORITES

TO SOME, A "SLOW-COOKED" MEAL MEANS setting aside precious weekend hours to spend time in the kitchen, tending and stirring a hearty braised roast or a rich, satisfying stew. To others, it means plugging in a slow cooker and getting dinner on the table without the labor or the baby-sitting required by traditional cooking methods. When the crockpot (a term coined by the Rival company) hit the culinary scene in the early 1970s, the allure of its catchphrase, "cooks all day while the cook's away," sent the appliance flying off store shelves. This original slow cooker offered busy families the promise of a slow-cooked labor of love, without the fastidious monitoring required for traditional stovetop preparations.

Many of the recipes that appeared in accompanying manuals cut a few too many culinary corners in the interest of speed. Canned soups, dehydrated broths, and overcooked vegetables did little to convince the savvy cook that the slow cooker warranted valuable real estate on a kitchen counter that was getting crowded with a microwave, food processor, and other new appliances (each with its own set of timesaving promises). One reason for the setback of slow cookers was the notion that all meat can cook for an indefinite period of time "while the cook's away." As we discovered early on in our testing, not everything can "cook all day" with good results.

Eventually, many of these avocado green and harvest gold appliances were relegated to the back of a closet, destined for the next tag sale. But culinary trends, ever fickle, have come full circle. Slow cookers are making a comeback, and with good reason. Busy cooks have realized that slow-cooker recipes, when made with quality ingredients and time-honored cooking techniques, can be as full flavored and well developed as their stovetop counterparts. Our goal was to develop recipes that could be started in the early morning (or better still, the night before) and be ready to serve by dinnertime. We also wanted the recipes to be suitable for a family-friendly weeknight supper or worry-free dinner party.

Today's sleek new slow cookers are much like the original crockpots, but come in a handier oval shape with removable inserts, and many have programmable features that you may or may not care to use. All the recipes in this chapter were designed for use in a 6-quart oval slow cooker.

Beef, chicken, pork, lamb, and vegetables all respond differently to the enclosed, moist-heat environment of the slow cooker and, as a result, have widely different cooking times. The wide window of cooking times for the same types of meat that were given in many slow-cooker recipes also perplexed us. How could it be that some pot roasts were done in seven hours, while others took 10 to 12 hours on the same setting? To solve the mystery, we conducted tests to determine the cooking characteristics of eight models of slow cookers. As it turns out, every slow cooker is different, and some models seem to run hotter than others—in fact, some cook hotter on low than others cook on high. (For more information on slow cookers, see page 299.) The recipes in this chapter all have a range of cooking times (for both high

SLOW-COOKER TIMER

WHEN TESTING SLOW COOKERS, WE FOUND that a timer and keep-warm function were valuable features, especially if you like to use your slow cooker when you're at work. Without these features, a traffic jam might mean overcooked pot roast or bloated baked beans. Unfortunately, several of our favorite models did not have these features. But Rival (inventor of the original crockpot) sells a separate timer that works with most slow-cookers, including the one you may already own.

Here's how the Smart-Part Programmable Module ($15) works. Simply plug the slow cooker into the Smart-Part, plug the Smart-Part into the wall outlet, and then program the Smart-Part. Cooking times are limited to four or six hours on high and eight or ten hours on low. Still, a restrictive timer is better than none, and this device will automatically turn the slow cooker to "warm" once the set time has elapsed.

and low where appropriate) based on our testing. Establishing cooking times for slow-cooker recipes is not an exact science, so take our guidelines as a good approximation of how long the cooking will likely take rather than as an absolute. The bottom line is that you need to get to know your slow cooker by trying it with a variety of recipes, in order to determine reliable cooking times. Tougher, well-marbled cuts of beef like chuck turned meltingly tender and flavorful after nine or ten hours on low heat in the slow cooker and proved to be ideal candidates for this appliance. Chicken, tender and lean by nature, was best when cooked on low heat, for only four to five hours. For this reason, our chicken recipes are more suitable for those who work at home, or for weekends when you are apt to be around in the afternoon to start the slow cooker. Pork and lamb fell in the middle of the road. Lean pork loin (see Braised Pork Loin with Sweet Potatoes, Orange, and Cilantro, page 314) was able to withstand six to seven hours on low heat. High heat toughened the meat and dried

EQUIPMENT: Slow Cookers

The slow cooker (better known as a crockpot, a name trade-marked by the Rival company) may be the only modern kitchen appliance that saves the cook time by using more of it rather than less. But gone are the days of merely picking out what size you need. We found 40 different models online, which begs the question, Is one slow cooker better than another? To find out, we rounded up eight leading models and put them through some very slow tests in the kitchen.

We prepared a simple beef chili on low temperature for six hours in each model and frankly, each chili was pretty good. We also prepared our Italian-Style Pot Roast (see the recipe on page 305) on high temperature in each model, leaving the meat in the cooker until the roast maintained an internal temperature of 200 degrees for an hour. All but one slow cooker managed this task, albeit at times ranging from seven to nine hours. Time, however, is not really the name of this game. It turns out that size matters, at least with our pot roast recipe. We recommend buying a slow cooker with a minimum capacity of 6 quarts. Anything smaller and you won't be able to fit a modest 5-pound roast, pork loin, or brisket.

Shape also matters. We found the round crock styles to be deeper than the oval crocks, and they heated more evenly. Such was the case with the Proctor Silex 7-quart round slow cooker ($39.95); a bare bones model (lacking a timer and power light) with a performance that outweighed its short-comings. That said, while the depth and shape of these round cookers made them perfect for submerging a roast in braising liquid, it proved a hindrance with recipes that required bulky, layered ingredients. Oval-shaped slow cookers, such as the Farberware Millennium 6-quart oval ($29.99) and the West Bend Versatility Cooker 6-quart oval ($39.99), proved to have the perfect amount of surface area for cooking layered split chicken breasts and large chunks of vegetables.

In addition to differences in size and shape, we noted a variety of features on slow cookers, some of which are quite helpful. A "keep warm" setting is sensible (it turns the heat down once the food is done), but only when paired with a timer. This way, if you are late getting home from work, dinner will still be fine. Without a timer, the keep warm function seems kind of useless. (See page 298 for information about a separate timer that most any slow cooker can be plugged into.) An "autostart" setting brings the crock up to temperature quickly before settling back into low temperature. We also liked models with power lights—without one, it's hard to tell if the slow cooker is on. As might be expected, a dishwasher-safe crock and lid are another plus; however, these weren't offered by our two favorite oval cookers, the Farberware and the West Bend.

Although we didn't find the perfect slow cooker, we did find some models good enough to recommend. Perhaps best of all, we found that spending more money didn't necessarily buy a better slow cooker.

THE BEST SLOW COOKER
The Farberware Millennium 6-quart oval ($29.99) won for its shape, performance, and modest price.

it out. Fattier pork cuts, like country-style ribs (see Country-Style Pork with Beans and Sausage, page 315) had a wider window of seven to eight hours on low or five to six hours on high. Our Asian-Spiced Pork Ribs (page 317), however, took a mere four hours to become tender.

PRACTICAL TIPS FOR SLOW-COOKER SUCCESS

- Use a 6-quart slow cooker to easily accommodate meat and vegetables that will serve at least six people.

- Trim as much excess fat as possible from meat.

- Brown meats thoroughly in a heavy-bottomed skillet or Dutch oven first for maximum flavor.

- Feel free to assemble and brown the ingredients the day before. Just cover and refrigerate meat and vegetables separately.

- Place hard or whole vegetables toward the edge of the cooker (where the heating elements reside) so that the vegetables will cook through, especially in chicken recipes (where the cooking time is short).

- Don't lift the lid during cooking: doing so extends the cooking time significantly.

- Stir in delicate fresh herbs in at the end of the cooking time to preserve their flavor.

- Make sure the electrical cord of your slow cooker does not touch the outside of the base unit, since it gets very hot.

As for the vegetables, we discovered several tricks to cooking them so that they were still flavorful and recognizable. We found that with long-cooking recipes (like our beef stew and pot roast recipes) the vegetables became mushy and almost unrecognizable after more than seven hours. The solution was to cut them into larger chunks to begin with or, in the case of potatoes, leave them whole (when using small red potatoes) and then cut them and stir them into the stew before serving. When we began testing the chicken dishes, which could withstand only four to five hours in the slow cooker, we found that we ended up with the reverse problem: crunchy vegetables. For these recipes, we solved the problem by arranging the vegetables carefully around the perimeter of the cooker, rather than mixing them in with the chicken and sauce. Since most slow cookers house the electrical elements around the side of the base unit, arranging the vegetables there gave them the added heat needed to cook through by the time the chicken was tender.

In addition to sorting out how various meats and vegetables would fare in the slow cooker, we realized in our initial testing that classic cooking techniques, however time consuming, are needed to produce a dinner worth coming home to. Many recipes simply dumped raw ingredients into the cooker and dismissed the important steps of browning ingredients and deglazing the pan, steps that we found were crucial for an intensely flavored braising medium. Without this, recipes like beef stew and pot roast were watery and flavorless. Browning meat serves two purposes in a recipe destined for a stovetop or the slow cooker: It gives the meat an attractive caramelized exterior, and it sets the stage for a flavorful foundation for the braising liquid. The more flavor you can coax from ingredients at the onset of cooking, the more rewarding your final meal will be. Using a heavy hand with spices and adding fresh herbs at the end of the cooking time to preserve their flavor can make a big difference in the level of flavor that ends up on your plate. If the thought of searing meat and sautéing vegetables before the sun comes up leaves you cold, the good news is that with a little organization, the majority of the work can be done the night before. In the morning, all you need to do is assemble the prepped ingredients in the slow cooker and plug it in.

The time constraints that changed the way Americans viewed cooking years ago have only intensified. In fact, given today's fast-paced world, the efficiency and reliability of the slow cooker is what sustains its popularity. The question "What's for dinner?" needn't haunt you all day when, with a minimum of advance planning and preparation, the flavors of an old-fashioned meal can be waiting for you when you come home from a long day at work. The culinary aromatherapy that wafts through the house might be reason enough to make use of your slow cooker. What may have been relegated to the back of your storage closet deserves a second look, and could very well re-emerge as a busy cook's best friend.

SLOW-COOKER SAFETY

FOOD SAFETY EXPERTS, INCLUDING THE USDA, state that meats must reach 140 degrees within two hours in order to be out of the danger zone. Most slow-cooker manuals (as well as many cookbooks) ignore this recommendation in their recipes. We believe that searing large cuts of beef or pork before placing them in the slow cooker mitigates this safety issue since most bacteria reside on the exterior of the meat. With chicken, however, this is not true, which is why we have chosen to use chicken parts only, not whole chickens, in our recipes. As for the autostart feature on some cookers, while it is true that they can jumpstart the cooking process by getting things hotter sooner, in our testing we found that it still took four hours to bring a roast out of the danger zone (40 to 140 degrees). In short, while we feel our techniques and choices of cuts of meat make these recipes as safe as possible, if food safety is your primary concern, then a slow cooker should not be your appliance of choice.

GUINNESS BEEF STEW

A GREAT BEEF STEW REQUIRES LONG HOURS of slow and steady moist-heat cooking to tenderize the meat and marry the flavors of the vegetables and broth. The cooking time required to make beef stew means that for most of us, it's relegated to weekends when there's more time to spend in the kitchen. That is, unless you have a slow cooker, which, with its moist-heat environment and steady temperatures, is perfect for delivering a great beef stew any night of the week.

The problems with the slow-cooker beef stew recipes we tested were numerous. Some recipes cooked the stew on low for six hours, others on low for 12 hours, both with disastrous results. The beef in these recipes ranged from tough and dry to tender but flavorless. And the accompanying broths were either pale and pasty, or flavorless with the viscosity of dishwater. We were determined to develop a robust and flavorful beef stew that could be put together with a minimum of fuss and would be ready and waiting after a long day at work. We also wanted to resolve the timing mystery: How long does it really take to cook a beef stew that is tender, flavorful, and moist?

We began our testing with the goal of developing a hearty beef stew in the Irish tradition; that is, using Guinness Stout instead of wine and parsnips in addition to potatoes. First we focused on which cut of beef would work best in the slow cooker. We quickly ruled out top and bottom round as too lean because they yielded dry, tough meat when stewed. Our next options were beef chuck and prepackaged beef chunks labeled "beef for stew" at the supermarket. The chuck roast, which we cut up ourselves, was flavorful, tender, and juicy. After many hours in the slow cooker, the "beef for stew" meat was either stringy and chewy, or just plain bland. The reason for this is simple. Prepackaged stewing beef is often made up of irregularly shaped end pieces from different cuts of meat that can't be sold as steaks or roasts. As a result, they may vary in texture and size and so cook inconsistently, giving you little control over the quality of your final stew. So with chuck roast as our cut of choice, we began examining recipes that had failed in our initial tests because they delivered pale and flavorless stews.

Most of the beef stew recipes we found simply dumped the beef and vegetables into the slow cooker and skipped the step of browning the beef and sautéing the vegetables first. All the recipes that had skipped this browning step were lackluster, to say the least. While we recognized that slow-cooker meals were meant to be easier to prepare and more convenient, in our estimation, these dump-and-cook recipes weren't worth the bother or the expense. We knew that there had to be a better approach. Searing meat takes only minutes (and can be done the night before) and builds the flavor foundation of the stew by leaving caramelized bits on the skillet bottom that can then be incorporated into the stew by a quick deglazing with broth or wine. This adds both flavor and valuable color to the stew, and is a step that we think is key.

Satisfied that we had a solid beginning for the stew, we turned our attention to the vegetables. Onions and carrots are essential to a beef stew in our opinion, and we decided to add parsnips as well, which gave the dish a nutty, sweet flavor that tasters liked. Next we tackled the potatoes, since any Irish stew worth its salt absolutely must have them. When we cut them into chunks and added them to the stew, they were watery and nearly broken apart by the time the stew was cooked. We were after a stew that was packed with tender but substantial chunks or wedges of potatoes, so we tried adding them whole to the stew and then cutting them up just before serving. This worked perfectly, and we found that they cooked through just fine and retained their creaminess and integrity.

Next we focused on the quantity of Guinness to add to the stew. With its characteristic malty flavor, Guinness can turn a sauce or stew bitter if used in excess. So we started with three 12-ounce bottles and then gradually worked our way down to just two. The only problem was that the bitterness of the stout still overshadowed the flavors of the root vegetables and the beef. To counteract the bitterness, we tried adding molasses to the stew but found its taste too strong. Brown sugar, however, provided just the right touch of caramelized sweetness and proved to be the right foil for the strong taste of the stout. To augment the Guinness and give the stew the right amount of liquid, we added beef broth, but found its flavor left a tinny aftertaste. Using equal parts of beef broth and chicken broth gave us the beefy flavor we were seeking, without the tinny taste. To add more complexity to the broth we added rosemary, thyme, and bay leaves in our initial tests. Rosemary turned bitter after hours of cooking, imparting a medicinal flavor to the stew, but thyme and bay leaves held up well after long periods of time in the slow cooker and flavored the stew just perfectly.

Our last challenge was to thicken the stew. With a slow cooker, moisture from the meat and vegetables is released during the long cooking time and trapped in the enclosed environment. So it made sense to us that instead of adding a thickener at the beginning of the cooking process, as many stovetop recipes do, we should add it at the end of the cooking time, when it was easier to determine accurately how much thickening the stew would require. Cooking the potatoes whole, then quartering them and stirring them back into the stew gave us a jumpstart on the thickening process by releasing starch and absorbing liquid. But the stew still needed further thickening, so we tested slurries made from a mixture of flour and beef broth, and cornstarch and beef broth. The stew thickened with the cornstarch had an unappealing and slippery texture. Tasters preferred the stew that was thickened with the slurry of flour and broth, which made it just thick enough to coat a spoon without being either pasty or slimy. It took ½ cup of flour mixed with ½ cup of broth to make a slurry that could thicken the stew to the proper consistency.

To clarify the right cooking time for the stew, we tested recipes cooked on low for six, eight, 10, and 12 hours. After six and eight hours, the beef was still a bit tough and chewy. At nine to 10 hours in the slow cooker, the meat was tender and the vegetables were soft and flavorful. And since we wondered how forgiving this slow-cooker favorite would be if you happened to get stuck in traffic, we tested it after 11 hours and it still tasted great (although the vegetables were quite soft).

Guinness Beef Stew

SERVES 6 TO 8

TIME: 9 to 10 hours on low or 6 to 7 hours on high

There is usually a lot of fat and gristle to trim away from a chuck roast, so don't be surprised if you trim nearly 1½ pounds off the roast. Guinness is a traditional Irish stout; however, any stout can be used.

5	pounds boneless chuck-eye roast, trimmed and cut into 1½-inch cubes (see the illustrations on page 148)
	Salt and ground black pepper
2	tablespoons vegetable oil
2	medium onions, chopped medium
3	cups Guinness Stout
1	tablespoon light or dark brown sugar
1	teaspoon dried thyme
2	bay leaves
2	cups low-sodium chicken broth
2	cups low-sodium beef broth
5	medium carrots, peeled and cut into 1-inch chunks
1	pound parsnips, peeled and cut into 1-inch chunks
2	pounds Red Bliss potatoes (about 6 medium), scrubbed
½	cup all-purpose flour
2	tablespoons minced fresh parsley leaves

1. Dry the beef thoroughly with paper towels, then season generously with salt and pepper. Heat 2 teaspoons of the oil in a 12-inch skillet over medium-high heat until just smoking. Distribute half of the beef evenly in the skillet and cook, without stirring, until well browned on one side, about 4 minutes. Stir the meat and continue to cook, stirring occasionally, until completely browned, 4 to 6 minutes longer. Transfer the beef to a slow cooker. Return the skillet to medium-high heat and heat 2 more teaspoons oil until just smoking. Brown the remaining beef and transfer it to the slow cooker.

2. Return the skillet to medium heat and heat the remaining 2 teaspoons oil until shimmering. Add the onions and ¼ teaspoon salt; cook, stirring occasionally, until the onions are softened and lightly browned, about 5 minutes. Add the stout, brown sugar, thyme, and bay leaves; turn the heat to high and bring to a boil, scraping the browned bits off the skillet bottom. Pour into the slow cooker.

3. Stir the chicken broth and 1½ cups of the beef broth into the slow cooker. Add the carrots and parsnips to the slow cooker. Nestle the carrots, parsnips, and potatoes around the edges of the slow cooker (see the illustration on page 323). Cover and cook, on either low or high, until the meat is tender, 9 to 10 hours on low or 6 to 7 hours on high.

4. When the meat is tender, remove the potatoes using a slotted spoon and transfer them to a carving board; allow them to cool slightly. Set the slow cooker to high (if necessary). Whisk the flour with the remaining ½ cup beef broth until smooth, then stir it into the slow cooker. Quarter the potatoes and return them to the slow cooker. Continue to cook on high until the sauce is thickened and no longer tastes of flour, 10 to 15 minutes longer. Stir in the parsley. Season to taste with salt and pepper before serving.

➤ VARIATION

Hearty Beef Stew

TIME: 9 to 10 hours on low or 6 to 7 hours on high

To keep the potatoes from falling apart during the long cooking time, put them into the slow cooker whole and nestle them around the edges of the cooker, where the heating coils reside.

5	pounds boneless chuck-eye roast, trimmed and cut into 1½-inch cubes (see the illustrations on page 148)
	Salt and ground black pepper
2	tablespoons vegetable oil
2	medium onions, chopped medium
3	medium garlic cloves, minced or pressed through a garlic press
1	cup dry red wine
2	cups low-sodium chicken broth
2	cups low-sodium beef broth
1	teaspoon dried thyme
2	bay leaves
2	pounds Red Bliss potatoes (about 6 medium), scrubbed

5   medium carrots, peeled and cut into 1-inch
     chunks
½   cup all-purpose flour
1   cup frozen peas, thawed
2   tablespoons minced fresh parsley leaves

1. Dry the beef thoroughly with paper towels, then season generously with salt and pepper. Heat 2 teaspoons of the oil in a 12-inch skillet over medium-high heat until just smoking. Distribute half of the beef in the skillet and cook, without stirring, until well browned on one side, about 4 minutes. Stir the meat and continue to cook, stirring occasionally, until completely browned, 4 to 6 minutes longer. Transfer it to a slow cooker. Return the skillet to medium-high heat and heat 2 more teaspoons oil until just smoking. Brown the remaining beef and transfer it to the slow cooker.

2. Return the skillet to medium heat and heat the remaining 2 teaspoons oil until shimmering. Add the onions and ¼ teaspoon salt; cook, stirring occasionally, until the onions are softened and lightly browned, about 5 minutes. Add the garlic and cook until fragrant, about 30 seconds. Add the red wine; turn the heat to high and bring to a boil, scraping the browned bits off the skillet bottom. Pour into the slow cooker.

3. Stir the chicken broth, 1½ cups of the beef broth, thyme, and bay leaves into the slow cooker. Following the illustrations on page 323, nestle the potatoes and carrots around the edges of the slow cooker. Cover and cook, on either low or high, until the meat is tender, 9 to 10 hours on low or 6 to 7 hours on high.

4. When the meat is tender, remove the potatoes using a slotted spoon and transfer to a carving board; allow them to cool slightly. Set the slow cooker to high (if necessary). Whisk the flour with the remaining ½ cup beef broth until smooth, then stir into the slow cooker. Quarter the potatoes and return them to the slow cooker. Continue to cook on high until the sauce is thickened and no longer tastes of flour, 10 to 15 minutes longer. Stir in the peas and parsley. Season to taste with salt and pepper before serving.

ITALIAN-STYLE POT ROAST

POT ROAST RECIPES APPEAR IN EVERY COOK-book featuring slow cookers and are highlighted as "starter" recipes in the ubiquitous manuals that accompany the appliance. Touted as the ultimate one-pot meal, few warrant ever making again. After testing many of these recipes, what we encountered were pitifully small chunks of pallid meat floating in a watery liquid with hopelessly overcooked vegetables bobbing on the surface. Many pot roasts were cooked on low for a mere five or six hours, resulting in rubbery, tough meat. Others were cooked for so long on low that they literally fell apart when we tried to lift them from the pot. Our goal was a tender piece of beef (large enough to feed six) with a full-flavored and substantial gravy. We also wanted to put a bit of an Italian spin on the traditional American pot roast recipe by using red wine, oregano, tomatoes, and dried porcini mushrooms.

The slow cooker seemed to us to be the perfect environment for essentially braising a pot roast until fork-tender. The meat for a tender, flavorful pot roast should be well marbled, with enough fat and connective tissue to provide the dish with flavor and moisture. After testing cuts from the sirloin, round, and chuck, we chose the boneless chuck-eye roast. Unlike the other cuts tested, the chuck-eye roast was moist and flavorful and had none of the unpleasant dry, tough qualities of the others.

Next we needed to address the liquid that would serve as the braising medium for the pot roast. To get the most flavor from the beef and create a solid foundation for the braising liquid, we knew that browning the meat first in a little oil over high heat was all that was needed. This step caramelized the exterior of the beef and lent the gravy the flavor and color we were looking for. To the browned bits that we had created in the skillet, we added red wine, broth, tomatoes, and tomato paste. This enhanced the flavor profile by adding texture and acidity to the broth. For herbs, we chose bay leaf, dried oregano (fresh herbs just disappeared after long cooking), and red pepper flakes for heat. At this point in our testing, the broth was tasty but not as deeply flavored as we were hoping for. In our quest for deeper flavor, we tried adding smoky bacon to our skillet after browning the meat, and then browning the onion, carrot, and garlic in the rendered fat. One taster suggested adding dried porcini mushrooms, since their robust flavor would likely add a depth of flavor to the dish that could withstand the long hours in the slow cooker. Generally, dried porcinis are soaked in hot water or broth before being used in any recipe, both to clean and to soften them. But in this case (where the porcinis would have plenty of time to soften up during the long cooking process) we simply rinsed them and added them directly to the slow cooker; this worked just fine.

During our testing process, we cooked more than 100 pounds of beef chuck roast, and it became clear to us that we needed to begin with a roast that weighed more than 3½ pounds. By the time a 3½-pound roast was tender, we were left with barely enough meat to serve four people. Testing showed that the average chuck roast shrank by as much as two pounds during the prolonged cooking time. To compensate for this we decided on a starting weight of 5½ to six pounds. Previous pot roast tests had shown that reaching and sustaining an internal temperature of 200 to 210 degrees was necessary for a meltingly tender piece of meat. To determine how long it would take a 5- or 6-pound roast to reach that point in the slow cooker, we conducted tests using temperature probes inserted into the center of roasts cooked on both high and low. The ideal time turned out to be nine to 10 hours on low, or six to seven hours on high.

Confident that weight, time, and temperature were accurate, we moved on to the component that promised to make this dish worth coming to the table for: the gravy. The braising liquid had great flavor and was a good jumping-off point for the final gravy. The only problem was that it was too thin to earn to earn the title of gravy. We wanted it to coat the sliced meat and be thick enough to fill the well in our mashed potatoes. First we tried straining the cooking liquid, discarding the vegetables, and adding a mixture of flour and water to the pot. This thickened the juices but left behind the sort of pasty-textured gravy that we were trying to avoid. One test cook suggested that the vegetables that had been discarded might well serve as a thickener for the broth in place of the flour. After removing the pot roast from the slow cooker, we pureed the vegetables and broth (an immersion blender made this task very easy) and then finished the resulting gravy with a generous amount of fresh parsley. We suggest slicing the roast thin, across the grain, and serving it with either garlic mashed potatoes or polenta. And, of course, lots of gravy!

Italian-Style Pot Roast

SERVES 6 TO 8

TIME: 9 to 10 hours on low or 6 to 7 hours on high

Our favorite cut for pot roast is a chuck-eye roast. Many markets sell this roast with elastic netting, which should be removed. Re-tie the roast using heavy-duty butcher's twine. Leftover pot roast can make a great second meal if you shred the meat and toss it with the leftover gravy and some egg noodles.

8	ounces (about 8 slices) bacon, chopped
	Vegetable oil
I	boneless chuck-eye roast (5 to 6 pounds), tied
	Salt and ground black pepper
2	medium onions, chopped medium
4	medium carrots, peeled and cut into 1-inch chunks
6	medium garlic cloves, sliced thin
I½	cups dry red wine
2	tablespoons tomato paste
½	ounce dried porcini mushrooms, rinsed
½	teaspoon red pepper flakes
2	teaspoons dried oregano leaves
2	bay leaves
I	(28-ounce) can crushed tomatoes
I¾	cups low-sodium beef broth
2	cups low-sodium chicken broth
4	tablespoons chopped fresh parsley leaves

1. Cook the bacon in a 12-inch skillet over medium heat, stirring occasionally, until brown and crisp, about 5 minutes. Remove the bacon with a slotted spoon, drain it briefly on paper towels, and then transfer it to a slow cooker. Pour off and reserve the bacon fat. (You should have at

least 4 teaspoons. If not, substitute vegetable oil for the missing bacon fat.)

2. Dry the roast thoroughly with paper towels, then season generously with salt and pepper. Return the skillet to high heat and heat 2 teaspoons of the reserved bacon fat until just smoking. Brown the roast thoroughly on all sides, reducing the heat if the fat begins to smoke heavily, 8 to 10 minutes. Transfer to the slow cooker.

3. Return the skillet to medium heat and heat the remaining 2 teaspoons reserved bacon fat until shimmering. Add the onions, carrots, and garlic; cook, stirring occasionally, until the vegetables are lightly browned, about 4 minutes. Add the wine, tomato paste, porcini mushrooms, red pepper flakes, oregano, and bay leaves, scraping the browned bits off the skillet bottom; turn the heat to high and simmer until the wine has reduced by half, 8 to 10 minutes. Add the tomatoes and bring to a boil. Pour the sauce into the slow cooker.

4. Add the beef and chicken broths to the slow cooker. Cover and cook, on either low or high, until the meat is tender, 9 to 10 hours on low or 6 to 7 hours on high. Transfer the beef to a carving board and tent loosely with foil to keep warm. Allow the cooking liquid to settle for about 5 minutes, then use a wide spoon to skim the fat off the surface. Discard the bay leaves. Puree the liquid and vegetables, in batches, in a blender or a food processor fitted with the steel blade until smooth. (Alternatively, use an immersion blender and puree in the slow-cooker insert until smooth.) Stir in the parsley and season to taste with salt and pepper. Slice the roast into ½-inch-thick slices, arrange on a warmed serving platter, and pour ½ cup of the sauce over the meat. Serve, passing the remaining sauce separately.

> VARIATION

Country-Style Pot Roast with Gravy

TIME: 9 to 10 hours on low or 6 to 7 hours on high

Boneless chuck roast is essential for tender meat. In most markets, you will have to order a large 5- to 6-pound chuck roast. Alternatively, use two 3-pound roasts.

I	boneless chuck-eye roast (5 to 6 pounds), tied
	Salt and ground black pepper

4	teaspoons vegetable oil
3	medium onions, chopped medium
I	large celery rib, chopped medium
4	medium carrots, peeled and cut into 1-inch chunks
6	medium garlic cloves, minced or pressed through a garlic press
I	cup dry red wine
I	(28-ounce) can crushed tomatoes
2	cups low-sodium chicken broth
1¾	cups low-sodium beef broth
½	teaspoon red pepper flakes
I	teaspoon dried oregano
3	bay leaves
I	teaspoon dried thyme
2	tablespoons chopped fresh parsley leaves

1. Dry the roast thoroughly with paper towels, then season generously with salt and pepper. Heat 2 teaspoons of the oil in a 12-inch skillet over medium-high heat until just smoking. Brown the roast thoroughly on all sides, reducing the heat if the fat begins to smoke heavily, 8 to 10 minutes. Transfer it to a slow cooker.

2. Return the skillet to medium heat and heat the remaining 2 teaspoons oil until shimmering. Add the onions, celery, and carrots; cook, stirring occasionally, until the vegetables are lightly browned, 4 minutes. Stir in the garlic and cook until fragrant, about 30 seconds. Add the wine, scraping the browned bits off the skillet bottom, and cook until almost dry, 8 to 10 minutes. Add the tomatoes, broths, red pepper flakes, bay leaves, and thyme; bring to a boil. Pour into the slow cooker.

3. Cover and cook, on either low or high, until the meat is tender, 9 to 10 hours on low, or 6 to 7 hours on high. Transfer the beef to a carving board and tent loosely with foil to keep warm. Allow the cooking liquid to settle for about 5 minutes, then use a wide spoon to skim the fat off the surface. Discard the bay leaves. Puree the liquid and vegetables, in batches, in a blender or a food processor fitted with the steel blade until smooth. (Alternatively, use an immersion blender and puree in the slow-cooker insert until smooth.) Stir in the parsley and season to taste with salt

and pepper. Slice the roast into ½-inch-thick slices, arrange on a warmed serving platter, and pour ½ cup of the sauce over the meat. Serve, passing the remaining sauce separately.

BRAISED BRISKET WITH ONION GRAVY

BEEF BRISKET IS BY NATURE A FLAVORFUL BUT tough cut of meat that requires hours of slow, even cooking to make it palatable. This quality alone made it a shoo-in for our slow-cooker chapter, and we found plenty of recipes that extolled the virtues of brisket in the slow cooker. The problems became apparent after the first test, which delivered dry, stringy meat that was more often than not battleship gray. Sauces ranged from flavorless and watery to achingly sweet with ketchup, molasses, or brown sugar. Cooking times ranged from eight hours to a whopping 18 hours on the low setting. What we wanted was a slow-cooked brisket that was juicy and tender with a rich, flavorful sauce.

Whole briskets weigh roughly 12 to 13 pounds, yet butchers usually sell them cut in half or even smaller. If cut in half, one end of the brisket is called the "first" or "flat" cut, and the other is called the "second" or "point" cut (see the illustrations on page 155). We prefer pieces from the second (point) cut because they tend to be thicker and more tender and flavorful. Braising requires that the meat lay flat in a covered pot, and our 6-quart oval slow cooker was the ideal vessel for our 3-pound brisket. (If the brisket folds up the sides a bit, don't worry. It will shrink quite a bit in the first few hours of cooking.) The method for starting a slow-cooker brisket is the same as for cooking on the stovetop or in the oven. To avoid the unappealing gray, boiled-meat color, the meat must first be well browned, which also sets up the foundation for the sauce.

Many brisket recipes we researched based the sauce on the flavor of caramelized onions. We gave this idea a try, finding it easy to lightly caramelize some onions in the drippings left over from browning the meat. To build a flavorful, well-rounded sauce around the onions, it was important to add both brown sugar and tomato paste to develop the sweet onion flavor. A combination of beef and chicken broth also proved crucial, as did the addition of red wine, garlic, bay leaves, and fresh thyme. A dash of cider vinegar in the sauce brightened the flavors and added a refreshing contrast to the sweetness of the onions and brown sugar. A light thickening of the liquid at the end of the cooking time with a slurry of flour and beef broth gave the sauce the body we were seeking. With an ample amount of sauce to serve alongside the thinly sliced beef, no one would ever complain that this slow-cooker brisket is stringy, dry, or flavorless.

Braised Brisket with Onion Gravy

SERVES 4

TIME: 8 to 9 hours on low or 5 to 6 hours on high

A whole brisket weighs roughly 12 to 13 pounds, but is usually sold cut in half or even smaller. We prefer to use the brisket half that's known as the second cut, or point cut, which tends to be thicker and more tender and flavorful.

I	beef brisket (about 3 to 3½ pounds), preferably point cut (see the illustration on page 155), trimmed of excess fat
	Salt and ground black pepper
4	teaspoons vegetable oil
4	large yellow onions, halved and sliced thin
6	medium garlic cloves, minced or pressed through a garlic press
½	cup dry red wine
1¾	cups low-sodium beef broth
I	cup low-sodium chicken broth
2	tablespoons brown sugar
I	teaspoon tomato paste
4	bay leaves
I	teaspoon dried thyme
¼	cup all-purpose flour
2	tablespoons cider vinegar

1. Dry the brisket thoroughly with paper towels, then season generously with salt and pepper.

Heat 2 teaspoons of the oil in a 12-inch skillet over medium-high heat until just smoking. Brown the brisket thoroughly on both sides, reducing the heat if the fat begins to smoke heavily, 8 to 10 minutes. Transfer it to a slow cooker.

2. Return the skillet to medium heat and heat the remaining 2 teaspoons oil until shimmering. Add the onions and ¼ teaspoon salt; cook, scraping the browned bits from the pan bottom, until the onions are softened and lightly browned, about 10 minutes. Stir in the garlic and cook until fragrant, about 30 seconds. Stir in the wine, scraping the browned bits off the skillet bottom, and cook until almost dry, about 1 minute. Add 1 cup of the beef broth, the chicken broth, brown sugar, tomato paste, bay leaves, and thyme; bring to a boil. Transfer to the slow cooker.

3. Cover and cook, on either low or high, until a dinner fork can be slid in and out of the brisket with little resistance, 8 to 9 hours on low or 5 to 6 hours on high.

4. Transfer the brisket to a carving board and tent loosely with foil to keep warm. Discard the bay leaves. Set the slow cooker to high (if necessary). Whisk the flour with the remaining ¾ cup of beef broth until smooth, then stir it into the slow cooker. Continue to cook on high until the sauce has thickened and no longer tastes of flour, 10 to 15 minutes longer. Stir in the vinegar and season with salt and pepper to taste. Slice the brisket thin across the grain. Arrange it on a warmed serving platter and pour about ½ cup of the sauce over the meat. Serve, passing the remaining sauce separately.

CHILI CON CARNE

SLOW-COOKER RECIPES SEEM TO BE DIVIDED on what style of chili is best: ground beef chili, or chunky-style beef chili. We made our decision for this slow-cooker version right off the bat. Ground beef chili takes a mere two hours on the stovetop, and although it can be done in the slow cooker, we wanted to develop a recipe for a hearty chili, with stew-size chunks of meat that would tenderize and develop full flavors in the time it takes to put in a full day at the office.

We followed a recipe with ingredients typical of many slow-cooker versions: beef stew meat (we chose beef chuck, based on results with our slow-cooker beef stew recipe), onions and garlic, canned chiles, tomato puree, chili powder, cumin, and water. The resulting chili was watery, flat, and harsh and lacked the authentic flavors we were seeking. We turned to a stovetop recipe for chili that featured bacon, two different chiles that were freshly roasted, and masa harina (ground corn flour) for thickener. This chili was spicy-hot, rich, and beefy, with a great smoky flavor. With this as our working recipe, we set out to adapt its flavors for the slow cooker.

We began by browning the bacon until it was crisp and all of the fat had been rendered. We then used that fat to sear the beef chuck and brown the onions, garlic, and fresh jalapeño chiles. For spices, we turned to ground options for speed, but missed the deep flavors of the roasted chiles. We found that by sautéing the chili powder and ground cumin with the onions, we were able to release their deep flavors without the time-consuming roasting and grinding required in our original stovetop recipe. We experimented with quantities of each spice and settled on 3 tablespoons of chili powder and 2 tablespoons of cumin. That may look like a heavy-handed amount, but we found that the intensity of ground spices diminished during the long cooking time, and a large quantity was definitely needed to compensate for that. To balance the slight bitterness of the chili powder, we added 2 teaspoons of sugar.

At this point the flavors were nearly there, but we felt the chili was still one-dimensional. We thought of the deep, smoky flavor of chipotles (smoked jalapeño peppers), which are available dried whole, powdered, canned in adobo sauce, or pickled. After trying them all, we found that we preferred the flavor of those in adobo sauce, which is made of tomato sauce, vinegar, and a blend of other spices.

For the tomato component of the chili, we tested diced tomatoes, tomato puree, and crushed tomatoes; the crushed tomatoes gave a much-needed boost to the body of the chili, without being intrusive. To strengthen the flavor, we replaced the water that had been present in our original test with chicken broth, with great results. But our chili was now soupier than we liked because in a slow cooker, the liquid has little opportunity to condense and concentrate the flavors. Since we had masa harina in the test kitchen, we used it to thicken the chili, and while it worked beautifully, we knew that it might not be something home cooks would be apt to find or buy, especially since it is only available in 5-pound bags. We tried ground tortilla chips, but they left a greasy film on the surface of the chili. Corn tortillas, which are made from masa harina, turned out to be the answer. They are available in the refrigerator section of most grocery stores in 6-inch rounds and, unlike the chips, are not deep fried. We first softened the tortillas in chicken broth, then ground the mixture in the food processor fitted with a steel blade and added this smooth puree to the chili at the end of the cooking time. But while this trick did thicken the chili, it gave it an unpleasant uncooked corn flavor. So we added it to the chili at the start of the cooking process instead, and it infused a subtle corn flavor throughout the chili and left us with one less thing to do to get dinner on the table.

Chili Con Carne

SERVES 6 TO 8

TIME: 9 to 10 hours on low or 6 to 7 hours on high

There is usually a lot of fat and gristle to trim away from a chuck roast, so don't be surprised if you trim off nearly 1½ pounds (see the illustrations on page 148). Serve with tortilla chips, corn tortillas or tamales, rice, biscuits, or plain crackers and top with chopped minced white onion, diced avocado, or shredded cheddar or Jack cheese.

8	ounces bacon (about 8 slices), chopped
	Vegetable oil
4	pounds chuck roast, trimmed and cut into 1½-inch cubes
	Salt and ground black pepper
1	medium onion, chopped medium
3	jalapeño chiles, stemmed, seeded, and minced
5	medium garlic cloves, minced or pressed through a garlic press
3	tablespoons chili powder
2	tablespoons ground cumin
1	(28-ounce) can crushed tomatoes
2	canned chipotle chiles in adobo sauce, minced to a paste
2	teaspoons sugar
6	(6-inch) fresh corn tortillas, torn into 2-inch pieces
4	cups low-sodium chicken broth
3	(15.5-ounce) cans red kidney or pinto beans, drained and rinsed (optional)
2	tablespoons lime juice
¼	cup chopped fresh cilantro leaves
1	cup sour cream

1. Cook the bacon in a 12-inch skillet over medium heat, stirring occasionally, until brown and crisp, about 5 minutes. Remove the bacon with a slotted spoon, drain it briefly on paper towels, and then transfer it to a slow cooker. Pour off and reserve the bacon fat. (You should have at least 2 tablespoons. If not, substitute vegetable oil for the missing bacon fat.)

2. Dry the beef thoroughly with paper towels, then season generously with salt and pepper. Return the skillet to medium-high heat and heat 2 teaspoons of the reserved bacon fat until just smoking. Distribute half of the meat evenly in the skillet and cook, without stirring, until well browned on one side, about 4 minutes. Stir the meat and continue to cook, stirring occasionally, until completely browned, 4 to 6 minutes longer. Transfer it to the slow cooker. Return the skillet to medium-high heat and heat 2 more teaspoons bacon fat until just smoking. Brown the remaining beef and transfer to the slow cooker.

3. Return the skillet to medium heat and heat the remaining 2 teaspoons bacon fat until shimmering. Add the onion, jalapeños, garlic, chili powder, and cumin; cook, stirring occasionally, until the onion is lightly browned, about 10 minutes. Stir in the tomatoes, chipotles, and sugar; turn the heat to high and bring to a boil. Pour into the slow cooker.

4. Combine the tortillas and 1 cup of the chicken broth together in a microwave-proof

309

bowl and heat in the microwave on high until mushy, 1 to 3 minutes. Puree the mixture in a blender or in a food processor fitted with the steel blade until smooth, about 1 minute. Stir into the slow cooker.

5. Add the remaining 3 cups chicken broth to the slow cooker and stir to combine. Cover and cook, on either low or high, until meat is tender, 9 to 10 hours on low or 6 to 7 hours on high. Stir in the beans (if using) during the last hour of cooking. Before serving, stir in the lime juice and cilantro, and season with salt and pepper to taste. Serve, passing the sour cream separately.

BEEF BARLEY SOUP

BEEF BARLEY SOUP IS THE PERFECT COLD-weather comfort food. What could be better than tender beef married with vegetables, flavorful broth, and toothsome barley? It is the ultimate "good for what ails you" soup. The problem with many recipes we tested was the palpable lack of flavor, minuscule amounts of beef, and textures ranging from gruel to sludge. We knew we'd need to come up with a recipe that yielded lots of beef, an intensely flavored broth, and just the right amount of barley to make this a satisfying one-pot meal.

We started with a hefty 3-pound chuck roast that we thoroughly trimmed and cut into bite-size (½-inch) cubes. We found it necessary to sear the meat in batches in a hot skillet. If too much meat was added to the skillet at once, or if the skillet was not sufficiently hot, the beef released moisture and began to steam in its own juices. After cooking the meat in two batches, we were left with a satisfying brown fond from which to continue to build our soup. We added onions and carrots to the skillet to brown and contribute more flavor to the foundation in place. We then deglazed our pan with a good-quality dry red wine and scraped up the tasty browned bits from the bottom. Then we added diced tomatoes and turned our attention to the remaining liquid component of our soup, which in many recipes had been water.

A great soup deserves good stock, not water, but because of the time involved in making home-made stock, it was not an option. As this was a beef soup, we naturally tested canned beef broth, but disliked its tinny aftertaste. When we combined it with an equal amount of chicken broth, the results were far better. Chicken broth, beef broth, and the flavor added by the well-browned beef and vegetables gave us the deep flavors we wanted.

The final component to add to our soup was barley. Pearl barley, the most commonly available variety, has had its tough outer hulls removed, which makes it a fairly quick-cooking grain. Since pearl barley can absorb two to three times its volume of cooking liquid, we knew that we needed to be judicious in the quantity we added to the soup. After all, we were making soup, not a side dish. After some experimenting, we found that ⅔ cup was the ideal amount to lend a pleasing texture to the soup without overfilling the slow cooker with swollen grains. A final sprinkling of fresh parsley added a bright finish to this simple yet satisfying soup.

Beef Barley Soup
SERVES 6 TO 8
TIME: 7 to 8 hours on low or 5 to 6 hours on high

The barley, cooked over a long period of time, adds body as well as a nutty flavor to the soup. This soup is often seasoned with dill; simply replace the parsley with 2 tablespoons minced fresh dill.

3	pounds chuck roast, trimmed and cut into ½-inch cubes (see the illustrations on page 148)
	Salt and ground black pepper
2	tablespoons vegetable oil
2	medium onions, minced
2	medium carrots, peeled and chopped fine
½	cup dry red wine
2	(14.5-ounce) cans diced tomatoes
1	teaspoon dried thyme
4	cups low-sodium beef broth
4	cups low-sodium chicken broth
⅔	cup pearl barley
¼	cup minced fresh parsley leaves

1. Dry the beef thoroughly with paper towels, then season generously with salt and pepper. Heat 2 teaspoons of the oil in a 12-inch skillet over medium-high heat until just smoking. Add half of the meat to the skillet and cook, without stirring, until well browned on one side, about 4 minutes. Stir the meat and continue to cook, stirring occasionally, until completely browned, 4 to 6 minutes longer. Transfer it to a slow cooker. Return the skillet to medium-high heat and heat 2 more teaspoons oil until just smoking. Brown the remaining beef and transfer it to the slow cooker.

2. Return the skillet to medium heat and heat the remaining 2 teaspoons oil until shimmering. Add the onions, carrots, and ¼ teaspoon salt; cook, stirring occasionally, until softened, 3 to 5 minutes. Stir in the wine, scraping the browned bits off the skillet bottom, and cook until almost dry, about 1 minute. Add the tomatoes and the thyme; bring to a boil. Pour into the slow cooker.

3. Stir the beef and chicken broths and the barley into the slow cooker. Cover and cook, on either low or high, until the beef is tender, 7 to 8 hours on low or 5 to 6 hours on high. Before serving, stir in the parsley and season with salt and pepper to taste.

LAMB VINDALOO

VINDALOO HAS ITS ROOTS IN GOA, A REGION on India's western coast that was once a Portuguese colony. Many local dishes, including vindaloo, are a blend of Indian and Portuguese ingredients and techniques. Vindaloo is made most often with pork, but sometimes with chicken, lamb, beef, or vegetables. The word *vindaloo* is derived from a combination of Portuguese words—*vinho*, for wine vinegar, and *allios*, for garlic. This stew is usually made with a mixture of warm spices (such as cumin and cardamom), chiles (usually in the form of cayenne and paprika), tomatoes, mustard seeds, and vinegar.

When this stew is correctly prepared, the meat is tender, the liquid is thick and deep reddish-orange in color, and the flavors are complex. Onions and garlic add pungency, while the heat of the chiles is tamed by the sweetness of the aromatic spices and the acidity of the tomatoes and vinegar.

We decided to start our testing with the meat component of the dish, and then test the flavoring options. Various cuts of lamb are available in the supermarket; kidney or loin chops, boneless leg, shoulder chops, and packages of pre-cut "lamb for stew" are the most prevalent. Given the leanness and exorbitant price of kidney or loin chops, we decided to test the leg, shoulder chops, and stew meat. Not surprisingly, the pre-packaged stew meat was disappointing. The pieces were irregularly sized and seemed to have come from several parts of the animal. The resulting stew had some pieces that were dry and others that were overcooked. The shoulder chops were tender, juicy, and flavorful after the long cooking process, but required a significant time investment to separate the meat from the fat and bone. Boneless leg of lamb that we trimmed and cubed ourselves, although more pricey, was the easiest to deal with, given the large quantity that we needed.

As expected, we found that browning enhanced the flavor of the lamb and the stewing liquid. We did find it necessary to sear the meat in two batches to avoid steaming the meat in its own juices. Having garnered as much flavor as possible by carefully browning the meat, we added onions, and a hefty quantity of garlic for authenticity and flavor. Next, we moved on to the spices, the cornerstone of lamb vindaloo.

Classic recipes include a combination of sweet and hot spices. Many use small amounts of many spices. We had the best results using hefty amounts of a few key spices. For chile flavor we used sweet paprika and cayenne. To give the stew its characteristic earthy qualities, we added cumin and cardamom. The cardamom is sweet and aromatic, while the cumin hits lower, earthier notes. Bay leaves brought a deep herbaceous flavor to this stew, and a hit of cilantro just before serving added freshness.

With our meat and spices chosen, we turned to the liquid element of our stew. Most of the recipes we uncovered in our research called for water. Given the moist environment of the slow cooker, we questioned whether broth might be a better option for this medium. We prepared two batches: one with water and the other with chicken broth. Tasters felt that the chicken broth added fullness to the stew without overpowering the complexity of the spices.

Sweet and sour flavors are the final component of this stew. Diced canned tomatoes, with their juices, were far less work than the fresh tomatoes we tested, and performed admirably. Two tablespoons of red wine vinegar and 1 teaspoon of sugar provided just the right balance of sour and sweet. We tried adding the vinegar at the end of the cooking time, but tasters felt this stew was harsh. The vinegar needed time to soften and meld with the other flavors. To finalize the texture, we thickened the stew with a slurry of flour and chicken broth.

Although vindaloo is not fiery, it is spicy and therefore best served over rice to help temper the intensity of flavors. Basmati rice is the ideal partner for this dish, but steamed long-grain white rice is also a nice accompaniment.

Lamb Vindaloo

SERVES 6 TO 8

TIME: 6 to 7 hours on low or 4 to 5 hours on high

Boneless leg of lamb is easy to trim and cut into pieces; however, trimmed lamb shoulder chops will also work nicely. Serve with basmati rice or couscous.

I	boneless leg of lamb (about 5 pounds), trimmed and cut into 1½-inch cubes
	Salt and ground black pepper
2	tablespoons vegetable oil
3	medium onions, chopped medium
8	medium garlic cloves, minced or pressed through a garlic press
2	tablespoons sweet paprika
I	tablespoon ground cumin
½	teaspoon ground cardamom
¼	teaspoon cayenne pepper
2½	cups low-sodium chicken broth
I	(14.5-ounce) can diced tomatoes
2	bay leaves
2	tablespoons red wine vinegar
I	teaspoon sugar
¼	cup all-purpose flour
¼	cup chopped fresh cilantro leaves

1. Dry the lamb thoroughly with paper towels, then season generously with salt and pepper. Heat 2 teaspoons of the oil in a 12-inch skillet over medium-high heat until just smoking. Add half of the lamb to the skillet and cook, without stirring, until well browned on one side, about 4 minutes. Stir the meat and continue to cook, stirring occasionally, until completely browned, 4 to 6 minutes longer. Transfer it to the slow cooker. Return the skillet to medium-high heat and heat 2 more teaspoons oil until just smoking. Brown the remaining lamb and transfer it to the slow cooker.

2. Return the skillet to medium heat and heat the remaining 2 teaspoons oil until shimmering. Add the onions and ¼ teaspoon salt; cook, scraping the browned bits off the pan bottom, until the onions are softened and lightly browned, about 10 minutes. Add the garlic, paprika, cumin, cardamom, and cayenne; cook until fragrant, about 30 seconds. Add 2 cups of the chicken broth, the tomatoes, bay leaves, vinegar, and sugar, scraping the browned bits off the pan bottom; turn the heat to high and bring to a boil. Transfer to the slow cooker.

3. Cover and cook, on either low or high, until the lamb is tender, 6 to 7 hours on low or 4 to 5 hours on high.

4. Discard the bay leaves. Set the slow cooker to high (if necessary). Whisk the flour with the remaining ½ cup chicken broth until smooth, then stir into the slow cooker. Continue to cook on high until the sauce is thickened and no longer tastes of flour, 10 to 15 minutes longer. Before serving, stir in the cilantro and season with salt and pepper to taste.

BRAISED PORK LOIN WITH SWEET POTATOES

BONELESS PORK LOIN SEEMED AT THE OUTSET to be a problematic cut of meat for the slow cooker. With little internal fat and connective tissue to keep it juicy, the meat served up by many of the recipes we tried was dry and sandy. After eight to 10 hours on low in the slow cooker (some recipes called for six to eight hours on high), the meat was falling apart, but not in a tender, good way. What we wanted was a pork roast that was juicy and flavorful. We wanted it to be tender, but not disintegrating into shreds, with a rich sauce that would enhance this popular, yet bland, "other white meat."

We focused our attention on time and temperature, which we knew would be key to the success of a perfectly cooked pork loin. We started by browning the pork roast well and smothering it in a spicy blend of onions, jalapeño chiles, garlic, and tomatoes. We added enough broth to partially submerge the roast, inserted a temperature probe through the lid of the slow cooker and into the roast, and monitored the progress. In the dry environment of the oven, the test kitchen recommends cooking pork loin to 135 degrees, counting on the internal temperature rising to a final temperature of 145 degrees while the meat is out of the oven and resting. We were assuming that, in accordance with most of the slow-cooker pork recipes that we found, our roast would take at least six hours to reach that temperature when set on low. To our surprise and dismay, the pork loin reached our target temperature in less than three hours, disqualifying it as a meal that one could leave in the slow cooker for an extended period of time. The meat was somewhat juicy, but extremely tough.

On the verge of abandoning pork loin for a fattier cut, we decided to try cooking the pork loin to 135 degrees, and then let it cook longer to see what would happen. We inserted the temperature probe into the meat and charted the progress for six hours, at which point the roast was at 170 degrees. Much to our surprise, the meat was not dried out and tough but more tender and flavorful than it was in our original test after three hours of cooking. Theorizing that more must be better, we cooked another roast, this time for over seven hours, or until an internal temperature of 200 degrees was reached. At this point, we had definitely gone too far! The meat was as dry and sandy as it was in the recipes we had tried in the beginning of our testing. We tested cooking the roast on high until the same temperature was reached, but the pork turned out tough. It seemed that slow and low was the key to tender, juicy slow-cooker pork. Our roast could survive for six hours on low in the slow cooker, but no longer without sacrificing quality.

The braising liquid for the pork, tasty from the chiles, garlic, and tomatoes, needed a flavor boost to balance the heat of the chiles. We added orange juice for sweetness and a long strip of orange peel for flavor. Tasters liked the deep smoky flavor of chipotle chiles; cumin and oregano rounded out the Southwestern theme. At this point, the flavors were good but the liquid needed body. We wanted it to have more of a gravy consistency, so we tried adding potatoes to the cooker, counting on their starchy qualities for thickening. White potatoes seemed out of place with what was emerging as a Southwestern-style dish. We thought of sweet potatoes, and tried adding them to the slow cooker at the onset of cooking. The sweet potatoes broke down during cooking, which helped to thicken the sauce, and enhanced the sweetness of the orange. To make a more substantial gravy, we pureed the braising liquid and sweet potato solids for a naturally thickened sauce that could evenly coat the sliced pork loin. Sour cream, flavored with fresh cilantro and lime, added a refreshing topping to complement the richness of the pork, and tame the heat of the jalapeño-spiced sweet-potato gravy.

Boneless pork loin fares well in the slow cooker as long as it is cooked on low and the internal temperature does not exceed 175 degrees. We recommend that you begin monitoring the temperature after four hours with an accurate instant-read thermometer.

Braised Pork Loin with Sweet Potatoes, Orange, and Cilantro

SERVES 4 TO 6

TIME: 5 to 6 hours on low

Canned chipotles in adobo sauce are available in most supermarkets.

PORK LOIN

1	boneless center-cut pork loin roast (about 4½ pounds), tied at even intervals along the length with butcher's twine
	Salt and ground black pepper
4	teaspoons vegetable oil
2	medium onions, halved and sliced thin
3	jalapeño chiles, stemmed, seeded, and minced
6	medium garlic cloves, minced or pressed through a garlic press
1	tablespoon ground cumin
1	teaspoon dried oregano
1	(14.5-ounce) can diced tomatoes
1	cup low-sodium chicken broth
1	cup orange juice
1	(6-inch) strip orange peel, from 1 orange
2	canned chipotle chiles in adobo sauce, minced to a paste
1½	pounds sweet potatoes (about 2 medium), peeled and cut into ½-inch chunks
¼	cup chopped fresh cilantro leaves

CILANTRO SOUR CREAM

1	cup sour cream
2	tablespoons chopped fresh cilantro leaves
1	tablespoon lime juice
	Salt and ground black pepper

1. FOR THE PORK: Dry the roast thoroughly with paper towels, then season it generously with salt and pepper. Heat 2 teaspoons of the oil in a 12-inch skillet over medium-high heat until just smoking. Brown the roast thoroughly on all sides, reducing the heat if the fat begins to smoke heavily, 8 to 10 minutes. Transfer it to a slow cooker.

2. Return the skillet to medium heat and heat the remaining 2 teaspoons oil until shimmering. Add the onions, jalapeños, and ¼ teaspoon salt;

cook, stirring occasionally, until softened, about 5 minutes. Stir in the garlic, cumin, and oregano; cook until fragrant, about 30 seconds. Stir in the tomatoes, chicken broth, orange juice, orange peel, and chipotles, scraping up any browned bits off the skillet bottom; increase the heat to high and bring to a boil. Transfer to the slow cooker.

3. Following the illustrations on page 323, nestle the sweet potatoes into the slow cooker around the edges. Cover and cook on low until the pork roast is tender and registers between 165 and 175 degrees on a thermometer, 5 to 6 hours.

4. Transfer the pork to a carving board and tent loosely with foil to keep warm. Allow the cooking liquid in the slow cooker to settle for about 5 minutes, then use a wide spoon to skim the fat off the surface. Puree the liquid and vegetables in batches in a blender or food processor fitted with the steel blade until smooth, and return to the slow

EQUIPMENT: Instant-Read Thermometers

There are two types of commonly sold hand-held thermometers: digital and dial face. While they both take accurate readings, we prefer digital thermometers because they register temperatures faster and are easier to read. After testing a variety of digital thermometers, we preferred the Thermapen ($80) for its well-thought-out design—a long, folding probe and comfortable handle—and speed (just 10 seconds for a reading). If you don't want to spend so much money on a thermometer, at the very least purchase an inexpensive dial-face model. There's no sense ruining an expensive roast because you don't own even a $10 thermometer.

THE BEST INSTANT-READ THERMOMETER
The Thermapen ($80) is our top choice for its pinpoint accuracy and quick response time.

cooker. (Alternatively, use an immersion blender and puree directly in the slow cooker.) Stir in the cilantro and season with salt and pepper to taste.

5. FOR THE CILANTRO SOUR CREAM: Mix the sour cream, cilantro, and lime juice together and season with salt and pepper to taste. Slice the roast into ½-inch-thick slices, arrange on a warmed serving platter, and pour ½ cup of the pureed sauce over the meat. Serve, passing the remaining sauce and cilantro sour cream separately.

PORK AND BEANS WITH SAUSAGE

OUR GOAL FOR PORK AND BEANS WAS FAR FROM the syrupy sweet canned versions available in supermarkets. We wanted something more like French bistro fare: not too sweet, mildly spicy, and with lots of tender meat. Many of the slow-cooker versions we encountered dished up greasy, bland stews with beans that had passed their point of perfection hours before the allotted time was reached. We wanted pork and sausage to be the dominant forces in this stew, surrounded by soft, creamy beans stewed for hours in a flavorful broth.

Our first question was: Which bean would work best? Given the fact that the lucky legume would be spending hours in the slow cooker, we knew that it had to be a sturdy variety. We tested navy beans and cannellini beans and found that they burst open during cooking, rendering them mushy and waterlogged. The great northern bean was our next choice. Sturdier than navy and cannellini beans, great northern beans delivered the creamy texture we wanted, and held their own for the duration of cooking. An overnight soak in water gave them a head start on slowly absorbing the moisture they needed to cook evenly. It also served to keep the beans from splitting open during the long cooking process.

Looking for a cut of pork that would be moist, tender, and flavorful for the stew, we started with pork shoulder. We peeled, boned, trimmed, and cubed this gargantuan cut of pork into stew-size pieces, a process that took quite a bit of time and yielded quite a bit of waste. While the end product

of this stew was tender, the preparation time that was involved sent us in search of a speedier alternative. Pork butt seemed a good choice for its high fat content, but it too required butchering that we weren't willing to do. We settled on country-style pork ribs, which are available bone-in and boneless. Leaving the meat on the bone added more flavor to the stew and kept the meat in recognizable portions. The meat turned out moist, flavorful, and required no advance preparation save the trimming of excess fat. We browned the ribs to get a flavorful start for our stew, then added an onion and a generous quantity of garlic. Next we added white wine, tomato paste, fennel, thyme, and a bay leaf to the skillet and scraped up all of the browned bits to add to the slow cooker.

The last important component in question for the stew was sausage. We tested Italian sausage, chorizo, and kielbasa and preferred the latter for two reasons. Not only did it contribute a smoky flavor to the stew, it seemed to retain its flavor throughout the cooking process. Others seemed to release their flavors into the stew and end up as rubbery, flavorless chunks of meat by the end of the long cooking time. Diced tomatoes went in next, followed by chicken broth.

This stew is hearty and full flavored without being fussy to prepare. The combination of meaty ribs, spicy kielbasa, and creamy beans give it great flavor and heft, and it's perfect for either a busy weeknight or weekend since it can be left alone to cook nearly all day.

Country Style Pork with Beans and Sausage

SERVES 6

TIME: 7 to 8 hours on low or 5 to 6 hours on high

Great northern beans are large, hard beans that hold up well in the slow cooker. If unavailable, substitute kidney or red beans.

1	pound dried great northern beans, rinsed, sorted, and soaked in cold water to cover for at least 8 hours or up to 24 hours
3	pounds country-style pork ribs (about 12 ribs), trimmed of excess fat

Salt and ground black pepper
2   tablespoons vegetable oil
1   medium onion, chopped medium
6   medium garlic cloves, minced or pressed
    through a garlic press
1   cup dry white wine
2   tablespoons tomato paste
1   teaspoon fennel seed
1   teaspoon dried thyme
1   bay leaf
1   pound kielbasa, sliced 1 inch thick
2   (14.5-ounce) cans diced tomatoes
2¾ cups low-sodium chicken broth
¼   cup chopped fresh parsley leaves

1. Drain the beans and transfer them to a slow cooker. Dry the ribs thoroughly with paper towels, then season generously with salt and pepper. Heat 2 teaspoons of the oil in a 12-inch skillet over medium-high heat until just smoking. Add half of the ribs and brown on all sides, 5 to 7 minutes. Transfer them to the slow cooker. Return the skillet to medium-high heat and heat 2 more teaspoons oil until just smoking. Brown the remaining ribs and transfer them to the slow cooker.

2. Return the skillet to medium heat and heat the remaining 2 teaspoons oil until shimmering. Add the onion and ¼ teaspoon salt; cook, stirring occasionally, until beginning to brown, about 2 minutes. Add the garlic and cook until fragrant, about 30 seconds. Add the wine, tomato paste, fennel seed, thyme, and bay leaf, scraping up the browned bits from the bottom of the skillet; turn the heat to high and bring to a boil. Transfer the onion mixture to the slow cooker.

3. Add the kielbasa, tomatoes, and chicken broth to the slow cooker. Cover and cook, on either low or high, until the meat is tender, 7 to 8 hours on low or 5 to 6 hours on high. Before serving, discard the bay leaf, stir in the parsley, and season with salt and pepper to taste.

ASIAN SPICED PORK RIBS WITH NOODLES

BABY BACK RIBS ARE A STAPLE OF BACKYARD barbecues, tailgate parties, and chain restaurant menus across the country. Whether rubbed with secret spices, slathered in sticky sauce, or smoked over designer hardwoods, pork ribs are an item that few can resist. Creating a rib recipe for the slow cooker, without the advantages of a super-hot grill or arid oven, proved to be a challenge. Slow-cooker ribs are braised, low and slow. They can be tender and delicious, but they lack the sexy exterior that other cooking mediums can provide. We set out to create a slow-cooker rib recipe that would make up in flavor for what it lacked in beauty.

The problem we encountered with most slow-cooker rib recipes was that they were more often than not swimming in thick barbecue sauces or watery marinades. Also, the ribs were cooked for such a long period of time that the bones were left bobbing in the sauce, while the meat (albeit tender) lay floating alongside. What we wanted were tender, pull-apart ribs that were Asian-inspired, slightly sweet and spicy without a sticky tomato-based barbecue sauce.

Testing began with baby back ribs as opposed to spareribs, for the simple reason that they fit into the slow cooker more easily than the relatively unwieldy pork spareribs. Our standard procedure for every recipe up until this point had been to brown the meat before adding it to the slow cooker to reap the benefits of the fond left behind on the skillet bottom. We tried browning the ribs, only to discover that coaxing color out of a curved piece of meat (or in this case, curved bones) was next to impossible. Conceding that the ribs had to be added au naturel the pot, we cut them into more manageable portions and set them in the pot. Then we turned our attention to creating a braising liquid that we knew would have to have intense flavors to make amends for the lack of browning.

We started with soy sauce, cornstarch (for added thickness), and hoisin sauce, a sweet-spicy barbecue sauce that added a deep, dark reddish color to the braising liquid. Next, dark brown sugar and rice vinegar were added for the sweet-and-sour component we were looking for; chicken stock enhanced the flavor and diluted the saltiness of both the soy and the hoisin. We cooked the ribs for six hours on low, as directed by many rib recipes, and we were left with overcooked ribs. The braising liquid, however, showed promise. To the existing braising liquid, we added orange zest and five-spice powder, which is a Chinese blend of star anise, cinnamon, cloves, fennel, and Szechwan pepper. Keeping with our Asian theme, we sautéed shiitake mushrooms, onion, garlic, jalapeño, and fresh ginger and added them all, plus a generous splash of sherry to the slow cooker.

After four hours, the ribs were fork-tender and beginning to pull away from the bone, but still had enough structural integrity to make it from the slow cooker to serving platter. (Cooked any longer than four hours, the ribs resembled the disintegrating ribs we ended up with in the first few recipes we tested.) There were, however, parts of the ribs that were not fully submerged in the braising liquid, so they were unevenly cooked. Cutting each rack of ribs into just two sections enabled us to fit them neatly to the curve of the slow cooker with a minimum of liquid. By stacking them on top of each other, we were able to fit enough ribs to serve six.

The resulting braising liquid was rich and flavorful, and the abundant broth and braised vegetables were enough to leave us wondering if we might somehow be able to put them both to good use. More than one taster commented that although the ribs were tender and flavorful, it would be helpful to suggest an accompanying starch or vegetable that could turn this dish into a complete meal. Plain white rice would be a traditional accompaniment, but we wondered if noodles, coated in some of the braising liquid, could be integrated into the dish. Without the luxury of stovetop controls, a slow cooker would not be the ideal vessel for cooking pasta. To solve the problem, we cooked the pasta separately when the ribs were close to being done, then strained the braising liquid through a sieve to trap the solids. Then we then combined the strained solids with the pasta. After removing some of the grease from the braising liquid, we added it to the braised vegetables and pasta on the stovetop and simmered the mixture until the juices formed a velvety gravy that would coat the pasta. To add texture and create a complete, one-pot meal, we tossed in some finely shredded cabbage, colorful scallions, and fresh cilantro.

This is not your average slow-cooker meal. It's a bit more complicated than most and deserving, we thought, of an upscale presentation. Serving this recipe from the slow-cooker insert is an option, but we liked a presentation where the noodles and vegetables are piled high on a large platter with the tender ribs arranged around the edge.

Asian Spiced Pork Ribs with Noodles

SERVES 4 TO 6

TIME: 4 hours on low

The cooking liquid remaining after the ribs are done is used as a sauce for the accompanying noodles. Figure on serving roughly ½ rack of ribs per person. For spicier ribs, increase the amount of Tabasco. Hoisin sauce and toasted sesame oil can be found in Asian food aisle of the supermarket.

3	racks baby back ribs or loin back ribs (about 5 pounds total), each cut in half
I	cup soy sauce
I	tablespoon cornstarch
½	cup hoisin sauce
2	teaspoons Tabasco sauce
I	teaspoon toasted sesame oil
I	cup dark brown sugar
I	cup rice vinegar
I	cup low-sodium chicken broth
I	teaspoon five-spice powder
2	tablespoons vegetable oil
10	ounces shiitake mushrooms, brushed clean, stems discarded, and quartered
	Salt
I	large onion, halved and sliced thin
3	jalapeño chiles, stemmed, seeded, and minced
6	medium garlic cloves, sliced thin
I	(2-inch) piece fresh ginger, peeled and grated
½	cup dry sherry
½	pound spaghetti

¼   head Napa cabbage, shredded fine

2   bunches scallions, sliced thin

¼   cup chopped fresh cilantro leaves

1. Stack the ribs in a slow cooker. Whisk the soy sauce and cornstarch together in a medium bowl until smooth. Add the hoisin, Tabasco, sesame oil, brown sugar, rice vinegar, chicken broth, and five-spice powder and whisk to combine; set aside.

2. Heat 1 tablespoon of the vegetable oil in a 12-inch skillet over high heat until shimmering. Add the mushrooms and ¼ teaspoon salt; cook, stirring occasionally until they have released their moisture and are dry and brown, 7 to 10 minutes. Add the remaining tablespoon vegetable oil, the onion, and jalapeños; cook, stirring occasionally, until softened and beginning to brown around the edges, 3 to 5 minutes. Stir in the garlic and ginger; cook until fragrant, about 30 seconds. Add the sherry and cook, scraping the browned bits from the bottom of the skillet, until almost dry, about 1 minute. Quickly whisk the soy mixture to re-combine, and stir into the skillet; bring to a boil. Pour into the slow cooker.

3. Cover and cook on low until the meat is tender, about 4 hours.

4. Bring 4 quarts of water to a boil in a large pot. Add 1 tablespoon salt and the pasta and cook, stirring often, until al dente. Drain the pasta and return it to the pot. While the pasta is cooking, transfer the ribs to a carving board and tent loosely with foil to keep warm. Strain the cooking liquid, reserving the strained vegetables, and set aside. Add the cabbage, scallions, cilantro, and strained vegetables to the pasta and toss, adding the strained cooking liquid as needed for sauce.

5. Pile the noodles in the center of a large, warmed platter and arrange the ribs around the edges. Serve immediately, passing the extra sauce separately.

CHOPPING CHILES SAFELY

Cleaning and cutting up very hot fresh chiles such as jalapeños or habaneros with bare hands can cause burning sensations in hands and, if you touch them, eyes. Here's a tip for minimizing discomfort:

1. Turn a plastic zipper-lock bag inside out to use it as a glove. It's helpful to secure the bag with a rubber band around your wrist.

2. The bag can then be turned right side out to store leftover chiles.

CHICKEN CHASSEUR

CHICKEN CHASSEUR, OR HUNTER-STYLE CHICKEN, is the French equivalent of chicken cacciatore, a simple, peasant-style braise enriched by the deep, woodsy flavors of mushrooms, smoky bacon, red wine, and herbs. It differs from cacciatore in that it uses white wine instead of red and features a punchier sauce that includes red onion and red pepper flakes. Many of the recipes for this dish feature generic, pasty sauces and chicken that emerges dry and stringy after a long day in the slow cooker. We were hunting for tender, discernible pieces of moist chicken with a robust sauce that would be easy to assemble for the slow cooker.

We settled on bone-in chicken breasts right away since boneless breasts cooked much too quickly (and did not retain their shape). As with our other slow-cooker recipes, we wanted to brown the chicken first to begin the foundation for the stew. This time, instead of using oil for the browning, we cooked bacon until the fat had rendered, transferred the bacon to the slow cooker, and then used the rendered fat to brown the chicken. To deglaze the skillet, we used a dry red wine but were unhappy with the bruised color the red wine deposited on the chicken breasts. We switched to a dry white wine, added chicken broth, and cooked the stew using a temperature probe to monitor the internal temperature of the chicken breasts with a goal of 165 degrees. The chicken was tender and still attached to the bone after four hours, but still bore a dark mottled look that seemed to have come from the mushrooms. As a result, we opted to leave the skin on during cooking to provide a barrier against off colors and then remove it just before serving. We were concerned that leaving the skin on during cooking would make for a greasy sauce, but as it turned out, the preliminary browning had rendered enough of the fat into the skillet to keep it out of the stew.

At this point, the flavor of the stew was weak, and the broth was much too thin. We added diced tomatoes and tomato paste for body, and fresh thyme, bay leaf, and red pepper flakes for a flavor boost. This helped, but tasters were clamoring for more mushroom flavor. Increasing the amount of fresh mushrooms from 10 to 20 ounces was a start, but we still wanted more mushroom essence. So we turned to a flavor trick that we had used before: dried porcini mushrooms. The porcinis provided a huge boost to the flavor of the braise, but the color of the liquid was now a muddied brown. On a tip from our science editor, we switched from white onions to red and were surprised at the dramatic change in color. As it turns out, anthocyanin, the water-soluble pigment found within the cell walls of the red onions, had leached into the sauce, reacted with the acidity of the wine, and turned the sauce a rich mauve color. This added to the aesthetic appeal of the finished dish and completed the flavor profile we had been striving for.

When the chicken was done, we removed it to a serving platter, thickened the sauce with a slurry of flour and chicken broth, and then finished it with fresh parsley for flavor.

Chicken Chasseur

SERVES 6

TIME: 4 to 5 hours on low

Dried porcini mushrooms are usually sold in ¼-, ⅓-, or ½-ounce packages. If you prefer dark meat, you can substitute 12 bone-in, skin-on chicken thighs for the chicken breasts (use paper towels to remove the skin after browning). Cooking on the high setting will yield tough, stringy meat. We recommend cooking chicken exclusively on the low setting.

8	ounces (about 8 slices) bacon, chopped
	Vegetable oil
6	bone-in, skin-on split chicken breasts (about 4 pounds)
	Salt and ground black pepper
1¼	pounds cremini mushrooms, brushed clean and quartered
1	large red onion, minced
4	medium garlic cloves, minced or pressed through a garlic press
½	teaspoon red pepper flakes
1½	cups dry white wine
2	tablespoons tomato paste
¼	ounce dried porcini mushrooms, rinsed thoroughly and chopped fine
4	sprigs fresh thyme
2	bay leaves
2	cups low-sodium chicken broth
1	(14.5-ounce) can diced tomatoes
¼	cup all-purpose flour
¼	cup minced fresh parsley leaves

1. Cook the bacon in a 12-inch skillet over medium heat, stirring occasionally, until brown and crisp, about 5 minutes. Remove with a slotted spoon, drain briefly on paper towels, and then transfer to a slow cooker. Pour off and reserve the bacon fat. (You should have at least 2 tablespoons. If not, substitute vegetable oil for the missing bacon fat.)

2. Dry the chicken thoroughly with paper towels, then season generously with salt and pepper. Return the skillet to medium-high heat and heat 2 teaspoons of the reserved bacon fat until just smoking. Carefully lay 3 of the chicken breasts in the skillet, skin-side down, and cook

until golden, about 6 minutes. Flip the chicken over and continue to cook until the second side is golden, about 3 minutes. Transfer the chicken to the slow cooker. Return the skillet to medium-high heat and heat 2 more teaspoons bacon fat until just smoking. Brown the remaining chicken and transfer it to the slow cooker.

3. Return the skillet to medium heat and heat the remaining 2 teaspoons bacon fat until shimmering. Add the cremini mushrooms, onion, and ¼ teaspoon salt; cook, stirring occasionally, until the mushrooms have released their moisture and are dry and browned, 10 to 12 minutes. Add the garlic and red pepper flakes; cook until fragrant, about 30 seconds. Add the wine, tomato paste, porcini mushrooms, thyme, and bay leaves, scraping the browned bits off the bottom of the pan. Turn the heat to high, bring to a simmer, and cook until the wine has reduced by roughly half, 6 to 8 minutes. Transfer to the slow cooker.

4. Add 1½ cups of the chicken broth and the diced tomatoes to the slow cooker. Cover and cook on low until the chicken is tender but not falling apart, 4 to 5 hours.

5. Transfer the chicken to a carving board, remove the skin, and tent loosely with foil to keep warm. Discard the bay leaves and thyme sprigs. Set the slow cooker to high. Whisk the flour with the remaining ½ cup chicken broth until smooth, then stir into the slow cooker. Continue to cook on high until the sauce is thickened and no longer tastes of flour, 10 to 15 minutes longer. Stir in the parsley and season with salt and pepper to taste. Return the chicken to the slow cooker and allow to heat through before serving.

CHICKEN WITH WHITE WINE AND TARRAGON

CHICKEN WITH WHITE WINE, TARRAGON, AND cream sounds like a company-worthy dish, and we wondered if it could be replicated in a slow cooker. Our objective was to find a way to end up with tender chicken breasts braised in a wine-and-herb-infused sauce that was rich and creamy

enough to serve over rice. We wanted it to be simple to prepare, yet elegant enough for a special occasion.

We started our testing by browning bone-in chicken breasts with their skin on. This helped to render the chicken fat and added extra flavor to the dish as well. We then added white button mushrooms, onion, and garlic to the skillet with a small amount of salt to draw moisture out of the mushrooms. To deglaze the skillet, we used a dry white wine, scraping up the browned bits from the skillet. Then we added chicken broth, fresh tarragon, and heavy cream. We transferred it all to the slow cooker. After four hours the chicken was tender, but we were hardly impressed with the resulting sauce. The mushrooms had turned gray and slimy, the aromatic tarragon had all but disappeared, and the heavy cream had separated, leaving us with a curdled, watery sauce.

The mushroom and tarragon issues were easy to fix. Cremini mushrooms, which are baby portobello mushrooms, weathered the braise far better than white button mushrooms. Because of their firmer, meatier texture, they were better able to withstand the long cooking time without breaking down and becoming mushy. To keep the tarragon flavor from waning, we decided to stir it into the sauce right before serving.

To address the broken sauce, we tried adding the cream after the chicken had finished cooking, and had good results, but the sauce was still thin. We next tried making a slurry with cream and flour, stirring it into the pot after the chicken had been removed. The resulting sauce was the perfect consistency, light and creamy, with a delicate tarragon flavor. Finished with a splash of fresh lemon juice and served over steaming rice, this is a great "company's coming for dinner" recipe, any night of the week.

Chicken with White Wine, Tarragon, and Cream
SERVES 6
TIME: 4 hours on low

If you prefer dark meat, you can substitute 12 bone-in chicken thighs for the chicken breasts (use paper towels to remove the skin after browning). If cremini mushrooms are unavailable, substitute portobello mushrooms, dark gills removed and cut into 1-inch chunks. Cooking on the high setting will yield tough, stringy meat. We recommend cooking chicken exclusively on the low setting.

6	bone-in, skin-on split chicken breasts (about 4 pounds)
	Salt and ground black pepper
2	tablespoons vegetable oil
1¼	pounds cremini mushrooms, brushed clean and quartered
1	medium onion, chopped medium
4	medium garlic cloves, minced or pressed through a garlic press
1¾	cups dry white wine
4	sprigs fresh thyme
1	bay leaf
6	medium carrots, peeled and cut into 3-inch chunks
1	cup low-sodium chicken broth
1	cup heavy cream
¼	cup all-purpose flour
¼	cup chopped fresh tarragon leaves
1	tablespoon lemon juice

1. Dry the chicken thoroughly with paper towels, then season generously with salt and pepper. Heat 2 teaspoons of the oil in a 12-inch skillet over medium-high heat until just smoking. Carefully lay 3 of the chicken breasts in the skillet, skin-side down, and cook until golden, about 6 minutes. Flip the chicken over and continue to cook until the second side is golden, about 3 minutes. Transfer the chicken to a slow cooker. Return the skillet to medium-high heat and heat 2 more teaspoons oil until just smoking. Brown the remaining chicken and transfer it to the slow cooker.

2. Return the skillet to medium heat and heat the remaining 2 teaspoons oil until shimmering. Add the mushrooms, onion, and ¼ teaspoon salt; cook, stirring occasionally, until the mushrooms have released their moisture and are dry and browned, 10 to 12 minutes. Add the garlic and cook until fragrant, about 30 seconds. Add the wine, thyme, and bay leaf, scraping up any browned bits off the skillet bottom; turn the heat to high, bring to a simmer,

and cook until reduced by about half, 8 to 10 minutes. Transfer the mixture to the slow cooker.

3. Following the illustrations on page 323, nestle the carrots into the slow cooker around the edges and add the chicken broth. Cover and cook on low until the chicken is tender but not falling apart, about 4 hours.

4. Transfer the chicken to a carving board and tent loosely with foil to keep warm. Discard the bay leaf and thyme sprigs. Turn the slow cooker to high. In a small bowl, whisk the cream and flour together until smooth, then stir into the slow cooker. Continue to cook on high until the sauce thickens and no longer tastes of flour, 10 to 15 minutes longer. Stir in the tarragon and lemon juice; season with salt and pepper to taste. Return the chicken to the slow cooker and allow to heat through before serving.

MOROCCAN SPICED CHICKEN STEW

MOROCCAN CUISINE OFFERS A FEAST FOR THE senses. Drawing on influences from diverse surrounding cultures, Moroccan stews (or tagines, as they're commonly called) are highly aromatic and flavorful. Characterized by brilliant, earthy hues and a blend of sweet and savory ingredients, they can be at once intriguing, yet intimidating. Traditional ingredient lists are often quite extensive, calling for cumin, saffron, coriander, and chiles of all sorts, in addition to complex, robust spice pastes that require shopping reconnaissance missions just to get started. Our plan for this recipe was to duplicate the flavors of a traditional Moroccan tagine in the slow cooker, without using a laundry list of exotic ingredients.

We started by browning chicken thighs, which we chose because their flavor is more robust than that of white chicken meat. Next we added onions and garlic to the skillet. Knowing that the choice of spices would be critical, we started with three that are common in many Moroccan recipes: cardamom, cinnamon, and hot paprika. Cardamom is a pungent, aromatic spice with lemony undertones and is available in whole pods or in ground form, which we used for this recipe, just to keep things simpler. Cinnamon stick (which is the bark of a tropical evergreen tree) added a warm contrasting flavor, balancing nicely with the cardamom. As for the paprika, a spice made from dried, ground red pepper, we had a range of choices before us since it's available in many varieties, which range in potency from sweet to hot. Knowing that we wanted a stew with a vibrant and piquant flavor, we chose hot paprika.

To temper the sharp spices, we added dried apricots for their sweetness and used chicken broth as our stewing medium. Now we had a stew packed with great flavors and a balanced contrast between hot and sweet undertones. For contrasting texture, we turned to chickpeas (or garbanzo beans), a common ingredient in Moroccan cuisine. Their firm but creamy texture and nutty flavor added yet another dimension to the stew. Since dried chickpeas were not an option, given the cooking time, we decided to use canned chickpeas. When added to the slow cooker at the onset of cooking, the chickpeas absorbed the complex flavors of the stew, but their firm texture was compromised by long cooking. Added during the last hour of cooking, the chickpeas retained their integrity yet still had ample opportunity to attract the full spectrum of flavors from the braising liquid. Finishing the stew with fresh cilantro and lemon juice gave it the sharp, bright flavor we sought. With its exotic flavors and heady aromas, this simple stew has all the intrigue and complexity of a Casablanca classic, without being daunting. It is perfect served over couscous or fragrant basmati rice.

Moroccan Spiced Chicken and Apricot Stew

SERVES 6

TIME: 4 to 5 hours on low

Prunes or raisins can be substituted for the apricots. If you are unable to find hot paprika, substitute sweet paprika and add cayenne pepper to taste. Cooking on the high setting will yield tough, stringy meat. We recommend cooking chicken exclusively on the low setting.

12	bone-in, skin-on chicken thighs (about 4½ pounds), trimmed of excess fat
	Salt and ground black pepper
2	teaspoons vegetable oil
2	medium onions, chopped fine
6	medium garlic cloves, minced or pressed through a garlic press
I	cinnamon stick
½	teaspoon ground cardamom
1½	teaspoons hot paprika
8	ounces dried apricots (about I cup), cut in half
3	cups low-sodium chicken broth
I	(15.5-ounce) can chickpeas, drained and rinsed
3	tablespoons all-purpose flour
¼	cup minced fresh cilantro leaves
2	tablespoons lemon juice
I	lemon, cut into wedges

1. Dry the chicken thoroughly with paper towels, then season generously with salt and pepper. Heat the oil in a 12-inch skillet over medium-high heat until just smoking. Carefully lay 6 of the chicken thighs into the skillet, skin-side down; cook until golden, about 6 minutes. Flip the chicken over and continue to cook until the second side is golden, about 3 minutes. Transfer the chicken to a slow cooker. Using paper towels, remove and discard the browned chicken skin. Pour off all but 2 teaspoons of the fat left in the skillet and return to medium-high heat until just smoking. Brown the remaining chicken, transfer it to the slow cooker, and discard the skin.

2. Pour off all but 2 teaspoons of the fat left in the skillet and return to medium heat until shimmering. Add the onions and ¼ teaspoon salt; cook, scraping the browned bits off the bottom of the skillet, until the onions are soft and translucent, about 4 minutes. Add the garlic, cinnamon, cardamom, and paprika; cook until fragrant, about 30 seconds. Add the apricots and 2½ cups of the chicken broth, scraping up any browned bits from the bottom. Turn the heat to high and bring to a boil. Transfer the mixture to the slow cooker.

3. Cover and cook on low until the chicken is almost tender, about 3 to 4 hours. Quickly stir in the chickpeas, replace the cover, and cook until the chicken is tender but not falling apart, about 1 hour longer.

4. Transfer the chicken to a carving board and tent loosely with foil to keep warm. Discard the cinnamon stick. Set the slow cooker to high. Whisk the flour with the remaining ½ cup chicken broth until smooth, then stir it into the slow cooker. Continue to cook on high until the sauce is thickened and no longer tastes of flour, 10 to 15 minutes longer. Stir in the cilantro and lemon juice. Season with salt and pepper to taste. Return the chicken to the slow cooker and allow to heat through before serving. Serve with lemon wedges.

CURRIED CHICKEN WITH POTATOES

AN INDIAN CHICKEN CURRY SHOULD HAVE complex layers of flavor but at the same time be light and clean tasting. Many of the chicken curries that we tried had overpowering amounts of spice and cloyingly thick sauces. We wanted a mild but flavor-packed curry, with a light but substantial sauce that would hold its own when served over couscous or rice.

We chose chicken thighs for this stew and began by browning them with the skin on. This added fond to the skillet, giving us a good foundation for building multiple layers of flavor in the curry. Discarding the skin after browning eliminated its rubbery texture from the final stew. We then added onions, carrots, garlic, ginger, and jalapeño chiles and cooked them until the aromatics were translucent and the chiles and ginger were fragrant. Curry powder and cayenne went into the skillet next. Frying the spices encouraged their flavors to bloom, and infused the stew with complex flavors. We then scattered these aromatics on top of the now-skinless chicken in the slow cooker.

To continue to build the flavors, we returned the skillet to the stove and added diced tomatoes with their juice, but the resulting stew had a diluted flavor that tasters disliked. We tried crushed tomatoes and "stir fried" them in the hot skillet in the hopes of coaxing out more flavor. The crushed tomatoes added deep flavor and body to the stew, and the frying process served

two purposes. It intensified the tomato flavor and it reduced the liquid, enabling us to use less thickener at the end of the cooking process. Coconut milk, a star ingredient in curries of many origins, adds an incredible richness to a stew, but because of its relatively high fat content, we were reluctant to add it at the beginning of the cooking process. When exposed to high heat, the fat in coconut milk has a tendency to separate, leaving behind an oily slick. Fortunately, the moderate temperature of a slow cooker set on low proved to be the ideal environment for the coconut milk. Because coconut milk is so rich and thick, we found that we needed to add chicken broth to the stew to temper the richness.

We wanted potatoes with our curry, but in our first attempts to add them, the chicken was done before the quartered potatoes (which we had added to the bottom of the slow cooker) were soft enough to be edible. Placing whole Red Bliss potatoes toward the outer edge of the slow cooker solved the problem. Nestled next to the heating elements, the potatoes softened thoroughly as the chicken cooked. After four hours, when the chicken was tender, we removed the potatoes with a slotted spoon, quartered them, and then

ARRANGING VEGETABLES IN A SLOW COOKER

In recipes where the meat is only in the slow cooker for 4 to 5 hours, it is important to arrange the vegetables around the edges of the slow cooker, nearer the heating elements, so that they will cook evenly. Also, this technique is useful in recipes like Beef Stew (page 303) and Curried Chicken, where potatoes are added whole to the stew.

stirred them back into the stew. The cut potatoes absorbed the flavors of the stew and began to thicken the broth with their starch. To augment the thickening process, we stirred in a slurry of flour and reserved chicken broth. To brighten the flavors and enhance the muted colors, we finished this classic Indian curry with green peas, fresh cilantro leaves, and lemon juice.

Curried Chicken Thighs with Peas and Potatoes

SERVES 6

TIME: 4 to 5 hours on low

Serve this dish with a basmati pilaf or couscous. Cooking on the high setting will yield tough, stringy meat. We recommend cooking chicken exclusively on the low setting.

12	bone-in, skin-on chicken thighs (about 4½ pounds), trimmed of excess fat
	Salt and ground black pepper
1	tablespoon vegetable oil
1	medium onion, halved and sliced thin
4	medium carrots, peeled and chopped medium
4	large garlic cloves, minced or pressed through a garlic press
1	(1½-inch) piece fresh ginger, peeled and minced
1	jalapeño chile, stemmed, seeded, and minced
4	teaspoons curry powder
¼	teaspoon cayenne pepper
1	cup canned crushed tomatoes
1	(13.5-ounce) can coconut milk
2½	cups low-sodium chicken broth
1	cinnamon stick
1	bay leaf
½	cup currants or golden raisins
2	pounds Red Bliss potatoes (about 6 medium), scrubbed
¼	cup all-purpose flour
2	cups frozen peas, thawed
¼	cup chopped fresh cilantro leaves
1	tablespoon lemon juice
1	lemon, cut into wedges

1. Dry the chicken thoroughly with paper towels, then season generously with salt and pepper.

Heat 2 teaspoons of the oil in a 12-inch skillet over medium-high heat until just smoking. Carefully lay 6 of the chicken thighs in the skillet, skin-side down; cook until golden, about 6 minutes. Flip the chicken over and continue to cook until the second side is golden, about 3 minutes. Transfer the chicken to a slow cooker. Using paper towels, remove and discard the browned chicken skin. Pour off all but 2 teaspoons of the fat left in the skillet and return to medium-high heat until just smoking. Brown the remaining chicken, transfer it to the slow cooker, and discard the skin.

2. Pour off all but 2 teaspoons of the fat left in the skillet and return to medium heat until shimmering. Add the onion, carrots, garlic, ginger, jalapeño, and ¼ teaspoon salt; cook, scraping the browned bits off the bottom of the skillet, until the onion is soft and beginning to brown, 5 to 7 minutes. Stir in the curry and cayenne; cook until fragrant, about 30 seconds. Transfer to the slow cooker.

3. Return the skillet to high heat and heat the remaining teaspoon oil until shimmering. Add the crushed tomatoes and cook until they begin to brown, about 1 minute. Add the coconut milk, 2 cups of the chicken broth, the cinnamon stick, bay leaf, and currants, and bring to a boil. Transfer the mixture to the slow cooker.

4. Following the illustration on page 323, nestle the potatoes around the inside edges of the slow cooker. Cover and cook on low until the chicken is tender but not falling apart, 4 to 5 hours.

5. Transfer the chicken to a carving board and tent loosely with foil to keep warm. Transfer the potatoes to a large bowl and set aside. Discard the cinnamon stick and bay leaf. Set the slow cooker to high. Whisk the flour with the remaining ½ cup chicken broth until smooth and stir it into the slow cooker. Quarter the potatoes and return them to the slow cooker. Continue to cook the sauce on high until it has thickened and no longer tastes of flour, 10 to 15 minutes longer.

6. Stir in the peas, cilantro, and lemon juice and season with salt and pepper to taste. Return the chicken to the slow cooker and allow to heat through before serving. Serve with lemon wedges.

INDEX

Z

Ziti, baked, 21–24
  with Eggplant and Smoked
    Mozzarella, 23–24
  with Italian Sausage, 22–23
  with Tomatoes and Mozzarella,
    21–22
Zucchini:
  Chicken Casserole with Summer
    Squash, Sun-Dried Tomatoes,
    and Basil, 62–63

Zucchini *(cont.)*
  Chicken Tagine with Olives,
    Honey and, 203
  Lasagna with Roasted Eggplant
    and, 40
  Penne with Summer Squash,
    Tomatoes, Basil and, 26–29,
    99
  Ratatouille, Oven-Baked,
    253–54
  shingling technique for, 55

Zucchini *(cont.)*
  size of, for pasta sauce, 28
  summer squash casserole
    with Feta, Lemon, and Oregano,
      249
    Provençal, 247–49
  Vegetable and Bean Tamale Pie,
    141–42

A Note on Conversions

SOME SAY COOKING IS A SCIENCE AND AN art. We would say that geography has a hand in it, too. Flour milled in the United Kingdom and elsewhere will feel and taste different from flour milled in the United States. So we cannot promise that the loaf of bread you bake in Canada or England will taste the same as a loaf baked in the States, but we can offer guidelines for converting weights and measures. We also recommend that you rely on instincts when making our recipes. Refer to the visual cues provided. If the bread dough hasn't "come together in a ball," as described, you may need to add more flour—even if the recipe doesn't tell you so. You be the judge. For more information on conversions and ingredient equivalents, visit our Web site at www.cooksillustrated.com and type "conversion chart" in the search box.

The recipes in this book were developed using standard U.S. measures following U.S. government guidelines. The charts below offer equivalents for U.S., metric, and Imperial (U.K.) measures. All conversions are approximate and have been rounded up or down to the nearest whole number. For example:

1 teaspoon = 4.9292 milliliters, rounded up to 5 milliliters

1 ounce = 28.3495 grams, rounded down to 28 grams

Volume Conversions

U.S.	METRIC
1 teaspoon	5 milliliters
2 teaspoons	10 milliliters
1 tablespoon	15 milliliters
2 tablespoons	30 milliliters
¼ cup	59 milliliters
½ cup	118 milliliters
¾ cup	177 milliliters
1 cup	237 milliliters
1¼ cups	296 milliliters
1½ cups	355 milliliters
2 cups	473 milliliters
2½ cups	592 milliliters
3 cups	710 milliliters
4 cups (1 quart)	0.946 liter
1.06 quarts	1 liter
4 quarts (1 gallon)	3.8 liters

Weight Conversions

OUNCES	GRAMS
½	14
¾	21
1	28
1½	43
2	57
2½	71
3	85
3½	99
4	113
4½	128
5	142
6	170
7	198
8	227
9	255
10	283
12	340
16 (1 pound)	454

Conversions for Ingredients Commonly Used in Baking

Baking is an exacting science. Because measuring by weight is far more accurate than measuring by volume, and thus more likely to achieve reliable results, in our recipes we provide ounce measures in addition to cup measures for many ingredients. Refer to the chart below to convert these measures into grams.

INGREDIENT	OUNCES	GRAMS
1 cup all-purpose flour*	5	142
1 cup whole-wheat flour	5½	156
1 cup granulated (white) sugar	7	198
1 cup packed brown sugar (light or dark)	7	198
1 cup confectioners' sugar	4	113
1 cup cocoa powder	3	85
Butter†		
4 tablespoons (½ stick, or ¼ cup)	2	57
8 tablespoons (1 stick, or ½ cup)	4	113
16 tablespoons (2 sticks, or 1 cup)	8	227

*U.S. all-purpose flour, the most frequently used flour in this book, does not contain leaveners, as some European flours do. These leavened flours are called self-rising or self-raising. If you are using self-rising flour, take this into consideration before adding leavening to a recipe.

† In the United States, butter is sold both salted and unsalted. We generally recommend unsalted butter. If you are using salted butter, take this into consideration before adding salt to a recipe.

Oven Temperatures

FAHRENHEIT	CELSIUS	GAS MARK (IMPERIAL)
225	105	¼
250	120	½
275	130	1
300	150	2
325	165	3
350	180	4
375	190	5
400	200	6
425	220	7
450	230	8
475	245	9

Converting Temperatures from an Instant-Read Thermometer

We include doneness temperatures in many of our recipes, such as those for poultry, meat, and bread. We recommend an instant-read thermometer for the job. Refer to the table at left to convert Fahrenheit degrees to Celsius. Or, for temperatures not represented in the chart, use this simple formula:

Subtract 32 degrees from the Fahrenheit reading, then divide the result by 1.8 to find the Celsius reading.

EXAMPLE:

"Roast until the juices run clear when the chicken is cut with a paring knife or the thickest part of the breast registers 160 degrees on an instant-read thermometer." To convert:

160° F − 32 = 128°
128° ÷ 1.8 = 71° C (rounded down from 71.11)